Context

Berlin • Brandenburg
Mecklenburg-Vorpommern

Grund- und Leistungskurs

Vokabeltrainer-App

Verfügbar für: iOS, Android und Windows Phone

Cornelsen

Context • Berlin, Brandenburg, Mecklenburg-Vorpommern Grund- und Leistungskurs

Im Auftrag des Verlages herausgegeben von
Dr. Annette Leithner-Brauns, Dresden; Ingrid Becker-Ross, Krefeld; Prof. Hellmut Schwarz, Mannheim

Erarbeitet von
Irene Bartscherer, Bonn; Ingrid Becker-Ross, Krefeld; Friederike von Bremen, Hannover; Ulrike Elsäßer, Stuttgart; Gerit Fredrich, Meiningen; Prof. Dr. Britta Freitag-Hild, Potsdam; Veronika Gastpar, Mainburg; Dr. Peter Hohwiller, Landau; Markus Hözel, Köln; Ulrich Imig, Wildeshausen; Elke Jentsch, Reichenbach im Vogtland; Dr. Annette Leithner-Brauns, Dresden; Sylvia Loh, Esslingen; Dr. Paul Maloney, Hildesheim; Markus Marzinzik, Landau; Claudia Meixner, Erlangen; Christina Pape, Jork; Neil Porter, Tel Aviv; Birgit Rietgraf, Weissach; Angela Ringel-Eichinger, Bietigheim-Bissingen; Victoria Schoeneberg, Köln; Dr. Andreas Sedlatschek, Esslingen; Claudia Spieler, Gießen; Marcel Sprunkel, Köln; Sabine Struß, Verden; Michael Thürwächter, Heidelberg; Inga Wittbrodt, Sankt Augustin

unter beratender Mitwirkung von
Martina Baasner, Berlin; Dr. Sabine Buchholz, Hürth; Bernd Koch, Marburg; Claudia Krapp, Geestland; Jochen Lüders, München; Gunthild Porteous-Schwier, Moers; Sieglinde Spranger, Chemnitz

in Zusammenarbeit mit der Englischredaktion
Elke Lehmann *(Projektleitung)*; Aryane Beaudoin; Dr. Marion Kiffe, Laura Morgenthal, Dr. Georg-Christian v. Raumer, Ingrid-Maria Sauer, Anna Schwarz, Hartmut Tschepe, Ralph Williams sowie Katrin Gütermann, Berlin, und Neil Porter, Tel Aviv

Layoutkonzept
zweiband.media, Berlin

Layout und technische Umsetzung
designcollective, Berlin

Umschlaggestaltung
axeptDESIGN, Berlin; Michaela Müller für agentur corngreen, Leipzig

Weitere Bestandteile des Lehrwerks

- E-Book zum Schülerbuch (978-3-06-036480-0)
- Workbook (978-3-06-031667-0)
- Abi to go · VOCABI (978-3-06-033490-2)
- Abi to go · SKILLS (978-3-06-033858-0)
- Abi to go · GRAMMAR (978-3-06-034842-8)
- Audio-CDs (+ MP3) (978-3-06-033487-2)
- Video-DVD (978-3-06-033488-9)
- Lehrerfassung des Schülerbuchs (978-3-06-036479-4)
- Handreichungen für den Unterricht (978-3-06-036476-3)
- UMA und Begleitmaterialien auf USB-Stick (978-3-06-036477-0)
- Vorschläge zur Leistungsmessung (978-3-06-033590-9)
- More Speaking Practice (Rollen- und Bildkarten) (978-3-06-031504-8)
- Geschlossene Aufgaben zum Hör- und Hörseh-verstehen (978-3-06-035306-4)
- Geschlossene Aufgaben zum Leseverstehen (978-3-06-035456-6)

www.cornelsen.de

Die Webseiten Dritter, deren Internetadressen in diesem Lehrwerk angegeben sind, wurden vor Drucklegung sorgfältig geprüft. Der Verlag übernimmt keine Gewähr für die Aktualität und den Inhalt dieser Seiten oder solcher, die mit ihnen verlinkt sind.

1. Auflage, 2. Druck 2021

Alle Drucke dieser Auflage sind inhaltlich unverändert und können im Unterricht nebeneinander verwendet werden.

© 2019 Cornelsen Verlag GmbH, Berlin

Druck und Bindung: Livonia Print, Riga

ISBN 978-3-06-036475-6

Contents

PART ONE: Individual and Society

Chapter 1 — Living One's Life – Individuals in Society

Page	Function	Part of chapter/Level/Title	Text type/Media	Communicative and language skills	Text type to be produced
14	Lead-in				
16	Words in Context	Young people in a multi-faceted society	Informative text 🎧	Vocabulary skills Language awareness Writing	Comment
	Part A	Future success			
18	***	A1 Successful children *Amy Chua*	Non-fictional text	Language awareness Speaking Writing	Discussion Email Comment
21		A2 Growing up queer in 2018 *Arianna Balderrama*	Magazine article	Language awareness Speaking	Discussion
23		A3 Stereotypes in Los Angeles *Paul Haggis*	Screenplay ▶	Viewing Language awareness Writing	Discussion
26	Focus on Skills	Resolving a heated argument		SPEAKING	Role-play
27	Culture Spot	Graffiti and street art	Photos	Speaking	
	Part B	Getting involved			
28	*	B1 Young people raising their voices	Photos, quotes	Speaking	
29		B2 It could have been me	Radio interview 🎧	Listening	
29		B3 Volunteering in Germany *Sophia Seiderer*	German online article	Mediation G–E Speaking Writing	Email Discussion
31		B4 An individual in a utopian society	Film trailer Film clips ▶	Viewing Speaking	Discussion
32	Fact File	From utopia to dystopia	Informative text		
33	Chapter Task	Getting your message across	▶	Viewing Speaking	Vlog Discussion

Chapter 2 — The Power of Words – from Shakespeare to Today

Page	Function	Part of chapter/Level/Title	Text type/Media	Communicative and language skills	Text type to be produced
34	Lead-in				
36	Words in Context	The power of the spoken word	Informative text 🎧	Vocabulary skills Language awareness Writing	Comment
	Part A	Shakespeare's power of language			
38	*	A1 William Shakespeare: the man, his work and his time	Keywords Mindmap		Presentation
39	***	A2 Lady Macbeth persuades her husband (Macbeth *William Shakespeare*)	Drama extract	Language awareness Writing	Summary
41	Focus on Skills	Reading for analysis (drama extract)		READING Writing	
42	***	A3 Richard courts his enemy (Richard III *William Shakespeare*)	Drama extract	Language awareness Speaking	Performance of a dialogue

Text level: * basic, *** advanced

Contents

Page	Function	Part of chapter/Level/Title	Text type/Media	Communicative and language skills	Text type to be produced
	Part B	Shakespeare's words updated			
45	***	B1 My future wife (The Taming of the Shrew *William Shakespeare*)	Drama extract	Language awareness Speaking Writing	Cartoon/ comic strip/ short dialogue Discussion Storyboard
47	Focus on Skills	Evaluating a modern Shakespeare adaptation	🎬	VIEWING	Evaluation
48		B2 Responding to a sonnet (Sonnet 116 *William Shakespeare*, Marital Sonnet 4 *James Simmons*)	Poems	Speaking Writing	Discussion Summary Email/letter/ comment/ short poem/ …
49	Culture Spot	Shakespeare for the masses	Photo	Speaking	Creative design
	Part C	The powerful words of today's poets			
50	Fact File	Performance poetry	Informative text		
50		C1 Performance poetry (Dis Poetry *Benjamin Zephaniah*, Famous for what? *Hollie McNish*)	Film clips, 🎬 poems, audio text 🎧	Listening Viewing Mediation G–E Writing	Discussion Review Letter/lines of poetry
52		C2 The psychological power of words (The right word *Imtiaz Dharker*)	Poem, audio text 🎧	Listening Reading	Inter- pretation
53	Chapter Task	Writing a review		Writing	Review

PART TWO: National and Cultural Identity

Chapter 3 — The UK – a Kingdom United?

Page	Function	Part of chapter/Level/Title	Text type/Media	Communicative and language skills	Text type to be produced
54	Lead-in				
56	Words in Context	Character of a country	Informative text 🎧	Vocabulary skills Language awareness	Advertising slogan
	Part A	A crowned nation			
58		A1 Dangerous books *Alan Bennett*	Novel extract	Language awareness Speaking Writing	Discussion Story/ dialogue
60	Fact File	The British system of government	Informative text		
61	Focus on Skills	Listening for gist and detail		LISTENING	
62		A2 Does Britain still need the monarchy?	Podcast 🎧	Listening	Discussion
63	*	A3 The British and their tea	Podcast 🎧	Listening	
63	Culture spot	The Fourth Plinth	Photos	Speaking	

Contents

Page	Function	Part of chapter/Level/Title	Text type/Media	Communicative and language skills	Text type to be produced
	Part B	The multicultural face of the UK			
64	Fact File	From Empire to Commonwealth – Britain as a multicultural society	Informative text		Comment
65		B1 The British Empire report	Short documentary 🎬	Viewing Writing	Video script
66		B2 Between two cultures *Mike Bartlett*	Drama extract	Language awareness Writing	Email/ dialogue Comment
69		B3 A closer look at Britain's Muslims *Harriet Sherwood*	Newspaper article	Reading	Presentation
	Part C	Where do we go from here?			
70	***	C1 Before the EU referendum	Political speech 🎧	Listening	
70		C2 Trying to understand the Brexit vote *Catherine Hickley*	Statistics, graphs, newspaper article	Mediation G–E	Comment
72	*	C3 Reactions to the referendum	Cartoon		
73	Chapter Task	A podcast on British culture	🎧	Listening Writing	Podcast

Chapter 4	India – a Kaleidoscope

Page	Function	Part of chapter/Level/Title	Text type/Media	Communicative and language skills	Text type to be produced
74	Lead-in		Photos	Speaking	
76	Words in Context	India then and now	Informative text 🎧	Vocabulary skills Language awareness	
	Part A	India's past: echoes and reflections			
78	*	A1 India's UNESCO World Heritage sites	Photos		Timeline Presentation
79	***	A2 Colonizers and colonized	Speech (extract) Photo	Speaking	Oral statement
79	***	A3 The British Empire from an Indian perspective *Gurcharan Das*	Non-fictional text	Mediation E–G	Discussion
81	Fact File	Gandhi and India's struggle for independence	Informative text	Speaking	One-minute speech
81		A4 Gandhi remembered *Chetan Bhagat*	Fictional letter	Language awareness Writing	Blog entry/ comment
84	Focus on Skills	Listening to a radio interview	🎧	LISTENING	
	Part B	Tales from modern India			
85		B1 Urbanization in India: the big picture	Graph		Discussion
85		B2 Life in a megacity	Film poster	Writing	Creative Writing
86	Focus on Skills	Watching a film trailer	🎬	VIEWING	Discussion
87		B3 Celebrating Indian culture	Film extract, 🎬 German-language interview	Viewing Mediation G–E	Email
88	Culture Spot	Indian truck art	Photos Web text		

Contents

Page	Function	Part of chapter/Level/Title	Text type/Media	Communicative and language skills	Text type to be produced
	Part C	Indians abroad			
89		C1 The Indian diaspora		Speaking	Presentation
89		C2 A taste of the Indian diaspora *Michelle Warwicker*	Online article	Speaking	Discussion
90		C3 English lessons *Shauna Singh Baldwin*	Short story	Language awareness Writing	Letter
93	Chapter Task	Presenting India			Presentation

Chapter 5 — The USA – Still the Promised Land?

Page	Function	Part of chapter/Level/Title	Text type/Media	Communicative and language skills	Text type to be produced
94	Lead-in				
96	Words in Context	A country like no other	Informative text 🎧	Vocabulary skills Language awareness Writing	Comment
	Part A	The American dream			
98		A1 Unlike other nations *David Kamp*	Magazine article	Language awareness Speaking	Discussion
99		A2 Reinventing the American dream *June Sochen*	Newspaper article	Reading Writing	Mindmap Comment
102		A3 The danger to the dream *Barack Obama*	Speech extract 🎧	Listening	Oral report
103		A4 How to become homeless	Film extract 🎬	Writing Viewing Speaking	Oral report
103	Fact File	Home ownership	Informative text		
104	Culture Spot	Flag (1954) *Jasper Johns*	Painting 🎧	Speaking Listening	
	Part B	Dealing with diversity			
105	Fact File	Ethnic neighbourhoods	Informative text		
105		B1 The new neighbours *Bruce Norris*	Drama extract 🎧	Listening Speaking	Discussion
108		B2 Integration or frustration? *Stefanie Mitchell, Orlando Patterson*	Interview	Reading	Comment
110		B3 The changing face of America *William J. Clinton*	Speech extract	Reading	Summary
112	Focus on Skills	Speaking in front of an audience		SPEAKING	Speech
	Part C	The United States' place in the world			
114	*	C1 Facts and figures	Statistics	Speaking	Discussion
114		C2 The German view *Michael Hochgeschwender*	German podcast 🎧	Listening Mediation G–E	Email
115	***	C3 The end of the American era? *Eliot A. Cohen*	Magazine article	Language awareness Speaking	Summary Discussion
117	Chapter Task	Giving a speech on why you would like to visit the USA		Speaking	Speech

PART THREE: One World

Chapter 6 — Beyond the Nation – Europe and a Globalized World

Page	Function	Part of chapter/Level/Title	Text type/Media	Communicative and language skills	Text type to be produced
118	Lead-in				
120	Words in Context	Globalization: Europe, the world	Informative text 🎧	Vocabulary skills Language awareness Mediation E–G	Oral presentation
	Part A	European integration as a model?			
122	***	A1 A great achievement of the past *Herman Van Rompuy*	Speech 🎧	Listening Language awareness Speaking	Presentation
124		A2 Europe's lost generation *Anna Isaac*	Newspaper article	Speaking	Speech
126		A3 Hunting for personnel *Sascha Schmierer*	German newspaper article		
127	Focus on Skills	Mediating texts in oral communication		MEDIATION G–E	Role-play
	Part B	Chances and risks of globalization			
128	*	B1 How big is the impact?	Film clip 🎬	Viewing Speaking	Comment/presentation
129		B2 The need for a new label *Lucy Siegle*	Newspaper article	Writing	Clothing label Magazine article
130	***	B3 The return of the nation state *Larry Elliott*	Newspaper article		
132	Focus on Skills	Using reading strategies (non-fictional texts)	Online article	READING Writing	Summary
	Part C	English as a global language			
133		C1 Keeping the accent *Aoife Mannix*	Poem	Reading Language awareness Writing	Short story/dramatic scene
134	*	C2 English as a global language *David Crystal*	Interview 🎧	Listening	Discussion
134		C3 Linguistic diplomacy: the Eurovision Song Contest *R.L.G.*	Newspaper article	Mediation E–G	Discussion
136	Culture Spot	Keeping our language clean?	Song 🎧	Listening Mediation G–E	
137	Chapter Task	'Slavery? Not today, not in Germany!' Preparing an exhibition	Pictures	Speaking	Presentation

Chapter 7 — Science – Enhancing Life?

Page	Function	Part of chapter/Level/Title	Text type/Media	Communicative and language skills	Text type to be produced
138	Lead-in				
140	Words in Context	Science – motor of progress?	Informative text 🎧	Vocabulary skills Language awareness	Description

Contents

Page	Function	Part of chapter / Level / Title	Text type / Media	Communicative and language skills	Text type to be produced
	Part A	**The genetic engineering debate**			
142		**A1 A saviour sibling** *Laura Roberts*	Newspaper article	Language awareness Speaking	Discussion Description
144	**Fact File**	**Ethics in science**	Informative text		
144		**A2 You are mine to kill** *Nick Dear*	Drama extract	Speaking	Discussion
146	*	**A3 Designer people**	Cartoon	Speaking	Discussion Short presentation
147	**Culture Spot**	**The Long Awaited (2008)** *Patricia Piccinini*	Sculpture	Writing	Email
148	***	**A4 Animals with bonus features** *Bob Holmes*	Magazine article	Speaking	Discussion
149	**Focus on Skills**	**Using reading strategies (scientific text)**		READING	Diagram, flowchart
	Part B	**Modifying mankind**			
150		**B1 A brain-enhancing pill**	TV news report ▶	Viewing Mediation E–G Writing	(Written) Discussion
151	***	**B2 Can this woman cure ageing with gene therapy?** *Dara Mohammadi and Nicola Davis*	Newspaper article	Language awareness Writing	Comment
	Part C	**Quenching the thirst for energy**			
155	*	**C1 The global demand for energy**	Graphs	Analysing graphs and charts Speaking	Discussion
156		**C2 The future of energy in Germany**	Informative text	Reading	Short written presentation
157	**Focus on Skills**	**Mediating written texts**		MEDIATION G–E	Summary
158		**C3 A possible future**	Interview 🎧	Listening Speaking	Discussion
158	*	**C4 Biofuels – the green alternative?**	Film clips ▶	Viewing Speaking	Discussion
159	**Chapter Task**	**Doing a WebQuest**		Speaking	Presentation

Chapter 8	Work and Business – Careers and Perspectives				
Page	Function	Part of chapter / Level / Title	Text type / Media	Communicative and language skills	Text type to be produced
160	**Lead-in**		Photos	Speaking	
162	**Words in Context**	**The world of work and business**	Informative text 🎧	Language awareness Vocabulary skills Speaking	
	Part A	**The right to a job – the right job**			
164	***	**A1 The second Bill of Rights** *Franklin D. Roosevelt*	Speech ▶	Language awareness Speaking Writing	Comment/ speech
165		**A2 More work, fewer workers** *Catherine Clifford*	Online article		

Contents

Page	Function	Part of chapter/Level/Title	Text type/Media	Communicative and language skills	Text type to be produced
167		**A3 Income inequality and guaranteed income** *Felix Oberholzer-Gee*	German newspaper article	Mediation E–G Writing	Article
168	**Fact File**	**Minimum wage and unconditional basic income**	Informative text	Speaking	
169		**A4 Teenagers' career aspirations** *Kirstie Donnelly*	Survey Preface	Writing	Argumentative text
170	**Focus on Skills**	**From informal to formal dialogues**		SPEAKING	Role-play
172		**A5 Do you love your job?** *Uwe Jean Heuser*	German newspaper article	Mediation G–E	Summary Role-play
173	**Culture Spot**	**Corporate Head (1991)** *Terry Allen, Philip Levine*	Sculpture Poem		
	Part B	**Stepping into the world of work**			
174		**B1 Mitch's first glimpses of the world of work** *Carl Deuker*	Novel extract	Writing	Email
176		**B2 Ten things not to say in a job interview** *Mark King*	Online article	Speaking	Discussion
177	*	**B3 Help wanted in Paradise** *Sarah Butler*	Newspaper article	Speaking	Discussion
179	**Focus on Skills**	**Writing a letter of motivation**		WRITING	Letter of motivation
180		**B4 Surviving a telephone interview**	Audio text 🎧	Listening Speaking	Role-play
180		**B5 Look them in the eye – the job interview**	Video clip ▶	Viewing	
181	**Chapter Task**	**Writing your personal statement**		Writing	Personal statement

PART FOUR: Challenges of the Present

Chapter 9 — Modern Media – Tools or Tyrants?

Page	Function	Part of chapter/Level/Title	Text type/Media	Communicative and language skills	Text type to be produced
182	**Lead-in**		Pictures, cartoon	Speaking	
184	**Words in Context**	**Living interactive lives**	Informative text 🎧	Vocabulary skills Language awareness	Discussion
	Part A	**Dis-connected**			
186		**A1 Lonely friends** *Ms Moem*	Poem ▶	Viewing Language awareness Mediation E–G Writing	Discussion Comment
187	**Culture Spot**	**New media art: *Viewpoint of Billions with Google Glass* (2013)** *David Datuna*	Photo Film clip ▶	Speaking	Discussion
188	***	**A2 Online learning in 2044** *Ernest Cline*	Novel extract	Language awareness Writing	Analysis
190	**Focus on Skills**	WRITING **Writing an argumentative text**		WRITING	Argumentative text
192	*	**A3 Digital media at school** *Gerhard Witossek*	German online article	Mediation G–E Speaking	Presentation

9

Contents

Page	Function	Part of chapter / Level / Title	Text type / Media	Communicative and language skills	Text type to be produced
	Part B	**Being on display**			
194	*	**B1 Should classrooms have video cameras?**	Online comments	Speaking Language awareness	Discussion Presentation
195	Fact File	**CCTV (Closed-Circuit Television)**	Informative text		Discussion
196	***	**B2 9/11 – a game changer** *Barack Obama*	Speech 🎧 Cartoon	Reading Speaking	Presentation
	Part C	**Truth and lies in modern media**			
198	***	**C1 The future of fake news: don't believe everything you read, see or hear** *Olivia Solon*	Newspaper article	Language awareness Writing	Guideline for a newsletter
201	Chapter Task	**Discussing the pros and cons of modern media**		Speaking Writing	Presentation Argumentative text

Chapter 10 — Urban, Suburban and Rural Life

Page	Function	Part of chapter / Level / Title	Text type / Media	Communicative and language skills	Text type to be produced
202	Lead-in		Photos	Speaking	
204	Words in Context	**The world becomes urbanized**	Informative text 🎧	Language awareness Vocabulary skills Speaking	
	Part A	**Big-city life**			
206		**A1 Living in London, New York, Rio de Janeiro** *Carlene Thomas-Bailey*	Online article	Speaking	Comment Speech
208	Focus on Skills	**Speaking in a panel discussion**		SPEAKING	Panel discussion
209	Fact File	**Changing urban lifestyles**	Informative text	Writing	Summary
210		**A2 Urban transformation**	Radio debate 🎧	Listening	
211		**A3 Urban decay, urban renewal** *Katja Kullmann, Alexandra Rotter*	German-language newspaper interview	Mediation (G–E) Writing	Email
212	***	**A4 Why US talent is moving to Detroit**	Film clip ▶	Viewing	
213	Culture Spot	**The Shard**	Photo Quotations		Discussion
	Part B	**In suburbia**			
214		**B1 The American suburb, then and now** *Leigh Gallagher*	Online article		
216		**B2 A suburban street** *John Lanchester*	Novel extract		
	Part C	**Take me home, country roads**			
218	*	**C1 Country life**	Painting Poem	Speaking	Poem
219		**C2 Small-town stories** *Garrison Keillor*	Preface		
221	Chapter Task	**A panel discussion**		Speaking	Panel discussion

Contents

222	Context Task

Support Pages

224	Chapter 1	236	Chapter 6
226	Chapter 2	238	Chapter 7
230	Chapter 3	240	Chapter 8
231	Chapter 4	242	Chapter 9
233	Chapter 5	244	Chapter 10

Reference Section

Language Practice

246		**Focus on Grammar**
246	LP 1	Simple and progressive verb forms
247	LP 2	Present tense or future?
248	LP 3	Simple present and present perfect
249	LP 4	Present perfect and simple past
250	LP 5	Infinitive or gerund after certain verbs
251	LP 6	Infinitive or gerund after certain nouns
252	LP 7	The passive
253	LP 8	Conditional sentences
254	LP 9	Articles, quantifiers and countability
255	LP 10	Using adjectives and adverbs
256		**Focus on Style**
256	LP 11	Using the right register
256	LP 12	Avoiding German-sounding sentence patterns
257	LP 13	Placing emphasis on key points 🎧
259	LP 14	Linking words and phrases
261	LP 15	Connecting your thoughts (sentence structure)
262		**Focus on Vocabulary**
262	LP 16	Avoiding Germanisms
263	LP 17	Spelling
263	LP 18	Writing about texts
264	LP 19	Collocations
266	LP 20	Word formation

Everyday English

268	EE 1	Eating in and out
268		Fact File: Eating out – American style
269	EE 2	Planning a trip using the internet
270	EE 3	Dealing with medical emergencies 🎧
270		Fact File: Getting medical assistance
271	EE 4	Making phone calls
272	EE 5	Watch your valuables!

Communicating across Cultures

273	CC 1	Cultural awareness
274	CC 2	The language of politeness
275	CC 3	Polite behaviour
275	CC 4	Meeting and greeting
276	CC 5	Making small talk 🎧
276	CC 6	Talking about sensitive issues 🎧
277		Fact File: Political correctness
277	CC 7	Making polite complaints 🎧

Language Awareness

279	LA 1	Varieties of English
280	LA 2	Communication problems and compensation strategies
281	LA 3	Similarities and differences of languages
282	LA 4	Influencing through language

Skills File

284		**Language learning and study skills**
284	SF 1	Dealing with unknown or new words
286	SF 2	Using a dictionary and a grammar book
287	SF 3	Doing research
288	SF 4	Doing project work
289	SF 5	Structuring information and ideas: visual aids and outlines
290	SF 6	Paraphrasing
291	SF 7	Working with closed test formats
292	SF 8	Learning languages with electronic devices
293	SF 9	Assessing yourself and giving feedback
294	SF 10	Finding and developing your individual language learning skills
295		**Text skills**
295	SF 11	Analysing pictures
295	SF 12	Analysing charts and graphs
297	SF 13	Analysing cartoons
300	SF 14	Reading strategies
301	SF 15	Marking up a text / Making and taking notes
302	SF 16	Identifying text types (non-fiction)
303	SF 17	Analysing stylistic devices
305	SF 18	Analysing non-fiction
306	SF 19	Analysing narrative prose
307	SF 20	Analysing drama
309	SF 21	Analysing poetry
311		**Listening and viewing skills**
311	SF 22	Listening
312	SF 23	Analysing a film ▶

Contents

314	**Speaking skills (monologues and dialogues)**	
314	SF 24	Giving a presentation
316	SF 25	Giving a speech
318	SF 26	Taking part in an interview
318	SF 27	Having a discussion
320	SF 28	Having a debate
322	**Writing skills**	
323	SF 29	Writing a formal letter or email
324	SF 30	Writing an application
326	SF 31	Writing a summary
327	SF 32	Writing a review
330	SF 33	Writing a report
331	SF 34	Argumentative writing
333	SF 35	Writing a character profile
335	SF 36	Writing a text analysis
336	SF 37	Doing a creative writing task
337	SF 38	Writing a well-structured text
338	SF 39	Quoting a text
340	SF 40	Proofreading
341	**Mediation skills**	
341	SF 41	Mediation of written and oral texts

Exam Practice		
343	EP 1	How to do exams in general
344	EP 2	Working with texts
352	EP 3	Mediation
354	EP 4	Listening and viewing
356	EP 5	Speaking
359	EP 6	Closed test formats

360	**Glossary**
377	**Historical Documents**
382	**Charts**
384	**Verbs for Tasks ('Operatoren')**
386	Acknowledgments

About the photograph on the cover of this book

The cover photo, taken in April 2013 near the junction of St Mary Axe and Leadenhall Street in London, shows a number of well-known buildings in the City of London's 'Tower Cluster' zone:

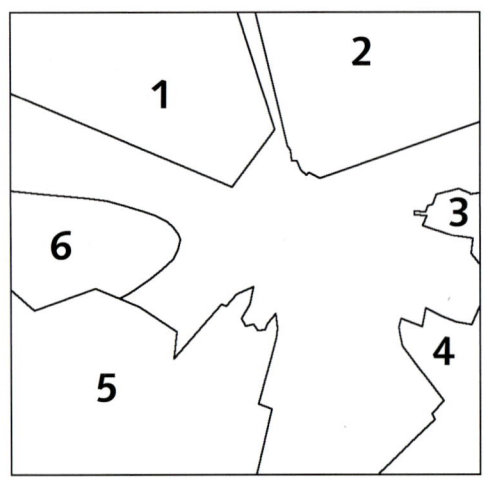

1 *St Helen's*, 1 Undershaft, Gollins Melvin Ward Partnership 1969, 28 storeys

2 *The Leadenhall Building (the Cheesegrater)*, 122 Leadenhall Street, Rogers Steark Harbour + Partners 2013, 48 storeys

3 *Lloyd's building*, 1 Lime Street, Richard Rogers 1986, 14 storeys

4 *Willis Building*, 51 Lime Street, Foster + Partners 2007, 26 storeys

5 *St Andrew Undershaft*, 1532

6 *30 St Mary Axe (the Gherkin)*, Foster + Partners 2003, 41 storeys

Abbreviations and labels used in *Context*

adj	adjective
adv	adverb
AE/BE	American English / British English
ca. *(Latin)*	circa = about, approximately
cf.	confer (compare), see
derog	derogatory *(abfällig, geringschätzig)*
e.g. *(Latin)*	exempli gratia = for example
esp.	especially
et al. *(Latin)*	et alii = and other people/things
etc. *(Latin)*	et cetera = and so on
f./ff.	and the following page(s)/line(s)
fml/infml	formal/informal English
i.e. *(Latin)*	id est = that is, in other words
jdm./jdn.	jemandem/jemanden
l./ll.	line/lines
n	noun
pt(s)	point(s)
p./pp.	page/pages
pl	plural
sb./sth.	somebody/something
sing	singular
sl	slang
usu.	usually
v	verb
vs. *(Latin)*	versus *(gegen, im Gegensatz zu)*

CC	Communicating across Cultures
EE	Everyday English
EP	Exam Practice
LA	Language Awareness
LP	Language Practice
SF	Skills File
PREVIEW	refers to the advance organizer (chapter preview) in the Lead-in of each chapter.
LANGUAGE AWARENESS	gives you information about a wide range of phenomena of the English language.
LANGUAGE HELP	gives you ideas, words and phrases to get started on tasks.
TROUBLE SPOT	points out language difficulties and common mistakes.
CHALLENGE	marks a more difficult task.
SUPPORT	refers you to the Support Pages (pp. 224–245) where you can find more help to do the assignment.
YOU CHOOSE	lets you decide which of the two given assignments you would like to do.
BASIC	marks a task that tests language skills you should already be familiar with.
***metaphor**	indicates that a word or expression (here: *metaphor*) is explained in the Glossary (pp. 360–376).
▶ **SF 21**	directs you to the Skills File (here: Skill 21).
▶ **LP 7**	directs you to the Language Practice section (here: Language task 7).
🎧 **CD2** 04	indicates that the sound file can be found on the accompanying audio CD (here: CD2, track 4).
🎬 **DVD**	indicates that the film or video clip can be found on the accompanying video DVD.
👆 **Webcode**	can be entered at www.cornelsen.de to connect you to a website with additional material or support.

A detailed list of sources and acknowledgements can be found on pp. 386ff. of this book.

1 Living One's Life – Individuals in Society

A

B

C

D

E

F

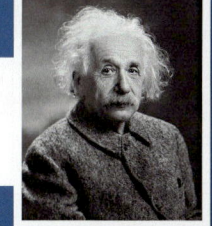

It is only to the individual that a soul is given.
ALBERT EINSTEIN

There is no such thing as society: there are individual men and women, and there are families.
MARGARET THATCHER

A hero is an ordinary individual who finds the strength to persevere and endure in spite of overwhelming obstacles.
CHRISTOPHER REEVE (ATTRIBUTED)

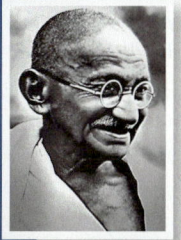

We but mirror the world. All the tendencies present in the outer world are to be found in the world of our body. If we could change ourselves, the tendencies in the world would also change.
MAHATMA GANDHI

You grown ups say you love us, but I challenge you, please make your actions reflect your words.
SEVERN SUZUKI

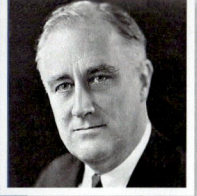

True individual freedom cannot exist without economic security and independence. People who are hungry and out of a job are the stuff of which dictatorships are made.
FRANKLIN D. ROOSEVELT

Ask not what your country can do for you – ask what you can do for your country.
JOHN F. KENNEDY

1 The individual and society

a Describe one of the pictures and note down what words, phrases and concepts come to mind when you look at it. Make a list or mind map.
b Now read the quotations. Comment on the one that speaks to you most.
c Match one quotation and one illustration. Explain your decision.

2 Famous individuals

a Work in groups of four. Each group picks one of the people quoted above. Do some research on their lives and find out what they did for society.
b Present your findings to other groups.

Download a list of chapter vocab here: 🖑 **Webcode** context-71

▶ SF 11: Analysing pictures

▶ SF 3: Doing research

PREVIEW

In this chapter you will reflect on your own role in society, consider how people view each other, and discuss ideas for getting involved in society and making a difference.

Main topics
- Identity and goals .... p. 18
- Stereotypes and prejudice .... p. 23
- Getting involved and making a difference ... p. 28

Focus on Skills: SPEAKING
- Resolving a heated argument .... p. 26
Chapter Task: Making a vlog about your own aims and ambitions or about an issue that matters to you .... p. 33

CD1 06
Listen to an audio version of the text on the CD or download it here:
 Webcode context-07

Young people in a multifaceted society

A generation full of hope

Today's young generation has lots of ideas about how to improve our world. Young people are often full of hope and creativity and have an incredible energy. They are not afraid to try something new, to get involved in big issues and to fight for what they want or believe in. They take part in demonstrations against war and discrimination and for equality and education. They use the internet as a means of communication as well as for political purposes. Many young people commit themselves to improving their communities and to making a difference to our world. They volunteer or work for charities, often helping people on the fringes of society like the disabled and homeless or collecting money for victims of natural disasters throughout the world. Today's teens are able to stand up for their beliefs and basic rights, and are smart and strong enough to shape the future of society for the better.

The media and youngsters

Nevertheless, at the same time, the media often paint a grim picture of the younger generation, appealing to stereotypes of young anti-social troublemakers. They are depicted as individuals who indulge in criminality, or who are obsessed by selfies and their self-image, or they may be depicted as alienated and socially impaired computer nerds with no time for real interaction with others. Age-based prejudice distorts the reality of the generation that will deal with the problems the older generation leaves behind.

Finding one's identity

Just like other generations, today's teens are not a uniform group. They do not all share a collective identity or share common experiences. Our individual character and our social background influence our identity. Family, education, culture and religion all have an influence on our moral values, attitudes and habits. Our sense of identity accounts for how we perceive ourselves and also how we are perceived and positioned by others. Our identities do not just determine our personal style but affect the opportunities we are given and our access to power, status, education and wealth. Like generations before them, young people must find out who they are and who they want to be in a diverse and ever-changing society. Unlike other generations, young people today have access to an immense variety of individual lifestyles. This opens up new possibilities for them to choose and construct their own identities, but it can also lead to conflicts and divided loyalties.

An unknown future

Living in a 'me-first' society and globalized world, young people are going to face big challenges in the future. Social inequality and unemployment, political instability and terrorism as well as environmental problems are just some of the pressing issues they will have to deal with. At the same time, the world is getting closer. With communication increasing, young people from different countries may be able to find creative solutions together to the most urgent problems.

5

10

15

20

25

30

35

40

45

1 Definitions

Match the definitions below to highlighted words and phrases from the text.
1 engage in
2 way of interacting with other people
3 speak or act in support of
4 constantly changing or developing
5 thinking only of yourself
6 important issues requiring immediate attention or action

2 Word formation and word families

Find the missing word. Use a dictionary if necessary.

verb	noun	adjective
improve		
volunteer		
	value	
	belief	
shape		
	stereotype	
		alienated
		moral
perceive		
	access	

▶ SF 1: Dealing with unknown or new words

▶ LP 20: Word formation

3 Words in use

a Complete each sentence with a verb from the grid.
  1 Young people are often … as troublemakers.
  2 Our identities are … by the people around us.
  3 Young people are concerned about how society … and … them.
  4 Many young people … family and friendship over having lots of money.

b **CHALLENGE** ▶ Activate your vocabulary – translate the following sentences. Pay special attention to the underlined expressions, which are highlighted in the text.
  1 Die großen Herausforderungen unserer vielschichtigen Welt erfordern kreative Lösungen und vor allem engagierte Individuen.
  2 Viele junge Leute sind heute bereit, sich einzubringen und sich für die Verbesserung der Lebensbedingungen von Menschen in den unterschiedlichen Teilen der Erde einzusetzen.
  3 Unsere Werte, Einstellungen und Gewohnheiten werden maßgeblich von unserer sozialen Herkunft geprägt.
  4 Häufig wird die Wahrnehmung anderer Menschen beeinflusst durch Stereotypen, Sichtweisen und Vorurteile, die das soziale Miteinander belasten.

▶ LP 16: Avoiding Germanisms

4 Writing

Outline how you see your own generation and what you think are the greatest challenges your generation has to face. Write a short comment.

▶ SF 38: Writing a well-structured text

▶ SF 34: Argumentative writing

Future success

A1 Successful children *Amy Chua*

· With a partner, discuss what your aims in life are, where these aims come from, who supports you on your way, and what helps you to achieve your aims.

Amy Chua, a professor of law at Yale University, is the child of Chinese immigrants and is herself the mother of two daughters. In her book Battle Hymn of the Tiger Mother *(2011) she describes her strict parenting techniques, which she thinks make children successful.*

A lot of people wonder how Chinese parents raise such stereotypically successful kids. They wonder what these parents do to produce so many math whizzes and music prodigies, what it's like inside the family, and whether they could do it too. Well, I can tell them, because I've done it. Here are some things my daughters, Sophia and Louisa, were never allowed to do: 5

· attend a sleepover
· have a playdate
· be in a school play
· complain about not being in a school play
· watch TV or play computer games   10
· choose their own extracurricular activities
· get any grade less than an A
· not be the #1 student in every subject
  except gym and drama
· play any instrument other than the piano   15
  or violin
· not play the piano or violin.

I'm using the term 'Chinese mother' loosely. I recently met a supersuccessful white guy from South Dakota (you've seen him on television), and after comparing notes we decided that his working-class father had definitely been a Chinese mother. I know   20
some Korean, Indian, Jamaican, Irish, and Ghanaian parents who qualify too. Conversely, I know some mothers of Chinese heritage, almost always born in the West, who are not Chinese mothers, by choice or otherwise. [...]

What Chinese parents understand is that nothing is fun until you're good at it. To get good at anything you have to work, and children on their own never want to work,   25
which is why it is crucial to override their preferences. This often requires fortitude on the part of the parents because the child will resist; things are always hardest at the beginning, which is where Western parents tend to give up. But if done properly, the Chinese strategy produces a virtuous circle. Tenacious practice, practice, practice is crucial for excellence; rote repetition is underrated in America. Once a child starts to   30
excel at something – whether it's math, piano, pitching, or ballet – he or she gets praise, admiration, and satisfaction. This builds confidence and makes the once not-fun activity fun. This in turn makes it easier for the parent to get the child to work even more. [...]

I think there are three big differences between the Chinese and Western parental   35
mind-sets.

---

2 **whizz** *(infml)* person who is very good at sth.
22 **conversely** [kɒnˈvɜːsli] *(adv) (fml)* umgekehrt
26 **crucial** extremely important
override sth. reject sth., cancel sth.
fortitude strength of mind
29 **tenacious** [təˈneɪʃəs] not giving up; persistent
30 **rote repetition** method of learning sth. by repeating it continually
31 **pitching** *(in baseball)* throwing the ball at the batter

First, I've noticed that Western parents are extremely anxious about their children's self-esteem. They worry about how their children will feel if they fail at something, and they constantly try to reassure their children about how good they are notwith-
40 standing a mediocre performance on a test or at a recital. In other words, Western parents are concerned about their children's psyches. Chinese parents aren't. They assume strength, not fragility, and as a result they behave very differently.

For example, if a child comes home with an A-minus on a test, a Western parent will most likely praise the child. The Chinese mother will gasp in horror and ask what
45 went wrong. If the child comes home with a B on the test, some Western parents will still praise the child. [...] If a Chinese child gets a B – which would never happen – there would first be a screaming, hair-tearing explosion. The devastated Chinese mother would then get dozens, maybe hundreds of practice tests and work through them with her child for as long as it takes to get the grade up to an A. Chinese parents
50 demand perfect grades because they believe that their child can get them. If their child doesn't get them, the Chinese parent assumes it's because the child didn't work hard enough. That's why the solution to substandard performance is always to excoriate, punish, and shame the child. The Chinese parent believes that their child will be strong enough to take the shaming and to improve from it. [...]
55 Second, Chinese parents believe that their kids owe them everything. [...] Anyway, the understanding is that Chinese children must spend their lives repaying their parents by obeying them and making them proud. By contrast, I don't think most Westerners have the same view of children being permanently indebted to their parents. Jed [Amy Chua's husband] actually has the opposite view. 'Children don't
60 choose their parents,' he once said to me. 'They don't even choose to be born. It's parents who foist life on their kids, so it's the parents' responsibility to provide for them. Kids don't owe their parents anything. Their duty will be to their own kids.' This strikes me as a terrible deal for the Western parent.

Third, Chinese parents believe that they know what is best for their children and
65 therefore override all of their children's own desires and preferences. That's why Chinese daughters can't have boyfriends in high school and why Chinese kids can't go to sleepaway camp. It's also why no Chinese kid would ever dare say to their mother, 'I got a part in the school play! I'm Villager Number Six. I'll have to stay after school for rehearsal every day from 3:00 to 7:00, and I'll also need a ride on weekends.'
70 God help any Chinese kid who tried that one.

Don't get me wrong: It's not that Chinese parents don't care about their children. Just the opposite. They would give up anything for their children. It's just an entirely different parenting model. I think of it as Chinese, but I know a lot of non-Chinese parents – usually from Korea, India, or Pakistan – who have a very similar mind-set,
75 so it may be an immigrant thing. Or maybe it's the combination of being an immigrant and being from certain cultures.

From: *Battle Hymn of the Tiger Mother*, 2011, pp. 3–6, 47–48, 56–59

COMPREHENSION ◀

1 Examining parental styles
Describe the two contrasting parenting styles Chua refers to.

ANALYSIS ◀

2 Examining a book title
Analyse the title of Chua's book and explain what it tells us about her parenting philosophy.

39 **notwithstanding** in spite of
40 **mediocre** [ˌmiːdiˈəʊkə] not very good, (only) average
42 **fragility** [frəˈdʒɪləti] weakness
52 **excoriate sb.** (*fml*) criticize sb. severely
61 **foist sth. on sb.** force sth. on sb.

▶ LP 8: Conditional sentences

■ **LANGUAGE AWARENESS**

Influencing through language
By using rather formal style and language in your text, you create an atmosphere that has an impact on the readers (here: a 'no-nonsense' style of language that reflects the proposed educational style). Generally, you can use a specific style in order to support a particular view you want to express.

▶ LA 4: Influencing through language

▶ SF 34: Argumentative writing

■ **LANGUAGE HELP**

- If I were you, I'd …
- The best thing to do is …
- I don't think it's advisable to …
- It might be better to …
- You definitely should/ought to …
- If you ask me, I would/ wouldn't …

▶ CC 6: Talking about sensitive issues

▶ SF 27: Having a discussion

— **LANGUAGE AWARENESS** ◀

3 What if …?

a Read ll. 43–53 again and identify the grammar construction used extensively in these lines. Analyse its function and explain why the writer uses it. SUPPORT ▶ p. 224

b Find other verbal and stylistic elements in the text that contribute to its style and atmosphere.

— **BEYOND THE TEXT** ◀

4 YOU CHOOSE ▶ Examining statements

a Choose one or more of Amy Chua's statements and comment on them from your own point of view.

OR

b Discuss one of the following statements, referring to Chua:
- Parents can never be friends with their children.
- The stricter the parents, the sneakier the child
- A child simply needs – and profits from – discipline

5 Giving advice

a Imagine that Chua's daughter, 17-year-old Louisa, is a friend of yours and rebels against her mother's strict parenting style. Discuss with a partner what advice you would give her. Try to see both sides.

b Now write a longer email to Louisa, giving your advice. ▶ LANGUAGE HELP

6 A mother-daughter argument

a Louisa refuses to obey her mother and they have an argument. Divide the class in two halves. One half prepares Louisa's arguments, the other half Amy's. You may take notes on little cue cards.

b Pair up with another student from the other side and start your argument.

c Tell the others in class about your argument. How did it end? Could you solve the conflict? Why (not)?

A2 Growing up queer in 2018 *Arianna Balderrama*

· PLACEMAT ACTIVITY

Before you read the text below, form groups of four around a large sheet of paper. In your corner of the paper, write down ways in which people your age style their appearance. When everyone is finished, compare your answers. In the centre of the page, write down reasons why teens are often concerned with the image they project.

'Fag!' The word flew out the driver's side window of a beat up, dark car. I lifted my head from looking at my shoes and saw that the word had come screeching out of a painfully average man, who had a child in the backseat. It festered in the air for a moment, followed by the sound of low tires traveling away. I wasn't sure if it was
5   directed to me or the friend beside me.

I examined my friend, a male with black hair pointing east, wearing activewear. Clearly, he was male-presenting, whereas I wore a button-up closed to the top. The shirt that once gained me compliments and boosted my confidence now felt stained, dirty, and vacant. My hair was shaved on the left only, and on the right side it was
10 tucked behind my ear.

The confusion lifted. Obviously, it was to me.

I cut my hair short for the first time after not attending school because of too much stress. Watching the curls fall out of my head, then burning the remaining strands straight, felt liberating. This was what I desired for years on end, and I was finally
15 comfortable enough to do it without thinking about the opinions of others. Compliments for the unfamiliar were scribbled upon me in school.

Burning my hair to a crisp every morning sure gave me an overwhelming confidence boost. Running my hands to the shaven side was a new habit I had picked up. I felt better.
20 Middle school is a bright time for insecurities to shine. The new change of my outward appearance felt mundane at the time, but now, the backlash of the encounter from a vehicle was ghastly. In that moment, I was thinking perhaps I should have never cut it off, or worn a more feminine top? Maybe I could have gotten ready, instead of throwing on some clothes and rushing to school.
25 I like to think I live my life pretty okay, about a C- on the grade scale. It's not good, but I'm passing. Being 15 and identifying as queer has not left me with many difficulties, as it would have in previous years. I'm constantly complimented for my short hair and sense of style. I'm aware that I am able to express who I am to so many people, freely.
30 Personally, I have come to realize many teens my age are not bothered much about sexuality or identity. They are accepting and open minded. That's not to say acceptance is 100 percent, but it's getting there.

The difference between the past and today is discussion. Living in a time where digital technology is glued to people my age, information is spread rapidly.
35 The internet has given me news updates and profiles of queer youth around the world. To an extent, I am granted a sense of ease. That ease also comes from how young people view the world and have the determination to change it. It fuels me with motivation to create positive change for my future. Social media fills younger folks like myself with comfort that solitude is not possible. Knowing I am not alone with
40 my ideas is enough to propel me to become a better person.

I do not pursue communicating with others through social media. Rather, I enjoy exploring the profile set ups of individuals and reading their publicized thoughts. It's

······▶

1 **fag** (AE, derog) homosexual male
2 **screech** (v) scream
3 **fester** eitern
6 **activewear** sportswear
7 **button-up** button-up shirt
8 **stained** (adj) having dirty spots on it
9 **vacant** empty
10 **tuck sth.** etwas stecken
13 **strand** piece of hair
14 **for years on end** for a very long time
16 **scribble sth.** write sth. hastily
17 **burn sth. to a crisp** heat sth. until it is burnt and stiff
20 **insecurity** lack of confidence
21 **mundane** unspectacular
backlash aftereffect
22 **ghastly** horrible
25 **grade** (AE) = **mark** (BE)
26 **identifying as queer** openly showing that you are not heterosexual
30 **be bothered about sth.** regard sth. as a problem
34 **be glued to sb.** be closely linked to sb.
36 **to an extent** gewissermaßen
be granted sth. be given sth.
ease (n) state of being without worry
39 **solitude** feeling of being alone
40 **propel sb.** [- '-] motivate sb.
41 **pursue sth.** actively seek sth.

■ LANGUAGE AWARENESS

Using politically correct language
Being 'politically correct' means that you notice expressions and actions that may exclude, marginalize, or offend a particular group of people. When it comes to language, it means that you should avoid disrespectful remarks or jokes that refer to someone's gender, race, culture, religion or sexual orientation. Staying respectful helps promote understanding and equality.

▶ LA 2: Communication problems and compensation strategies

43 **the beauty** the good thing about it
45 **inevitable** [- '---] unavoidable
47 **appreciate sth.** [ə'priː.ʃeɪt] be thankful for sth.
48 **like-minded** thinking the same way
50 **across the board** from a wide variety of backgrounds
51 **the luxury** the advantage
54 **realm** [relm] world
   thrive gedeihen
55 **empowerment** control over one's life
56 **degrading** (adj) abusive
   advocate sth. speak out in favour of sth.
57 **jerk** (sl) unpleasant person
   rock sth. (sl) wear sth. (an item of clothing)
   mating call Lockruf
48 **heteronormative** making heterosexuality the norm

both personal and public. The beauty is that you can say anything, and at least one person will connect with you.

I'm fearful of what others think of me, but I know judgement is inevitable. I personally do not enjoy sharing fragments of my life too often through social media; however, I appreciate that others do. Twitter threads of personal experiences and Instagram pictures of trips are all openly shared between like-minded people. Social media platforms have assisted us in being able to voice our thoughts and find counter-arguments and agreements from people across the board. 50

My school labels itself as a safe space, and so far, the term is fitting. The luxury lies within the group of girls promoting self love, or perhaps in the teachers motivating students to become a better version of themselves. My personal surroundings are a positive realm to thrive in, and the difficulty is minimal.

As a queer female, empowerment from others, both personally and through social 55 media, is much needed. Degrading terms are avoided and love is advocated.

And to the jerk in the beat up car, I have short hair and rock button ups as a mating call for girls, not to fit in your heteronormative world, jerk.

From: 'Growing up queer in 2018', *Out Front Magazine*, 12 January 2018

COMPREHENSION

1 Appearance and self-image
  a Describe how Arianna changed her image in middle school and how she felt about it at the time.
  b Explain why she was confused when a stranger shouted abuse at her and a friend.

ANALYSIS

2 Examining the writer's attitude
  a Point out statements that describe Arianna's feelings toward the society she lives in. SUPPORT ▶ p. 224
  b Analyse the reasons she names for her assessment.

LANGUAGE AWARENESS

3 Connotation
  a Arianna uses many words that convey a positive or negative feeling ('connotation'). Group the following words from the text into two groups words with a positive connotation / words with a negative connotation.
  fester (l. 3) – *boost* (l. 8) – *accepting* (l. 31) – *comfort* (l. 39) – *empowerment* (l. 55) – *degrading* (l. 52) – *heteronormative* (l. 58)
  b Find four more words from the text and add them to your lists. Then compare results with a partner.

BEYOND THE TEXT

4 Thinking about your own school
  a Arianna's school calls itself a 'safe space' (l. 51) for all students regardless of their sexual orientation. Rank the school you go to on a scale from 1 to 6 (school marks) based on the degree of acceptance among the students.
  b Form groups of four or five. Compare your rankings and discuss the reasons for your assessments.

A3 Stereotypes in Los Angeles *Paul Haggis*

The film Crash *(2004) tells the interwoven stories of several individuals in Los Angeles and portrays the racial and social tensions between them.*

· Look at the film stills below and speculate about the characters, their personalities and the relationships between them. How might the lives of the two young men and the couple collide?

Scene 1: Ext.   Westwood – Night

Italian restaurant. Anthony flies out the door, Peter just one step behind him. They're in their early twenties, young, hip, well-dressed men, friends since third grade. They button their jackets as they head down the sidewalk.

1 **Ext.** exterior
Westwood district of Los Angeles
16 **size sb. up** *(infml)* decide quickly what another person is like
17 **tip (sb.)** *(jdm.) Trinkgeld geben*
21 **kinda** *(infml)* kind of

5 ANTHONY   You see any white people in there waiting an hour and thirty-two minutes for a plate of spaghetti? Huh? And how many cups of coffee did we get?

PETER   You don't drink coffee and I didn't want any.

ANTHONY   That woman poured cup after cup to every single white person around
10   us. Did she even ask you if you wanted any?

PETER   We didn't get any coffee that you didn't want and I didn't order, and this is evidence of racial discrimination? Did you happen to notice our waitress was black?

ANTHONY   And black women don't think in stereotypes? When's the last time you
15   met one who didn't think she knew everything about your lazy ass before you even opened your mouth? That waitress sized us up in two seconds. We're black, and 'black people don't tip' so she wasn't gonna waste her time; someone like that, nothing you can do to change their mind.

20 PETER   So how much did you leave her?

ANTHONY   You expect me to pay for that kinda service?

Peter laughs; Anthony doesn't.

ANTHONY   ... What? What?

PETER   Nothing, nothing.

25 *Rick & Jean Cabot, white, early 40s, head for their car. Jean pulls her jacket closed as they walk.*

RICK   You're seriously jealous of Karen??

JEAN   Hardly. I'd just like to see you get through a meal without calling her, or someone else at your office.

30 RICK   See this? Off. No more calls tonight.

·····▶

A **stereotype** is a fixed, over-generalized belief about a particular group of people. One advantage of a stereotype is that it enables us to respond quickly to situations because we may have had a similar experience before. One dis-advantage is that it makes us ignore differences between individuals, so that we end up making simplistic generaliza-tions about individuals or groups.

Prejudice is an unjustified or incorrect attitude that is usually negative towards an individual based solely on the individual's membership of a social group. For example, a person may hold prejudiced views towards a certain race or gender, etc.

Discrimination is negative behaviour or action towards an individual or group of people due to their sex/race/social class, etc.

Microaggressions are often unintended racist or sexist comments that make a person feel underestimated on the basis of their colour or gender.

---

38 **UCLA** (abbr) University of California, Los Angeles
43 **trigger-happy** (infml, disap-proving) willing and quick to use violence, esp. a gun
44 **LAPD** (abbr) Los Angeles Police Department
45 **Int.** interior
47 **locksmith** person who repairs locks (= Schlosser/in)
52 **pantry** small room next to a kitchen where food is stored
64 **patronize sb.** ['pætrənaɪz] treat sb. like a child

Jean notices Anthony and Peter and takes Rick's arm.

JEAN	Ten bucks says she calls on the car phone.
ANTHONY	You see what that woman just did?
PETER	She's cold.
ANTHONY	She got colder as soon as she saw us.	35
PETER	Here it comes.
ANTHONY	Look around! You couldn't find a whiter, safer or better-lit part of this city. But this white woman sees two black guys who look like UCLA students strolling down the sidewalk, and her reaction is blind fear. I mean, look at us. Are we dressed like gangbangers? Do we look threat-ening? No. Fact, if anybody should be scared around here, it's us: the only two black faces surrounded by a sea of over-caffeinated white people patrolled by the trigger-happy LAPD. So, why aren't *we* scared?	40

Scene 2: Int. Rick & Jean's Home – Night

Jean's feet descend the stairs to the expensive kitchen, where Daniel, the Hispanic 45
locksmith, re-keys the door. He's twentyish, close-cropped hair, baggy pants, tattoos.

JEAN	How much longer are you going to be?
DANIEL	This is the last door.
JEAN	Thanks.

She exits, walking through the pantry into the dining room where several staff members 50
work. She turns into the living room, where Rick and two aides work up strategy.

JEAN	*(interrupting)* I need to talk to you for a second.

She exits without waiting for a response. Rick turns to Karen, his top aide (young, black, brilliant).

RICK	Just find Flanagan.	55

Karen dials as Rick exits to the [...] hall off the kitchen where Jean waits, arms crossed so tightly they're squeezing all the air out of her lungs.

JEAN	I want the locks changed again in the morning.
RICK	Honey, why don't you go to bed? Did you check on James?
JEAN	Of course I checked on James. I've checked on him every five minutes since we've been home, don't patronize me! I want the locks changed again in the morning!	60
RICK	Shhh, it's ok. You just need to lie down.
JEAN	Didn't I just ask you not to treat me like a child? [...] I want the locks changed again in the morning. And you could mention that we'd appreci-ate it if next time they didn't send a gang member.	65
RICK	*(lowering his voice)* You're talking about that kid in there?
JEAN	Shaved head, pants down around his ass, prison tattoos!
RICK	Oh for Christ sakes, those aren't prison tattoos!
JEAN	Right, and he isn't going to sell our key to one of his gangbanger friends the moment he's out the door.	70
RICK	Jean, it's been a tough night. Why don't you go upstairs and …
JEAN	… wait for them to break in? *(in a rage)* I just had a gun pointed in my face.
RICK	You lower your voice.
JEAN	And it's my fault because I knew it was going to happen. But if a white person sees two black men walking towards them and turns and walks the other way, she's a racist, right? Well, I got scared, and I didn't say anything and ten seconds later I had a gun in my face.	75

---

80 Now, I'm telling you that your amigo in there is going to sell our house key to one of his homies! And this time it would be really fucking nice if you acted like you actually cared!!

Jean turns and storms into the kitchen. Rick stares at her as she makes a show of wiping down the counter.

From: *Crash. Draft with Final Revisions*, 2004, pp. 8–10, 29–32

80 **homie** *(infml)* member of the same gang

COMPREHENSION ◀

1 Knowing what happened

Something happened between these two scenes. What was it?

1 Rick and Jean's house was broken into, and most of the jewellery and computers were stolen.

2 Jean discovered that Rick is having an affair with Karen.

3 Daniel meets Anthony and Peter and they discuss how to rob rich people's houses.

4 Rick and Jean were assaulted by Anthony and Peter, who stole their car, their money and their house keys.

▶ SF 7: Working with closed test formats

2 Understanding disagreements

a Summarize Anthony and Peter's conversation.

b Then write a summary of Jean and Rick's argument at home.

▶ SF 31: Writing a summary

LANGUAGE AWARENESS ◀

3 Spoken language

Find words and phrases in the two scenes which show typical features of conversations. Discuss which of these words and phrases are acceptable in a written document, too, and which should be reformulated.

▶ SF 20: Analysing drama
▶ LP 11: Using the right register

■ LANGUAGE AWARENESS

Spoken and written English
Similar to many other languages, there are specific differences between spoken and written English, such as different lengths of utterances, short forms vs. long forms, colloquial vs. more formal phrases, or paratactical vs. hypertactical constructions.

ANALYSIS ◀

4 Examining the characters

a Describe the characters, their different views, their use of language and their behaviour.

b Now view the two film scenes. Analyse the characters' facial expressions, gestures and voices. How do these elements add to their characterization?

c Discuss your personal reaction to the characters with a partner and comment on the characters' views and behaviour.

▶ LA 1: Varieties of English

 DVD

▶ SF 23: Analysing a film

5 Examining stereotypes

a Explain what stereotypes are, and give examples from each scene. Use the Fact File (p. 24) for help.

b Analyse the role stereotypes and prejudice play in the dialogues in the text, reflecting on how the characters perceive each other and the influence this has on their relationships.

BEYOND THE TEXT ◀

6 YOU CHOOSE ▶ Stereotypes in everyday life

a Describe a situation in which you were or somebody else was confronted with stereotypes. Tell a partner about it and reflect about your experiences.

 OR

b Discuss the function of stereotypes in everyday life: how they influence our perception of others and how we deal with them. SUPPORT ▶ p. 225

■ **LANGUAGE AWARENESS**

Verbal and non-verbal communication
Non-verbal features such as volume, facial expressions and gestures play an important part in face-to-face conversation. Pay attention to and control your body language, especially when you want to solve a conflict.

▶ LA 4: Influencing through language

▶ SF 37: Doing a creative writing task

▶ LP 11: Using the right register
▶ SF 27: Having a discussion

SPEAKING FOCUS ON SKILLS

Resolving a heated argument

When people have opposing points of view or interests, they may start to argue. Everybody – willingly or not – uses different strategies to heat up or cool down a conflict. Usually, people feel offended if somebody orders them around ('Stop this now.'), threatens them ('If you don't …, I will …'), blames them ('You are always …'), evaluates their behaviour ('You're always trying to …'), or shouts at them. A set of communicative strategies can be helpful to solve a conflict.

1 Strategies to cool down a conflict
Choose five of the strategies below and rank them according to their importance. Exchange your ideas with a partner and try to agree on a list of the five most effective strategies. Present your results to the rest of the class.
1 Respect the other person.
2 Try to find a win–win resolution.
3 Relax. Take a deep breath. Speak slowly and softly.
4 Listen carefully to what the other person is saying.
5 Use 'I' messages. Such as: 'I feel bad when you do that.'
6 Put what the other person said in your own words to make sure you understand. ('I understood … Is that what you meant?')
7 Watch your language and use words like 'maybe' and 'perhaps'.
8 Ask for a break if you need to collect your thoughts or release stress.

2 Analysing and solving a conflict
a Go back to p. 66. Describe and analyse the conflict between Rick and Jean. Pay special attention to their language and behaviour.
b Discuss what Rick and Jean might have done to achieve better communication. Which of the strategies could each of them use?
c Rewrite parts of the dialogue between Rick and Jean to make it end in a positive way.

3 Dealing with aggression
a List a few everyday conflicts between, for example, parents and children, men and women, or friends, in which people become aggressive.
b Together with a partner, role-play a few of these situations. One partner is verbally aggressive, while the other partner tries to calm the other by stating his or her observations, feelings, needs and requests. Here is how it might go:
1 'I noticed you …' (observation).
2 'When you did that, I felt …' (feeling).
3 'I need …' (need)
4 'therefore, I'm hoping you'll …' (request)
c Change roles so that each of you can try out the observation-feeling-need-request method.
d Report back to the group what you think about this way of reacting to aggression.

⦿ CULTURE SPOT

Graffiti and street art

'Imagine a city where graffiti wasn't illegal, a city where everybody could draw whatever they liked. Where every street was awash with a million colours and little phrases. Where standing at a bus stop was never boring. A city that felt like a party where everyone was invited, not just the estate agents and barons of big business. Imagine a city like that and stop leaning against the wall – it's wet.'

From: Banksy, *Wall and Piece*, 2014

1   Look at the street art by the British artist Banksy in the photos. Describe the images and say why you think they were made.

2   State which ones you like, and why.

3   Discuss which ones should be saved.

4   Most art can be bought and sold at a price. Discuss who owns street art.

5   Comment on Banksy's statement.

Getting involved

B1 Young people raising their voices

1 Young people making a difference

a **EXPERT GROUPS** Get together in groups of four. Each student has a number (1–4). Each group researches one of the three young people featured below. Individually, find information about them, their lives, their stories and their achievements, then compare your results in your group.

Emma Gonzalez

'All of these people are getting paid to do nothing about guns, and we as a people are doing nothing in response, so that's our fault. It's the people's fault for not doing something.'

Quoted in: Wesley Lowery, 'Emma González hated guns before. Now, she's speaking out on behalf of her dead classmates', *The Washington Post*, 21 February 2018

Malala Yousafzai

'Let us pick up our books and our pens. They are our most powerful weapons. One child, one teacher, one book and one pen can change the world.'

Quote from the speech that Yousafzai gave to the United Nations on 12 July 2013

Boyan Slat

'I never felt youth to be a dis-advantage. With age often comes prior knowledge, which may be limiting. Because I had no clue of all the reservations that could be brought up against my idea, I went ahead and started working on it. I may not have done so if I had been older.'

Quoted in: Avital Andrews, 'Boyan Slat's plan to clean Earth's oceans', *Pacific Standard*, 12 June 2017

b **JIGSAW GROUPS** Form new groups with the students who have the same number as you. As an expert, present 'your' young person to the others. In the end, everyone in your new group should be well informed about each of the three young people.

2 Visions and ideas

a Discuss which of the three young people (including their work and vision) you find most interesting and why.

b **CHALLENGE** **HOT SEAT** Act the part of one of the young people in question. Answer questions from the rest of the class on your ideas, motives and beliefs.

3 Raising your voice

Apart from children's rights, what do you think are pressing issues that should be discussed and that people should raise their voices for?

■ **LANGUAGE AWARENESS**

Using quotations
When introducing yourself, another person or an important topic, it can be very effective to use a short, but expressive or perhaps humorous quotation – but don't overdo it. Make sure that you use a reliable source to quote from.

▶ LA 4: Influencing through language

▶ SF 26: Taking part in an interview

B2 It could have been me

In the early morning hours of 12 June 2016, more than 300 people were having a good time at the Pulse nightclub in Orlando, Florida, a popular meeting place for gays, when a gunman entered and opened fire. Before he was killed by the police he had murdered 49 people and injured 53 others. Eddie Meltzer talked to NPR's Ari Shapiro about what he did later that day.

Find a link to the interview here:
Webcode context-72

1 Listening for gist

Listen to the interview (00:47–06:21). Choose the correct statement from the three below.

1 Eddie volunteered to help because he was an eye-witness to the shooting.
2 Eddie volunteered to help because he is bilingual.
3 Eddie volunteered to help because he knew a lot of the victims personally.

▶ SF 22: Listening

2 Listening for detail

a Listen to the interview again and take notes on the following aspects:
 – people who needed special help
 – being prepared for a crisis situation
 – Eddie's personal loss
 – his motivation for getting involved
b Compare notes with a partner.

3 Getting involved

In a small group, make a list of other emergency situations that can occur. Discuss the reasons why people spontaneously offer their help.

B3 Volunteering in Germany *Alexandra Mankarios*

A friend of yours in California is active in a number of volunteer organizations. You have been discussing volunteering in the USA compared to Germany. You come across the following article about volunteer work in Germany.

Sie lesen Kindern vor, begleiten Sterbende, sammeln Unterschriften gegen Tierversuche oder retten unvorsichtige Badeurlauber vor dem Ertrinken. Sie löschen Brände, unterstützen Flüchtlinge oder organisieren Tauschbörsen in der Nachbarschaft. Etwas freiwillig für die Gesellschaft zu tun, ist ein Trend in Deutschland geworden:
5 Über ein Drittel der Bundesbürger engagiert sich ehrenamtlich in Vereinen, Initiativen oder anderen Gruppen. Und ihre Zahl wächst.

Der Hauptgrund für den Dienst an anderen ist keineswegs immer die Selbstlosigkeit, fand das Deutsche Zentrum für Altersfragen im Freiwilligensurvey, einer repräsentativen Umfrage zum Bürgerschaftlichen Engagement in Deutschland
10 heraus. Das Engagement soll vor allem Spaß machen und einem selbst neue Freundeskreise eröffnen. Erst an zweiter Stelle steht das Bedürfnis, anderen zu helfen, an dritter folgt die Aussicht, zum Gemeinwohl beizutragen und vielleicht sogar dabei ein bedeutendes soziales Zeichen zu setzen.

Keine Frage – nicht jede kleine Nachbarschaftsinitiative sitzt ein Jahr nach ihrer
15 Gründung bereits am runden Tisch mit der Lokalpolitik und berät im übernächsten Jahr die Vereinten Nationen. Aber viele soziale Organisationen, die heute weltweit Einfluss auf Politiker und Wirtschaftsunternehmen ausüben, haben einmal ganz klein angefangen [...] So ging etwa ab 1989 eine Gründungswelle der Obdachlosen-

zeitungen um die Welt. Und rund 900 Tafeln versorgen heute Menschen in ganz Deutschland mit Lebensmitteln, die früher im Müll gelandet wären. Die Idee [20] entstand 1993 in Berlin. Sowohl die Macher der Obdachlosenzeitungen als auch die Betreiber der Tafeln verstehen sich nicht nur als Hilfsorganisationen, sondern nehmen auch politisch Einfluss.

Parallel zur rasanten Verbreitung dieser Erfolgsprojekte lässt sich in Deutschland ein zweiter Trend beobachten: wachsende Politikverdrossenheit. Seit Anfang der [25] 1990er Jahre sinken die Mitgliederzahlen der Parteien von Jahr zu Jahr, seit 1998 nimmt auch die Wahlbeteiligung bei der Bundestagswahl kontinuierlich ab. 1997 lautete das Wort des Jahres „Reformstau". Anfang des neuen Jahrtausends wehte mit der Agenda 2010 ein deutlich kälterer Wind als bisher durch das Sozialsystem.

Beide Entwicklungen gehören zusammen. Das Vertrauen der Bürger in den Staat [30] nimmt ab. Was liegt also näher, als die Geschicke der Gesellschaft eben selbst in die Hand zu nehmen? Allerdings nicht als aufopferungsvolle Lückenbüßer, sondern als aktive Mitgestalter. Die Folge: Im so genannten Dritten Sektor, dem Bereich des Bürgerschaftlichen Engagements, ist mehr Bewegung denn je zu spüren.

36 Prozent der Deutschen engagieren sich freiwillig, 27 Prozent sind nicht dazu [35] bereit, so der Deutsche Freiwilligensurvey. Die übrigen 37 Prozent sind eine Art „Schläfer": Sie engagieren sich zwar aktuell nicht, sind aber dazu bereit. Vor allem Zeitmangel und Mobilität werden als Gründe genannt, warum sich Menschen nicht so stark engagieren, wie sie gern würden. Anderen fehlt möglicherweise einfach die Inspiration, aus den unzähligen Vereinen, Initiativen, Organisationen und kirch- [40] lichen Angeboten das passende zu wählen.

Hier können Freiwilligenagenturen Abhilfe schaffen. Seit der Gründung der ersten Agentur dieser Art 1988 in Berlin ist kaum ein Flecken in Deutschland übrig geblie- ben, dessen soziale Organisationen nicht von den Freiwilligen-Netzwerken erfasst sind. Der Service führt heute meist sogar per Mausklick [45] zum Ziel: Wer sich engagieren möchte, kann sich online in den Datenbanken der Agenturen über lokale Organisationen informieren und erfahren, wo welche Art der Unter- stützung gebraucht wird. Von Alkoho- [50] lismus bis Zivilschutz steht eine breite Themenpalette zur Auswahl, die Tätig- keiten reichen vom einmaligen Anpacken bis hin zum langfristigen, qualifizierten Engagement. [55]

From: 'Wecke den engagierten Bürger in dir', *Stern*, 29 November 2014

▶ SF 41: Mediation of written and oral texts

▶ SF 27: Having a discussion

COMPREHENSION ◀

1 Mediation (German → English)

You and your Californian friend have been discussing how and why people get involved. Write her or him an email outlining what you have learned from this article about volunteer work in Germany. **SUPPORT** ▶ p. 225

BEYOND THE TEXT ◀

2 To volunteer or not to volunteer

  a With a partner, discuss the question whether the two of you should join a volunteer organization or not. One of you wants to, the other does not. You may make notes on little cue cards.

  b Tell the class about your discussion and your decision.

B4 An individual in a future society

▶ SF 23: Analysing a film

Taking a stand

You are going to watch the trailer for the 2012 blockbuster film The Hunger
Games, *based on the novel by Suzanne Collins and starring Jennifer Lawrence.*

> **TROUBLE SPOT**
>
> **star** = *die Hauptrolle spielen*
> **star sb.** = *jdn. in einer Haupt-
> rolle zeigen*

─────────────────────── COMPREHENSION ◀

1 Viewing for information
Make notes on the characters, setting, plot and main themes of the film as
can be derived from the trailer.

🎬 **DVD**

tribute ['trɪbjuːt] person who
fights in the Hunger Games
odds *(pl)* Gewinnchancen
victor winner

─────────────────────── ANALYSIS ◀

2 A volunteer
  a The protagonist Katniss Everdeen offers herself as a volunteer. Explain what
    her volunteering means in the context of the film.
  b Explain how Katniss's volunteering relates to the concept of volunteering
    as presented in this chapter. **SUPPORT** ▶ p. 225

3 Advertising
Identify and analyse the means of advertising the trailer uses.

A disturbing future

In this section you will watch an episode from the beginning of the film The
Hunger Games.

─────────────────────── COMPREHENSION ◀

1 Layers of society
In groups of three, outline how the different groups of society – the tributes,
the audience and the game makers – are portrayed.

─────────────────────── ANALYSIS ◀

2 Examining the social structure
Read the Fact File (cf. p. 32).
  a Assess which elements of a dystopian society are visible in the film.
  b **CHALLENGE** ▶ Examine what aspects of present-day society the film may
    reflect and criticize. Report to the class.

🎬 **DVD**

glimpse *(n)* quick look
overstate sth. exaggerate sth.
goosebumps *Gänsehaut*
have the odds in your favour
be lucky

FACT FILE

From utopia to dystopia

The term 'utopia' comes from Greek and means both 'no-place' and 'good place'. In 1516 the English lawyer, philosopher and
5 adviser to the king, Thomas More, wrote a work of fiction called *Utopia*, describing a paradise-like place and society on an island of the same name. From then on, the term was used to refer to imaginary, paradise-like
10 places, but also came to describe a particular kind of narrative, known as utopian literature.

In the course of the 20th century, former utopian ideals seemed absurd. Moreover, totalitarianism often led to the establishment of oppressive dictatorships
15 instead of better societies. As a consequence, the belief in heaven on earth turned into a nightmarish vision:

Sir Thomas More (ca. 1478–1535)

the term 'utopia' was replaced by 'dystopia', meaning 'bad' or 'hard' or – to put it simply – a utopia gone wrong. The main aim of a dystopia is to portray images of the future 20 as realistic and threatening possibilities. In the 20th century, dystopia became the main form of visionary literature, mirroring society's failures and projecting today's divisive issues (such as capitalism, con- 25 sumerism, self-indulgence, the power of science and technology and globalization) into the future. Often the true purpose of a dystopia is to make us aware of problems our society is facing.

Talk to a partner: What utopian or dystopian novels or films do you know? How do they portray the future?

▶ DVD

starve die because you do not have enough food

The issues

Watch two further episodes.

──────────────────────────── COMPREHENSION ◀

1 A dystopian society

Make notes on further elements of *characterization, costume design and *setting that are indicative of a dystopian society.

──────────────────────────────────── ANALYSIS ◀

2 Violence

a Evaluate the use of violence in the scenes you watched.

b Assess which contemporary issues are dealt with in *The Hunger Games*.

──────────────────────────── BEYOND THE TEXT ◀

3 YOU CHOOSE ▶ Watching the film

a If you have not seen the film, get together with others who have not seen it either and discuss whether or not you would like to watch the whole film. Keep notes of your discussion so that you can present your findings to the class.

OR

b If you have seen the film, discuss Katniss's role within her society.

Getting your message across

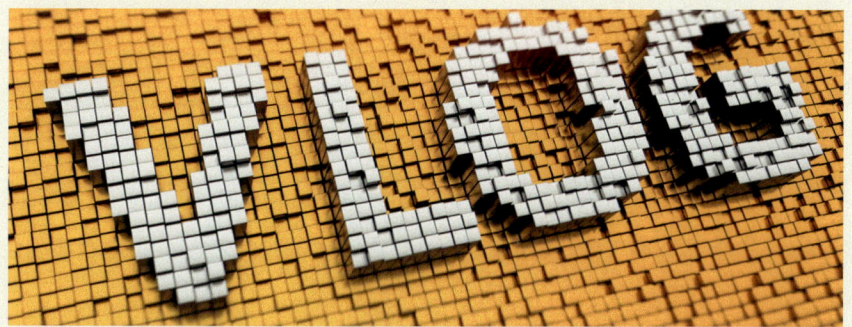

In this section you are going to create a vlog. A vlog is a video blog post or video podcast. Vloggers make videos of themselves or certain events and then upload them to the internet. Vloggers use video to express their thoughts, opinions and interests and to get their messages across. A vlog can be topical, instructional or entertaining.

1 Examine a video campaign or vlog

Across the world, web video has become a medium to give people a voice concerning political and social issues. The United Nations, for example, created a YouTube channel called 'Raise your voice and change climate change!', where you can find a lot of videos made by people who wanted to speak their minds, among them Desmond Tutu, a South African social rights activist and first black Archbishop of Cape Town, and numerous young people from all over the world.

a Watch Tutu's video. Describe your impressions of the video, and how Tutu tries to convey his message.

b Find other videos from the campaign, and discuss whether such video campaigns can make a difference.

2 YOU CHOOSE **Create your own vlog**

a Present yourself in a vlog. You may refer to some of the following aspects:

· your aims and ambitions
· voluntary work you do
· your philosophy of life
· a person that impresses you and could be a role model to others
· a thing that is worth fighting for

OR

b Produce a video on an issue that matters to you. If you are uncertain, here are a few subjects you can choose from:

· environment
· education
· children's/women's/men's rights
· freedom and human rights
· homelessness

3 Choose the class's favourite vlog

Get into groups of six and present your vlogs to each other. Choose one to be presented to the entire class. Be prepared to give reasons for your choice. In class, watch the videos you have chosen and discuss them. With the assessment sheet your teacher will give you, evaluate the vlogs and vote for the video you want to win the class contest.

 DVD

▶ SF 23: Analysing a film

With a video camera or a mobile phone everyone can become a vlogger.

2 The Power of Words – from Shakespeare to Today

Lacklustre tennis tournament keeps fans away

Suspect leads police on wild goose chase

Cruise ship returns to port a sorry sight

Priest and pop star make strange bedfellows

Referees urge fair play at World Cup

William Shakespeare (based on the Chandos portrait)

5 ways for shy people to break the ice

Download a list of chapter vocab here: 👆 **Webcode** context-73

▶ LP 1: Simple and progressive verb forms

1 Examining powerful language

a Work with a partner. Translate the headlines, each of which contains a phrase that was first used or coined by Shakespeare. Use a dictionary if necessary.

b Choose two of the phrases that you find particularly effective. Take turns explaining to each other what is so powerful about them that they are still being used in modern English.

2 Writing a *news story

Choose one of the headlines and write a short text about what you imagine is the story behind the headline. Write about 60 words.

3 Thinking about poetic word power

a Read the lines on the following page above, which are taken from poems that you will find in this chapter. With a partner decide on the two that appeal to you most.

b With your partner, decide what it is about the phrases that suggest they come from a poem.

c Share your ideas with other couples who have chosen different phrases. Compare the different ways in which poetic words appealed to you.

she wished she had shaped lips that kissed like Kim Kardashian

bigger boobs and Big Brother

de tongue fires a riddim dat shoots like shots

Love is not love Which alters when it alteration finds

Let's call this love, that alters when it finds

Alteration, the marriage of two minds

Are words no more than waving, wavering flags?

4 Using powerful words in politics and society

In class, collect, display and analyse famous lines, quotes and slogans from politics, literature, society and advertising that make use of the power of words.

PREVIEW

In this chapter you will learn about the power of poetic language from Shakespeare to today.

Main topics

- Shakespeare: Using word power to persuade .... p. 38
- Adapting Shakespeare's words to create new art .... p. 45
- Modern-day poets' use of words, sound and imagery .... p. 50

Focus on Skills: READING and VIEWING

- Reading for analysis (drama extract) .... p. 41
- Evaluating a modern Shakespeare adaptation .... p. 47

Chapter Task:

Writing a review of a film or text you have seen or read .... p. 53

CD1 09

Listen to an audio version of the text on the CD or download it here:

Webcode context-11

▶ SF 1: Dealing with unknown or new words

The power of the spoken word

The importance of the spoken word in Shakespeare's time

In Shakespeare's time people went to the theatre to 'hear' a play. The stage was equipped with only the most necessary props. The actors used body language and gestures, but the visual aspect was not so important for the overall dramatic impression. The most important element was the language, the words spoken by the actors. Sometimes we even speak of word-scenery, as the characters often describe the scenery for the audience. Shakespeare included many scenes in his plays in which a character uses words to persuade other characters to do things they might not want to originally do. Quite a few plays rely on quick verbal exchange, in which characters reply to each other in witty comments. Sometimes the word-fights are playful, sometimes they contain an element of challenge and sometimes they are cynical or evil. All of them demonstrate Shakespeare's mastery of language, as well as his enjoyment at creating these scenes.

Shakespeare's themes and language in our time

Since Shakespeare's time, the English language has developed considerably, while the themes of his plays have remained relevant up to this day. That is why there is such a wealth of adaptations of the plays both in writing and in films. Sometimes, it is just the main theme that has been adapted, as in the musical *West Side Story* (1957), which is based on Shakespeare's play *Romeo and Juliet*. Here, the language has been changed to fit the setting of New York in the 1950s. Occasionally there are filmed versions of his plays that keep Shakespeare's language but are set in a different location. *William Shakespeare's Romeo and Juliet* (1996), for example, is set in a fictitious modern American city called 'Verona Beach', complete with skyscrapers, large cars, and armed gangs – and yet the characters speak in Shakespeare's iambic pentameters. The film *Richard III* (1995) is set in a 1930s dictatorship. The popularity of these films shows that Shakespeare's language is still understandable when accompanied by images that we can relate to.

Poetry as drama

To this day, more than 400 years after his death in 1616, Shakespeare is not only remembered for his plays, but also for his poetry. His cycle of 154 sonnets deals in different ways with love, the passing of time, and death. While drama is no longer written in verse, poetry itself has remained popular. Poets of every age have found new ways of exploring the power of words to express feelings, attitudes and experiences in different types of verse. Sometimes they return to writing traditional formats such as sonnets, sometimes they write free verse that has no clear patterns either of rhyme or rhythm. One tendency in the 21st century is to perform poetry to an audience, thus lifting it off the page and making interaction between the poet and his or her listeners possible. Performance poetry can be said to create a link between Shakespeare's drama in verse and poetry of the 21st century.

5

10

15

20

25

30

35

40

1 Performance words

List words from the text that you could use when talking about
a what you can see
b what you can hear
during the performance in a theatre. Add short definitions to each word.

2 Collocations

a Collocations are words that often 'go together'. Find as many collocations as possible in the boxes below. In some cases you may have to add an article, a pronoun or a preposition.

find	elements
contain	scenery
write	mastery
describe	verse
express	ways
perform	poetry
create	link
demonstrate	feelings

b Use at least four collocations to write a short text about a poem, play or song that you like.

3 Phrasal verbs

A phrasal verb consists of a verb and an adverb or preposition. Fill the gaps with the correct phrasal verbs. Look at the text again for help.
1 While Shakespeare's theatres had little scenery, today's theatres are … up-to-date video and sound projectors.
2 Many of Shakespeare's plays have been … the big screen.
3 Shakespeare is best … his plays and sonnets.
4 The novel, which … a romance between an Englishman and a Lithuanian immigrant, is … a seaside town in England.
5 The reason why Shakespeare is still popular today is because people can still … his ideas and characters.
6 The play, which is … an old legend, has been updated to a modern setting.

4 Word families

a Find the corresponding nouns to these verbs and adjectives. Look at the text for help or use a dictionary.

1 be set in	4 adapt sth.	7 interact with sb./sth.
2 express sth.	5 popular	8 persuade sb. to do sth.
3 perform sth.	6 relevant	9 equip sb./sth. with sth.

b Write a sentence with each of the nouns.

5 Writing

Write an email to a friend telling him or her why you are (not) looking forward to seeing a Shakespeare play with your class. Include as many words and phrases from the text as possible.

▶ SF 3: Using a dictionary and a grammar book

▶ LP 19: Collocations

▶ SF 3: Using a dictionary and a grammar book
▶ LP 20: Word formation

Find an online dictionary here:
 Webcode context-52

Shakespeare's power of language

A1 William Shakespeare: the man, his work and his time

Form six groups and pick one of the topics below. Research your topic carefully. You can use the keywords in the boxes as guidelines. Remember to write down your sources. In your group, decide how you want to present your findings in class (handout, poster, digital slide show, etc.). SUPPORT ▶ p.226

Shakespeare's life

1564–1616 • Stratford-upon-Avon • 'small Latin, less Greek' • Ann Hathaway • seven lost years • actor and playhouse owner • 'second-best bed'

CHALLENGE ▶ **Shakespeare and Germany**

puppet theatre • translation vs. adaptation • influential for German drama • sonnet translations • Goethe, Schiller, Schlegel, Tieck, Günther, …

London and the Elizabethan theatre

metropolis • bankside • open playhouses • platform stage • male actors • the Lord Chamberlain's Men • the King's Men • entertainment business • Globe Theatre

Shakespeare's works

comedies, tragedies, histories, romances • sonnet cycle • verse epic • blank verse • comic relief • word play • imagery • tradition and innovation • Folio edition

CHALLENGE ▶ **Shakespearian English**

Early Modern English • major linguistic changes • flexible system • words from different origins • no fixed rules • neologisms

The Elizabethan world view

Henry VIII • Elizabeth I • Golden Age • the Great Chain of Being • dei gratia (Lat) • microcosm and macrocosm • time of upheaval • new discoveries • geocentric vs. heliocentric model • religious changes

When you have reached the end of Part B (p. 49), assess which of the aspects collected in this task have helped you to understand Shakespeare's texts better, which ones are interesting but do not really contribute to your understanding of the texts and which ones were missing.

A2 Lady Macbeth persuades her husband

William Shakespeare

In Shakespeare's play Macbeth, *Macbeth has told his wife about prophecies he heard promising him he will become king of Scotland. When the present king, Duncan, honours them with a visit, they plan to murder him so that Macbeth can become his successor. In a *soliloquy immediately before the passage printed below, Macbeth conscience has warned him not to go ahead with the plan. His wife interrupts his thoughts at this point.*

LADY MACBETH	He has almost supped: why have you left the chamber?
MACBETH	Hath he asked for me?
LADY MACBETH	Know you not he has?
MACBETH	We will proceed no further in this business:
	He hath honoured me of late; and I have bought 5
	Golden opinions from all sorts of people,
	Which would be worn now in their newest gloss,
	Not cast aside so soon.
LADY MACBETH	Was the hope drunk
	Wherein you dressed yourself? Hath it slept since? 10
	And wakes it now, to look so green and pale
	At what it did so freely? From this time
	Such I account thy love. Art thou afeard
	To be the same in thine own act and valour
	As thou art in desire? Wouldst thou have that 15
	Which thou esteem'st the ornament of life,
	And live a coward in thine own esteem,
	Letting 'I dare not' wait upon 'I would',
	Like the poor cat i' the adage?
MACBETH	Prithee, peace: 20
	I dare do all that may become a man;
	Who dares do more is none.
LADY MACBETH	What beast was't, then,
	That made you break this enterprise to me?
	When you durst do it, then you were a man; 25
	And, to be more than what you were, you would
	Be so much more the man. Nor time nor place
	Did then adhere, and yet you would make both:
	They have made themselves, and that their fitness now
	Does unmake you. I have given suck, and know 30
	How tender 'tis to love the babe that milks me:
	I would, while it was smiling in my face,
	Have plucked my nipple from his boneless gums,
	And dashed the brains out, had I so sworn as you
	Have done to this. 35
MACBETH	If we should fail?
LADY MACBETH	We fail!
	But screw your courage to the sticking-place,
	And we'll not fail. When Duncan is asleep –
	Whereto the rather shall his day's hard journey 40
	Soundly invite him – his two chamberlains

1 **supped** finished supper
5 **honoured me of late** showed me respect lately
7 **would be worn** should be enjoyed
8 **cast aside** thrown away
13 **Such I account thy love** I consider your love to be like that
14 **to be the same … as thou art in desire** to be as brave in what you do as in what you are wishing for
16 **esteem'st** (v) consider
17 **esteem** (n) great respect, admiration
18 **dare** be brave enough to do sth.
   wait upon be a servant to
19 **adage** ['ædɪdʒ] proverb, saying; (here) 'A cat likes to eat fish, but doesn't like to get its feet wet.'
20 **Prithee, peace** please be quiet
25 **durst** (*past tense*) dared
27 **Nor time … adhere** neither the time nor the place were right then
28 **make both** force both to be right
29 **have made themselves** have offered themselves
   fitness suitability, being right for sth.
30 **give suck** breastfeed a baby
33 **plucked** pulled away
   boneless gums toothless mouth
38 **screw your courage to the sticking-place** get your courage up (image taken from the tuning of a violin: the player tightens each string until it produces the right note and then fixes it)
40 **Whereto … invite him** to which his long travels will lead him soon
41 **chamberlain** ['tʃeɪmbəlɪn] *Kammerdiener*

⁴² **wassail** ['wɒseɪl] ale, spiced beer
⁴³ **warder** guard
⁴⁴ **fume** alcoholic steam
receipt of reason [rɪ'siːt] brain
⁴⁵ **limbeck** *Destillierkolben*
⁴⁶ **drenched** drunk
⁴⁹ **spongy** ['spʌndʒi] like a sponge, soaked with liquid, (here) drunk
bear take, stand
⁵⁰ **quell** (*n*) killing, murder
⁵² **undaunted mettle** fearless character

> Will I with wine and wassail so convince
> That memory, the warder of the brain,
> Shall be a fume, and the receipt of reason
> A limbeck only: when in swinish sleep 45
> Their drenched natures lie as in a death,
> What cannot you and I perform upon
> The unguarded Duncan? What not put upon
> His spongy officers, who shall bear the guilt
> Of our great quell? 50
>
> MACBETH Bring forth men-children only;
> For thy undaunted mettle should compose
> Nothing but males.

From: *Macbeth*, Act 1, Scene 7

COMPREHENSION ◀

1 Understanding the conflict
   a An argument is taking place between Macbeth and Lady Macbeth. Collect keywords that underline the position of each character.
   b Write a short summary of each of the speeches in modern English.
   c State what Lady Macbeth is trying to persuade her husband to do.

LANGUAGE AWARENESS ◀

2 Analysing ways of addressing
   a Study how Macbeth and Lady Macbeth address each other.
      Read the language awareness box on the left and explain what their ways of addressing mean.
   b In one part of the dialogue, Lady Macbeth changes the form of address. Identify the change and discuss what may have caused it.

3 Rewriting Shakespeare's questions
Look at how Shakespeare formed questions. Instead of the modern use of the modal verb *do* he used a different form of question. Identify those questions and rewrite them in modern English.

16th-century English
In Shakespearean times there were two forms of *you*:
- *thou* (object form *thee*; possessive form *thy/thine*), used similarly to German *du*
- *ye/you*, used as a term of respect or as the plural form (cf. the old German use of *Ihr*)

By using either the one or the other of these forms one could express different relations of power and authority.

Verbs following *thou* ended in *-st*, e.g. *didst, camest, hast*. The second-person singular form of *be* was *art*: *thou art = you are* (careful: not *your art*). Misunderstandings can result when hearing words that are now obsolete and whose meaning may have changed. The third-person singular verb often ended in *-th*, e.g. *doth (does), hath (has), seemeth (seems)*.

▶ LA 1: Varieties of English
▶ LA 4: Influencing through language

Cawdor Castle, where Shakespeare's Macbeth *is set*

FOCUS ON SKILLS

Reading for analysis (drama extract)

*Look at **A2** again. Now you are going to analyse how the writer has made the content interesting by using the sound of the words, stylistic devices, metaphorical language and forms of characterization.*

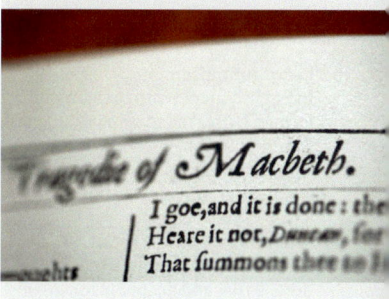

1 Reading aloud: The rhythm of the text

a Read the text aloud to get a feeling for its *metre.

b Read the Fact File on the right. Then count the syllables and the metric feet in ll. 1–22 of the extract from *Macbeth*.

c Work with a partner. Read parts of the dialogue out loud again. Pay attention to the speakers completing the blank verse for each other.

2 Understanding *stylistic devices

a Read Lady Macbeth's speeches and identify which form of punctuation appears a lot. Name the stylistic device and explain its purpose here.

b Note down words that are repeated in the text and in which lines they occur. Describe the effect of their repetition.

c Write a statement explaining what both stylistic devices tell you about the argumentation of both Macbeth and Lady Macbeth.

3 Analysing *images

When reading, you should always try to visualize what the words are telling you and which mental images are created.

a Read ll. 4–6 again. Macbeth speaks about 'buying golden opinions' that he wants to 'wear in their newest gloss': Apparently he sees 'opinions' as new clothes. Explain what that tells you about his character.

b Lady Macbeth responds by using imagery herself. Read ll. 9–12 and explain how she takes up her husband's image and expands it.

c In l. 23 Lady Macbeth mentions a 'beast'. Explain what she is referring to.

4 Understanding *characterization

a Lady Macbeth's passage from ll. 30–35 gives us a good idea of the kind of woman she is. Read the passage out loud. Explain the image she uses and what it tells you about her character.

b Read the extract either aloud or in silence slowly and purposefully. Compare lengths, content and messages of the speakers' passages. Draw conclusions about the characters.

c FREEZE-FRAME Work with a partner. Imagine how the actor and actress would perform the dialogue and create a freeze-frame. Get together with another pair. Present your freeze-frame and let them guess which moment you have chosen.

d Write an analysis about the couple Macbeth and Lady Macbeth on the basis of the complete passage. Write at least 150 words.

▶ SF 17: Analysing stylistic devices
▶ SF 20: Analysing drama

■ FACT FILE

Blank verse
The type of verse used most often by Shakespeare is called blank verse. It consists of iambic pentameters, which are five iambs. An iamb is an unstressed syllable followed by a stressed syllable, which sounds like 'dah DUM'.
Note: Shakespeare's rhythm is varied, lively and never monotonous, because his characters are saying important things. That is why not all lines in the excerpt can be spoken in the 'dah DUM' rhythm.

■ LANGUAGE AWARENESS

Influencing through speech rhythm
Being particularly close to normal English speech rhythm, blank verse is highly flexible, which was probably what made it so popular in poetry and drama in Shakespeare's time.
*Rhythm and *metre can have a considerable effect on the audience and make a speech more memorable. How you pronounce something or the rhythm you use has an impact on your audience, their attention and their mood.

▶ LA 4: Influencing through language

▶ SF 35: Writing a character profile

A3 Richard courts his enemy *William Shakespeare*

In Richard III *Richard, Duke of Gloucester, has killed his enemies King Henry VI and his son Edward Plantagenet. He wants to become king himself, and decides to marry Edward's widow Anne to strengthen his position. In this scene Richard approaches Anne as she accompanies the body of her father-in-law, Henry VI, to his burial place. Read the extract to see how Richard tries to persuade Lady Anne that he is courting her out of love. Try to visualize the scene, imagining how the two characters interact with each other.*

LADY ANNE	Didst thou not kill this king?	
GLOUCESTER	I grant ye.	
LADY ANNE	Dost grant me, hedgehog? then, God grant me too	
	Thou mayst be damned for that wicked deed!	
	O, he was gentle, mild, and virtuous!	5
GLOUCESTER	The fitter for the King of heaven, that hath him.	
LADY ANNE	He is in heaven, where thou shalt never come.	
GLOUCESTER	Let him thank me, that holp to send him thither;	
	For he was fitter for that place than earth.	
LADY ANNE	And thou unfit for any place but hell.	10
GLOUCESTER	Yes, one place else, if you will hear me name it.	
LADY ANNE	Some dungeon.	
GLOUCESTER	Your bed-chamber.	
LADY ANNE	Ill rest betide the chamber where thou liest!	
GLOUCESTER	So will it, madam till I lie with you.	15
LADY ANNE	I hope so.	
GLOUCESTER	I know so. But, gentle Lady Anne,	
	To leave this keen encounter of our wits,	
	And fall somewhat into a slower method,	
	Is not the causer of the timeless deaths	20
	Of these Plantagenets, Henry and Edward,	
	As blameful as the executioner?	
LADY ANNE	Thou art the cause, and most accursed effect.	
GLOUCESTER	Your beauty was the cause of that effect;	
	Your beauty: which did haunt me in my sleep	25
	To undertake the death of all the world,	
	So I might live one hour in your sweet bosom.	
LADY ANNE	If I thought that, I tell thee, homicide,	
	These nails should rend that beauty from my cheeks.	
GLOUCESTER	These eyes could never endure sweet beauty's wreck;	30
	You should not blemish it, if I stood by:	
	As all the world is cheered by the sun,	
	So I by that; it is my day, my life.	
LADY ANNE	Black night o'ershade thy day, and death thy life.	
GLOUCESTER	Curse not thyself, fair creature; thou art both.	35
LADY ANNE	I would I were, to be revenged on thee.	
GLOUCESTER	It is a quarrel most unnatural,	
	To be revenged on him that loveth you.	
LADY ANNE	It is a quarrel just and reasonable,	
	To be revenged on him that slew my husband.	40

2 **grant** admit, allow
6 **the fitter** the better
8 **holp** *(past tense)* helped
  thither there
12 **dungeon** ['dʌndʒən] dark underground prison
14 **Ill rest betide the chamber** may there be no peace and quiet to be had in the room
18 **keen encounter of our wits** our fierce argument
20 **timeless** too early
23 **accursed** damned
25 **haunt** follow, chase, stalk
29 **rend** rip, pull
30 **endure** tolerate
31 **blemish** ['blemɪʃ] ruin
40 **slew** *(past tense)* killed

GLOUCESTER	He that bereft thee, lady, of thy husband,	
	Did it to help thee to a better husband.	
LADY ANNE	His better doth not breathe upon the earth.	
GLOUCESTER	He lives that loves thee better than he could.	
LADY ANNE	Name him.	45
GLOUCESTER	Plantagenet.	
LADY ANNE	Why, that was he.	
GLOUCESTER	The selfsame name, but one of better nature.	
LADY ANNE	Where is he?	
GLOUCESTER	Here.	50

She spitteth at him.

	Why dost thou spit at me?	
LADY ANNE	Would it were mortal poison, for thy sake!	
GLOUCESTER	Never came poison from so sweet a place.	
LADY ANNE	Never hung poison on a fouler toad.	55
	Out of my sight! thou dost infect my eyes.	
GLOUCESTER	Thine eyes, sweet lady, have infected mine.	
LADY ANNE	Would they were basilisks', to strike thee dead!	
GLOUCESTER	I would they were, that I might die at once;	
	For now they kill me with a living death.	60
	Those eyes of thine from mine have drawn salt tears,	
	Shamed their aspect with store of childish drops: [...]	
	I never sued to friend nor enemy;	
	My tongue could never learn sweet smoothing word;	
	But now thy beauty is proposed my fee,	65
	My proud heart sues, and prompts my tongue to speak.	
	Teach not thy lips such scorn, for they were made	
	For kissing, lady, not for such contempt.	
	If thy revengeful heart cannot forgive,	
	Lo, here I lend thee this sharp-pointed sword;	70
	Which if thou please to hide in this true bosom.	
	And let the soul forth that adoreth thee,	
	I lay it naked to the deadly stroke,	
	And humbly beg the death upon my knee.	
	Nay, do not pause; for I did kill King Henry,	
	But 'twas thy beauty that provoked me.	
	Nay, now dispatch; 'twas I that stabb'd young Edward,	
	But 'twas thy heavenly face that set me on.	

Here she lets fall the sword.   80

Take up the sword again, or take up me.

From: *Richard III*, Act 1, Scene 2

The scene ends with Anne allowing Richard to place his ring on her finger and agreeing to meet him after the burial of Henry VI.

41 **bereft thee of sb.** made you lose sb.
55 **toad** *Kröte*
58 **basilisk** ['bæzɪlɪsk] mythical animal with the power to cause death by looking at a person
62 **shamed ... of childish drops** made me feel ashamed as I cried like a child
63 **sued to** [su:d] appealed to, was attractive to
64 **smoothing** ['smu:ðɪŋ] nice, flattering
65 **fee** reward
67 **scorn** ridicule, sarcasm
68 **contempt** hate, disrespect
70 **Lo** Look!
74 **humbly** modest, moderately
77 **nay** no
dispatch go ahead; kill me

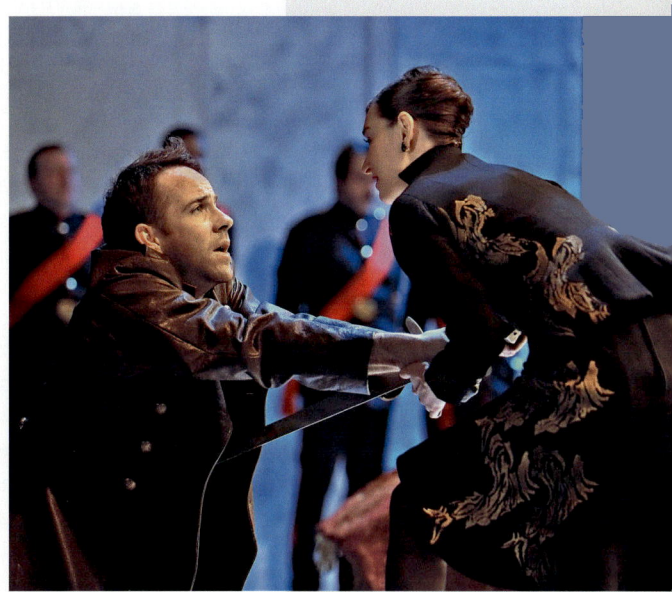

The opening of Richard III in the First Folio of Shakespeare, 1623

The Tragedy of Richard the Third:
with the Landing of Earle Richmond, and the
Battell at Bosworth Field.

Actus Primus. Scœna Prima.

Enter Richard Duke of Gloster, solus.

Ow is the Winter of our Discontent,
Made glorious Summer by this Son of Yorke:
And all the clouds that lowr'd vpon our house

That waites vpon your Grace?
Cla. His Maiesty tendring my persons safety,
Hath appointed this Conduct, to conuey me to th'Tower
Rich. Vpon what cause?
Cla. Because my name is *George.*
Rich. Ala---

COMPREHENSION ◄

1 Understanding the content
  a Outline the gist of the fight between Lady Anne and Gloucester.
  b Describe Lady Anne's feelings for her dead husband and for Gloucester.

ANALYSIS ◄

2 A word fight
  a Look closely at how one speaker takes up a particular word or concept from the other and changes it according to their own purposes. Make notes.
  b Discuss your findings with a partner or in class.

3 Working with imagery
Work with a partner. Identify the *images each speaker uses. Explain them with the help of the annotations and from the context they are used in.
SUPPORT ▶ p. 228

4 Persuasive words and actions
  a Note down words and phrases that Gloucester uses to change Lady Anne's feelings towards him.
  b Examine if her reactions show the desired effect.
  c Explain the effect of Gloucester offering Lady Anne his sword to kill him on the spot.

5 Understanding character
On the basis of your analysis, describe the speakers' characters.
SUPPORT ▶ p. 228

▶ SF 35: Writing a character profile

LANGUAGE AWARENESS ◄

6 Forms of address
Look at the language awareness box on p. 40 again. Analyse the use of *thou* and *you* forms as an indicator of the relationship of the speakers. Interpret their forms of addressing each other.

BEYOND THE TEXT ◄

7 Performing the scene
  a Discuss how the characters could be presented on stage.
  b In small groups, practise reading the dialogue out loud with appropriate *emphasis and gestures. Then perform your reading in front of the class.

Shakespeare's words updated

B1 My future wife *William Shakespeare*

The following extract is taken from William Shakespeare's The Taming of the
Shrew. *Petruchio has gone to Padua to find a wealthy wife. On hearing of the
shrewish elder daughter of the wealthy Baptista Minola, who so far has driven
any potential husband away with her sharp tongue, he decides that she is just
the right woman for him. The following extract is from their very first meeting.*

PETRUCHIO	Good morrow, Kate; for that's your name, I hear.	
KATHARINA	Well have you heard, but something hard of hearing:	
	They call me Katharina that do talk of me.	
PETRUCHIO	You lie, in faith; for you are called plain Kate,	
	And bonny Kate and sometimes Kate the curst;	5
	But Kate, the prettiest Kate in Christendom	
	Kate of Kate Hall, my super-dainty Kate,	
	For dainties are all Kates, and therefore, Kate,	
	Take this of me, Kate of my consolation;	
	Hearing thy mildness praised in every town,	10
	Thy virtues spoke of, and thy beauty sounded,	
	Yet not so deeply as to thee belongs,	
	Myself am moved to woo thee for my wife.	
KATHARINA	Moved! In good time: let him that moved you hither	
	Remove you hence: I knew you at the first	15
	You were a moveable.	
PETRUCHIO	Why, what's a moveable?	
KATHARINA	A joined-stool.	
PETRUCHIO	Thou hast hit it: come, sit on me.	
KATHARINA	Asses are made to bear, and so are you.	20
PETRUCHIO	Women are made to bear, and so are you.	
KATHARINA	No such jade as you, if me you mean.	
PETRUCHIO	Alas! good Kate, I will not burden thee;	
	For, knowing thee to be but young and light –	
KATHARINA	Too light for such a swain as you to catch;	25
	And yet as heavy as my weight should be. [...]	
She strikes him.		
PETRUCHIO	I swear I'll cuff you, if you strike again.	
KATHARINA	So may you lose your arms:	
	If you strike me, you are no gentleman;	30
	And if no gentleman, why then no arms. [...]	
PETRUCHIO	[...] 'Twas told me you were rough and coy and sullen,	
	And now I find report a very liar;	
	For thou are pleasant, gamesome, passing courteous,	
	But slow in speech, yet sweet as spring-time flowers:	35
	Thou canst not frown, thou canst not look askance,	
	Nor bite the lip, as angry wenches will,	
	Nor hast thou pleasure to be cross in talk,	
	But thou with mildness entertain'st thy wooers,	
	With gentle conference, soft and affable. [...]	40

shrew *widerspenstige, zänkische Frau*

2 **something hard of hearing**
you must be slightly deaf
5 **bonny** beautiful
curst *(participle)* cursed
7 **dainty** sweet
8 **dainties are all Kates** a pun on
'cate', an Elizabethan sweet
9 **consolation** *Trost*
11 **sounded** proclaimed, reported
13 **woo sb.** *jdn. umwerben*
14 **hither** to this place, here
15 **hence** away from here
18 **joined-stool** piece of furniture
20 **ass** donkey
bear *Lasten tragen; gebären*
22 **jade** worthless person
23 **Alas!** [əˈlæs] expression of
sadness, *Ach!*
25 **swain** lover, wooer (cf. l. 13)
28 **cuff sb.** hit sb.
29 **arms** *Wappen*
32 **coy** shy
sullen unfriendly
34 **gamesome** [ˈɡeɪmsəm] playful
passing very, exceedingly
courteous [ˈkɜːtɪəs] polite
36 **frown** [fraʊn] look displeased
askance [əˈskæns] *verächtlich*
37 **wench** girl
40 **conference** conversation
affable [ˈæfəble] likeable

42 **dowry** [ˈdaʊri] *Mitgift*
'greed agreed
43 **will you, nill you** if you want or not
44 **for your turn** just right for you
50 **conformable** [kənˈfɔːməbl] *angepasst, fügsam*
household Kates wives by the name of Kate
51 **make denial** [dɪˈnaɪəl] refuse

Thus in plain terms: your father hath consented
That you shall be my wife; your dowry 'greed on;
And, will you, nill you, I will marry you.
Now, Kate, I am a husband for your turn;
For, by this light, whereby I see thy beauty,   45
Thy beauty, that doth make me like thee well,
Thou must be married to no man but me;
For I am he am born to tame you Kate,
And bring you from a wild Kate to a Kate
Conformable as other household Kates.   50
Here comes your father: never make denial;
I must and will have Katharina to my wife.

From: *The Taming of the Shrew*, Act 2, Scene 1

COMPREHENSION ◀

1 **YOU CHOOSE** ▶ **Understanding the dialogue**

a Create a cartoon or a comic strip summarizing the scene. Draw 1–2 frames with speech bubbles and captions.

 OR

b Write a short modern English version of the dialogue. Practise reading it with a partner, and then present it to the class.

ANALYSIS ◀

2 **Comparing dialogues**
Compare the way Petruchio woos Katharina to the way Gloucester woos Anne (**A3**, pp. 42–43). Evaluate what each man reveals about himself and how effectively they each use words to achieve their aims. **SUPPORT** ▶ p. 228

LANGUAGE AWARENESS ◀

3 **Playing with words**
a Look at ll. 7–31 again. Describe the changes in meaning, grammar or form that occur to certain words.
b Translate those words into German. Explain why in some cases the word-play does not work and why in others it works the same as in English.
c Think of three more words that have at least two meanings. Write six appropriate sentences.

BEYOND THE TEXT ◀

4 **Modernizing the play**
a Imagine the scene is going to be adapted for a modern film version. With a partner, discuss a suitable setting and which actors should take the leading roles. Consider in particular which elements from the original scene should be kept and which removed. Share your ideas in class.
b **CHALLENGE** ▶ Create a storyboard for the scene you are planning.

▶ SF 37: Doing a creative writing task

▶ LA 4: Influencing through language

▶ SF 37: Doing a creative writing task

■ **LANGUAGE AWARENESS**

Homonyms, i.e. two or more words that have the same spelling or pronunciation but different meanings, are often used for word play in literature or in jokes because they can be the source of comic misunderstandings or puns, which is appealing to an audience

VIEWING FOCUS ON SKILLS

Evaluating a modern Shakespeare adaptation

Kate in a Lift
The film sequence you are about to watch is from a BBC series in which Shakespeare plays were modernized. It represents the same scene from The Taming of the Shrew that you have studied in **B1**.

1 Before viewing
Before watching the film excerpt, speculate which aspects might have been modernized. Look at your notes from **B1**, task **3** again.

2 Viewing without sound
You will watch the film extract without sound. Split the class in two groups, with one half doing task **a** and the other doing task **b**.
a Concentrate on the places shown in the scene. While viewing, make notes on them and the atmosphere they create. Explain why the director may have chosen them.
b Examine the body language and facial expressions of the two main characters. While viewing, make notes about what they tell you about their characters.
c Share your findings first with a partner, then report them to the class.

3 Viewing with sound
a Watch the film with sound. With your partner from task **2**, discuss if you get new information from the dialogue. List elements of the dialogue that surprised you.
b View the extract again and concentrate on the music. Describe how it is used, and to what effect.

4 Viewing for the final time
Before viewing the extract for the final time, look at ▶ SF 23 Analysing a film on p. 313. Then, in groups of four, examine the camera work. Two of you concentrate on the part in front of the flat, the other two on the part in the lift. Explain how the camera work affects you as a viewer. Share your findings in your group, then in class.

5 Evaluation
Evaluate how successful the director has been in adapting the material. Name the elements that were changed and the effect the scene has on you.
SUPPORT ▶ p. 229

▶️ **DVD**

quid *(BE sl)* British pound
clap eyes on sb. see sb. for the first time
trout *(infml)* unpleasant woman
chord *Akkord*
take the mick (out of sb.) *(BE infml)* make fun of sb.
certifiable lunatic [ˌsɜːtɪˈfaɪəbl ˈluːnətɪk] crazy person
bugger sth. up *(sl)* ruin sth.
put your cards on the table say what you really want
alluring *(adj)* attractive
arousing *(adj)* sexy
snarl make an angry noise when talking
lewd [luːd] sexually vulgar
obnoxious very annoying
plucky having courage and spirit

▶ SF 23: Analysing a film

B2 Responding to a sonnet

APPOINTMENT TASK
· Make an appointment card with the names of three partners.
· With your partners, discuss the statements on the right and make notes on your appointment card.
· Discuss your conclusions in class.

1 *Love for someone does not change, even if the person you love changes.*
2 *Love can be between any-one, no matter what age, gender, race or religion.*
3 *Love is not a physical but a spiritual experience.*

Now read the sonnets. Concentrate on the different images the words create in your mind.

Sonnet 116   *William Shakespeare*

Let me not to the marriage of true minds
Admit impediments. Love is not love
Which alters when it alteration finds,
Or bends with the remover to remove:
O no! It is an ever-fixèd mark   5
That looks on tempests and is never shaken;
It is the star to every wandering bark,
Whose worth's unknown, although his height be taken.
Love's not Time's fool, though rosy lips and cheeks
Within his bending sickle's compass come: 10
Love alters not with his brief hours and weeks,
But bears it out even to the edge of doom.
If this be error and upon me proved,
I never writ, nor no man ever loved.

1 **Let me not** May I never
2 **admit** accept
impediment [ɪm'pedɪmənt] *Hindernis*
3 **alter** ['ɔːltə] change
4 **remover** person who goes away
5 **mark** landmark or star that helps a sailor to navigate
6 **tempest** storm
7 **wander** ['wɒndə] travel
bark ship
10 **bending** curved
sickle *Sichel*
compass ['kʌmpəs] *Reichweite*
12 **bear sth. out** endure sth.
edge of doom end of time
13 **upon** against
14 **writ** (have) written

In 1971, Northern Irish poet James Simmons (1933–2001) wrote a series of 'Marital Sonnets'. No. 4 reads like a modern response to Shakespeare's Sonnet 116.

Marital Sonnet 4   *James Simmons*

We murmured passionate language in that trance
when each was famished for the mutual kiss;
but we have altered, and it spoils all chance
of happiness, comparing that with this.
Displays of fireworks were put on by lust,   5
romantic symphonies, unholy wars:
now contraceptives, unworn, gather dust,
in which we once soared gleaming towards the stars.
In age's Leamington our joys last longer,
the libraries are good, the tea-rooms neat,   10
good arguments aren't broken off by anger,
new appetites are fed, we are replete.
Let's call this love, that alters when it finds
alteration, the marriage of two minds.

2 **famished** ['fæmɪʃd] very hungry
mutual *gegenseitig*
7 **contraceptive** *Verhütungsmittel*
8 **soar** rise high
gleam (v) shine
9 **Leamington** ['lemɪŋtən] a spa town in Warwickshire, England
12 **replete** [rɪ'pliːt] very full

From: *Poems 1956–1986*, 1986, p.77

COMPREHENSION ◀

1 Brief summaries
Summarize each poem's message in one sentence.

ANALYSIS ◀

2 GALLERY WALK **Comparing the sonnets**
Compare the two sonnets. Examine structure, development of the idea and style. Present your findings on posters and evaluate the posters in a gallery walk. SUPPORT ▶ p. 229

▶ SF 21: Analysing poetry

Find a tool to make your poster here: 🖐 **Webcode** context-50

BEYOND THE TEXT ◀

3 Creative writing
Write a response to one of the sonnets. This can take the form of an email or a letter to a friend, a comment, or even a short poem. Refer to your notes from the pre-reading discussion.

▶ SF 29: Writing a formal letter or email
▶ SF 34: Argumentative writing
▶ SF 37: Doing a creative writing task
▶ SF 38: Writing a well-structured text

📍 CULTURE SPOT

Shakespeare for the masses

WILL POWER

1 Explain the wordplay on the T-shirt. Consider what wearing this T-shirt would mean to you.

2 What do objects like this tell you about Shakespeare's place in British culture?

3 Design a Shakespeare object. Choose a picture, pun, quote or slogan and present your idea to the class.

▶ SF 24: Giving a presentation

Part C

The powerful words of today's poets

C1 Performance poetry

Benjamin Zephaniah

■▶ DVD

> ■ FACT FILE
>
> **Performance poetry**
> During the 1980s, the term 'performance poetry' came into popular usage to describe poetry written or
> 5 composed for performance before an audience rather than for print distribution. Before the invention of the printing press, all poetry was performed orally, and in many
> 10 cultures outside our Western traditions, oral poetry and storytelling are still more important than reading. In the West poetry has become a very individual form of
> 15 culture. With the rise of new media and technology, the interest in poetry on the page faded, but the spoken word remained important. Punk, reggae and hip hop all had an effect on how the spoken word 20 was perceived. Many contemporary poets took up these influences and started to 'perform' their poetry rather than just read it.
>
> 1 *State why you think oral poetry came into existence and what role it has played in society.*
>
> 2 *Do you prefer to listen to poetry or to read it? Give reasons for your answer.*

Dis poetry   *Benjamin Zephaniah*

Benjamin Zephaniah is well known in Britain for his oral renditions of his poems.

— COMPREHENSION ◀

1 First impressions
  a Watch the performance. Make notes of your first impression and of what you hear. Exchange notes with a partner. ▶ LANGUAGE HELP
  b Listen and watch again. Add to your notes.

2 A first attempt at understanding
Choose the sentences that correspond with how you understand the poem.
  A The speaker is saying that his poetry is an essential part of his life.
  B The speaker is saying that rhythm is all that matters.
  C The speaker is saying that poetry needs to be written with love.
  D The speaker is saying that poetry needs to be chanted.

3 Understanding the poem
Your teacher will give you the text. Read the poem.
  a List the various descriptions of 'dis poetry' given in the poem.
  b Sum up what his poetry means for the poet himself.

— ANALYSIS ◀

4 Looking at the language
Explain why the poet decided to spell some of the words as he did.

5 Looking at rhythm and rhyme
One of the keywords of the poem is 'riddim'. Analyse how the length of the lines and the *rhymes contribute to the *rhythm.

6 The meaning of the poem

With a partner, discuss the meaning of the last seven lines. Use your findings to write down your interpretation of the poem.

BEYOND THE TEXT ◀

7 Reviewing a poetry performance

Watch the performance again. Pay special attention to the speaker's gestures. Then write a review for the English pages of your school magazine.

SUPPORT ▶ p. 229

▶ SF 32: Writing a review

Famous for what? *Hollie McNish*

Discuss what being famous means to you.
Then watch Hollie McNish perform her poem.

🎬 DVD

COMPREHENSION ◀

1 Discussing your first reactions

Discuss your first impressions of the performance. Consider aspects like the poet herself, the manner of delivery, the type of poem, and the poem itself.

2 Understanding the poem

Describe the situation in the poem briefly and state what you think the message is.

3 Re-examining the message

Your teacher will give you the text. Read the poem and then look at your answer to task **2** again. If necessary, change your statement.

ANALYSIS ◀

4 Analysing the style

Explain what makes this a poem. Examine the *rhythm, sound of words, *rhyme and *imagery.

▶ SF 21: Analysing poetry

BEYOND THE TEXT ◀

5 Mediation (German ➜ English)

Imagine that an English friend sent you a link to Hollie McNish performing her poem. You want to show him or her that Germans do poetry performances too. You have come across the poetry performance that you can hear on the CD. Tell your friend what the subject of the poem is and how it is similar or different to the performance by Hollie McNish. Write about 150 words.

🎧 CD1 10
▶ SF 41: Mediation of written and oral texts

6 YOU CHOOSE ▶ **Creative writing**

a Imagine you are a careers advisor at school. Write a letter to the girl addressed in Hollie McNish's poem.

 OR

b Imagine the person addressed in Hollie McNish's poem was a boy. What parts of the poem would have so be changed? Rewrite those lines using new phrases and ideas.

▶ SF 29: Writing a formal letter or email
▶ SF 37: Doing a creative writing task

🎧 CD1 11

Imtiaz Dharker

C2 The psychological power of words

All poets rely on the power of their words to make an impression on listeners and readers. On a different level, some poets write directly about the impact of words in our lives. The following poem not only relies on the power of words but directly writes about the impact words have in our lives.

The right word   *Imtiaz Dharker*

Listen to Imtiaz Dharker reading her poem.

COMPREHENSION ◀

1 Giving an initial reaction

  a Talk about your impression of the poem with a partner.

  b Agree on one sentence that states the message of the poem.

  c Now read the poem.

Outside the door,
lurking in the shadows,
is a terrorist.

Is that the wrong description?
Outside that door,   5
taking shelter in the shadows,
is a freedom fighter.

I haven't got this right.
Outside, waiting in the shadows,
is a hostile militant.   10

Are words no more
than waving, wavering flags?
Outside your door,
watchful in the shadows,
is a guerrilla warrior.   15

God help me.
Outside, defying every shadow,
stands a martyr.
I saw his face.

No words can help me now.   20
Just outside the door,
lost in shadows,
is a child who looks like mine.

One word for you.
Outside my door,   25
his hand too steady,
his eyes too hard
is a boy who looks like your son,
too.

I open the door.   30
Come in, I say.
Come in and eat with us.

The child steps in
and carefully, at my door,
takes off his shoes.   35

From: *The Terrorist at My Table*, 2006, pp. 25–26

2 Understanding the general idea

  a List the different descriptions of the people standing outside the speaker's door. **SUPPORT** ▶ p. 229

  b Add *connotations that go with each description as well as the mental image it conveys. **SUPPORT** ▶ p. 229

  c In one sentence, state the idea that the speaker is developing in the course of the poem.

ANALYSIS ◀

3 Analysis and interpretation

Interpret the poem by analysing its structure and images. Evaluate whether the speaker gives an answer to her question about words being 'no more than waving, wavering flags' (ll. 11–12). Conclude your interpretation by considering whether she found 'the right word'.

'I can't wait to see the reviews in the newspaper to find out whether I like the movie or not.'

Writing a review

Reviews are written by critics to inform other people about the positive and negative aspects of a particular book, film, etc. But increasingly ordinary people write reviews on the internet not just about films and books, but also about general products.

For the task at hand, you are going to be the critic of a weekly magazine for young adults. You have been asked to hunt for some 'good stuff' in literature or film and write a review explaining to readers of your own age group why you like the material you have chosen.

When you have finished the task, your teacher will give you an assessment sheet.

1 Get hold of one of your literary favourites. This can be a novel, a short story, a play (that you have either read or watched on stage), a poem or a collection of poems, a song or a film. Take a fresh look at your chosen material and read/ view it for analysis.

2 Make an outline for your review and structure your material.

3 Write a catchy beginning for your review.

4 State what the text/film is about and what happens. Don't reveal anything that might ruin the pleasure for someone else (e.g. the ending).

5 Write the main body, which includes the reasons why you have chosen this particular book or film. Include quotes from the text/film that reveal the power of its language.

6 Write a suitable ending in which you recommend your item.

7 a GALLERY WALK When you are satisfied with your review, type a neat copy and present it in a gallery walk.
　 b Move around and read all the reviews. Your teacher will give you an assessment sheet. Take a vote on which three should be printed.

▶ SF 19: Analysing narrative prose
▶ SF 20: Analysing drama
▶ SF 21: Analysing poetry
▶ SF 23: Analysing a film
▶ Focus on Skills: Reading for analysis (drama extract), p. 41
▶ SF 5: Structuring information and ideas: visual aids and outlines
▶ SF 32: Writing a review

▶ SF 40: Proofreading

3

The UK – a Kingdom United?

BBC
Adele
roast
beer
pudding
terraced
houses

politeness
GB **pride**
Ed Sheeran
Queen
lawn

Benedict
Cumberbatch
cricket
peas

rowdy
loyalty
fairness

Download a list of chapter vocab here: **Webcode** context-74

▶ SF 2: Using a dictionary and a grammar book

1 Getting to know the British

a Choose four red words and four blue words from the flag. Explain them to a partner and say why you think they are part of 'Britishness'.

b Choose four words you do not know and look them up in a monolingual dictionary. Guess why these words are considered typically British.

c Find three words on the flag that you do not think are typically British. Compare your words with those chosen by a partner.

2 Looking at your own country

What's typically German? Collect your ideas and make up a German flag in the same way as the British flag above. Present your German flag to your partner. Explain your choices and discuss the words that are different.

benefits

Harry and Meghan

haggis

The Beckhams

rugby   fish & chips

hypocrisy   Oxbridge

Ascot

booze

House of Lords

Traditions

fashion

newspaper

The Empire

Wales

kilt

choir singing

crisps

The Beatles

monarchy

James Bond

Marmite

Giant's Causeway

football   pubs

boarding schools

humour   culture   Kate and William   Bed & Breakfast

weather   good   England   cuppa   Northern Ireland

manners

aristocracy   posh   class   queuing   Commonwealth

integrity   tea   Shakespeare   pound sterling   NHS

Stonehenge

bank holiday   Keira Knightley   Eurotunnel   accents

Scotland   irony   Plymouth

cider

heritage   rationalism   Rolls Royce   left-hand driving

prude   Monty Python   Downton Abbey

Westminster

J. K. Rowling   multiculturalism   Union

community   resilience   xenophobia   Wimbledon

PREVIEW

In this chapter you will gain an insight into British culture and learn about problems faced by people in Britain today.

Main topics

- Politics and traditions .... p. 60
- Multiculturalism in the UK .... p. 63
- Future challenges .... p. 70

Focus on Skills: LISTENING

- Listening for gist and detail......................... p. 61

Chapter Task:

Listening to a podcast and using it as a model to make a podcast of your own............ p. 73

Download an audio version of the text here:

Webcode context-75

Character of a country

A political state

The terms Great Britain, Britain, England and the UK are often mistakenly used as synonyms. Great Britain is the largest island of the British Isles (and also the largest island in Europe); England is a country on this island.
The United Kingdom (also called 'Britain') includes England, Scotland, Wales and Northern Ireland and is a state with a population of about 62 million people.
The Union Flag, also known as the Union Jack, has been the national flag of the United Kingdom since 1908 and represents the powerful community and strong individual identities of the different nations.
Characteristically, Scotland has always been seen as a separate nation and since the late 20th century, many Scots have wanted to be fully independent. However, in a 2014 referendum, 55% of the voting population voted to stay in the UK.
Even in the 21st century, the royal family remains a very important British institution. Events like the opening ceremony of the 2012 Olympic Games (in which one scene showed the Queen jumping out of a helicopter with James Bond), the Queen's Diamond Jubilee, Prince William's marriage to Kate Middleton and the birth of Prince George all saw the British population celebrate the fresh and modern image portrayed by their monarchy.

Multiculturalism

As head of the British Empire, the UK was once a colonial super-power with territories in many countries, like India, Australia, New Zealand and small island nations like the Seychelles, Mauritius and the Maldives. Today there is still a strong bond between many former states of the British Empire and most of these nations are members of the Commonwealth of Nations. Together, they work towards world peace, promotion of democracy worldwide, and ending racism, sexism, poverty, ignorance, and disease.
Partly due to its history, immigrants from all over the world have settled in the UK, shaping the culture and adding to the nation's diversity with their food, religions and music. The result is a very multicultural society with the aim that everyone, regardless of colour, race or culture, should feel at home.

An uncertain future

The UK plays a significant role in world politics and has permanent representation on the UN Security Council and in NATO. Furthermore, the UK has one of the largest and most influential economies in the world.
However, the financial crisis of 2007–2008 did not leave the UK unaffected and has led to economic problems, increased unemployment, social inequality and poverty. Added to this, anti-immigration feeling increased in some parts of the population, and politicians who opposed the EU and Britain's membership in the EU became more and more popular. This development culminated in a referendum held on 23 June 2016 with a majority voting for leaving the European Union. The future position of the UK both in relation to the EU and in the world is, as yet, unclear.

5

10

15

20

25

30

35

40

45

▶ SF 1: Dealing with unknown or new words

1 Using your own knowledge

For each of the three parts of the text, try to think of one piece of information which is not mentioned. Write them down and compare your findings with a partner.

2 Words in use

a Find a highlighted expression from the text that describes or names the following:

1 the name of the national flag of the UK
2 a person who joins a team, a union or an organization
3 relatives of the monarch of the United Kingdom
4 something that connects people or things, keeping them firmly together
5 a country that governs many other countries
6 an institution made up of countries that were once under the leadership or control of the British crown
7 having a strong effect on somebody or something

b Give definitions or use examples to explain the following terms from the text:

1 multicultural society	5 former
2 referendum	6 diversity
3 image	7 crisis
4 shape	8 social inequality

In the 2016 referendum a majority voted for the UK to leave the European Union.

3 Phrases into English

In each of the following sentences, a useful phrase from the text is missing. Copy and complete the sentences. If you aren't sure how to translate the German words, look at the text again.

1 The royal family aims to (*ein frisches, modernes Erscheinungsbild vermitteln*).
2 People with roots all over the world (*tragen zur Vielfalt der Nation bei*).
3 Everyone should feel safe in the country they live in (*unabhängig von Hautfarbe, Rasse oder Kultur*).
4 Events that began on Wall Street in New York (*haben das Vereinigte Königreich nicht unberührt gelassen*).
5 Politicians (*die die EU ablehnen*) have been gaining more popularity in some parts of the UK.

▶ LP 16: Avoiding Germanisms

4 GALLERY WALK Writing

Create a slogan for an educational course on the UK's history and traditions, culture or politics. Write a short explanation for your slogan and use as many highlighted words from the text above as possible. Present your slogans in a gallery walk and decide on the best three.

> ■ FACT FILE
>
> **Slogans** should be easy to understand and be memorable. Good slogans play with language (e.g. rhyme or rhythm and puns) to make you think.
>
>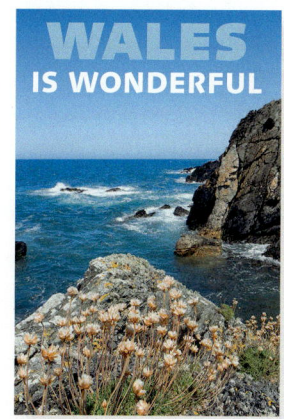
> **WALES IS WONDERFUL**

A crowned nation

A1 Dangerous books *Alan Bennett*

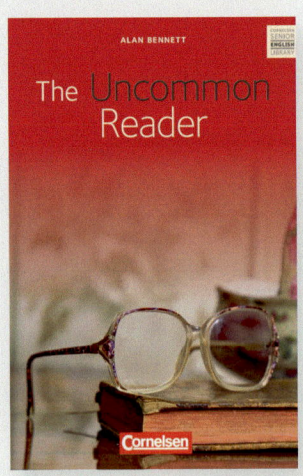

- In three sentences, state why you think reading is or isn't important. Share your answers in class.
- Discuss whether you think reading plays a part in a typical day in the Queen's life. What other duties might be on her agenda?

In the following extract from the novel The Uncommon Reader, *the Queen has developed an intense passion for literature. This starts to affect the way she carries out her public duties and what people think of her.*

One of the Queen's recurrent royal responsibilities was to open Parliament, an obligation she had never previously found particularly burdensome and actually rather enjoyed: to be driven down the Mall on a bright autumn morning even after fifty years was something of a treat. But not any more. She was dreading the two hours the whole thing was due to take, though fortunately they were in the coach, not the open ⁵

carriage, so she could take along her book. She'd got quite good at reading and waving, the trick being to keep the book below the level of the window and to keep focused on it and not on the crowds. The duke didn't like it one bit, of course, but goodness it ¹⁰ helped.

Which was all very well, except it was only when she was actually in the coach, with the procession drawn up in the palace forecourt and ready for the off, that, as she put on her glasses, she realised she'd ¹⁵ forgotten the book. And while the duke fumes in the corner and the postillions fidget, the horses shift and the harness clinks, Norman is rung on the mobile. The Guardsmen stand at ease and the procession waits. The officer in charge looks at his watch. Two minutes late. Knowing nothing displeases Her Majesty more and knowing nothing of the book, he does not look forward to the ²⁰ repercussions that must inevitably follow. But here is Norman, skittering across the gravel with the book thoughtfully hidden in a shawl, and off they go.

Still, it is an ill-tempered royal couple that is driven down the Mall, the duke waving viciously from his side, the Queen listlessly from hers, and at some speed, too, as the procession tries to pick up the two minutes that have been lost. ²⁵

At Westminster she popped the offending book behind a cushion in the carriage ready for the journey back, mindful as she sat on the throne and embarked on her speech of how tedious was the twaddle she was called on to deliver and that this was actually the only occasion when she got to read aloud to the nation. 'My government will do this ... my government will do that.' It was so barbarously phrased and wholly ³⁰ devoid of style or interest that she felt it demeaned the very act of reading itself, with this year's performance even more garbled than usual as she, too, tried to pick up the missing couple of minutes.

It was with some relief that she got back into the coach and reached behind the cushion for her book. It was not there. Steadfastly waving as they rumbled along, she ³⁵ surreptitiously felt behind the other cushions.

The Queen and the Duke of Edinburgh making a journey in the royal carriage

² **burdensome** implying hard work
³ **the Mall** [mæl] road leading to Buckingham Palace
¹⁴ **draw up** position yourself
ready for the off ready to go
¹⁶ **fume** be very angry
¹⁷ **postillion** [pɒˈstɪliən] driver of a coach with horses
fidget [ˈfɪdʒɪt] make nervous movements
Norman fictional character in *The Uncommon Reader* who works as the Queen's servant
¹⁸ **stand at ease** relax *(military)*
²¹ **repercussion** [ˌriːpəˈkʌʃn] negative consequence
skitter run in a funny way
²⁴ **vicious** [ˈvɪʃəs] angry
listless without energy or enthusiasm
²⁸ **twaddle** [ˈtwɒdl] *(infml)* silly speech
³⁰ **barbarous** very unpleasant
³¹ **devoid of sth.** without sth.
demean sth. make people have less respect for sth.
³⁶ **surreptitious** [ˌsʌrəpˈtɪʃəs] subtle

'You're not sitting on it?'

'Sitting on what?'

'My book.'

40 'No, I am not. Some British Legion people here, and wheelchairs. Wave, for God's sake.'

When they arrived at the palace she had a word with Grant, the young footman in charge, who said that while ma'am had been in the Lords the sniffer dogs had been round and security had confiscated the book. He thought it had probably been 45 exploded.

'Exploded?' said the Queen. 'But it was Anita Brookner.'

The young man, who seemed remarkably undeferential, said security may have thought it was a device.

The Queen said: 'Yes. That is exactly what it is. A book is a device to ignite the 50 imagination.'

The footman said: 'Yes, ma'am.'

It was as if he was talking to his grandmother, and not for the first time the Queen was made unpleasantly aware of the hostility her reading seemed to arouse.

'Very well,' she said. 'Then you should inform security that I shall expect to find 55 another copy of the same book, vetted and explosive free, waiting on my desk to-morrow morning. And another thing. The carriage cushions are filthy. Look at my gloves.' Her Majesty departed.

'Fuck,' said the footman, fishing out the book from where he had been told to hide it down the front of his breeches. But of the lateness of the procession, to everyone's 60 surprise nothing was officially said.

From: *The Uncommon Reader*, 2008, pp. 32–35

COMPREHENSION ◀

1 Identifying key points

  a Point out how the Queen's reading habit interferes with her duties.

  b Compare the Queen's day as shown in the passage to your initial ideas about a typical day in her life.

LANGUAGE AWARENESS ◀

2 Analysing direct speech

Analyse the language used in direct speech by the Queen, the duke and the footman. Assess its effect on your impression of their characters.

ANALYSIS ◀

3 Analysing humour

Analyse the *humour in this passage. Take into consideration how the *plot, certain aspects of the language and the *imagery contribute to the humorous effect.

BEYOND THE TEXT ◀

4 YOU CHOOSE ▶ **Creative writing**

  a Imagine another situation (e.g. naming a ship / attending a pop-concert / being on a state visit) in which the Queen does not fulfil her duties because of her new hobby and write a similar passage. Try to include elements of *humour.

  OR

  b After the incident, the footman tells his wife about his encounter with the Queen. Write their dialogue and include the events that probably took place while the Queen was opening the Parliament.
SUPPORT ▶ p. 230

---

40 **British Legion** ['liːdʒn] organization that helps ex-soldiers
44 **confiscate sth.** take sth. away
46 **Anita Brookner** (1928–2016) British novelist and art historian
47 **undeferential** [ˌʌndɪfə'renʃl] showing no respect
49 **ignite sth.** *etwas entzünden*
55 **vet sth.** check sth.
59 **breeches** ['brɪtʃɪz] (pl) *Reiterhose*

■ LANGUAGE AWARENESS

Using direct speech
Integrating direct speech, e.g. by quoting somebody or by reflecting (parts of) a conversation, is an effective stylistic device when producing a prose text such as a speech, a written discussion or even a novel. It can lend credibility to what you are saying, but also evoke a certain atmosphere, thus conveying authenticity and a special mood.

▶ LA 2: Communication problems and compensation strategies
▶ LA 4: Influencing through language

▶ SF 19: Analysing narrative prose
▶ LP 18: Writing about texts
▶ SF 37: Doing a creative writing task
▶ CC 6: Talking about sensitive issues

Find out more about the British royal family here:
 Webcode context-14

■ FACT FILE

The Palace of Westminster, London

The British system of government

The head of state is the king or queen, who has many ceremonial functions and social duties but no real power. The monarch's duties include opening Parliament and officially appointing the Prime Minister after his or her election.

The UK Parliament is known as the 'Mother of Parliaments' because it has served as a model for many governments all over the world. It dates back to the year 1215, when a group of noblemen forced King John of England to respect certain rights. Among these, set down in the Magna Carta, was their

A session of the English Parliament, ca. 1690

right to be consulted before the king could make them pay new taxes. Over the centuries, this group of noblemen evolved into today's Parliament.

The two houses of Parliament, the House of Lords and the House of Commons, meet in the Palace of Westminster. Thus journalists often refer to 'Westminster' when they mean Parliament, especially if they are talking about the House of Commons. There are currently over 700 members of the House of Lords, but their power is limited. Although both houses of Parliament must, in theory, approve laws before they are submitted to the king or queen, the Lords can only delay a bill that has passed in the House of Commons. Traditionally, a committee of the House of Lords was also the highest court in the land, but that function has been moved to the newly created Supreme Court.

Real power lies with the House of Commons, which is elected for up to five years (although the Prime Minister can call a general election any time before that). Each Member of Parliament (MP) represents one of 650 constituencies (electoral districts) in the UK. In each constituency, the candidate with the most votes wins, and that person then sits in the Commons. In the

UK's so-called 'first-past-the-post' system, all other votes are worthless. This effectively prevents smaller parties being elected to Parliament and can potentially lead to a majority in Parliament that does not always reflect the total number of votes. For example, in the 2005 general election, the Labour party won 55% of the seats in the House of Commons with just 35% of the votes.

Her Majesty's Government consists of the Prime Minister (PM) and the Cabinet, which is made up of the MPs who run the different government departments. The most important ministers are the Chancellor of the Exchequer, who is in charge of finance, the Foreign Secretary and the Home Secretary, who is responsible for the country's internal affairs. In the press, the Prime Minister's office is often referred to as 'Number 10', after its address at 10 Downing Street, and the ministries are known as 'Whitehall', after the street in London where most of them are located.

1 *Describe the roles of the following people and groups to a partner using one sentence for each*:
Partner A: the Prime Minister • the Cabinet
Partner B: an MP • the monarch

2 *In a table, list what you now know about one of the houses of the UK Parliament. Present your list to your partner.*
Partner A: The House of Lords
Partner B: The House of Commons

3 *List differences and similarities to the German system of government.*

▶ The British System of Government, p. 388

Listening for gist and detail

Listening is the key to successful oral communication. It requires focus, preparation and practice.

What do the British think of the royal family?

1 Before listening
You are going to hear two short interviews about people's opinions of the British monarchy. What might people say? Write 2–3 sentences.

2 Dealing with different accents
When listening to native English speakers, you will often hear people speak with different accents. When somebody's accent is difficult to understand, you should focus on words you can understand and use the context to figure out the rest of the sentence. As you listen, you will probably get used to the accent.
a Listen to a short excerpt of an interview. The interviewer and the interviewee have different accents. Try to write down exactly what both men say, then compare your answers with a partner.
b Discuss which man was easier to understand and why.

3 First listening: listening for gist
a Skim through the task below and note down keywords that you can listen out for. Compare your notes with a partner.
b Listen to the extract, then choose the right answers.
1 The first interviewee …
… considers the institution of the monarchy a brilliant idea.
… isn't really sure what he thinks about the monarchy.
… completely rejects the monarchy.
2 The young couple …
… think the royal family should be abolished.
… have generally positive opinions about the royal family.
… think the royal family is mainly a bad thing for the UK.

4 Second listening: listening for detail
Again, skim through the questions to find out what specific information you will have to listen out for.
a Listen to the first interview again. Are the sentences below true or false? Correct the false answers.
1 The first interviewee understands why some people would like to have an elected president instead of a monarch.
2 The Queen is his favourite member of the royal family.
3 He was born during the Queen's reign.
4 He does not think that Charles will become King.

Buckingham Palace, home of the Queen in London

b Listen to the second interview and finish the sentences.
1 The young woman says that the royal family does a lot of good for …
2 The young man mentions … as two examples of the stereotypical English image.
3 The young man says that the … has been lost.
4 The young man's favourite member of the royal family is …
5 The young man thinks that Kate has …
c Compare and discuss your results with a partner.

5 Evaluating the listening procedure
a Compare your initial expectations which you wrote for Task **1** with what you actually heard.
b Discuss the listening procedure with a partner. To what extent were your anticipations useful? Which tip or strategy was most helpful to you?

A2 Does Britain still need the monarchy?

COMPREHENSION ◀

🎧 **CD1** 15

▶ SF 22: Listening
▶ SF 7: Working with closed test formats

1 Listening for gist
Listen to part two of the podcast and decide which of the following statements best expresses the main ideas of the speakers.
a 1 The first interviewee would keep the monarchy, but doesn't like it very much.
2 The first interviewee thinks the media hate the royal family.
b 1 The second interviewee quite likes William and Harry.
2 The second interviewee thinks Australia should no longer be a member of the Commonwealth.

▶ SF 7: Working with closed test formats

2 Listening for detail
Listen to the first interview again. Match the arguments given in the list below to those of the interviewee. There are more arguments than needed.

do a lot of charity • very expensive • outdated institution • symbol of Britain • attracts tourists • good role model • a tradition to keep • too many scandals • arrogant and snobby family • close to the people • loved by the media

BEYOND THE TEXT ◀

3 Preparing for a discussion
a Look again at the arguments put forward by all of the speakers in both parts of the podcast. Divide their arguments into two columns: 'in favour of' and 'against' the monarchy.
b Together with a partner, add further arguments to your list.

4 Having a discussion
a In groups of 4–5, discuss whether the monarchy in Britain should be abolished. ▶ LANGUAGE HELP
b CHALLENGE ▶ Take notes of the different arguments raised during your discussion and present the three most convincing ones to the rest of the class.

A3 The British and their tea

The British are famous for their love of tea. In the following podcast, you will get to know more about this tradition.

- Before listening, brainstorm in class what you know about the British tradition of drinking tea.

COMPREHENSION ◀

1 Listening for gist
In one sentence, summarize what the podcast is about.

2 Listening for detail
  a Complete the following statements about the history of tea.
  1 The British made their first cup of tea sometime in the middle of the … century.
  2 In the 19th century, tea became popular among … people.
  3 Tea drinking has a much longer history in …, where people have drunk tea for thousands of years.
  4 Nearly everyone in Britain puts … in their tea, and about a third of people add … to make the tea sweet.
  b **CHALLENGE** ▶ While working on **2a**, take notes on how to make a nice cup of tea the British way.

3 Analysing style
How does the speaker of the podcast try to hold the audience's attention and entertain his listeners? **SUPPORT** ▶ p. 230

▶ SF 22: Listening

🎧 **CD1** 16
rich *(here)* dark; strong

┌─ **TROUBLE SPOT** ─────┐
drunk *(v)* = getrunken
drunk *(adj)* = betrunken
drunk *(n)* = Betrunkene/r
└──────────────────┘

▶ EE 1: Eating in and out

▶ SF 17: Analysing stylistic devices

📍 CULTURE SPOT

The Fourth Plinth is one of four pillars in Trafalgar Square in London, which was built in 1840. As there wasn't enough money to make a statue for it, it stood empty for 150 years. In 1999 a commission decided to display contemporary artworks on it.

In 2015 the artwork Gift Horse by German-born artist Hans Haacke was unveiled.

The Fourth Plinth

1 Comment on the idea of using the Fourth Plinth as a display for art.

2 Research other artworks that have been featured on the Fourth Plinth. Present the one you like best to the class. Give reasons.

▶ S3: Doing research

The multicultural face of the UK

■ FACT FILE

From Empire to Commonwealth – Britain as a multicultural society

The British Empire was once the largest colonial empire in the world, covering nearly one fifth of the land worldwide during the late 19th and early 20th centuries.

Beginning in the 16th century, Britain started to establish colonies all over the world, including settlement colonies like Canada, Australia and New Zealand; trading colonies (e.g. in North America, India and Africa); as well as strategically important naval bases in the Mediterranean (e.g. Gibraltar). Around 1920, Britain ruled over approximately 20% of the world's population. It was said that the sun never set on the Empire because its economic and political power as well as territory were so great. English was the language used to administer this vast empire, a language that thus became deeply rooted worldwide.

In the aftermath of World War I, colonies started to seek autonomy and political independence. This led to a decline of the British Empire. In 1931 the Commonwealth of Nations was founded. Hong Kong was the last colony to become independent in 1997.

Today the Commonwealth of Nations is a voluntary association of 53 sovereign countries of the former British Empire. It includes about two billion people, or 30% of the world's population. The ceremonial Head of the Commonwealth is the British monarch. The states are united by the important role English plays in each of them, by common cultural elements, history and shared values such as the promotion and protection of democracy, development (with respect to economy, sustainability, health and education), the rule of law and the guarantee of human rights. In 1961, for example, the members of the Commonwealth united against South Africa's apartheid regime.

However, promoting democracy is a work in progress, in the course of which the Commonwealth has faced challenges and seen setbacks. Not surprisingly, the Commonwealth has its critics who believe that it offers the appearance of legitimacy, even if some member nations have corrupt governments, flawed democracies or authoritarian regimes. Membership can be, and in fact has been, suspended in several cases. Suspended

Queen Victoria (1819–1901) ruled over almost a quarter of the world's population by the end of her reign.

countries can remain members unless they choose to leave. Fiji, independent since 1970, was suspended from the organization for various crimes against humanity in 2009. Pakistan or Nigeria, on the other hand, have returned after their suspension.

Every four years, athletes from 70 nations and territories take part in the Commonwealth Games, which include classic Olympic sports as well as typical sports played in Commonwealth countries (e.g. netball). The three key values of the Commonwealth Games movement are humanity, equality and destiny.

Throughout the age of Empire and Commonwealth, people have migrated to Britain. After World War II, Britain needed workers, so it encouraged Commonwealth citizens (e.g. from India, Pakistan and the Caribbean) to come to Britain, granting them the right to live and work there without restrictions. However, once the job situation changed and the number of immigrants coming to Britain increased, racial tensions and riots developed. The 1960s, however, marked a change in immigration policies. In 1962, the Commonwealth Immigrants Act was passed to restrict immigration. More immigration acts as well as anti-discrimination acts followed in order to ensure equal rights for all citizens. Immigration has been strictly controlled, but people from all over the world have continued to migrate to Britain (e.g. refugees from the former Soviet Union in the 1990s and East-Europeans from 2004 onwards).

The question of whether or not (and how) to restrict immigration – even from EU countries – continued to be debated and arguably tipped the scales in the 2016 EU referendum, when a close majority of Britons voted 'Leave'. It remains to be seen whether the UK will stay the open, multicultural society that it has been for so long.

Comment on the quote 'The sun never sets on the British Empire'.

State possible connections between imperialism, immigration and the development of English as a world language.

B1 The British Empire report

The video you are about to watch presents the rise, dominance and fall of the British Empire.

1 Before viewing

Before you watch the video, speculate about how the filmmaker might deal with the subject of colonialism. Take into consideration the Fact File 'From Empire to Commonwealth'.

— **ANALYSIS** ◀

2 Viewing for the first time

Watch the video and describe it with two adjectives which you find most suitable: e.g. funny, informative, exaggerated, annoying, innovative, childish, surprising, etc. Explain your choices.

3 Examining how material is presented

a Watch the video for a second time. Examine the different methods that are used to present information. Consider how the events are visualized and supported by film excerpts, still pictures, sound effects and music.

b Compare your findings and discuss their effect on the viewer. To what extent do the presenter and the different material that is shown support the viewer's understanding of the Empire's history?

— **BEYOND THE TEXT** ◀

4 Beyond the video

a List five important dates and events in German history. With a partner compare your lists and decide on the four most important events.

b **CHALLENGE** Write the script for a video report aimed at an English audience in which you show and comment on important dates in German history. If you want to, you can use *irony and *humour or you can make it informative and objective.

▶ SF 23: Analysing a film

DVD

peak highest point
leap big jump
shift sth. move sth.
spell trouble be a problem

▶ SF 37: Doing a creative writing task

Map of the world showing in red the extent of the British Empire in 1907

3

Part B

B2 Between two cultures   *Mike Bartlett*

In the play Artefacts *by Mike Bartlett, Kelly is a teenage girl living in Great Britain with her mother Susan. Her father left the family when Kelly was little to live in his home country Iraq. In the following scenes, she meets her father Ibrahim for the first time since he left.*

- Read the two extracts and imagine what the scenes would look like on a stage.

Extract 1

IBRAHIM	Do you think we look alike?	
KELLY	You and my uncle?	
IBRAHIM	You and me.	
KELLY	Uh … No.	
IBRAHIM	You're passionate.	5
KELLY	I'm English.	
IBRAHIM	You are half Iraqi. You can have an Iraqi passport now.	
KELLY	That's not much use.	
IBRAHIM	Would you prefer it if I had been an American?	
KELLY	No.	10
	Well, yeah. That would be better though, wouldn't it? Cos an American passport's worth loads. I could go there and work and stuff. But I told you I'm not going to go to Iraq, am I?	

After a short pause when Kelly's mother Susan enters, Kelly continues.

KELLY	This afternoon when I was bored I looked in the mirror cos, apparently, I'm half Iraqi.	15
SUSAN	Are you sure you're both all right?	
KELLY	But which bits?	
SUSAN	Up here?	
KELLY	Hips. Hands.	20
IBRAHIM	Kelly?	
KELLY	I've got English legs. Iraqi breasts.	
IBRAHIM	I wish we could've met earlier.	
KELLY	But my stomach is slightly potted.	
IBRAHIM	Kelly? […]	25
KELLY	I have a little pot belly. Maybe this is the point they mix. The two countries. Where my genes got confused. This belly is not Iraqi or English. It's Engraqi. Iringlish. I like my belly. Yeah. […] Am I what you expected?	
IBRAHIM	I tried not to expect anything.	30
KELLY	But you did.	
IBRAHIM	I imagined you might look like Kate Winslet.	
KELLY	This isn't going very well, is it?	
IBRAHIM	I don't know.	
KELLY	Bit of a fucking disappointment for you.	35
IBRAHIM	No.	
KELLY	If you were after –	
IBRAHIM	You are better than Kate Winslet.	
KELLY	What do you want?	
IBRAHIM	You are you.	40
KELLY	Why are you here? Now, what do you *want*?	

11 **cos** [kɒz] *(infml)* because
24 **potted** *(here)* larger than usual

■ **LANGUAGE AWARENESS**

Language reflecting the world
The central conflict of the play *Artefacts* – the question 'Where do I belong?' – is also reflected in the language used. In a mixture of Iraqi and English, Kelly ironically describes herself as 'Engraqi' or 'Iringlish'. Word formations react to changes in the world but can also cause serious misunderstandings, especially when it comes to the sensitive issues of ethnicity and race, cf. so-called 'hyphenated ethnicities' such as *Anglo-Saxons* or *Afro-Caribbeans* as well as terms like *African Americans* (i.e. Americans of African descent); or the German nicknames *Wessi, Ossi* and *Wossi*.

▶ LA 1: Varieties of English
▶ LA 4: Influencing through language

IBRAHIM	That we meet.
KELLY	Just that.
IBRAHIM	Yes.
45 KELLY	You don't want money?
IBRAHIM	I run the National Museum of Iraq. In Baghdad. A number of our artefacts were stolen. During the war. I was invited to come and give a lecture at the British Museum about the current state of our collection. That is where I have been today.
50 KELLY	So I'm not actually sure why you came at all.
IBRAHIM	It is expensive to fly here. I will probably never come back to Britain. So I thought it best we meet.

Extract 2

On her first visit to Iraq, Kelly meets her father's other family. One of Ibrahim's daughters has been kidnapped and Kelly asks her father about this incident.

IBRAHIM	Why? Why are you asking? Why do you want to know?
KELLY	I've got a right to know.
55 IBRAHIM	A right? You have no right to know about my family.
KELLY	She's my sister.
IBRAHIM	And I'm your father.
KELLY	Apparently.
IBRAHIM	You should trust me that I will do the right thing. But you don't. Do you?
60	You think you know better. You have not been here a day yet. What makes you think you will know better than me?
KELLY	Maybe I don't trust you. Not hard to work out why, is it? [...]
IBRAHIM	What makes you think what I am doing is a mistake?
KELLY	You are that kind of man.
65 IBRAHIM	Weak.
KELLY	Careless.
IBRAHIM	And why do you think I am *careless*? I will tell you.
KELLY	Yeah, all right then, tell me what I think.
IBRAHIM	You come here and you see this city and you see me and my normal
70	house. You see how poor we are and we don't have things you have. And you see on your news how the country is fighting itself. And you think we are all careless. No, not just careless, you think we are stupid. So this is why you're asking what is going on, because you want to make sure that I am being civilised in what I am doing. That I am being
75	intelligent – *reasonable* in how I am behaving. Because we Iraqis, you think, we tend to get things wrong all the time. We allow our girls to be kidnapped. We tend to mess things up. That is really why you do not trust me.
80 KELLY	Cos I'm racist.
IBRAHIM	Because you are English. And you don't know any better. When you are a child in England you are still taught underneath that you should rule the world. How in the end Britain has always made the world better.
KELLY	You told me I'm half Iraqi.
85 IBRAHIM	I hoped you were.
KELLY	I am. Whether I like it or not. I can't choose.
IBRAHIM	Yes, you can. You can choose where you belong.

From: *Artefacts*, 2008, pp. 8, 41–42

Actress Lizzie Watts performing in a production of Artefacts *at the Bush Theatre in London*

■ LANGUAGE AWARENESS

Layout

In printed texts the typography (*italics*, **bold face**) is often used to underline/point out what would have been stressed if it had been spoken. It thus works as an implicit stage direction and influences the readers because it ironically turns what is said/written into the opposite, questions what is said or simply emphasizes its message. In digital messages or texts emoticons are often used in a similar way.

▶ LA 4: Influencing through language

76 **tend to do sth.** do sth. regularly
78 **mess sth. up** do sth. very badly

Part B

► SF 20: Analysing drama
► LP 18: Writing about texts

■ **LANGUAGE AWARENESS**

Colloquialism
In literature, colloquialism is the use of informal words and expressions in conversations to underline the speaker's social status, level of education, relationship with others, etc.
The opposite of colloquialism is standard or formal English.
Examples:

wanna	want to
gonna	going to
go nuts	go insane

Both varieties of English can be used intentionally to create am impression of belonging to the same peer group or showing respect.

► LA 1: Varieties of English
► LA 4: Influencing through language
► SF 37: Doing a creative writing task
► SF 27: Having a discussion

► LP 13: Placing emphasis on key points
► SF 34: Argumentative writing

COMPREHENSION ◄

1 Looking for the main idea
a Describe how Kelly tries to find out which culture she belongs to.
b Point out which prejudices towards the Iraqi and English cultures are discussed in the text.

ANALYSIS ◄

2 Analysing character relationships
Analyse the relationship between Kelly and her father Ibrahim. Reflect on what they talk about and how they speak to each other.
SUPPORT ▶ p. 230

LANGUAGE AWARENESS ◄

3 Studying colloquial language
a Read the explanation of colloquialism on the left and find examples of colloquial language in the conversation between Kelly and Ibrahim.
b Rewrite the examples you found in the text in formal English.

BEYOND THE TEXT ◄

4 YOU CHOOSE ▶ Creative writing

a Write an email Kelly sends to her best friend in Britain after she has met her father in Iraq. **OR** b Together with a partner, write a dialogue between Kelly's father Ibrahim and her mum Susan after the first meeting of father and daughter.

5 Thinking about cultural identity
a Together with a partner, discuss whether 'You can choose where you belong' (l. 88). Who or what influences you in your choice? Think about family, culture, education and list concrete examples for and against the quote.
b **CHALLENGE ▶** Write a *comment on Ibrahim's idea that 'You can choose where you belong.' (l. 87)

B3 A closer look at Britain's Muslims *Harriet Sherwood*

The election of Sadiq Khan as Mayor of London in 2016 seemed to demonstrate that British Muslims have definitely entered the mainstream. A recent survey adds some surprising nuances to the popular image.

Muslims in the UK attach more importance to being British than the general population, according to a report. They also place greater emphasis on education, and identify more strongly with their religious identity than their non-Muslim peers. [...]

Eighty-five percent said they felt they belonged to Britain. More than half (55%)
5 said their national identity was important, compared with 44% of the general population.

Religious identity is extremely or very important to 94%, and more than half pray at least five times a day or engage in worship of some kind. Asif Aziz, the chairman of the Aziz Foundation, which commissioned the report with the Joseph Rowntree
10 Charitable Trust, Barrow Cadbury Trust and Unbound Philanthropy, said: 'While British Muslims identify strongly with their religious identity, they are also staunchly British.'

Muslim children have high aspirations for their educational achievement, with 56% saying it was very likely they would go to
15 university, compared with 38% of non-Muslim children. More Muslim girls than boys expected a university education.

Celebrating Eid ul-Fitr in London

More than 7% of Muslims are unemployed, compared with 4% of the UK population as a whole.

Almost two-thirds of Muslims said they think different
20 religious and ethnic groups should mix more. A majority of Muslims of all ages wear a poppy on Remembrance Day and almost three-quarters said they always or sometimes send Christmas cards.

Forty-five percent of Muslims under 24 said at least half their
25 friends are from outside their ethnic group. Those in London are more likely to have a diverse group of friends than Muslims in the rest of the country.

Muslims tend to have more conservative social attitudes than the general population, the report said. Half of Muslim men and one-third of women believe wives should obey their husbands, and 38% of men said it is acceptable for a British Mus-
30 lim to have more than one wife. A majority said homosexuality should not be legal.

From: 'Muslims place greater importance on national identity, finds UK study', *The Guardian*, 21 March 2018

---

8 **engage in sth.** do sth.
  worship *(n)* prayer
9 **commission sth.** *etwas in Auftrag geben*
11 **staunch** [stɔːntʃ] very firm
13 **aspiration** ambition
20 **mix** *(v)* have social contact
21 **poppy** *Mohnblume*
  Remembrance Day 11 Nov., the day on which people remember the victims of the First World War (1914–18). In the UK, the poppy is the symbol of Remembrance Day.
26 **diverse** [daɪˈvɜːs] mixed

COMPREHENSION ◀

1 Organizing information
  a Collect information from the text in two lists under the headings 'Ways in which British Muslims are like other UK citizens' and 'Ways in which British Muslims and other UK citizens differ'.
  b Outline those pieces of information in the text that are most surprising to you.

ANALYSIS ◀

2 Talking about statistics
  a Collect words and phrases from the text that can be used for talking about groups.
  b Conduct a survey on social attitudes in your class. Use the phrases you have collected to summarize your results.

▶ SF 15: Marking up a text / Making and taking notes

🎧 **CD1** 17

disillusionment [ˌdɪsɪˈluːʒnmənt]
state of no longer feeling
enthusiasm
ensure sth. [ɪnˈʃʊə] make sure
that sth. happens

▶ SF 12: Analysing charts
  and graphs
▶ SF 22: Listening

Where do we go from here?

C1 Before the EU referendum

Listen to a speech made in 2013 by David Cameron, British Prime Minister 2010–2016. Cameron talks about the UK's membership in the EU.

────────────────────────────────── **COMPREHENSION** ◀

1 Listening for gist
Which of these topics does David Cameron talk about?
1 reasons for the British to be sceptical about the EU
2 arguments why he wants a referendum right now
3 the right time for a referendum

2 Listening for detail
a Complete the sentences taken from Cameron's speech.
1 They resent the … in our national life by what they see as unnecessary rules and …
2 But I don't believe that to make a … at this moment is the right way forward, either for Britain or for Europe as a …
3 And when the referendum comes let me say now that if we can … such an arrangement, I will … for it with all my heart and …
b **CHALLENGE** ▶ Explain the reasons for the anti-EU feeling mentioned by Cameron in your own words.

────────────────────────────────────── **ANALYSIS** ◀

▶ SF 17: Analysing stylistic
  devices

3 Analysing style
Listen again. Analyse how Cameron tries to convince his listeners of his views. Focus on language and content. Is he successful? **SUPPORT** ▶ p. 231

C2 Trying to understand the Brexit vote *Catherine Hickley*

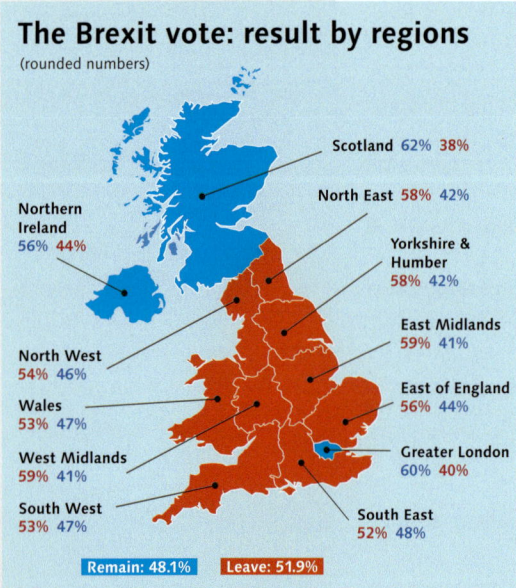

The Brexit vote: result by regions
(rounded numbers)

Scotland 62% 38%
North East 58% 42%
Northern Ireland 56% 44%
Yorkshire & Humber 58% 42%
East Midlands 59% 41%
North West 54% 46%
East of England 56% 44%
Wales 53% 47%
Greater London 60% 40%
West Midlands 59% 41%
South West 53% 47%
South East 52% 48%

Remain: 48.1%   Leave: 51.9%

Source: BBC

Eight months after the referendum on EU membership, British journalist Catherine Hickley examines the motives behind anti-EU sentiment in the UK.

Am Morgen nach dem 23. Juni 2016 war ich eine von vielen fassungslosen ungläubigen Remainern. […] Für mich war das Ergebnis ebenso rätselhaft wie für viele Deutsche. In den Monaten, die seit dem ersten Schock vergangen sind, habe ich versucht, die Brexitbefürworter, die Brexiteers, zu verstehen, von denen es auch in meiner Familie welche gibt. […] 5

Rund 3,5 Millionen Einwohner Großbritanniens sind nicht-britische EU-Bürger. Die meisten sind mit der Osterweiterung ab 2004 ins Land gekommen. Damals hatte Großbritannien – anders als Deutschland – den Menschen in den neuen EU-Staaten vollständigen Zugang zu seinem Arbeitsmarkt gewährt. Mittlerweile gibt es mehr gebürtige Polen in Großbritannien als Inder. Seit 2009 kamen dann zunehmend EU-Immigranten aus Spanien, Griechenland und Portugal ins Land. 10 15

Am Anfang wurde diese Zuwanderung positiv gesehen. Die vielen jungen Polen und Ungarn, die in Pubs, Restaurants, Shops und Pflegeheimen arbeiteten, galten
20 als Zeichen für eine florierende, attraktive Wirtschaft. [...]

Doch in der Wahrnehmung der Briten hat sich spätestens seit der Finanzkrise etwas verschoben. Es ist der Eindruck entstanden, Großbritannien platze aus allen Nähten; das Bevölkerungswachstum sei untragbar, die Lebensqualität verschlechtere sich ohne Aussicht auf Besserung. So kam es zur gefühlten Notwendigkeit, die „Kon-
25 trolle zurückzugewinnen", wie ein Slogan der Leave-Kampagne lautete. [...]

Den Briten geht es um viel praktischere Probleme, wie beispielsweise die über-forderte öffentliche Infrastruktur und der überteuerte Wohnungsmarkt. Wer schon einmal in der Rushhour mit der U-Bahn gefahren ist, die Nase in die Achselhöhle eines anderen gequetscht, kann mit den Londonern fühlen, die das zweimal täglich
30 tun. Berufspendler, die auf die desaströsen südlichen und südöstlichen Bahnstrecken angewiesen sind, kennen die endlosen Verspätungen und die häufigen Zugausfälle. Die Londoner haben zwar dafür gestimmt, in der EU zu bleiben, aber die südöst-lichen Regionen, in denen viele leben, die sehr lange in die Stadt pendeln müssen, waren zu 51,8 Prozent für den Brexit.

35 Außerdem haben viele Briten die ewigen Krisen im staatlichen Gesundheitswesen und der überfüllten Schulen satt. Eine Bekannte hat für den Brexit gestimmt, weil ihre Tochter keinen Platz an einer guten staatlichen Schule bekommen hatte. [...]

Ein chronisches, krasses Missverhältnis zwischen Angebot und Nachfrage hat außerdem den britischen Wohnungsmarkt zerstört. Der durchschnittliche
40 Wohnungspreis beträgt acht durchschnittliche Jahreseinkommen – ein Rekord. Seit 1997 hat sich dieses Verhältnis verdoppelt. Immer mehr junge Menschen in London sind deshalb gezwungen, ein Zimmer mit einem Fremden zu teilen, um die Miet-kosten zu senken. Wohl gemerkt, es handelt sich dabei nicht um Studenten, sondern um Arbeitnehmer.

45 Man kann nicht leugnen, dass die Einwanderung die Wohnungsnot in Großbritan-nien verschärft hat, auch wenn das nur einer von vielen Faktoren ist. Und es hilft nicht, diejenigen, die der Einwanderung die Schuld für ihre unmittelbaren Sorgen geben, als Rassisten abzutun, was zu viele im Remain-Lager getan haben. Das soll allerdings nicht heißen, dass es keine Fremdenfeindlichkeit in Großbritannien gibt.
50 Zahlreiche Menschen haben das Referendum genutzt, um ihren persönlichen Hass an unschuldigen Litauern und Slowaken abzureagieren.

Es ist aber unwahrscheinlich, dass der Brexit diese Probleme lösen wird.

From: 'Das Empire ist längst Geschichte', *ZEIT online*, 20 February 2017

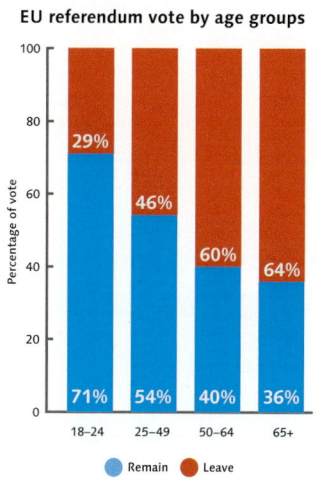

EU referendum vote by age groups

Source: yougov.com

1 Mediation (German → English)
Your English friend George, who voted for the UK to remain in the EU, can't understand why so many people in his country support Brexit. You find this article online and summarize for him the reasons the author names for the majority decision in favour of leaving the EU.

▶ SF 41: Mediation of written and oral texts

2 Writing
Based on the graphs on this page and on the previous page, analyse the result of the Brexit referendum. Compare this result with your personal position on Brexit. **SUPPORT** ▶ p. 231

■ TROUBLE SPOT
Brexit (without 'the')
= *der Brexit*
'Are you for or against **Brexit**?'
(But before another noun:)
the Brexit *referendum*, **the Brexit** *vote*, **the Brexit** *chaos*

C3 Reactions to the referendum

In September 2017, about a year after the Brexit referendum, Trevor White published the following cartoon.

COMPREHENSION ◀

1 Describing a cartoon

Describe the cartoon. Include the topic it addresses, who drew it, the time of publication and a systematic outlining of the elements it makes use of.

▶ LANGUAGE HELP

ANALYSIS ◀

2 Colours and symbols

Examine Trevor White's view of the situation after the Brexit referendum and the means he employs to express this view in the cartoon.

BEYOND THE CARTOON ◀

3   YOU CHOOSE ▶   Practising speaking

a Compare the outlook expressed by the cartoonist with that of the Brexiteers as described by Catherine Hickley (cf. **C2**, pp. 70–71).	**OR**	**b** CHALLENGE ▶ Prepare a monologue on whether leaving the EU presents a chance or a great risk to the UK. If possible include information on recent political developments and decisions.

■ **LANGUAGE HELP**

- eddy
- St. George's Cross
- English flag
- panic
- compare sth. with/to

A podcast on British culture

In this Chapter Task you will listen to a report on a British TV show and use what you learn to create your own podcast on an aspect of British culture.

> ■ **FACT FILE**
>
> ***Downton Abbey*** is a well-known and popular British TV series that is broadcast by ITV in the UK and PBS in the USA. The period drama series, set in Yorkshire, England, follows the wealthy Crawley family through life's events as they are impacted by history. Some of the major historical events include the sinking of the Titanic, World War I and the Spanish influenza pandemic. Julian Fellowes is the creator, executive producer and writer of this series that is co-produced by Carnival Films and Masterpiece. *Downton Abbey* has won several awards, including a Golden Globe and a Primetime Emmy.

1 Understanding an example podcast

a Read the Fact File and look at the picture. Collect ideas about the setting of the series.

b Listen to the podcast and complete the sentence: In the interview …
   1 … the executive producer summarizes the plot of *Downton Abbey* for those who do not know the series.
   2 … *Downton Abbey's* success in the UK and worldwide is mentioned.
   3 … the executive producer announces the final season of the series and gives hints about its ending.

c Listen again. Which statements are true? Correct the wrong statements.
   1 *Downton Abbey* is set around the time of the Second World War.
   2 *Downton Abbey* is a uniquely English *genre that cannot be produced anywhere other than in Great Britain.
   3 *Downton Abbey* portrays the class system and shows how aristocrats lived in a very contemporary way.
   4 The fourth series and the Christmas special have to be cancelled since many key stars are leaving the series for Hollywood.

2 Thinking about podcasts

Collect ideas about what makes a podcast interesting.

3 Creating a podcast

Go back to the flag on the Lead-in pages (pp. 54–55). Choose a topic connected to the UK and discuss it in your own short podcast, between three and four minutes long. Organize your work, make an outline, write your script, practise and record it.

4 Evaluating a podcast

Present your podcast to the class. While listening to your classmates' podcasts, take notes on their content as well as their strengths and weaknesses. Give feedback, praising the aspects that you liked and giving clear, constructive advice for the aspects your classmates could improve. Your teacher will give you an assessment sheet.

🎧 **CD1** 18

expressly definitely
reverential [ˌrevəˈrenʃl] very serious
life blood sth. that is necessary for success and survival

▶ SF 22: Listening

▶ SF 4: Doing project work
▶ SF 5: Structuring information and ideas
▶ LP 13: Placing emphasis on key points

4 India – a Kaleidoscope

A

- India is the largest democracy, the 2nd most populous country and the 9th largest economy in the world.

- Four world religions originated in the Indian subcontinent: Hinduism, Buddhism, Jainism and Sikhism.

- 50 % of all Indians are below the age of 25.

B

Download a list of chapter vocab here: (🔊) **Webcode** context-76

▶ SF 11: Analysing pictures

1 A first glimpse of India: photos and facts

Work with a partner. Choose one picture and speculate about the people you see and where and when the photo might have been taken. Link your photo to the facts about India. Present your picture in class, saying what you find most interesting and surprising.

2 Presenting India

Form groups. Imagine you are going to produce a short video clip about India for a multicultural festival at your school. Brainstorm ideas about what your audience might want to know about India, and discuss how you would present them in your clip. Share your ideas in class. Use them when you work on the Chapter Task (cf. p. 93).

C

D

- The literacy rate in India is 65% among women and 82% among men.

- India is about 31% urban (as compared to 82.4% in the USA and 75% in Germany).

- Mumbai (21 million), Delhi (16 million) and Kolkata (14 million) are among the world's biggest metropolitan areas.

literacy ['lɪtərəsi] ability to read and write

$$(2 \times 3)2 + 4 = 16$$

$$(3 \times 3) + 6 = 15$$

E

PREVIEW

In this chapter you will learn about India as a modern society and about its history. You will gain an insight into India's development from a former British colony into an independent nation and learn about Indian communities abroad.

Main topics

- India's past, the legacy of the British Empire and Mahatma Gandhi .... p. 78
- Aspects of Indian life today .... p. 85
- Indians abroad .... p. 89

Focus on Skills: LISTENING and VIEWING

- Listening to a radio interview .... p. 84
- Watching a film trailer .... p. 86

Chapter Task: Putting together a multi-media presentation about India for a multicultural festival at your school .... p. 93

*Download an audio version
of the text here:*

Webcode context-77

TROUBLE SPOT

Hindi = one of the official
languages spoken in India
Hindu (l. 27) = a person whose
religion is Hinduism

---

*The emperor Akhbar with
his cavalry (Moghul painting,
ca. 1590)*

*Jawaharlal Nehru (left) and
Mahatma Gandhi (1946)*

India then and now

India before the arrival of the Europeans

Mark Twain once referred to India as 'the cradle of the human race'. Indeed,
India can look back on a long history. As early as 2500 BC large cities emerged
along the Indus River. This civilization traded with Mesopotamia and Egypt and
developed a distinctive culture, from which Hinduism emerged. The Mauryan   5
Empire, the first and largest empire on the Indian subcontinent, reached its
peak in the 3rd century BC. Under its ruler Ashoka, Buddhism spread throughout the region. Arts and science flourished again in the 4th century AD during
the Golden Age of the Gupta emperors. The concepts of zero and infinity are
believed to have been developed by Indian mathematicians during this era.   10
In the 12th century AD Islamic invaders conquered northern India. Islamic rule
reached its zenith during the Mughal period, which began in 1526 and led to
the unification of large parts of India. It was during the Mughal era that many
magnificent buildings such as the Taj Mahal were built.

India and the British Empire   15

When European trading companies arrived in India in the early 17th century to
gain access to the country's wealth, the decline of the Mughal empire was
accelerated. A century later, the British East India Company had become the
dominant force in the subcontinent. After a massive revolt against the British in
1857 the last Mughal emperor was deposed and the British Crown took over   20
control, turning India into the largest and most profitable colony of its empire,
its 'Jewel in the Crown'. British rule in India, also known as 'the Raj', lasted
until 1947. During this era, the British modernized the country, but mis-
management, food shortages and diseases also led to the deaths of millions of
people and resentment against the colonial power. The Indian struggle for   25
independence, led by Gandhi and Nehru, culminated in 1947, when the former
colony was divided into two separate countries, Hindu-dominated India and
Muslim-dominated Pakistan. After Partition widespread displacement of Hindus
and Muslims and sectarian violence between the two groups followed. To this
day, the relationship between India and Pakistan remains tense.   30

India today

India is often described as a land of contrasts and paradoxes. It is home to an
estimated 330,000 millionaires, but also to one third of the world's poor. It is
the world's largest democracy, but millions of its citizens are still illiterate. India
is the largest country in southern Asia, yet it is densely populated with a   35
population exceeding 1.3 billion people, half of them under the age of 25. India
is also one of the world's most promising new markets, but the benefits of
economic growth have not yet reached all Indians. In fact, India's growth poses
many new challenges. India will need to feed, house and educate the next
generation of Indians, who will both contribute to and benefit from the   40
country's success. In the next two decades, India will see a massive migration
from rural areas to the cities. The demand for energy will increase as future city
dwellers will need electricity, water and mass transit. Today 400 million Indians
are not connected to the electricity grid. The Indian government aims to
increase power generation by 700% in the next 25 years. Will the new India   45
manage to meet these challenges successfully?

1 Paraphrasing key terms

Paraphrase the following key terms, which are used frequently when talking about India:

1	Indian subcontinent	4	the Raj
2	colonial power	5	Independence
3	the Jewel in the Crown	6	Partition

▶ SF 1: Dealing with unknown or new words

2 Words in use

Find the highlighted words in the text to match the definitions:

1 the act of joining parts of a country together
2 a situation when people do not have enough to eat
3 the act of forcing people to leave the area where they live
4 a violent confrontation between different groups in society
5 increase in business activities
6 movement of a large number of people

3 Prepositions

Complete the following sentences about India with the correct prepositions. Look at the text if necessary:

1 Gandhi united millions of Indians in their struggle … independence.
2 India is home … about 330,000 millionaires.
3 There is great demand … highly-skilled IT professionals.
4 Indian citizens have started to show growing resentment … inequality.

▶ LP 19: Collocations

4 Verbs and nouns

a Many verbs in English have a tendency to form partnerships with nouns (as in *make a decision* or *find a solution*). These are called 'collocations'. Scan the text for the noun *challenge*: which verbs does *challenge* collocate with?

b Search for more examples of verbs collocating with *challenge* using a mono-lingual dictionary or a corpus, e.g. the British National Corpus (BNC). Illustrate each collocation with an example sentence.

c Do the same for the nouns *access* and *control*.

▶ LP 19: Collocations

5 Images of India

India has been described as 'the cradle of the human race' and as 'a land of contrasts and paradoxes'. Write two paragraphs in which you explain the two images. Choose appropriate vocabulary from the text and the tasks above.

▶ SF 38: Writing a well-structured text

India's past: echoes and reflections

A1 India's UNESCO World Heritage sites

The following WebQuest will take you on a virtual journey across India through time and space.

Qutb Minar

Mountain Railways of India

Sanchi

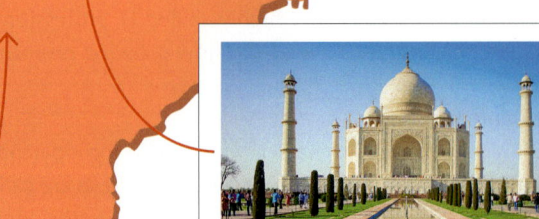
Taj Mahal

I N D I A

Ellora Caves

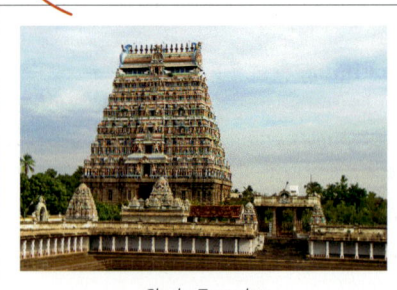
Chola Temples

▶ SF 3: Doing research
▶ SF 24: Giving a presentation

A WebQuest

a Form six groups. Each group works on one site. Go to the UNESCO World Heritage website and find information, videos, etc. there about the history and cultural significance of your site. Present your findings in class, explaining what makes them places of outstanding universal value.

b Together create a timeline of Indian history based on the information you have collected.

A2 Colonizers and colonized

> To feel that somewhere among those millions you
> have left a little justice or happiness or prosperity,
> a sense of manliness or moral dignity, a spring of
> patriotism, a dawn of intellectual enlightenment
> 5 or a stirring of duty where it did not before exist –
> that is enough, that is the Englishman's justification
> in India.
>
> Lord Curzon, Viceroy of India from 1899 to 1905, in his
> farewell speech on leaving India

ANALYSIS ◀

Comparing a quote and a photo

Study the photo and the quote carefully. Then prepare an oral statement in
which you explain what they tell you about the relationship between the British
and the Indians during the British Raj. **SUPPORT** ▶ p. 231

A3 The British Empire from an Indian perspective

Gurcharan Das

*In this text you will learn about the impact of the British Empire from an Indian
perspective. Certain parts of the text have been left out (cf. gap A, etc.) – don't
worry about them on your first reading.*

[A] Britain gave us democracy, the rule of law, an independent judiciary and a free
press. It built railways, canals, and harbors, but it could not bring about an industrial
revolution. It could not raise economic growth or lift people out of poverty. It could
not avert famines. The truth is the Raj was economically incompetent. It just did not
5 know how to 'develop' a country. Had it known it, Britain could have gained much
from having a larger market for its manufactures. It introduced modern education
and helped create a small middle class, but it did not educate the mass of the people.
This was its other failure and linked to the first, for development is not possible without mass literacy.

10 [B] Had India remained united, billions could have been saved in defense expenditures and invested instead in improving the lives of ordinary people in both countries. Whether an undivided India could have survived the Muslim-Hindu animosity
is another counterfactual of history.

[C] Many Indians despair over the divisiveness of caste and would prefer to wish it
15 away. However, the hold of the Indian way of life is also a bulwark against
the onslaught of the global culture. The British gave us the English language,
which allowed us to converse with our compatriots in a country with 16 official
languages. However, English also divided us into two nations – the 10 percent elite
who learned English and shut out the 90 percent who did not. Knowing English today,
20 though, gives Indians a competitive advantage in the global economy and is an
important factor in our nascent success in the information economy.

[D] In school we had learned that the Indian subcontinent was a triangle with the
Himalayas, the Arabian Sea, and the Bay of Bengal as its sides. The Himalayas ran
from east to west and cut off the cold winds from the north. This allowed agriculture

---

4 **dawn** time of day when light
first appears
enlightenment process of
understanding sth.
5 **stirring of sth.** ['stɜːrɪŋ]
beginning of sth.
viceroy ['vaɪsrɔɪ] person
representing the British monarch
in India

▶ SF 11: Analysing pictures

1 **judiciary** [dʒuˈdɪʃəri] *Gerichtsbarkeit*
4 **avert sth.** [əˈvɜːt] prevent sth.
famine ['fæmɪn] long period of
time without food
6 **manufactures** (here) goods
made in large numbers
10 **expenditure** [ɪkˈspendɪtʃə]
amount of money spent
12 **animosity** [ˌænɪˈmɒsəti] strong
feeling of hatred
13 **counterfactual** sth. that has not
happened but might have under
different conditions
14 **divisiveness** [dɪˈvaɪsɪvnɪs] force
that splits people into different
groups
15 **bulwark** ['bʊlwək] *(fml)* person
or thing that protects or defends
sth.
17 **16 official languages**
23 languages are now recognized
for official use at state level
21 **nascent** ['neɪsənt] beginning
to exist

27 **Aryans** ['eərɪənz] ancient race that moved into India from Central Asia around 1500 BC
Mughals ['muːɡɑːlz] Muslim dynasty that conquered northern India in the 16th century

31 **infuriating** (adj) making you extremely angry

to prosper and created wealth, but it also attracted barbarian invaders from the north. 25
It gave us a warm climate so that no one who came wanted to leave. First came the
Aryans, then the Turks, the Afghans, and the Mughals. They came, they stayed, and
they merged and became Indian. To accommodate them we merely created a new sub-
caste each time and they became part of our diversity. The British did not. But now
that they have been gone for more than fifty years, our confidence is restored, espe- 30
cially among the young. Our infuriating diversity may also be of some value. Because
we have always learned to live with pluralism, it is possible that we might be better
prepared to negotiate the diversity of the global economy.

From: *India Unbound*, 2001, pp. 14–15; letters in brackets added for didactic reasons

▶ SF 7: Working with closed test formats

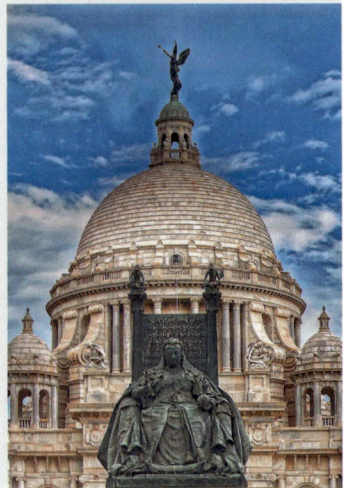

Statue of Queen Victoria in front of the Victoria Memorial, Kolkata

COMPREHENSION ◀

1 Filling in the gaps

Four passages from the text above have been omitted. For each of the four
gaps (A, B, C, D) select the most appropriate passage from the list below.
Note that there are six passages to choose from. Compare with a partner.

1 Although Indians gloss over it, the British Raj was the most important
event in the making of modern India – for better and for worse.

2 As a subdivisional officer, my father was an important official of the
British Raj.

3 The British gave us a hundred years of peace – the so-called Pax Britannica
– but they also consciously pursued a divide-and-rule policy which made
Hindus and Muslims conscious of their separate identities. This led to a
tragic division of the country.

4 The British were different from our other invaders. They did not merge
with us and remained aloof* to the end. This shook our self-confidence.

*aloof distant, impersonal

5 The Raj gave us modern values and institutions, but it did not interfere
with our ancient traditions and our religion. India has therefore preserved
its spiritual heritage and the old way of life continues.

6 Western education provided the stimulus for the most dramatic change
in the minds of Indians in a thousand years.

2 Aspects of British rule

List the positive and the negative aspects mentioned by Gurcharan Das
about British rule in India.

▶ SF 41: Mediation of written and oral texts

3 Mediation (English ➜ German)

In your History class, you are discussing the legacy of colonialism. You have
read this text and offer to summarize the main points raised in the text in
German. Make notes and practise your talk.

ANALYSIS ◀

▶ SF 6: Paraphrasing

4 A critical view of British rule in India

Work with a partner. Explain the following quotes from the text and point
out what they tell you about the legacy of the British Raj.

1 'The Raj was economically incompetent.' (l. 4)

2 'Had India remained united, billions could have been saved in defense
expenditures.' (ll. 10–11)

3 'English … divided us into two nations.' (l. 18)

4 'Our infuriating diversity may … be of some value.' (l. 32)

(All quotes from: Gurcharan Das, *India Unbound*, 2001, pp. 14–15)

─── BEYOND THE TEXT ◀

5 `CHALLENGE▶` **The legacy of the Raj**

Discuss whether the British Raj was beneficial for India, both during the time of the Raj itself and following Independence. Justify your opinion by referring to the texts you have examined. `SUPPORT▶` p.232

A4 Gandhi remembered *Chetan Bhagat*

- 3–2–1 BRAINSTORMING Write down three things you know about Mahatma Gandhi, two reasons why he is considered very important today, and one question you have about him. In class, share your ideas and create a mind map about Gandhi.

■ **FACT FILE**

Gandhi and India's struggle for independence

Mohandas Karamchand Gandhi was born in Porbandar in Gujarat in 1869 to Hindu parents. At the age of 19, he was sent to London to become a barrister.

He returned to India in 1891 to practice law. Two years later, he moved to
5 Durban, South Africa, where he accepted a job at an Indian law firm.

Gandhi was shocked at the way Indians were treated there. He became actively involved in fighting for their rights and developed his philosophy of non-violence, *satyagraha* ('devotion to truth'). After 20 years of fighting for the rights of Indians and Africans, Gandhi returned to India in 1915.
10 Gandhi continued his fight against colonial rule in India by organizing peaceful protests.

Millions of Indians followed him. His campaigns for independence ultimately led the British to withdraw from India in 1947.

But independence from British rule came at a price: the Partition of the sub-
15 continent. In 1948 Gandhi, who had been opposed to Partition, was shot by a young Hindu fanatic who was angry at him for his tolerance towards Muslims.

Gandhi's philosophy of non-violent resistance has inspired millions of people around the world, and even today the Mahatma ('Great Soul') is admired for his courage, will-power, strength and determination in fighting for a just cause.

1 *Add more details to your mind map.*
2 *Use the mind map to give a one-minute speech about Gandhi.*

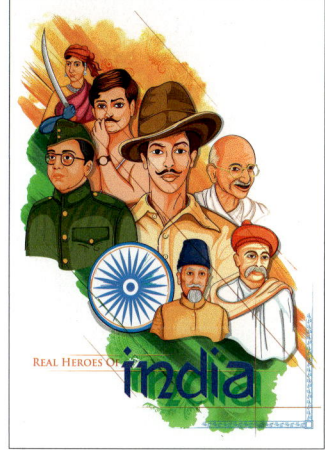

Celebrating Indian national independence

■ **TROUBLE SPOT**

fanatic (l. 16) = *noun (person who is extremely enthusiastic about sth.)*
fanatical = *adjective (enthusiastic)*

In 2012, Chetan Bhagat, one of the most popular Indian novelists writing in English today, wrote the following fictional letter to Gandhi.

Dear Gandhiji,

You left us more than sixty years ago. If you were still around, you would have been more than 140 years old. However, we have not forgotten you. You are on every banknote and most stamps. There are many statues of you. Prestigious roads in almost
5 every city are named after you. Our politicians try to model themselves on you. They wear the fabric you promoted, they quote you at every instance, they've got a photograph of you in their offices and some even eat and live like you. There are books, TV programmes and movies about you. Seriously, you'd be impressed at how much we still adore you. However, there are things that won't make you feel proud. The India
10 you spent all your life making free is far from free. True, the white guys are gone. But there are still millions of poor people. After sixty-plus years, we are still among the poorest nations on earth. This lack of money leads to a lot of problems in healthcare, infrastructure and education. Many children still don't go to a good school. Those who

1 **Gandhiji** in many Indian languages '-ji' can be added to names to show respect

---

■ **TROUBLE SPOT**

fabric ['fæbrɪk] (l. 6) = *material from which clothes are made*
Fabrik = *company, firm*

■ **TROUBLE SPOT**

programme (l. 8) = *sth. that people watch on TV or listen to on the radio*
Fernsehprogramm, -kanal = *TV channel*

Election campaign in India

do don't get into good colleges. And those who go to college don't get good jobs. We need to get rich, and fast. Not only to make more schools and colleges, but also because most Indian problems are linked to the lack of money. Yet, it is considered un-Indian to think that way. The young generation, which thinks like that, is considered materialistic and greedy. The older generation takes the moral high ground – slowness in work is termed patience, non-stop discussion and no action is called careful consideration and lack of improvement in standards of living is countered with claims about the need to live with austerity. And yes, in many cases, politicians who speak like this claim to be your fans.

The younger generation wishes you could come down for one day and clarify these points. Is progress un-Indian? Is change bad? Is a desire to see my country as rich as some other nations materialistic? Is getting things done fast impatience? If you blessed our purpose of building a developed India, the job would become so much easier.

The young generation needs you down here for something else, too. We have a new battle here just like the one you fought with the British. The enemy is not as clear as it was in your case – the white people. Our enemy is the old school of thought, or rather, the people who defend the old school of thought. They do this in the name of antique Indian policies, culture and values. You could help identify this enemy more clearly. Many people who are at the helm of affairs now have served India for decades, maybe with good intentions.

But obviously they don't want to accept they screwed up. We wish they would, though, and we'd have a national day of shame. It won't be easy, but from there we could make a new beginning. But they won't, for they are in power. And to defend themselves and their ways, they don't mind crushing the aspirations, ideas and talent of an entire generation.

Yes, there is a lot of talk of India being a young nation and about youth power. However, youth power is the biggest myth going around India right now. Of course, the youth has spending power – we can buy enough SIM cards, sneakers and fizzy drinks to keep many MNCs in business. But we do not have the power to change things. Can the youth get a new college set up? Can the youth ask the government to provide tax incentives to MNCs to relocate jobs to smaller towns? No way. We are wooed, used, but seldom heard. If you came down, you could unite us. You used religious festivals as social events and propagated your cause. You understood that people need entertainment to bind them. Perhaps we could integrate colleges in the same way, link all colleges maybe for their annual festivals and the message of change could be channelled through them. We have amazing technology such as the Internet now. You would use it so well. If the youth unites, there could actually be youth power.

With our purpose blessed, enemy identified and youth united, we could take the first steps towards the new Indian revolution. After all, China had one and only after that did they get on the path of true progress.

15
20
25
30
35
40
45
50
55
60

19 **lack of sth.** state of not having sth.
23 **greedy** wanting more money
take the moral high ground claim that your arguments are morally better than other people's arguments
29 **austerity** [ɒsˈterəti] situation when people do not have a lot of money
42 **at the helm of sth.** in charge of sth.
44 **screw up** (infml) do sth. badly
52 **MNC = multinational company** company operating all over the world
53 **tax incentive** [ˌɪnˈsentɪv] Steueranreiz
54 **woo sb.** try to get sb.'s support
56 **propagate your cause** [ˈprɒpəɡeɪt] spread your ideas

65 But if it is not feasible for you to come back, we'll have to try to bring about change ourselves. If we can be inspired to do that, we can say we have not forgotten you and understand the meaning of your birthday. We hope you had a good one up there! Lots of love, The Younger Generation[1]

64 **feasible** that can be achieved

COMPREHENSION ◀

1 True/false statements
Write six true/false statements on a piece of paper. Swap your statements with a partner. Check your partner's statements, correct the false ones and check each other's solutions.

▶ SF 7: Working with closed test formats

2 Finishing sentences
Finish the sentences with ideas from the text.
1 If Gandhi lived in India today, he would be shocked to hear that …
2 Young Indians need Gandhi to …
3 Gandhi's message to young Indians would be …

LANGUAGE AWARENESS ◀

3 Informal style
Chetan Bhagat often uses informal language in his letter.
a Put the following examples[1] of informal English into formal English:
1 'If you were still around.' (l. 2)
2 'True, the white guys are gone.' (l. 10)
3 'But obviously they don't want to accept they screwed up.' (l. 44)
4 'No way.' (l. 54)
b Scan the letter for at least three more examples of informal style and put them into formal style.
c Explain why Bhagat uses informal diction in this text.

■ LANGUAGE AWARENESS
Writing letters
When writing a letter it is especially important to adapt your style and register to the recipient. This is because your letter will always have a particular purpose: you may want to convince somebody of your feelings, complain about something, get access to information or to a job, etc. Carefully assess the communicative situation and adopt a style and register (formal or informal) that fits with the situation.

▶ LA 4: Influencing through language

▶ LP 11: Using the right register

BEYOND THE TEXT ◀

4 ▶YOU CHOOSE▶ **Youth empowerment**
Choose one of the following writing tasks. ▶ LANGUAGE HELP

a An Indian newspaper has asked young people to write about their Indian dream and contribute a text for their online *blog. Imagine you are a teenager growing up in India. Write a blog entry. Use ideas for your blog from Bhagat's letter. You could start like this: 'I dream of an India that …, a country that stands up to …, an India Mahatma Gandhi would be proud of …'

OR

b '[Young people] do not have the power to change things.' (l. 52)[1] Comment on this statement with reference to the community *you* live in.

■ LANGUAGE HELP
- What I would like to see is …
- If we put all our efforts together …
- We have the potential to …
- One major obstacle is …
- If we want to see improvements, we have to …
- Our main contribution could be …

▶ SF 37: Doing a creative writing task

▶ SF 38: Writing a well-structured text

[1] Text and quotes from: Chetan Bhagat, 'Letter to Bapu from Generation Next on His Birthday', *What Young India Wants*, 2012, pp. 127–130

🎧 **CD2** 03

Ela Gandhi

▶ SF 22: Listening

Nelson Mandela (1918–2013) was a civil rights activist in South Africa who fought against apartheid. Inspired by Gandhi, he became a leader of the African National Congress (ANC) and was sent to prison after protesting against racial inequality. When he was released in 1990 after 27 years in prison, he continued his fight – and succeeded. In the 1994 presidential elections all races were finally allowed to vote, and Nelson Mandela won the election and became president. Like Gandhi, Mandela is regarded as a role model of tolerance and reconciliation around the world today.

LISTENING FOCUS ON SKILLS

Listening to a radio interview

In this section you are going to focus on how to listen to a radio interview. Ela Gandhi, Mahatma Gandhi's granddaughter, is a peace activist and politician. She grew up in Durban, South Africa, and knew both Mahatma Gandhi and Nelson Mandela personally. You are going to listen to part of a radio interview with her.

1 Before listening

Sometimes you may have an idea what a radio report or an interview you are about to listen to might be about. In this case it is useful to collect some words that you might expect to hear. This will make it easier to understand the interview.

Before you listen to the interview with Ela Gandhi, read the Fact File below left and brainstorm what an interview with someone who knew both Gandhi and Mandela might be about. Make a list of keywords you expect to hear.

2 Listening for gist

Listen to the interview for the first time to get the gist. Before you do, read the task below carefully so you know what information to listen out for.

> What is Ela Gandhi speaking about? Choose the correct answers:
> Ela Gandhi is speaking about:
> 1 Her childhood memories in South Africa.
> 2 Nelson Mandela's visit to India.
> 3 Similarities between Mahatma Gandhi and Nelson Mandela.
> 4 The situation in South Africa when Mandela was released from prison.
> 5 The political situation in South Africa after Nelson Mandela's death.

3 Listening for detail

Listen to the interview again and pay attention to details. In the task below you will be asked to complete sentences while listening. When doing a task like this, you are usually not expected to write down exactly what you have heard. You may use your own words to show that you have understood that particular part of the text.

> Listen again and complete the sentences:
> 1 Gandhi and Mandela were capable of inspiring people because …
> 2 Both Gandhi's and Mandela's ideal was to …
> 3 When Mandela visited Gandhi's home in India, he refused to … because …
> 4 The fact that Nelson Mandela invited the man who had demanded the death penalty for him symbolizes …
> 5 When Mandela was released from prison, South Africans hoped that … despite the fact that … .

Tales from modern India

B1 Urbanization in India: the big picture

net new employment *Nettoneu-beschäftigung (= Differenz aus der Anzahl neu geschaffener Arbeits-plätze und der Anzahl beendeter Arbeitsverhältnisse)*
residential space area consisting of houses rather than offices

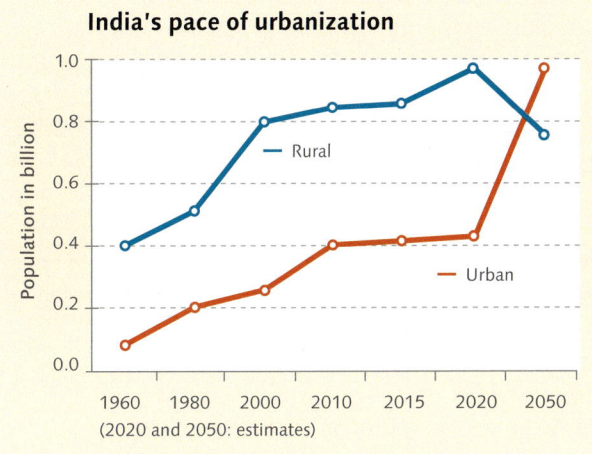

India's pace of urbanization

(Y-axis: Population in billion, 0.0 to 1.0)
Rural
Urban

1960 1980 2000 2010 2015 2020 2050
(2020 and 2050: estimates)

FACT FILE

India in 2030
- **590 million** people will live in cities, nearly twice the population of the USA today.
- **70%** of net new employment will be generated in cities.
- **91 million** urban households will be middle-class, up from **22 million** today.
- **68** cities will have a population of 1 million plus, up from **42** today; Europe has 35 today.
- **700–900 million m²** of commercial and residential space will be built – or a new Chicago every year.
- **2.5 billion m²** of roads will be built, 20 times the amount added in the past decade.
- **7,400 km** of metros and subways will be constructed – 20 times the capacity added in the past decade.

───────────────────────────────── COMPREHENSION ◀

1 Indian urbanization
Use the chart above to describe the process of urbanization in India.
SUPPORT ▶ p. 232

▶ SF 12: Analysing charts and graphs

───────────────────────────────── ANALYSIS ◀

2 Key figures
Work with a partner and analyse the consequences of urbanization for the future of India. One partner focuses on the opportunities that urbanization provides, one on the dangers. Use the key figures provided in the Fact File as a starting point. Exchange your ideas with each other afterwards and discuss them.

B2 Life in a megacity

Kolkata is one of the fastest-growing megacities in the world. The poster on the right is of the documentary film The Revolutionary Optimists *(2013), which follows several young children growing up in Kolkata.*

───────────────────────────────── ANALYSIS ◀

1 The poster
Study the poster. Speculate about the girl: who is she, what may she be doing? Use the data and facts from **B1**.

───────────────────────────────── BEYOND THE TEXT ◀

2 Creative writing
Use your ideas to write down what the girl may be saying.

HOW FAR WOULD YOU GO TO CHANGE YOUR WORLD?

THEREVOLUTIONARYOPTIMISTS

▶ SF 11: Analysing pictures
▶ SF 37: Doing a creative writing task

Part B

 DVD

feature film main film with a story

▶ SF 23: Analysing a film

VIEWING FOCUS ON SKILLS

Watching a film trailer

In the previous section you examined a poster. Now you are going to watch the trailer for the documentary film The Revolutionary Optimists *(2013).*
A film trailer is a short film advertising a feature film or documentary. A trailer introduces audiences to the film it advertises and tries to get them interested in watching the whole film. Trailers use various techniques to create interest and grab the viewers' attention. When dealing with a film trailer you should therefore pay special attention not only to the story of the film and the actors, but also to camera work, visual elements, sound and music.

1 Before viewing
Before you watch the trailer for *The Revolutionary Optimists*, speculate about what you expect to see in it and how the subject matter might be presented. Use the notes you made when you discussed the poster (cf. p. 85).

2 While viewing: first impressions
a While watching the first time, take notes on the following aspects:
- *characters and *setting (who do you see? where are they?)
- actions (what are people doing in the film?)

Share your findings.
b What would you say the documentary film is about?

3 While viewing: camera work
a Watch the trailer again, this time without sound so that you can concentrate on the camera work. Choose the correct answers:

1 The field size predominantly used in the trailer is			
a long shots	b full shots	c medium shots	d close-ups

2 The camera angle predominantly used in the trailer is		
a high angle	b low angle	c eye level

3 The type of camera movement predominantly used in the trailer is			
a zooming	b tilting	c tracking	d panning

b Explain the function of each of these techniques in this trailer.

4 Analysing the voice-over
Watch the trailer a third time, this time with sound. Concentrate on the intertitles and the voice-over. Make notes on the information they provide and explain how they contribute to the trailer.

5 Evaluating the trailer
Look through your findings in tasks **1–4** and discuss whether the trailer is successful in creating interest in the film.

B3 Celebrating Indian culture

Sanjeev Bhaskar is a well-known British comedian and broadcaster. In 2007
he made a four-part television series for the BBC, India with Sanjeev Bhaskar,
in which he travelled back to the country of his ancestors.

BEFORE VIEWING ◀

1 PLACEMAT **Festivals**
Think of festivals you are familiar with (rock festivals, carnival …). Why are
festivals so popular? How do they differ from everyday life? Collect your
ideas in a placemat activity; the mind map below can help you to get started.

▶ CC 1: Cultural awareness

COMPREHENSION ◀

2 First viewing: no sound
You are going to watch a scene from *India with Sanjeev Bhaskar* showing
Bhaskar celebrating Holi. Watch the clip without sound first and take notes
on how Holi is celebrated.

3 Second viewing: with sound
Watch the clip again, now with sound, and take notes on how Bhaskar
explains the importance of Holi today.

ANALYSIS ◀

4 Third viewing: analysing camera work and sound
Watch the clip for a third time and analyse how the camera work and the
soundtrack contribute to creating Bhaskar's perspective of Holi.

BEYOND THE TEXT ◀

5 The meaning of Holi
Research the religious side of Holi and explain its origins and meaning.

6 Mediation (German ➜ English)
Holi has become a global phenomenon in recent years. It is even celebrated
in Germany today. An Indian friend of yours wants to know why. You have
come across the following interview with Maxim Derenko (cf. p. 88), who
started organizing Holi festivals in Germany in 2011. Based on this interview,
write an email to your friend answering his question. **SUPPORT** ▶ p. 232

🎬 **DVD**
▶ SF 23: Analysing a film

▶ SF 3: Doing research

▶ SF 41: Mediation of written
and oral texts

Part B

Wie kam die Idee, das indische Holi-Festival in Deutschland zu veranstalten?
Mein Kollege und Mitveranstalter, Jasper Hellmann, war 2011 in Indien auf Durch-
reise. Er war beim ursprünglichen Holi-Festival selbst vor Ort und war total begeis-
tert davon. Bei seiner Rückkehr steckte er mich und Max Riedel, den dritten Mann
im Bunde, mit der Idee an, ein Holi-Festival in Deutschland zu veranstalten. 5

In Indien ist das Holi-Fest ein hinduistisches Frühlingsfest. Wie kommt es, dass es trotz
fehlenden traditionellen Hintergrunds in Deutschland so gut aufgenommen wird?
Die Reaktionen und Erfahrungen aus dem letzten Jahr haben gezeigt, dass die
Kernelemente des Holi-Festes [...] bei den Leuten gut ankommen. Bei dieser Fest-
lichkeit steht die Gleichheit aller Menschen im Vordergrund, denn in Indien werden 10
die sogenannten Kasten aufgehoben. In Deutschland gibt es zwar keine Kasten, jedoch soziale Unterschiede. Des Weiteren wird Toleranz und gegenseitiger Respekt
großgeschrieben. Die vielen bunten Farben spielen einen weiteren Faktor beim
Festival. Die Symbolik für die Gleichheit und die Besonderheit dieses Festivals sind
die Farben, diese sollen alle Menschen gleich (bunt) machen. 15

Habt ihr mit dem Erfolg der ersten Holi-Festivals im letzten Jahr gerechnet?
Wir haben natürlich nicht mit einem so durchschlagenden Erfolg gerechnet. Eigentlich war die Idee ein kleines Open-Air-Festival für einige Leute zu machen, in diesem
Bereich haben wir auch schon Erfahrungen in Berlin gesammelt. Ein solches Festival gab es zuvor noch nie in Deutschland. [...] 20

Wird sich das Holi-Festival etablieren können oder handelt es um einen aktuellen Trend?
Die Resonanz des letzten Jahres hat gezeigt, dass der Hype ungebrochen ist und die
Nachfrage immer noch sehr hoch ist. Wir haben unsere Tour für dieses Jahr durch-
geplant und waren innerhalb weniger Stunden in fast allen Städten ausverkauft.

From: Carolin Roder / Sandra Kurz / Maxim Derenko, 'Holi Festivals – der neue Trend?!',
ARTikel, 1 July 2013

📍 CULTURE SPOT

'[Indian truck art is] an art form that makes
journeys through the dusty highways of India
incredible in more ways than one. With a kaleidoscope of bright paints, motifs, typography
and some unique *couplets, these Indian trucks
take you on a rather colourful journey of
diverse cultures and beliefs of the country.'

From: the website of *Horn Please*, 2012

Indian truck art

1 Describe the trucks in the photos.

2 Explain how Indian truck art relates to what you have
learned about India in this chapter so far.

Indians abroad

C1 The Indian diaspora

1 BRAINSTORMING **Moving to foreign countries**
Work in pairs and brainstorm possible reasons why people move to foreign countries today.

2 Locating the Indian diaspora
The word *diaspora* describes communities of people who live outside their country of origin. India has the second largest diaspora comprising around 30 million ethnic Indians living in more than 100 countries.

a Work in pairs. Each pair focuses on one of the regions or countries on the right. Research the history, size and role of the Indian diaspora in the area you are dealing with and make a poster summarizing your findings.
SUPPORT ▶ p. 232

b GALLERY WALK Present your posters in a gallery walk activity.

> **Countries/regions**
> - United Kingdom
> - United States
> - Canada
> - The Middle East (UAE, Saudi Arabia, Oman, Kuwait)
> - South Africa
> - East Africa (Tanzania, Kenya)
> - South-East Asia (Malaysia, Singapore)
> - South America and the Caribbean (Guyana, Suriname, Trinidad)
> - Pacific Islands (Fiji)
> - Indian Ocean Islands (Mauritius, Reunion)
>
> *Find a map showing the regions here:*
>
> **Webcode** context–17

C2 A taste of the Indian diaspora   *Michelle Warwicker*

When it comes to food, the Indians of the diaspora have not only absorbed influences from the countries they live in but have also influenced the cuisine of their new countries.

Bunny chow has nothing to do with rabbits. [...] It is made with a half or a quarter loaf of bread, hollowed out and filled with steaming curry cooked with meat or beans. A traditional bunny chow (or simply 'bunny' if you are in Durban in South Africa where the dish origi-
5 nated) is made with mutton, chicken, mince, lamb or kidney beans. The loaf is crusty enough to hold the saucy filling in a parcel, and the bread from the centre is placed on top to keep the curry warm and provide diners with something to scoop with. Cheap, tasty and filling, bunny chow is one of the most popular takeaway meals in its home city. It is sold in
10 small diners and takeaway kiosks and is rarely even served with a fork. [...]
   Durban is home to a very large population of people of Indian ethnic origin, and the dish fuses Indian and African influences. Bunny chow may owe its origins to the Indian immigrants who arrived in South Africa in the second half of the 19th century to be put to work on sugar plantations. One theory is that they began to use a sturdy
15 bread loaf so they could transport curry to the plantations to eat during the day. Today bunny chow has spread to other South African cities, but the original and for many people the best is still found in Durban.

From: 'What is bunny chow?', BBC, 20 January 2014

Bunny chow

1 **chow** [tʃaʊ] *(sl)* food

> ■ LANGUAGE AWARENESS
> **The language of food and cooking**
> When it comes to food, language has always been very productive. Food-related terms have migrated around the world, sometimes merging with native words. The English word beef is an example: it was derived from the Old French word buef (modern French boeuf) as early as the Middle Ages. In today's globalized world, such borrowings and influences are common.
>
> ▶ LA 3: Similarities and differences of languages
> ▶ EE 1: Eating in and out

— COMPREHENSION ◀

1 Thinking about food and culture
Outline how bunny chow reflects the Indian diaspora experience.

— BEYOND THE TEXT ◀

2 Fusion cuisine
Discuss to what extent fusion food is an integral part of modern society.

Part C

C3 English lessons *Shauna Singh Baldwin*

Shauna Singh Baldwin is an Indo-Canadian author. Born in Montreal, she grew up in Delhi and went to the USA to study. The following short story is about an Indian woman who has moved to the USA.

I told Tony – that is what he likes me to call him in America – I told Tony I will take English lessons till my green card comes. Valerie says there are English teachers who will teach me for free and she will find a good one who will come to the apartment so that I do not have to go outside. Tony says OK, and then he leaves for work at the cardboard factory. 5

I pick up the breakfast dishes and Suryavir's toys. No one can say his name here – I will tell them at the school to call him Johnny, like Tony's Johnny Walker whisky.

The phone rings and my heart starts to pound – *dharak dharak*. Our answering machine message has Valerie's voice, and I follow the words with her accent.

'We're naat here right naow, but if you leeev a mehsej, weell get right baak to you.' 10
But it is only Valerie herself. 'Pick up the phone, Kanwaljit. I want to know if you're home so I can drop the kids off for the day.'

'Hello,' I say. 'I am here. You come.'

Valerie is a nice person, but you cannot be too careful. Tony says we cannot meet anyone from India till my green card comes, so Valerie is the only one who sees me. 15
I call her Grocery Store Valerie to myself, because she answered my card in the grocery store, and now I babysit her two strong and unruly boys. What farmers they would have made in Punjab. My son is not so strong. More than two years of women's company. I spoilt him while we were waiting for Tony to get his citizenship, but what was I to do? If I had disciplined him, Tony's parents would have been 20
angry – he is their only grandson.

Valerie's boys don't listen to love or scolding. But they go to school, and Valerie says it is the law. I have to send Suryavir to school. So I went there with her to register him and on the form I wrote the address I had memorized from Valerie's cheques, not ours. Still, Tony was worried in case anyone who might report us saw me. He makes 25
me dress in pants so that I look Mexican, and says it is only a short while now. I hope so.

But first I will learn English. It's not that I don't understand it, but it has too many words. Get it. Put it. I am stuffed. Pick up your stuff. On the other hand. Hand it to you. I learned English in school, passed my matriculation examination, too. We 30
learned whole passages of translation by heart – I had a good memory. Now Tony says I must speak English to pass my immigration interview and to memorize my amnesty story.

A knock. Someone is standing far away from the peephole – why are they doing that? Oh, it's Valerie; she was bending down to tie a shoelace for little Mark. 35

'Hello, hello. Come in. How are you?'

Valerie has found an English teacher who will come to the apartment and teach me for free. But Tony and I are afraid. This English teacher is from India and we didn't want to meet any people from India.

Valerie said she told the teacher I am Tony's girlfriend and that Suryavir is our son. 40
She said the English teacher was surprised. Indian couples do not usually live together, she told Valerie. Tony says to tell Valerie we don't need this teacher. But I took her phone number to please Valerie. I may call her just to speak in Punjabi for a while.

I told Valerie I will change my name. I asked her to call me Kelly. No one here can say Kanwaljit. And Kanwaljit is left far away in Amritsar before the fire. 45

2 **green card** ['– –] document that allows sb. to work legally in the USA

7 **Johnny Walker whisky** US brand of whisky

18 **Punjab** [pʌn'dʒɑːb] region in north-western India, largely populated by Sikhs

22 **scold sb.** speak angrily to sb. who has misbehaved

29 **stuffed** *(adj)* full from eating

30 **matriculation examination** exam taken in the final year of school

Some nights I lie next to Tony, here in America where I live like a worm avoiding the sunlight, and I wonder if he knows. And is it only because it was his brother that he does not sense that another man's body has come between us, or is it that he cannot remember the fire we felt in those early days? We only had three weeks in which
50   Suryavir was made. Then he was gone.

If I had been able to return to my parents until he told me to come to America, I would not have been so weak. But to do so would have smelled of disgrace, and I am not shameless. Nor was it a matter of a month or two. Tony told me after six months, when I was becoming big with his son; it would take him two more years.

55   I tell myself it is not only another man's body that invades our bed, but another woman's too. And yet, that is different. I hear her tearful voice on our answering machine. Her anger follows us from city to city – Fremont, Dallas, Houston, Miami, New York, Chicago – threatening to report us to Immigration. He lived with her for two years, shared her bed, paid her our life savings for a marriage certificate. I will ask
60   the English teacher how to say, 'Is not two years of our life enough? Is not my worm existence, my unacknowledged wifehood, enough for you? Enough that I call myself his girlfriend, my son his bastard?'

But she does not have form, no substance in our bed, I cannot imagine him with her black body – and if I can, what of it? Many men pay prostitutes. This one's price
65   was higher and she lasted longer. And he got his green card after two years. Thus am I here.

The other man in bed with us – he has form. He looks like Tony, only younger. And he still laughs at me, waving pictures of Tony with her. Telling me Tony left me for an untouchable, a *hubshi*. Threatening to tell my parents if I would not open my legs to
70   him.

I did. *Rubba-merey*, I did.

I thought some force would come upon us then and tear him from my flesh before the act was done. Save me, as the virtue of Dropadi was saved. And it did. Too late for virtue but soon enough for vengeance.

75   The police came looking for him. Oh, not for my protection – no. They were rounding up all Sikh boys between the ages of fifteen and twenty-five for 'questioning'. Tony's parents knew what was in store and they hid him in the servant's quarter, a concrete room on the flat roof of the house.

They told the police he was with Tony in America. That made them angry. One
80   sinewy fellow with a whisky smell took a can of gasoline and slowly, as we marched from the rooms around, and as Suryavir's eyes grew larger, poured it in a steady dribble all round the centre courtyard. They all walked to the door and, almost as an afterthought, the sinewy policeman threw a lit match and the world exploded from silence into horror.

85   I took no chances. I gave Suryavir to Tony's mother and then climbed out of the back window. His father was blinded by tears and I pushed him after them. Then I ran up the narrow steep staircase to the servant's quarter on the roofs.

And I locked it.

And ran back through lung-searing smoke and purifying flame. I was given venge-
90   ance, and I took it as my due. But still he comes between us – the half-dead only half a world away.

I called the English teacher today. She speaks Punjabi with a city accent. I will have to ask Tony, but I think it will be, like Americans say, 'fine, fine' for her to come and teach me.

■ **FACT FILE**

The Sikhs
Since the formation of India, many Sikhs (l. 76) have demanded a separate Sikh state in Punjab. During the 1980s militancy reached a peak, leading to an attack by Indian forces on the Golden Temple of Amritsar, Punjab (l. 45) – the Sikhs' holiest temple – and the subsequent assassination of the prime minister, Indira Gandhi.

Sikhs at a religious ceremony

---

52   **disgrace** loss of respect
61   **unacknowledged** *(adj)* not publicly recognized
69   **hubshi** (here) black (originally Punjabi/Hindi for 'Ethiopian')
71   **rubba-merey** (Punjabi/Hindi) oh my God
73   **Dropadi** popular heroine in Hindu mythology who is regarded as a role model of virtue, bravery and resilience
74   **vengeance** ['vendʒəns] revenge
80   **sinewy** ['sɪnjuːi] having a thin body
89   **searing** *(adj)* so strong that it burns you
89   **purify sth.** make sth. pure

LANGUAGE AWARENESS

Language and culture
Studying a foreign language is more than just learning words and grammar, it includes immersing oneself into a different culture and thereby at least slightly changing one's own identity. Think about how using another language might affect your attitude and the way you sound or appear.

▶ LA 1: Varieties of English
▶ LA 3: Similarities and differences of languages

96 **Gurdwara** building in which Sikhs worship
100 **Keogh** ['kiːəʊ]
106 **pry** try to find out things about other people's private lives
109 **Holiday Inn** US hotel chain

Her family on her father's side is from Rajasansi, just outside Amritsar. And she is married to a white guy so she is probably not part of the Gurdwara congregation; they have all heard of Tony's Green-Card Wife. (These matters travel faster than aeroplanes fly between cities.) I will tell Tony I will take English lessons, and that she will be my teacher. 95

Tony was finishing breakfast when Mrs Keogh, the English teacher, arrived. She knocked and I let her in. Then I asked her to sit down, offered her some tea and listened while she and Tony spoke English. 100

'Thank you very much. My girlfriend is just new from India. As soon as her green card comes we will be getting married, so till then I think English lessons will help her pass the time.' 105

The English teacher did not remark on 'my girlfriend'. Good. Not a prying woman. She said, 'I am glad to help you and your fiancée.'

Tony continued, 'I will not like it if you teach her more than I know. But just enough for her to get a good-paying job at Dunkin' Donuts or maybe the Holiday Inn. She will learn quickly but you must not teach her too many American ideas.' 110

The English teacher smiled at me.

Tomorrow, I will ask her where I can learn how to drive.

From: *English Lessons, and Other Stories*, 1996, pp. 129–134

COMPREHENSION ◀

1 Characters and plot
  a Read up to l. 45 and collect facts about the narrator, her husband, her son and Valerie.
  b Read on up to l. 91 and summarize what the narrator's dark secret is.
  c Read the last part of the story and point out the meaning of the English lessons for the narrator and for her husband.

ANALYSIS ◀

▶ SF 19: Analysing narrative prose

2 The protagonist's identity
  a Work with a partner and examine the different facets of Kanwaljit's identity. Consider the following aspects: her personality, family, friends, relationships, cultural background, feelings and thoughts, language. Use visual aids to present your findings.
  b **CHALLENGE** ▶ Compare Kanwaljit's and Tony's migrant experiences. Consider their hopes for and expectations of living in the USA.

▶ SF 3: Doing research

LANGUAGE AWARENESS ◀

▶ LP 2: Present tense or future?
▶ LP 3: Simple present and present perfect
▶ LP 4: Present perfect and simple past

3 The use of tenses
Oral and written storytelling is traditionally done in the past tense. This story also uses the present tense and the future for narration. Analyse the use and functions of the different narrative tenses in the story.
SUPPORT ▶ p. 233

BEYOND THE TEXT ◀

▶ SF 37: Doing a creative writing task

4 Writing a letter about your life
Imagine you are Kanwaljit in three years' time. Write a letter to your parents in which you tell them about your new life.

Presenting India

After working on this chapter, gather ideas for a multimedia presentation on the topic 'India – a kaleidoscope' for a multicultural festival at your school.

▶ SF 4: Doing project work
▶ SF 24: Giving a presentation

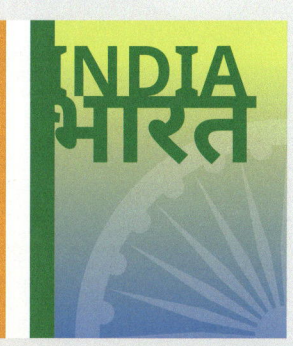

1 Form groups. Each group picks one topic. You could include some of the following aspects in your presentation:
Germans in India – the Indian diaspora in Germany – the global importance of India in the 21st century – Indian festivals – Indian foods – Indian classical and popular music – Indian literature – Indian movies – reasons to visit India – traces of India in your community (e.g. food, music, clothes) – ways to promote intercultural relations between India and Germany (e.g. exchange programmes, business cooperation, etc.)

2 Think about interesting ways of presenting *your* topic, e.g. interviews, slide shows, showing a film, making your own film, or reading out poetry or stories you like. Use ideas from this unit and choose at least one audio file (e.g. a radio interview or report) or video clip (e.g. an excerpt from a feature film or documentary, a trailer, song) for your presentation.

3 Prepare your presentation. Make sure work is distributed equally among the group and agree on a project schedule.

4 On the day of your presentation, come prepared and give your presentation.

5 With the use of an assessment sheet, which your teacher will give you, evaluate the work of the different groups.

5 The USA –
Still the Promised Land ?

A

B

C

Download a list of chapter vocab here: **Webcode** context-78

Download a detailed timeline as well as further information and tasks based on the pictures:
Webcode context-79

1 GROUP PUZZLE **The American experience**

a Form six groups. Give each group a letter A–F.
In your group, talk about the picture that matches your letter:
What situation does it show? What do you know about this episode in US history? Share your knowledge.

b Use the webcode to access further information on the story behind your picture. Share the new information in your group.

c Form new groups of at least six members each; all six letters must be represented in each group. Tell each other about your pictures. Discuss what makes them part of the American experience.

Timeline of American history

| 1775–1783 | 1789 | 1861–1865 | 1890 |

1607 1620   4 July 1776   1803

1989–1991   2001   2006   2008

1955
1954
1945
1941
1929
1919
1917

D

E

F

2 Putting yourself in the picture

a Choose one person from any of the six pictures.
Write an *interior monologue for your person: How (or why) did you get into your present situation? How do you imagine your future?

b Form groups of 4–5. Read your monologues to each other. The listeners try to guess which person you have chosen.

c Discuss the different motives of the people you have talked about, and how they are connected with the idea of America as 'the Promised Land'.

TROUBLE SPOT

The term 'America' is often used to refer to the USA (rather than the entire American continent). Strictly speaking this is not correct. If you do use the term, make sure the meaning is made clear by the context.

PREVIEW

In this chapter you will examine the image of the USA at home and abroad and learn more about some of the challenges facing the United States today.

Main topics
- The American dream today .... p. 98
- The challenge of diversity .... p. 105
- Equality and inequality .... p. 106
- The United States' role in the world .... p. 114

Focus on Skills: SPEAKING
- Speaking in front of an audience .... p. 112

Chapter Task: Giving a speech in which you explain why you would like to be given the opportunity to visit the USA .... p. 117

Download an audio version of the text here:

 Webcode context-80

A country like no other

A nation founded on principle

Most nations are held together by a common history, language and culture. The USA is different: it is a nation united solely by the shared values of equality, democracy, and individual freedom. The Founding Fathers, inspired by the ideas of the Enlightenment, created a self-governing republic without social barriers. The crowned heads of Europe expected the young nation to collapse in chaos; instead, it grew and prospered, ultimately rising to the status of a world power.

'Remember, gentlemen, we aren't here just to draft a constitution. We're here to draft the best damned constitution in the world.'

Land of opportunity

While the promise of freedom from religious and political persecution played and continues to play a major role in attracting immigrants to America's shores, it became clearer as the United States expanded westward that the continent also held vast stores of natural resources. In the first half of the 19th century, it was mainly the availability of cheap farmland that drew millions to try their luck in the New World; later, huge supplies of coal and iron ore powered the growth of industry, attracting further waves of immigration. The economic vitality of the young nation gave rise to the material side of the American dream, expressed in slogans like 'from rags to riches' or 'the sky's the limit'. In a country so rich in opportunity, success was believed to lie in the hands of the individual. A culture arose that honoured personal material success; as long as upward mobility guaranteed equality of opportunity for all, the majority felt that the self-made millionaire had a right to his wealth.

The American century – and beyond

The 20th century saw the United States rise to a position of economic and military leadership in the world. America viewed itself as a beacon of democracy, which it strove to export to other countries. With the collapse of the Soviet Union and the end of the Cold War (1989), the USA was seemingly the only remaining superpower. Yet since the turn of the century, America has increasingly been forced to cope with doubts and difficulties. The terrorist attacks of 11 September 2001, economic turmoil, the massive loss of jobs in the manufacturing sector, the widening gap between rich and poor, the unsolved problem of racism – all of these factors have contributed to a deep-rooted feeling of insecurity that finds its expression in populist movements and an increasing polarization of public opinion. On the international level, America is faced with a confusing number of new challenges on multiple fronts that defy simple solutions. It remains to be seen whether the US will live up to its role as 'world policeman' or withdraw into a phase of self-absorbed isolationism.

5

10

15

20

25

30

35

40

■ TROUBLE SPOT
the USA (l. 32) + *singular verb*
The USA is/was/has ...

▶ SF 1: Dealing with unknown or new words

1 Words in use

Replace the underlined words with highlighted expressions from the text:
1 In the 20th century the United States became the most powerful country in the world.
2 Americans believe in giving everyone the same chance in life.
3 We don't know yet if the USA will remain the leading world power.
4 The availability of cheap land was an important factor attracting Europe's rural poor to America's shores.
5 There's a growing difference between rich and poor.

2 Collocations with prepositions

▶ LP 19: Collocations

a Complete the underlined collocations with the correct prepositions. If you need help, look at the text again:
1 By 1900, the USA had risen … the status of a major industrial country.
2 The United States of America became known as the land of promise, a country rich … opportunity.
3 Hundreds of different ethnic groups have all contributed … American culture.
4 Stories of successful immigrants gave rise … the saying that in America the streets were paved with gold.
5 For many European Jews, freedom … persecution made the USA the new Promised Land.
6 America has been forced to cope … many difficulties.
b Find four more collocations with prepositions in the text and write a quiz for your partner. Then do the quiz your partner gives you.

3 Connotation

Most people react positively to the word *freedom* and negatively to *slavery*. This emotional aspect of language is called *connotation.
a Sort the words in the list on the right into two groups (positive/negative connotation). Compare results with your partner.
b Together, find three more words from the text for each of the two groups.

values • persecution • doubts • prosper • opportunity • insecurity • collapse • equality

4 General terms ('Oberbegriffe')

a Find general terms to describe each of the five (groups of) examples. Choose the terms from the highlighted expressions in the text.
1 George Washington and Benjamin Franklin
→ **general term:** *the Founding Fathers*
2 coal, oil, water, farmland → **general term:** …
3 Free public schools are available to everyone. → …
4 A factory worker rises to become the director of a large firm. → …
5 Only landowners are allowed to vote. → …
b Choose three more general terms from the highlighted words in the text. Write an example illustrating each of them. Swap examples with a partner and find the correct terms from the text.

5 Your view

The USA – still 'a beacon of democracy' (ll. 30–31) for the rest of the world? State your opinion in a short text (ca. 200 words).

▶ LP 14: Linking words and phrases

The American dream

A1 Unlike other nations   *David Kamp*

The term 'American dream' first appeared in historian James Truslow Adams's book The Epic of America *in 1931. Writer and editor David Kamp examines the ideas that Adams encapsulated in a phrase that became a national catchword.*

James Truslow Adams (1878–1949), American historian and author of numerous popular history books

encapsulate sth. summarize sth. in a word or phrase
catchword word or phrase that everyone knows
1 **proper** real, genuine
2 **trace sth.** follow sth. to its origin
5 **rank** *Rang*
6 **get-go** ['--] *(infml)* beginning
egalitarian [i,gælɪ'teəriən] based on equality
7 **fled** past tense of the verb 'flee'
persecution *Verfolgung*

Adams's goal wasn't so much to put together a proper history of the US as to determine, by tracing his country's path to prominence, what makes this land so unlike other nations, so uniquely *American*. [...] What Adams came up with was a construct he called 'that American dream of a better, richer, and happier life for all our citizens of every rank.'   5

From the get-go, Adams emphasized the egalitarian nature of this dream. It started to take shape, he said, with the Puritans who fled religious persecution in England and settled New England in the 17th century. '[Their] migration was not like so many earlier ones in history, led by warrior lords with followers dependent on them,' he wrote, 'but was one in which the common man as well as the leader was hoping for   10 greater freedom and happiness for himself and his children.' [...]

America was truly a new world, a place where one could live one's life and pursue one's goals unburdened by older societies' prescribed ideas of class, caste, and social hierarchy. Adams was unreserved in his wonderment over this fact. Breaking from his formal tone, he shifted into first-person mode in *The Epic of America*'s epilogue,   15 noting a French guest's remark that his most striking impression of the United States was 'the way that everyone of every sort looks you right in the eye, without a thought of   20 inequality.' [...]

It's also worth noting that Adams did not deny that there is a material compo-   25 nent to the American Dream. *The Epic of America* offers several variations on Adams's definition of the dream (e.g., 'the American   30 dream that life should be made richer and fuller for everyone and opportunity remain open to all'), but the word 'richer' appears in all of them, and he wasn't just talking about richness of experience. Yet Adams was careful not to overstate what the dream promises. In one of his final iterations of the 'American Dream' trope, he described it as 'that dream of a land in which life should be better and richer and fuller for every   35 man, with opportunity for each according to his ability or achievement.'

13 **prescribed** *vorgeschrieben*
14 **unreserved** frank, open
wonderment ['wʌndəmənt] *(fml)* amazement
33 **overstate sth.** exaggerate sth.
34 **iteration** [,ɪtə'reɪʃn] repetition
trope *(technical term)* theme
37 **temper sth.** *etwas abschwächen*
38 **shrewd** clever
41 **stupendous** [stjuː'pendəs] spectacular

That last part – 'according to his ability or achievement' – is the tempering phrase, a shrewd bit of expectations management. A 'better and richer life' is promised, but for most people this won't be a rich person's life. 'Opportunity for each' is promised, but within the bounds of each person's ability; the reality is, some people will realize   40 the American Dream more stupendously and significantly than others.

From: 'Rethinking the American Dream', *Vanity Fair* (magazine), 5 March 2009

COMPREHENSION ◀

1 The essence of the dream

a Make notes on the content of Adams's concept of the American dream.

b Compare notes with your partner; make corrections if necessary.

2 The uniqueness of the American experiment

David Kamp writes that in Adams's view, 'America was truly a new world' (l. 12; 'Rethinking the American Dream', *Vanity Fair*, 5 March 2009). Point to arguments that justify this claim.

ANALYSIS ◀

3 The writer's opinion

In most cases, Kamp writes objectively on Adams and his views. Examine the text for places where the writer makes his own opinion clear.

▶ SF 14: Reading strategies

BEYOND THE TEXT ◀

4 Different dreams

Compare Adams's concept with other popular versions of the American dream. **SUPPORT** ▶ p. 233

5 The historical context

a Adams's book was published in 1931, at the beginning of the worst economic crisis in US history. Find out more about the Great Depression and present your findings to your class.

▶ SF 3: Doing research

b Discuss how the historical context might have inspired Adams to create his vision of a national dream.

▶ SF 27: Having a discussion

6 An egalitarian society?

a Which is the proper goal of society: to give everyone an equal chance of success (even if the result is extreme inequality), or to guarantee that everyone has enough to live a decent life (even if it means taking money from the rich and giving it to the poor)? Write down your ideas on a piece of paper.

b Find someone who has chosen the opposite view. Exchange opinions.

c Which type of society would you prefer to live in? Evaluate the pros and cons of the two policies described in **6a**.

▶ SF 34: Argumentative writing

A2 Reinventing the American dream *June Sochen*

• Speculate on the title of the following text. Why might the author, a former professor of history, think that the American dream needs reinventing?

Certain parts of the text have been left out (cf. gap 1, etc.) – don't worry about them on your first reading.

Given the uncertain economic conditions, a contentious presidential campaign and the high cost of a college education, it is difficult to know how the traditional definition of the Dream can be applied for the younger generation. [1] Answering the question looking backward is easier than looking forward.

5   For the generation that fought to free the American colonies from Great Britain, it meant freedom of religion and speech and the liberty to pursue your own path. Contrary to the experience of most people across the Atlantic in the 1700s, Americans looked to a bright future. Children benefited from public school education, hardworking parents, and seemingly endless land to be purchased and cultivated.

1 **contentious** full of conflict
8 **benefit** ['benɪfɪt] *(v) profitieren*
9 **purchase sth.** ['pɜːtʃəs] *(fml)* buy sth.
10 **favorable** *(AE)* = *(BE)* **favourable** *günstig*
11 **hitch your wagon** (here) attach your wagon to horses

Part A

If things were not favorable for you in Boston, you could pack your belongings, hitch your wagon, and take your family to the West. [...]   10

The popular press and penny novels heralded the 'rags to riches' stories of ordinary Americans. This country could fulfill both the ideals and the material aspirations of all newcomers, or so the rhetoric promised. For much of the 19th Century, upward mobility became a constant theme in all political pronouncements, sermons, and   15 business proposals. If you worked hard, you could achieve the American Dream of more education than your parents, greater economic success than your parents, and a larger home than your parents.

There were enough measurable examples of success to make most Americans believe that the American Dream was attainable for them. [2] Though the Civil War   20 surely set back the hopes and plans of a generation, the post-war generation looked forward to a brighter future.

The 20th Century, though promising much of the same, had more obstacles in its path. Two world wars, the worst depression in American history, the Cold War, Korea and Vietnam all slowed down the belief, and the actuality, of inevitable progress   25 toward everyone's fulfillment of the American Dream. Indeed, the seeming certainty that each generation would do better than the last one, has been dashed in recent years.

The 21st Century started with a new threat: September 11, 2001 and the attack on the World Trade Center. [3] The dot.com bubble burst early in the century followed   30 by the Great Recession of 2007; though the recession is formally over, it has left us five years later with high unemployment and great uncertainty about the future.

The divide between the generations is dramatic. [4] Recent college graduates find their career hopes unrealized in the current job market. Wages have stagnated in the last 30 years with manufacturing and service industries going overseas.   35

Only a small segment of the economy – the banks and insurance companies, for example – seem[s] to be thriving.

[5] This country remains a desirable destination for immigrants from all over the world. Just as new immigrants believe in the American Dream, most Americans, according to the polls, also appreciate the multiple benefits offered by this country   40 and have no desire to live elsewhere. The current economic troubles are seen as challenges to overcome, not as insuperable obstacles. Home ownership remains a goal as does job security.

Despite our troubles, the original meaning of the Dream, the ideological portion, remains vibrant while the material promises are harder to obtain. The freedoms   45 enjoyed in this country cannot be taken for granted as there are still many places on the globe where repression describes daily life for many people. Though surely the material aspect of the Dream continues to be a goal – a home [...], a yearly vacation, and a job that pays all the bills – preserving the ideals of the American Dream is more important than ever before.   50

From: 'The American Dream revisited', *Naples Daily News*, 8 August 2012 (figures in brackets added for didactic reasons)

12 **herald sth.** ['herəld] (*v, fml*) call attention to sth.
14 **rhetoric** ['retərɪk] (*fml*) (here) speech-making
15 **pronouncement** public statement
16 **proposal** plan, idea
20 **attainable** within reach
21 **set sth. back** *etwas zurück-werfen*
23 **obstacle** ['ɒbstəkl] sth. that is in the way
25 **inevitable** [ɪn'evɪtəbl] *unvermeidlich*
27 **dash sth.** destroy sth.
30 **dot.com bubble** period from ca. 1997–2000, when the value of internet start-ups rose sharply and then collapsed
33 **divide** (*n*) gap
38 **desirable** [dɪ'zaɪərəbl] attractive
40 **appreciate sth.** [ə'priːʃɪeɪt] know the value of sth.
   benefit (*n*) advantage
42 **insuperable** [ɪn'suːpərəbl] (*fml*) *unüberwindlich*
45 **vibrant** ['vaɪbrənt] alive
46 **take sth. for granted** *etwas als selbstverständlich ansehen*
47 **repression** *Unterdrückung*

▶ SF 7: Working with closed test formats

COMPREHENSION ◀

1 Filling in the gaps

a Five sentences have been removed from the text; the gaps are marked and numbered. Choose the right sentence for each gap from sentences A–G below (there are two sentences that don't belong to the text):

A Workers over 50 who lost their jobs may never recover the earnings and positions they once had.

Chapter 5   The USA – Still the Promised Land?

B But the American Dream continues to live.

C In particular, African Americans and many women felt excluded from the Dream.

D There was little government on any level to help or hinder individual accomplishment.

E Americans have always believed in the power of the individual to shape his or her own life.

F Indeed, all future generations may have to reinterpret the Dream.

G International terrorism became a new concern.

b Compare solutions with your partner and discuss points where you differ.

2 The main idea

Sum up the main reasons Sochen gives why the American dream needs to be reinvented. Compare her reasons with the ideas your class had before reading the text.

— ANALYSIS ◀

3 Exploring the American dream

a Form small groups. Each group will need a blank poster. Your task is to present the information on the American dream contained in the text in the form of a clearly structured mind map. Follow these steps:

1 Divide the subtopics from the list on the right among the members of your group. Each member makes notes on their subtopic.

2 Pool your results and create a mind map that presents your information in a clearly structured form.

b Display your posters on the walls of your classroom. Compare the mind maps created by your classmates and discuss their pros and cons.

— BEYOND THE TEXT ◀

4 YOU CHOOSE ▶ Comparing interpretations

a Write a comment comparing James Truslow Adams's and June Sochen's interpretations of the American dream (**A1**, **A2**). Point to similarities and differences.

 OR

b Write a comment relating June Sochen's views on the American dream (**A2**) to the cartoon below.

■ **LANGUAGE AWARENESS**

Using time references
In order to support your line of argument, it is helpful to refer to historical events and establish a timeline by using a lot of time references. This way you make your arguments plausible and objective.

▶ LA 4: Influencing through language

Find a mindmapping tool here:
 Webcode context-53

- *political ideals*
- *economic opportunity*
- *upward mobility*
- *threats to the dream*
- *state of the dream today*

▶ SF 34: Argumentative writing
▶ SF 13: Analysing cartoons
▶ SF 18: Analysing non-fiction

Part A

Barack Obama, 44th President of the USA (2009–2017)

🎧 **CD2** 07

premise ['premɪs] assumption
(*cf. German Prämisse*)
land-grant college college
funded with money from the sale
of state-owned land
bust (*v*) break up
Medicare, Medicaid state-
supported healthcare programs
**New Deal, War on Poverty,
Great Society** slogans of social
policy under (F. D.) Roosevelt and
Johnson
prosperity [prɒ'sperəti]
Wohlstand
confine sb. to sth. limit sb. to
sth.
blue-collar job factory job
debt [det] money you owe sb.
consistently [kən'sɪstəntli]
regularly
unravel [ʌn'rævl] fall apart
automate ['ɔːtəmeɪt] become
automated
leverage [*AE*: 'levərɪdʒ, *BE*:
'liːvərɪdʒ] negotiating power
begrudge sth. *etwas missgönnen*
aspire to sth. strive to reach sth.
handsomely ['hænsəmli]
generously
offend sb. upset sb.

A3 The danger to the dream *Barack Obama*

The extract you are about to hear is taken from a speech made by Barack Obama (US President 2009–2017) at a community centre in a poor neighbourhood in Washington, D.C., on 4 December 2013.

◀ **COMPREHENSION**

1 Listening for gist
After listening to the excerpt once, decide which of the following statements best summarizes the main idea:
1 America has always rewarded success.
2 The present imbalance between poor and rich threatens the American dream.
3 The task of the government is to ensure that everyone has a fair share of the United States' wealth.

2 Listening for detail
YOU CHOOSE ▶ Together with your partner, choose either task **a** or task **b** before listening to the speech a second time.

a Looking backward
1 Obama begins by pointing to four former presidents: Abraham Lincoln, Theodore ('Teddy') Roosevelt, Franklin D. Roosevelt ('FDR'), and Lyndon B. Johnson ('LBJ'). Take notes on each of them while listening.
2 Compare notes with your partner. Together, decide what these presidents had in common and why Obama mentions them.
3 Link up with a pair that chose task **b**. Tell each other what you have learned.

OR

b Then and now
1 Take notes on the following points:
- the American attitude to success
- upward mobility
- factors that limited upward mobility in the past
- the threat to upward mobility in the present.
2 Compare notes with your partner. Make any necessary additions or corrections.
3 Link up with a pair that chose task **a**. Tell each other what you have learned.

◀ **BEYOND THE TEXT**

3 More success stories
Choose one American person who you regard as a success story. Research this person's *biography and report back to your class.

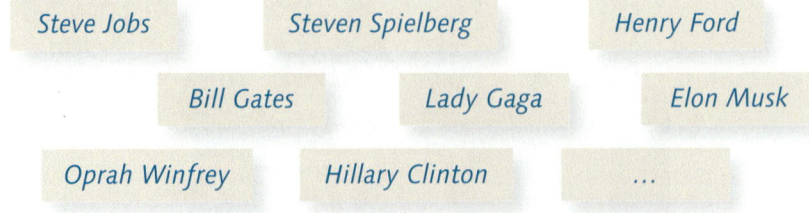

Steve Jobs   Steven Spielberg   Henry Ford

Bill Gates   Lady Gaga   Elon Musk

Oprah Winfrey   Hillary Clinton   …

A4 How to become homeless

You are going to watch an excerpt from the 2009 documentary Capitalism: A Love Story. *In it, film-maker Michael Moore explains how millions of Americans lost their homes following the financial crisis of 2008.*

■ DVD

FACT FILE

Home ownership
Since only few people can afford to pay cash for a house, the usual procedure is to borrow the money
5 you need from a bank. The so-called **mortgage** ['mɔːɡɪdʒ] (a kind of loan) can have either a fixed **interest rate** (e.g., for a 10-year

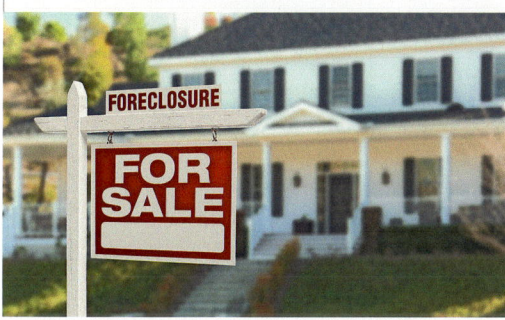

period) or a floating rate that varies with the money market. If the
10 borrower cannot pay the monthly rate, the bank **forecloses**, meaning it cancels the mortgage and tries to sell the house to get its money back. In a **boom market**, this is
15 usually no problem, but if housing prices fall, the bank can be left with a loss.

*Make sure you understand the four terms **in bold print**. Then shut your book. Together with your partner, take turns asking each other to explain each of the terms in bold.*

hunky-dory *(infml)* state in which everyone is happy
tap sth. *etwas anzapfen*
home equity ['ɛkwəti] net value of your house
refinance your home pay back old loans by taking out new ones
scam dishonest plan for making money
down payment *Anzahlung*
approved [əˈpruːvd] accepted (as customers)
demeanor *(AE)* = *(BE)* **demeanour** way sb. looks or behaves
pitch sales talk
subprime used to describe loans to people who are considered bad risks
on disability receiving disability payments *(Erwerbsunfähigkeitsrente)*
foreclosure notice letter stating that your mortgage has been cancelled

◀ COMPREHENSION

1 Writing conference: first reactions (first viewing)
Form small groups. Write down your first reaction to the video. Then pass your paper to the right. Add comments to the papers you are given.

2 Understanding the background
Copy and complete the following text using words from the list on the right:

US *homeowners* were persuaded to … from banks to finance … The new … had a … interest rate. When the interest rate …, many … were unable to pay the … rates. They lost the … of their houses and were forced to ….

borrow money • consumer spending • floating • homeowners • monthly • mortgages • move out • owners • ownership • rose

◀ ANALYSIS

3 Film technique (second viewing)
While watching the film for the second time, make notes on the effect it has on you. Fill in the missing information on the worksheet that your teacher will give you.

▶ SF 23: Analysing a film

◀ BEYOND THE TEXT

4 Discuss how effective the film is at helping people to understand the housing crisis.

5 **YOU CHOOSE** **Michael Moore: an American institution**

a Research Moore's career and report back to your class. b Read a few online reviews of *Capitalism: A Love Story* and report back to your class: What did the critics praise or criticize about the film?

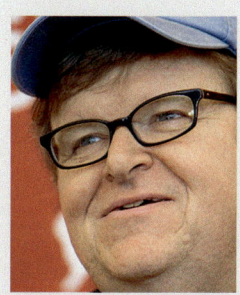
Film-maker Michael Moore

⦿ CULTURE SPOT

Flag (1954)

is a painting by the American artist Jasper Johns (born 1930). It is on display at the Museum of Modern Art in Manhattan, New York City.

▶ CC 1: Cultural awareness

1 Describe your reaction to the work of art above. Would you react the same way to a painting of the German flag in a German art museum? Explain.

🎧 **CD2** 05

2 Listen to a recording of two US teenagers talking about the picture. How do their views influence your reaction to the painting?

3 The photo on the right shows a small section of the painting in detail. Describe what you can recognize in the painting, and discuss why you think the artist chose this technique.

4 Jasper Johns's 'Flag': a statement on the American dream? Discuss.

For another work of art based on the Stars and Stripes, see p. 187.

Dealing with diversity

■ FACT FILE

Ethnic neighbourhoods

Because of its history, the USA is a racially and ethnically diverse nation. With immigrants pouring in from all over the world, it was only natural that new-
5 comers to America's shores flocked to neighbourhoods where they could speak their own language and live their culture. They often had networks of friends and relatives from the Old World who helped them find work and a place to live. By 1900, Polish,
10 Irish, Italian, German, Jewish and Asian quarters had arisen in virtually every city in the US.

Although **ghetto** is technically just another word for 'ethnic neighbourhood', in the USA it is used mainly for the – usually undesirable – quarters of a city in

which African Americans formerly were forced to live. 15
Black families wishing to move to a better part of town found that no landlord would rent them an apartment and no bank would give them credit to buy a house. White homeowners feared that the appearance of black faces in their street would send 20
property values into a downward spiral. It was only after the Civil Rights Act of 1968 prohibited discrimination in housing that the situation of African American families slowly began to improve.

List the 'push and pull factors' that lead to the creation of ethnic neighbourhoods. Do they exist in Germany too?

B1 The new neighbours   *Bruce Norris*

September 1959. *Karl comes to visit his neighbours Russ and Bev, who have just sold their inner-city house (where the scene takes place) and bought a new one in the suburbs. Jim is a young clergyman who has come to talk to Russ. Ted Driscoll is the real estate agent who has sold the house for Russ and his wife. Betsy is Karl's wife.*

- While you are reading the dialogue, form a mental image of the situation, i.e. the characters and what they may be doing while they are speaking.

Suburban street (1950s)

KARL [...] I take it, Russ, you're
aware that the Community
Association meets the first
Tuesday of each month? And
5 as I'm sure you know, Don
Skinner is part of the steering
committee. And somehow it
came to Don's attention at
this late juncture that Ted
10 Driscoll had found a buyer for
this house and I have to say it
did come as something of a
shock when Don told us what
sort of people they were.
15 RUSS What sort of people are they?
(Beat. Karl stares at Russ.)
KARL Well. *(Chuckles.)* Uhh ... Huh.
I suppose I'm forced to
consider the possibility that
20 you actually don't *know*.

RUSS Don't know *what*?
KARL Well, I mean. That
they're colored.
RUSS Who are?
KARL The family. It's a colored   25
family.
(Pause.)
So: I contacted the family –
JIM Wait wait wait.
KARL *(To Russ.)*   30
You're saying Ted never
bothered to tell you?
RUSS We, uhh ... sort of gave Ted
free rein on the –
JIM I don't think you're right on   35
this one, Karl.
KARL Oh, but I am. Oh, I've spoken
with the family.
RUSS Bev?
JIM On the *telephone*?   40

real estate agent *Immobilienmakler/in*
1 **I take it** *(infml)* I assume
6 **steering committee** [kəˈmɪti] *Steuerungskomitee*
9 **juncture** [ˈjʌŋktʃə] *(fml)* moment in time
16 **beat** *(n)* brief pause
17 **chuckle** laugh briefly and quietly
25 **colored** *(AE)* = *(BE)* **coloured** *(used for black people until the late 1950s, now an old-fashioned or offensive word)*
32 **bother to do sth.** [ˈbɒðə] think it necessary to do sth.
33 **give sb. free rein (on sth.)** [reɪn] *jdm. freie Hand geben (in einer Sache)*

45 **c'mere** = come here

65 **Negro** *(used for black people up until 1966, now an old-fashioned or offensive word)*

▶ **CC6: Talking about sensitive issues** (Fact File: Political correctness)

69 **common courtesy** ['kɜːtəsi] standard politeness

70 **interchangeable** *austauschbar*

73 **conduct one's business** [kən'dʌkt] behave

78 **pull a stunt** *(infml)* play a trick

88 **one hundred percent** (here) pure African American

93 **unsavory** *(AE)* = *(BE)* **unsavoury** unpleasant looking

117 **love thy neighbor** *(AE)*/**neighbour** *(BE)* *allusion to the Bible („Liebe deinen Nächsten")

119 **principled** basing our behaviour on moral principles

KARL Oh, no. As a matter of fact, Betsy and I've just come directly from … *(Beat, for effect.)* well, from *Hamilton Park.*

BEV *(To Russ.)* What is it?

45 RUSS C'mere a second.

KARL Now, Russ. You know as well as I do that this is a progressive community.

BEV *(To Russ as she joins them.)* What's he talking about?

50 KARL If you take the case of Gelman's grocery: That's a fine example of how we've all embraced a different way of thinking –

RUSS Slow down a second. Bev, get Ted

55 Driscoll on the phone.

BEV *(To Russ.)* What for?

RUSS Karl says. Karl is *claiming* –

KARL Russ, I have met *personally* with the family, and –

60 BEV What family?

RUSS He claims this family. The family to whom Ted sold the house.

KARL It's a colored family. *(Jim shakes his head.)*

65 JIM *(To Karl.)* Sorry, don't we say *Negro,* now?

KARL *(Irritated.)* I *say* Negro. –

JIM *(Overlapping.)* Well, it's only common courtesy, and I'm –

70 KARL *(Continuous.)* – I say them inter-changeably –

JIM *(Overlapping.)* – not trying to tell you how to conduct your business.

KARL *(Continuous.)* – and of course I said

75 *Negro* to them – No I think we both know what you're doing.

JIM And furthermore, I don't think Ted would pull a stunt like that.

KARL Yes. We all admire Ted. But I don't

80 think any of us would accuse him of putting the community's interests ahead of his own. [...]

BEV Waitwaitwait. Karl, are you *sure?*

KARL I was sitting with them not two

85 hours ago.

BEV But isn't it possible that they're … I don't know, *Mediterranean,* or – ?

KARL Bev, they are *one hundred percent.* And I don't know how much time any of

90 you have spent in Hamilton Park, but Betsy was waiting in the car and I can tell you, there are some *unsavory* characters. [...]
Now, some would say change is

95 inevitable. And I can support that, if it's change for the better. But I'll tell you what I *can't* support, and that's disregarding the needs of the people who *live* in a community.

BEV But don't they have needs, too? 100

KARL Don't who?

BEV The family.

KARL Which family?

BEV The ones who –

KARL The *purchasers?* 105

BEV I mean, in, in, in, in *principle,* don't we *all* deserve to – shouldn't we *all* have the opportunity to, to, to –

KARL *(Chuckles with amazement, shakes his head.)* Well, *Bev.* 110

JIM In *principle,* no question.

KARL But you can't *live* in a principle, can you? Gotta live in a *house.*

BEV And so do they.

KARL Not in *this* house, they don't. 115

JIM But here's the real question:

KARL And what happened to *love thy neighbor?* If we're being so principled.

BEV They would *become* our neighbors.

KARL And what about the neighbors you 120
already *have,* Bev?

BEV I care about them, too!

KARL Well, I'm afraid you can't have it both ways.

RUSS Okay. Assuming – 125

BEV Wait. Why not? [...]

JIM But the key question is this:

BEV No. Why *not* have it both ways?

KARL Darling, I came to talk to Russ. [...]

BEV Why not, if it would *benefit* someone? 130

JIM But *would* they benefit?

BEV If we could make them our *neighbors.*

KARL But they won't be *your* neighbors, Bev. *You're* the ones moving *away!*

From: *Clybourne Park,* 2010 – Act One, pp. 27–30

COMPREHENSION ◀

1 The topic

Sum up the main topic of the conversation in one sentence.

2 True or false?

Check each of the following statements. If you think the statement is true, point to evidence in the dialogue. If you think it is false, correct it.

1 A black family has bought Ted Driscoll's house.
2 Karl has just phoned the people who bought the house.
3 Russ didn't know that the house had been sold to African Americans.
4 Karl is upset about a black family moving into the neighbourhood.
5 Karl thinks that Hamilton Park is a progressive community.
6 Bev believes that everyone should be given a chance.

ANALYSIS ◀

3 Working with a *dramatic text

a In groups of four, each of you chooses one of the four roles in the scene. Listen to a recording of the text and concentrate on 'your' character while listening. Try and imagine what your character is doing, and where he/she is standing, etc.

b PLAYBACK In your group, decide where you want to stand while you are playing your roles. Then practise playing your part in pantomime while the recording is on.

4 Examining the *characters

Copy and complete the table. For the second column, choose phrases from the box on the right, or make up your own. ▶ LANGUAGE HELP

	Behaviour / character traits	Evidence from text (line numbers)
Karl		
Russ		
Bev		
Jim		

5 The dramatic conflict

At the heart of every drama is a conflict that is usually embodied by two of the characters. Choose the two characters that you think most clearly embody conflict in this scene. Contrast their points of view in a text of 100–150 words.

BEYOND THE TEXT ◀

6 The other side of the coin   SUPPORT ▶ p. 234

Form groups of four. Two of you are Bev and Russ, the other two are the African American couple who have bought the house in Clybourne Street. Imagine that after Karl has left, the black couple come to look at the house. How would Russ and Bev behave? How might the black couple explain their wish to move to an all-white neighbourhood? Discuss the issues at hand, then prepare role cards for your parts. Practise the scene, then perform it for your class.

■ **LANGUAGE AWARENESS**

Political correctness in language

Talking about ethnicities can be a sensitive issue. In the text "The new neighbours", a number of different terms referring to African Americans can be found. Not all of them are considered politically correct today. Whether a particular term is appropriate or not may depend on whether it is used by somebody who belongs to the ethnic community in question or not. Added to that is the fact that terms may have a different connotation in two different languages or countries.

▶ LA 1: Varieties of English
▶ LA 3: Similarities and differences of languages
▶ LA 4: Influencing through language
▶ SF 7: Working with closed test formats

 CD2 06

▶ SF 22: Listening

■ **LANGUAGE HELP**

- naïve
- shocked
- angry
- hypocritical
- idealistic
- wants to appear liberal
- self-confident
- tries to mediate
- embarrassed
- bossy

▶ SF 20: Analysing drama

B2 Integration or frustration?

Stefanie Mitchell, Orlando Patterson

In response to violent protests in several American cities, the Kerner Commission was created in 1967 to investigate the causes of racial unrest. 50 years later, African-American sociologist Orlando Patterson was asked how much progress racial integration has made in the meantime.

- Form three groups. Each is given one of the following topics: (A) 'The Civil Rights Movement', (B) 'Segregation and desegregation', (C) 'Black culture'. Research your topic and present your results to the rest of the class.

[...] In 1968, the Kerner Report concluded that 'the nation was moving toward two societies, one black, one white – separate and unequal.' What is your assessment of the situation 50 years later?

PATTERSON: Since then, there have been very important changes, but also some disappointments. There is no doubt that in the public sphere, particularly in the political realm, there have been substantial improvements. A good example is the election of a black president, but we should see this simply as the result of major changes in our political system that allowed blacks to be elected as mayors, congressional and senatorial representatives, and the occasional governor in the past 50 years. The Obama election didn't mark a post-racial era. That's an exaggerated and absurd claim. It's nonsense. 5

We all know that the major disadvantages that African Americans face have roots in their enslavement. For most of the time African Americans have lived in this country, they have been viewed as the quintessential outsiders, as people who didn't belong to the dominant political or moral community. That was reflected in the absence of blacks in important political positions but also in the national conversation, up to about the 1960s. That has changed completely. In addition to that, there are some important economic changes, and this shouldn't be sniffed at. There is a genuine black middle class. Finally, there is also the strong influence of blacks in the cultural life of the country. But in spite of their presence in the public sphere, black Americans still remain quite segregated in their private lives. 15

What are the factors that allowed segregation to continue? Some experts argue that segregation is almost as bad as before, or perhaps even worse.

PATTERSON: [...] There have been some changes in education at the elite level. But by and large this has been a major area of disappointment. The number of black students in overwhelmingly majority-black schools is as great as it was when the report came out. That, of course, is related to housing segregation. Now, blacks can afford good schools if they can afford to live in places that have such schools. [...] Those at the bottom, the black poor, are not seeing much change. In relative terms, the black poor may even be slightly worse off. They certainly are as segregated as they ever were, and the violence in the inner cities has increased substantially since the Kerner Report. 25 30

The report blamed 'structural racism' created by 'white institutions' and 'white society' for the violence and the conditions of the ghettos and the inner cities. One of its recommendations was to improve the conditions of the ghettos or simply get rid of them. Why has it been hard to accomplish this? 35

in response to sth. as a reaction to sth.
6 **substantial** fairly large
14 **quintessential** most obvious
16 **national conversation** public discussion (in the media etc.)
18 **sniff at sth.** *(infml)* regard sth. as trivial
30 **be worse off** *(infml)* schlechter dran sein
35 **accomplish sth.** manage to do sth.

many, having a black community ensures black cultural and communal life, both of which could dissipate if blacks are integrated in the broader white community. I dis-
40 agree. Ghettos never worked.

When people say that black neighborhoods are needed for black culture to live on, I point to the Jews, because even as they integrated, they preserved their culture. All other groups in America recognize that staying clustered in ghettos is not good. That was true of Jews. It's been true of Asians. That's also true of Irish and Italians, and
45 more recently it's been true of Hispanics. There is a growing Hispanic middle class that is very integrated. I don't see why black Americans can't do the same. Research-ers found that blacks who moved to better neighborhoods were better off than those who stayed in their neighborhoods with similar resources.

What other factors have prevented integration from happening?

50 PATTERSON: There has always been right-wing and racist opposition to any government attempt at integration. [...] But there is also the hypocrisy and the 'not-in-my-backyard' view of many middle- and upper-middle-class people, including white liberals, who have strongly resisted attempts at building moderate-income and low-income housing in the suburbs. [...] But the main reason for the lack of integration is that blacks don't
55 have the income to integrate; they can't afford to live in the suburbs or send their kids to private schools. Some can do it, and that's some progress, but it's not enough.

Some are saying it's time for a new report on the racial divide in the U.S. Do we need a new version of the Kerner Report?

PATTERSON: It can do no harm, but I don't think it would be effective. Bill Clinton tried
60 a National Conversation on Race, and it didn't lead to much. What I think is more important is that the leadership within both the black and the liberal communities work together to improve the situation in the inner cities. Right now, people are fully aware of the despair and pessimism that exist in the black community, especially in regard to black youth, police brutality, black unemployment, and mass incarceration,
65 which is an abomination. One in three black youth is likely to risk imprisonment. That's an abomination for all Americans.

We know what the solutions are: integration, education, and decent jobs. Whether we need another commission to say that again, I don't think so. There has to be a joint effort of all communities and a massive infusion of support at the local, state, and
70 federal level to provide better education in the inner cities because this goes beyond providing jobs. The jobs are not coming back even for white people in the Midlands, and I don't expect them to come back in the inner cities.

From: 'The Kerner Report on Race, 50 Years on', *The Harvard Gazette*, 21 March 2018

---

38 **ensure sth.** guarantee sth.
39 **dissipate** disappear
50 **right-wing** very conservative
64 **incarceration** imprisonment
65 **abomination sth.** that cannot be tolerated
71 **Midlands** in the USA, region formed by New Jersey, Pennsylvania, Delaware and Maryland

In this photo from 2017, former US Senator Fred Harris of Oklahoma is holding a copy of the Kerner Report as he discusses the 50th anniversary of the Kerner Commission. Harris is the last surviving member of the Kerner Commission.

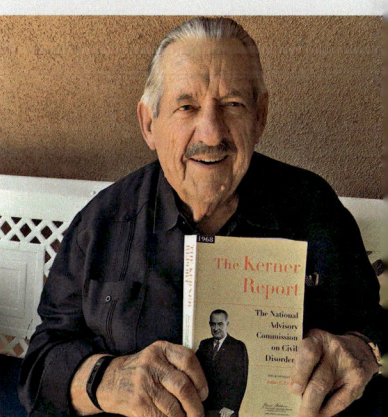

COMPREHENSION ◀

1 Collecting information

a Outline the areas in which Patterson sees progress in racial integration and those which are still problem areas.

b Compare lists with your partner; add any missing information.

ANALYSIS ◀

2 Analysing the argumentation

Examine the reasons Patterson names why many black people in the US feel 'despair and pessimism' (l. 63) and the measures he recommends to improve the situation.

BEYOND THE TEXT ◀

3 Integration – a desirable goal?

Patterson is opposed to ghettos, yet he also admits that some black leaders speak out in their favour (cf. ll. 36–40). Comment on the question whether or not it is good for a minority to preserve its culture by living together in one neighbourhood.

B3 The changing face of America   *William J. Clinton*

Looking back on history of the USA at the end of the 20th century, Clinton, President of the United States from 1993–2001, points out how the lessons of the past can help the United States cope with the challenges of the future. His message still sounds true in the second decade of the 21st century. Clinton made the *speech from which this excerpt is taken to graduating students at Portland State University.

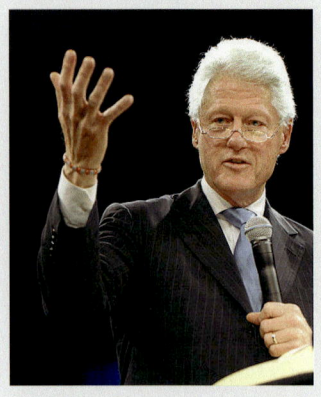

Bill Clinton, 42nd President of the USA (1993–2001)

2 **strengthen sth.** make sth. stronger

7 **ensure** make sure *(sicherstellen)*

8 **the brass ring** *(AE, infml)* the opportunity to be successful

14 **industrious** [ɪnˈdʌstriəs] hard-working

15 **heritage** [ˈherɪtɪdʒ] cultural tradition

26 **magnitude** *Größenordnung*

29 **unequivocally** [ˌʌnɪˈkwɪvəkli] *unmissverständlich*

30 **revitalize sth.** [ˌriːˈvaɪtəlaɪz] give sth. new life

32 **energize sth.** [ˈenədʒaɪz] give sth. energy

Today I want to talk to you about what may be the most important subject of all, how we can strengthen the bonds of our national community as we grow more racially and ethnically diverse. [...]

The driving force behind our increasing diversity is a new, large wave of immigration. It is changing the face of America. And while most of the changes are good, they do present challenges which demand more, both from new immigrants and from our citizens. Citizens share a responsibility to welcome new immigrants, to ensure that they strengthen our Nation, to give them their chance at the brass ring. In turn, new immigrants have a responsibility to learn, to work, to contribute to America. If both citizens and immigrants do their part, we will grow ever stronger in the new global information economy.

More than any other nation on Earth, America has constantly drawn strength and spirit from wave after wave of immigrants. In each generation, they have proved to be the most restless, the most adventurous, the most innovative, the most industrious of people. Bearing different memories, honoring different heritages, they have strengthened our economy, enriched our culture, renewed our promise of freedom and opportunity for all. [...]

But now we are being tested again by a new wave of immigration larger than any in a century, far more diverse than any in our history. Each year, nearly a million people come legally to America. Today, nearly one in ten people in America was born in another country; one in five schoolchildren are from immigrant families. Today, largely because of immigration, there is no majority race in Hawaii or Houston or New York City. Within five years, there will be no majority race in our largest State, California. In a little more than 50 years, there will be no majority race in the United States. No other nation in history has gone through demographic change of this magnitude in so short a time.

What do the changes mean? They can either strengthen and unite us, or they can weaken and divide us. We must decide.

Let me state my view unequivocally. I believe new immigrants are good for America. They are revitalizing our cities. They are building our new economy. They are strengthening our ties to the global economy, just as earlier waves of immigrants settled the new frontier and powered the Industrial Revolution. They are energizing our culture and broadening our vision of the world. They are renewing our most basic values and reminding us all of what it truly means to be an American. [...]

settled the new frontier and powered the Industrial Revolution. They are energizing our culture and broadening our vision of the world. They are renewing our most basic values and reminding us all of what it truly means to be an American. [...]

35 My fellow Americans, we descendants of those who passed through the portals of Ellis Island must not lock the door behind us. Americans whose parents were denied the rights of citizenship simply because of the color of their skin must not deny those rights to others because of the country of their birth or the nature of their faith.

We should treat new immigrants as we would have wanted our own grandparents
40 to be treated. We should share our country with them, not shun them or shut them out. But mark my words, unless we handle this well, immigration of this sweep and scope could threaten the bonds of our Union.

Around the world, we see what can happen when people who live on the same land put race and ethnicity before country and humanity. If America is to remain the
45 world's most diverse democracy, if immigration is to strengthen America as it has throughout our history, then we must say to one another: Whether your ancestors came here in slave ships or on the Mayflower, whether they landed on Ellis Island or at Los Angeles International Airport, or have been here for thousands of years, if you believe in the Declaration of Independence and the Constitution, if you accept the
50 responsibilities as well as the rights embedded in them, then you are an American. Only that belief can keep us one America in the 21st century.

From: 'Commencement Address at Portland State University', 13 June 1998

COMPREHENSION ◀

1 Clinton's message

Summarize Clinton's position on diversity in no more than four sentences.

LANGUAGE AWARENESS ◀

2 Political vocabulary

a Clinton's speech contains many words and phrases related to the idea of a country and the people who live in it, e.g. *our national community* (l. 2). Collect more examples from the text.

b Compare lists with a partner and add any words or phrases that are missing from your list.

c Examine the connotations of the words and phrases.

d 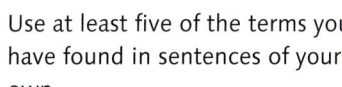 YOU CHOOSE ▶

| Arrange the terms you have found in the form of a mind map. | **OR** | Use at least five of the terms you have found in sentences of your own. |

■ **TROUBLE SPOT**

treat sb. (l. 40) = *jdn. behandeln (auch als Arzt/Ärztin)*
deal with a topic = *ein Thema behandeln*
handle a situation/problem (l. 41) = *mit einer Situation / einem Problem o. Ä. umgehen, zurechtkommen*

35 **descendant** [dɪˈsendənt] *Nachkomme*
36 **Ellis Island** N.Y. centre for new immigrants, 1892–1954
38 **faith** religion
40 **shun sb.** avoid sb.
41 **sweep, scope** *Größenordnung*
44 **ethnicity** [eθˈnɪsəti] *ethnische Zugehörigkeit*

■ **LANGUAGE AWARENESS**

Denotation and connotation
Denotation is the literal meaning of a word as you might find it in a dictionary (e.g. *spider* = a creature with eight legs), while *connotation* refers to the associations or the emotional colouring some or many people connect to that word (e.g. *spider* > small, wriggly, agile, scary, …). When using a word, you should be aware of both its denotation and its connotation

▶ LA 1: Varieties of English
▶ LA 4: Influencing through language

SPEAKING **FOCUS ON SKILLS**

Speaking in front of an audience

*Before you speak in front of an audience, you should consider how to make your speech more effective. Analysing a professional speech is a good way to examine *stylistic devices and their effect.*

Analysing a speech

1 Analysing the structure

a Identify the following parts of Clinton's speech (pp. 110–111) by putting them in the correct order and giving line numbers:

1 Statement of the main topic
2 Appeal to the audience to be fair in dealing with the consequences
3 Appeal to the audience to make a commitment
4 Description of historical developments
5 Statement of the challenge
6 Description of the present situation
7 Statement of opinion

b Examine how Clinton links the parts of his speech to make it easier for his listeners to follow his ideas. List the different ways of linking ideas for your own later use.

2 Analysing the *stylistic devices

a Examine the language of the speech. Point out passages where Clinton

- catches his listeners' attention
- emphasizes his message
- creates a feeling of unity with his audience
- reveals a positive or negative attitude to his topic
- appeals to his listeners' sense of fairness.

Make notes on your findings (including line numbers).

b Compare notes with your partner. Analyse your examples and explain the techniques used. The terms you may need are in the list on the left.

c Team up with another pair and give Clinton's speech an 'effectiveness rating' (on a scale from 1 to 6).

*alliteration • *anaphora [ə'næfərə] • comparative/superlative • *connotation • *contrast • *direct address • *enumeration • *emphasis • *metaphor •*parallelism • personal pronoun • *repetition • *rhetorical question • *simile • *wordplay

Preparing your own speech

1 Choosing a topic

Choose one of the following topics to prepare and deliver your own speech modelled on the one you have just analysed:

- *Living together in our multicultural school*
- *The world is changing – let's change with it!*
- *The challenges of freedom in a diverse society*

2 Collecting and organizing ideas

a Brainstorm what ideas/associations/aspects of your topic come into your head.

b Sort the ideas, keeping in mind that your speech will need a clear structure.

c Prepare an outline that includes suitable linking phrases and signpost words, e.g. 'for one thing …', 'In addition …', 'above all …'.

▶ SF 5: Structuring information and ideas
▶ LP 14: Linking words and phrases

3 Writing a first draft

a Decide on a good opening sentence. Choose from the following list, or phrase your own:

- *Today I would like to talk to you about what we can do to make life easier for all of us at this school.*
- *Last night I went to a multicultural community event, and that gave me the idea of talking to you about how our world is changing and what we can do to change our attitudes.*
- *The other day I saw a sign that said 'Freedom is never free', and I started thinking about the price of freedom in our democracy. Today I would like to tell you my thoughts on this subject.*

b Remember to use stylistic devices like those you identified in Clinton's speech in order to

- catch your listeners' attention: *Do you know how many nations are represented by the students at our school?*
- emphasize your message: *Cheap air travel, the internet, the end of the Cold War – all of these developments have made our world smaller and more connected than it has ever been before.*
- create a feeling of unity with your audience: *Together, we can find a solution.*
- convey a positive or negative attitude: *Tolerance and respect lead to understanding and cooperation; intolerance and distrust to conflict and violence.*
- appeal to your listeners' sense of fairness: *Imagine how you would feel if this happened to you.*

c Take special care with your closing sentence(s), because this is what will stick in your listeners' minds.

4 Revising your draft

Read your draft aloud to a partner to test its effect as a spoken text. Mark the passages that don't 'work' and note what changes you want to make. Then write a revised version, always keeping in mind that it is a speech with which you want to make an impact on your listeners.

Rehearsing and delivering your speech

1 Decide how you want to deliver your speech, and take the necessary precautions to ensure you don't get mixed up and can be seen and understood clearly:

Method	Position
Speaking freely from notes on index cards	Standing in front of the class
Reading aloud from a manuscript	Sitting at a desk in front of the class

2 Practise your speech until you feel comfortable with it. You can make a recording of the speech and then listen to yourself speaking to get an 'outside impression'. Practise speaking in front of a full-length mirror to monitor your eye contact and body language. Refer to the Skills File (pp. 317–318) for additional tips on how to deliver a speech.

▶ SF 25: Giving a speech

> **TROUBLE SPOT**
>
> **actual** ['æktʃuəl] (l. 39) = *real, concrete*
> But: *aktuell* = **current, topical**

▶ LP 13: Placing emphasis on key points

> **LANGUAGE AWARENESS**
>
> **Emphasizing your message: using literary devices**
> In discussions and speeches, but also in written texts, you can support and stress what you want to say by using literary devices like repetition, imagery and rhetorical questions, thus adding atmosphere and emotion.

▶ LA 4: Influencing through language

The United States' place in the world

C1 Facts and figures

	USA	China	Germany	Brazil	India	Russia
1 GDP	19,390,604	12,237,700	3,677,439	2,055,505	2,597,491	1,577,524
2 Military spending	597,178	228,173	43,023	25,751	59,757	55,327
3 Balance of trade	−568,439	210,728	281,389	30,177	−73,362	83,886

All figures are in millions of US dollars and are from 2017. Sources: World Bank (GDP and balance of trade), SIPRI (military spending).

■ **FACT FILE**

GDP (**Gross** [grəʊs] **Domestic Product**) is defined as the total value of goods and services produced in a country. The **balance of trade** is the difference between the total value of exports from a country and imports into the same country. A negative balance (**deficit** ['defɪsɪt]; opposite: **surplus** ['sɜːpləs]) means the country imports more than it exports.

▶ SF 12: Analysing charts and graphs

■ **LANGUAGE AWARENESS**

Emphasizing your message: using facts and figures
Underlining your ideas with facts and figures conveys objectivity and helps you to convince your readers or audience.

▶ LA 4: Influencing through language

 CD2 08

COMPREHENSION

1 Understanding the figures
    a Write eight sentences comparing the figures in the table. **SUPPORT** ▶ p. 234
    b Compare sentences with your partner. Check each other's information to make sure you have both got the facts right.

BEYOND THE TEXT

2 The facts behind the figures
Link up with another pair and discuss what influence the facts from the table above could have on the balance of power in the world.

C2 The German view   *Michael Hochgeschwender*

In the podcast you are about to hear, historian Michael Hochgeschwender is asked if the USA is still the leading world power. When you mention this interview to your American e-pal, she wants to know what the professor says about the USA's status in the world. You will hear the interview twice.

COMPREHENSION

1 While listening
Listen to what Hochgeschwender says about the position of the USA in the world. Take notes on the following aspects:
- what the historian says about the world status of the United States,
- his reasons for his opinion,
- his views on the future development of the United States' role.

▶ SF 22: Listening

2 After listening
Compare notes with your partner.

BEYOND THE TEXT

▶ SF 41: Mediation of written and oral texts
▶ CC 6: Talking about sensitive issues

3 Mediation (German ➜ English)
    a Use your notes to write an email of about 150 words explaining Hochgeschwender's position to your e-pal.
    b **CHALLENGE** ▶ Add a further paragraph to your email from **a** in which you comment on the historian's views and ask your American e-pal for her opinion.

C3 The end of the American era? *Eliot A. Cohen*

The 2016 election victory of a presidential candidate who promised 'America first' gave rise to worldwide fears that the US could withdraw from its position of world leadership. In the following text, a foreign-policy expert examines possible consequences of the Trump presidency.

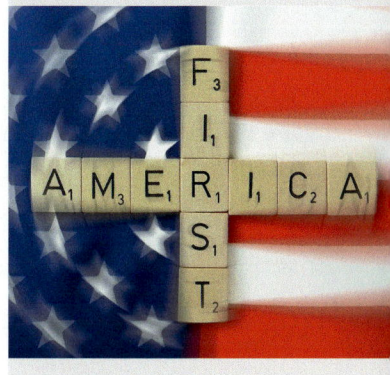

Donald Trump was right. He inherited a mess. In January 2017, American foreign policy was, if not in crisis, in big trouble. Strong forces were putting stress on the old global political order: the rise of China to a power with more than half the productive capacity of the United States (and defense spending to match); the partial recovery of
5 a resentful Russia under a skilled and thuggish autocrat; the discrediting of Western elites by the financial crash of 2008, followed by roiling populist waves, of which Trump himself was part; a turbulent Middle East; economic dislocations worldwide. [...]

These circumstances would have caused severe headaches for a competent and
10 sophisticated successor. Instead, the United States got a president who had unnervingly promised a wall on the southern border (paid for by Mexico), the dismantlement of long-standing trade deals with both competitors and partners, a closer relationship with Vladimir Putin, and a ban on Muslims coming into the United States. [...]

On issues that are truly global in scope, Trump has abdicated leadership and the
15 moral high ground. The United States has managed to isolate itself on the topic of climate change, by the tone of its pronouncements no less than by its precipitous exit from the Paris Agreement. As for human rights, the president has taken only cursory notice of the two arrests of the Russian dissident Alexei Navalny or the death of the Chinese Nobel Prize winner and prisoner of conscience Liu Xiaobo. Trump did not
20 object after Turkish President Recep Tayyip Erdoğan's security detail beat American protesters on American soil, in Washington, D.C. In April, he reportedly told Filipino President Rodrigo Duterte, who has used death squads to deal with offenders of local narcotics laws, that he was doing an 'unbelievable job on the drug problem'. Trump's secretary of state, Rex Tillerson, made it clear in his first substantive speech to State
25 Department employees that American values are now of at best secondary importance to 'American interests', presumably economic, in the conduct of foreign policy. [...]

This dangerous and dispiriting chapter in American history will end, in eight years or four – or perhaps in two or even one, if Trump is impeached or removed under the Twenty-Fifth Amendment. But what will follow? Will the United States recover within
30 a few years, as it did from the disgrace of Richard Nixon's resignation and the fecklessness of Jimmy Carter during the Iranian hostage crisis? Alas, that is unlikely. Even barring cataclysmic events, we will be living with the consequences of Trump's tenure as chief executive and commander in chief for decades. Damage will continue to appear long after he departs the scene.

35 Americans, after trying every other alternative, can always be counted on to do the right thing, Winston Churchill supposedly said. But who will count on that now, after the victory of a man like Trump? Other countries interpret Trump's election as America's repudiation of its role as guarantor of world order. Canadian Foreign Minister Chrystia Freeland put it bluntly in a speech in June: 'The fact that our friend and ally
40 has come to question the very worth of its mantle of global leadership puts into sharper focus the need for the rest of us to set our own clear and sovereign course.'

Indeed, that is what is happening. Trump is not entirely a historical fluke, and it is reasonable to see his foreign policy as reflecting some Americans' attitudes toward the outside world. Our politicians and our foreign-policy establishment – the former

1 **inherit sth.** *etwas erben*
5 **resentful** angry
   thuggish behaving like a criminal
6 **roiling** rapidly moving
7 **dislocation** sudden, unexpected change
10 **sophisticated** experienced
   successor *Nachfolger/in*
   unnerving *beunruhigend*
11 **dismantlement** *Abbau*
14 **scope** importance
   abdicate sth. abandon sth. (esp. power)
16 **precipitous** [-'--] hasty
17 **cursory** superficial
20 **security detail** *Sicherheitskräfte*
22 **death squad** *Killerkommando*
23 **narcotics** drugs
24 **substantive** [-'--] (*adj*) important
27 **dispiriting** discouraging
28 **impeach sb.** remove sb. from office
30 **resignation** act of quitting your job
   fecklessness weak, irresponsible behaviour
31 **alas** (*old use*) unfortunately
32 **bar sth.** regard sth. as unlikely to happen
32 **cataclysmic** catastrophic
   tenure *Amtszeit*
38 **repudiation** (*fml*) rejection
   guarantor [ˌɡærənˈtɔː] *Garant, Bürge*
39 **bluntly** openly
   ally ['ælaɪ] *Verbündete(r)*
40 **mantle** (*figurative*) office, position
42 **fluke** accident

₄₆ **prudent** wise
₄₉ **civic** public
₅₂ **resilience** ability to deal with stress
₅₅ **stunted** weakened
₅₇ **failing state** country whose government has lost control

consumed by domestic matters, the latter largely by technocratic concerns – have lost the ability to make the case to the country for prudent American management of an international system whose relative peace for 70 years owes so much to Washington's leadership. Americans who oppose Trump may conclude (also reasonably) that the country's internal problems, including the fundamentals of its civic culture, demand their attention. They too may turn inward, not least because they have lost confidence in the strength of political institutions and the competence of the political class. [...] 45 50

America's astonishing resilience may rescue it once again, particularly if Trump does not finish his first term. But an equally likely scenario is that Trump will leave key government institutions weakened or corrupted, America's foreign-policy establishment sharply divided, and America's position in the world stunted. An America lacking confidence, coupled with the rise of undemocratic powers, populist movements on the right and left, and failing states, is the kind of world few Americans remember. It would be like the world of the late 1920s or early 1930s: disorderly and unstable, but with much worse to follow. 55

From: 'How Trump is ending the American era', *The Atlantic*, October 2017

COMPREHENSION ◀

1 Understanding the text
  a Outline the writer's argumentation by summarizing each of the paragraphs in one sentence.
  b Compare your results with your partner. Discuss any points on which you disagree.

ANALYSIS ◀

2 The writer's bias
  a Collect examples that show where the writer stands regarding Donald Trump and the politics he represents.
  b Analyse the writer's standpoint, referring to your examples from **2a**.

3 Collocations: the language of politics
Many common political terms are collocations of adjectives and nouns (e.g. 'presidential election') or two nouns ('trade deal'). Find the English equivalent of each of the following in Cohen's text:
(1) Außenpolitik (2) Verteidigungsausgaben (3) Finanzkrise (4) enge Beziehung (5) politische/r Gefangene/r (6) wirtschaftliche Interessen (7) globale Führungsrolle (8) innenpolitische Angelegenheiten (9) politische Einrichtungen (10) populistische Bewegung

LANGUAGE AWARENESS ◀

4 Persuading the reader
The writer is not only convinced of his point of view – he wants to convince his readers as well. Point out ways in which Cohen tries to influence the reader to accept his views and identify the language structures he uses for this purpose. **SUPPORT** ▶ p. 235

BEYOND THE TEXT ◀

5 America's role in the world
  a Since the end of World War II, the USA has seen itself as the 'guarantor of world order' (l. 38). In groups of four or five, point to examples that illustrate this role.
  b Discuss whether the global community needs a 'world policeman' and whether America is the country that should play this role.

Giving a speech on why you would like to visit the USA

Imagine you discover this advert on the internet:

The Chance of a Lifetime!

The German-American Friendship Organization is offering ten stipends for German teenagers aged 18 or older. Winners will spend three months in the United States, living with American families, visiting schools, businesses and places of interest, talking to politicians, business people, and just plain Americans of all ages.

To apply to our program, send us a video of not more than five minutes in which you make a speech on the subject: 'Why I want to learn more about the United States of America.'

Excited at the prospect of an all-expenses-paid stay in the USA, you decide to apply.

1 Getting started

Collect your ideas using a suitable method: What do you find fascinating, irritating, or intriguing about the USA and about Americans? What kinds of people would you like to talk to? What questions would you ask them?

▶ SF 25: Giving a speech

2 Writing your speech

a Organize your ideas in the form of an outline. Use the outline to write a first draft.

b Read your drafts aloud in small groups and discuss them, suggesting improvements where needed.

c Prepare a revised version. Make sure it does not take longer than five minutes. Practise reading your speech in front of a friend or a mirror until you feel confident with it. Then make a video of yourself delivering your speech.

3 Evaluation

Form small groups. In your group, let the others watch your video (or you can deliver it 'live'). The others give you feedback. They fill in assessment sheets given out by your teacher.

6 Beyond the Nation – Europe and a Globalized World

Download a list of chapter vocab here: **Webcode** context-81

▶ CC 1: Cultural awareness

▶ SF 41: Mediation of written and oral texts

▶ SF 24: Giving a presentation

1 Displaying one's national identity

During great sports events, above all soccer world championships, people often display their national identity and patriotism by carrying flags or singing their national anthem.

a THINK Describe your attitude to this behaviour, referring to the pictures above and your own experience.

b PAIR Compare and discuss your ideas with a partner.

c SHARE Present your most interesting findings to the class.

2 YOU CHOOSE **Researching flags and anthems**

a Use German sources to find out about the history of the German flag and the national anthem. Prepare a short presentation for English-speaking visitors to your school.

OR

b Choose a country and do some research into the history of its anthem and flag. Present your findings to the class.

3 Understanding national symbols

Define the function of national symbols such as flags and anthems.

4 Finding out about international institutions

a Find out about the roles of the following institutions: UN, UNESCO, WHO, Commonwealth, EU. Describe and explain their logos.

b Say why institutions that cut across national boundaries might be necessary.

5 Thinking about your sense of identity

a Complete this sentence: 'I rather see myself as (1) a German or other national citizen, (2) a European, (3) a cosmopolitan citizen, (4) none of the above.' Say why.

b Find out how the majority of your class see themselves and why.

PREVIEW

In this chapter you will learn what living in a globalized world means for the individual and the world.

Main topics

- Personal identities in a global world .... p. 118
- The historical peacekeeping merits of the EU and its current challenges .... p. 122
- Promises and challenges of globalization .... p. 128
- The role of English in a global world .... p. 133

Focus on Skills: MEDIATION and READING

- Mediating texts in oral communication .... p. 127
- Using reading strategies .... p. 132

Chapter Task:

Preparing an exhibition on the topic 'Slavery? Not today, not in Germany!' .... p. 137

CD2 09

Listen to an audio version of the text on the CD or download it here:

Webcode context-23

> **TROUBLE SPOT**
>
> *Preis* = **prize** (award given to sb. for an achievement)
> *Preis* = **price** (the money you have to pay for sth.)

Globalization: Europe, the world

European integration as a model?

Political experts say that the power of nation states has been declining and that today the most important decisions are taken on an international level. The European Union, which connects independent nation states, is a good example. The two principal purposes of the European Union (and of its predecessors) are to secure peace and promote economic growth. In 2012, the European Union was awarded the Nobel Peace Prize for overcoming the hostility among European countries after the Second World War and for advancing reconciliation and peace. At the moment of the award, however, Europe was and still is challenged by a monetary crisis, which forced many member states to make massive cuts in their budgets. As a result, unemployment rates increased and many young people, especially those from Spain or Greece were forced to leave their countries and find occupation elsewhere.

Chances and risks of globalization

Globalization can be described as a process in which barriers, especially trade barriers, between nations are removed. This process accelerated when modern communication technologies came into play and transport costs decreased. It made international collaboration and competition possible: Companies in the developed countries were able to outsource their production and services to countries whose labour force was prepared to work for significantly lower wages.

This international division of labour may have freed many people in the developing countries from extreme poverty; however, many of them have to work under poor working conditions with low safety standards. In the traditional industrialized countries, globalization has resulted in redundancies in the domestic workforce.

GLOBALIZATION MEANS WHEN YOUR EMAIL ACCOUNT IS FULL WITH SPAM FROM COUNTRIES YOU'VE NEVER HEARD OF...

The threats and opportunities of globalization can be illustrated well through the example of international sports. Top soccer clubs pay enormous sums for the best players from all over the world, allowing for extraordinary labour mobility. Yet, only the richest clubs can participate in this 'leg-drain' and if players are frequently being bought and sold they may feel uprooted and unable to develop a sound sense of identity.

English as a global language

The cultural impact of globalization is illustrated most clearly by the role of English as a global language. Today, English is not only the native language of more than 360 million speakers worldwide, but it is also used as a lingua franca between non-native speakers of English in international business, science and technology, and popular culture. On the one hand, this makes international communication easier, but on the other hand, it threatens local languages and thus cultural and linguistic diversity.

5

10

15

20

25

30

35

40

▶ SF 1: Dealing with unknown or new words

1 Words in use: synonyms

Find a <mark>highlighted</mark> word or expression that means the same as …
1 the aim or function of something.
2 the percentage of people in a country without a job.
3 the readiness of people to work in different places.
4 not feel at home anywhere.
5 give a job to external workers, often in another country.
6 language spoken all over the world.

2 Word formation

For each gap in the sentences below choose a suitable word from the list on the right, turn it into the required word class (e.g. a verb into a noun) and adjust its grammatical form if necessary (e.g. the plural form).
1 Some European countries had an extremely … relationship for centuries.
2 With the Treaty of Friendship (1963) France and Germany were officially …
3 In our times of globalization, individuals world-wide have to … and …
4 Since the EU was …, lasting peace has been one of its aims.
5 Today, the EU is facing great …

*collaboration ·
competition · challenge ·
foundation · hostility ·
reconciliation*

▶ LP 20: Word formation

3 Activating your vocabulary

Translate the following passage. The <u>underlined</u> words and phrases are taken from the text, but you should try to translate them without looking at the text again. Paraphrase if you do not know the exact word or expression. Revise your version with the help of the text and a dictionary.

▶ SF 6: Paraphrasing
▶ SF 2: Using a dictionary and a grammar book

Globalisierung ist ein Prozess <u>voller Chancen und Risiken</u>. Kritiker befürchten, dass sie Arbeitsplätze in den <u>traditionellen Industrieländern</u> gefährdet und Arbeiter in den <u>Entwicklungsländern</u> ausbeutet, die oft unter sehr <u>schlechten Arbeitsbedingungen</u> arbeiten müssen. Befürworter der Globalisierung glauben, dass sie <u>extreme Armut</u> in vielen Ländern besiegen kann. Der Abbau von <u>Handelsschranken</u> sei von Vorteil für alle.

▶ LP 16: Avoiding Germanisms

4 Mediation (English ➜ German)

You are asked to briefly inform your politics course in German on the future of nation states as described in this text. Prepare and give a short oral presentation. Make visual aids if necessary.

▶ SF 41: Mediation of written and oral texts
▶ SF 5: Structuring information and ideas: visual aids and outlines
▶ SF 24: Giving a presentation

Part A

Nobel Peace Prize medal

▶ SF 11: Analysing pictures
▶ SF 22: Listening
▶ SF 7: Working with closed test formats

🎧 **CD2** 10, 11, 12, 13

Herodotus [həˈrɒdətəs] (ca. 484–425 BC) Greek historian
Winston Churchill (1874–1965) British Prime Minister (1940–1945 and 1951–1955)
founder person who starts an institution or organization
ceasefire [ˈsiːsfaɪə] time when enemies stop fighting
reconciliation [ˌrekənsɪliˈeɪʃn] situation where two people or groups become friendly again after a disagreement
Konrad Adenauer (1876–1967) first post-war Chancellor of West Germany (1949–1963)
Treaty of Rome founding document of the European Economic Community from 1957
Willy Brandt (1913–1992) German Chancellor (1969–1974)
Gdansk Danzig, Polish seaport
François Mitterand (1916–1996) French President (1981–1995)
Helmut Kohl (1930–2017) German Chancellor (1982–1998)
Tallin, Riga, Vilnius capitals of the Baltic states Estonia, Latvia and Lithuania, respectively
Jean Monnet (1888–1979) French diplomat, considered to be one of the founding fathers of the European Union
perpetual [pəˈpetʃuəl] continuing for a long period of time with no interruption
Srebrenica town in Bosnia, site of a massacre during the Balkan War (1995)
Abraham Lincoln [ˈlɪŋkən] (1809–1865) President of the United States (1861–1865)

European integration as a model?

A1 A great achievement of the past   *Herman Van Rompuy*

Since 1901 the Nobel Peace Prize has been awarded annually (with few exceptions) to individuals and institutions who have sought to establish or keep peace. During the award ceremony, the winner is required to give the Nobel Lecture, a lecture on a subject related to the topic of the prize. When in 2012 the European Union was awarded the prize, the Nobel Lecture was given by Herman Van Rompuy, President of the European Council, and José Manuel Barroso, President of the European Commission.

1   Before listening
Look at the picture on the right and describe the setting and the general atmosphere of the ceremony.

Hermann Van Rompuy gives his Nobel Lecture.

◀ COMPREHENSION ◀

2   Listening for gist
Listen to the audio file, which contains Van Rompuy's part of the Nobel Lecture. From the following statements choose the one that best describes the speaker's message.
1   Peacekeeping is Europe's ongoing goal.
2   Lasting peace has been established in Europe.
3   Current challenges are threatening to seriously destabilize the EU.

3   Listening for detail: part 1
Listen to the first part of the speech, then decide whether the following statements are true or false according to the speaker.
1   The Nobel Prize belongs to Europe's political elite, who united Europe after World War II.
2   War used to be a constant feature of European history.
3   Van Rompuy still has wartime memories of his own.
4   Europe would not have gained peace without the European Union.
5   Konrad Adenauer was awarded a French medal in 1951.

4 Listening for detail: part 2

Say which historical events depicted in the photos are mentioned by Rompuy. Give the photos headings.

A

B

C

D

E

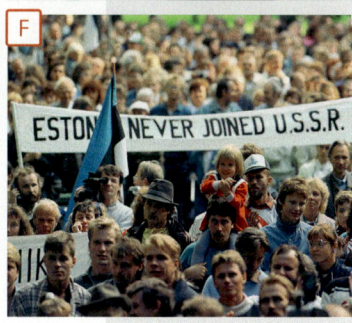
F

5 Listening for detail: part 3

Choose the correct statement.

a Rompuy mentions the example of Srebrenica to prove that …
  1 … there is no European post-war generation.
  2 … there was war in Europe not very long ago.
  3 … Soviet rule in Eastern Europe was responsible for massacres.

b According to the speaker, the economic crisis …
  1 … does not put the European Union to the test.
  2 … mainly affects young academics.
  3 … reduces the feeling of solidarity.

— LANGUAGE AWARENESS ◄

6 A non-native accent

a Listen to the speech once more and examine Van Rompuy's English. Identify elements that show that English is not his native tongue.
  ▶ LANGUAGE HELP

b Do you think it's a disadvantage to speak with an accent? Say why or why not.

— BEYOND THE TEXT ◄

7 YOU CHOOSE Research on the EU

Do some research on one of the topics below, then present your results:

a Describe the status of English in the European institutions. Discuss whether the use of other languages, e.g. German, should be promoted within European institutions.

OR

b Outline the events that led to European unification and describe their context and consequences. Add more 'historical moments' that helped to unite Europe.

■ LANGUAGE AWARENESS

English as a lingua franca
In particular contexts, such as foreign policy and in the world of finance, English is the most important lingua franca or bridge language. This means that for the people involved, English is no longer a foreign language. It has acquired the status of a second language, even though you can hear from people's accents and command of English that they are not native speakers.

▶ LA 1: Varieties of English

■ LANGUAGE HELP

- pronounce … as … / say … instead of …
- not pronounce … properly
- use voiceless/voiced consonants
- long/short vowel / diphthong

▶ SF 24: Giving a presentation

A2 Europe's lost generation *Anna Isaac*

Beginning in 2010, several member states of the Eurozone had trouble financing their national debt. New mechanisms were installed to stabilize the euro. Eight years later, journalist Anna Isaac looks at the price some countries have paid for stability.

Outside a McDonald's in Latina, Italy, the city's teens are clutching cigarettes and milkshakes while engrossed in a passionate debate about identity.

The discussion taking place under the golden arches that are perhaps the most recognisable symbol of globalisation is about whether or not a local park named after Mussolini should no longer bear the name of Italy's wartime fascist leader. 5

This is Europe's lost generation, weighed down by endemic youth unemployment. Now, after a decade of austerity and stagnation, some are reawakening the ghosts of their fascist forefathers as they search for meaning and occupation in an age of economic disruption.

A new wave of citizens are questioning whether, after the global financial crisis of 10 2008, the Eurozone bond crisis of 2012 and the migration crisis of 2015, the EU can deliver on its core promise to 'enhance economic, social and territorial cohesion' between its 28 members.

This should not come as a surprise. It is now six years since the former Greek finance minister Yanis Varoufakis warned that the Brussels and Berlin-backed auster- 15 ity imposed on Greece would turn the EU's economic periphery into 'Bailoutistan'.

Mr Varoufakis warned that the handouts ensured that an economic gulf would emerge between Germany and France, and everyone else within the euro and the wider union. Young workers, he said, were inevitably going to pay the greatest price for the bailout. 20

'A generation was sacrificed in the crisis,' he tells The Telegraph. 'They either went abroad to find work, or those left behind were condemned to live with low expectations.'

In economics, there is a phenomenon known as hysteresis, in which long-term unemployment acts as a brake on growth, leaving part of the labour market perma- 25 nently ossified. [...]

This is the crisis now facing parts of Europe. Aside from the individual human costs, this hysteresis has major implications for the long-term economic health of the bloc's southern Mediterranean countries, making it one of the EU's greatest economic challenges as the gap between Europe's richest and poorest grows. 30

But it is one that the power centres of the European Union, whose attentions have been focused on keeping its strongest economies afloat and growing emerging markets in the east, may have left too late to tackle.

Outside McDonald's in Latina, 16-year-old Marco tells the story of his 26-year-old brother, who has struggled to find permanent work for nearly five years. He had hoped 35 a relative could swing him a job in a small packaging company in Atessa on the eastern side of the country, only to be disappointed when the factory was relocated to Slovakia to access cheaper labour.

It is far from an isolated case. Whirlpool, the white-goods maker, also announced earlier this year it would move production from Turin to Slovakia as it chased greater 40 efficiencies, leaving 500 out of work.

Italy's productivity growth in recent years has been outpaced by Germany by 20 per cent, while its economic output is still smaller than before the 2009 downturn.

---

1 **clutch sth.** hold sth. tightly
2 **be engrossed in sth.** [ɪnˈɡrəʊst] *in etwas versunken sein*
5 **Mussolini** Benito Mussolini (1883–1945), Fascist prime minister of Italy (1922–43)
6 **endemic** [enˈdemɪk] widespread
7 **austerity** [ɒˈsterəti] economic policy aimed at reducing spending
9 **disruption** continual disturbance
11 **bond crisis** *Anleihenkrise, die zu Rettungsmaßnahmen der EZB für hochverschuldete EU-Staaten führte*
12 **enhance sth.** make sth. stronger
   cohesion [kəʊˈhiːʒn] *Zusammenhalt*
16 **Bailoutistan** play on words from 'bailout' (= a situation in which sb. is saved from bankruptcy)
17 **gulf** gap
19 **inevitable** [ɪnˈevɪtəbl] unavoidable
26 **ossified** *(fml)* no longer functioning
32 **afloat** functioning
33 **tackle sth.** deal with sth.
36 **swing sb. a job** *(infml)* use one's influence to get sb. a job
38 **access sth.** [ˈækses] *(v)* have access to sth.
39 **white goods** *weiße Ware (Küchengroßgeräte)*
42 **outpace sth.** *etwas übertreffen*

At the same time, all the Eastern European states boast higher GDP growth than
45 their southern Mediterranean counterparts, confirming Marco's place at the bottom
of the EU's economic heap.

After a decade of relative decline, Europe's youth are ripe for exploitation by populist and anti-democratic forces that are now shaking the Continent's foundations. [...]

The fact that the economic prospects of member states are diverging, not converg-
50 ing, presents a serious long-term risk to the cohesion of the European project.

It has always been one of the core promises of the European Union that membership would bring states together – with the richer countries investing in the poorer
states in order to even things out, for the common benefit of all.

Earlier this year, the former European commissioner and current head of the World
55 Bank, Kristalina Georgieva, admitted that that process, fuelled by the transfer of
so-called 'structural funds' from richer to poorer states via the EU's budget, was starting to stall. 'The convergence machine still works,' she said. 'But it is not working for
everyone.'

That shift, which is leaving young men like Marco behind, is the underlying force
60 that is firing up the neo-fascist and populist forces that are now causing deep political and economic stresses in the Union.

From: 'Future of Europe: Can the EU save a lost generation left fighting for its life in an
economic maelstrom?', *The Telegraph*, 13 September 2018

COMPREHENSION ◄

1 The lost generation
  a Explain why Isaac speaks of a 'lost generation' in Europe.
  b Outline the causes of the 'lost generation' according to the author.

ANALYSIS ◄

2 The text type
  a Examine how the writer begins her text and the effect this creates.
  b Consult the Glossary (Non-fictional texts, pp. 368–370) and determine the
    text type of this text.
  c Examine the text again and point out further evidence to support your
    choice.

3 Figurative language
Isaac often uses figurative language (metaphors and similes) to make her
style more vivid (e.g., l.6, 'weighed down by endemic youth unemployment'). Find more examples and analyse their effect. **SUPPORT** p.236

4 Economic jargon ['dʒɑːgən]
Because her text deals with the economy, Isaac uses many words that are
found mostly in economics texts. This kind of language is called **jargon**. Find
the English expression for each of the following:
a) *konvergieren* b) *Jugendarbeitslosigkeit* c) *Finanzkrise*
d) *Produktivitätszuwachs* e) *Wirtschaftsleistung* f) *langfristiges Risiko*

BEYOND THE TEXT ◄

5 The writer's message
Isaac suggests that there is a connection between the high unemployment
among young people in some EU countries, globalization, the fundamental
goals of the EU, and the rise of populistic and anti-democratic movements in
Europe. In a small group, create a poster showing the connections between
these factors. Explain your poster to your class.

---

44 GDP = Gross [grəʊs] **Domestic Product** (*Bruttosozialprodukt*)
47 exploitation [ˌeksplɔɪˈteɪʃn] *Ausbeutung*
53 even sth. out (v) bring sth. to the same level
common benefit [ˈbenɪfɪt] *gemeinsamer Nutzen*
55 fuel sth. (v) *etwas antreiben*
57 stall (v) stop functioning

■ **TROUBLE SPOT**
that [ðət] (ll. 48, 60) = relative pronoun ('der/die/das')
that [ðət] (ll. 49, 51, 55) = conjunction ('dass')
that [ðæt] (ll. 55, 59) = determiner ('diese/r/s')

■ **FACT FILE**
The term **lost generation** was originally applied to the young men who were killed in World War I. So many young men lost their lives that almost a full generation was lost. More widely the term is applied to the generation of men and women who grew up during or after the war and who suffered emotional damage and social disadvantages as a result.

▶ SF 16: Identifying text types (non-fiction)

▶ SF 17: Analysing stylistic devices

▶ SF 1: Dealing with unknown or new words

▶ SF 5: Structuring information and ideas: visual aids and outlines

A3 Hunting for personnel   *Sascha Schmierer*

In some European countries many young people face the problem of unemployment. In others, employers in some areas have great difficulty filling their job vacancies. Read this text from a German newspaper about a way to solve both problems.

Es steht nicht zu befürchten, dass die Krankenschwestern im Ludwigsburger Klinikum ihre Patienten beim Weckruf am Morgen künftig mit einem fröhlichen „Buenos Días" begrüßen. Und das Küchenteam wird statt leckerer Tapas wohl auch weiterhin salzarm zubereitete Krankenhauskost servieren. Dennoch bricht für den Klinikenverbund Ludwigsburg-Bietigheim nächsten Mittwoch eine „spanische Ära" an.   5

Pünktlich um 9.30 Uhr wird die Medizindirektorin Andrea Grebe im Konferenzraum an der Erlachhofstraße mehr als 30 neue Pflegekräfte von der Iberischen Halbinsel begrüßen. Nach einem ambitionierten Sprachkurs sollen die hoch qualifizierten neuen Mitarbeiter den eklatanten Personalmangel in der Intensivmedizin in den   10 drei Häusern in Ludwigsburg, Bietigheim und Neuenbürg beheben – olé im OP sozusagen.

„Fachkräfte für Intensivstationen und den OP-Bereich sind in Deutschland fast nicht zu finden, der Markt ist leergefegt", erklärt der Kliniken-Sprecher Alexander   15 Tsongas den für ein schwäbisches Spital bisher noch eher ungewöhnlichen Schritt. Weil bei der Suche nach qualifiziertem Personal allerdings weder regionale Berufsmessen noch die Werbeaktionen in angrenzenden Bundesländern erfolgreich waren, wichen die Stellenbesetzer des   20 Kliniken-Verbunds nach Südeuropa aus.

Auf die in Spanien geschalteten Anzeigen für OP-Pflegekräfte meldeten sich binnen weniger Tage zahlreiche Bewerber, mit 60 Kandidaten führten die Personalchefs ein Vorstellungsgespräch.   25

Ergebnis ist, dass bereits nächste Woche mehr als 30 spanische Pflegekräfte ihren Dienst in Ludwigsburg antreten. Bevor die neuen Mitarbeiter – bis auf wenige Ausnahmen handelt es sich um junge Frauen – auf die Tochterkliniken verteilt werden, steht ein je nach Vorkenntnissen zwischen vier und sechs Monaten   30 dauernder Intensivsprachkurs auf dem Lehrplan. Parallel zum Deutschlernen sind Arbeitspraktika in den Krankenhäusern vorgesehen. Für das erste halbe Jahr sind die neuen Pflegekräfte mit einem Praktikantenvertrag ausgestattet. Nach der Probezeit winkt ein unbefristeter Arbeitsvertrag – schließlich hofft die Chefetage des Kliniken-Verbunds, dass die neuen Mitarbeiter aus dem Süden im kalten Deutschland nicht   35 gleich das Weite suchen.

From: 'Olé im OP: Kliniken suchen in Spanien fehlendes Personal', *Stuttgarter Nachrichten*, 12 October 2012

▶ LP 6: Infinitive or gerund after certain nouns

■ TROUBLE SPOT

jdn. / etwas pflegen
= (a sick person) *nurse sb. / care for sb.*
= (an animal) *look after sth.*
= (a garden, a plant) *tend sth.*

MEDIATION **FOCUS ON SKILLS**

Mediating texts in oral communication

Imagine the following situation: While on holiday in Italy, you have a talk (in English) with a young Italian named Ornella Conti, who helps out as a waitress at the hotel where you are staying. She tells you that she has trained as a nurse, but cannot find work in her profession in Italy. You remember the article about job vacancies in Germany (cf. A3, p. 126) and decide to tell her about it.

▶ SF 41: Mediation of written and oral texts

1 Choosing the relevant information

a Look at the following keywords from text **A3**. Which of them do you think would be relevant to Ornella Conti?

■ TROUBLE SPOT
information (sing)
Not: ~~informations~~

1 Um 9.30 werden die neuen Pflegekräfte in Ludwigsburg begrüßt.	4 In Deutschland gibt es nicht genügend Pflegekräfte für Intensivstationen.
2 Auf Messen und durch Werbeaktionen konnte kein zusätzliches Pflegepersonal gewonnen werden.	5 Die neuen spanischen Pflegekräfte sind vor allem Frauen.
3 Pflegekräfte müssen einen Sprachkurs absolvieren.	6 Sie sind zunächst als Praktikant/innen angestellt.

b Note down any other information you consider useful to Ornella.

2 Explaining specific terms

When mediating information from German into English, you will have to paraphrase or explain words, either because you (or the person you are talking to) don't know their English equivalents or because your partner has a different cultural background.

a Which of the words below would you explain to Ornella Conti? Say why.

■ LANGUAGE AWARENESS

Explaining or paraphrasing
When mediating or explaining culture-specific concepts to someone from a different cultural background, you can either give a definition ('A … is sth. that …') or use a paraphrase (A … is something like a …. It also has …). This can also help to clear up misunderstandings or misinterpretations in conversations.

1 *Intensivstation*	4 *Praktikantenvertrag*
2 *Arbeitspraktikum*	5 *unbefristeter Arbeitsvertrag*
3 *Sprachkurs*	6 *Probezeit*

b Paraphrase or explain the words from **a**.

▶ LA 2: Communication problems and compensation strategies

▶ SF 6: Paraphrasing

▶ LP 11: Using the right register

3 Choosing the correct register

The place where a conversation takes place and your relationship to the addressee influence the way you speak to them. Read the two beginnings of the conversation with Ornella Conti and decide which of them would be more appropriate in the given situation. Say why.

'Well, actually, I read an article just a few days ago and I think it might interest you. Basically it was all about how Germany really needs nurses and …'

'Bearing in mind the situation you have been telling me about I would like to inform you about the opportunities that have opened in Germany for qualified nurses.'

4 Speaking to the addressee

a Structure your ideas and prepare your side of the conversation, bearing in mind your results from tasks **1–3**.

b Work with a partner to role-play the conversation. Answer their questions and pay attention to their facial expression or gestures to find out whether they have understood you. Rephrase your statements if necessary. Then swap roles.

▶ CC 4: Meeting and greeting

▶ LP 12: Avoiding German-sounding sentence patterns

▶ LP 16: Avoiding Germanisms

Chances and risks of globalization

B1 How big is the impact?

Globalization is a complex process that affects various aspects of life. The video you are going to watch explains how it works.

1 Identifying the players in globalization
Describe the aspects of globalization that are presented in the picture below. Based on what you already know about globalization try to say how they are connected.

► LP 7: The passive

COMPREHENSION ◄

2 Defining globalization
a Watch the video and note down the main topics mentioned in it. Compare notes with a partner.
b Watch the video for a second time and add information on the topics from **a**.
c Compare your notes in a group and add to them if necessary.
d As a group give a short presentation on globalization with each group member contributing 1–2 sentences on each topic.

ANALYSIS ◄

3 Examining the video
Describe the devices that are employed in the video and explain their function. ► LANGUAGE HELP

BEYOND THE TEXT ◄

4 YOU CHOOSE Illustrating globalization

a Comment on the quotation below and find examples that illustrate it further.

OR

b Find a picture that illustrates your personal view on the impact that globalization has on people. If necessary, collect background information about it. Present your findings in class.

> 'Globalization isn't something that just happens to economies. It happens to people.'
> *Kelsey Timmerman*

DVD

► SF 15: Marking up a text / Making and taking notes

► SF 24: Giving a presentation

► SF 23: Analysing a film

LANGUAGE HELP
- explainer video / instructional video
- hand-crafted drawings showing … / scraps of paper
- put sth. on screen / remove sth.
- use audio effects to …

B2 The need for a new label   *Lucy Siegle*

- What information might be missing on the labels on the right?

Imagine a label, one that reads: 'An actual, living, breathing human used their own hands to help make this product.' This is just what the (western) world needs, a label affixed to consumer goods. We need this urgent reminder because in those seconds when we decide to purchase another piece of life's apparatus we are strikingly effect-
5 ive at suppressing any ethical doubt over its provenance.
   The first thing we do (with varying levels of awareness) is convince ourselves that – from the hottest bits of sleek hi-tech gadgetry to highly embellished fashion garments – these were made by very clever robot arms that can apply toxic chemicals to a touch screen or expertly sew a sequin or bead. But as today's Observer report on
10 Apple products lays bare, our consumer goods still arrive courtesy of the blood, sweat and tears of many human beings. [...] The habitual use of unpaid, enforced overtime is common across many sectors. In the fashion industry, garment workers are effect-ively set up to fail. When a multinational places an order at the behest of a buyer the workers are set quotas to meet the order. Professor Doug Miller, an expert on the
15 garment supply chain and workers' rights, has identified a discrepancy between the estimated and real time taken for a garment worker to complete an order. So the multinational buyer's calculations are based on standard minute values (SMVs) – virtual minutes based on a factory that operates at near 100% efficiency. However, in countries such as Cambodia (the British high street is heavily reliant on Cambodian
20 production), the efficiency of factories rarely rises above 30%. Garment workers can therefore work flat out without any hope of meeting their targets within their paid working hours. At this point, they are forced to work overtime and sometimes gates may be shut or locked (including the fire escapes). [...] As consumers, we still tend to be most receptive to the voices of brand spokespeople. Time after time, we trust their
25 soothing words: 'We're working on these challenges', 'We've been let down badly by a supplier', 'These are not our values' etc. and placated by their corporate social responsibility reports. Robert Reich warns in his recent book, *Supercapitalism*, corporate social responsibility is 'as meaningful as cotton candy'. But Reich's ultimate position is that we should stop expecting corporations to do the right thing. And I can't
30 see any way of absolving the consumer of responsibility. I used to advocate going through a sort of consumerist catechism before making any consumer purchasing decision. Who made this product? Why did they make it? Why do I need it? I feel as if I urgently need to return to this way of buying. An understanding of the provenance of the product is key.

From: 'Were humans harmed in the making of your shiny gadget?', *The Guardian*, 1 May 2011

COMPREHENSION ◀

1 Collecting information
Collect information from the article about the situation in the garment industry, how we consumers deal with it and what we *should* do. Write down 5–9 keywords for each of these topics, then present your results.

ANALYSIS ◀

2 Examining the text
Analyse the tone of the text.

BEYOND THE TEXT ◀

3 Promoting transparent labelling   SUPPORT   ▶ p. 236
   a Design a clothing label that helps buyers make responsible choices.
   b Write an article for a magazine in which you promote this new label.

---

5 **provenance** ['prɒvənəns] place that sth. has come from
7 **sleek** elegant, shiny
   gadgetry collection of modern devices/tools
9 **sequin** ['siːkwɪn] small shiny disc sewn onto clothes as deco-ration
   bead small piece of wood or glass that can be put on a string and worn as jewellery
10 **lay sth. bare** *(fml)* make sth. known that was a secret
   courtesy of sb./sth. ['kɜːtəsi] as the result of sb./sth.
11 **overtime** time that you spend at your job after the normal work hours
13 **at the behest of sb.** because sb. has ordered it
14 **quota** amount of sth. that sb. needs to achieve
21 **flat out** *(adv)* completely
26 **supplier** Lieferant/in
   placate sb. [plə'keɪt] make sb. worry less about something
28 **cotton candy** Zuckerwatte
30 **absolve sb.** [æb'sɒlv] state formally that sb. is not respon-sible for sth.
   advocate sth. ['ædvəkeɪt] advise/recommend sth.
31 **catechism** ['kætəkɪzəm] set of questions and answers used to instruct people about Christian beliefs

▶ SF 18: Analysing non-fiction

▶ SF 37: Doing a creative writing task

₂ **schlep** (v, infml) travel
₃ **host sth.** (Veranstaltung) ausrichten
₄ **besiege sth.** [bɪ'siːdʒ] etwas belagern
₅ **away fixture** (n) meeting held abroad
₆ **take a dim view of sth.** not tolerate sth.
₉ **disrupt sth.** disturb sth.
₁₀ **balaclava** [ˌbælə'klɑːvə] Sturm-haube, Mütze mit Öffnungen für Augen und Mund
₁₇ **embrace sth.** etwas bejahen, etwas akzeptieren
₂₄ **constrain sth.** limit sth.

B3 The return of the nation state *Larry Elliott*

- Skim the text in 1–2 minutes to find out the gist. Compare first impressions with a partner.

The election of Donald Trump in 2016 marked a turning point in global trade. Proclaiming 'America First', Trump imposed tariffs on imported goods to protect American workers. Larry Elliot, economics editor of the Guardian, *suggests that there are good reasons for taking Trump's position seriously.*

Once every three years the International Monetary Fund and the World Bank hold their annual meetings out of town. Instead of schlepping over to Washington, the gathering of finance ministers and central bank governors is hosted by a member state. Ever since the 2000 meeting in Prague was besieged by anti-globalisation rioters, the away fixtures have tended to be held in places that are hard to get to or where the regime tends to take a dim view of protest: Singapore, Turkey, Peru. 5

This year's meeting will take place in a couple of weeks on the Indonesian island of Bali, where the IMF and the World Bank can be reasonably confident that the meetings will not be disrupted. At least not from the outside. The real threat no longer comes from balaclava-wearing anarchists throwing Molotov cocktails but from within. 10 Donald Trump is now the one throwing the petrol bombs and for multilateral organisations like the IMF and World Bank, that poses a much bigger threat.

The US president put it this way in his speech to the United Nations on Tuesday: 15 'We reject the ideology of globalism and we embrace the doctrine of patriotism.' For decades, the message from the IMF has been that 20 breaking down the barriers to trade, allowing capital to move unhindered across borders and constraining the ability of governments to 25 regulate multinational corporations was the way to prosperity. Now the most powerful man on the planet is saying something different: 30 that the only way to remedy the economic and social ills caused by globalisation is through the nation state. Trump's speech was mocked by fellow world leaders, but the truth is that he's not a lone voice.

₃₁ **remedy sth.** ['remədi] cure sth.
 ills (fml) problems
₃₂ **mock sth.** laugh at sth.
₃₅ **Xi Jinping** (born 1953) President of the People's Republic of China since 2013
₃₆ **stupendous** [stjuː'pendəs] enormous
 post sth. announce sth. publicly or officially
₃₈ **frown upon sth.** [fraʊn] regard sth. critically
₃₉ **subsidy** ['sʌbsədi] money given by the government to a private firm

The world's other big economic superpower – China – has never given up on the nation state. Xi Jinping likes to use the language of globalisation to make a contrast 35 with Trump's protectionism, but the stupendous growth posted by China over the past four decades has been the result of doing the opposite of what the globalisation textbooks recommend. The measures traditionally frowned upon by the IMF – state-run industries, subsidies, capital controls – have been central to Beijing's managed capitalism. China has certainly not closed itself off from the global economy but has 40

engaged on its own terms. When the communist regime wanted to move people out of the fields and into factories it did so through the mechanism of an undervalued currency, which made Chinese exports highly competitive. When the party decided that it wanted to move into more sophisticated, higher-tech manufacturing, it insisted
45 that foreign companies wishing to invest in China share their intellectual property.

This sort of approach isn't new. It was the way most western countries operated in the decades after the second world war, when capital controls, managed immigration and a cautious approach to removing trade barriers were seen as necessary if governments were to meet public demands for full employment and rising living standards. The
50 US and the EU now say that China is not playing fair because it has been prospering with an economic strategy that is supposed not to work. There is some irony in this.

The idea that the nation state would wither away was based on three separate arguments. The first was that the barriers to the global free movement of goods, services, people and money were economically inefficient and that removing them would lead
55 to higher levels of growth. This has not been the case. Growth has been weaker and less evenly shared.

The second was that governments couldn't resist globalisation even if they wanted to. This was broadly the view once adopted by Bill Clinton and Tony Blair, and now kept alive by Emmanuel Macron. The message to displaced workers was that the power of
60 the market was – rather like a hurricane or a blizzard – an irresistible force of nature. This has always been a dubious argument because there is no such thing as a pure free market. Globalisation has been shaped by political decisions, which for the past four decades have favoured the interests of capital over labour.

Finally, it was argued that the trans-national nature of modern capitalism made the
65 nation state obsolete. Put simply, if economics was increasingly global then politics had to go global, too. There is clearly something in this because financial markets impose constraints on individual governments and it would be preferable for there to be a form of global governance pushing for stability and prosperity for all. The problem is that to the extent such an institutional mechanism exists, it has been
70 captured by the globalists. That is as true of the EU as it is of the IMF.

So while the nation state is far from perfect, it is where an alternative to the current failed model will inevitably begin. Increasingly, voters are looking to the one form of government where they do have a say to provide economic security. And if the mainstream parties are not prepared to offer what these voters want – a decently paid job,
75 properly funded public services and controls on immigration – then they will look elsewhere for parties or movements that will. This has proved to be a particular problem for the parties of the centre left – the Democrats in the US, New Labour in Britain, the SPD in Germany – that signed up to the idea that globalisation was an unstoppable force.

80 Jeremy Corbyn certainly does not accept the idea that the state is obsolete as an economic actor. The plan is to build a different sort of economy from the bottom up – locally and nationally. That's not going to be easy but beats the current, failed, top-down approach.

From: 'The truth is that Trump has a point about globalisation',
The Guardian, 26 September 2018

---

42 **undervalued** *unterbewertet*
43 **currency** *Währung*
44 **sophisticated** [səˈfɪstɪkeɪtɪd] complex
   insist *darauf beharren, darauf bestehen*
46 **approach** strategy
52 **wither (away)** [ˈwɪðə] gradually disappear, become weaker
58 **broadly** generally speaking
   Clinton, Bill (born 1946) US President (Democratic Party), 1993–2001
   Blair, Tony (born 1953) UK Prime Minister (Labour Party), 1997–2007
59 **Macron, Emmanuel** (born 1977) French President since 2017
   displaced unemployed
65 **obsolete** [ˈɒbsəliːt] outdated
67 **impose constraints on sb.** *jdm. Beschränkungen aufzwingen*
68 **governance** [ˈɡʌvənəns] government
69 **to the extent** *in dem Maße, soweit*
72 **inevitable** [ɪnˈevɪtəbl] unavoidable
   look to sb. to do sth. *(fml)* rely on sb. or expect sb. to do sth.
73 **have a say** *ein Mitspracherecht haben*
77 **New Labour** the Labour Party since Tony Blair
80 **Corbyn, Jeremy** (born 1949) British politician, Leader of the Labour Party and Leader of the Opposition since 2015

■ TROUBLE SPOT

Stress on first syllable:

argument	**de**mocrat
barrier	**me**chanism
capital	**in**terest
communist	**pla**net
contrast *(n)*	**pro**test *(n)*

▶ LP 5: Infinitive or gerund after certain verbs

▶ SF 14: Reading strategies

READING FOCUS ON SKILLS

Using reading strategies (non-fictional texts)

Reading strategies help you to read more effectively. They can help you to find information quickly, to see if a text is relevant for you or to come to an in-depth understanding of the content.

*Before actually reading the text **B3**, you were asked to skim it to find out what it's about. Now practise your scanning and close-reading techniques.*

1 Scanning

a Scan the text on pp. 130–131 to find the answers to the following questions. For each question, decide in advance what keyword, name or number you are going to look out for in the text.
1 What is China's relationship to the idea of the nation state?
2 What happened in Prague in 2000?
3 What is Trump's position on globalization?

b Locate the following ideas in the text and say in which order they appear. What keyword, name or number are you going to look for?
1 Bill Clinton and Tony Blair shared a fatalistic view of globalization.
2 China doesn't play by the rules of globalization.
3 Globalization has not led to economic growth.
4 The EU and the IMF are dominated by globalists.
5 In the postwar era, most western countries did what China is doing now.

2 Close reading I: content and structure

a Read the text carefully and make notes on the content of each paragraph.
b Write a summary of the text.
c Read the text again and examine its structure. Add the words below to your notes from **a** where they fit. You can also add your own categories.

background information • cause • conclusion • detail • example • opposite viewpoint • outlook • result quotation • thesis • …

3 Close reading II: identifying the text type
Explain what type of text this is and analyse its *tone.

▶ SF 31: Writing a summary

▶ SF 16: Identifying text types (non-fiction)

English as a global language

C1 Keeping the accent   *Aoife Mannix*

- What do you expect after reading the title of the poem?

> The barman makes me repeat my order
> three times before he finally understands me.
> Heads turn and stare, I can feel my hands sweat
> and my throat close over the way it did years ago.
> Then he tells me my accent is so cute,   5
> he's going to give me one of the drinks for free.
> And all the people at the bar smile at me.
> And it doesn't make up for the way
> they laughed at me at school,
> repeating how I said the word potato   10
> over and over like a needle in my ear,
> or Alexis Fortgang dropping a worm in my hair
> and telling me to fuck off back to the little hole
> in the ground I crawled out of.
> But still, now that the way I speak is sweet,   15
> I swallow my bitterness
> and try not to think about how opening my mouth
> used to feel like a betrayal.
> The words sounding out of tune,
> a fork dropped on a china plate.   20
> Suddenly it's interesting and cool
> and everyone wants to go there.
> But I still hide behind my pride,
> the way I used to long to talk
> like everybody else.   25

From: *The Elephant in the Corner: New & Selected Poems*, 2005, p. 54

COMPREHENSION ◀

1 Understanding the situation
Describe the speaker's experience in the bar and the memories it provokes.

LANGUAGE AWARENESS ◀

2 Examining the present participle
  a Identify the present participles in ll. 8–14, then reformulate these lines without using participles.
  b Compare with the original and explain why the participle constructions are especially helpful in the poem.

ANALYSIS ◀

3 Examining the poem
  a Subdivide the poem by introducing *stanzas, which may vary in length. Explain the structure you have chosen. Compare it to the original version.
  b Examine the *stylistic devices used in this poem to highlight the speaker's attitude towards her accent. Focus on the choice of words and the *imagery used.

■ FACT FILE

The term ***third culture kid*** (TCK) is applied to children who spend a considerable time of their childhood or adolescence outside their parents' home country, usually because their parents work abroad. Third culture kids experience the culture they are living in plus the culture from which their parents originated – without really belonging to either of them: they belong to a third culture, which is a mix of the other two cultures. In the era of modern globalization, the number of third culture kids has increased: global job mobility, proximity to neighbouring countries, international school attendance, multi-ethnic homes and worldwide adoption are on the increase and bring with them not only cultural, but also linguistic opportunities and challenges.

Compile possible advantages and challenges of early cross-cultural education.

Aoife ['ifə]
1 **order** *(n)* request for food or drinks in a pub or restaurant
4 **throat** *Kehle*
  close over become very narrow
5 **cute** sweet, nice
8 **make up for sth.** do sth. that corrects a bad situation
19 **out of tune** containing wrong notes and therefore sounding unpleasant
20 **fork** *Gabel*
  china ['tʃaɪnə] *Porzellan*

▶ LP 18: Writing about texts
▶ LP 15: Connecting your thoughts (sentence structure)

■ LANGUAGE AWARENESS
Accents
An accent may be regional or it may indicate somebody's socio-economic status. Speakers may be proud of their accent because it shows where they are from and where they belong, or they may choose to suppress it and opt for a neutral way of speaking.

▶ LA 1: Varieties of English
▶ SF 21: Analysing poetry
▶ SF 17: Analysing stylistic devices

▶ SF 37: Doing a creative writing task

— BEYOND THE TEXT ◀

4 YOU CHOOSE ▶ **Creative writing** SUPPORT ▶ p. 236

a Write a *short story based on the poem.

 OR

b Write a dramatic *scene based on the poem.

C2 English as a global language   *David Crystal*

- Try to define the term *global language* and collect reasons why a language might become a global language.

— COMPREHENSION ◀

1 Understanding the main idea

Listen to David Crystal and decide which statement fits the text best:

1 English-speaking nations are powerful because they speak the global language English best.
2 Throughout the centuries people have had the power to decide which language is the global language.
3 The global language is the language of the people who have the most power globally.

2 Connecting language and power

Listen again and describe the connection between power and language as seen by Crystal.

— BEYOND THE TEXT ◀

3 Thinking about global languages of the future

Discuss when and how the four types of power mentioned by David Crystal might one day be dominated by other languages. Which languages might they be? Justify your answer by giving examples.

C3 Linguistic diplomacy:
the Eurovision Song Contest   *R. L. G.*

- Do you prefer listening to songs in English or in your mother tongue? Explain what difference it makes to you.

Last Saturday saw Denmark win the Eurovision Song Contest, the country's third win in the contest's history. A prototypically apple-cheeked blonde took the trophy for her country, but she did so with the rather un-Danish name of Emmelie de Forest and the equally un-Danish title, 'Only Teardrops'.

The contest has always been about more than music. Every year comes a slew   5
of articles about the political nature of the voting. Countries that share ethnic or political friendships routinely give each other high marks: Greece and Cyprus typically give each other the maximum of 12 points while stiffing Turkey with nul points, for example. Estonia and Latvia this year gave Russia 12 points, no doubt because those countries' large Russian populations voted for their neighbour.   10

Language, of course, plays a role in this as well. 'Ethnicity' in Europe is often linguistic: an ethnic Russian is not apparent on the streets of Riga until he opens his mouth. Linguistic neighbours will tend to be generous to one another. Finland and Estonia are friendly not only because they are nearby but because their Finno-Ugric languages resemble each other, while being utterly unrelated to their neigbours'.   15
(Hungarian is also Finno-Ugric.) Each country can give 12 points to only one other

---

DVD

▶ SF 22: Listening
▶ SF 7: Working with closed test formats

■ **LANGUAGE AWARENESS**

Language and power

By the 15th century, the influence of French on the English language had more or less ceased and English had effectively become the national language. As England's power and influence grew and spread throughout the world, so did that of the English language, which became a world language – a status it has retained to this day, long after the end of the British Empire.

▶ LA 1: Varieties of English
▶ LA 4: Influencing through language

---

2 **apple-cheeked** having cheeks (= *Wangen*) the colour of apples
5 **slew** (infml) large number
8 **stiff sb. with sth.** (here) reject / mildly insult sb.
  nul points [nyl pwɛ̃] (*French*) nil (= *no*) points
11 **ethnicity** [eθ'nɪsəti] fact of belonging to a particular race
12 **Riga** capital of Latvia

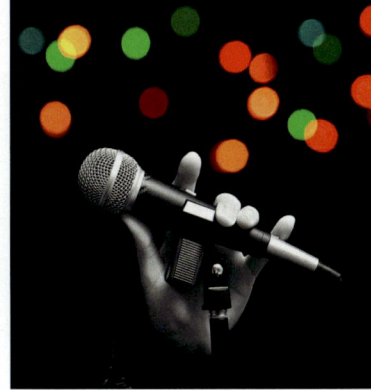

country, and this year Denmark and Sweden gave their 12's to Norway, Norway its 12 to Sweden, as befits the Scandinavian language continuum.

20 But the Scandinavians share something else besides apple-cheeked blondes and North Germanic languages: their tendency to sing in English. In that, they are like most countries nowadays. But some interesting variation clouds the picture.

The French, of course, overwhelmingly prefer French. (France has, however, sent two entries in Corsican and one, in 2008, mostly in English.) Spain nearly always opts for Spanish, and Italy for Italian. But it isn't true that big countries sing in their

25 own languages while small ones opt for English. Germany has sung just one German title ('Frauen regieren die Welt', or 'Women Run the World') in the past ten years. And a few small countries opted for linguistic pride over Anglophone Euro-cheer this year. Iceland's EyþórIngi offered up a dreary ballad in Icelandic, the perfect accompaniment to an official video in which he glumly fillets a fish in the rain. The highest-rank-

30 ing song not sung in English this year was technically Greece's 'Alcohol is Free', an upbeat ska tune in which the verses were in Greek and only the three-word chorus in English. It came in 6th place. The highest-ranking song entirely devoid of English was Italy's 'L'Essenziale' (7th).

Songs mostly in English have won 24 times, while songs in French have won 14.

35 That leaves just about a third of the contests won in any other language. This is despite two periods (1956–1965 and 1977–1999) in which contest rules required countries to sing in their own languages. [...]

It is clear that pop is just another area in which English is taking over Europe, alongside business and the politics of the European Union. French is holding a solid second

40 place, as it does elsewhere. The rest of Europe's many language communities divide up what remains. Whether you find this linguistic convergence cheerful as an Abba foot-stomper or depressing as an Icelandic fishing trip will say as much about your politics as it will about your views on language.

From: 'English atop the Eurovision pile, yet again', *The Economist*, 20 May 2013

COMPREHENSION ◀

1 Understanding the content
Structure the text (introduction, main body, conclusion), then make notes on the content of each part.

2 Mediation (English ➜ German)
You are watching the song contest together with a friend who claims that language does not play any role in the ESC today since almost all songs are sung in English. In German, tell him why he is not quite right using information from the text.

ANALYSIS ◀

3 Examining the tone
a Analyse which elements contribute to the neutral *tone of the text.
b Identify the text type.

BEYOND THE TEXT ◀

4 Reacting to a statement
Explain the last sentence and comment on it.

5 Discussion **SUPPORT** ▶ p. 237
In groups of five prepare and hold a panel discussion in which you discuss the question of whether each country should be obliged to enter songs in their national language only. One student is the moderator, the others argue either for or against the topic.

---

18 **befit sb.** (*fml*) be suitable for sb.
21 **cloud sth.** make sth. unclear
23 **entry** (here) song that takes part in a competition
24 **opt for sth.** choose sth.
28 **dreary** sad and boring
accompaniment music that is played to support singing
29 **glum** quiet, sad, unhappy
31 **upbeat** (*infml*) cheerful/enthusiastic
ska fast and rhythmic music, related to Reggae
chorus part of a song that is sung after each verse
32 **devoid of sth.** without sth.
41 **convergence** [kən'vɜ:dʒəns] process of moving towards each other and meeting at a point
ABBA Swedish pop band that won the ESC in 1973
42 **foot-stomper** lively music that makes you move your feet

---

▶ SF 15: Marking up a text / Making and taking notes

▶ SF 41: Mediation of written and oral texts

▶ SF 18: Analysing non-fiction
▶ SF 16: Identifying text types

▶ SF 27: Having a discussion

⚲ CULTURE SPOT

Keeping our language clean?

🎧 CD2 14

1 You're Skyping with an Irish friend of yours and talking about music. She has just come across a song by the a cappella group Wise Guys that she doesn't understand. Listen to the song, then tell her what it's about and what message you think it conveys.

2 Collect other examples of English (or pseudo-English) words often used in German. State for each example whether you accept it and use it or whether you avoid using it.

3 What does this use of English tell you about the role of English in German culture?

4 Radio stations, e.g. in France and Italy, are obliged to play a considerable number of songs in French or Italian, respectively. What do you think of this attempt to promote the native language?

'Slavery? Not today, not in Germany!' Preparing an exhibition

For the project week at your school, you are preparing an exhibition on the topic 'Slavery? Not today, not in Germany!' As a lot of visitors from your foreign partner schools will be attending, posters and presentations will be in English.

Work in groups of five.

1 Planning your work
   a Do some research to get a general idea of the topic and to identify suitable subtopics. `SUPPORT` ▶ p. 237
   b Divide the work up among yourselves.

▶ SF 4: Doing project work

2 Preparing your poster
   a Research your part. Make sure to use German publications too. Notes, articles, books or worksheets you read at school, including in other subjects like History or Latin, may also be helpful. Make notes.

▶ SF 3: Doing research

   b Organize your findings and prepare your poster. `SUPPORT` ▶ p. 237
   c In your group, swap posters and check each other's.

▶ SF 5: Structuring information and ideas: visual aids and outlines
▶ SF 40: Proofreading

3 Preparing and giving your presentation
   a In your group, organize and practise your presentation.
   b Give your presentation in class.

▶ SF 24: Giving a presentation

4 Assessing presentations
   Using the assessment sheet your teacher will give you, assess the other groups' posters and presentations. In class, discuss how they might be improved.

7 Science – Enhancing Life?

Biofuel

Transhumanism
human advancement
through technology

Gene therapy
modifying human DNA
to treat disease

Genetic engineering
manipulation or modifi-
cation of organisms using
biotechnology

Energy transition
the path to a sustainable
economy, e.g. by using
biofuels

Gene pharming
the use of genetically
modified organisms to
produce pharmaceutical
products

*Download a list of chapter vocab
here:* **Webcode** context-70

1 Identifying current trends in science

  a Study the pictures, then match them to one of the topics in the box.

  b THINK Pick the photo you find most interesting and speculate about which
development in modern science it depicts.

  c PAIR Find a partner who chose the same photo. Exchange your ideas, and
on the basis of your findings make a chart outlining chances and risks
these developments might have for the future.

  d SHARE With your chart, move around the classroom. Find a couple who
made a chart based on a different picture. Discuss your charts and decide
together whether the developments you have discussed will have a positive
or negative impact on the future.

E

F

G

H

2 A look into the future

Predicting the future is difficult, if not impossible. Use your imagination and look into the future.

YOU CHOOSE Examining new technology

a Choose a modern form of technology (such as Google Glass, 3D printers, driverless cars, etc.) and say why you think it has the capability to transform our society in the future. In small groups present and discuss your ideas.

OR

b Make a ranking of new technologies according to their importance to you. In small groups compare your lists and together choose the three technological inventions that have the biggest potential in the future.

▶ SF24: Giving a presentation

PREVIEW

In this chapter you will learn about attempts to improve human life through genetic engineering and technological advancements. You will also examine the challenges of acquiring energy.

Main topics

- Genetic engineering .... p. 142
- Mind- and body-enhancing drugs .... p. 150
- Gene therapy .... p. 151
- Future energy policy .... p. 155

Focus on Skills: READING and MEDIATION

- Using reading strategies (scientific text) .... p. 149
- Mediating written texts .... p. 157

Chapter Task: Doing a WebQuest on genetically modified food .... p. 159

CD1 04

Listen to an audio version of the text on the CD or download it here:

 Webcode context-04

Science – motor of progress?

Feeding the world, healing deadly diseases and finding renewable sources of energy are some of the challenges we have to meet in the 21st century if we want to continue to live well. It is probably in the fields of science and technology that we will find answers to these problems.

Genetic Engineering   5

Scientists are now able to map the DNA sequence of the genes of many plants, animals and humans. They hope to use this information to improve the robustness or yield of crops and livestock and to cure human diseases. Genetic engineering (GE) is the process by which the sequence of an organism's DNA is altered by technological means, e.g. by inserting   10
a foreign gene to produce a more desirable result.

In order to provide food for an increasingly faster growing world population the commercial use of GE in farming may help increase food production. The first genetically modified (GM) crop was introduced in 1995   15
– the slow-softening tomato. Others have been made more insect-resistant or disease-resistant. In 2013, GM crops, including maize, cotton and rice, were being grown on more than 175 million hectares in 29 countries. In medicine, genetic engineering may one day be used to   20
repair defective genes.

A new widely-debated approach is gene pharming. Pharma crops are genetically modified plants like maize that produce much-needed medicines. The genes for human proteins like insulin could be transferred to   25
animals, which then produce the protein in their milk. However, there are ethical concerns about genetic engineering:

'They used to be called sheep, and they produced wool. Now they're some sort of bioengineered creatures, and they produce antibiotics.'

- **Risk and safety:** Transgenic plants or animals (i.e. containing one or more foreign genes) may in the end prove to be unhealthy or even dangerous.   30
- **Meddling with reproduction:** In vitro fertilization (IVF) offers the opportunity to preselect an embryo that is free from genetic disorders. Many fear this will lead to custom-made designer babies – children designed to have a particular eye colour or IQ.

These are reasons why GE requires public approval and careful regulation.   35

Quenching the thirst for energy

With the rise of emerging countries like Brazil and India the global thirst for energy is growing rapidly. Since the Fukushima nuclear disaster of 2011 many nations have agreed on a nuclear power phase-out. Even though renewable sources of energy like solar, wind and hydropower do not seem to be cost-   40
efficient at the moment, experts are researching ways to switch from finite energy sources such as coal, gas and petroleum to sources that are sustainable and more environmentally friendly. This is seen as an important step to reduce humanity's carbon footprint and to stop global warming.

Using plants like rapeseed or palm oil to produce biofuels is another way to   45
avoid using fossil fuels. However, environmental and ethical concerns about such technologies are growing.

▶ SF 1: Dealing with unknown or new words

1 Information Stock Exchange
a Choose two of the issues in the text that you feel well-informed about. Write them on green cards.
b Write two terms on red cards that you would like to find out more about.
c Walk around the classroom and find two people with green cards that match your red cards. Ask them to give you the information you want.
d Explain the terms on your green cards to two students.
e On the blackboard arrange your cards in three columns:
- Still lost: red cards with terms that still need clarifying
- Lost and found: green and red matches
- Information pool: green cards that were not talked about

2 Formal vs. informal language
Scientific reports strive for accuracy and precision, which is why they rarely use phrasal verbs. Try to substitute the phrasal verbs or informal expressions below with a formal verb from the text.

1 put sth. into sth.
2 move sth. from one place to another
3 make sth. different
4 make sth. less or smaller

▶ LP 11: Using the right register

> ■ **LANGUAGE AWARENESS**
>
> **Formal language** may be used in order to be accurate and precise (as e.g. in scientific or legal texts), but also to impress others or convey an atmosphere of respect and politeness, e.g. in a letter of application or when addressing somebody of higher authority. Be aware of the context your text is situated in and adapt your style and register accordingly.

3 Compound adjectives
Compound adjectives make texts more formal by condensing information.
a Find examples of compound adjectives such as *custom-made* (l. 33) in the text and categorize them according to their structure:
noun + adjective • noun + participle • adjective + adjective • adjective/adverb + participle
b Make these sentences shorter by forming compound adjectives.
1 Genetic engineering is a business that is growing fast.
2 GE companies hope to make progress at a speed that will break all records.
3 They hope to help farmers keep their fields free from pollution.
4 The development took ten years before GE crops could hit the market.

▶ LA 4: Influencing through language

▶ LP 10: Using adjectives and adverbs

> ■ **TROUBLE SPOT**
>
> Hyphenated compound adjectives are only used **before** nouns:
> *It was a well-written report.*
> ⟷ *The report was well written.*

4 Writing
Describe the picture and discuss it with reference to genetic engineering.

The genetic engineering debate

A1   A saviour sibling   *Laura Roberts*

Genetic screening is a new technology that has been helping families with genetically transmitted diseases.

sibling brother or sister
1 **tissue** ['tɪʃuː] *Gewebe*
2 **specifically** intended for a particular purpose
3 **disorder** *Störung*
4 **bone marrow** *Knochenmark*
donor *Spender/in*
7 **conception** *Empfängnis*
15 **suitability** [ˌsuːtəˈbɪləti] *Eignung*
16 **umbilical** [ʌmˈbɪlɪkl] **cord** *Nabelschnur*
32 **burden** sth. that gives a person a heavy responsibility
35 **bubbly** full of life and energy

Megan Matthews, nine, received tissue donated by her 18-month old brother Max who was created specifically so that he could aid her medical treatment. [...]

Megan, from King's Lynn, Norfolk, was born with a rare blood disorder which can cause bone marrow failure and a worldwide search for a suitable bone marrow donor failed. The condition, Fanconi Anaemia, meant she needed transfusions every few weeks and was unable to fight infections.   5

Her parents Katie and Andy Matthews wanted another child but natural conception would have provided only a one in four chance that the sibling would be a perfect tissue match. The new child could also have been born with the same life-threatening genetic disorder. To avoid this, Cambridge, Bristol and Nottingham medical teams   10 were involved in a treatment which used donated cells from the specifically created baby and taken to treat Megan's disorder.

Two embryos were implanted into Mrs Matthews by CARE Fertility in Nottingham after they were checked for transplant suita-   15 bility. Initially umbilical cord blood was saved and after Max was born an operation was carried out to take bone marrow. The tissue transplant took place in July this year at Bristol Royal Hospital for Sick Children.   20 Compared to her frequent and invasive hospital visits, Megan now only requires a weekly check-up at Addenbrookes hospital in Cambridge.

Simon Fishel, managing director of Care   25 Fertility, said that ethical concerns over creating children with specific genetic material were outweighed by the benefits. He said: 'The ethical issues are in favour of doing this work. We are trying to save the life of a child   30 and achieve a family without the enormous burden of a child with this disorder who would die.' Mrs Matthews also said she had no ethical problems with the treatment her family had received. She said: 'Max is loved for being him and not for what he has done. He has completed our family and now I have a bubbly and healthy girl.'   35

The use of genetically engineered children for medical treatment has been widely criticised. Josephine Quintavalle, Director of Comment on Reproductive Ethics told the BBC: '[Max] owes his life to his capacity to be of therapeutic use to his sick sister, otherwise he would not have been chosen in the first place. This is the big ethical problem.' Sufferers of Fanconi Anaemia may suffer long-term health problems and   40 Megan may require further treatment.

From: *'First complete "saviour sibling" transplant carried out in the UK'*,
Daily Telegraph, 22 December 2010

SAVIOUR SIBLINGS HOW IT WORKS

Woman is given fertility drugs.

Eggs are fertilized to produce embryos.

Multiple eggs are produced.

Embryos are analysed for genetic defects and tissue compatibility.

Only healthy embryos are injected into uterus.

Mother gives birth to genetically healthy baby.

Transfusion of umbilical cord blood to sick child

— COMPREHENSION ◀

1 Understanding the concept of saviour siblings

Choose the statement which fits best and give the line that provides evidence for your choice.

a A saviour sibling is a brother or sister …
  1 who has been specifically created for the purpose of curing a sick brother or sister.
  2 whose life was saved by receiving a transplant from a brother or sister.

b Without a transplant Megan would …
  1 have died within a short period of time.
  2 have had to go in and out of hospitals to receive transfusions.

c The use of IVF was necessary to …
  1 produce a healthy embryo.
  2 make sure that the baby would not suffer from Fanconi Anaemia.

d The procedure has been widely criticized as …
  1 human beings seem to have been reduced to commodities.
  2 embryos are killed in the process.

▶ SF 7: Working with closed test formats

2 Summarizing information

Use the drawing and the information from the text to explain how a saviour sibling is produced.

▶ SF 31: Writing a summary

— ANALYSIS ◀

3 Argumentative structure

a Look at the last sentence of the article and decide whether the writer is in favour of the use of saviour siblings, whether she is against their use or whether he takes a neutral position.

b Analyse the argumentative structure of the article, paying particular attention to the effect of the writer's use of direct and indirect speech.
  SUPPORT ▶ p. 238

▶ SF 18: Analysing non-fiction

— LANGUAGE AWARENESS ◀

4 Using the passive

a Scientific texts usually contain many passive constructions. Look at the use of the passive voice in ll. 2, 11, 13, 15, 16, 17–18, 28, 34, 36, 39, and analyse its effect. (Hint: it may help to transform one or two into the active voice to see the difference.)

b In German, active sentences with *man* are often used instead of a passive sentence. In which cases do you think *man* might be better than the passive voice if you were to translate the sentences?

▶ LP 7: The passive

■ LANGUAGE AWARENESS

Differences between languages
Grammatical constructions in other languages may not always have a close equivalent in your mother tongue (e.g. the English gerund compared to German). Even a concept as familiar as the passive may follow special rules (e.g. the English personal passive) and often cannot be translated word for word into German.

— BEYOND THE TEXT ◀

5 PLACEMAT ACTIVITY Case studies

Choose one of the cases below and use a placemat to note down the pros and cons for that case. Use the guidelines from the Fact File on p. 144 to consider the ethical dimensions of the topic. Discuss the issue with your group members and prepare a group statement in which you justify your position.

1 Megan's case (cf. text)

2 A pair of deaf parents wants to use genetic screening to ensure that their child is also deaf.

3 Parents who want to use genetic screening to test their foetus for genes that indicate a high risk of their child developing particular conditions, so that they can abort the foetus if they so wish.

▶ LA 1: Varieties of English
▶ LA 3: Similarities and differences of languages
▶ SF 24: Giving a presentation

FACT FILE

Ethics in science

Science is advancing at an ever-accelerating speed. New discoveries and new technologies are affecting all areas of our life. Many new
5 inventions or discoveries have sparked public discussions on whether their use is desirable or should be avoided.

In order to find out which course of action is the moral one, people turn to ethics. Ethics is
10 the branch of philosophy that studies the principles of what is morally right or wrong. When it comes to ethical decision making, the following questions can help you. You can use them to test whether your decision is morally acceptable: 15

- Are the rights of everyone involved respected?
- Which solution would be the most just, fair or responsible?
- Which solution will probably have the best overall consequences, even if it means that 20 some will not benefit from it?
- Which solution will be most sustainable and help everyone?
- Think of the wisest person you know. What would he or she do in this situation? 25

Read the Fact File and write down: 3 words or expressions that are new to you and worth adding to your word bank on genetic engineering; 2 ethical principles that are particularly important when it comes to ethical decision making; 1 reason why ethical decision making is important.

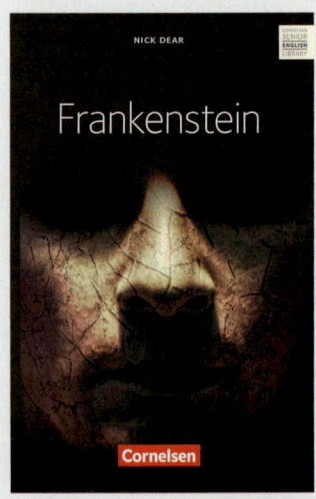

A2 **You are mine to kill** *Nick Dear*

The excerpt below is from Nick Dear's 2011 stage adaptation of Mary Shelley's novel Frankenstein *(1818). Considered by many to be one of the first horror stories, Shelley's gothic novel poses many moral and ethical questions about the role of science in a society that was beginning to change due to scientific advances. Victor Frankenstein, a young scientist, has succeeded in creating life. From dead bodies and with the help of newly-discovered electricity he has brought a creature to life. Appalled by its ugliness, he sends it away. After he learns that the creature has killed his brother William, he searches for it in the Arctic ice, where the creature has fled.*

- With a partner, come up with a list of guidelines that a responsible scientist should follow, e.g. whether they should make their findings publicly available.

There is a sound like a great exhalation of breath, as the glacier shudders and shifts. Through the snowstorm the Creature is suddenly visible, standing very still on the ice. He makes a great leap towards Victor.

VICTOR	My God! Muscular coordination – hand and eye – excellent tissue – perfect balance! And the sutures have held! I failed to make it handsome, but I gave it strength and grace. 5

Victor circles the Creature. The Creature swivels to keep an eye on him.

	What an achievement! Unsurpassed in scientific endeavour! God, the madness of that night – the heat, the sweat, the infusions, the moment when I saw it crawl towards me, and I – and I – 10
CREATURE	You ran away.
VICTOR	What?
CREATURE	You abandoned me.
VICTOR	*(stunned)* It speaks!
CREATURE	Yes, Frankenstein. It speaks. 15
VICTOR	You know my name?

5 **suture** ['suːtʃə] *Naht*
7 **swivel** ['swɪvl] turn round quickly
8 **unsurpassed** better or greater than any other
endeavour (n) [ɪn'devə] attempt to do sth. new and difficult
10 **crawl** walk on your hands and knees
13 **abandon sb.** leave sb. with no intention of seeing them again

The Creature hands Victor the tattered journal.

	My journal!
CREATURE	Why did you abandon me?
20 VICTOR	I was terrified – what had I done?
CREATURE	Built a man, and given him life –
VICTOR	Well, now I have come to take it away –
CREATURE	*(laughs)* Oh, have you?
VICTOR	I have come to kill you!
25 CREATURE	To kill me? Why then did you create me?
VICTOR	To prove that I could!
CREATURE	So you make sport with my life?
VICTOR	In the cause of science! You were my greatest experiment – but an experiment that has gone wrong. An experiment that must be
30	curtailed!

Victor runs at him and attacks him with his stick, but the Creature swiftly disarms him and throws him to the ground.

CREATURE	Be still, genius! I have a request.
VICTOR	Damn you, you can't have requests!
35 CREATURE	Oh, I can! Listen to me. It's your duty.
VICTOR	I have no duty to a murderer.

From: *Frankenstein*, 2001, pp. 38–39

30 **curtail sth.** [–ˈ–] (here) bring sth. to an end
31 **disarm sb.** take a weapon away from sb.

The National Theatre's production of Nick Dear's Frankenstein

---

COMPREHENSION ◀

1 Creature and creator

Describe the situation as presented in this scene.

ANALYSIS ◀

2 Responsible or irresponsible scientist?

Examine the attitude of Victor Frankenstein to his creation. Use your list from above to judge whether his attitude shows him to be a responsible or an irresponsible scientist.

BEYOND THE TEXT ◀

3 CHALLENGE ▶ The experiment

Creature or human? Comment on this question taking into consideration ethical and legal aspects and the character of the Creature. Discuss the consequences this decision will have for the Creature and for possible punishments regarding Williams's death.

4 FOUR-CORNERS ACTIVITY **Discussing statements**

Assign each of the four positions below to a corner in your classroom. Then stand next to the statement that comes closest to your own opinion. With the others in your corner discuss the reasons why you each chose that position.

'We've created a teenager.'

▶ SF 27: Having a discussion

| Scientists should have complete freedom in their research and not be controlled by the government. | Science creates more problems than it solves. | Whenever there is a discovery, somebody immediately uses it for their own gain. | It is not for humans to create life forms and use them for their own purposes. |

A3 Designer people

'It's your mother. You're being recalled for the correction of a minor defect.'

—————————————————————————— COMPREHENSION ◀

1 Describing a cartoon

Describe the cartoon and identify the topic the cartoon addresses.

—————————————————————————— ANALYSIS ◀

2 Examining a cartoon

Analyse the means the cartoonist employs to make his point.

—————————————————————————— BEYOND THE CARTOON ◀

3 Comparing texts

Comment on how the topic of the cartoon is similar or different to the dilemma dealt with in *Frankenstein* (cf. **A2**).

4 YOU CHOOSE ▶ Practising speaking

When doing the following task, use the guidelines from the Fact File (cf. p. 144) to include the ethical dimension of the topic.

a Prepare a monologue on whether designer babies are desirable or not. 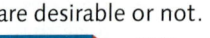 **OR**	**b** Find a partner and discuss in front of the class whether designer babies are desirable or not, with one of you being in favour and one against.

SUPPORT ▶ p. 238

▶ **LANGUAGE HELP**

▶ SF 13: Analysing cartoons

▶ SF 24: Giving a presentation
▶ SF 27: Having a discussion

Find a tool for improving your speaking skills here:
Webcode context-51

⦿ CULTURE SPOT

The hyperrealistic sculptures by Australian contemporary artist Patricia Piccinini address ethical issues of genetic engineering in an often disturbing or provocative way.

The Long Awaited (2008)

Silicone, fibreglass, human hair, plywood, leather, clothing. 152 x 80 x 92 cm high.
Courtesy of the artist and Tolarno and Roslyn Oxley9 Galleries

Patricia Piccinini on *The Long Awaited*:

'Empathy is at the heart of my practice. I don't think that you really can – or indeed should – try to understand the ethics of something without emotions [...]. It is one thing to argue for or against cloning when it is just an intellectual issue. However, things change if you have a mother or son who might need it. I like to think that my work understands that the point at which "good" becomes "bad" does not stand still, which is why it is so difficult to find.'

From: patriciapiccinini.net/writing/41/232/29#, 23 January 2019

1 Study the sculpture. Then discuss your reactions to it with a partner. Choose the adjectives from the list below to describe the sculpture and its effect on you.

aesthetic · calming · delightful · disturbing · embarrassing · harmonious · interesting · loving · obnoxious · quaint · shocking · supportive · tasteless · touching · tranquil · understanding · unsettling · warm

2 Analyse the relationship between the boy and the creature on the bench. Explain to what extent the sculpture illustrates Piccinini's comment.

3 Write a formal email to Patricia Piccinini in which you comment on *The Long Awaited* as a statement on genetic engineering.

A4 Animals with bonus features — *Bob Holmes*

- FOUR-CORNERS ACTIVITY **Animal rights**
  Read the four statements displayed in four corners of your classroom, then stand next to the one you can identify with most. Explain why.
  1 Through breeding and selection humans have always changed domestic animals. Genetic engineering is basically no different.
  2 The genetic engineering of animals should be forbidden as it violates animal rights and is potentially harmful to the animal.
  3 Using genetically engineered animals to produce drugs is acceptable if it reduces severe human suffering.
  4 Animals with human DNA should be entitled to special rights.

The text below examines the genetic engineering of animals so that they may benefit humans in more ways than they do today.

6 **tedious** ['tiːdiəs] taking a long time and requiring a lot of work
18 **jumping gene** gene that can insert copies of itself into other DNA sites in the same cell
25 **omega-3** ['əʊmɪɡə] type of fatty acid
32 **tack sth. on** add sth.
34 **antibody** *Antikörper*

Unless you live in Europe, your last meal probably contained genetically modified ingredients – 80 per cent of soya grown worldwide is now genetically engineered, for instance. Yet while modified plants are rapidly taking over the planet's farms, the same cannot be said for GM animals. [...]

The main reason is that the genetic engineering of animals – with the exception of mice – has been a slow, tedious process needing a lot of money and not a little luck. Behind the scenes, though, a quiet revolution has been taking place. Thanks to a set of new tricks and tools, modifying animals is becoming a lot easier and more precise. That is not only going to transform research, it could also transform the meat and eggs you eat and the milk you drink. The first transgenic animals were produced by injecting DNA into eggs, implanting the eggs in animals and then waiting weeks or months to see if any offspring had incorporated the extra DNA. Often fewer than 1 in 100 had, making this a long, expensive process. [...]

In mice, geneticists found a way round this problem: producing cells with the desired modification first, before growing entire animals. [...] At the same time, biologists have developed more efficient ways of adding DNA to cells, by hijacking natural genetic engineers such as viruses, and jumping genes capable of 'copying and pasting' themselves. All these advances mean the effort and cost needed to produce GM animals has decreased a hundredfold. [...] The ability to easily and precisely modify animals will undoubtedly lead to huge pay-offs in research and medicine. [...]

Genetically modified farm animals could provide us with more nutritious meat, milk and eggs, while causing fewer pollution problems, and perhaps suffering less too. Pigs whose muscles are enriched with omega-3s have already been created, and researchers are exploring similar options with milk. [...]

Genetic engineering is now a standard technique in the production of many protein-based drugs. Human insulin, for example, has long been produced by cultures of bacteria carrying the human insulin gene. Pharmaceutical companies are eager to turn animals into drug factories, too. That's because animal cells alter many of their proteins by tacking on sugars and other 'decorations', an extra step that bacteria cannot perform. As a result, many proteins – most importantly, antibodies – work much better if they are made in animal cells.

35 One such animal-produced protein has already been approved for clinical use by the US Food and Drug Administration. An anticoagulant called antithrombin III is purified from the milk of genetically engineered goats created by GTC Biotherapeutics, a biotech company in Framingham, Massachusetts. Many others are under development. [...] Open Monoclonal Technology of Palo Alto, California, has engineered
40 rats to produce human antibodies. Its first product, an anti-cancer antibody for treating lymphoma, should be in clinical trials within two to three years.

From: 'Altered animals: creatures with bonus features', *The New Scientist*, 14 July 2010

36 **anticoagulant** [ˌæntɪkəʊˈægjələnt] *Gerinnungshemmer*
41 **lymphoma** [lɪmˈfəʊmə] *Lymph-drüsenkrebs*

READING FOCUS ON SKILLS

Using reading strategies (scientific texts)

Scientific texts are challenging both in terms of content and language. The tips below can help you to get a detailed and thorough understanding of such texts.

1 Understanding the gist
Skim text **A4** on the previous page quickly to get a basic understanding of what the text is about. The first sentence of a paragraph is usually the topic sentence that states the main idea of the paragraph. Summarize to a partner what you think the text is about.

▶ SF 14: Reading strategies

2 Reducing the complexity of the text
Focus on the most relevant pieces of information only. Often it is not necessary to understand a sentence or paragraph word for word.
a Add headlines to the paragraphs to mark what they are about in general.
b The second and the third paragraphs deal with the advancements made in changing the genetic makeup of animals. In order to understand what these are, identify words that describe the development so that you will be able to explain it. (Hint: you can ignore technical details.)

LANGUAGE AWARENESS

Lingua franca
English is considered *the* modern lingua franca or bridge language. In the past, Latin was the European lingua franca, something you can still notice in scientific fields. In many languages, a basic understanding of Latin can help to navigate complicated texts and to decode unknown terms.

3 Dealing with hard words
a Scientific texts are full of technical terms. Often they are of Latin or Greek origin and are similar to German words, e.g. 'precise' *(präzise)* in l. 8. Find more examples in the text and explain their meaning.
b Scientific texts aim for accuracy. They use *formal instead of *informal style. Use the context to find the equivalent of these words in the text:

> change sth. • put sth. into sth. • include sth. • being able • go down •
> offer sth./make sth. available • do sth. • accept • make sth. cleaner •
> create/design sth.

c Often the meaning becomes clear when you look at the word family, e.g. *purify* (v) – *pure* (adj). Now use this strategy to find the meaning of 'engineer' (l. 2), 'nutritious' (l. 22) and 'enrich' (l. 24).

▶ LA 1: Varieties of English
▶ LA 2: Communication problems and compensation strategies
▶ LA 3: Similarities and differences of languages

▶ SF 1: Dealing with unknown or new words
▶ LP 11: Using the right register

▶ LP 20: Word formation

4 Relating information
It is helpful to draw diagrams or flowcharts in order to understand processes. Try to draw a simple diagram or flowchart to illustrate the process of creating a transgenic animal as described in the second paragraph.

▶ SF 5: Structuring information and ideas: visual aids and outlines

Part B

DVD

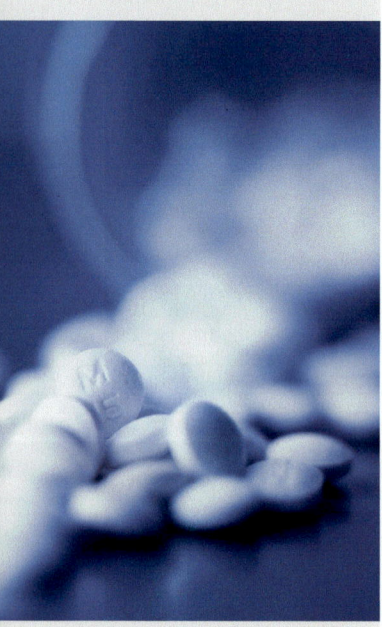

modafinil

▶ SF 41: Mediation of written and oral texts

▶ SF 23: Analysing a film

Modifying mankind

B1 A brain-enhancing pill

Watch the short *news report on the use of Modafinil.

———————————————————————— COMPREHENSION ◀

1 Understanding the effects of a neuro-enhancing drug
Describe the positive and negative effects of the neuro-enhancing pill as mentioned in the video. Outline why the drug is popular despite the risks that come with it.

2 Mediation (English → German)
A fellow student of yours believes that it's impossible to get such a drug without a prescription. Tell him or her (in German) what you have found out.

———————————————————————————————— ANALYSIS ◀

3 Examining the tone
Choose adjectives from the list below to describe the *tone of the report. Provide evidence for your opinion from the news report.

objective · neutral · biased · sensational · critical · exaggerated

—————————————————————————— BEYOND THE TEXT ◀

4 SILENT-WRITING DISCUSSION What if there were 'smart pills'?
   a Get together in groups of four (students A–D). Look at the questions below. Write your question at the top of a piece of paper, then answer it. Then pass the paper on to the student to your right. Add your answer to the next question on the paper you receive. Continue until every student has the paper again that he or she started with.

Student A:	Student B:
Imagine there were pills that could really make people smarter. Should those pills be given to everyone for free?	Imagine there were pills that could really make people smarter. If people took such pills before an exam, would you consider it to be cheating?

Student C:	Student D:
Imagine there were pills that could really make people smarter. Should parents be allowed to give such pills to school-age children?	Imagine there were pills that could really make people smarter. Would taking such pills to enhance your brain power be any different from drinking coffee or energy drinks, taking vitamins or going for a run?

   b Now read the responses and sum up the comments for your group members.
   c Discuss the impact of neuroenhancers on society and recommend how society should deal with them.

B2 Can this woman cure ageing with gene therapy?

Dara Mohammadi and Nicola Davis

The following article looks at an astonishing announcement made by Elizabeth Parrish, CEO of a biotech company, who claims to have found a way of curing ageing with gene therapy.

- Before reading the article, briefly discuss with a partner what you imagine your lives to be like when you're getting old. Would you like to live forever?

Elizabeth Parrish is CEO of BioViva, a Seattle-based biotech company working to develop treatments to slow the ageing process. In April, the company revealed that Parrish herself had undergone 'the first gene therapy successful against human ageing'. The treatment, it claimed, had reversed the biological age of her immune cells
5 by 20 years.

'There are a lot of fantastic conclusions that [people] can jump to,' says Parrish – 'defeating death, or people becoming immortal, or things like that. What we're trying to do is hit the biggest point of suffering right now in the industrialised world, which is the diseases of ageing.'

10 In September 2015, Parrish, then 44, flew to Colombia to receive two experimental gene therapies. One was a myostatin inhibitor, a drug that is being tested as a treatment for muscle loss. The other was a telomerase gene therapy – the drug that BioViva claims has reversed her cells' biological age, by lengthening parts of her genetic material called telomeres.

15 Genes are held in twisted molecules of DNA called chromosomes. At the ends of these chromosomes are stretches of DNA called telomeres. Telomeres protect the important genetic material from damage
20 that can lead to disease-causing malfunction or cell death. Telomeres also allow the cell and its DNA to divide, but as cells divide a portion of the telomeres is lost until, after a finite number of divisions, the cell dies, a
25 process that might contribute to the human ageing process.

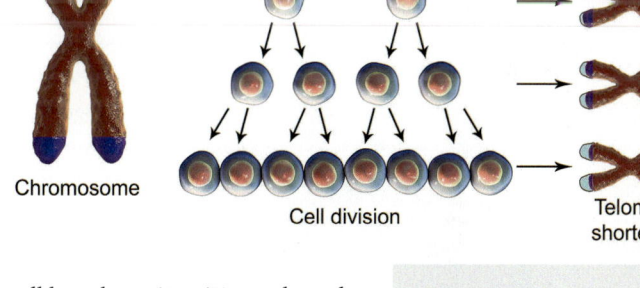

If a cat has nine lives, then a dividing human cell has about 50 to 70 – unless, the thinking goes, you lengthen the telomeres to extend the cell's lifespan and increase its ability to withstand damage. The gene therapy that Parrish received is designed to
30 do just that by encouraging the cell to produce telomerase, a protein that repairs telomeres.

The treatment is highly controversial. Because BioViva had not done the necessary pre-clinical work to progress to human studies, the US Food and Drug Administration did not authorise Parrish's experiment – hence her trip to an unnamed clinic in
35 Colombia.

BioViva claims that six months after treatment the telomeres in Parrish's white blood cells had lengthened by 9%. It was an announcement met by a mixture of derision and incredulity by many scientists, who cited the lack of proper scientific procedure. 'We used third-party testing for everything,' asserts Parrish. 'We used
40 a standard telomere testing system that doctors sell and patients can buy over the

Elizabeth Parrish

20 **malfunction** *(n)* failure to work correctly
38 **derision** strong feeling that sb./ sth. is ridiculous, shown by laughing at sb./sth. in an unkind way

68 **pseudoscience** [ˈsjuːdəʊ] false science, pretended science

71 **rigour** [ˈrɪɡə] strictness, thoroughness, paying great attention to detail

73 **pan out** *(infml)* develop in the expected positive way, succeed

internet. By that test, it said my telomeres in my [white blood cells] extended by the equivalent of 20 years.'

The scientists' scepticism goes further than the reliability of the company's testing systems. On its website, BioViva claims that its work builds on that of María Blasco, director of the Spanish National Cancer Research Centre. In a 2012 study, Blasco's findings suggested that a similar telomerase gene therapy could increase the median lifespan of mice by around 20%. Her work since has focused on assessing whether the technology can improve outcomes in mice with heart and blood diseases that originate in very short telomeres.   45

Blasco does not associate herself with BioViva's work and she has no relation with the company or with Parrish. 'Clinical validation of our telomerase gene therapy strategy, as with any other therapies, should be achieved through rigorous trials validated and backed by the regulatory agencies,' she says.   50   55

On her company profile Parrish describes herself as a 'humanitarian, entrepreneur and innovator' and 'a leading voice for genetic cures'. Absent from that list is the word 'scientist'. She also describes herself as 'patient zero' for these treatments – a term some would take issue with. 'Patient zero' is typically used to describe the first patient in an infectious disease outbreak, rather than the first patient to have received a treatment. A better description, some would argue, is that hers was an n = 1 study (a study on only one person).   60   65

'Perhaps she is patient zero, but only for the spread of the pseudoscience that's going to grow from her story,' says Timothy Caulfield, a professor in the Faculty of Law and the School of Public Health at the University of Alberta. Caulfield is concerned that Parrish's work lacks scientific rigour and is at risk of being picked up by unscrupulous practitioners aware of the selling power of anti-ageing treatments. 'People forget that most clinical trials don't pan out,' he says. 'Drugs often look really promising in mice but don't pan out in people – they're different animals.'   70   75

But Parrish, who says she has already had people contact her to ask if they can try her anti-ageing gene therapy, argues that enough animal studies have been conducted to move to humans. 'I think we are doing things wrong. We should be able to say, 'This looks promising, it didn't kill mice, it doesn't kill human cells.' So what we said [when deciding to test her company's treatments] was, 'Let's just run a test; let's see if this stuff is safe.''   80

Parrish and her team say they plan to explore the effects of the gene therapy in other cells in her body, and to assess the effect of the muscle-loss treatment. Meanwhile, they are looking to test the treatments in more people, but first they need to find a country with less stringent requirements than the US. 'We are still looking for a faster route,' says Parrish. 'We have gone from country to country, with groups who are asking these countries to re-regulate. They will come in with new regulatory standards ... with a fast track to get the most life-saving therapeutics to humans as fast as possible.'   85

90　While Caulfield admits that the drug development process is strict, he argues that
it needs to be to maintain scientific rigour. 'Sure, we're all looking at ways to get effective drugs to clinics quicker but this idea of foreign shopping until you can find the
regulatory framework that is most friendly to your idea about how science should be
done is a terrible mistake,' he says. 'Good science should be universal.'

95　Quick to distance himself from BioViva was George M Martin, professor of pathol-
ogy at the University of Washington. Martin had agreed to be an adviser to the
company after being visited at his university by Parrish but relinquished that role on
hearing the news of Parrish's self-experiment. 'I resigned only weeks after accepting
the invitation, I never attended a board meeting and I certainly had no inkling of her
100　plans to carry out human interventions without any pre-clinical work,' he says.

George Church, professor of genetics at Harvard Medical School and another of the
BioViva's advisers, is wary of the idea that he has 'ties' with the company. 'I wouldn't
call them ties,' he says. 'I advise people who need advice and they clearly need advice.'
Church says he advised the company to go through proper regulatory channels and
105　to do the required pre-clinical work. 'If you just let people run loose without any
advice, especially if they don't have training in medical research, then you're inviting
consequences.'

It's a point, he notes, that was tragically highlighted by a gene therapy trial in France
that is believed to have caused cancer in two participants in 2003, and the 1999 death
110　of Jesse Gelsinger, the first person to die in a clinical trial for the therapy. Both failures, he says, set back the whole field. 'Since then, the field has improved tremen-
dously and is much safer but new drugs have to be tested in placebo controlled trials
with animal testing first.'

And it's not just scientists who are cautious about how advanced therapeutics such
115　as gene therapies or those that use stem cells are handled. The public and policymak-
ers, whose attitudes can either help or hinder potential medical advances, are also
twitchy about science that tinkers with the inner workings of life. If the debate around
the powerful new genome-editing tool, Crispr/Cas9, is anything to go by, Parrish's
approach to combating ageing won't roll out without significant scrutiny.

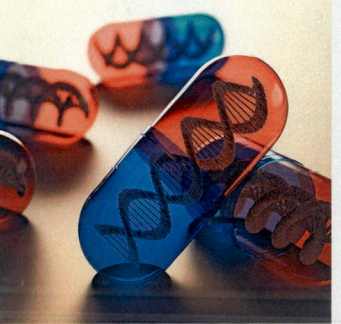

120　Duncan Baird is a professor of Cancer and Genetics at Cardiff University's School
of Medicine. He urges caution over Parrish's impatient approach to unearthing treatments. 'Life and ageing are too biologically complicated to start boiling it all down to
these entities at the ends of chromosomes [telomeres],' he says. 'To pick out one
particular phenomenon of telomere length as a key determinant of ageing and say
125　that if you're going to lengthen telomeres you're magically going to cure ageing,
I think that's fanciful.'

Without a much greater understanding of the biological processes that underlie
ageing, such tampering can be dangerous, says Baird. One of the reasons telomeres
have evolved to be the length they are, he says, is to limit the number of times a cell
130　can proliferate and thus to limit its potential to be cancerous. 'Meddling with a funda-
mentally important tumour-suppressive mechanism that has evolved in long-lived
species like ours doesn't strike me as a particularly good idea.'

Attempts to combat ageing, and its myriad manifestations, do not belong to Parrish
alone. Around the world, teams of dedicated researchers are doing the painstakingly
135　thorough work needed to unpick the biological mysteries of ageing and, maybe one
day, figure out how to tackle it. But, as so often with science, it seems success might
lie in the very thing that Parrish refuses to accept: time itself.

From: 'Can this woman cure ageing with gene therapy?', *The Guardian*, 24 July 2016

99　**inkling** slight idea, notion
117　**twitchy** *(infml)* nervous, anxious
　tinker with sth. make small changes in order to improve or repair sth.
121　**unearth sth.** [ʌnˈɜːθ] discover, reveal, find sth.
128　**tampering** *(n)* attempt to change sth. without permission
130　**proliferate** [prəʊˈlɪfəreɪt] rapidly increase in number
133　**myriad** extremely large number, innumerable
134　**painstaking** *(adj)* extremely careful, with attention to detail

Part B

1 Reading for gist

Skim the text, then state which of the following sentences summarizes the article best.

a The text outlines Elizabeth Parrish's approach to developing an anti-ageing gene therapy, which is regarded with scepticism by various scientists.

b The text deals with the risks and benefits of BioViva's recently tested anti-ageing gene therapy.

c The text describes the efforts of BioViva CEO Elizabeth Parrish to develop a gene therapy in order to cure ageing.

2 Reading for detail

Scan the text and find out …

Partner A:

- how Parrish wants to extend a cell's life span,
- what problems Parrish has to face and how she wants to avoid or solve them.

Partner B:

- what Parrish hopes to achieve,
- how other scientists react to Parrish's approach.

Make notes and present your findings to each other.

3 Pros and cons

List arguments given in the text for and against an anti-ageing gene therapy.

4 Argumentative structure

a Analyse the argumentative structure of the text.

b Find elements in the text that reveal the writers' position regarding the validity of the anti-ageing gene therapy.

5 Direct and indirect quotations

The text contains a lot of direct and indirect quotes.

a Find at least four examples and analyse their grammatical form.

b Explain the function of these quotes.

6 Discussing pros and cons

In pairs, discuss the pros and cons of an anti-ageing gene therapy. Use the arguments you collected in task **3** and add your own ideas.

7 YOU CHOOSE ▶ Writing a comment

Choose one of the following and write a comment. SUPPORT ▶ p.239

a 'Nothing could be more desirable than living forever.' OR b 'Genetic engineering and gene therapy have been (illegally) used by athletes to improve their performance, but why not?' OR c 'What we're trying to do is hit the biggest point of suffering right now in the industrialized world, which is the diseases of ageing.' (ll.6–7)[1]

[1] From: Dara Mohammadi / Nicola Davis, 'Can this woman cure ageing with gene therapy?', *The Guardian*, 24 July 2016

LANGUAGE AWARENESS

Intended readership

A text is effective if it addresses and activates a specific group of readers. Aspects of language such as style, register or certain sentence constructions can help to reach those readers, so can a particular layout or well-chosen illustrations. Use these elements in your own texts to make them more effective. Equally, be aware of such elements when reading the texts of others.

▶ LA4: Influencing through language

▶ SF24: Giving a presentation
▶ SF27: Having a discussion

Quenching the thirst for energy

C1 The global demand for energy

With an ever-increasing world population and the economic progress of emerging nations, the global demand for energy poses a challenge that includes environmental, political and technological aspects.

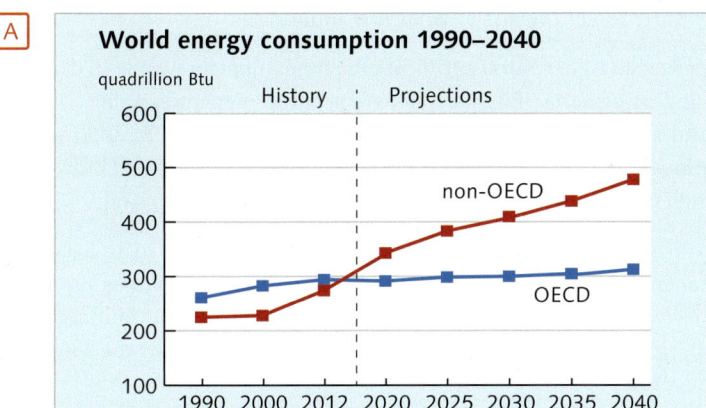

A

World energy consumption 1990–2040

quadrillion Btu

History | Projections

non-OECD

OECD

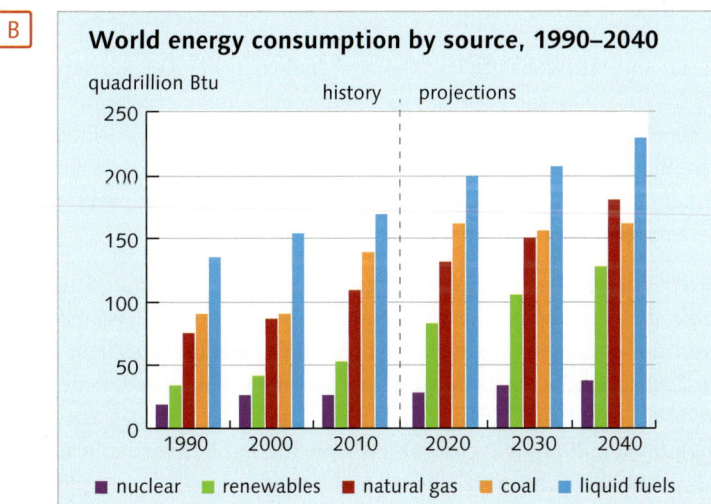

B

World energy consumption by source, 1990–2040

quadrillion Btu

history | projections

■ nuclear ■ renewables ■ natural gas ■ coal ■ liquid fuels

From: *EIA, International Energy Outlook 2018*

quadrillion [kwɒˈdrɪljən]
a thousand trillion (= 10^{15})
Btu = British thermal unit
unit of energy, ca. 1055 joules
OECD = Organization for Economic Cooperation and Development intergovernmental organization with 36 member countries

■ **LANGUAGE AWARENESS**

Numbers and dates
Although numbers and dates appear to be objective and factual in their message, they can also cause misunderstandings between speakers of different languages, e.g.:

German	English
1,0	1.0 ('one point oh')
1.000 = 1000	1,000 = 1000
Null/null	zero, oh (*BE also:* nought, nil)
Milliarde	billion [ˈbɪljən]
Billion	trillion [ˈtrɪljən]
03.04.2018	03/04/2018 *(BE)* 04/03/2018 *(AE)*

▶ LA 2: Communication problems and compensation strategies

▶ LA 3: Similarities and differences of languages

───────────────────── COMPREHENSION ◀

1 Understanding graphs
Study the graphs and state what information they give about future trends of energy consumption. ▶ LANGUAGE HELP

───────────────────── BEYOND THE TEXT ◀

2 Thinking about future trends
  a In small groups discuss the positive or negative consequences these trends might have.
  b Suggest ways how to tackle the problematic aspects that these trends could cause.

▶ SF 12: Analysing charts and graphs

■ **LANGUAGE HELP**
• The line graph/bar chart is about .../deals with ...
• The chart gives/compares/ explains ...
• The size/The number of ... has increased sharply/ significantly.
• Whereas in 2000 ...
• In comparison with .../ Compared to ...

C2 The future of energy in Germany

*You are taking part in an international youth conference about how different
countries are reacting to environmental awareness. The conference intends to set
up a website for young people dedicated to showing recent changes in global
energy policies. You are to present the German* Energiewende *in a text of about
200 words, explaining the German position and the aims of the* Energiewende.
*While searching for information you have come across the following text. Skim
the text in order to get the gist of what it is about.*

Die Energiewende ist der Kurzbegriff für eine fundamentale Wende in der Energieversorgung: Das bisherige Energiesystem, das auf Kernenergie, Kohle, Öl und Gas
beruht, wird abgelöst von einer neuen Energieversorgung auf Basis Erneuerbarer
Energie (EE) – Windkraft, Sonnenenergie, Wasserkraft, Biomasse und Erdwärme. Die
wesentlichen Gründe für diese Wende in der Energieversorgung sind: 5

- Risikovorsorge: Die Risiken der Kernenergie sind prinzipiell nicht beherrschbar.
  Dies haben die Reaktorkatastrophen in Tschernobyl und Fukushima gezeigt.
  Zudem ist der hochradioaktive Abfall aus Kernkraftwerken für Hunderttausende
  von Jahren äußerst giftig, ohne dass bisher eine Lösung für die Endlagerung
  gefunden wäre.   10
- Klimaschutz: Bei der Verbrennung von Kohle, Öl und Gas entstehen klimaschäd-
  liche Treibhausgasemissionen, die die Hauptverursacher für den Klimawandel
  sind.
- Knappe Ressourcen: Kohle, Öl und Gas sind endlich. Je knapper sie werden, desto
  teurer wird ein auf fossile Energieträger basierendes Energiesystem.   15
- Wertschöpfung vor Ort: Während ein großer Teil der bisherigen Energieträger
  (insbesondere Öl, Gas, Uran und Steinkohle) importiert wird, sind die Erneuerbaren Energien heimische Energien, die somit die Wertschöpfung vor Ort erhöhen
  und die Importabhängigkeit reduzieren.

Die Frage der Energieversorgung war lange ein zentraler politischer Streitpunkt –   20
insbesondere die Nutzung der Kernenergie war über Jahrzehnte Gegenstand hefti-
ger Auseinandersetzungen. Seit den Beschlüssen des Bundestages vom Juni 2011
existiert in Deutschland jedoch ein parteiübergreifender Konsens, dass der Weg der
Energiewende beschritten werden soll. So sind sowohl der Ausstieg aus der Kernenergie bis zum Jahr 2022 als auch konkrete Ziele für den Ausbau der Erneuerbaren   25
Energien im Strombereich gesetzlich festgeschrieben. [...]

Was sind die zentralen Themen und Herausforderungen?
Stromerzeugung und -verbrauch haben eine besondere Bedeutung für die Energiewende, da die Erneuerbaren Energien hier die riskanten beziehungsweise CO_2-inten-
siven Energieträger Kernenergie, Braun- und Steinkohle ersetzen müssen. Zudem   30
werden mittelfristig immer größere Anteile des Wärme- und Verkehrsbedarfs durch
Strom bereitgestellt werden. Die Energiewende-Ziele im Stromsektor lauten:
- Erneuerbare Energien: mindestens 80 Prozent Anteil Erneuerbarer Energien an
  der Stromversorgung bis spätestens 2050 mit den Zwischenzielen von 40 Prozent
  bis 2025 und 55 bis 60 Prozent bis 2035.   35
- Energieeffizienz: Reduktion des Stromverbrauchs um 10 Prozent bis 2020 und 25
  Prozent bis 2050 gegenüber dem Niveau von 2008.

From: *agora-energiewende, 2014*

MEDIATION FOCUS ON SKILLS
Mediating written texts

When mediating a text from one language into another, you always have to take into consideration the following aspects.

1 Content: What information do you want to get across?
Remember that when you are mediating, the final text is always shorter than the original text, as you are only mediating the important or necessary information.
Read the task in the introduction to text **C2** (cf. p. 156) again. What do you have to focus on?
Look at the statements below. Which are correct and which are incorrect?

> 1 I have to summarize all the information in the text.
> 2 I need to include the dates by which time goals must be met.
> 3 I have to explain why the *Energiewende* took place.
> 4 I can show what the aims are by also explaining what Germany intends to stop doing.
> 5 I need to discuss why it will be a challenge to meet the aims.
> 6 I need to discuss the political background.
> 7 I need to point out the future goals of the German energy policy.

▶ SF 41: Mediation of written and oral texts

2 Recipient: Who are you mediating for?
Decide who you are mediating for, and in which medium. Are you writing for people who speak English well? Are they experts on the matter?

3 Language: What style of language should you use?
  a After deciding who your audience is, consider how this may affect the style and structure of your text. Is the style of the original text formal or informal? Should it be retained in your text? What about the vocabulary?
  b In the text there are many words which you don't know in English. Try to translate or explain the following terms in English: *Erdwärme, Biomasse, Treibhausgas, Wasserkraft*. Check your results with a dictionary afterwards. For your audience, how might it be best to mediate theses terms?
  c Are there any structural features (e.g. bullet points, boxes, headlines) that you need in your text?

▶ LP 11: Using the right register

▶ SF 6: Paraphrasing

4 Intercultural aspects: Which aspects of the text might be hard to understand for people from a different culture?
Sometimes you have to explain things that are easy for you to understand but hard for other people, because they are specific to your culture.
  a Think of the term *Energiewende*. Describe it in a way that would make its meaning clear to somebody with no idea what it is.
  b Find other aspects in the text that would have to be adapted, stressed or explained, e.g. when mediating for someone from a country with energy resources very different from your own.

5 Write your text.

6 Peer Assessment
In groups of four evaluate your texts using the assessment sheet your teacher will give you.

▶ CC 1: Cultural awareness

■ LANGUAGE AWARENESS
Bridging intercultural differences
When being faced with intercultural differences, be it in direct conversation or when mediating difficult concepts, you have to choose the right register and style. You also have to decide which aspects need further explanation and background information so that a reader or listener can understand you and your message.

▶ LA 2: Communication problems and compensation strategies

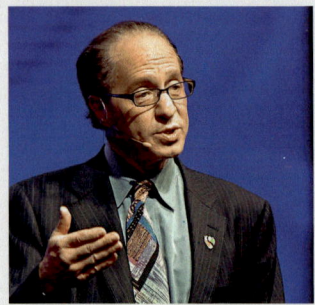

🎧 **CD1** 05
▸ SF 22: Listening
▸ SF 7: Working with closed test formats

Raymond Kurzweil

🟥 **LANGUAGE AWARENESS**

Speaking convincingly
Experts convince their audience through their professional knowledge and experience. When presenting their ideas they can also gain more credibility by using certain rhetorical strategies like providing and explaining their knowledge in a lucid and understandable way, establishing contact with their audience by showing emotions or even using humour. Look for signs of this in the given interview.

▸ LA 2: Communication problems and compensation strategies

📽 **DVD**
▸ SF 23: Analysing a film

🟥 **FACT FILE**

Biofuels are a type of energy derived from renewable plant and animal materials. Approximately 100 billion litres of biofuel are produced each year. Biofuels provide about 3% of the world's fuels for road transport.

▸ SF 3: Doing research
▸ SF 28: Having a debate

C3 A possible future

— COMPREHENSION ◀

1 Understanding an expert's perspective
Listen to the following interview with Raymond Kurzweil, an expert on technology, and say which of the following statements he made and which he did not.
1 Fossil fuels should be taxed to reflect the true cost they have on the environment.
2 Wind energy will be the most used renewable energy.
3 Within 14 years 100% of our energy needs will come from renewable sources.
4 Governments are unable to aid the change to renewable energies.

— BEYOND THE TEXT ◀

2 Examining predictions
a The interview was made in 2008. Discuss to what extent Kurzweil's predictions have come true.
b Discuss how relevant his perspective is today.

C4 Biofuels – the green alternative?

The European Union has committed itself to producing at least 27% of its energy from renewable sources of energy by 2030. One way of achieving this goal is through the use of biofuels. This concept has been met with both approval and rejection.

— COMPREHENSION ◀

1 Arguments for and against
Watch the two video clips about biofuels and note down arguments for and against biofuels.

— ANALYSIS ◀

2 Comparing films
a Explain which of the two clips you found more convincing.
b Examine how the use of music, light, cinematic devices and the voiceover contributed to the ideas in the one you found most convincing.

— BEYOND THE TEXT ◀

3 Having a debate
In two groups find arguments in favour of and against biofuels. The motion could be as follows: 'Governments should subsidize biofuels.'
SUPPORT ▸ p. 239

'No you can't turn your vegetables into bio-fuel.'

Doing a WebQuest

A supermarket in your hometown has announced their decision to stock genetically modified (GM) foods. The public is concerned.

- Do a quick opinion poll to find out what your class thinks about this issue.

In order to decide whether or not to take action, a Committee of Concerned Citizens agrees to consult experts: a scientist, a farmer, an environmentalist, and a nutritionist.

1 Get together in groups of four. Each of you researches the topic from the point of view of one of the experts (cf. the cards below). Make sure to also use German sources.

> As the **scientist**, you investigate the process of creating GM foods. You need to consider the following questions:
> - How are GM foods produced?
> - Is there a danger that this process might lead to unsafe products?
> - What safeguards should be installed to prevent unsafe products?

> As the **environmentalist**, you investigate the environmental aspects of GM foods. You need to consider the following questions:
> - What environmental problems might be caused by GM foods?
> - What safeguards should be installed to minimize these problems?

> - As the **farmer**, you think of the consequences for farmers like yourself. You need to consider the following questions:
> - What consequences will GM foods have for farmers (their health, cost of seeds, etc.)?
> - What experiences have farmers had with GM foods so far?

> As the **nutritionist** you investigate the nutritional aspects of GM foods. You need to consider the following questions:
> - Do GM foods have the same nutritional value as natural foods?
> - Could there be any nutritional problems or long-term health effects involved in eating GM foods?

2 In your group, exchange the results of your research. Decide whether or not to recommend stocking GM foods.

3 Prepare a presentation for the Committee in which you give a recommendation and justify your opinion (no longer than ten minutes). Make sure your listeners can follow your arguments – they are no experts on the matter!

▶ SF 24: Giving a presentation

4 Give your presentation.

5 After each group has given their presentation, the Committee (i.e. the class) discusses the recommendations and decides whether to take action.

▶ SF 27: Having a discussion

6 Repeat the opinion poll you conducted before the WebQuest.

7 Evaluate the presentations with the assessment sheet your teacher will give you.

8 Work and Business –
Careers and Perspectives

WHEREVER YOU GO

GO WITH YOUR HEART

Download a list of chapter vocab here: **Webcode** context-82

▶ SF 11: Analysing pictures
▶ SF 13: Analysing cartoons

1 Talking about pictures

a Choose one of the pictures A–E. Think about the situation it shows and prepare to talk about your response to it. Find other students who have picked the same picture and exchange your thoughts. Select one spokesperson for your group to report back to your class.

b Work with a partner and choose another picture. Think of a question raised by this picture and write it on the board or on a strip of paper that you attach to the board. Take a class vote about the two most interesting questions and start discussing them.

C

D

'I love your business model!'

E

'I really enjoyed my job. Management found out about it and fired me.'

Career decisions: priorities and consequences

You enjoy doing it.

Poor but happy

Just a dream

The perfect job

You're good at it.

Rich but unfulfilled

It's well-paid.

FACT FILE

Venn diagrams – named after John Venn (1834–1923), a British logician, philosopher and mathematician – use overlapping circles to illustrate all possible logical relations between a number of sets.

2 Talking about charts and diagrams

With a partner, explain the Venn diagram above with regard to business and entrepreneurs. Try and find an example of a person and a business idea that fits the field in the centre.

▶ SF 12: Analysing charts and graphs

PREVIEW

In this chapter you will learn about today's challenges and prospects of entering the world of work and business.

Main topics

- Work and business then and now .... p. 164
- Job aspirations and job satisfaction .... p. 169
- Applying for your first job .... p. 176
- Job interviews by telephone or face-to-face .... p. 180

Focus on Skills: SPEAKING and WRITING

- From informal to formal dialogues .... p. 170
- Writing a letter of motivation .... p. 179

Chapter Task:

Writing an application letter (a 'personal statement') to a university .... p. 181

🎧 **CD3** 02

*Download an audio version of the
text here:*

 Webcode context-26

The world of work and business

The right to a job – the right job

World economy has two faces. Many countries are recovering from a difficult
period of recession. In many countries, average wages have risen so that
many people have been lifted out of poverty. Despite minimum wage and
unconditional basic income being under discussion, there is a global rise in
income inequality – the rich are getting richer, and the poor are getting poorer. 5
The fact that budget cuts have claimed many jobs makes the situation even
more tense: people collecting unemployment benefits often have to face
tough odds.

Stepping into the world of work
10
Building a career is not always easy nowadays. In some university courses
competition among students is unusually high – for some the job hunt is
already on. And once people get into their dream job, more often than not
they are expected to move around the world and to adapt to new situations
quickly. Furthermore, it is not unusual to change jobs often. 15

To get your career on track, it is therefore essential
to access career advice and gain work experience.
Career advisers can do you a huge service, e.g. by
telling you which applicants are really needed out
there because they are in short supply. Too often there 20
is a massive mismatch between young people's
career expectations and the realities of the market.
In a paid or unpaid internship you can catch up on missing
experience: schools do not, for example, tell you how to
deal with difficult customers – this is what you learn best 25
in an internship. Once you know that you have a head for,
say, numbers, or that you have a passion for languages,
you can narrow down your job sector or employment area.

Applying for a job

Research the companies that have caught your interest 30
and start your application. For example, report on your
ability to solve problems and showcase your skills in a
professional letter of motivation.

Job interviews

Even though face-to-face interviews are still most popular, 35
you might also be invited for a telephone interview or
to an assessment centre. As applicants come from a wide
range of backgrounds, it is important that you
leave a positive impression on the interviewer.
Successful candidates convince employers not only 40
with their interview responses but with professional
body language and demeanour too. Don't spoil your
chances by asking about the salary package right away!

▶ SF 1: Dealing with unknown or new words

1 Words and phrases

Complete these phrases (1–6) with the help of the <mark>highlighted</mark> words from the text and match them with the correct German equivalent (a–f).

1	income …	a	Durchschnittsgehalt
2	… package	b	Etatkürzungen
3	job…	c	Berufsberatung
4	… advice	d	Arbeitserfahrung
5	… cuts	e	Gesamtgehalt
6	average …	f	Einkommensgefälle

2 Prepositions

Test yourself: do you know the right prepositions?

- recover … recession
- be lifted … poverty
- a rise … inequality
- be … short supply
- deal … customers
- report … your skills
- a mismatch … expectations and reality

▶ LP 19: Collocations

3 Opposites

Find the opposites of these words and expressions:

- have no particular talent for sth.
- employee
- do sb. a disservice
- hide sb./sth.

4 Collocations

From the three words offered, choose the correct one.

- make/build/form a career
- gain/make/find work experience
- from a big/great/wide range of backgrounds
- the elected/successful/winning candidate

> ■ LANGUAGE AWARENESS
>
> **Collocations** are combinations of two or more words which are often used together in a way that sounds natural and whose meaning is sometimes difficult to guess. Collocations are often specific to a particular language and can usually not be translated literally.

5 The situation in Germany

Using the text as background information, describe the situation for (young) job hunters in Germany. You may draw on the experiences of people you know.

▶ LA 3: Similarities and differences of languages

▶ LP 19: Collocations

6 Showcase your skills

Think about a talent that you have, or that you have always dreamed of possessing. Talk to your partner about how you can use this talent to start a unique career.

'I see under "special talents" that you always land on your feet. Tell me about that.'

🎬 DVD

▶ Historical documents:
The Bill of Rights (1791), p. 378

2 **necessitous** *(fml)* [nəˈsesɪtəs]
poor, needy
5 **self-evident** [ˈevɪdənt] obvious,
needing no proof or further
explanation
7 **prosperity** success, material or
financial well-being
station *(fml)* social position
9 **remunerative** *(fml)*
[rɪˈmjuːnərətɪv] well-paid
11 **recreation** [ˌrekriˈeɪʃn] *Freizeit,
Erholung*
13 **decent** [ˈdiːsnt] of a sufficient
standard or quality

The right to a job – the right job

A1 The second Bill of Rights *Franklin D. Roosevelt*

In his State of the Union address of 11 January, 1944, US President Franklin D. Roosevelt suggested that an 'economic bill of rights' be adopted to complement the political rights guaranteed by the US Constitution and the Bill of Rights of 1791.

We have come to a clear realization of the fact that true individual freedom cannot exist without economic security and independence. 'Necessitous men are not free men.' People who are hungry and out of a job are the stuff of which dictatorships are made.

In our day these economic truths have become accepted as self-evident. We have 5
accepted, so to speak, a second Bill of Rights under which a new basis of security and prosperity can be established for all – regardless of station, race, or creed.
Among these are:

- The right to a useful and remunerative job in the industries or shops or farms or mines of the nation; 10
- The right to earn enough to provide adequate food and clothing and recreation;
- The right of every farmer to raise and sell his products at a return which will give him and his family a decent living;
- The right of every businessman, large and small, to trade in an atmosphere of freedom from unfair competition and domination by monopolies at home or 15 abroad;

- The right of every family to a decent home;
- The right to adequate medical care and the opportunity to achieve and enjoy good health;
- The right to adequate protection from the 20 economic fears of old age, sickness, accident, and unemployment;
- The right to a good education.

All of these rights spell security. And after this war is won we must be prepared to move forward, 25 in the implementation of these rights, to new goals of human happiness and well-being.

America's own rightful place in the world depends in large part upon how fully these and similar rights have been carried into practice for 30 all our citizens.

For unless there is security here at home there cannot be lasting peace in the world.

From: the website of the Franklin D. Roosevelt Presidential Library and Museum

F. D. Roosevelt giving his State of the Union address on 11 January 1944

26 **implementation** realization of
sth. that has been officially
decided
28 **rightful** correct, appropriate,
legal

COMPREHENSION ◀

1 Looking at the text
  a In your own words, give a brief description of each of the eight rights that Roosevelt wants guaranteed.
  b Outline what Roosevelt means by 'People who are hungry and out of a job are the stuff of which dictatorships are made' (ll. 3–4).

LANGUAGE AWARENESS ◀

2 Finding the 'right' constructions

a Collect all the expressions from the text which contain the word 'right' followed by a preposition. Write them down in a table like this:

the right of ... to + *verb*	the right to + *noun (phrase)*
the right of every farmer to raise	the right to a useful and remunerative job ...
...	

b Find a simple rule explaining how you can use the prepositions *of* and *to* in connection with the noun *right*.

ANALYSIS ◀

3 Examining the text

a Analyse how Roosevelt attempts to convince his audience of his idea of economic fairness. Consider the language and the line of argument.

b Explain why the realization of the rights listed is essential for Roosevelt.

BEYOND THE TEXT ◀

4 Reacting to the text

Choose the three rights which you consider most important and explain your choice to your partner. After listening to your partner's reasons, work together to decide which in your opinion are the three most important rights.

5 **YOU CHOOSE ▶** Commenting or giving a speech

'Necessitous men are not free men.' (ll. 2–3; from the website of the Franklin D. Roosevelt Presidential Library and Museum)

a Prepare a three-minute speech on the basis of this quote. **OR** **b** Write a *comment of 200–300 words.

A2 More work, fewer workers *Catherine Clifford*

Globalization and technology have had dramatic effects on the world of work, and there is more to come, according to experts.

Donald Trump got elected in part by appealing to blue-collar America, blaming the loss of US jobs on immigration and bad trade deals with China, and pledging to improve the situation.

He largely ignored one key issue: automation.

5 'They are not talking about technology, robots and automation and factories, but that is a big part of it,' says Martin Ford, the author of [...] *Rise of the Robots: Technology and the Threat of a Jobless Future*, in a phone conversation with CNBC. [...]

Although conventional wisdom holds that manufacturing in the United States is in decline, in fact it's been growing steadily.

10 The production of manufactured goods in the U.S. has been 'on a steady and long-term growth path' as measured in inflation-adjusted dollars in recent decades, according to a report on the evolution of the sector from Ball State University. 'The notion that manufacturing in the United States is in decline is factually incorrect,' the report states. Even through the Great Recession, manufacturing grew in the US. From 2006

15 to 2013, manufacturing grew by 17.6 percent, or at roughly 2.2 percent per year.

But, even as manufacturing production has grown, employment in the sector 'has largely stagnated,' the Ball State report says. That is due to increases in productivity of each worker thanks to technology. [...]

■ LANGUAGE AWARENESS —

Prepositions

Prepositions can have a lot of different meanings. Using them correctly can be difficult – the ten prepositions *at, by, for, from, in/into, of, on, to* and *with* are said to have more than 200 different meanings. Differences between English and German may be slight, but all the more confusing, cf. *auf dem Bild* – in the picture, *an der Wand* – on the wall etc. As for prepositional phrases, make sure to check them, as they tend to differ from German.

▶ LA 3: Similarities and differences of languages

▶ SF 2: Using a dictionary and a grammar book

▶ LP 19: Collocations

▶ SF 17: Analysing stylistic devices

▶ SF 25: Giving a speech

▶ SF 25: Giving a speech

▶ SF 34: Argumentative writing

▶ LP 14: Linking words and phrases

1 **blue-collar** (*attr.*) relating to factory work
2 **pledge sth.** promise sth.
8 **conventional wisdom** what most people think is true
hold sth. (*fml*) claim, say
11 **inflation-adjusted** (*adj*) *inflationsbereinigt*
12 **notion** idea, statement
15 **roughly** circa

19 **require sb./sth.** need sb./sth.
25-26 **susceptible to sth.**
[sə'septəbl]] *anfällig für etwas*
28 **transition** *Übergang*
29 **disrupt sth.** destroy sth.
30 **substitute sth.** replace sth.
33 **accelerate** [ək'seləreɪt] move faster, increase one's speed
33-34 **intensify sth.** make sth. more intense
34 **pace** speed
35 **phase sth. out** *etwas auslaufen lassen*
36 **at risk** in danger
38 **from scratch** *von Grund auf*
40 **AngelList** name of an internet platform for startups

As machines get better, in other words, factories require fewer workers.

'We are already seeing the impact of technology on the job market and that is something that is going to get worse,' says Ford.   20

One 2013 study written by Oxford University's Carl Frey and Michael Osborne estimates that 47 percent of the U.S. jobs could be replaced by robots and automated technology in the next 10 to 20 years. And a 2016 analysis from the World Bank estimated that roughly two-thirds of all jobs in developing nations around the globe are susceptible to replacement by automation.   25

While new technologies have always eliminated some jobs while creating others, that transition takes time.

'Technological change disrupts labor markets and can hurt individuals whose skills are substituted by technology, because they often do not have the skills required in many of the new jobs,' according to the World Bank report on the digital state of the world. 'Even for those who stay within the same occupations, jobs will be transformed, requiring modern skills. The speed of these changes appears to be accelerating, intensifying creative destruction and the pace of labor market changes.'   30

Currently, factory and office jobs are being phased out, and other low-skilled jobs, like those at Wal Mart and McDonald's, may also soon be at risk, says Ford.   35

For example, San Francisco-based robotics company Momentum Machines has built a robot that can make a hamburger from scratch. No human labor required. The technology is more sanitary and faster than human cooks are, and the product is fresher, the company claims on its AngelList page.   40

From: 'The real reasons for disappearing jobs isn't trade – it's robots', *CNBC*,
21 November 2015

COMPREHENSION ◄

1 True or false?
  a Decide whether the following statements are true or false. Correct the false statements.
    1 In his campaign speeches, Donald Trump criticized the effects of automation on the job market.
    2 Manufacturing in the US has declined since 2000.
    3 During the same time period, employment in manufacturing has remained at the same level.
    4 In the next 10–20 years, one of two US jobs could be lost to automation.
    5 Workers who lose their jobs will be given new ones.
    6 Office jobs are not threatened by automation.
  b Compare results with your partner.

ANALYSIS ◄

2 Examining the writer's position
  a Decide which of the following statements best describes the writer's position.
    1 The writer criticizes US politicians for ignoring the impact of automation.
    2 The writer cites a number of different sources to document a trend.
    3 The writer warns her readers about the effects of automation in the near future.
  b Analyse the text and collect evidence to support your choice.
  c Consult the Glossary (pp. 360ff.) and decide which text type the given text belongs to. Think about the purpose of the text and why it has been written.

► BEYOND THE TEXT ◄

3 Looking into the future

a Form groups of 5–6. Each student is given a small card. On your card, write the name of a job. Put the cards face down in the centre. **SUPPORT** ► p. 240

b Each student chooses one card. Tell the others in your group what job you have chosen and whether you think this job will be replaced by a robot or a computer some day. Name reasons for your opinion. **SUPPORT** ► p. 240

c Together with the rest of the class, make two lists: jobs that will disappear in the next ten years / jobs that are not threatened by automation. Discuss the points you don't agree on.

A3 Income inequality and guaranteed income

Felix Oberholzer-Gee

The idea of an unconditional basic income has many supporters in western Europe, but also among US Americans. Felix Oberholzer-Gee, professor at Harvard Business School, seeks an explanation for this.

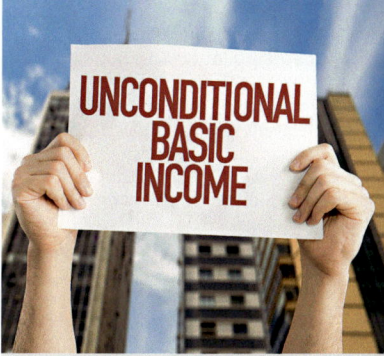

In Western Europe, there is a lively debate about proposals to guarantee every citizen a basic income. The idea, which has a long history dating back to the 1920s (at least), is increasingly popular in policy circles and the broader population. The German and Spanish parliaments explored it. The Swiss will soon vote on an initiative that would
5 guarantee everyone $2,800 each month — no questions asked, irrespective of whether a person works. Early polls indicate that more than 45 percent of Swiss voters will support the initiative.

The supporters of a guaranteed income are a varied lot. They range from unreconstructed communists to humanists with a strong sense of dignity and the
10 wealthy. One concern that many of them share, however, is the global rise in income inequality. In the past few decades, economic growth lifted hundreds of millions out of poverty. But, at the same time, the distribution of income became increasingly skewed in favor of wealthy individuals.

The current situation is exceptional from a historical point of view. For example, the
15 top 10 percent of earners in the U.S. captured 35 percent of income through the 1950s and 1960s. Today, this share stands at 50 percent. Rising inequality reflects gains at the top in all sources of income: salaries and business income, as well as capital income and capital gains.

There are many reasons why income inequality has risen. One is technology, which
20 tends to benefit the well-educated. Machines increasingly take over routine tasks, leaving low-paid service jobs for unskilled workers. As a result, U.S. employment and wages tend to grow at the very bottom and at the very top of the distribution in skills. The middle is hollowed out.

Import competition from poorer countries is a second reason. Chinese imports, for
25 example, explain about one quarter of the decline in U.S. manufacturing from 1990 to 2007.

Third, globalization produces so-called superstar effects. In a flat world, top talent is handsomely rewarded for its broad appeal. The Brazilian soccer player Pelé, the best ever, earned $1.1 million in 1960 (adjusted for inflation). The Portuguese forward
30 Cristiano Ronaldo made $17 million this past year. Pelé played for 350,000 television sets in Brazil. At the [2010] World Cup, 700 million people watched Ronaldo, as Eduardo Porter writes in *The Price of Everything*.

From: 'Will a guaranteed income ever come to America?', *PBS Newshour*, 7 April 2014

FACT FILE

In his bestselling book *The World Is Flat: A Brief History of the Twenty-First Century* (2005), Thomas L. Friedman analyses the globalization of markets and the resulting challenges and opportunities both for societies and for individuals. The term **flat world** has become a widely-used catchphrase.

---

5 **irrespective of sth.** regardless of sth.
9 **unreconstructed** *(adj) (derog)* hartnäckig, unverbesserlich
dignity ['dɪgnəti] sense of your own importance
13 **skewed** *(adj)* not accurate or correct, distorted
23 **hollow sth. out** *(fig)* diminish sth.
27 **flat world** cf. Fact File above

▶ SF 18: Analysing non-fiction

COMPREHENSION ◀

1 Looking at the text

a Outline the concept of an unconditional basic income.

b Point out what information is given in the text in connection with these countries: Brazil, China, Germany, Portugal, Spain, Switzerland, the USA.

c Using keywords, sum up the three reasons given for the United States' current problem of income inequality.

ANALYSIS ◀

2 Money and motivation

Analyse how the *article presents the idea of an unconditional basic income. Pay special attention to the writer's line of argumentation and *stylistic devices and use the information in the Venn diagram on p. 161 as a backdrop to your analysis.

BEYOND THE TEXT ◀

3 Mediation (English → German)

The topic of income inequality comes up in your Social Studies class. You offer to give a talk in German about the situation in the USA and its causes as presented in this article. Sum it up for a presentation of about three minutes. Make notes and practise the talk.

4 An unconditional basic income for all?

Suppose Germany adopted the concept of an unconditional basic income for all citizens. Think of possible consequences …

a … for employees.

b **CHALLENGE** ▶ … for self-employed people and businesses.

Write an article for your school magazine.

■ **LANGUAGE AWARENESS**

Use of numbers and dates
Writers often support and prove their argumentation by quoting a lot of facts, numbers and dates in order to be convincing. This is especially relevant for texts about finance and money.

▶ LA 4: Influencing through language

▶ SF 24: Giving a presentation

▶ SF 41: Mediation of written and oral texts

■ **FACT FILE**

The concepts of **minimum wage** and an **unconditional basic income** (UBI) are essentially different from each other. While one stipulates a certain level of pay
5   to all employees, the other guarantees an income to all, whether they are currently holding a job or not, in addition to any other income they might receive. In Switzerland, there have been initiatives for
10   both concepts. In May 2014, a majority of voters rejected the proposal for a minimum wage of 22 Swiss francs per hour. Preparations for another, more far-reaching referendum began in
15   September 2013, when activists advocating the introduction of UBI collected around 130,000 signatures from supporters. The referendum was held on 5 June 2016, with a majority of 76.9 %
20   voting against an unconditional basic income.

Make appointments with two students and exchange your views about the idea of an unconditional basic income.

Basic-income activists dumped eight million Swiss coins – one for each citizen – in front of the parliament building in Bern in the autumn of 2013.

A4 Teenagers' career aspirations *Kirstie Donnelly*

A survey published in 2015 by skills development organization City & Guilds Group looked at young Britons' job ambitions. Perhaps not surprisingly, expectations and reality do not entirely match, as Kirstie Donnelly, MBE, Managing Director City & Guilds Group, points out in the preface to the study.

Welcome to our most recent piece of research, an exploration into the career aspirations of 14–19 year olds at one of the most crucial deci-
5 sion making crossroads in their lives. The 3,154 young people we surveyed are making decisions now that will shape their futures. But do they have all the information they
10 need to make informed choices that will give them the best chance of thriving in the workplaces of today and tomorrow? [...] The findings of the research are concerning
15 but not entirely unexpected. Young

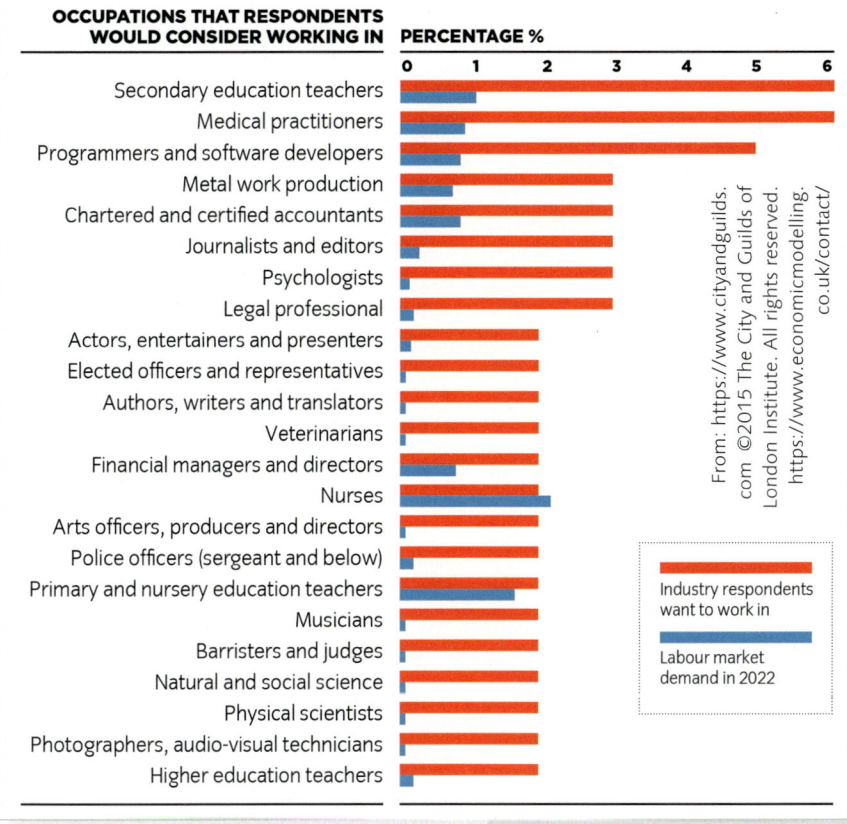

people are optimistic but often not prepared for the realities of the UK jobs market. Salary expectations are high, often career aspirations don't match demand in the workplace and young people aren't generally aware of what employers are looking for. They have great expectations now but their dreams are likely to be dashed if they carry
20 on along their current trajectory. The research backs up what we've been saying for some time: young people need better and more consistent exposure to employers and the workplace throughout their education. This includes the chance to undertake work experience, hear from employers about the range of jobs available and get inspired to work in previously unimagined areas. It is this early understanding of the
25 workplace that can help young people secure that all important first step on the career ladder. There also needs to be a recognition from parents, young people and teachers that whilst university can be an amazing route to a great career it is not the only route and is not always the best one. Our research shows that the vast majority of young people want to go to university despite many not knowing what they want to study.
30 With EMSI telling us that under a third of the available jobs between 2015 and 2022 are predicted to be graduate roles and the average debt on leaving university now standing at £44,000 that's a pretty significant gamble. This single minded focus on university is in part thanks to the poor quality advice young people are receiving about the workplace. Rather than giving careers advice based on real local labour market
35 intelligence, 14–19 year olds are being exposed to a narrow range of careers, with a one-size-fits-all education route to get there. While steps are being taken to improve careers advice for those still in education, much more needs to be done. We need to

······▶

■ LANGUAGE AWARENESS

Politically correct language
In the context of job and professional functions, gender mainstreaming is a question of language. Some, but not all professions have a male and a female version. Sometimes speakers or writers resort to neutral versions (e.g. chairman/chairwoman → chairperson) to avoid any form of language that violates equality.

▶ LA 4: Influencing through language

skills development organization
Organisation für fachliche Aus- und Weiterbildung
20 **trajectory** direction
30 **EMSI** US labour market analyst

change our education system to make it truly responsive to employer needs and ensure that every young person has the chance to follow their own path to career success. ⁴⁰

COMPREHENSION ◀

1 Popular jobs

a The bar chart on page 169 shows the jobs young Britons aged 14–19 would most consider working in. The chart also shows the actual demand for these jobs in 2022, the year the young people complete their training. Talk to a partner about things you find surprising.

b Carry out a class survey: What kind of job(s) do you want to do later? Make a list, ranking jobs according to popularity. Then compare the results with the UK survey, pointing out similarities and differences.

2 Choosing a career

a Outline how, according to Kirstie Donnelly, these young people arrived at their career decisions.

b List the suggestions she makes to support young people in this process.

ANALYSIS ◀

3 Style and language

The study was commissioned by the City & Guilds Group, an organization promoting vocational education and training. Find elements in the text that reflect this connection.

BEYOND THE TEXT ◀

4 Writing

Should you pursue the career of your dreams or should you consider only those careers where job demand is fairly certain?

Write an argumentative text in which you consider both sides, including aspects both may be missing. State your own views. **SUPPORT** ▶ p. 240

▶ SF 14: Reading strategies

▶ SF 15: Marking up a text / Making and taking notes

▶ SF 34: Argumentative writing
▶ LP 15: Connecting your thoughts (sentence structure)

YOUR NEW CAREER

▶ CC 5: Making smalltalk

▶ SF 14: Reading strategies

SPEAKING FOCUS ON SKILLS
From informal to formal dialogues

In any form of successful conversation, you should stick to the topic and contribute to a pleasant atmosphere. Moreover, you should adapt your style, vocabulary and your reactions to the situation in general and to the other person's social and professional standing. Sometimes you can be informal and sometimes you have to be more formal, depending on the situation.

1 An informal conversation

a Imagine you meet somebody your age at a party. You talk to each other about your career aspirations and your dreams about the future.
Before you start, scan **A4** (cf. pp. 169–170) again for phrases and words you might need for this conversation. Then talk to a partner for at least three minutes.

b You probably talked to your partner in a rather colloquial way.

THINK Assess your conversation and make notes on the following aspects:
- style of language
- phrases that you used repeatedly
- sentence structures
- the way you adapted to the given situation
- problems, mistakes, breaks

PAIR Exchange your findings with your partner and add to your notes and your list of phrases.

SHARE Share your most interesting findings with your class. Explain how you could have improved your conversation.

2 A formal conversation

a Imagine you have to have a similar conversation in a more formal context and with somebody older than you and in a different position, e.g. a guidance counsellor at school, an advisor at university or a board member of an organization that awards scholarships, internships or something else you are very interested in. What would you have to change in this form of discourse? Make notes.

b Match the following sentences and phrases with the stages of a formal conversation in the box below. Pick out the ones you consider too blunt or even impolite to be used in such a conversation.

Bye. – It's very convenient for me to meet you here. – I absolutely hate that kind of job. – I actually think I am quite good at working in a team as … – Oh, really, you studied at ABC University! I have heard a lot about it. – I don't think I'm qualified for such a career. – Excuse me for taking up some of your time, but … – Hi, my name is Tom. – It was very nice talking to you. Thank you for devoting some of your time to me. – I actually always wanted to talk to you in person. – I don't care for other people's experience. – You can't be serious! – It was a pleasure meeting you. Thank you very much for your advice. – Would you mind me asking you a few questions?

> - Introducing yourself
> - Getting into the conversation
> - Showing interest in the other person
> - Talking about your qualities, likes and dreams
> - Expressing dislikes and rejections politely
> - Saying thank you and goodbye

In groups of 3–4, collect more ideas and phrases and add them to your list.

3 Role-play

Talk to a partner about your plans and career aspirations as described in task **2** for at least five minutes.

Partner A: You are a student. You have plans and career aspirations, but you are not sure how to go about them.

Partner B: You are an influential older person and you are willing to give Partner A some help or advice.

After five minutes swap partners and take over the other role.

■ LANGUAGE AWARENESS

Using formal English
In some situations formal English tends to be used because there is an imbalance of authority or power, for example in a job interview or in a conversation where one ranks higher in hierarchy than the other.

▶ LA 1: Varieties of English
▶ LA 4: Influencing through language

▶ CC 1: Cultural awareness
▶ CC 2: The language of politeness
▶ CC 3: Polite behaviour
▶ CC 5: Making smalltalk
▶ LP 11: Using the right register

A5 Do you love your job?   *Uwe Jean Heuser*

In a job interview you may be asked about your ideas of your future workplace and how you can achieve satisfaction at work. The following excerpt from an *article in the German weekly DIE ZEIT *gives an insight into job satisfaction and its implications.*

Lange gingen Ökonomen davon aus, dass Arbeit reine Last sei: Statt ihre Freizeit zu genießen, litten die Menschen acht oder zehn Stunden am Tag – und für dieses Übel würden sie bezahlt. Eine traurige Theorie war das und gottlob eine falsche. Heute erforschen Wirtschaftswissenschaftler, in welchem Maße der Beruf ihr Lebensglück beeinflusst und wie zufrieden Menschen sind. Und siehe da: Menschen, die sich als 5 hochzufrieden bezeichnen, werden von anderen auch so wahrgenommen. Sie sind offener für positive Einflüsse, nehmen leichter Kontakt auf und blicken optimistischer in die Zukunft. Sogar ihre Immunabwehr ist besser, sie sind selten krank. [...]

Nach einer Umfrage der Beratungsfirma Gallup sind mehr als 90 Prozent der Arbeitnehmer mit ihrem Job zufrieden, aber fast 25 Prozent spüren keine innere 10 Bindung an ihr Unternehmen. Manchmal liegt das an ihnen, oft aber an Firmenkultur und Chefs. Wo Kollegen kooperationswillig sind, wo Führungskräfte schwelende Konflikte rasch lösen und die Mitarbeiter beruflich unterstützen, entsteht Zufriedenheit. Umgekehrt geht es den meisten auf die Nerven, wenn Streitigkeiten ungelöst bleiben, niemand Apathie oder Mobbing entgegentritt. Noch schlimmer ist es nur, 15 wenn Angestellte – zu Recht oder Unrecht – ihren Job permanent für gefährdet halten und keine Möglichkeit für einen Wechsel sehen.

Produktiv ist dieses Gefühl des Ausgeliefertseins nicht, auch wenn umgekehrt ein Wohlgefühl bei den Angestellten noch keine gute Leistung garantiert. Die Wirtschaft braucht eine Atmosphäre, in der sich zufriedene Mitarbeiter über den Dienst nach 20 Vorschrift hinaus engagieren. Und sie schafft umso mehr Wohlstand, je treffsicherer sich die Menschen erst ihren Beruf und später ihre Jobs aussuchen.

Die Bedingungen in der Wirtschaft ändern sich heute rasant, also müssen sich Erwerbstätige öfter fragen, ob die Arbeit ihre Erwartungen erfüllt. Gerade diejenigen, die sich im Job aufzehren, stellen sonst irgendwann fest, dass das übrige Leben leidet. 25 [...] Kein Wunder, dass auch flexible Tätigkeiten und Phasen von Teilzeit das Glück des Einzelnen beflügeln. Und sei es nur, weil er merkt: Ich habe mein Leben selbst in der Hand.

From: 'I love my work', *DIE ZEIT*, 24 Oktober 2013

1 Translating or paraphrasing?

Not every word or phrase can be directly rendered in another language; sometimes you have to find a paraphrase.

a Find out whether *luck* or *happiness* are both good equivalents of *Glück* in the context of this article (cf. l. 26). Likewise, check whether *binding* for 'Bindung' (l. 11), and *wellness* for 'Wohlgefühl' (l. 19) are suitable equivalents.

b Describe in German what is meant by the following expressions, then paraphrase them in English: 'dieses Gefühl des Ausgeliefertseins' (l. 18), 'Dienst nach Vorschrift' (ll. 20–21), 'sich im Job aufzehren' (l. 25).

2 Mediation (German → English**)**

An English friend of yours thinks that the importance of job satisfaction is overrated. Sum up the main ideas of the article for her in English (ca. 150 words).

▶ SF 2: Using a dictionary and a grammar book

▶ LP 16: Avoiding Germanisms

▶ SF 6: Paraphrasing

▶ SF 41: Mediation of written and oral texts

3 A tricky question in your job interview

a Some of the aspects of job satisfaction mentioned by Heuser should not be brought up in a job interview. List them, then compare with your partner.
SUPPORT ▶ p. 240

b Work with your partner again. One of you acts as the interviewer and asks 'How can you contribute to a healthy working atmosphere?', the other tries to answer this question. Then swap roles and ask or answer the question again.

📍 CULTURE SPOT

Corporate Head (1991)

The joint work of Terry Allen (sculpture) and Philip Levine (*poem on the plaque next to the sculpture), 'Corporate Head' is located outside the Los Angeles offices of the professional services firm EY (previously Ernst & Young).

They said
I had a head
for business.
They said
to get ahead
I had to lose
my head.
They said
be concrete
& I became
concrete.
They said,
go, my son,
multiply,
divide, conquer.
I did my best.

1 Describe 'Corporate Head'.

2 How do the sculpture and the poem relate to the topic of this chapter?

3 Discuss why the company EY may have commissioned 'Corporate Head'.

Stepping into the world of work

B1 Mitch's first glimpses of the world of work
Carl Deuker

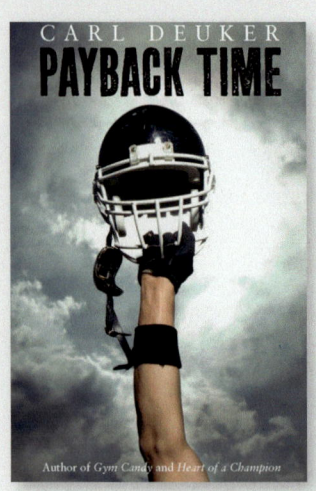

In the novel Payback Time *(2010), Mitch True, a not-too-popular high-school student, is a reporter for the school magazine. He has reluctantly accepted the responsibility for the sports section. In the following excerpt, Mitch is on his way to his first interview with the coach of the Lincoln Mustangs – his former PE-teacher McNulty.*

I parked my mom's Ford Focus by the gym, eased out of the front seat, and looked around. When I spotted McNulty loading tackling sleds into a school van, I tensed. To him, I'd always be a fat loser and nothing more. But a reporter has to have the courage to approach people, ask them questions, and get them to talk. 'I'm Mitch True,' I said as I neared him. 'I'm the school sports reporter. I'd like to ask you some questions.'   5

'I was hoping you'd come around,' he said. 'Step into my office.'

I gaped, dumbfounded. He was hoping I'd come around? When I recovered, I nearly had to run to catch up as he strode across the field and into the coaches' office in the gym. He took a seat behind a neatly organized desk while I squeezed into a wobbly blue plastic chair across from him.   10

'What's your name again?'

I told him again.

'You were in my gym class last year, right?'

'Two years ago.'

'Well, Mr. True, you are now an important member of the Lincoln Mustang football   15
family.'

I smiled.

'What's funny?' McNulty said, his blue-gray eyes glittering like shiny stones.

Like an idiot, I patted my jiggly belly. 'Me? An important member of the football family. How?'   20

He leaned forward, pointing his pencil at me. 'You are the person who sends in a game recap to the Seattle Times. You write exciting articles, and the Times will push them to the top of the high school page. That happens, and other newspapers will pick them up, which translates into publicity for the players and for me. It also means a byline for you, some cash, and a summer internship to boot. You remember last year's   25
sports writer, Boyd Harte. He interned at the Bellevue Journal.'

I hadn't thought about the connections I'd be making, but as a sports stringer, I'd be dealing with editors of real newspapers, something that would not have happened if I'd remained the news reporter for the Lincoln Light – unless the big dailies suddenly become interested in the accomplishments of Lincoln High's chess club.   30
'Sounds great,' I said. 'In fact, it sounds fantastic.'

McNulty leaned back. 'See. We're all part of one big family.'

I cleared my throat. 'How about we get started? I've got some questions. First –'

'No, no, no,' McNulty said, pointing the pencil at me again. 'No questions – not today, not ever. This job takes forever and pays peanuts. Here's how it works. You write   35
down or tape what I tell you. When I'm done, jazz it up whatever you want, but never make me, my coaches, or my players look bad. Understand?'

---

2 **tackling sled** *Gewichtsschlitten (Trainingsgerät im American Football)*
7 **gape** *(v)* stare with your mouth open
   dumbfounded [dʌmˈfaʊndɪd] *(adj)* very surprised and unable to speak
19 **pat sth.** touch sth. gently
22 **game recap** summary of a game
24 **translate into sth.** change into sth.
25 **byline** line at the beginning or end of a newspaper article that gives the writer's name
   to boot *(adv) (old-fashioned/humorous) obendrein*
26 **intern** [ˈ--] *(v)* be on an internship *(Praktikum)*
27 **stringer** [ˈstrɪŋə] freelance journalist
36 **jazz sth. up** *(infml)* make sth. more interesting or attractive

Mr. Dewey had warned us about people like McNulty, but this was my first time dealing with one. 'A reporter who lets himself be pushed around is a traitor to his
40 profession.' That's what Dewey had said.

I could feel myself trying to say: 'Coach, I will ask the questions I want to ask, and I will write what I want to write.'

In the classroom, practicing with bald, bowtied Mr. Dewey, I had spit out similar words like a machine gun spits out bullets. But McNulty's eyes were scary. I squirmed
45 as he stared at me, feeling like a snot-nosed preschooler who'd been caught marking a wall with crayons. 'Understood?' he said again, a threat in his voice, as though he might force me to do cartwheels in front of the football team if I argued.

'Yes, sir!'

From a drawer he took three sheets of paper covered with black type and showed
50 them at me. 'Here's the information for the football preview. Horst Diamond will be the focus, and you'll be leading every game story with his name, too. He's a lock for a D-I scholarship. UW is drooling over him, but he's got a shot at a bigger school – Notre Dame, or even USC. Your job is to get him publicity.'

I scanned the three sheets. 'But what if somebody else has a better game?'

55 'Nobody's going to have a better game. Run or pass – everything we do goes through Horst. I want a swarm of college coaches around here. They'll see him, and they'll see me and the program I run. I do not intend to spend my life coaching high school.'

McNulty stood. 'Read those pages, prepare a few questions, and before practice tomorrow you can interview Horst. He'll be at the field fifteen minutes early. Have
60 your photographer come along for that.' He paused. 'You've got a photographer, right?'

'A photographer?'

'Every sports story needs pictures. Either you've got to take them yourself, or you've got to get a photographer. Didn't you know that?'

From: Payback Time, 2010, pp. 22–25

TROUBLE SPOT

intern ['--] (n) = Praktikant/in
intern [''--] (v) (l. 26) = ein Praktikum machen
internship ['---] (l. 25) = Praktikum
apprentice = Auszubildende/r, Lehrling
apprenticeship = Ausbildung, Lehre
trainee [-'-] = Auszubildende/r, Trainee
hand = Helfer/in (z.B. in einer Fabrik)
employee [--'-] = Mitarbeiter/in, Angestellte/r
employer = Arbeitgeber/in
superior [suː'pɪərɪə] = Vorgesetzte/r
boss = Chef/in, Vorgesetze/r
chief = Leiter/in, Chef/in

43 **bowtied** [ˌbəʊˈtaɪd] (adj) wearing a bow tie (Fliege)
44 **squirm** sich winden
46 **crayon** ['kreɪən] Buntstift
51 **lock** (n) (infml) sure thing, certainty
52 **D-I = Division I** in the USA, highest level of college and university athletics
UW – University of Washington
drool over sb./sth. für jdn./ etwas schwärmen
53 **USC** = University of Southern California

► SF 14: Reading strategies
► SF 19: Analysing narrative prose
► SF 35: Writing a character profile

COMPREHENSION ◄

1 Who said it?

Using the text, point out who says the following and what is being talked about or what is happening at this particular moment: 'I'd like to ask you some questions.' / 'What's funny?' / 'Sounds great.' / 'How about we get started?' / 'Understood?' / 'Nobody's going to have a better game.'

ANALYSIS ◄

2 Power relations

Work on your own first, then tell each other about your findings.

SUPPORT ► p. 241

Partner A: Analyse the meeting between Mitch and McNulty and explain how one of them shows his power and superiority through non-linguistic means (e.g. facial expressions).

Partner B: Analyse the meeting between Mitch and McNulty and explain how one of them uses language to demonstrate his power and superiority.

BEYOND THE TEXT ◄

3 Writing about Mitch's experiences

a Outline what Mitch has learned about the world of work. Make notes.

b In an email to a friend Mitch writes about the experience he has gained. Write his email using your notes from **a**.

LANGUAGE AWARENESS

Verbal and non-verbal means of communication
In a conversation, power may be exerted by language as well as by non-verbal means. But since both function differently in various cultures, they can both be the cause of intercultural misunderstandings. For example, the distance people expect you to keep when talking with them may differ from culture to culture.

► LA 2: Communication problems and compensation strategies
► LA 4: Influencing through language
► SF 15: Marking up a text/ Making and taking notes
► SF 37: Doing a creative writing task
► LP 11: Using the right register

B2 Ten things not to say in a job interview *Mark King*

Getting invited to an interview is a big step on the way to getting a job. Now it's important not to spoil one's chances by saying something stupid. The Guardian's *Mark King has some useful advice.*

With the jobs market more competitive than ever it can be hard work just to get an interview, so once you're actually in front of potential employers you don't want to ruin your prospects with an ill-chosen comment.

Sadly, some job hunters still do speak before they think. Corinne Mills, managing director of Personal Career Management, says she can recall many instances of inter- 5 viewees saying the wrong thing. 'I remember when one man was asked why he wanted the job, he replied, "Because my mum thought it was a good idea",' she says.

She adds that some job hunters have also been known to say they've applied for a job 'because it will pay the rent while I look for a job I really want to do', and a common response to a question about what candidates like to do in their spare time 10 is 'go to the pub'.

Richard Nott, website director at CWJobs.co.uk, says candidates should avoid discussing religion and politics. 'Employers like people who can talk passionately about their own interests as it helps them to get to know you as a person. But we would always advise against sharing your views on these two topics without knowing if the 15 interviewer shares that point of view.'

We asked Nott, Mills and Nik Pratap of Hays Senior Finance for their list of the top things to avoid saying at a job interview:

1. 'Sorry I'm late.' It goes without saying that punctuality is key. Your interviewer doesn't want you to arrive for work 20 minutes late every morning. 20
2. 'What's your annual leave and sickness policy?' It doesn't look good if, before you've even been hired, you're planning your absence from the company.
3. 'I'll just take this call.' Mills says a large number of candidates think it is OK to take telephone calls, texts etc. during an interview. It isn't.
4. When asked, 'Where do you see yourself in five years?' never say, 'Doing your job.' 25 As much as this might be a genuine answer, Nott says candidates should 'try to build a response around the experience they would like to have gained and the level of responsibility they'd like to have, rather than threatening the interviewer's job.'
5. 'My previous employer sucked.' No matter how mind-numbingly boring those 30 roles might have been, 'speaking badly of a previous employer is not only unprofessional, but also reflects on your character,' Pratap says. Your new employer will contact your former employer for references following an interview, so it's never wise to burn your bridges.
6. 'You make widgets? I thought you made cricket bats.' Failing to research your 35 prospective employer fully is a big faux pas. 'Saying you've looked at their website is only marginally better – employers expect far more research,' Mills explains.
7. 'Bloody hell.' Never swear in your interview. It can happen, especially if your interviewer is themselves prolific with the profanities, but don't let them set the standard of the interview and remain professional at all times. 40
8. 'I was very good at sorting out PEBs by using ARCs.' Don't fall into the industry jargon of your previous employer or assume the interviewer knows anything about your experience, Pratap advises. Instead, speak clearly about your skills and experience to avoid any confusion or misunderstanding.

45 9. 'Do I really have to wear that uniform?' Any criticism of staff uniform will go down like a lead balloon. Do you think your interviewer enjoyed wearing that fluorescent green ensemble when they performed your role?

10. When asked, 'What do you expect to enjoy most about this role?' never reply with any of the following: the perks, the pay, lunchtimes, my co-workers or the holidays,
50 Nott says.

From: *The Guardian*, 10 May 2012

47 **ensemble** [ɒnˈsɒmbl] set of clothes that are worn together
49 **perk** (*usu. pl.*) Vergünstigung

COMPREHENSION

1 Understanding the rules

In groups of three or four, quickly decide which of the mistakes in the list (cf. ll. 19–50) are ones that are easily made and which ones you are sure you would never make.

ANALYSIS

2 The language of the text

a Explain how King tries to amuse the reader. **SUPPORT** ▶ p. 241

b Explain how King makes his advice easy to understand and to remember.

▶ SF 17: Analysing stylistic devices

BEYOND THE TEXT ◀

3 Your five golden rules

King gives tips for people being interviewed – but what about those asking the questions? In a group, think of five golden rules for interviewers.

▶ CC 3: The language of politeness
▶ CC 4: Meeting and greeting

B3 Help wanted in Paradise *Sarah Butler*

Do you ever dream about escaping to a romantic South Seas island? Then perhaps this would be the right job for you.

Wanted: barefoot bibliophile willing to punt Daniel Defoe to rich, modern-day Robinson Crusoes at a luxury desert island resort.

5 Philip Blackwell, scion of the bookseller family, needs a Man Friday for possibly the world's most remote bookshop, based in the luxury eco resort of Soneva Fushi in the Maldives.

10 'The pay is derisory but the fringe benefits unparalleled,' Blackwell said. 'The role will evolve and it is in part up to you to make the most of this unique opportunity. It's a dream job for many people. If I was 25 again I would do it.'

The successful applicant will be expected to sign up for a minimum of three months, during which time they must write 'an entertaining and lively blog that
15 captures the exhausting life of a desert island bookseller'. Oh, and mingle with A-list celebrities and their friends.

They should have 'a passion for books, the ability to engage guests of all ages', be able to entertain children with storytelling and host creative writing courses for guests.

20 'We want someone on the ground who is creative and inspiring and can maybe get more people to share the pleasure of reading, which is what people enjoy doing on holiday,' Blackwell said.

1 **bibliophile** [ˈbɪbliəfaɪl] person who loves books
2 **punt sth.** (*here*) sell sth.
Daniel Defoe (c. 1660–1731) English novelist, author of Robinson Crusoe (1719)
4 **resort** [rɪˈzɔːt] area reserved for holidaymakers
5 **scion** [ˈsaɪən] (*fml*) Spross, Nachkomme
6 **bookseller family** Blackwell's, famous UK bookseller, founded by Benjamin Blackwell in 1879
7 **Man Friday** allusion to Robinson Crusoe's native servant
9 **eco** [ˈiːkəʊ] based on ecological principles
Maldives [ˈmɔːldiːvz] Malediven
10 **derisory** [dɪˈraɪsəri] (*fml*) ridiculously low
fringe benefits Lohnzusatzleistungen, Sondervergünstigungen
unparalleled without equal
15 **mingle with sb.** [ˈmɪŋɡl] have social contact with sb.
A-list list of the most important or successful people
17 **engage sb.** win sb.'s attention
18 **host sth.** direct sth.
20 **on the ground** vor Ort

24 **foliage** [ˈfəʊliːdʒ] Gebüsch
25 **reserve** (n) land that has been set aside
28 **mansion** [ˈmænʃn] large house
   spa Wellnessbereich
30 **stock sth.** have sth. ready to sell
32 **enquiring** asking questions
37 **tricky** difficult
38 **source sth.** find sth.
41 **game reserve** Wildreservat
42 **reference library** library containing dictionaries, encyclopedias, etc.
45 **over-endowed** [ɪnˈdaʊd] überversorgt

▶ SF 14: Reading strategies

■ **TROUBLE SPOT**

the Maldives + sing v = die Malediven + Pluralverb
The Maldives has a tropical climate.
in the Maldives = auf den Malediven

▶ SF 14: Reading strategies

▶ SF 27: Having a discussion

They will also live near the exclusive resort, which is described as lying 'among dense foliage on beaches with sand as soft as snow,' within the Baa Atoll biosphere reserve.   25

Villas at the resort range in price from about $2,000 a night for a one-bed property up to nearly $26,000 for the nine-bedroom Private Reserve, described in promotional material as a 'playful deserted-island mansion', with its own swimming pool, spa, sauna and steam room. [...]

The shop will stock a mix of books that reflect the local environment, including the   30
colourful marine life, as well as titles that reflect the interests of the wealthy tourists. 'They are highly educated, enquiring people who want to relax and get away from things but also think a bit and better themselves,' Blackwell said.

The bookshop is a new experiment for Blackwell, who gave up running the British bookshop chain that bears his name in 2006 after the family sold the business. The   35
resort shop is an extension of his Ultimate Library business, which he set up almost accidentally while travelling the world after leaving Blackwell's. Finding it tricky to source suitable reading matter on his holidays, he came up with the idea of creating library collections for resort hotels. He now has more than 250 projects around the world, including more than 30 luxury hotels and resorts as well as a cruise ship, a   40
Kenyan game reserve and a London private members' club.

For every hotel library supplied, the company also helps donate a reading and reference library to a local institution that can benefit those who live nearby.

'It's a gap year project that's still going on,' Blackwell joked. If it is a commercial success, he says he may consider opening more: 'The Maldives is not over-endowed   45
with bookshops.'

From: 'Best job in the world? Luxury resort in Maldives seeks bookseller', *The Guardian*, 19 August 2018

--- COMPREHENSION ◀

1 The origin of the idea
Explain how Blackwell got the idea of opening a bookshop on a remote Pacific island.

2 Organizing information
Collect information about the job presented in the article. Use the terms below to organize the facts.
a) duties   b) qualifications   c) pay   d) fringe benefits

--- ANALYSIS ◀

3 Comparing reactions
a Analyse your reaction to this job offer by making two lists:
   a) what you find attractive about the job; b) what you dislike about the job.
b Compare lists with a partner and discuss your reactions.

4 Social classes
Examine the text for information about the social class Philip Blackwell belongs to. **SUPPORT** ▶ p. 241

--- BEYOND THE TEXT ◀

5 Taking a decision
Imagine that you are offered the choice between taking the job of island bookseller and working with poor children at a school in the Maldives. Which would you choose? Form small groups. Discuss your decisions and the reasons behind them.

WRITING FOCUS ON SKILLS

Writing a letter of motivation

When applying for any type of position – an internship, a place at a university, a job – you are usually expected to write a letter of motivation, in which you explain why you are interested and what recommends you for the position. Such letters, which may also be called personal statements, cover letters, statements of purpose or letters of intent, are mostly formal letters.

*Imagine you want to apply for the job of bookseller in a luxury resort in the Maldives (cf. **B3**, pp. 177–178).*

1 Thinking about your motivation
  a Reread the article on pp. 177–178.
  b THINK List three reasons that motivate you to apply for this job.
  c PAIR AND SHARE Work with one or two partners and exchange your ideas. Add convincing ideas to your list.

2 Presenting your assets
  Of course, it is not enough to just write that you have all the requirements as listed in the job description – you must prove it, either by presenting convincing evidence or by handing in relevant certificates.
  a List arguments and certificates showing that you are qualified for the position.
  b Work with a partner who knows you well. Exchange your lists and give each other feedback.

3 Writing your first draft
  a Turn your lists from 1 and 2 into a text. Stick to the conventions of formal letters.
  b Add typical application phrases to your text. ▶ LANGUAGE HELP

4 Typing your final version
  a Reread your first draft after a day or two.
  b Type it up on a computer and use your spellchecker to correct it.

5 A winning application
  A modern alternative to the letter of motivation is an application video. Watch the video made by Elisa, a young woman who applied for (and was given) 'the best job in the world', and discuss the relative merits of a letter of motivation and an application video.

▶ LP 11: Using the right register
▶ CC 2: The language of politeness

◼ LANGUAGE HELP

- I have a strong interest in …
- I was particularly impressed by …
- I understand that this position requires …
- I have demonstrated the desired qualities through …
- I would value the opportunity to gain experience in …
- I am very keen to …
- I see that this position offers … In respect to this, one of my key strengths is the ability to … I recently demonstrated this quality through …
- This experience taught me the importance of …
- I have developed skills in …
- My experience in …
- As you can see from the attached CV …
- In addition, my role as …
- My responsibilities included …

▶ SF 29: Writing a formal letter or email
▶ SF 30: Writing an application

▶ SF 40: Proofreading

▶ DVD

take a leap of faith *(idiom)* try one's luck
'roo *(infml)* kangaroo
fervent sincere, dedicated
anthropologist sb. who studies the human race

▶ SF 23: Analysing a film

B4 Surviving a telephone interview

Telephone interviews have become increasingly popular in the business world. Easy as they might seem, there are practical dos and don'ts applicants should be aware of, as the audio explains.

▸ EE 4: Making phone calls

COMPREHENSION ◀

1 Expectations
Before listening, arrange the following headings in the order of appearance you expect from the listening text:
Thank your interviewer / Research the company / Practise responses for your phone interview / Keep notes about your work experience / Be friendly during the phone interview
Then listen to the audio and check whether you were right.

▸ SF 22: Listening

 CD3 03

sophisticated *(here)* intelligent, complex
résumé *(AE)* = *(BE)* **CV / curriculum vitae**

ANALYSIS ◀

2 After listening
Explain the functions of the following in the context of a telephone interview: *paper, sticky tape, voice recorder, water, letter.*

BEYOND THE TEXT ◀

3 Act out an interview
  a Here are some typical questions asked by interviewers. With a partner, add three more questions:
    What is important to you in a job? How would you describe your present workplace? How do you handle stress and pressure? What motivates you? Where do you see yourself in three years' time? In what kind of company do you enjoy working? What does success mean to you?
  b Let your partner interview you.

▸ SF 26: Taking part in an interview

B5 Look them in the eye – the job interview

Though the most frequent type of interview, a face-to-face meeting between an employer and a job seeker has its pitfalls. This video gives helpful advice.

▸ SF 11: Analysing pictures

COMPREHENSION ◀

1 Do's and don'ts
Watch the video. With your partner, list and rank the given dos and don'ts of job interviews. SUPPORT ▸ p. 241

⊡ **DVD**

non-negotiable *(here)* obligatory
succinct short and precise
jack of all trades *Alleskönner/in*
unruly disorderly

BEYOND THE TEXT ◀

2 Body language
  a Compare Lauren Ferrara's body language to that of the presenter.
  b Take your own pictures in which you show good and bad examples of body language in job interviews and/or the oral exams of the *Abitur*. Evaluate the body language and rank the pictures from good to bad.

▸ SF 26: Taking part in an interview

3 Surprising advice
Which piece of advice given in the video did you find surprising?

Writing your personal statement

'Personal statement' is the term commonly used for a letter of motivation that you send to the university at which you want to study. In this letter you present yourself and explain why the university should offer you a place to study. A standard text type in the English-speaking world, personal statements are becoming increasingly popular with German universities too. They may also be required when applying for an internship, for volunteer work or for a year abroad.

1 Think about yourself

a Imagine you want to apply to a university for a particular course or subject. Alternatively, think of what kind of internship or volunteer work you are interested in.
Then study the table below and make notes on the points in the left column ('What?').

▶ SF 15: Marking up a text / Making and taking notes

Your personal statement	
What?	**How?**
• reasons why you are choosing higher education • reasons for your interest in the subject • things you already know about your subject • the subject and its connection to your education, work experience and to your hobbies	• catchy introduction • coherent main part • concise conclusion • max. 600 words • perfect grammar, spelling and punctuation • reader-friendly layout

b Add some notes as to why you think you should be offered a place. Describe your skills, your knowledge and your experience.
c Finally, add any other achievements and attributes that you might mention in your personal statement.

2 Ask for feedback

Work with a partner you know well. Let your partner read your notes and ask if there are any aspects of your personality that you forgot to mention. Then swap roles.

3 Get down to work

Now write out your personal statement for a course of your choice. Make use of your partner's advice, of the tips in the table above ('How?') and of the phrases given on p. 179 (Language help). Your teacher will give you an assessment sheet.

▶ SF 30: Writing an application

9 Modern Media – Tools or Tyrants?

Download a list of chapter vocab here:
 Webcode context-68

retard ['riːtɑːd] (*taboo, sl*)
stupid person

▶ SF 13: Analysing cartoons

BEiNG FiVE *A kid who blogs using voice recognition software* by GEORGE SFARNAS © 2014 beingfive.blogspot.com

I'M A DIGITAL NATIVE, WHICH MEANS I WAS BORN IN THE AGE OF TECHNOLOGY...SO IT COMES NATURAL TO ME!

MY PARENTS ARE DIGITAL IMMIGRANTS, WHICH MEANS THEY CAN LEARN TECHNOLOGY, BUT THEY HAVE TO WORK AT IT!

AND MY GRANDPARENTS ARE DIGITAL RETARDS, WHICH MEANS THEY BARELY KNOW HOW TO USE A TOASTER!

1 Talking about a cartoon
a THINK Make a few notes on the message of the cartoon above.
b PAIR With a partner, collect examples to illustrate the degree of media literacy that is to be expected of each of the three groups referred to in the cartoon.
c SHARE Present your findings in class. Focusing on your peer group, agree on the three types of media you use most.

hashtag

Let's Player

influencer

streaming

user-generated content

social media

VR

smart TV

2 MARKETPLACE (MILLING-AROUND ACTIVITY) The digital age

a Walk around your classroom. As soon as your teacher tells you to stop, explain to each other one or two of the terms above. Tell each other whether the term in question is relevant to you or not. Take notes. When your teacher gives you a signal, swap partners. Repeat this activity until everyone has explained each of the terms.

b Present and evaluate the results of your discussions in class.

PREVIEW

This chapter invites you to explore the impact of modern media on our lives now and in the future.

Main topics
- Pleasures and problems of interactive internet use .... p. 186
- Surveillance media – pros and cons .... p. 194
- Truth and lies in modern media .... p. 198

Focus on Skills: WRITING
- Writing an argumentative text .... p. 190

Chapter Task:
Discussing the impact of the media on our future lives .... p. 201

*Download an audio version
of the text:*
 Webcode context-69

Living interactive lives

Connected

In recent years a great many social networks have been developed to cater for people of different age groups and interests. Not only do they offer an easy way of staying in touch with friends and acquaintances, they also provide a platform to 'meet' like-minded people, exchange ideas and material, seek advice and 5
collaborate on a private and professional level. However, people's 'likes' and 'dislikes' are carefully stored, along with a great number of other details gathered about the users, to be exploited by businesses or political organizations. This pool of information allows for personalized ads as well as effective campaigning, but with it comes the danger of subtle manipula- 10
tion. Despite warnings as to the potential abuse of data inadvertently revealed, social networks continue to grow in popularity, especially among younger people, who have embraced a virtual lifestyle from an early age on and are therefore used to 15
sharing their everyday lives with an online community.

Digital media has also had a major impact on the educational system. Though banned or at least restricted at first, its 20
potential for supporting self-initiated learning has by now been recognized, turning it into a valuable teaching tool for research, cooperative learning and self-study, to name but a few of its 25
numerous uses. With the demand for media literacy increasing in every type of job and schools responding to the requirements of the 21st century, there has been a shift to a more media-based way of 30
teaching, which is more able to integrate students with special needs.

Surveillance

Digital media gives users access to a huge amount of unfiltered information. However, it also reveals details about individual users, be it 35
intentionally or by chance. Hence secret services have benefitted greatly from sophisticated surveillance technology. Moreover, CCTV is starting to be used in schools, both as a security measure and a means of quality control.

Trust in media

New technologies bring about new opportunities as well as challenges. The 40
importance of social media platforms such as Facebook, Twitter and Instagram has rapidly grown because they provide new ways for people to get involved, whether it be social, democratic or political engagement. However, recent surveys worldwide show an erosion of trust in social media. People are afraid of believing fake news, or being exposed to unethical or illegal behaviour. They 45
seem far more willing to trust the journalism in newspapers and online media than what they read on Facebook or Twitter.

■ TROUBLE SPOT

the media (l. 34) + *singular
verb or plural verb*
***Digital media gives/give …
The media has/have …***

▶ SF1: Dealing with unknown or new words

1 Words in use

Find the <mark>highlighted</mark> words or phrases in the text that match these definitions:

1 engage in a way of life that is centred on the internet
2 encourage independent studying
3 make something available
4 the process of gradually destroying sth. or of gradually being destroyed
5 work and study together
6 friends or contacts you don't know very well
7 show something that is usually hidden
8 unintentionally

2 Improving your style

a Gather phrases from the text that express the idea of 'a lot of'. Go beyond the highlighted words.

b Collect linking words from the text. Classify them in three categories according to their meaning:

▶ LP 14: Linking words and phrases

Adding a similar aspect	Introducing a contrast	Drawing a conclusion

c Fill in additional linking words that you know. Compare your results with those of your partner and present them in class.

3 Grammar and style: Participle constructions

a Rewrite the underlined clauses using participle constructions.
   1 People who use smartphones sometimes seem to become addicted to them
   2 As they are afraid that they might miss out on something, they constantly check their digital device.
   3 They often annoy their parents or even friends by the fact that they are glued to their screen while they are having a conversation.
   4 Although they realize that they may get into trouble if they use their phone in class, some of them just can't stop playing with their mobile anyway.

▶ SF2: Using a dictionary and a grammar book

▶ LP 15: Connecting your thoughts (sentence structure)

b How is the following participle construction different from the others in the text? How would you translate *with* here?
   With the demand for media literacy increasing in every type of job and schools responding to the requirements of the 21st century, there has been a shift to a more media-based way of teaching, which is more able to integrate students with special needs. (ll. 26–32)

▶ LP 16: Avoiding Germanisms

c Rewrite this sentence, using *with* followed by a participle construction.
   As the rules at school strictly forbid the use of mobile phones in class, teachers are required to take action against mobile phone use in their classrooms.

4 Discussion

Is digital media replacing traditional forms of communication and information? Discuss this question with a partner, using as many of the <mark>highlighted</mark> words from the text as possible.

Dis-connected

A1 Lonely friends *Ms Moem*

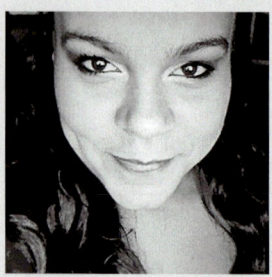

Ms Moem

Ms Moem is a contemporary English poet, who writes poems, rhymes and verses on all topics. She has her own poetry blog website.

▪ Watch and listen to Ms Moem's poem 'Connected' – a poem about Facebook, Twitter, YouTube and social media in general.

COMPREHENSION ◀

1 First impressions

   a Make notes on the effect of listening to the poem and watching its words unfold in the video clip. Then compare your experiences in class and discuss your first understanding of the content of the poem.

   b Sum up the essence of this poem as a Twitter message of no more than 140 characters.

2 Understanding the speaker's attitude towards social media

   a List the aspects that are important for the speaker with regard to social networks.

   b State how important the speaker considers her own role as a social media user. Give evidence from the text.

3 Mediation (English ➜ German)

Your friend is fascinated with social networks and has shared Ms Moem's video clip with you and other friends on a social networking site. He recommended it because he feels it reflects his positive attitude towards social media. Outline to him in German what the poem actually says about social media.

ANALYSIS ◀

4 Poetic devices

Examine which means the poet uses to draw our attention to the influence of social media on our lives. **SUPPORT** ▶ p. 242

5 The message

Interpret what impact the internet has had on human relationships according to Ms Moem's poem.

BEYOND THE TEXT ◀

6 Creating images

In small groups, discuss how you could underline the message of the poem with video sequences or stills instead of showing the words in the video clip. You may also include ideas for background music. Present your ideas to each other.

7 Writing a comment

'Oh why can't we turn the time back.
It was simpler when we could just be friends, and that didn't depend on whether someone had accepted your friend request.'
Write a short comment in which you state why you do or do not agree with this statement from Ms Moem's poem. ▶ LANGUAGE HELP

▶ **DVD**

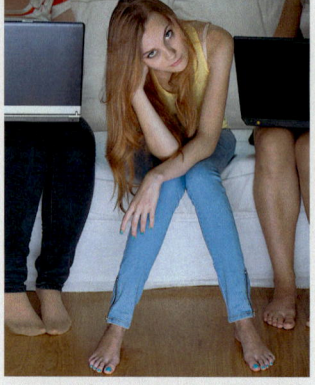

▶ SF 41: Mediation of written and oral texts
▶ SF 21: Analysing poetry

■ LANGUAGE AWARENESS

Using verbal means of argumentation

In any form of argumentative discourse, you should try to convince others not only by *what* you say but also by *how* you are saying it. E.g., make your attitude clear by the careful use of either positive or negative adjectives and adverbs – cf. LANGUAGE HELP below.

▶ LA 4: Influencing through language

■ LANGUAGE HELP

- win a friend ⟷ lose a friend
- make friends with sb. = forge/form/develop/build a friendship with sb.
- cultivate a friendship
- a close/special/intimate ['ɪntɪmət]/trusted/loyal/true/lifelong/long-time/long-lost/new-found friend
- a fair-weather friend (= sb. who will let you down when you are in need)
- a casual acquaintance [əˈkweɪntəns] (= a person you don't know very well)

CULTURE SPOT

New media art:
Viewpoint of Billions with Google Glass *(2013)*

- *American artist David Datuna was the first to incorporate internet-connected smartglasses ('wearable computing') into a piece of modern art.*
- *Four interactive cameras were built into a 12-foot (3.67 m) flag of the United States of America. These automatically connected with viewers wearing Google Glass.*
- *Photos, newspaper clippings and videos of famous moments in US history had been placed behind thousands of optical lenses. They were projected to the wearer's 'third eye' when they looked at the artwork.*
- *For up to three minutes viewers had a unique experience, e.g. they could answer questions posed by Glass and had their responses and experiences recorded and uploaded onto the artist's website, YouTube and Tumblr.*

▶ DVD Watch a video on David Datuna's interactive installation 'Viewpoint of Billions with Google Glass'.

1 Describe David Datuna's art installation. How is art created with new media?

2 Explain the title of the installation. Work in pairs and exchange your opinions on this work of art.

3 Discuss in class whether or not you would like to contribute to Datuna's interactive installation.

For another work of art based on the Stars and Stripes, see p. 104.

A2 Online learning in 2044   *Ernest Cline*

The following text is an extract from a science-fiction *novel. It's the year 2044, and Wade Watts, the teenaged *protagonist, escapes his depressing reality by spending his waking hours immersed in the OASIS, a virtual utopia where you can be anything you want to be on any of ten thousand planets, if you can pay for it.

I'd attended school in the real world up until the sixth grade. It hadn't been a very pleasant experience. I was a painfully shy, awkward kid, with low self-esteem and almost no social skills – a side effect of spending most of my childhood inside the OASIS. Online, I didn't have a problem talking to people or making friends. But in the real world, interacting with other people – especially kids my own age – made me a nervous wreck. I never knew how to act or what to say, and when I did work up the courage to speak, I always seemed to say the wrong thing. 5

My appearance was part of the problem. I was overweight, and had been for as long as I could remember. My bankrupt diet of government-subsidized sugar and starch-laden food was a contributing factor, but I was also an OASIS addict, so the only exercise I usually got back then was running away from the bullies before and after school. To make matters worse, my limited wardrobe consisted entirely of ill-fitting clothes from thrift stores and donation bins – the social equivalent of having a bull's-eye painted on my forehead. 10

Even so, I tried my best to fit in. Year after year, my eyes would scan the lunchroom like a T-1000, searching for a clique that might accept me. But even the other outcasts wanted nothing to do with me. I was too weird, even for the weirdos. And girls? Talking to girls was out of the question. To me, they were like some exotic alien species, both beautiful and terrifying. Whenever I got near one of them I invariably broke out in a cold sweat and lost the ability to speak in complete sentences. 15 20

For me, school had been a Darwinian exercise. A daily gauntlet of ridicule, abuse, and isolation. By the time I entered sixth grade, I was beginning to wonder if I'd be able to maintain my sanity until graduation, still six long years away.

Then, one glorious day, our principal announced that any student with a passing grade-point average could apply for a transfer to the new OASIS public school system. 25

The real public school system, the one run by the government, had been an underfunded, overcrowded train wreck for decades. And now the conditions at many schools had gotten so terrible that every kid with half a brain was being encouraged to stay at home and attend school online. I nearly broke my neck sprinting to the school office to submit my application. It was accepted, and I transferred to OASIS Public School #1873 the following semester. 30 35 40

Prior to my transfer, my OASIS avatar had never left Incipio, the planet at the center of Sector One where avatars were spawned at the time of their creation. There wasn't
45 much to do on Incipio except chat with other noobs or shop in one of the giant virtual malls that covered the planet. If you wanted to go somewhere more interesting, you had to pay a teleportation fare to get there, and that cost money, something I didn't have. So my avatar was stranded on Incipio. That is, until my new school e-mailed me a teleportation voucher to cover the cost of my avatar's transport to Ludus, the planet
50 where all of the OASIS public schools were located.

There were hundreds of school campuses here on Ludus, spread out evenly across the planet's surface. The schools were all identical, because the same construction code was copied and pasted into a different location whenever a new school was needed. And since the buildings were just pieces of software, their design wasn't
55 limited by monetary constraints, or even by the laws of physics. So every school was a grand palace of learning with polished marble hallways, cathedral-like classrooms, zero-g gymnasiums, and virtual libraries containing every (school board-approved) book ever written.

On my first day at OPS #1873, I thought I'd died and gone to heaven. Now, instead
60 of running a gauntlet of bullies and drug addicts on my walk to school each morning, I went straight to my hideout and stayed there all day. Best of all, in the OASIS, no one could tell that I was fat, that I had acne, or that I wore the same shabby clothes every week. Bullies couldn't pelt me with spitballs, give me atomic wedgies, or pummel me by the bike rack after school. No one could even touch me. In here, I was
65 safe.[1]

43 **incipio** (*Latin*) I am beginning, I begin
44 **spawn sth.** produce sth.
45 **noob** (*sl*) a person that has just started doing sth. and is very inexperienced in it
49 **ludus** (*Latin*) game, school
55 **monetary constraint** financial restriction
57 **school board-approved** accepted by the institution in charge of local schools
63 **pelt sb. with sth.** attack sb. by throwing things at them
give sb. atomic wedgies (*infml*) pull sb.'s underwear up forcefully as a kind of bullying, usually performed on male victims
64 **pummel sb.** ['pʌml] keep hitting sb.

————————— COMPREHENSION ◀

1 Understanding the situation
  a Name Wade's reasons for wanting to attend the new OASIS public school.
  b Describe the schools on Ludus.
  c Point out what makes OPS #1873 so much better in Wade's opinion.

————————— ANALYSIS ◀

2 Telling names
  Refer to the annotations and analyse what the names reveal about the
  *character and the *setting. **SUPPORT** ▶ p. 242

————————— LANGUAGE AWARENESS ◀

3 Telling images
  a Study the following (parts of) sentences in their contexts and paraphrase their meaning.[1]
    1 'My bankrupt diet of government-subsidized sugar and starch-laden food was a contributing factor […]' (ll. 9–10)
    2 '[…] the social equivalent of having a bull's-eye painted on my forehead.' (ll. 13–14)
    3 'For me, school had been a Darwinian exercise. A daily gauntlet of ridicule, abuse, and isolation.' (ll. 21–22)
    4 'The real public school system, the one run by the government, had been an underfunded, overcrowded train wreck for decades.' (ll. 26–30)
  b The sentences in **a** all contain *images. Interpret what they tell you about the protagonist.
  c **CHALLENGE** ▶ Write an analysis of the telling *images in the text, taking further examples into account.

▶ SF 6: Paraphrasing

■ **LANGUAGE AWARENESS**
Using figurative language
By choosing particular names for their characters and by using figurative language, writers may convey a particular atmosphere, conjure up certain images in the mind of their readers and generally influence the way their readers understand their texts.

▶ LA 4: Influencing through language

[1] Text and quotes from: *Ready Player One*, 2012, pp. 30–32

▶ SF 5: Structuring information and ideas

▶ SF 34: Argumentative writing

Means of argumentation
Your line of argument is convincing if it consists of a *statement*, which is supported by *evidence* and by *examples* from personal experience as well as common sense. Carefully choose *connecting words* and use the right *register* adapted to your intended audience.

▶ LA 4: Influencing through language

WRITING   FOCUS ON SKILLS

Writing an argumentative text

In argumentative writing, we present arguments for and against a topic in order to convince others of our point of view. Writing an argumentative text is often a requirement in both school-leaving and international language proficiency examinations. You usually have a time limit and must keep within a certain number of words.

A typical assignment could be:
'Discuss whether attending OASIS public school will solve Wade's problems.'

1 Examining the task
Before gathering any arguments, make sure you are familiar with the meaning of the keywords of the task, i.e. *OASIS public school* and *Wade's problems*. (Refer to your work on text **A2**, p. 189.)

2 Collecting arguments
Divide the class into two groups. One half of the class has to find at least three reasons why OASIS might be considered the perfect school for Wade, the other half has to collect at least three arguments supporting the idea that his problems will remain. Work on your own and make notes.

3 Developing a thesis and an antithesis
Arrange a central meeting point in the classroom, the so-called database. As soon as you have finished collecting your arguments, go to the database and pair up with a student from the other group. Exchange your arguments. Discuss and reach an agreement on how to answer the topic question. The position you support is called the thesis ['θiːsɪz], the one you reject is called the antithesis [æn'tɪθəsɪs].

4 Composing the argumentative text
 1 Introduction
 Start your text with an interesting example, quote, definition or statistic related to your topic in order to grab your reader's attention. Then introduce the topic itself with a clear statement or *rhetorical question. Compare and evaluate the following three introductions:

▶ SF 38: Writing a well-structured text

A   *Online schooling is a type of distance learning. You take courses without attending an actual school. Students and teachers interact via the internet, rather than meeting face-to-face. Wade sees this aspect as a big improvement on his old school. But will changing schools really solve his problems?*

B   *'On my first day at OPS #1873, I thought I'd died and gone to heaven.'[1] This is Wade's first impression of his new online school, after leaving the bullies of his old school behind. But will his opinion change as he gets to know his new school better?*

C   *Statistically, one in four students is regularly bullied at school in the USA. So there are lots of real-life Wades looking for a way out of their difficult situation. Wade chooses to attend an online school to escape his problems at school. But will online-education really turn out to be a positive alternative for Wade?*

[1] Ernest Cline, *Ready Player One*, 2012, p. 32

Either choose one of these introductions for your argumentative text or create your own.

2 Main part

On the basis of your notes from **3** on the opposite page, compose the main part of your argumentative text. Remember to start a new paragraph for every part of your text and avoid using contracted forms like *there's, she's, he'll*, etc.

Use some of the linking words from **Words in Context** to connect your ideas. Here are some additional phrases to help you structure your text:

▶ LP 11: Using the right register

▶ LP 14: Linking words
and phrases

▶ LP 15: Connecting your thoughts
(sentence structure)

Presenting various options	*on the one hand – on the other hand* *not only – but also* *either – or*
Giving reasons	*because* *as* *since ('da', 'weil')*
Giving examples	*for example (e.g.)* *for instance* *such as*

Complete the following sentences and add your own reasons and examples illustrating your arguments:

On the one hand, Wade's difficult situation may improve for a while because …
On the other hand, online education is unlikely to completely solve his problems as …

3 Conclusion

The purpose of the conclusion is to round off your argumentative text. For this reason you should not present any new arguments but rather draw a logical conclusion from your line of arguments in order to support your thesis, for example predict what will happen to Wade.

Summing up	*In brief ('kurz gesagt'), …* *To sum up, …* *In conclusion, I would like to say that …* *In the final analysis ('letztendlich', 'alles in allem'), …*

Complete the following conclusion by briefly stating your view and adding your own idea of how Wade might overcome his problem.

To sum up, in my opinion Wade's escape into the virtual world will only create more problems. Instead of trying to avoid all human interaction, he should rather …

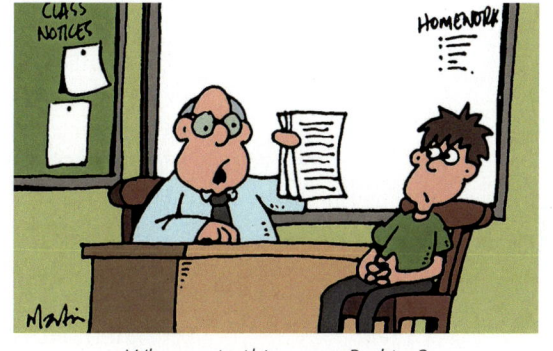

Who wrote this essay, Perkins?
You or Google?

A3 Digital media at school *Gerhard Witossek*

The following text is from the home page of a German educational institution. It includes information on the kinds of devices and services that are suitable for school, their benefits and potential drawbacks.

Digitale Medien im Lehr- und Lernprozess

Im Wandel

Ist von digitalen Medien im Unterricht die Rede, heißt das in vielen Schulen die Nutzung von Internet, Lernplattformen und Beamern. Diese sind in die Klassenräume eingezogen und sind weitgehend Bestandteil modernen Unterrichts.

In den letzten Jahren hat sich die Veränderungsdynamik deutlich beschleunigt: In 5
der gegenwärtigen Diskussion geht es um die Nutzung von „interaktiven White-
boards", „Clouds", „Tablet-PCs" und „Smartphones". Insbesondere die Tablet-PCs, großformatige Smartphones und die Arbeitsmöglichkeiten in der Cloud entwickeln sich rasant weiter.

Dabei stellt sich die Frage, wie diese Medien zielgerichtet im Unterricht eingesetzt 10
werden können. Digitale Medien sollen nicht zum Selbstzweck werden, sondern den Lehr-Lern-Prozess fördern. Darüber hinaus soll den Schülerinnen und Schülern ein sinnvoller und reflektierter Umgang mit den neuen Technologien vermittelt werden. Es gilt also, mediendidaktische, medienerzieherische und mediengestalterische Kompetenzen zu entwickeln und miteinander in Einklang zu bringen. 15

Im Unterricht

Digitale Medien sicher zu beherrschen, die neuen Entwicklungen zu verfolgen und sinnvoll in den Lehr-Lern-Prozess zu implementieren, stellt für die einzelne Lehrkraft eine große Aufgabe dar. Neben anderen und bewährten Medien und Methoden sollen digitale Medien den Unterricht bereichern: Veranschaulichung, Handlungs- 20
orientierung oder die Förderung sozialer Kompetenzen sind nur einige Anfor-
derungen an den Unterricht, die leichter mit digitalen Medien erfüllt werden können.

Die Arbeit mit digitalen Medien ermöglicht auch neue Unterrichtsstrukturen. Die üblichen 45-Minuten-Einheiten können besser verbunden werden. An Kreidetafeln lebte das erarbeitete Ergebnis bislang meist nur in den Heften der Schüler fort. Bedient man sich digitaler Tafeln oder Lernplattformen zur Sicherung der Ergebnisse, können diese wieder gezeigt, verändert und weiterentwickelt werden. Der „rote Faden" einer 30 Unterrichtssequenz wird da-
durch deutlicher und die Entwicklungsschritte im Unter-
richt greifbarer.

Digitale Medien können 35 Schülerinnen und Schülern auch ein anderes Lernen außerhalb der Schule ermöglichen. Beispielsweise können Unter-
richtsmaterialien in die Cloud gestellt, in-
teraktive Übungen im Internet genutzt oder Apps sinnvoll eingesetzt werden. [...]

False friends

Beamer
= video projector
Handy = mobile phone/
cellphone
(Lautsprecher-)Box
= (loud)speaker

Die Chancen

Der Einsatz digitaler Medien im Unterricht ist integraler Bestandteil zeitgemäßen
45 pädagogischen Handelns. Schülerinnen und Schüler wachsen mit den neuen
Technologien auf, sie gehören zu den Kulturtechniken unserer Gesellschaft. Deshalb
liegt es auch in der Verantwortung der Schule, dazu beizutragen, dass Kinder und
Jugendliche Medienkompetenz entwickeln können. Es darf auch nicht vergessen
werden, dass Jugendliche bereits von sich aus digitale Medien für die Schule nutzen.
50 Beispielsweise recherchieren sie mit Hilfe des mobilen Internets, tauschen sich per
Facebook über Unterrichtsinhalte aus oder stellen sich in der Cloud gegenseitig
Arbeitsmaterialien bereit. Diese generelle Bereitschaft zum Umgang mit digitalen
Medien kann für den Unterricht produktiv genutzt werden.

Digitale Medien können auch die Lehrkraft entlasten. Im Internet finden sich Un-
55 terrichtsmaterialien, Freeware, Apps oder Lernplattformen, die schnell verfügbar und
benutzerfreundlich sind. Zum Beispiel können der Tafelanschrieb am interaktiven
Whiteboard abgespeichert, interaktive Übungen nach Hause mitgegeben oder Ar-
beitsblätter online zur Verfügung gestellt werden.

Die Nutzung neuer Medien im Unterricht bereitet Jugendliche auf ihr Arbeits-
60 leben vor: In fast allen Berufen ist der Computer das Arbeitsmittel schlechthin. Die
hohe Veränderungsdynamik sorgt auch hier für schnelle Entwicklungen, auf die
Schülerinnen und Schüler vorbereitet werden müssen.

Die Risiken

Jugendliche werden häufig als „digital natives" bezeichnet, also als eine Generation,
65 die mit neuen Medien aufwächst und in deren Alltag die Nutzung digitaler Medien
ganz normal ist. Dies führt allerdings nicht automatisch zu einem reflektierten und
bedachten Umgang mit den Möglichkeiten der digitalen Welt. Beschäftigt man sich
im Unterricht näher mit dem Schutz persönlicher Daten in sozialen Netzwerken, so
zeigt sich sehr schnell, dass längst nicht alle Schülerinnen und Schüler die Risiken
70 überblicken.

From: *Münchner Kommunaler Bildungsserver*, October 2014

Mediation (German → English)

Imagine you are spending a school year as an exchange student at a high school
in Oregon, USA. Your exchange school is about to introduce a new media
concept. In order to incorporate a wide range of ideas, all of its exchange
students are asked to outline the role of digital media at school in their home
countries. Use the German article as the basis for your English presentation to
the school board. Make some notes.

"Can't I just email you a link to my blog, miss?"

LANGUAGE AWARENESS

Addressing an intended target audience
Most texts are directed at a particular audience. Keep this in mind when mediating and trying to overcome cultural differences. Avoid misunderstandings by adapting your style and register to your intended audience.

▶ LA 4: Influencing through language

▶ SF 41: Mediation of written and oral texts
▶ SF 24: Giving a presentation

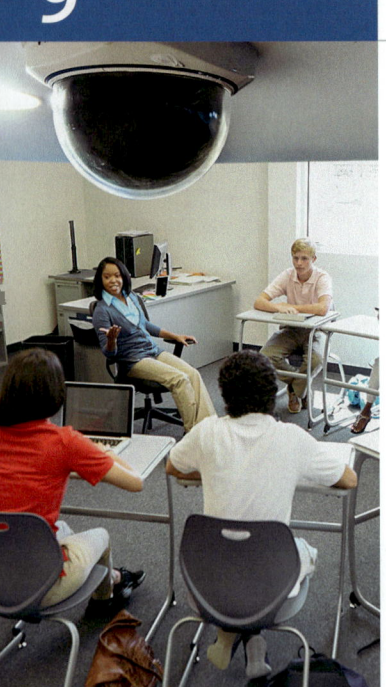

Being on display

B1 Should classrooms have video cameras?

- Work in pairs. Partner A deals with text **1** (T1), partner B with text **2** (T2). Read your text and take notes of the arguments you find.

T1	YES

Cameras are needed for protection
Everybody seems to feel okay about video cameras in public places like subway stations and shopping malls, where they make people feel safer. So why shouldn't cameras be installed in classrooms? Schools are public places too; that's why they're called *public* schools. Anybody who doesn't like this can transfer to a private school.   5

Classroom cameras would protect the rights of students and teachers. Like, if some student thinks his teacher has got something against him, he can refer to the video recording as proof. In the same way, it would protect students who might otherwise become victims of bullying. It would also be a great help for a teacher who is wrongly accused of misconduct in class.   10

Of course, there's a privacy issue here as well, but there is no reason why it can't be solved. The recordings would be kept locked away in the Principal's office, with limited access for other people. After 24 hours they would be automatically deleted. All in all, I would say video surveillance is a help, not   15
a hazard.

T1
11 **misconduct** wrong behaviour
16 **hazard** risk, danger

T2
6 **unbearable** intolerable

COMPREHENSION ◀

1 Collecting arguments
Share your arguments with your partner and discuss which ones you consider most convincing.

LANGUAGE AWARENESS ◀

▶ LP 11: Using the right register

2 Using more formal language
Texts T1 and T2 contain some elements of informal language. In an argumentative text, you should aim at using more formal language. Rewrite the underlined sentences or parts of these sentences using a more formal *register:
1 Everybody seems to feel okay about video cameras in public places like subway stations and shopping malls. (T1, l. 2)
2 Like, if some student thinks his teacher has got something against him, he can refer to the video recording as proof. (T1, ll. 7–9)
3 This is really bad for a place where you are supposed to be able to trust other people. (T2, ll. 11–12)
4 Most bullies aren't that dumb—they don't bully when adults are watching. (T2, ll. 13–14)

■ FACT FILE

CCTV (closed-circuit television) is a system in which television signals are not publicly broadcast but are monitored only by those people who have access to the system's content 5 (**'closed circuit'** ['sɜːkɪt]). The primary purpose of CCTV is to reduce crime and anti-social behaviour, especially in public places and shops. With around 4.2 million CCTV cameras 10 (one for every 14 people), Britain has become the most watched country in the world, a **'surveillance society'**.

What would be your immediate reaction to CCTV cameras in your classroom? Make notes and discuss them with a partner.

NO 👎 **T2**

Cameras do more harm than good
I do not believe that cameras would create an atmosphere of trust and security in the classroom. The opposite is true. Both students and teachers would have the feeling that they are being watched all the time (whether 5 or not this is actually true). Many students have trouble talking in front of others. Cameras would make the situation unbearable for them. Teachers might be afraid to say anything meaningful to a student because the recording could be used against them (by the school administration or by a lawyer representing the student's family, for example). Presumably both 10 students and teachers would feel like inmates in a prison with cameras watching them. This is really bad for a place where you are supposed to be able to trust other people. It's also naïve to think that cameras can stop bullying. Most bullies aren't that dumb—they don't bully when adults are watching. Cameras would just push bullying out of sight, into cyberspace or 15 the toilet stalls. That is why I think classroom cameras are a bad idea.

■ TROUBLE SPOT

actual ['æktʃuəl] = *tatsächlich, wirklich, konkret*
actually (l. 5) = *eigentlich, wirklich*
But: *aktuell* = **topical, current**

▶ LP 16: Avoiding Germanisms

■ LANGUAGE AWARENESS

Recognizing false friends
When translating from German into English, beware of Germanisms and outright mistakes by watching out for false friends. For examples, see the TROUBLE SPOTs above and on p. 196. Other examples:
prägnant ≠ **pregnant**
Kittchen ≠ **kitchen**
bekommen ≠ **become**
Gymnasium ≠ **gymnasium**

▶ LA 3: Similarities and differences of languages

BEYOND THE TEXT ◀

3 Discussing the pros and cons of surveillance at school
Get together in groups of four and do the following task:
As there have been some cases of bullying and vandalism at your school, the school board wants to introduce CCTV cameras inside and outside the school building (except for the private toilet cubicles) to monitor and protect the students.
As student representatives you are on a committee that will be heard before the school board's final decision.
a Discuss the pros and cons of the proposed idea.
b Develop a concept that you consider acceptable for your school.
c Present your concept to the school board (i.e. the class).

SUPPORT ▶ p. 242

CD1 03

game changer sth. that changes a
situation completely

B2 9/11 – a game changer   *Barack Obama*

*The following extract is taken from remarks on US intelligence programmes by
US President Barack Obama on 17 January 2014.*

- Study the word cloud below, which contains the most frequently used
  words in Obama's remarks. The size of the letters indicates the frequency
  of the words. Work with a partner and speculate on the general content
  of Obama's remarks, using as many words from the cloud as possible.

---

1 **intelligence** [ɪnˈtelɪdʒəns]
secret information about an
enemy
2 **President Truman (Harry S.
Truman)** 33rd US President
(1945–1953)
4 **avert sth.** [əˈvɜːt] prevent sth.
6 **anchor sth.** [ˈæŋkə] fix sth.
firmly
7 **checks and balances** mutual
control

> **■ TROUBLE SPOT**
>
> **ordinary** [BE: ˈɔːdnri,
> AE: ˈɔːrdneri] (ll. 7–8)
> = *gewöhnlich, durchschnittlich*
> But: *ordinär* = **vulgar** [ˈvʌlgə]

9 **informer** sb. who gives away
secrets, usually for money
13 **revelation** [ˌrevəˈleɪʃn] act of
disclosing secrets
15 **twilight** (here) final stage of sth.
when it becomes weaker or less
important than it used to be
18 **emerge** [ɪˈmɜːdʒ] appear, to
become known
19 **proliferation** [prəˌlɪfəˈreɪʃn]
rapid increase

Throughout American history, intelligence has helped secure our country and our
freedoms. [...] (I)n the early days of the Cold War, President Truman created the
National Security Agency, or NSA, to give us insights into the Soviet bloc, and provide
our leaders with information they needed to confront aggression and avert catastrophe.

Throughout this evolution, we benefited from both our Constitution and our tradi-   5
tions of limited government. U.S. intelligence agencies were anchored in a system of
checks and balances – with oversight from elected leaders, and protections for ordinary citizens. Meanwhile, totalitarian states like East Germany offered a cautionary
tale of what could happen when vast, unchecked surveillance turned citizens into in-
formers, and persecuted people for what they said in the privacy of their own homes.   10

In fact, even the United States proved not to be immune to the abuse of surveillance. And in the 1960s, government spied on civil rights leaders and critics of the
Vietnam War. And partly in response to these revelations, additional laws were established in the 1970s to ensure that our intelligence capabilities could not be misused
against our citizens. In the long, twilight struggle against Communism, we had been   15
reminded that the very liberties that we sought to preserve could not be sacrificed at
the altar of national security.

If the fall of the Soviet Union left America without a competing superpower, emerging threats from terrorist groups, and the proliferation of weapons of mass destruction placed new and in some ways more complicated demands on our intelligence   20
agencies. Globalization and the Internet made these threats more acute, as technology erased borders and empowered individuals to project great violence, as well as
great good. Moreover, these new threats raised new legal and new policy questions.

For while few doubted the legitimacy of spying on hostile states, our framework of
laws was not fully adapted to prevent terrorist attacks by individuals acting on their
own, or acting in small, ideologically driven groups on behalf of a foreign power.

The horror of September 11th brought all these issues to the fore. Across the political spectrum, Americans recognized that we had to adapt to a world in which a bomb
could be built in a basement, and our electric grid could be shut down by operators
an ocean away. We were shaken by the signs we had missed leading up to the attacks
– how the hijackers had made phone calls to known extremists and traveled to suspi-
cious places. So we demanded that our intelligence community improve its capabilities, and that law enforcement change practices to focus more on preventing attacks
before they happen than prosecuting terrorists after an attack.

It is hard to overstate the transformation America's intelligence community had to
go through after 9/11. Our agencies suddenly needed to do far more than the traditional mission of monitoring hostile powers and gathering information for policy-
makers. Instead, they were now asked to identify and target plotters in some of the
most remote parts of the world, and to anticipate the actions of networks that, by their
very nature, cannot be easily penetrated with spies or informants.[1]

---

24 hostile [BE: 'hɒstaɪl, AE: 'hɑːstl]
belonging to the enemy
26 on behalf of as a representative of
27 bring sth. to the fore gain public attention for sth.
38 plotter sb. making secret plans to harm others

◼ **FACT FILE**

9/11 refers to September 11th, 2001. On this date four planes were hijacked by terrorists in the USA. One plane crashed in Pennsylvania, one destroyed part of the Pentagon in Virginia, and two flew into the World Trade Center, New York City. About 3,000 people were killed in these attacks which were conducted by the ex-treme Islamic group Al Qaeda [æl'kaɪdə].

▶ SF 38: Writing a well-structured text

COMPREHENSION ◀

1 The structure of the text
  a Divide this extract into parts and give headings to each part.
  b Outline Obama's argumentation in your own words.

ANALYSIS ◀

2 Understanding the title
Explain why 9/11 can be considered a 'game changer' with regard to US security policy.

▶ SF 17: Analysing stylistic devices
▶ Glossary, p. 360

3 Analysing stylistic devices
  a The phrases in the box on the right are quotes[1] from the text. Explain their meaning.
  b Point out what *stylistic device is used in all of these phrases and analyse the effect achieved by employing it.
  c Go over the text again and find at least one example of an *antithesis. Describe its effect on the reader.

- 'U.S. intelligence agencies were anchored in a system of checks and balances' (ll. 6–7)
- 'states like East Germany offered a cautionary tale' (ll. 8–9)
- 'the very liberties that we sought to preserve could not be sacrificed at the altar of national security' (ll. 16–17)

BEYOND THE TEXT ◀

4 Evaluating a cartoon
  a Analyse the cartoon on the right, keeping in mind some of the information presented in Obama's speech.
  b **CHALLENGE** ▶ 'It is hard to overstate the trans-formation America's intelligence community had to go through after 9/11.' (ll. 35–36)[1]
Look for a cartoon on the internet that expresses the idea of the quote, print it and bring it along to class. Tape it to the wall of your classroom and analyse it orally with your classmates as they walk from cartoon to cartoon.
After examining all the cartoons, stand next to the one you prefer in order to select the most popular cartoon. Be prepared to justify your choice.

▶ SF 13: Analysing cartoons

---

[1] Text and quotes from 'Remarks by the President on Review of Signals Intelligence', official website of the White House, 17 January 2014

Part C

Truth and lies in modern media

C1 The future of fake news: don't believe everything you read, see or hear *Olivia Solon*

'Fake news' – how is it produced, how can we avoid being fooled by it?
The following article looks at some recent technological developments.

- Have you ever been tricked by fake news or manipulated pictures on the internet or in social media? Before reading the text, talk to a partner and tell each other about your experiences.

In an age of Photoshop, filters and social media, many of us are used to seeing manipulated pictures – subjects become slimmer and smoother or, in the case of Snapchat, transformed into puppies.

However, there's a new breed of video and audio manipulation tools, made possible by advances in artificial intelligence and computer graphics, that will allow for the creation of realistic looking footage of public figures appearing to say, well, anything. Trump declaring his proclivity for water sports. Hillary Clinton describing the stolen children she keeps locked in her wine cellar. Tom Cruise finally admitting what we suspected all along … that he's a Brony. 5

This is the future of fake news. We've long been told not to believe everything we read, but soon we'll have to question everything we see and hear as well. 10

For now, there are several research teams working on capturing and synthesizing different visual and and audio elements of human behavior.

Software developed at Stanford University is able to manipulate video footage of public figures to allow a second person to put words in their mouth – in real time. Face2Face captures the second person's facial expressions as they talk into a webcam and then morphs those movements directly onto the face of the person in the original video. The research team demonstrated their technology by puppeteering videos of George W Bush, Vladimir Putin and Donald Trump. 15

On its own, Face2Face is a fun plaything for creating memes and entertaining late night talk show hosts. However, with the addition of a synthesized voice, it becomes more convincing – not only does the digital puppet look like the politician, but it can also sound like the politician. 20

A research team at the University of Alabama at Birmingham has been working on voice impersonation. With 3–5 minutes of audio of a victim's voice – taken live or from YouTube videos or radio shows – an attacker can create a synthesized voice that can fool both humans and voice biometric security systems used by some banks and smartphones. The attacker can then talk into a microphone and the software will convert it so that the words sound like they are being spoken by the victim – whether that's over the phone or on a radio show. 25 30

Canadian startup Lyrebird has developed similar capabilities, which it says can be used to turn text into on-the-spot audiobooks 'read' by famous voices or for characters in video games.

Although their intentions may be well-meaning, voice-morphing technology could be combined with face-morphing technology to create convincing fake statements by public figures. 35

You only have to look at the University of Washington's Synthesizing Obama project, where they took the audio from one of Obama's speeches and used it to

6 **footage** ['fʊtɪdʒ] *Film(material)*
7 **proclivity for sth./for doing sth.** natural tendency to do sth. that is mostly bad
9 **Brony** *(derog)* fan of the show *My Little Pony*
17 **morph sb./sth. into sb./sth.** change the shape or character of sb./sth. into sb./sth. else, especially by means of computer-generated animation
18 **puppeteer** person who performs with puppets to entertain people
20 **meme** [miːm] *(here)* amusing or interesting picture, video, etc. that is spread widely through the internet
25 **impersonation** act of pretending to be another person (in order to trick people or entertain them)

40 animate his face in an entirely different video with incredible accuracy (thanks to training a recurrent neural network with hours of footage), to get a sense of how insidious these adulterations can be.

Beyond fake news there are many other implications, said Nitesh Saxena, associate professor and research director of the University of Alabama at Birmingham's depart-45 ment of computer science. 'You could leave fake voice messages posing as someone's mum. Or defame someone and post the audio samples online.'

These morphing technologies aren't yet perfect. The facial expressions in the videos can seem a little distorted or unnatural and the voices can sound a little robotic.

But given time, they will be able to faithfully recreate the sound or appearance of a person – to the point where it 50 might be very difficult for humans to detect the fraud.

Given the erosion of trust in the media and the rampant spread of hoaxes via social media, it will become even more important for news organizations to scrutinize content that looks and sounds like the real deal.

55 Telltale signs will be where the video or audio was created, who else was at the event and whether the weather conditions match the records of that day.

People should also be looking at the lighting and shadows in the video, whether all of the elements featured in the 60 frame are the right size, and whether the audio is synced perfectly, said Mandy Jenkins, from social news company Storyful, which specializes in verifying news content.

Doctored content might not pass the scrutiny of a rigorous newsroom, but if posted as a grainy video to social 65 media it could spread virally and trigger a public relations, political or diplomatic disaster. Imagine Trump declaring war on North Korea, for example.

'If someone looks like Trump and speaks like Trump they will think it's Trump,' said Saxena.

70 'We already see it doesn't even take doctored audio or video to make people believe something that isn't true,' added Jenkins. 'This has the potential to make it worse.'

From: 'The future of fake news: don't believe everything you read, see or hear', *The Guardian*, 26 July 2017

HOW TO SPOT FAKE NEWS

CONSIDER THE SOURCE
Click away from the story to investigate the site, its mission and its contact info.

READ BEYOND
Headlines can be outrageous in an effort to get clicks. What's the whole story?

CHECK THE AUTHOR
Do a quick search on the author. Are they credible? Are they real?

SUPPORTING SOURCES?
Click on those links. Determine if the info given actually supports the story.

CHECK THE DATE
Reposting old news stories doesn't mean they're relevant to current events.

IS IT A JOKE?
If it is too outlandish, it might be satire. Research the site and author to be sure.

CHECK YOUR BIASES
Consider if your own beliefs could affect your judgement.

ASK THE EXPERTS
Ask a librarian, or consult a fact-checking site.

IFLA
International Federation of Library Associations and Institutions

COMPREHENSION ◀

1 Words and ideas

Step 1 On your own, write the following terms on cards and sort them on two piles: one with terms that you can easily explain with reference to the text and one with terms you are not sure about.

> *adulteration • doctored content • erosion of trust • fake news • hoaxes • manipulated pictures • meme • morphing technology • news organizations • political or diplomatic disaster • public figures • public relations • realistic looking news footage • real time • scrutinize • telltale signs • voice impersonation*

Step 2 With a partner, talk about the terms on your second pile. Make sure that you can explain them to each other. Use the text or a dictionary.

Step 3 Each partner takes one complete set of cards and arranges them in a way which shows best how they can be related to each other.

Step 4 Present and explain your arrangements to each other. Discuss differences and ask and answer questions.

—————————————————————————————— ANALYSIS ◀

2 What makes the text appealing?
Analyse the methods used to make the text appealing.
SUPPORT ▶ p. 243

—————————————————————————— LANGUAGE AWARENESS ◀

3 Inversion
a Look at ll. 22–23 again. Explain why the auxiliary *does* comes before the subject in the first half of the sentence *(does the digital puppet look)* while the auxiliary *can* comes after the subject in the second half *(it can also sound)*.
b CHALLENGE ▶ Write three more sentences about the future of fake news that start with *Not only … (but …)*.

4 Diction
The writer uses many terms and expressions that refer to deceit. Check the use of the words below in a monolingual dictionary. Make sure you understand their implications and then try and sort them according to the intensity of their meaning (from the weakest / most neutral to the strongest) into four groups.

rather neutral			very strong

*fake • fraud • deceit • hoax • adulteration • manipulation •
impersonation • trick*

—————————————————————————————— BEYOND THE TEXT ◀

5 YOU CHOOSE ▶ **Fake news**

a Write a guideline for the school magazine in which you inform students about recent technical developments and also give advice. You may want to refer to the illustration on page 199 for ideas.
SUPPORT ▶ p. 243

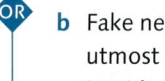

b Fake news – mass hysteria or utmost damage to public trust in the media? Discuss.
SUPPORT ▶ p. 243

LANGUAGE AWARENESS —

Using a word in its correct context
The better you know in what kind of different contexts a particular word can be used, the better you understand what implications that word has and the more effectively can you use it. It helps to carefully study the sample sentences in dictionary entries.

▶ LA 1: Varieties of English
▶ LA 2: Communication problems and compensation strategies

Discussing the pros and cons of modern media

Write a text on the following topic:

Will the media change our lives for better or worse over the next ten years? Discuss.

"PLEASE DON'T JUDGE ME BY MY YOUTUBE VIDEOS!"

Instructions

1   Create four posters to place along the walls of your classroom. Each poster will have one of the following headings: **the internet – digital image processing – school/work – surveillance**. Divide the posters vertically into two parts for the positive and negative aspects of the headings.

The internet	**Digital image processing**	**School/Work**	**Surveillance**
positive	positive	positive	positive
negative	negative	negative	negative

2   Choose one expert per poster.

3   The rest of the class walk from poster to poster, suggesting their ideas for each of the topics to the experts, who are to write down the entries on the posters.

4   Stand next to the poster which you would like to use as the basis for your text.

5   Discuss with your classmates who have chosen the same poster as you which aspects on the poster you consider most important.

6   Check Focus on Skills (pp. 190–191) and write an argumentative text, narrowing down the topic ('Will the media change our lives for better or worse over the next ten years?') to the heading of your chosen poster.

▶ SF 34: Argumentative writing

7   Having finished this task, exchange your text with a classmate who has chosen the same topic. Your teacher will give you an assessment sheet to fill work. Evaluate each other's work, keeping in mind what you have learnt in this chapter.

▶ SF 40: Proofreading

10 Urban, Suburban and Rural Life

A

B

Download a list of chapter vocab here: **Webcode** context-27

1 Different places
a THINK Describe the five photos A–E. Imagine what kind of lives people may lead there (e.g. family size, profession, housing, leisure activities).
b PAIR Compare your ideas with a partner.
c SHARE Compare your ideas with another pair. As a group, agree on which one of the above locations you would most like to live in.

 CD3 04
▶ SF 22: Listening

2 Different lifestyles
a Listen to the five statements and match them to the photos. Give reasons for your choices.
b Listen to the statements again, this time taking notes. Point out advantages and disadvantages of living in each place.

C

D

E

3 Should I stay or should I go?

▶ SF 24: Giving a presentation

a Prepare a two-minute presentation on the place where you live.
Make notes, e.g. on index cards or in a mind map.

b Listen to some of the presentations.

c With a partner, talk about why you are planning to stay in your town or area
in the future – or, alternatively, why you would like to move elsewhere.

PREVIEW

In this chapter you will learn about trends and developments of different living spaces and lifestyles in big
cities, suburbs, small towns and rural areas.

Main topics

- Urban change .... p. 206
- Suburban life .... p. 214
- Living in the country .... p. 218

Focus on Skills: SPEAKING

- Speaking in a panel discussion .... p. 208
Chapter Task: Having a panel discussion on
the pros and cons of living in a city, a suburb
or the country .... p. 221

CD3 05

Listen to an audio version of the text on the CD or download it here:

 Webcode context-28

The world becomes urbanized

The rapid growth of cities

In 2007, for the first time in history, more people worldwide were living in towns and cities than in rural areas. In many developing countries, cities continue to grow so rapidly that these developing countries are catching up with developed countries when it comes to urban living. As developing countries become more urbanized and young people worldwide continue to seek employment and social opportunities that only city life can provide, urban sprawl will simply continue to spread in the years to come. The major challenge that lies ahead for both developed and developing countries is keeping pace with this continuing urbanization. A basic infrastructure, complete with sanitation facilities, access to safe drinking water, adequate housing and education, an efficient transportation network and adequate recreational amenities is necessary for the sustainable growth of a city.

The changing face of western cities

The urban landscape changes with the expansion of cities, as well as with the movement of people within these cities. Sprawling suburbs call for new solutions to provide sustainable living for everybody. A well-developed infra-structure, as well as ample job opportunities, are needed to prevent expanding cities from deteriorating. Due to job opportunities still mostly being found in the city centre, a high number of jobholders who live in suburban areas spend a lot of time commuting to and from work on a daily basis. Thus, a major challenge for big cities is how to cope with the rising number of commuters. One of the most urgent problems in this respect is air pollution, which is a direct result of increased traffic and the corresponding clogged streets and traffic jams. Possible solutions could include carpooling, car sharing and/or more efficient public transportation networks. The relocation of people from the outer suburbs to near and around the city centre (usually in order to reduce travel time and cost) seems to be a new trend. There is a whole new breed of city dwellers, found in the young affluent professionals who are drawn to city centres and their trendy lifestyles. As a result, these inner-city areas benefit from urban revitali-zation; whereas, in juxtaposition, other city areas might slowly decay and end up in a state of degradation (as is sometimes the case with the development of city slums).

Suburbs, small towns and rural areas

Due to urban growth, rural areas and small towns are facing a decline in population. City migrants leave an aging rural population behind. Opportunities for employment as well as other incentives are needed to encourage the inhabitants to stay in their native rural surroundings or to attract newcomers to a life in the countryside.

1 Words in use: Comprehension

a Find highlighted words or phrases in the text that describe or name the following:

1 make progress at the same rate as somebody or something else
2 the basic systems and services needed for a city to run smoothly
3 facilities for people's enjoyment when they are not working
4 travelling to and from work
5 decline naturally or economically
6 the central section of a large city
7 all the people who live in the countryside

b Give definitions or use examples as in **a** to explain the following highlighted terms from the text

1 urban sprawl   3 affluent
2 housing   4 city dweller

▶ SF 1: Dealing with unknown or new words

▶ SF 6: Paraphrasing

2 Word families

a Copy out and complete the table below. Use your dictionary if necessary.

Verb	Noun	Adjective	Participle
			urbanized
		sustainable	
	sprawl		
commute			

▶ SF 2: Using a dictionary and a grammar book

▶ LP 20: Word formation

b Choose three more highlighted words from the text, add them to your table and form word-families.

3 Collocations

a Each of the verbs on the right can be used with all of the words or phrases in each group below. Some of the collocations are in the text on the opposite page.

1 … jobs, entertainment, accommodation, a better life
   … sustainable living, opportunities, more space, better conditions
2 … infrastructure, measures, facilities, knowledge
   … rush-hour traffic, unnecessary travel time, mistakes
   … bigger, urbanized, a centre, a crucial issue

b Use each of the verbs from **a** in a collocation and write meaningful sentences.

avoid • become • provide • require • seek

▶ LP 19: Collocations

4 Cartoon

Describe and analyse the cartoon on p. 204. Use as many of the highlighted phrases from the text in your description as possible.

▶ SF 13: Analysing cartoons

Big-city life

A1 Living in London, New York, Rio de Janeiro

Carlene Thomas-Bailey

The following are excerpts from a series of interviews that the Guardian *conducted with young people around the world about how they feel about their home cities.*

- Before reading, collect information about London, New York and Rio de Janeiro and arrange it in a mind map ('Aspects of big-city life').

FACT FILE

A **neighbourhood** is a district or an area within a town or city. Apart from having a geographic meaning the term also refers to the people living in such a district and therefore has a social, people-oriented component.
See also the Fact File *Ethnic neighbourhoods* (p. 105).

10 **Brixton** district of south London, known for its multi-ethnic community

10 **racially profile sb.** categorize sb. according to their race or ethnicity
13 **CitiBike** bike sharing system in New York City

A **Aida Gugsa (18), Sydenham, south London**

I've been living in Sydenham all my life and everyone is very friendly, I know all the
5 neighbours, I feel safe. I had a small kitchen fire last year when I burned a pot and my neighbours came to help, called the fire brigade, got it all sorted. If someone loses their keys, one of us will have a spare
10 key, it's very friendly. Brixton, too, looks a lot better now it's had some special attention, it's really grown and adapted through the years. There is still a sense of community but it feels safer than it was before, and some will say it's lost its character but I think it's gained more
15 character. I think cutting the crime and cleaning up the area, it brightened up Brixton and more people come to the area and feel safe and get to experience the culture. [...] London is a beautiful city. Ideally, I would prefer to see less homelessness, more places to inspire young people to grow and find paths for their futures, a better education system that helped everyone
20 and gave equal opportunities and resources to school boroughs. I'd like better work experience opportunities, centres which can teach people how to use money wisely, and more outdoor activities for all ages.

B

Kafila Muhammad (16), Williamsburg, Brooklyn (NY)

How safe I feel depends on what neighborhood I am in. Some are worse than others – it depends on the demographics: if the community is
5 low-income or not, where it's located, how big the police presence is in the community. Sometimes if there is more police I feel safer, and sometimes I feel more threatened because there is also the chance of being racially profiled. [...] I
10 think that transportation in NYC is amazing because we don't have to have a car; you can get anywhere on a bike or the subway or buses, or even walking because of the bridges. In my neighborhood we have more bike lanes now, and the new CitiBikes are great too. I use so many apps daily to navigate the city – Hopstop [a transit directions app] is amazing if you want to get anywhere in NYC and you need a shortcut.
15

Michel Silva (19), Rocinha favela, southern zone of Rio de Janeiro C

Rocinha is a very good favela to live in. We don't need to go into another neighbourhood to buy a product. There are five public schools, community and private nurseries. There are thousands of shops selling fresh fruit and vegetables. In addition there are two large supermarkets and an appliance 5 and electronics store. There is shopping in Rocinha. Residents use the malls in the neighbourhoods around the favela, but feel discriminated against by their lack of material wealth. The locals are friendly and there is not much prejudice among Rocinha residents. The problem is the discrimination slumdwellers suffer from middle-class neighbourhoods looking 10 down on us. Formerly there was a prejudice towards young people; all young children were thought to be drug dealers. The reality has changed a lot; young people are more interested in leisure activities and learning. [...] I want a city with fewer cars and better public transport services. Less trash on the floor, better sanitation in the slums, the demilitarisation of culture 15 in the slums, more leisure options, less pollution on beaches and less dishonesty among top politicians.

From: 'Cities debate: teenagers talk London, New York, Johannesburg and Rio de Janeiro', *The Guardian*, 29 January 2014

FACT FILE
A **favela** *(Portuguese)* is a poor area within or on the outskirts of Brazil's large cities, especially Rio de Janeiro.

LANGUAGE AWARENESS
Regional varieties
Distinctive regional varieties of a language may contribute to the special character of a city or even a quarter or neighbourhood. In the UK, there are Cockney (the dialect spoken in parts of the City of London around St. Mary-le-Bow), Glaswegian ('Glasgow patter', a Scots dialect spoken in and around Glasgow), Mancunian (spoken in Greater Manchester) and many others.

▶ LA 1: Varieties of English

COMPREHENSION ◀

1 City life, pro and con

  a Form three groups. Each group is given a letter A–C. Collect positive and negative aspects of city life as presented by Aida (A), Kafila (B) and Michel (C). Arrange your findings in a table.

  b In your groups, add more arguments from your mind maps.

LANGUAGE AWARENESS ◀

2 Using linking words

  a Describe the style of the three texts.

  b Rewrite one of the texts, including a range of linking words.

    ▶ LANGUAGE HELP

BEYOND THE TEXT ◀

3 GROUP PUZZLE **Comparing cities**

Form new groups of 4–6 members. All three cities (cf. **1a**) should be represented in each group. Tell each other about the pros and cons of living in 'your' city.

4 YOU CHOOSE ▶ **Commenting or giving a speech**

London, New York, Rio or none of these – where would you like to work or study? Using your notes from the previous tasks,

  a … write a comment for a student magazine. **b** … prepare a three-minute speech.

LANGUAGE HELP
above all • although • at the same time • because • besides • consequently • first of all • furthermore • however • in addition • in fact • so

▶ LP 14: Linking words and phrases

▶ SF 34: Argumentative writing
▶ SF 25: Giving a speech

Part A

Speaking in a panel discussion

In a panel discussion, a group of experts or people with different opinions or from different backgrounds discuss a topic in front of an audience. An additional person not participating in the discussion serves as a moderator.

For the following role-play, imagine that you are at an international youth conference where you are going to take part in a panel discussion on the following topic: 'Big cities – attractive places for young people to live and study in?'

1 Preparing the discussion

a Form groups of 5–7 members. Each member chooses one of the following roles (cf. text **A1**, pp. 206–207):

1 Aida Gugsa's best friend,
2 a first-year-student in London,
3 a foreign-exchange student studying in New York City,
4 a young person from East Harlem, New York City,
5 Michel Silva's 16-year-old brother,
6 a German intern in Rio de Janeiro,
7 the moderator.

▶ SF 15: Marking up a text / Making and taking notes

b Individually, prepare your roles: what is your view of the topic under discussion? Make notes on role cards (see example on the right).

> *The moderator*
> - *is neutral,*
> - *does not judge the opinions of those on the panel,*
> - *knows the topic and the necessary vocabulary well,*
> - *prepares a short introduction,*
> - *prepares motivating questions.*

2 Collecting arguments

Re-examine text **A1** as well as your notes from the group puzzle (cf. **A1**, task **3**). Note down all the arguments that are appropriate to your role. Think of examples to illustrate your opinion. Your argumentation should be logical. Also think of possible arguments others might mention and how you might respond. Make notes.

I am …	*a first-year student in London.*
My view of the topic in short:	*Big cities are attractive and exciting. If only they weren't so expensive!*
Positive aspects of big cities:	*…*
Negative aspects:	*…*
My argumentation:	*…*

3 Practising interaction and discussion phrases

a Look up discussion phrases in the Skills File and note them down according to the following forms of interaction:

giving an opinion • asking for an opinion • agreeing • disagreeing • asking for clarification • adding a point • opening and closing a discussion

Add more phrases that you know. Compare your lists in your group.

▶ SF 27: Having a discussion

b Practise your discussions in your groups.

4 Holding the panel discussion

One of the groups is the panel and discusses the topic for 10 minutes, while the others listen, take notes and give feedback. Your teacher will give you an assessment sheet. Take turns.

■ **FACT FILE**

Changing urban lifestyles

Gentrification and hipsters

The term *gentrification* denotes a change in an urban neighbourhood, whereby more affluent residents move into a run-down inner-city area, causing property prices to rise and in turn attracting others with a similar income and lifestyle to follow. The new residents bring with them economic development and building activity as houses and flats are renovated and turned into upmarket accommodation. 'Hip' and trendy shops and restaurants open up. At the same time, the original residents are gradually forced out because they cannot pay the rising rents or property taxes. The term *hipsters* refers to an urban subculture which emerged among the millennial generation (see below). Hipsters are associated with a non-conformist, bohemian lifestyle.

Millennials

People who were teenagers around the year 2000 are sometimes referred to as *Millennials*, the *Millennial Generation* or as *Generation Y*. Compared to the generations before them, the Millennials seem to be not as well off economically and financially, although on average they are better educated than prior generations. *Internet Generation* is another name sometimes used for this age group which grew up during the early years of the internet and can hardly imagine a life without it. Millennials are very familiar with technology and love social media. Statistically, this generation is less likely to get married and form their own households before their early 30s.

Boomerang kids

Young adults of the Millennial Generation who return to the home of their childhood after living independently for some time are sometimes referred to as *boomerang kids*. Uncertain economic prospects and the high costs of living in a single household make them 'boomerang back' to the family nest. Other reasons for returning to the parental home are problems on the job market as well as rising rents and mortgages.

3–2–1 summary

Having read the texts above, write down
- *three important facts about urban lifestyles,*
- *two interesting ideas mentioned in the texts,*
- *one question that you have.*

Now share your ideas with a partner and try to answer each other's question.

■ **LANGUAGE AWARENESS**

A **neologism** is a word that is relatively recent, can often be attributed to a special event, fact or person and has not yet reached mainstream use. Digital media have sped up the creation and spread of neologisms. As lifestyles and generations have changed, terms naming them have appeared: *Lost Generation, Baby boomers, Millenials / Generation Y / Generation Me …*
Once a neologism becomes common and enters dictionaries, it loses its innovative character.

▶ LA 4: Influencing through language

🎧 **CD3** 06

flip the script *(infml)* digress from a topic *(vom Thema abschweifen)*
be a proxy for sth. *für etwas stellvertretend sein*
redlining *(n)* practice of denying certain services to (people living in) certain areas, esp. for racial reasons
tanning booth *(infml)* *Sonnenstudio*
tax abatement tax reduction

▶ SF 22: Listening

▶ SF 7: Working with closed test formats

▶ SF 15: Marking up a text / Making and taking notes

▶ SF 34: Argumentative writing

A2 Urban transformation

Many cities are undergoing economic change as new residents and businesses are moving in. The extract you are going to hear is from a radio debate titled 'Gentrification: progress or destruction?'.

— COMPREHENSION ◀

1 Listening for gist
Read the sentences below. Then listen to the audio, noting down for each sentence whether A, B, C or D is correct:

1 In the USA, gentrification is often not only a question of income but also of
   A religion
   B political views
   C race
   D health

2 Kevin Archer is not an example of a good
   A gentrifier
   B landlord
   C citizen
   D customer

3 John Murph claims that the incoming people
   A improve
   B colonize
   C beautify
   D vandalize
   the neighbourhood.

4 Lisa Sturtevant thinks that cities should encourage long-term residents to
   A stay
   B move away
   C pay higher rents
   D donate money

— ANALYSIS ◀

2 Listening for detail
   a Find a partner. Listen to the audio a second time. Find more information about the statements 1–4 listed above. Take notes.
   Partner A: Concentrate on sentences 1 and 2.
   Partner B: Concentrate on sentences 3 and 4.
   b Exchange your information with your partner.

— BEYOND THE TEXT ◀

3 What's your opinion?
   a With your partner, list positive and negative aspects of gentrification. State your own opinion.
   b **CHALLENGE**
   'Gentrification: progress or destruction?' Write a comment of about 200 words, discussing whether gentrification is beneficial or damaging to inner-city areas.

Next to be gentrified? Street in Brooklyn

A3 Urban decay, urban renewal

German essayist and journalist Katja Kullmann, author of the book Rasende Ruinen – Wie Detroit sich neu erfindet *(2012), was interviewed by Alexandra Rotter of the news magazine* Format. *Here is an excerpt.*

FORMAT · · · *Wie kam es dazu, dass Sie einen Monat lang in der „Shithole"
· · · · · · · · · · · genannten ehemaligen Autostadt Detroit gelebt haben? [...] Welche
· · · · · · · · · · · Erkenntnisse haben Sie durch den Besuch dieser schrumpfenden Stadt
· · · · · · · · · · · gewonnen?*

KULLMANN · Auch in Mitteleuropa gibt es Städte, vor allem in alten Industrie- · · 5
· · · · · · · · · · · zonen, die verwaisen, vergreisen und verarmen. Auf der anderen
· · · · · · · · · · · Seite steigen die Mieten in Städten wie Wien und Berlin. Im
· · · · · · · · · · · Grunde sind diese Entwicklungen zwei Seiten derselben Medaille.
· · · · · · · · · · · Vielleicht können wir in Detroit schon ein bisschen unsere
· · · · · · · · · · · Zukunft betrachten. · 10

FORMAT · · · *Eine düstere Zukunft?*

KULLMANN · Nein, nicht nur. Ein Beispiel: Jeder Dritte in Detroit lebt von
· · · · · · · · · · · Lebensmittelmarken. Daraus ist eine Non-Profit-Farming-
· · · · · · · · · · · Bewegung entstanden. Auf mehr als 70 Farmen in der Stadt wird
· · · · · · · · · · · Gemüse angebaut, Rezepte werden ausgetauscht. Das hat nichts · · 15
· · · · · · · · · · · mit Ökoträumerei zu tun – anders kommen die Menschen nicht
· · · · · · · · · · · zu Lebensmitteln. [...]

FORMAT · · · *Könnte man Städte wie Detroit nicht auch sterben lassen?*

KULLMANN · Man versucht, den Raum zu verkleinern, lässt bewusst Teile der
· · · · · · · · · · · Stadt sterben und gibt sie an die Natur zurück. Es wird versucht, · · 20
· · · · · · · · · · · Leute zu bewegen, ihre Häuser aufzugeben und in einen anderen
· · · · · · · · · · · Stadtteil zu ziehen. In der Innenstadt gibt es drei sogenannte
· · · · · · · · · · · *Demonstration Areas*: Dort werden Bushaltestellen erhalten und
· · · · · · · · · · · das Straßenlicht nicht abgedreht. Es sollen kleine Villages
· · · · · · · · · · · entstehen, wo wieder Bäcker oder Gemüseläden aufmachen. Für · · 25
· · · · · · · · · · · jene, die außerhalb dieser Viertel leben, ist es natürlich übel: Oft
· · · · · · · · · · · sind nicht einmal die Umzüge in Sozialwohnungen finanziert.
· · · · · · · · · · · Wenn es aber gelingt, die Stadt auf ein Drittel zu verkleinern,
· · · · · · · · · · · wäre Detroit eine grüne Stadt mit vielen Fahrradwegen.

FORMAT · · · *Was können andere Städte von Detroit lernen?* · · · · · · · · · · · · 30

KULLMANN · In Detroit gibt es dieselben Probleme wie in Europa und anderen
· · · · · · · · · · · Ländern: Die Schere zwischen Arm und Reich geht auf, die
· · · · · · · · · · · Jugend ist arbeitslos. Gerade die Jüngeren haben aber keine
· · · · · · · · · · · Scheu mehr, mit Leuten, die aus anderen Schichten kommen,
· · · · · · · · · · · zusammenzuarbeiten. Das macht die Welt von beiden Teilen · · · 35
· · · · · · · · · · · größer. Ich will nichts romantisieren, aber ich appelliere gegen
· · · · · · · · · · · die Statusangst, also die Angst, abzustürzen, denn sie macht die
· · · · · · · · · · · Welt noch ein bisschen feindlicher und neurotischer.

From: *Format*, 7 August 2013

Detroit – faces of a city

Mediation (German ➔ English)
Searching the internet for a school project on urban development in central Europe, you come across the above interview with Katja Kullmann. Write an email to an American friend, explaining what parallels there are between the situation in Detroit and that in other parts of the world.

▶ SF 41: Mediation of written and oral texts

DVD

▶ SF 23: Analysing a film

A4 Why US talent is moving to Detroit

Detroit, nicknamed the Motor City (cf. Fact File on the left), was always a centre of the automobile industry, with big employers such as General Motors or Chrysler based there. However, the city has undergone a dramatic change in recent decades.

─────────────────────────────── COMPREHENSION ◀

1 Challenge Detroit
Watch the video. Describe its content and state its purpose in one or two sentences.

2 Understanding the message
Watch the video again, taking notes on the following questions:
a What is Challenge Detroit? What are its goals and how is it financed?
b According to the video, what motivated urban planner Jason Zogg to come to Detroit?
c What is Zogg's building project about?
d How did Challenge Detroit fellow Marlo Staples become actively engaged in the project?
With a partner, take turns in answering the questions and adding to your partner's results.

─────────────────────────────────────── ANALYSIS ◀

3 How effective is it?
Form groups of four. Analyse how effective the video clip is. Observe the change of scenes as well as the effect the music may have on you.
SUPPORT ▶ p. 244

────────────────────────────── BEYOND THE FILM ◀

4 Pursuing a vision
Doyle Mosher, the president of Challenge Detroit, believes that an influx of bright young thinkers will create opportunities to revitalize Detroit's economy. Do you agree with him? Explain your answer.

CULTURE SPOT

For a number of years, London has been undergoing a major architectural transformation, perhaps the greatest since the Great Fire of 1666. London's skyline, instantly recognizable by such distinctive landmarks as Christopher Wren's Saint Paul's Cathedral (1711) and Sir Norman Fosters 'Gherkin' (2004), is changing rapidly by the addition of a great number of high-rise buildings. One of these is the skyscraper nicknamed 'The Shard' (2013). Reactions to the building have been rather mixed.

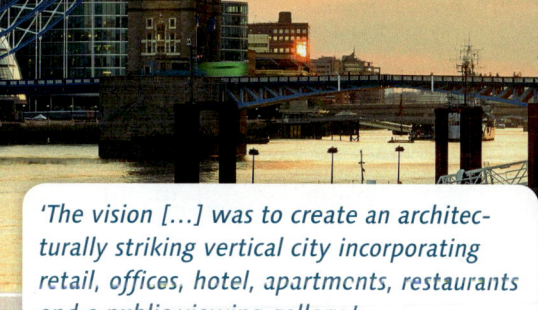

The Shard

'The vision [...] was to create an architecturally striking vertical city incorporating retail, offices, hotel, apartments, restaurants and a public viewing gallery.'
Irvine Sellar, developer

'... a colossal phallocentric monument, built by the rich-and-greedy, for the other rich-and-greedies ...'
Michele Hanson, *Guardian* columnist

London's 'tallest & most vulgar looking building. Serves no need or purpose ...'
Adel Darwish, London-based journalist

'For us – people living and working in Southwark – the Shard is not just a tall building. It has [...] brought new jobs, and symbolizes the emergence of south London as a part of the capital that punches at its weight.'
Peter John, leader of Southwark Council

1 Read the statements in the speech bubbles. Which of them – if any – do you identify or sympathize with? Why?

2 What's your opinion: Can modern high-rise buildings contribute to the attractiveness of urban skylines?

3 Can you think of other examples of controversial city architecture? Present them in your group.

In suburbia

B1 The American suburb, then and now   *Leigh Gallagher*

In her book The End of the Suburbs: Where the American Dream Is Moving *(2013), Leigh Gallagher traces the profound changes American suburbs and suburban life have been undergoing.*

- Before reading the following text, get into small groups and talk about what comes to your mind when you think of life in a US suburb.

Las Vegas suburbs

The American suburb used to evoke a certain way of life, one of tranquil, tree-lined streets, soccer leagues and center-hall colonials. Today's suburb is more likely to evoke endless sprawl, a punishing commute, and McMansions. In the pre-automobile era, suburban residents had to walk once they disembarked from the train, so houses needed to be located within a reasonable distance to the station and homes were built close together. Shopkeepers set up storefronts around the station where pedestrian traffic was likely to be highest. The result was a village center with a grid-shaped street pattern that emerged organically around the day-to-day needs and walking patterns of the people who lived there. Urban planners describe these neighborhoods, which you can still see in older suburbs, as having 'vibrancy' or 'experiential richness' because, without even trying, their design promoted activity, foot traffic, commerce and socializing. As sociologist Lewis Mumford wrote, 'As long as the railroad stop and walking distances controlled suburban growth, the suburb had form.'

Then came World War Two, and the subsequent housing shortage. [...] From then on, residential communities were built around a different model entirely, one that abandoned the urban grid pattern in favor of a circular, asymmetrical system made of curving subdivisions, looping streets and cul-de-sacs.

But in solving one problem – the severe postwar housing shortage – we unwittingly created some others: isolated, single-class communities. A lack of cultural amenities. Miles and miles of chain stores and Ruby Tuesdays. These are the negative qualities so often highlighted in popular culture, in TV shows like *Desperate Housewives*, *Weeds* and *Suburgatory*, to name just a few. [...]

There is still a tremendous amount of appeal in suburban life: space, a yard of one's own, less-crowded schools. I don't have anything against the suburbs personally – although I currently live in Manhattan's West Village, I had a pretty idyllic childhood growing up in Media, Pennsylvania, a suburb twelve miles west of Philadelphia. We are a nation that values privacy and individualism down to our very core, and the suburbs give us that. But somewhere between leafy neighborhoods built around lively railroad villages and the shiny new subdivisions in cornfields on the way to Iowa that bill themselves as suburbs of Chicago, we took our wish for privacy too far. The suburbs overshot their mandate. [...]

Whatever things look like in ten years – or twenty, or fifty, or more – there's one thing everyone agrees on: there will be more options. The government in the past created one American Dream at the expense of almost all others: the dream of a

5

10

15

20

25

30

35

40

1 **evoke sth.** *(fml)* bring a feeling, memory etc. to the mind
2 **tranquil** *(fml)* peaceful, quiet
3 **center-hall colonial** *(n)* American house type from colonial times to the 19th century
5 **McMansion** *(derog)* uniform, boring type of house
11 **grid** *Gitter, Raster*
16 **vibrancy** ['vaɪbrənsi] quality of being full of life and energy
22 **abandon sb./sth.** leave sb./sth. behind
23 **cul-de-sac** ['kʌl də sæk] street that is closed at one end
25 **amenity** [ə'miːnəti] sth. that makes a place pleasant and comfortable to live in
26 **Ruby Tuesday** US chain of restaurants
36 **bill yourself as sth.** call yourself sth.
37 **overshoot your mandate** ['mændeɪt] do more than your were meant to do

house, a lawn, a picket fence, two or more children, and a car. But there is no single American Dream anymore; there are multiple American Dreams, and multiple American Dreamers. The good news is that the entrepreneurs, academics, planners, home builders and thinkers who plan and build the places we live in are hard at work trying
45 to find space for all of them[1].

COMPREHENSION ◀

1 Outlining the writer's views

a Contrast US suburban life before and after the Second World War, as described by Gallagher.

b In one or two sentences, outline the new trend that US suburbs are facing at the beginning of the 21st century.

c Point out what, according to the writer, makes suburban life still attractive for Americans.

ANALYSIS ◀

2 Analysing style and figurative speech

a Analyse the sentence 'Today's suburb is more likely to evoke endless sprawl, a punishing commute, and McMansions.' (ll. 3–5)

b Explain what Gallagher means when she says 'The suburbs overshot their mandate.' (ll. 36–37)

LANGUAGE AWARENESS ◀

3 Using participles

a Rewrite the following expressions[1] using a relative clause instead of a participle.

Example: 'tranquil, tree-lined streets' (ll. 2) → tranquil streets that are lined with trees

   1 'a circular, asymmetrical system made of curving subdivisions' (ll. 22–23)

   2 'negative qualities so often highlighted in popular culture' (ll. 26 27)

   3 'leafy neighborhoods built around lively railroad villages' (ll. 34–35)

b Now rewrite these expressions[1] using a participle instead of the relative clause:

   1 'a village center with a grid-shaped street pattern that emerged organically' (ll. 11–12)

   2 'the day-to-day needs and walking patterns of the people who lived there' (ll. 12–14)

   3 'shiny new subdivisions in cornfields on the way to Iowa that bill themselves as suburbs of Chicago' (ll. 35–36)

c Compare the two versions of each of the expressions. Discuss with your partner which version you find better and why.

[1]Text and quotes from: 'The end of the suburbs', *Time*, 31 July 2013

BEYOND THE TEXT ◀

4 Sustainable living

a Read the Fact File on the right. Discuss with a partner what changes would have to be made to make suburbs more sustainable.

b **CHALLENGE ▶** How sustainable is the area where you live? Write an essay of about 200 words for a project on sustainable living in which you present your results.

■ LANGUAGE AWARENESS

Literary devices in non-fiction
Contrary to what you might expect, literary devices (e.g. figurative speech) are found not only in works of fiction but are also widely used in non-fiction as well as in everyday speech. They are used to evoke vivid images, to have an impact on the reader or the listener or to create a special atmosphere, e.g. in advertising, public speaking or journalism.

▶ LA 4: Influencing through language

■ FACT FILE

Sustainable living
To offer a good quality of life to both current residents and future generations cities need sustainable planning and development. This includes affordable homes, a lifestyle that is resource-efficient and environmentally-friendly, that recycles waste and uses renewable resources, that is energy efficient, provides an effective infrastructure and sufficient public transport. Open spaces and cultural amenities support a strong sense of community and contribute to an improved quality of life and to greater sustainability.

▶ SF 34: Argumentative writing

B2 A suburban street *John Lanchester*

The following excerpt is taken from John Lanchester's novel Capital, *which is set in a suburb in South London. Like the previous text (cf.* **B1**)*, it takes a long-term look at suburbia – with a slightly different twist.*

The properties in Pepys Road were built for a specific market: the idea was that they would appeal to lower-middle-class families willing to live in an unfashionable part of town in return for the chance to own a terraced house – a house large enough to have room for servants. For the first years they were lived in not by solicitors or barristers or doctors, but by the people who worked or clerked for them: the respectable, aspirational no-longer-poor. Over the next decades, the demographics of the street wobbled up and down in age, up and down in class, as it became more or less popular with upwardly mobile young families, and as the area did well or less well. The area was bombed in the Second World War, but Pepys Road was unaffected until a V-2 rocket hit in 1944 and destroyed two houses in the middle of the street. The gap stayed there for years, like a pair of missing front teeth, until a new property with balconies and French windows, looking very strange amid the Victorian architecture, was built there in the fifties. [...]

It would be hard to put your finger on the exact point when Pepys Road began its climb up the economic ladder. A conventional answer would be to say that it tracked the change in Britain's prosperity, emerging from the dowdy chrysalis of the late 1970s and transforming into a vulgar, loud butterfly of the Thatcher decades and the long boom that followed them. But it didn't seem quite like that to people who lived in the street – not least because the people who lived in the street changed too. As house prices slowly rose, the working classes, indigenous and immigrant, cashed in and moved out, usually looking to find bigger houses in quieter places, with neighbours like themselves. The new arrivals tended to be more middle-class, with husbands who worked at decently paid but not spectacular jobs, and wives who stayed at home and looked after the children [...].

People began to do up the houses, not in the ad hoc way of previous decades but with systematic make-overs in the open-plan style that became fashionable in the seventies and never really went away. [...] By late 2007, after many more years of a new

(line numbers in margin: 5, 10, 15, 20, 25)

Glossary

1 **Pepys** [pi:ps]
3 **terraced house** *Reihenhaus*
4 **solicitor, barrister** *(in Britain)* lawyer
6 **aspirational** *(fml)* socially ambitious
11 **property** building and the surrounding land
12 **French window** glass door leading outside, e.g. into a garden
15 **track sb./sth.** follow sb./sth. closely
16 **prosperity** economic success
dowdy boring, unattractive
chrysalis *(zoologisch)* Puppe
17 **Thatcher = Margaret Thatcher** (1925–2013) British Conservative prime minister 1979–1990
20 **indigenous** [ɪnˈdɪdʒənəs] *(fml)* belonging to a place, not coming from somewhere else
cash in take advantage of a situation by selling sth.

> ■ **TROUBLE SPOT**
> *wife* (sg) = *wives* (pl) (l. 23)

Terraced houses in Clapham, South London

boom, it was usual for two or three houses in the street to be undergoing some sort of major renovation at the same time. [...]

30 All this was part of a big change in the nature of Pepys Road. Over its history, almost everything that could have happened in the street had happened. [...]

Now, however, history had sprung an astonishing plot twist on the residents of Pepys Road. For the first time in history, the people who lived in the street were, by global and maybe even by local standards, rich. The thing which made them rich was 35 the very fact that they lived in Pepys Road. They were rich simply because of that, because all of the houses in Pepys Road, as if by magic, were now worth millions of pounds.[1]

32 **spring sth.** do sth. that sb. else was not expecting

COMPREHENSION

1 True or false?

  a Are the following statements true or false? Correct the false ones.

    1 The kind of people who live in Pepys Road have changed over the years.

    2 The street was entirely unaffected by the Second World War.

    3 Pepys Road developed from an unpopular to a favoured residential street.

    4 The street has always been popular with young families.

    5 Today the inhabitants of Pepys Road are considered to be rich.

  b Work with a partner. Write two more true/false statements about Pepys Road. Check and correct each other's sentences.

▶ SF 7: Working with closed test formats

2 Pepys Road then and now

Outline the change that Pepys Road has undergone in the years of its existence. Refer to both the people living there and the properties themselves.

ANALYSIS

3 Using language to create a vivid image

  a Examine the narrative perspective in this excerpt and the effect this perspective has on the reader.

  b Examine the author's use of *stylistic devices to convey an image of the street and its residents. Identify examples in the text and describe their effectiveness. **SUPPORT** ▶ p. 244

▶ SF 17: Analysing stylistic devices

4 In the light of this excerpt, explain the double meaning of the title of Lanchester's novel.

BEYOND THE TEXT

5 **YOU CHOOSE** **Pepys Road and on**

  a With a partner, write a description of what Pepys Road might be like in the year 2030. Discuss future demographic change, the development of architecture, etc. Give reasons for your opinion.

  b 'As house prices slowly rose, the working classes, indigenous and immigrant, cashed in and moved out, usually looking to find bigger houses in quieter places, with neighbours like themselves.' (ll. 19–22)[1] What factors would you consider when choosing a place to live? Write a short text of about 200 words. ▶ LANGUAGE HELP

[1] Text and quotes from: *Capital*, 2012, pp. 2–5

Part C

Take me home, country roads

C1 Country life

- With a partner, brainstorm your ideas about life in the country. Organize your ideas in a mind map. Then link up with another pair and exchange your views.

Look at the painting 'Clamdigger' (1935) by the American painter Edward Hopper (1862–1967).

Country living

It's grassroots
It's simple
It's basic, not plush
Uncomplicated
Uncluttered   5
Unhurried
Unrushed
It's relaxed,
Unpolluted,
Unequaled,   10
Unmatched.

From: Patricia Neely-Dorsey,
*Reflections of a Mississippi Magnolia
– A Life in Poems*, 2008

3 **plush** very comfortable
5 **uncluttered** *(adj)* not full of
things and people

▶ SF 11: Analysing pictures

LANGUAGE HELP

- The picture creates a/an …
- The atmosphere is … because the painter uses …
- It feels as if …
- The painting conveys … to the viewer …
- The light/pale/bright/dark/faint … colours emphasize …

---

1 **Setting and atmosphere**
Describe the *setting and the *atmosphere in the painting. How does Hopper achieve this particular atmosphere? ▶ LANGUAGE HELP

2 **Imagining**
What do you imagine the life of the man in the picture to be like? Discuss your ideas with your partner.

Now read the poem by Patricia Neely-Dorsey (see margin, above left).

COMPREHENSION ◀

3 **First reactions**
   a Say whether you like the poem and give reasons for your opinion. Consider the form of the poem as well as its content.
   b Outline what living in the country is like according to the poem.

ANALYSIS ◀

4 **Rearranging the lines of the poem**
   a Pair up with a partner. Arrange the lines of the poem in a different order and write them down.
   b Get together with another pair and compare your new versions of the poem. Explain what effect – if any – the changes have. Compare this with the sequence of words in the original poem and its effect.
      ▶ LANGUAGE HELP
   c Practise reading Neely-Dorsey's poem. Then read it to the class.

LANGUAGE HELP

- … affects / doesn't affect the meaning …
- … emphasizes …
- … changes the rhythm …
- … influences / doesn't influence the form …
- … reads more/less fluently …

▶ LP 20: Word formation

─────────────────────────────────── LANGUAGE AWARENESS ◀

5 Negative adjectives

a Which adjectives in the poem are formed the same way as 'uncomplicated' (l. 4)? Explain their construction.

b Find synonyms for the adjectives from **a**. Explain why the poet chose not to use these.

c Find English equivalents for the following German words: *ungewollt, unbekannt, ungeliebt, unerprobt, ungeeignet, unerforscht, ungeschlagen, ungeschrieben*.

── BEYOND THE TEXT ◀

6 YOU CHOOSE Your own poem or painting

a Use the mind map you drew at the start of **C1** and write your own poem about life in the country. You can create a poem like the one above or choose another form, e.g. an acrostic.

OR

b Think of a painting that would express your own ideas of country life. Describe what the painting would show and what colours you might use.

▦ LANGUAGE AWARENESS

Negation is the process of turning an affirmative (positive) statement into its opposite (a negative one). You can do this by changing the verb form (e.g. *They are* ➔ *aren't respectful*) or by adding prefixes or suffixes (*respectful* ➔ *disrespectful*; *useful* ➔ *useless*).

▶ LA 3: Similarities and differences of languages

▶ SF 37: Doing a creative writing task

C2 Small-town stories *Garrison Keillor*

The following text is an excerpt from a book about not just small but the very smallest towns in each of the US states, such as Delphos, Iowa, or Tenney, Minnesota.

- Before reading, brainstorm what you imagine life in a very small town to be like.

When we imagine the small American town, such as Anywhere, U.S.A., where John Doe lives at 1234 Maple Street, we imagine a town of at least two or three thousand souls, with a water tower, four or five church steeples, a 19th century Main Street with brick storefronts, a ball field, an old brick high school, a train depot, and hundreds of
5 white frame houses with picket fences. The Does grew up in Anywhere, but still, there are plenty of people here who don't know them [...]. In a one-dog town, it's different.

A town so small has precious few of the urban amenities and very little of the majestic privacy of life in the woods. You can't walk around the corner and find someone to cook your lunch for you or wash your clothes. There may not even be a corner to walk
10 around. But everyone in town has seen your underwear hanging on the clothesline and heard you snore, and if you like bourbon, they know how much. And when you go to church and kneel to confess your sins, everybody
15 else knows the sins you're thinking of and also which ones you're forgetting. They see the shoes
20 you're wearing and think that they like the ones you wore last Sunday better.

Garrison Keillor

1 **John Doe** *(AE)* name used for 'an average man' (cf. Jane Doe = an average woman)
4 **depot** ['depəʊ, *AE:* 'diːpoʊ] *(AE)* bus or train station
5 **frame house** *Holzhaus*
6 **one-dog town** very small town
7 **precious few** *(adv) (infml) herzlich wenige, nur eine Handvoll*
   amenity [ə'miːnəti] sth. that makes a place pleasant and comfortable to live in

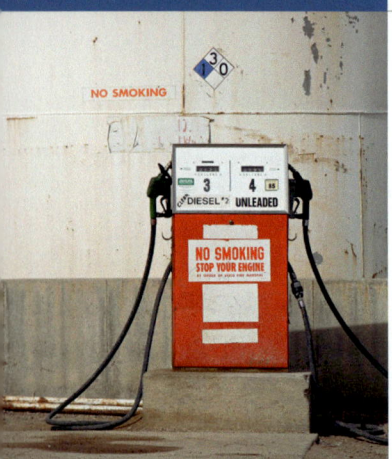

15 **stubbornness** *Sturheit, Dick-köpfigkeit*
16 **adhere to sth.** *(fml)* believe sth., support sth.
17 **Sun Belt** southern and south-western parts of the USA
18 **buckshot** *Schrotkugeln*
29 **go belly up** *(infml)* fail completely

These towns are monuments to the great American spirit of stubbornness. While the country as a whole follows trends, reads best-sellers, adheres to the current wisdom, and the population slips toward the cities and down to the Sun Belt like loose buckshot, some people simply don't do what everybody else does. [...] `25`

As isolated as their towns seem to be, a Delphosite or a Tennyan is apt to feel more connected to things than, say, a New Yorker does, who would hardly dare dream that he or she could make a big difference in the city, whereas in a one-dog town, every time you mow the grass, it's urban renewal. `30`

In a big city, it's easy to believe that the government is corrupt, and education is falling behind, and the church is pitifully irrelevant, and that society's decline is inevitable [...] but in a small town, you are deeply implicated in all institutions [...]. In a one-dog town, citizenship makes you a leader automatically. You are on all committees, and you can't sit in meetings and hope somebody else will speak up; you are going to have to do it and, if necessary, speak the inconvenient truth. Without it, the town may go belly up. Of course you can always blame the county, but you know what you know: your neighbors depend on you. [...] `35`

To outsiders, which we are, the one-dog town may appear vaguely silly and hopeless, a living failure, [...] but we may be wrong about this. Small-town people feel that they have escaped from the struggle for supremacy and found the secret of satisfaction. The philosophy of Good Enough, which is rare in mainstream America, is strong in the one-dog town. Elsewhere, people hate themselves for failing to be skinny enough, smart enough, sexy enough, rich enough, but perhaps in a Tenney, Minnesota, which never will be the Athens of the Midwest, [...] you can feel you are a good enough person for normal purposes and that life is good enough as it is. `40` `45`

From: Dennis Kitchen, *Our Smallest Towns*, 1995, introduction by Garrison Keillor, pp. 9–11

COMPREHENSION ◀

1 Small-town happiness
  a Identify different parts of the text and summarize each in one sentence.
  b Outline life in a very small town as described by Garrison Keillor.
  c Contrast the attitudes of small-town people to the ones living in bigger towns or in cities.

ANALYSIS ◀

2 Using descriptive language
  a Describe the *tone of the text. What effect does it have on you?
    ▶ LANGUAGE HELP
  b Examine the *stylistic devices the author uses to convey his message.
    `SUPPORT` ▶ p. 245

BEYOND THE TEXT ◀

3 `YOU CHOOSE` ▶ **Home is ...**

  a What does 'home' mean to you? Write a short essay of about 250 words. Discuss whether you would like to come back to your home town after university or training or whether you would prefer living somewhere else.

  b Your family has moved from the city to the country. Write an email to a friend and describe the new surroundings, your new life and your feelings.

▶ SF 37: Doing a creative writing task
▶ SF 34: Argumentative writing

A panel discussion

Some people want to live in the heart of a big city, others prefer to lead the quiet life that only a small town or the countryside can offer. But is everybody really free to choose their favourite place – and should they be? What about the problems of over-crowded megacities, what about depopulated regions lacking people and resources? Should there be incentives or regulations, making sure there is a healthy balance between town and country? But what exactly is this balance, and who gets to decide where people should live?

Conduct a panel discussion in which you exchange your views and arguments.

Tip: If you arrange for the panel discussion to be recorded, you can analyse and evaluate your performance afterwards.

Find a recording tool here:
Webcode context-56

1 Choosing a moderator
Choose somebody who opens, moderates and summarizes the discussion.
He or she also keeps track of whose turn it is to speak.

2 Deciding what your position is
Think about the question that is going to be discussed.
What is your own position, what are your preferences, i.e. where would you like to live, to study and to work in the future?

3 Collecting arguments
Collect arguments to support your position on each subtopic. Think of all the aspects you have dealt with in this chapter. Use the words and phrases you have learned as well as convincing examples to illustrate your point of view. Think of arguments for positions other than your own and of ways to answer them. Make notes.

4 Conducting the panel discussion
The moderator opens the discussion with a short intro-duction to the topic. He/she asks questions and coordinates the discussion.
Now it's your turn. Take an active part and prove that you can put forward your arguments in a convincing, but polite way.
At the end of the discussion (about 15 minutes in length) the moderator summarizes the arguments and closes the discussion.

5 Giving each other feedback
Your teacher will give you an assessment sheet.

global warming
qualification
literature
communication
nationalism
knowledge
civil rights
lingua franca
ethnicity
language awareness
skills
future plans
analysis
literacy
power
multiculturalism
happiness visions
culture
application
stereotypes morals
rhetoric
going abroad
role models
talents
word power
responsibility
disappointments
research
environmental awareness
immigration
intercultural learning
dreams globalization
leadership
identity

This context task gives you the opportunity to consider the topics you have dealt with in class again and to think about their relevance for your future life.

1 Giving a presentation I

Work on your own or in a group. Choose 3–5 items from the word cloud on the left and prepare a presentation on the topic 'Skills and insights I got from my English course that might be helpful for my future life'. Your presentation should be 5–7 minutes long if you are working on your own or 10–12 if you're in a group. You may want to add examples from your course work to illustrate your statements.

▶ SF 4: Doing project work
▶ SF 24: Giving a presentation

 OR ——————

2 Giving a presentation II

Work on your own. Think of 3–5 items that are not in the word cloud and use them as the basis of a presentation as explained in **1**.

▶ SF 24: Giving a presentation

 OR ——————

3 Making an advertisement

Work on your own, in pairs or in a group. Make an advertisement for your English class that tells younger students what to expect and/or what to look forward to. Choose a suitable form (e.g. leaflet, poster, electronic presentation, blog …) and present it in class (and, if possible, on the school website).

▶ SF 37: Doing a creative writing task

Find a tool to design your poster or flyer here:
 Webcode context-50

 OR ——————

4 Having a debate

Work in a group. Prepare and conduct a debate on the motion 'This house believes that English is the most important subject at school'.

▶ SF 28: Having a debate

 OR ——————

5 Writing a quiz

Work in a group.

a Choose five chapter topics or items from the word cloud and write a quiz consisting of three questions/tasks for each topic/item, e.g.
Example *lingua franca*:
1 Name three situations in which English is used as a lingua franca.
2 Why is a lingua franca so important in a country like India?
3 Name two possible disadvantages of using a lingua franca.

b Ask fellow students to do your quiz.

▶ SF 4: Doing project work

Support Pages

Chapter 1 Living One's Life – Individuals in Society

A1 Successful children   p.20

3 What if …?

a Read ll. 43–53 and say which type of conditional is being used. Here are some hints which will help you with conditional sentences of all three types:

- Conditional sentences type I refer to the future:
  - If her daughters are not honor students, Amy Chua will …
  - If Amy Chua ever has grandchildren, she will …
- Conditional sentences type II refer to present or future unreal situations.
  Using type II, Louisa might express her dreams and wishes:
  - If I had a part in the school play, I would …
  - If my mother were not a Chinese mother, I could …
- Conditional sentences type III refer to the past. Looking back, Amy Chua might think:
  - If my parents had not been Chinese immigrants, I would not have …
  - If I had been less strict with my daughters, they would never have …

Now go back to task **4** on p. 20.

A2 Growing up queer in 2018   p.22

2 Examining the writer's attitude

a Point out statements that describe Arianna's feelings toward the society she lives in.
You may refer to the following lines and statements:

- First paragraph (ll. 1–4): 'The word flew out', 'had come screeching', 'It festered'
- ll. 14–15: 'This was what I desired for years on end, and I was finally comfortable enough to do it without thinking about the opinions of others.'
- ll. 25–26: 'I like to think I live my life pretty okay, about a C- on the grade scale. It's not good, but I'm passing.'
- ll. 35–36: 'The internet has given me news updates and profiles of queer youth around the world. To an extent, I am granted a sense of ease.'
- l. 45: 'I'm fearful of what others think of me, but I know judgement is inevitable.'
- ll. 48–50: 'Social media platforms have assisted us in being able to voice our thoughts and find counter-arguments and agreements from people across the board.'
- l. 51: 'My school labels itself as a safe space, and so far, the term is fitting.'
- ll. 53–54: 'My personal surroundings are a positive realm to thrive in, and the difficulty is minimal.'
- ll. 57–58: 'And to the jerk in the beat up car, I have short hair and rock button ups as a mating call for girls, not to fit in your heteronormative world, jerk.'

Now go back to task **2b** on p. 22.

A3 Stereotypes in Los Angeles   p.25

6 Stereotypes in everyday life
  b Consider the following questions. This can also be done as pair or group work.
   1 How do stereotypes develop?
   2 How do they influence our perception of others, and what are the consequences?
   3 Are stereotypes only negative or can stereotypes be positive too?
   4 How should we deal with stereotypes?

B3 Volunteering in Germany   p.30

1 Mediation (German ➔ English)
How and why do people get involved?
  ▪ Read the German article, find keywords and note them down in English.
  ▪ Write an introductory sentence which tells your friend not only about the author, source and topic of the article at hand, but also about the writer's attitude towards his topic. You have to stay neutral and simply mediate the facts given in the text.
  ▪ With the help of your collection of keywords make your first draft. Concentrate on central statements.
  ▪ Revise your first draft. Improve its style by using participle constructions and connectives.
You may start your e-mail like this:
Dear …,

We recently discussed volunteer work and how and why people get involved at all. I have just read an interesting article in a German magazine and would like to tell you about it.

Now go back to task **2**, p.30.

B4 An individual in a future society   p.31

2 A volunteer
Explain how Katniss's volunteering relates to the concept of volunteering in this chapter.
  b 1 First of all, consider what volunteering is. You have already encountered it in this chapter, so look back at your work in **C1**, tasks **1** (if you have not done it, then look at the support information at **C2** above) and in **C3**, task **2a**, as well as the description of a volunteer in **C2**, in order to form a definition in your own words.
   2 Examine the word *volunteer*. Where does it come from and what different meanings does it have? In the extract Katniss says 'I volunteer'. What does she mean in the context of the film?
   3 Now relate the two ideas of volunteering: what qualities do they share?

Chapter 2   The Power of Words – from Shakespeare to Today

A1 William Shakespeare: the man, his work and his time   p.38

Shakespeare's life

Shakespeare was born in **Stratford-upon-Avon**, a small town south of Birmingham, in **1564**. We only know when he was baptized, not the exact date of his birth. He was the son of a glovemaker, a relatively wealthy businessman at the time. William attended local school, where – according to his own words – he learned '**small Latin and less Greek**', and there are no records that he went to university. At 18 he married **Ann Hathaway**, who was eight years his senior. They had three children; William's son Hamnet died as a child. In the mid-1580s Shakespeare 'disappeared' for about **seven years** which later led to the creation of rumours and legends trying to find explanations for the lack of any records. By 1592 he re-emerged in London as an **actor, playwright and shareholder** in London theatres. After a successful career he retired and went back to Stratford in 1614. He died there in **1616** leaving his **'second-best bed'** to his wife in his last will, which again led to considerable rumours about him disliking his wife, but was probably only a contemporary custom granting somebody a lifelong right to live in a house or room.

Suggestion for presentation: timeline

Shakespeare and Germany

The relation between Shakespeare and Germany has always been a fruitful, but also controversial one. In the beginning, Shakespeare's plays came to Germany as **puppet theatre**. Shakespeare in the original and early translations served as an example for many German writers, e.g. **Goethe** and **Schiller**, and fostered the development of a genuinely German national literature, especially in the field of drama. Not until 1741 (*Julius Caesar*) and 1758 (*Romeo and Juliet*) were the first plays translated into German. C.M. Wieland published the first more or less complete German edition of Shakespeare's plays. The most famous German version is probably the so-called 'classical' **Schlegel-Tieck translation** (1797–1840), which is still read and performed today. Yet their translation was not the product of collaborative work as the name would suggest, but rather the subject of a long-term argument between the writers. To date, Shakespeare's complete works have been rendered in German at least 40 times, including contemporary versions by Erich Fried and **Frank Günther**, along with countless versions of individual plays. All of them range in a wide field from **adaptations** to **'true' translations**, the latter being extremely hard to achieve for the multi-layered art of words used by Shakespeare. The sonnets in particular have been the focus of interest for many German writers and translators so that hundreds and hundreds of translated versions of these sonnets have been made.

Suggestion for presentation: general introduction and presentation of some translated parts, e.g. different versions of some lines of the same sonnet or part of a drama

London and the Elizabethan theatre

There were several playhouses in use during Shakespeare's time in London, e.g. The Theatre, The Rose, The Curtain, The Swan and **The Globe**. They were situated on the **bankside** of the river Thames next to prostitutes and bear-baiting arenas in a **metropolis** which was one of biggest and liveliest cities in the world. The playhouses were **open to daylight** and could therefore only be used in the warmer months. They were erected around a **platform stage**, used hardly any scenery, but did have spectacular period costumes. So-called groundlings were standing on three sides of the stage. The audience generally took a lively part by interacting with the **male-only actors** on stage. Shakespeare's main theatre, which he also part-owned, was The Globe. Actors were of low social status, so that they had to seek the patronage of a nobleman for financial as well as legal reasons. Shakespeare's theatre group was first called the **Lord Chamberlain's Men**. Later on they became known as the **King's Men** as after 1603 they earned the highest royal support for their performances. Theatres were a hugely popular form of **entertainment**, but also a very financially productive

business, with audiences up to 2500 people per performance. Theatres were disapproved of by city officials, who often petitioned to have them closed down.

Suggestion for presentation: illustration of an Elizabethan playhouse or contemporary sketch of the Thames bankside and explanations

The Elizabethan world view

The Elizabethan world view was based on traditional concepts and saw the earth as the centre of the cosmos **(geocentric)**. God and the church had the highest authority and followed the **'dei gratia'** model – every monarch was considered as established by God's grace as a wordly representative of divine power. **Elizabeth I** (1558-1603), daughter of **Henry VIII** and his second wife Anne Boleyn and last monarch of the Tudor line, was renowned as the 'Virgin Queen', as she never got married. Fixed ranks by birth were generally accepted as the basis of society which followed the **Great Chain of Being**, a strict hierarchical order of all matter and life. **Microcosm** and **macrocosm** were seen as corresponding, so whenever there was a disturbance in one of them, there was a reaction to it in the other. The Elizabethan Age is often remembered as a **Golden Age** because it was a flourishing time for culture, the arts, politics and international expansion. This quest and curiosity for **new discoveries**, and the struggle for power as well as **religious changes** (clashes between Catholic and Protestant beliefs) also caused growing **upheaval** in this society on the verge of modern times. There was a constant struggle for peace and stability against foreign influences as well as religious, social and political challenges at the local level.

Suggestion for presentation: several illustrations (Elizabeth I, Great Chain of Being, old sketches, etc.) to be explained or 10 theses describing the Elizabethan world view

Shakespearian English

Shakespearian or Elizabethan English are both included in what is called **Early Modern English**, replacing forms of Middle English, regional English dialects, and other languages like French and Latin. At this point the 'new' language still had a **flexible system** concerning structure and vocabulary, especially compared to Greek and Latin. Grammatical structures deriving from different systems existed side by side (cfwww. pronouns, word order, etc.). Rules which are clear today had not been fixed yet. English was undergoing **major linguistic changes**. Due to exploration and colonization, it was rapidly absorbing words from other languages. Writers and scientists expressed new ideas by inventing, borrowing or adopting words or phrases from other languages **(neologisms)**. In etymological dictionaries, many words which are still used today are attributed to Shakespeare. He may not have invented all of them, but was probably one of the first to write them down or use them publicly.

Suggestion for presentation: list of Shakespeare quotations showing some of the special words he 'invented' and used, including constructions typical for Elizabethan English

Shakespeare's works

More than 400 years after his death, Shakespeare is still seen as one of the most important – if not the most important – playwrights in the world. He wrote about **40 plays (comedies, tragedies, romances and history plays)** that are performed on stages around the world in many different languages. Shakespeare's oeuvre includes plays like *A Midsummer Night's Dream, Romeo and Juliet, Julius Caesar, Macbeth, Othello* and *The Tempest*, to name but a few. He also wrote a **sonnet cycle** set around a poet, his friend, a rival and a dark lady as well as different pieces of **verse epic**. In all his work, Shakespeare drew from **tradition** and was inspired by other forms of literature. He reinvented or reconstructed these ideas **innovatively** in his own individual way. His plays display a thought-provoking use of language, **word play** and **imagery**, combining tragic and comic elements, like the **comic relief** in his great tragedies, as well as a fascinating set of characters ranging from kings, murderers, witches and villains to innocent maidens, fairies and young lovers. Shakespeare may not have invented **blank verse** (an iambic pentameter without – i.e. 'blank of' – rhyme), but he made it popular for drama and thus served as an example for many European dramatists to follow in his footsteps. Only after his death did fellow actors and playwrights honour him by collecting the transcripts and (incomplete) texts of his plays in a first complete edition of his works, the so-called **First Folio edition** of 1623.

Suggestion for presentation: Ten examples taken from plays or performances to show the variety of his work

A3 Richard courts his enemy p.44

3 Working with imagery
Work with a partner. Identify the images each speaker uses. Explain them with the help of the annotations and from the context they are used in.
It is useful to become aware of your personal mental images when reading any text, and in particular a poetic passage like the one you are dealing with here. Consider
- names that Lady Anne calls Gloucester and whether these are straightforward or evoke certain images,
- personification of abstracts or of body parts,
- *similes,
- *metaphors.

5 Understanding character
On the basis of your analysis, describe the speakers' characters. Gloucester (= Richard) keeps twisting Anne's insults around to make them say something flattering
to her in response – which she does not seem to accept, at least verbally. In this context you have analysed her response to Richard's offering her his sword to kill him.
All these things are indicators of what kind of people these two dramatic characters are.
When describing them, consider
- what motivations they have for acting as they do,
- what emotions they display while they are speaking,
- what their actions reveal about them,
- whether their original emotions change and what that tells you about their characters.

B1 My future wife p.46

2 Comparing dialogues
Compare the way Petruchio woos Katharina to the way Gloucester woos Anne (**A2**, pp.79–81). Evaluate what each man reveals about himself and how effectively they each use words to achieve their aims. First look at your answers to **A2**, tasks **4** and **6** on p.81. Then
use the following questions to help you examine Petruchio.
1 How does Petruchio respond to Kate telling him that her name is Katharina? (ll.4–8)
2 What does he say he has heard about her from others? (ll.4–14)
3 How does he respond to her attempts to make fun of him? (ll.20–24)
4 How does Katharina come across?
5 How does Petruchio describe Katharina? (ll.34–40 and ll.49–50)
6 How does he propose to her? (ll.41–52)

Now consider what sort of person Petruchio is, and whether you think he is successful at wooing Katharina. Then find similarities and differences between Richard and Petruchio, considering the context of each man's wooing and the emotions involved. Finally, decide which of the two men will be more successful.

VIEWING FOCUS ON SKILLS   p.47

5 Evaluation
Evaluate how successful the director has been in adapting the material. Name the elements that were changed and the effect the scene has on you. Use the following categories to create a table in which you contrast the play and the film:
setting (*What is the setting in each genre?*) • **characters** (*How did they come across in the play/film?*) • **relationship** (*What was the characters' relationship like in each genre?*) • **changes** (*What elements were added to/missing in the film?*) • **extras** (*How did the film maker use lighting, music, noise?*)

B2 Responding to a sonnet   p.49

2 GALLERY WALK Comparing the sonnets
Compare the two sonnets. Examine structure, development of the idea and style. Present your findings on posters and evaluate them in a gallery walk. These steps may be useful:
1 Look at the structures of the poems by examining the rhyme scheme.
2 State the main idea presented in each poem.
3 Divide each poem up according to the images in it.
4 Examine how the idea of alteration is addressed in each poem.
5 Examine how Simmons uses phrases and ideas from Shakespeare in his own poem.

C1 Performance poetry   p.51

7 Reviewing a poetry performance
Watch the performance again. Pay special attention to the speaker's gestures. Then write a review for the English pages of your school magazine. In order to write a review, first consider what your opinion of the poetry performance is.
1 Describe the performance.
2 Decide what you think about how Zephaniah performs his poem.
3 Decide whether the performance helped you to appreciate the poem, or whether you would have preferred just reading it.
4 Write the review by following these steps:
  • Find a suitable introductory sentence.
  • When writing the body of the review, remember to combine elements of description and of comment, and consider both the poem itself and the performance by the poet.
  • Finish by giving either a recommendation or a short statement that summarizes why you are not recommending the poem or the performance.

C2 The psychological power of words   p.52

2 a + b Understanding the general idea
Draw a table like the one below. It will help you to examine the verbs and their connotations and to understand the images that the poem conveys.

Person	Verb/phrase	Connotation	Image
terrorist	lurk in the shadows	lie in wait, as if for an attack (negative)	dangerous person
freedom fighter …	take shelter …	wait somewhere safe until a danger has passed (neutral) …	person who needs safety and protection …

Chapter 3   The UK – a Kingdom United?

The royal carriage with footmen

A1 Dangerous books   p. 59

4 Creative writing

b Write the dialogue between the footman and his wife and
include the events that probably took place while the Queen
was opening the Parliament. The following questions might
help you to collect ideas:

- How did the footman experience the incident?
- What is probably the most important aspect for him?
- Imagine the footman's feelings during his encounter with the Queen.
  Do you think he was embarrassed, frustrated, angry, unhappy, etc.?
  How could he express this in his conversation with his wife?

Don't forget: You are going to write a dialogue. So the footman and his wife should refer to each other
and react to what the other person says.

A3 The British and their tea   p. 63

3 Analysing style

How does the speaker of the podcast try to hold the audience's attention and entertain his listeners?
First make notes on the following aspects of the podcast. What further examples can you find? What
effect do they have on you as a listener? Use your points to organize your analysis.

Aspect	Example	Effect
Statistics	By the end of the day, the counter will reach 165 million – that is three cups of tea per person per day.	…
Interesting facts	And it is well-known that the Queen likes a nice cup of tea, as well.	…
Personal facts	Yukk! I cannot stand tea with sugar!	…
Exaggeration	… in the interests of international harmony and understanding I shall now explain …	…

B2 Between two cultures   p. 68

2 Analysing character relationships

Analyse the relationship between Kelly and her father Ibrahim. Reflect on what they talk about and how
they speak to each other. Read the following quotes that Kelly and Ibrahim say to each other. How do you
imagine the actors are meant to say them? What emotions are being portrayed?

IBRAHIM   Would you prefer it if I had been an American? (l. 9)
IBRAHIM   I wish we could've met earlier. (l. 23)
IBRAHIM   I imagined you might look like Kate Winslet. (l. 32)
IBRAHIM   Because you are English. And you don't know any better. (l. 81)

KELLY   But I told you I'm not going to go to Iraq, am I? (ll. 12–13)
KELLY   This isn't going very well, is it? (l. 34)
KELLY   Why are you here? Now, what do you want? (l. 42)
KELLY   Yeah, all right then, tell me what I think. (l. 69)

All quotes from: Mike Bartlett, *Artefacts*,
2008, pp. 8, 41–42

C1 Before the EU referendum p.70

3 Analysing style

Listen again. Analyse how Cameron tries to convince his listeners of his views. Focus on language and content. Is he successful?

a First fill in the 'Explanation' column of the table. What are the different stylistic devices?

b List examples of the different devices you can hear in the text.

c Describe the effect they have on you as a listener.

d Use your points to organize your analysis of the speaker's style.

Stylistic device	Explanation	Example from the speech	Effect
Alliteration	▪ …	▪ Rules and regulations ▪ …	▪ …
Personal pronoun	▪ …	▪ …	▪ …
Antithesis, contrast	▪ …	▪ Some people say … but the question mark is already there. ▪ They say, but I don't believe	▪ …
Parallelism Repetition Anaphora	▪ The same word / structure is repeated	▪ It will be … ▪ …	▪ …
Rule of three	▪ …	▪ Weeks, years and months ▪ …	▪ …

C2 Trying to understand the Brexit vote p.71

2 Writing

Based on the graphs on p.71 and on p.70, analyse the result of the Brexit referendum. Compare this result to your personal position on Brexit.

a Examine the chart on p.71 and describe the general trend. Try and imagine reasons for this voting pattern.

b Analyse the map on p.70. Connect the outcome of the referendum and the regions of the UK.

c Now link these findings to your own view on the results of the referendum: which age group/region(s) do you sympathize with? Why?

Chapter 4 India – a Kaleidoscope

A2 Colonizers and colonized p.79

Comparing a quote and a photo

When studying the quote, you could consider the following:

▪ Who spoke the words?

▪ What is the speaker's view of colonialism?

▪ What is the speaker's view of the colonized people?

▪ What is the main message?

When studying the photograph, you should take the following aspects into account:

▪ When and where was the photo probably taken?

▪ Who can you see in the picture?

- What does body language reveal about the relationship of the people in the picture?
- What can you deduce from the picture about India under British rule?

A3 The British Empire from an Indian perspective   p.81

5 The legacy of the Raj

Discuss whether the British Raj was a good thing for India. Consider the following points in **A2**:
- What does Curzon say that he hoped he gave the Indians? Consider whether some of these might have been given to the Indians, and whether the Indians needed what he hoped to give.
- How might the Indians in the photos feel? Has their lives changed much since the Empire?

Also, consider the following points in text **A3**:
- the positive elements listed in ll. 1–2, 6–7, 16–21,
- the failures of the Empire in ll. 2–9, 10–14, 18–19.

B1 Urbanization in India: the big picture   p.85

1 Indian urbanization

When describing a graph, or diagram, start out by mentioning the topic, the type of presentation used (e.g. a bar chart, a line graph, etc.), the span of time it covers and its source and date of publication (if available). Then describe the diagram in detail by turning the graph into words. In the end summarize what you have learned.

Now go back to task **2** on p. 85.

B2 Celebrating Indian culture   p.87

6 Mediation (German ➔ English)

Before writing your email, have a look at the following opening and closing formulas and decide which of them are best used in formal, which ones in informal emails (or letters). Decide on the best for your email.

Dear Dr. Smith, • *Dear Madam,* • *Dear Ms. White,* • *Dear Prof. Smith,* • *Dear Sir or Madam,* • *Dear Mike,* • *Dear Sir(s),* • *Dearest* • *Hello, Mike!* • *Hey, babe!* • *Hi,* • *Tony,*	*Best regards* • *Best wishes* • *Hugs and kisses* • *Lots of love* • *Love* • *Regards* • *Sincerely yours* • *With best wishes* • *With kind regards* • *Yours ever* • *Yours faithfully* • *Yours sincerely* • *Yours truly* • *Yours*

Now choose the most appropriate opening and closing formulas for your email.

C1 The Indian diaspora   p.89

2 Locating the Indian diaspora

a When designing your poster, take the following points into consideration:
- Overall appearance: Does the poster attract your attention? Is it informative? How creative is the work that went into its making?
- Title: Does the poster have a title banner? Is the title clear? Is it eye-catching? Can it be read easily from 3 metres away?
- Layout: Is the text large enough to be read from 2 metres away? Is there sufficient 'resting space for the eye' (i.e. blank space)? Are colours and graphic highlighting used effectively? Are texts and illustrations/ photographs integrated in a meaningful way?
- Writing: Is the writing concise? Is the information included in the texts relevant? Can the texts be read easily? Is language used correctly (e.g. vocabulary, grammar, spelling)?

C3 English lessons p.92

3 The use of tenses

The following passages from 'English Lessons' illustrate the use of the narrative past, narrative present and narrative future tenses in the story:

> **narrative past:**
>
> The police came looking for him. Oh no, not for my protection – no. They were rounding up all Sikh boys between the ages of fifteen and twenty-five for 'questioning'. Tony's parents knew what was in store and they hid him in the servant's quarter, a concrete room on the flat roof of the house. (ll. 75–78)
>
> **narrative present:**
>
> The phone rings and my heart starts to pound – *dharak, dharak*. Our answering machine message has Valerie's voice, and I follow the words with her accent. (ll. 8–9)
>
> **narrative future:**
>
> I will tell Tony I will take English lessons, and that she will be my teacher. (ll. 98–99)

All quotes from: Shauna Singh Baldwin, 'English lessons', *English Lessons and Other Stories*, 1996, pp. 129–134

Find more examples like this in the story to illustrate each type of narration, then answer the following questions:
- Which type of narration lends the story a sense of immediacy?
- Which type of narration has a distancing effect?
- Which type of narration could be said to add a prophetic tone to the story?

Go back to 'English Lessons' and use your findings to interpret the story: Why are there so many tense switches in 'English Lessons'? What do they reveal about the first-person narrator? And what is their effect on the reader?

Now go back to task 4 on p.92.

Chapter 5 The USA – Still the Promised Land?

A1 Unlike other nations p.99

4 Different dreams

Compare Adams's concept with other popular versions of the American dream.

Examine the following quotes from American literature. Analyse the image they present of the American dream and compare it with Adams's.
- 'Remember that your future position depends mainly upon yourself, and that it will be high or low as you choose to make it.' (Horatio Alger, *Ragged Dick*, 1867)
- 'It [= America] is a fabulous country, the only fabulous country; it is the only place where miracles not only happen, but where they happen all the time.' (Thomas Wolfe, *Of Time and the River*, 1935)
- 'He had a good dream. It's the only dream you can have – to come out number-one man.' (Arthur Miller, *Death of a Salesman*, 1949)

B1 The new neighbours   p. 107

6 The other side of the coin

Form groups of four. Two of you are Bev and Russ, the other two are the African-American couple who have bought the house in Clybourne Street. Imagine that after Karl has left, the black couple come to look at the house. How would Russ and Bev behave? How might the black couple explain their wish to move to an all-white neighbourhood? Discuss the issues at hand, then prepare role cards for your parts.

Step 1: Give the black couple names (e.g. Francine and Albert). Each member of your group chooses one of the characters. Read the list below and decide whether the attitude would better fit the white couple or the black couple:

- a bit embarrassed by the situation
- looking forward to changing neighbourhoods
- want a better life for their children
- feel guilty about their behaviour
- worried about the reaction of the neighbours
- believe in equality and progress
- avoid talking about race and skin colour
- want their share of the American dream

Step 2: Now work together in 'couples' to prepare your role cards. Write down (in keywords) questions your person might ask and statements they might make.

Now practise the scene, then perform it for your class.

C1 Facts and figures   p. 114

1 Understanding the figures

a Compare the figures in the table by completing the eight sentences on the opposite page with phrases from the box. See also the Fact File on the top of the following page.

	USA	China	Germany	Brazil	India	Russia
1 GDP	19,390,604	12,237,700	3,677,439	2,055,505	2,597,491	1,577,524
2 Military spending	597,178	228,173	43,023	25,751	59,757	55,327
3 Balance of trade	−568,439	210,728	281,389	30,177	−73,362	83,886

1 The GDP of the USA is more than … as that of China, the country with the … largest economy.
2 The Russian GDP is only about … of China's.
3 China's GDP is … that of Germany, Russia and Brazil together.
4 Russia's GDP is … that of Brazil.
5 No country spends … money on the military as the USA.
6 In this table, Germany ranks only … in terms of GDP, but … in terms of balance of trade.
7 Russia has a healthy trade surplus, whereas India imports … it exports.
8 India's trade deficit is almost … Russia's trade surplus.

> an eighth • as large as • as much •
> first • larger than • more than •
> one and a half times as big •
> second • significantly less than •
> third

■ FACT FILE

GDP (**Gross** [grəʊs] **Domestic Product**) is defined as the total value of goods and services produced in a country. The **balance of trade** is the difference between the total value of exports from a country and imports into the same country. A negative balance (**deficit** ['defɪsɪt]; opposite: **surplus** ['sɜːpləs]) means the country imports more than it exports.

C3 The end of the American era? p. 116

4 Persuading the reader

The writer is not only convinced of his point of view – he wants to convince his readers as well. Point out ways in which Cohen tries to influence the reader to accept his views and identify the language structures he uses for this purpose.

Cohen uses irony, a certain word choice and selection of facts, rhetorical questions and judgemental adverbs and adjectives. Identify these devices in the highlighted passages of the text:

> [...] These circumstances would have caused severe headaches for a competent and
> 10 sophisticated successor. Instead, the United States got a president who had unnervingly promised a wall on the southern border (paid for by Mexico), the dismantlement of long-standing trade deals with both competitors and partners, a closer relationship with Vladimir Putin, and a ban on Muslims coming into the United States. [...]
> On issues that are truly global in scope, Trump has abdicated leadership and the
> 15 moral high ground. The United States has managed to isolate itself on the topic of climate change, by the tone of its pronouncements no less than by its precipitous exit from the Paris Agreement. As for human rights, the president has taken only cursory notice of the two arrests of the Russian dissident Alexei Navalny or the death of the Chinese Nobel Prize winner and prisoner of conscience Liu Xiaobo. Trump did not
> 20 object after Turkish President Recep Tayyip Erdogan's security detail beat American protesters on American soil, in Washington, D.C. In April, he reportedly told Filipino President Rodrigo Duterte, who has used death squads to deal with offenders of local narcotics laws, that he was doing an 'unbelievable job on the drug problem'. Trump's secretary of state, Rex Tillerson, made it clear in his first substantive speech to State
> 25 Department employees that American values are now of at best secondary importance to 'American interests', presumably economic, in the conduct of foreign policy. [...]
> This dangerous and dispiriting chapter in American history will end, in eight years or four – or perhaps in two or even one, if Trump is impeached or removed under the Twenty-Fifth Amendment. But what will follow? Will the United States recover within
> 30 a few years, as it did from the disgrace of Richard Nixon's resignation and the fecklessness of Jimmy Carter during the Iranian hostage crisis? Alas, that is unlikely.

From: 'How Trump is ending the American era', *The Atlantic*, October 2017

Now go back to task **5** on p. 116.

Chapter 6   Beyond the Nation – Europe and a Globalized World

A2 Europe's lost generation   p. 125

3 Figurative language

Isaac often uses figurative language (metaphors and similes) to make her text more vivid (e.g., l. 6, 'weighed down by endemic youth unemployment'). Find more examples and analyse their effect. Copy the table below, adding the missing information and two more examples from the text.

Example from text	Line(s)	Meaning
… some are reawakening the ghosts of their fascist forefathers …	7–8	
	17	a huge difference
keeping its strongest economies afloat		
	45–46	

B2 The need for a new label   p. 129

3 Promoting transparent labelling

a Design a clothing label that helps buyers make responsible choices.

1 Make a list of aspects that are important for responsible clothing production.

2 Choose the most important points and think of a system to evaluate them.

3 Write the text for a clothing label that contains information about these aspects.

Now go back to task **3b** on p. 129.

C1 Keeping the accent   p. 134

4   YOU CHOOSE   Creative writing

a Write a *short story based on the poem.

1 Outline the events and emotions you would like to include in your story.

2 Decide from which character's *point of view to tell the story – the *speaker of the poem, the barman or other people in the bar.

3 Decide what type of *narrator to use.

4 Start writing. Do not write an introduction, but start in the middle of the scene, e.g. 'I can feel their looks piercing my back'.

5 Do not write a clear, conclusive ending, but leave it open, even a bit vague.

6 Hold writing conferences among four or five students to improve your texts.

 OR

b Write a dramatic *scene based on the poem.

1 Decide on how you are going to convey the *speaker's feelings or memories. You might make her speak a *soliloquy or you might have a second actor who acts as the speaker's 'shadow', articulating her feelings and thoughts.

2 Write your scene, starting the action right in the middle of the action, e.g. with the barman saying 'Sorry, what was that?'.

3 Imagine the actors' gestures or movements and write stage directions.

C3 Linguistic diplomacy: the Eurovision Song Contest   p. 135

5 Discussion

In groups of five prepare and hold a panel discussion in which you discuss the question of whether each country should be obliged to enter songs in their national language only. One student is the moderator, the others argue either for or against the topic.

Moderator:

- Think of possible arguments and their counter-arguments.
- Collect questions or remarks that might make the participants put these arguments forward.

Discussion participants:

- Think of arguments for your position and collect examples to illustrate your point.
  Don't just talk about the very obvious topics, but search for arguments and examples the others might not have thought about.
- Collect arguments that your opponents might put forward and think about ways to refute them.

Chapter Task   p. 137

1 Planning your work

a Do some research to get a general idea of the topic and to identify suitable subtopics.

1 Don't forget to provide a definition of slavery.
2 Define the areas you want to focus on:
   a You might want to give a short historical survey of slavery. Consider e.g. the situation in Ancient Greece or Rome, the Middle Ages and/or the Americas.
   b You might also want to outline the grievances that have led to slave rebellions throughout history.
   c When considering modern-day slavery, think of e.g. the catering trade or agriculture, the construction industry, private households, the entertainment industry (football) or sexual slavery.
3 Decide whether you want to present a case study or general aspects of slavery.

Now go back to task **1b** on p. 137.

2 Preparing your poster

b Organize your findings and prepare your poster.
1 Structure your text and visual aids in a way that guides the reader of your poster through it: Use symbols, lines, arrows, colours, and fonts in a clear and meaningful way.
2 You may use pictures and/or quotations taken from films and/or literature dealing with slavery.

Now go back to task **2c** on p. 137.

Chapter 7   Science – Enhancing Life?

A1 A saviour sibling   p. 143

3 Argumentative structure

Analyse the argumentative structure of the text.

1 Structure the text by finding headlines for each paragraph (see example on the right).

2 Examine the direct quotes: Who is quoted and what do they say? Are the quotes in favour or against the procedure?

ll. 1–2	Introduction: sibling was saved
ll. 3–6	Medical history of first sibling
ll. 7–12	Problems facing a second sibling
ll. 13–23	Medical treatment

3 Examine the indirect quotes: Who is quoted and what do they say? Are the indirect and direct quotes from the same person? If so, decide how the direct quotes relate to the indirect quotes.

Now go back to task **4** on p. 143.

A3 Designer people   p. 146

4 Practising speaking

a Prepare a monologue on whether designer babies are desirable or not. Think of a catchy introduction to your speech, e.g. start with a provocative statement like 'designer babies are the future' or 'a child has to be smart, intelligent, healthy and cute'.

- State your opinion on the topic clearly: In my opinion …, The point is that …, The way I see it …, My point is …, What I'm trying to say is …
- Make sure you have at least three good arguments in favour of or against the topic:

  Pro: reduced risk of genetic diseases, better opportunities in life, the child can have better genes than his or her parents

  Con: imperfect embryos are killed, no more individuality, only the rich can afford the perfect child, altering a human being is unethical

- Summarize your points at the end of your speech and clearly state your opinion:
  To sum up …, That's why I think …, All things considered …, All in all …

B2 Can this woman cure ageing with gene therapy? p.154

7 YOU CHOOSE ▶ Writing a comment

Choose one of the following and write a comment.

In a comment you want to convince the reader of your own opinion on an issue (cf. SF 34 Argumentative writing, pp.331–333). The following questions might help you to decide for one of the topics and forming an opinion on them.

a 'Nothing could be more desirable than living forever.'

OR

b 'Genetic engineering and gene therapy have been (illegally) used by athletes to improve their performance, but why not?'

OR

c 'What we're trying to do is hit the biggest point of suffering right now in the industrialized world, which is the diseases of ageing.' (ll. 6–7)[1]

- Is living forever desirable?
- What do I personally consider desirable (or more desirable than something else)?
- Would I want to live forever? Why or why not?
- What could humanity have done or avoided if some individuals had lived forever?

- Is sports a topic I'm generally interested in?
- Do I know anything about genetic engineering and gene therapy, especially in connection with sports?
- What are potential dangers of these methods?
- Would I support these methods, would I use them myself, knowing about their dangers?

- What are age-related diseases?
- Are these diseases really the 'biggest point of suffering' and should science concentrate on dealing with these diseases or are they a luxury/first-world problem? Are there no other, bigger problems, both in the industrialized countries and worldwide?

[1] From: Dara Mohammadi/Nicola Davis, 'Can this woman cure ageing with gene therapy?', *The Guardian*, 24 July 2016

C4 Biofuels – the green alternative? p.158

3 Having a debate

Find arguments in favour of and against biofuels. The motion could be as follows: 'Governments should subsidize biofuels.'

Discussion boxes for a debate:

Agreeing with and supporting an argument

Exactly!
Definitely!
I couldn't agree more!
That's right!
I agree with …
What … said is (absolutely) right.
I'm of the same opinion (as …)
I would like to support what … said.
You've got a good point there.

Interrupting – Asking for clarification

Sorry to interrupt, but …
I would like to add something here.
What do you think about …?
What is your opinion on …?
Could you explain that again, please?

Disagreeing

I can't agree with you …
I think you're (absolutely) wrong there!
I (completely) disagree with you!
Do you really mean that?
But you just said that now.
I'm sorry, but that can't be right!
But what you've just said is …
I must contradict you …

Chapter 8   Work and Business – Careers and Perspectives

A2 More work, fewer workers   p. 167

3 Looking into the future

a If you cannot think of any jobs, here is a list to choose from:

> accountant • actor • actress • artist • author • poet • cleaner • construction worker • doctor •
> factory worker • firefighter • flight attendant • gardener • hairdresser • IT consultant • journalist •
> lawyer • lecturer • locksmith • nurse • pilot • policeman • policewoman • psychologist • scientist •
> social worker • soldier • speech therapist • teacher • waiter • waitress

Now go back to task **3 b** on p. 167.

b Here are some ideas for reasons why or why not certain jobs might disappear:

The job may disappear, because it …	The job is not threatened, because it …
• involves routine, repetitive tasks • can be organized along an assembly line • involves a lot of steps that can be supervised by computers • consists mainly of assembly work • is always done in the same place • involves easy manual labour or simply force	• requires soft or social skills like communication, empathy or compassion • is a job in the field of high-quality education and training • is a job in the field of developing IT, automation and technological innovation • needs a lot of creativity and imagination • involves problem solving or other complex skills • involves very refined and complex hand movements

Now go back to task **3 c** on p. 167.

A4 Teenagers' career aspirations   p. 170

4 Writing

Should you pursue the career of your dreams or should you consider only those careers where job demand is fairly certain? Write an argumentative text in which you consider both sides, including aspects both may be missing. State your own view. For ideas *for* wanting to pursue your preferred career / studies programme, i.e. *against* considering only those careers where job demand is projected, consider motivational aspects, your talents, achieving the goals you set yourself, potentially good results in examinations and if you are diligent and hardworking.

For ideas *against* wanting to pursue your preferred career / studies programme, i.e. *for* considering only those careers where job demand is projected, look for arguments, facts and figures from the article for support and think of the possibility of combining talents and interests with promising career paths.

A5 Do you love your job?   p. 173

3 A tricky question in your job interview

a Some of the aspects of job satisfaction mentioned by Heuser should not be brought up in a job interview. List them, then compare with your partner. Remember, for instance: Your future employer is interested in your well-being and job satisfaction, but also wants employees who can work in a team.

Now go back to task **3 b** on p. 173.

B1 Mitch's first glimpse of the world of work   p. 175

2 Power relations
Partner A: Analyse the meeting between Mitch and McNulty and explain how one of them shows his power and superiority through non-linguistic means (e.g. facial expressions). Focus and take notes on
- Mitch and McNulty on their way to the coach's office,
- where and how they are sitting in the office,
- McNulty's eyes and voice,
- McNulty's pencil.

Partner B: Analyse the meeting between Mitch and McNulty and explain how one of them uses language to demonstrate his power and superiority. Focus and take notes on
- who is asking the important questions,
- who is using imperatives,
- who is trying to be funny,
- who controls the conversation.

Now go back to task **3** on p. 175.

B2 Ten things not to say in a job interview   p. 177

2 The language of the text
  a Explain how King tries to amuse the reader. Consider the following *stylistic devices used by King: absurd example, exaggeration, metaphor. Find examples of these devices in lines 30, 35 and 46–47.

Now go back to task **2b** on p. 177.

B3 Help wanted in Paradise   p. 178

4 Social classes
Examine the text for information about the social class Philip Blackwell belongs to.
Find the answers to the following questions:
- What did Blackwell do after his family sold their business?
- Where did he spend his time?
- What sites did he choose for his new business idea?
- How does Blackwell describe the people who spend their holidays in luxury resorts?
Now think about your answers: what do they show you about Blackwell and the class he belongs to?

B5 Look them in the eye – the job interview   p. 180

2 Do's and don'ts
Watch the video. With your partner, list and rank the given dos and don'ts of job interviews.
Five of the following aspects are dealt with in the video:

1	conversation openers	5	no-go questions
2	dress code	6	professional documents
3	first impressions	7	punctuality
4	hairstyle	8	selling yourself and your strengths

Now go back to task **3** on p. 180.

Chapter 9 Modern Media – Tools or Tyrants?

A1 Lonely friends p. 186

4 Poetic devices
Examine the means the poet uses to draw our attention to the influence of social media on our lives. Poetic devices are tools used by the poet to emphasize the meaning of a poem. These questions might help you to do the task:

- What effect does the title have on the reader?
- What is striking about the endings of the lines?
- What means does the poet use to make the content appear more vivid and appealing to the reader?
- How does the poet involve the reader in the poem?
- What is the tone of the poem, and what effect does this tone have on the reader?

Now go back to task **5** on p. 186.

A2 Online learning in 2044 p. 189

2 Telling names
Refer to the annotations on pp. 20–21 and analyse what the names reveal about the *character and the *setting.

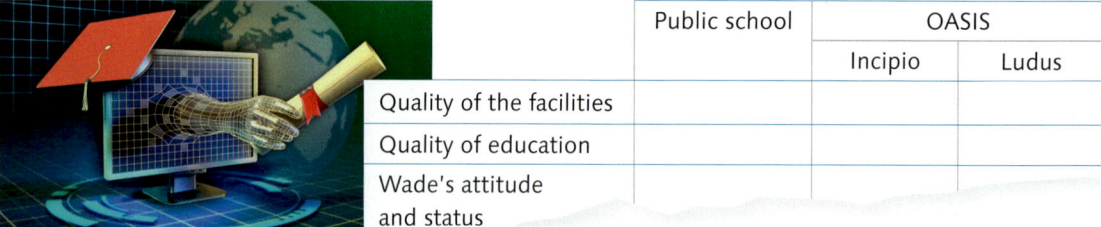

	Public school	OASIS	
		Incipio	Ludus
Quality of the facilities			
Quality of education			
Wade's attitude and status			

Step 1: Gather and structure the relevant information given in the text, using a grid like this one.
Step 2: Relate your findings to the names and explain their significance in the story.

Now go back to task **3** on p. 189.

B1 Should classrooms have video cameras? p. 195

3 Discussing the pros and cons of surveillance at school
c Present your concept to the school board (i.e. the class).
   Step 1: Make notes for each of the following steps.
      1 Address the members of the school board.
      2 State your group's attitude towards surveillance at school.
      3 Give reasons for your opinions and provide examples to illustrate your points. Present your concept in a clearly structured way with your most substantial argument at the end.
      4 Briefly sum up your main points.
      5 Invite the school board to ask questions or comment on your concept.
   Step 2: Plan how to present your reasons visually on the board / interactive whiteboard.
   Step 3: Use your notes to present your concept.

C1 The future of fake news: don't believe everything you read, see or hear   p. 200

2 What makes the text appealing?

Analyse the methods used to make the text appealing: Copy and complete the following table that helps you to identify possible elements of the text that address the reader.

Aspect	Example from the text	Function
Heading	• The future of fake news: don't believe everything you read, see or hear	Imperative form as a piece of advice → asks for action
Register	• Technical terms from the media world • Derogatory terms • …	
Stylistic devices	• Repeated use of we and us • Quotations • Open ending using a quotation • …	
Quotes	• Indirect quotation, l. 21 • Direct quotations by Saxena and Jenkins, starting l. 42 • Finishing quotes by both of them • …	
Writer's point of view	• Noticable bias towards dangers of doctoring content • (cf. e.g. last quotation) • …	

Now go back to task **3** on p. 200.

5 Fake news

a Write a guideline for the school magazine in which you inform students about recent technical developments and also give advice.

By carefully studying the task line, you can deduce the following tips for writing your text.

'inform' → **Tip 1:** You are supposed to inform, i.e. your introduction as well as your conclusion should explain and describe recent developments and potential risks.

'guideline' → **Tip 2:** By definition a guideline is a series of steps or a set of rules that help you to behave or proceed appropriately or that need to be carried out to reach a certain goal. This means that you are expected to write about three to five rules or directions to follow in order to avoid being manipulated by fake news. They could take the form of dos and don'ts, i.e. imperatives.

'school magazine' → **Tip 3:** This tells you something about your target audience. It consists of people your age, so you can address them in a style that matches your age. Don't forget to find a catchy headline.

b Fake news – mass hysteria or utmost damage to public trust in the media? Discuss.

The following aspects might serve as an inspiration:

*cyber attacks • fake news websites • bots • internet trolls • humorous use in satire shows • parody •
US presidential elections • The Daily Show • propaganda • international espionage • role of social media •
lying press (Lügenpresse) …*

Chapter 10   Urban, Suburban and Rural Life

A4 Why US talent is moving to Detroit   p. 212

3 How effective is it?

Analyse how effective the video clip is. Watching it a third time, observe the change of scenes, i.e. the change between people being interviewed, views of Detroit buildings, the inside of a school auditorium etc. Also pay attention to the effect the music has on you.

Use a table like the one below for taking notes.

Part of the clip	What you see	What you hear
Doyle Mosher (00:05–01:16)	▪ Derelict houses ▪ D.M. ▪ …	▪ D.M. talking ▪ …
Jason Zogg (01:17–01:53)		
Marlo Staples (01:54–02:26)		
…		

Now go back to task **4** on p. 212.

B2 A suburban street   p. 217

3 Using language to create a vivid image

b The following sentences are taken from the text. Each uses one or two of the stylistic devices listed in the box below. Match the appropriate term from the box to the sentences.

> A *contrast • B *enumeration • C *metaphor • D *parallelism • E *personification • F *repetition • G *simile

1 'For the first years they were lived in not by solicitors or barristers or doctors, but by the people who worked or clerked for them: the respectable, aspirational no-longer-poor.' (ll. 4–6)

2 'Over the next decades, the demographics of the street wobbled up and down in age, up and down in class, as it became more or less popular with upwardly mobile young families, and as the area did well or less well.' (ll. 6–8)

3 'The gap stayed there for years, like a pair of missing front teeth, until a new property with balconies and French windows, looking very strange amid the Victorian architecture, was built there in the fifties.' (ll. 10–13)

4 'It would be hard to put your finger on the exact point when Pepys Road began its climb up the economic ladder.' (ll. 14–15)

5 'A conventional answer would be to say that it tracked the change in Britain's prosperity, emerging from the dowdy chrysalis of the late 1970s and transforming into a vulgar, loud butterfly of the Thatcher decades and the long boom that followed them.' (ll. 15–18)

6 'The new arrivals tended to be more middle-class, with husbands who worked at decently paid but not spectacular jobs, and wives who stayed at home and looked after the children [...].' (ll. 22–24)

7   '[...] the people who lived in the street were, by global and maybe even by local standards, rich. The thing which made them rich was the very fact that they lived in Pepys Road. They were rich simply because [...]' (ll. 33–35)

Now go back to p. 217 and finish task **3b**.

C2 Small-town stories   p. 220

2 Using descriptive language

b Examine the stylistic devices the author uses to convey his message. Look for examples of these stylistic devices:

alliteration • *allusion* • *contrast* • *enumeration* • *exaggeration* • *metaphor* •
parallelism • *repetition* • *simile* • *symbol*

Now go back to task **3** on p. 220.

Language Practice

Focus on Grammar

LP 1 Simple and progressive
verb forms. 246

LP 2 Present tense or future?. 247

LP 3 Simple present and
present perfect 249

LP 4 Present perfect and
simple past 249

LP 5 Infinitive or gerund after
certain verbs 250

LP 6 Infinitive or gerund after
certain nouns 251

LP 7 The passive 252

LP 8 Conditional sentences 253

LP 9 Articles, quantifiers and
countability. 254

LP 10 Using adjectives
and adverbs 255

Focus on Style

LP 11 Using the right register 256

LP 12 Avoiding German-sounding
sentence patterns 256

LP 13 Placing emphasis
on key points 257

LP 14 Linking words and phrases. . . 259

LP 15 Connecting your thoughts
(sentence structure). 260

Focus on Vocabulary

LP 16 Avoiding Germanisms 262

LP 17 Spelling. 263

LP 18 Writing about texts 263

LP 19 Collocations 264

LP 20 Word formation 266

*Download the suggested
answers to the tasks here:*

 Webcode context-29

Focus on Grammar

▶ LP 1 Simple and progressive verb forms

1 **BASIC** Choose the right form of the verb for each of the sentences below (make sure you choose the correct tense).

1 A man came running out of the bank and (*jump*) into the waiting car.

2 Sorry, I can't talk now – I (*make*) dinner for the family.

3 Smoking (*cause*) over 600,000 deaths in the EU every year.

4 It was a cold evening, and a light drizzle (*fall*). When no one (*come*) to unlock the gates the crowd (*get*) restless.

5 The housing prices in London (*always be*) high, but at present they (*skyrocket*).

6 The last time I talked to her, she (*look*) for a new job.

Most English verbs can be used in all tenses in both the simple and the progressive form:
Jasmin practises *the piano three hours a day. She*'s practising *now for her concert on Saturday.*

Simple form	Progressive form
• For states[1]: Our house *needs* repainting. • For actions that follow a plan or physical law: *Our plane* leaves *at 8:05 am. Water* boils *at 100 °C.* • Actions in a series (narration) • Verbs that describe what the author of a text does: *The author* criticizes *the government's lack of initiative.*	• For actions that are taking place at the present moment or were taking place at a certain point in time in the past: *I've* been waiting *here all morning! When the police arrived, two men* were loading *boxes into a van.* • For trends and developments: *It's* becoming *more and more difficult to find a permanent job. It's* getting *dark – let's go home.* • For descriptions of circumstances (weather, clothing, etc.): *A cold wind* was blowing. *She* was wearing *a red woollen sweater over a plaid skirt.*

---

[1]**state** *Zustand*

Verbs that describe a state (i.e. not an activity) are called **state verbs**. Normally, they can only be used in the simple form:
I heard a voice. Someone needed help. I wanted to help them, but I didn't know how.
A few state verbs can also be used in the progressive form, but with a different meaning. Compare the sentences in the table below and explain the difference in meaning:

Simple form	Progressive form
What do you think of his decision?	What are you thinking about?
You look upset – what's the matter?	Why are you looking at me like that?
For her, success is all that counts.	We're counting on you to help us.
How do you feel about same-sex marriage?	He stayed at home because he wasn't feeling well.
Everybody has a bad day now and then.	We were having lunch when my phone rang.

2 Choose the right form of the verb for each of the sentences below:
1 I (*think*) you should go to her and tell her how you (*feel*) about what happened.
2 Lydia (*love*) going to parties, but she never (*feel*) like organizing one herself.
3 While I (*look*) at the photos on our website I (*have*) a great idea for our next campaign.
4 Everyone (*need*) the feeling that their life (*count*) for something.
5 The last time I (*see*) Bruce and Charlene they (*have*) a big argument about something .
6 When I visited Bob in hospital, I (*think*) he (*look*) awful, but he said that he (*feel*) better.

TROUBLE SPOT

With **everybody/everyone**, the plural form of the possessive pronoun is commonly used.

Special uses: the progressive form used for emphasis
- Some speakers use the progressive form of state verbs, especially in the present perfect, to underline their message: *'New York? I've been wanting to go there for ages!'* / *'I've been meaning to write to you since Christmas!'*
- In some situations, the progressive form of the verb *be* is used to refer to behaviour that is temporary and (perhaps) not genuine: *Why are you being so stubborn? – Ignore him; he's just being a trouble-maker again.*
- The slogan of a US fast-food chain (*I'm loving it!*) belongs to the same category: using the progressive form of the state verb *love* has the effect of underlining the message and makes the slogan more memorable.

▶ LP 2 Present tense or future?

1 **BASIC** Spot and correct the mistakes in the sentences below:
1 I don't know how he reacts when we tell him the truth.
6 'I need a can opener for this.' – 'No problem, I go look for one.'
3 Is it true that Kai goes abroad next year?
4 The weather forecast says there are scattered showers throughout the afternoon.
5 I'm sure my parents don't let me go to the rock festival.
6 The German students will wait at Stansted until their bus will come to collect them.

Generally speaking, English – like German – uses the **present tense to talk about the present** and the **future to talk about the future**. However, there are a few exceptions to keep in mind:

- In English, when offering to do something, the ***will*-future** is used (whereas the present tense would be used in German): *Hast du Durst? Ich hole uns etwas zu trinken. / Are you thirsty? I'll fetch us something to drink.*
- In German, it is possible to talk about the future in the present tense: *Wir fahren morgen an die See*. You can do this in English too, but only with the **present progressive** when you talk about plans for the future: *We're leaving* for the coast tomorrow. A sentence like *Morgen regnet es wieder* can only be expressed in the *will*-future: *It will rain again tomorrow*.
- **The future is not used** after *if, when, unless, until, as soon as,* etc., even when you are referring to the future: *Phone me as soon as you arrive. – You won't get tickets unless you book in advance.*

2 Use the keywords and phrases to make complete sentences. All verbs are in the present or the future:

1 There's someone at the door. You / please / go / see who it is?
2 The PM says / he / attend to the problem / as soon as / government report / published.
3 In the course of the week / temperatures / drop slightly.
4 By the time / we / arrive at the airport / it / be / too late.
5 The people next door / have / their house repainted / next month.
6 The assistant director says / he / talk to the staff / before / situation / escalate any further.

▶ LP 3 Simple present and present perfect

1 **BASIC** Decide which of the following sentences are correct. Correct the faulty ones:

1 I have wanted to meet her for as long as I can remember.
2 For the past three years, John is saving his money for a trip to New Zealand.
3 The author and her family live in London since 2006.
4 Four hundred years after his death, Shakespeare has continued to fascinate audiences around the world.
5 We are waiting for this bus for the last half an hour – I don't think it's coming.
6 Leonie has been an avid reader ever since she taught herself to read at the age of five.

The **present perfect** is used in English for actions and states that began in the past, but are still going on or hold true. German uses the present tense in such cases.

German	English
Hunneman leitet die Organisation seit 2008.	*Hunneman has led the organization since 2008.*
Rowling arbeitet seit drei Jahren an einem neuen Roman.	*Rowling has been working on a new novel for three years.*

The **present perfect** is closely connected with the present time. For that reason, English speakers often choose verbs in the present perfect where a German might use a different verb in the present.

German	English
Kennst du den Roman Doktor Faustus?	*Have you* ever *read* Doktor Faustus?
Ich kenne Bratislava *nicht.*	*I've* never *been* to Bratislava.
Weißt du, ob Justin heute da ist?	*Have you seen* Justin this morning?
Wissen die Praktikanten schon Bescheid?	*Have the interns been informed* yet?

2 Translate the following sentences into idiomatic English. Use the verb in brackets in the present perfect.

1 Kennst du den Film *Casablanca*? (see)
2 Kennst du Paris? (be)
3 Kennt ihr schon das neue türkische Restaurant am Zimmerplatz? (check out)
4 Ich bin noch nie Ski gelaufen. (try)
5 Weißt du über das Treffen heute Nachmittag Bescheid? (hear)
6 Kennst du dich mit 3D-Druckern aus? (use)

▶ LP4 Present perfect and simple past

1 **BASIC** Complete the sentences with the correct form of the verb (present perfect or simple past).

1 When … you last … Thomas? (see)
2 The centre … opened in 2004. (be)
3 Until today, no one … a cure for cancer. (discover)
4 Sarah … me the revised version of the text just five minutes ago. (hand)
5 We're still friends, although I … her since we graduated. (not see)
6 I … the book when it first came out, but I … it. (read; not like)
7 Julia and Tobias … at a youth camp in Ireland in 2012. They … in contact ever since. (meet; keep)
8 My brother … to New Zealand yesterday, but we … from him yet. (fly; not hear)

Present perfect (This tense refers to a time that has not yet ended.)	**Simple past** (This tense refers to a time that is over.)
Use this tense • to present results: *Engineers at the Wyss Institute have developed a new kind of biodegradable plastic.* • to talk about states that have existed since some time in the past: *How long have you lived in Germany?* • to talk about actions in the past without saying when they happened: *She's been there before.* • to talk about actions that have happened more than once (or never): *I've seen that film at least five times. I've never been to Denmark.*	Use this tense when talking about events that happened in the past: *When I was a student, I lived in Exeter.*
Examples of signal words and phrases: • *already, ever, never, yet, often* • time phrases with *since* and *for* (*since 2013, for ten years*)	Examples of signal words and phrases: • *before, yesterday* • time phrases of the past (*ten minutes ago, last June, in 2010*) • *When …?*

> **■ TROUBLE SPOT**
> Signal words of the past can **never** be used together with the **present perfect**. Sentences such as ~~When have you last talked to him?~~ and ~~I have seen her just a few minutes ago~~ are always wrong!

2 Choose the correct form of the verbs in brackets in the following text. You may use the present, the simple past or the present perfect:

Almost everyone (hear) of Stephen King, the best-selling author of dozens of horror stories. King (be) born in 1947 in Maine, USA, where many of his stories (be) also set. After graduating from the University of Maine in 1970, King (find) a teaching position at Hampden Academy. His first novel, Carrie, (be) published by Doubleday in 1973 and (bring) King national attention as well as financial independence. In the summer of 1999, King (be) walking down a road when he (be) hit by a car and badly injured. He (survive), but since his accident, he (write) much less. His son Joseph Hillstrom King, who (use) the pen name Joe Hill, (write) three novels and numerous stories, all of which (belong) to the genre fantasy/horror. Similar to his more famous father, Hill (win) numerous writing awards.

World-famous author, Stephen King

▶ LP 5 Infinitive or gerund after certain verbs

1 **BASIC** Choose the correct form of the verb complement (infinitive or gerund) in the following sentences:
1 You can leave as soon as you have finished (clean up).
2 Many people dislike (be told) what to do.
3 How long have you wanted (go) there?
4 I don't mind (get) my hands dirty.
5 As she had never intended (take) the job, Sandy was surprised (receive) an offer.
6 She hoped (get) a better offer from a firm in Shanghai.

Infinitive or gerund?	Verbs	Example
verb + **infinitive**	most verbs that can take a complement	I *want to go* to Hawaii. I *wish to speak* to your boss. I'm *planning to study* physics.
verb + **gerund**	admit, avoid, consider, deny, dislike, enjoy, finish, give up, imagine, include, involve, justify, keep, mention, mind, miss, practise, risk, suggest	I *dislike waiting* for the bus. I *miss going* to school. ■ **TIP** To avoid mistakes, try learning these verbs by heart and then use the infinitive with the rest.
verb + **gerund or infinitive** (same meaning)	love, like, hate, prefer, begin, start, continue	I *love to play* badminton. / I *love playing* badminton.

A small number of verbs have **different meanings** when they are used with an infinitive or a gerund. Compare the sentences in the table below. What does the verb mean in each case?

Verb	Used with a gerund	Used with an infinitive
stop	*Stop shouting* like that!	Let's *stop to have* a break.
remember	I don't *remember seeing* him at the meeting.	Did you *remember to lock* the door?
forget	I'll never *forget seeing* London for the first time.	I *forgot to buy* a litre of milk – sorry!
mean	Sustainability *means not using* more than we produce.	I didn't *mean to make* her upset.
try	If you have the hiccups – *try holding* your breath.	We *tried to make* him change his mind, but he wouldn't listen.

2 Decide between a gerund or an infinitive in the following sentences:

1 For Melissa, the job in Los Angeles was a dream come true, but it meant (leave) her family and friends behind.
2 If we don't stop (dump) waste into the world's oceans, it may soon be too late.
3 Suzie mentioned (go) on a date but avoided (tell) us with whom.
4 I tried (reach) you by mobile, but I only got your mailbox.
5 John stopped (read) the newspaper and missed the train.
6 Anthony considered (run) the red light but then imagined (cause) an accident.
7 Students often say that they forgot (do) their homework, but no one really believes them.

▶ LP6 Infinitive or gerund after certain nouns

1 **BASIC** Spot the mistakes in the following sentences and correct them. Careful: not all sentences are wrong.

1 I don't know why she entered the competition – she doesn't have a chance of winning.
2 I'm afraid we don't have time of discussing the matter any longer.
3 Mark Zuckerberg wasn't the first person who had the idea to create a social networking site.
4 Our plan of camping in the wild turned out to be completely unrealistic.
5 Rosa Parks was one of the first African Americans who had the courage of speaking out against racism.
6 After their traumatic experience, the victims had the need of talking to someone who could help them.
7 Students often face the problem to find affordable accommodations.
8 The stipend helped Jens of going to New York for a year.

In German, you can add information to any noun using an infinitive phrase: *der Wunsch, reich und berühmt zu sein*.

In English, generally an **infinitive** is used, a **gerund with *of***, or a ***that*-clause**:
the right *to state* your opinion
the dream *of becoming* a star
the fact *that she could speak five languages*.
However, these complements cannot be used interchangeably:

Infinitive or gerund?	Nouns	Example
noun + infinitive	*right, wish, desire, longing, will, courage, strength, decision, time, need, ability*	the *right to bear* arms, *time to say* good-bye, the *will to live*
noun + *of* + gerund	most other nouns	the *risk of getting* lost, the *fear of being left behind*
special cases	• *chance, opportunity, plan*: Either the infinitive or *of* + gerund can be used. • *a/any chance*: *of* + gerund is used more often. • *the chance*: The infinitive is used more often.	This is my *chance to earn* lots of money. / This is my *chance of earning* lots of money. *Any chance of seeing* him again? *The chance to win* this game is pretty slim.

There are a few **more special cases** worth remembering:
- The word *reason* can be used either with an infinitive or with *for* + gerund. When *reason* is followed by *for* + a person, an infinitive must be used: *There's no reason for us to give up without a fight.*
- The word *attempt* can be followed either by an infinitive or by *at* + gerund: *The government's attempt at covering up / to cover up the matter only made things worse.*
- The expression *(to) have trouble / difficulty* is used with a gerund without any preposition: *I had trouble starting the motor. Difficulty* can also be followed by *in* + gerund: *We had difficulty* (not: ~~difficulties~~) *in persuading her to come to the meeting.* Careful: In other contexts *difficulty* is treated like a normal noun (*of* + gerund): *the difficulty of living with a permanent disability.*

2 Put the verb in brackets into the correct form; in some cases there is more than one correct solution:
1. All our attempts (reach) an agreement have failed.
2. The dream (find) a better life was reason enough for millions of immigrants (leave) their homeland.
3. The producer had trouble (find) a child star who could both act and dance.
4. Steven spent his first weeks in Kerala learning (cope) with the difficulties (live and work) in India.
5. I would be interested in hearing your reasons (reject) the proposal.
6. You can't imagine the difficulty we had (locate) a garage in Sofia that could repair our car.

▶ LP 7 The passive

1 **BASIC** Make complete sentences in the passive using the keywords:
1. Fitzgerald's classic novel, *The Great Gatsby* / first publish / 1925
2. To date[1] / it / adapt for the screen / six times
3. The most recent version / released / 2013
4. It / be / the first screen adaptation / that / film (v) / in 3D format
5. The title role / play / Leonardo DiCaprio
6. The film / criticize / some critics / as a costume spectacle
7. Most of the scenes / shoot / in Australia, / where huge sets / build / for the film

Rules for using the passive	Examples
The passive in English is formed using the verb **(to) be** and the **past participle**.	*Tchaikovsky's ballet* Swan Lake *was first performed in 1877.*
Generally, the passive is used when the person who does an action is unknown or unimportant.	*Three paintings were stolen from the museum last weekend.*
If the person or force that does something (the 'agent') is named in the sentence, it is introduced using the preposition **by**.	*The tower was damaged by lightning in 1988.*
Verbs that use a preposition keep the preposition in the passive.	*discriminate against sb.* → *African Americans have often been discriminated against, not only in the past.*
If the so-called **personal passive** can be formed, it is usually first choice.	*We were given our ID cards at the main desk.* (The 'normal' passive would sound awkward here: *Our ID cards were given to us at the main desk.*)
Passive forms of the **infinitive** and the **gerund** can also be formed.	*(to) love* → *(to) be loved* *loving* → *being loved*

---

[1]**to date** *(adv) bisher, bis jetzt*

2 Use an infinitive or a gerund in the passive to rewrite the <u>underlined</u> parts of the following sentences. You may have to change the word order. Avoid using a *by*-agent.

1 After the flood <u>they had to rebuild</u> most of the houses in the village. *(After the flood most of the houses in the village had to …)*
2 Teenagers hate <u>it when adults treat them</u> like children.
3 Even in his darkest moments, Colin never gave up the hope <u>that he would be rescued</u>.
4 It was her fear <u>that people would laugh at her</u> that held her back.
5 She told her doctor that she wanted <u>him to tell her the truth</u>.
6 No one likes the feeling <u>that someone is discriminating against them</u>.

Special uses: the *get*-passive

In colloquial English, many speakers form the passive using **get** instead of **be**. Common phrases are *get hurt, get killed, get lost, get caught.*
The *get*-passive is also used to emphasize the difference between an action and a state:
We soon got lost in a maze of tiny alleyways that all looked the same.
I couldn't spot a single familiar landmark and finally had to admit that I was lost.

▶ **LP 8 Conditional sentences**

1 | BASIC | Complete the following sentences with the correct form of the verb in brackets:

1 If I discover a cancer cure, I (become) famous.
2 If I discovered a cancer cure, I (become) famous.
3 If I had discovered a cancer cure ten years ago, I (be) famous.
4 If someone (be) famous, everyone recognizes them on the street.
5 If Romeo (not crash) the Capulets' party, he might never have met Juliet.
6 If the sea level (rise) one meter, hundreds of coastal cities would be in danger.

A variety of conditional sentences are possible in English. Their use depends on the situation.	
An imagined condition in the **past** with an imagined consequence in the **past**.	*If Sheila had taken part in the competition, she might have won a prize.*
An imagined condition in the **past** with an imagined consequence in the **present**.	*If you hadn't wasted all your money, you could afford to go with us to Greece.*
An imagined condition in the **present** with an imagined consequence.	*If Sarah worked harder, she would get better marks.*
A possible condition in the **present** with a possible consequence.	*If you have trouble with the new software, Kevin can / will help you.*
A condition that can happen at any time and its consequence.	*If the polar ice caps melt, the sea level rises / will rise.*

2 The text below presents some facts concerning the settlement of North America and its consequences. Draw conclusions from the facts using conditional sentences.
Example: *If European settlers had not come to America, herds of buffalo might still roam the Great Plains.*

When the first European settlers arrived at the shores of the New World, there were about three million Native Americans living in North America. Having no natural immunity to European diseases, thousands of natives fell ill and died. As they moved farther west, the white settlers pushed the natives off their land, at the same time decimating[1] the large herds of buffalo that roamed[2] the Great Plains. The Native Americans, whose way of life depended on the buffalo, could no longer exist. Ancient grasslands disappeared as farms were followed by railroads, towns, highways and factories, further restricting the freedom of movement of the native tribes. An ecological balance between man and nature that had existed for thousands of years was destroyed within a few decades.

▶ LP9 Articles, quantifiers and countability

1 **BASIC** Translate the nouns and noun phrases in brackets, deciding whether you need a singular or a plural and whether or not the definite article is necessary.
1 *(Die menschliche Gesellschaft)* hasn't made *(viele Fortschritte)* in dealing with the forces of *(das Böse)*.
2 We found *(einige interessante Informationen)* on the internet concerning *(die Kunst)* of the Aborigines.
3 *(Die Wissenschaft)* can provide us with *(Erkenntnisse)*, but it can't give us any *(Ratschläge)* on how to use it.
4 Despite all the *(Forschungen)* on cancer, there has been relatively *(wenig Fortschritte)*.
5 Although she grew up in L.A., her *(Kenntnisse)* of *(die Natur)* and *(die Umwelt)* is really impressive.

> *Find more information on articles, quantifiers and countability here:*
> **Webcode** context-30

2 The table below shows which social networking site five young people regularly use:

	Sandy	Carol	Andrew	James	Marvin
Spacebook	X	X	X	X	X
Lightnigram	X		X	X	X
Chatter	X	X	X		
Mumblr			X		X
OurSpace					

1 Make four statements about the group. Example: *A few of them use Mumblr.*
2 Make two statements about Sandy and Carol: what have they got in common?

---

[1]**decimate sth.** kill large numbers of sth.   [2]**roam** walk around with no fixed goal

▶ LP 10 Using adjectives and adverbs

1 **BASIC** Put the words in brackets in the right form (adjective or adverb):

1 In science-fiction films, robots (traditional) appear in the role of (soulless) killing machines.
2 The engineers who develop robots for new applications (passionate) believe that they will make our lives (happy and safe).
3 For example, they will free us from (boring) tasks like cleaning the house or mowing the lawn.
4 Most of the (heavy) work in farming is already done (automatic) by machine.
5 (Remarkable) progress has been made in developing robots for a (large) number of everyday uses.
6 Ideas that sounded (impossible) only ten years ago are (rapid) becoming reality.
7 Perhaps someday we will be (complete) dependent on (intelligent) machines for almost everything.

Adjectives

Adjectives are used to modify (i.e. describe) a noun. They can be used directly before the noun (*a short holiday, a famous tourist spot*) or they are used after certain verbs:

Verbs of being, seeming, becoming, etc.	*Why are you sad? She seemed unhappy. Don't get nervous. Injustice always makes me angry.*
Verbs that describe sense impressions	*He looks nervous. That sounds wonderful. The soup smells great and it tastes great too. The stone felt cold to the touch.*

Adverbs

Adverbs of manner are made from adjectives by adding *-ly*. (Exceptions: *fast, hard, early* and *late* are used as both adjectives and adverbs.)
Adverbs modify verbs, adjectives, or other adverbs:

Adverb modifies **verb**.	*She got up quickly and ran to the window.*
Adverb modifies **adjective**.	*The team has been incredibly successful this season.*
Adverb modifies **adverb**.	*The experts worked extremely cautiously to defuse the bomb.*

Certain adverbs can also be used to modify a whole sentence. Such adverbs are known as **sentence adverbs.** They always stand at the beginning of the sentence and are often separated by a comma from the rest of the sentence.

Adverb modifies **sentence**.	*Fortunately, none of the passengers were seriously injured.*

Other common sentence adverbs: *actually, admittedly, apparently, consequently, eventually, evidently, hopefully, incidentally, luckily, obviously, presumably, surprisingly, ultimately, understandably*.

---

2 Use a sentence adverb instead of the underlined words in each of the sentences below:

1 More and more cars hit the road every year. <u>As a result</u>, the number of traffic jams also increases.
2 <u>A surprising fact is that</u> the interest in car ownership is declining.
3 <u>It seems that</u> many young urbanites regard a car as an unnecessary expense.
4 <u>It is easy to understand that</u> the interest in car ownership is lowest where cheap, reliable public transportation is available.
5 <u>In the course of time</u> cars may disappear altogether from our city streets.
6 <u>I hope that</u> this development will mean cleaner air in cities that presently have a huge smog problem.

Focus on Style

▶ LP 11 Using the right register

1 **BASIC** In the following excerpt from a student's film summary, the teacher has underlined some expressions in red to indicate that they are inappropriate. Rewrite the text, correcting the stylistic problems.

The film Outsourced *is about this guy named Todd Anderson. He works for an American firm that has outsourced its call centre to India to save money. Todd gets sent there to bring the Indian workers up to US standards. When he gets there, he's totally lost, cause he doesn't know the first thing about India. He tries to get the Indians to act like Americans, but it doesn't work out. He only starts getting somewhere when he begins listening to the Indians and taking them seriously.*

Like other languages, English has different registers for different situations:

Register	Typical situations	Typical features
Informal	Everyday communication between friends, spoken English	Short or incomplete sentences, short forms (*they've, gotta*), phrasal verbs, colloquial expressions (*make it big, chill out,* etc.)
Neutral	Articles and essays on subjects of general interest	Mix of short and more complex sentences, no short forms, words of the general vocabulary
Formal	Official documents and speeches, business letters	Complex sentences, specialized or technical words

When writing essays for school, use the neutral register. Some teachers allow you to use short forms of negations in your writing (*don't, can't,* etc.); ask if you aren't sure.

2 After finishing school in Germany, you apply to a College of Arts in the United States. One day you receive the following letter:

> On behalf of the Admissions Committee I am pleased to inform you that you have been offered a place in the incoming freshman class. Your application convinced us that you have the talent and motivation required for academic success. Furthermore, after careful review of your family's financial situation, we have decided to award you a full scholarship, comprising all tuition fees as well as room and board for the duration of your studies.
> All our students are guaranteed on-campus accommodation in our newly-renovated dormitories (dual occupancy). Furthermore, the College provides a comprehensive 24/7 meal service. Should you decide to accept our offer, please reply by June 10th.

Look up the words and expressions you don't understand; most of them belong to the vocabulary of formal correspondence. Then write an email to your former host family in the US, telling them about the letter and its contents and asking about points that are unclear to you. Use a *neutral or moderately informal* style.

▶ LP 12 Avoiding German-sounding sentence patterns

1 **BASIC** Find the mistakes in the following sentences and correct them.
   1 If you ask me, Roland paid for his new smartphone far too much.
   2 In 2010 was the number of severe storms higher than ever before.
   3 Many teenagers use every day the internet to communicate with friends.

4   I download always the latest version of the program.

5   The author writes that the USA ignores all too often the rest of the world.

6   She points out in her latest book the decline of America's influence in the world.

7   This last point illustrates the author with an anecdote.

8   The summer months can be in some parts of Germany quite cool.

You already know that in some ways German and English sentences are formed differently. Here are some points to observe when you are writing English:

German	English
Dependent infinitives and participles are placed at the end of the sentence *(Satzklammer)*: *Er kann* hervorragend *Klavier spielen.* *Er hat* neulich in der Aula *ein Konzert gegeben.*	A 'cluster' instead of a 'bracket' is used, i.e. closely connected words (subject, verb, object) stay together: *He can play the piano* marvellously. Recently *he gave a concert* in the school hall.
The subject moves to third position if there is an adverbial phrase at the beginning of the sentence: *Im November 1989 / wurden / die Übergänge zwischen Ost- und West-Berlin / überraschend freigegeben.*	The subject always comes before the verb; in other words, the word order (S–V) stays the same when an adverbial phrase is put at the beginning of the sentence: *In November 1989 / the checkpoints between East and West Berlin / were unexpectedly opened.*
Verb and object are often separated: *Thomas und Harald spielen jeden Mittwoch Tennis.*	Verb and object **must** stay together: *Thomas and Harald play tennis every Wednesday.*

Even if there is no two-part verb, Germans tend to form a 'bracket sentence': *Dies ist in einigen Fällen ein Problem.*

In English the sentence would sound strange: *This is in some cases a problem.*

> **■ TIP**
>
> Begin your sentences with an adverbial phrase. This helps you to avoid the monotony of sentences that all begin with the subject. *Friedman is an optimist in this respect.* → *In this respect, Friedman is an optimist.*

---

2 Rearrange sentences in the following text to make it more idiomatic:

Thomas L. Friedman and Michael Mandelbaum collaborated on the book *That Used to Be Us*, which in 2011 was published. The authors point out using numerous examples how the US in global competition has fallen behind. America has lost sight according to the authors of its traditional strengths and values. The authors make in the second half of the book a number of suggestions as to what should be done. Some of these suggestions sounded to a few of the book's critics quite unrealistic. The book was in spite of its gloomy message an instant bestseller.

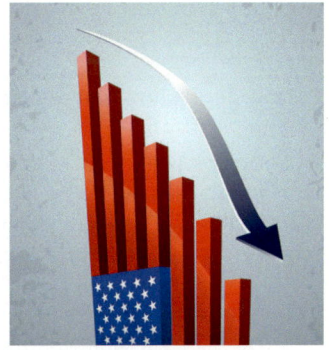

▶ **LP 13 Placing emphasis on key points** 🎧 CD3 07

1 **BASIC** Listen to three short conversations, then match them to the following techniques:

1   The important words in the sentence are stressed, i.e. spoken louder than the others.

2   The emphatic do-form of the verb is used.

3   The important word is made the subject of the reply.

> *Listen to the audio file on the CD or download it here:*
> **Webcode** context-31

Some of the techniques for emphasis that are used when speaking can also be used in written English; others sound rather formal in spoken English and are mainly used in writing:

Speaking/ Writing	Technique	Example
Speaking	Stressing the important words in the sentence, i.e. speaking them louder than the others	–
Speaking and writing	Using the emphatic *do*-form of the verb	I *do* think that's the wrong decision.
	Making the important word the subject of the reply	*Running* is the sport I love most.
Speaking (esp. in formal contexts) and writing	Special use of *very*	*Very* is used in English to modify words like *first* and *last*: In *the very first* scene of the film… • At *the very last* moment … It can also be used where in German you would use *gerade* or *genau* to emphasize something: *Gerade* die Anonymität des Internets … • *The very* anonymity of the internet …
	especially, in particular	Careful: Unlike *besonders*, you hardly ever find them at the beginning of a sentence: *Sitting still for 45 minutes can be a challenge, especially for young children.*
	Other expressions	German compound nouns like *Hauptgrund* or *Hauptfaktor* can be translated with *the main* reason, *the most important* factor, etc. To emphasize that you are naming the most important item in a list of facts or arguments, use *above all* or *most importantly* to introduce your sentence.

2 Now decide how you could reply emphatically to the following questions using one of the techniques in the table:

1 Do you like Indian cuisine? (You like some dishes, but not the really spicy ones.)
2 What would you like – apple juice or cola? (You choose.)
3 Didn't you read the novel over the weekend? (You didn't finish, but you read the first half.)
4 You're from Hamburg, right? (You went to school there, but you were born in Kiel.)

3 Translate these sentences into English:

1 Die Hauptursache von Hass ist Angst.
2 Besonders in den Entwicklungsländern haben viele Menschen keinen Zugang zu sauberem Wasser.
3 Wir erreichten unser Flugzeug in allerletzter Minute.
4 Vor allem gibt es eine wachsende Kluft *(a widening gap)* zwischen den armen und den reichen Ländern.
5 Schon im ersten Satz macht der Autor seine Meinung deutlich.
6 Die Hauptsache ist wohl die, dass es genug qualifizierte Arbeitskräfte *(workers)* gibt.

In written English, there are ways of structuring a sentence so as to emphasize a certain word or words:

Technique	Example	Comment
Using a subordinate clause that points to the most important idea in the sentence	*Ralph Nader first criticized the US automobile industry.* → *It was Ralph Nader who first criticized the US automobile industry. Society needs people who put the common good above personal gain.* → *What society needs is people who put the common good above personal gain.*	Pay attention to the forms of *be* used in the examples; why are they both in the singular?
Using a negation (*never, nowhere, not once,* etc.) or *only* + time phrase (e.g. *only later*) at the beginning of the sentence. The verb is put in the question form (inversion).	*Never before have young people had so many opportunities. Only then did she realize her mistake.*	This structure is common in political speeches.
Using contrast	*It was greed and arrogance, not simply bad timing, that led to the collapse of the bank. Unlike earlier SNS, Facebook appealed to users of all age groups. Compared with the US, China lacks a culture of creative entrepreneurship.*	

4 Rewrite the sentences to make them more emphatic, using the techniques from the table above.
1 Shared values hold a society together.
2 China's economy is growing rapidly; that of the EU isn't.
3 It has never before been so easy to communicate with people around the globe.
4 Western countries need a vision that includes the rest of the world.
5 Not lack of ambition, but fear of failure holds most people back.

▶ LP 14 Linking words and phrases

1 **BASIC** Complete the following text with suitable linking words or phrases from the choices below.

at the same time · for example · for one thing · furthermore · moreover · on the other hand · for instance

Are Americans environmentally friendly? There is no simple answer to this question. In a recent survey, … (1), 65% of American adults agreed that 'preserving the environment is very important.' … (2), 22% of consumers who remodeled their homes in the last 12 months said they had used environmentally friendly products for their renovation. … (3), data from the last five years indicate that consumers are now less willing to pay more or give up convenience for green products. … (4), the percentage of U.S. adults who agreed with the statement 'I am willing to give up convenience in return for a product that is environmentally safe' has declined 16% in the past five years, from 56% in 2007 to 47% in 2011.

… (5), there is definitely a trend among younger Americans toward more environmental awareness. … (6), consumers aged 18–24 are the only adult age group whose willingness to give up convenience or pay more for green products has held steady over the past five years. … (7), 53% of consumers aged 18–24 recycle products and 4% participated in environmental groups or causes in the past 12 months.

Statistics from: Bart King, 'American Environmentally Friendly Buying Habits', 6 April 2012

Linking words and phrases are the signposts of written and spoken communication; they help readers and listeners find their way through texts. Choosing the right phrases also helps you as a writer to think critically about the relationship between your sentences. The table below shows you a selection of useful phrases and their functions.

Use	Linking word or phrase
Stating your opinion	*In my opinion … • To my mind … • I think/feel/believe that …*
Listing facts, arguments, etc.	*First of all … • Firstly … • For one thing, …* *Secondly … • Furthermore … • What is more, … • Besides … • In addition … • Moreover …* *Finally … • Above all … • Most importantly …*
Giving an example	*for example … • for instance … • such as …*
Emphasizing	*In fact, … • As a matter of fact, … • Actually, …*
Contrasting	*On the one hand … On the other hand … • However … • … though … •* *Nonetheless … • Whereas … • Although … • In spite of …*
Conceding a point	*Of course … • Naturally … • Admittedly …*
Referring to a point in time or a development	*At the/that time … • In those days … • Eventually … • In the course of … •* *In the long run … • Meanwhile … • At the same time … • As a result …*
Coming to a conclusion	*All in all … • In the final analysis … • In conclusion … • Ultimately … • For the reasons mentioned above … • To sum up … • To conclude … • I would like to conclude by saying …*

2 In the following text, linking words and phrases have been left out. Decide where such 'signposts' are missing and choose appropriate ones from the table above. Then write an improved version of the text.

Google wants to change the world – again

Google revolutionized the way we use the Web in the 1990s with a new kind of search engine. Now it wants to change the way we navigate physical space. The California firm has developed a small
5 car that drives itself. The car is equipped with GPS and a host of sensors that collect information about the surroundings as it moves. There is a steering wheel and a brake (for emergencies), but the car is programmed to work without a
10 human driver.

Google is not interested in going into the car business. The real purpose is to change how we think about mobility. Why should you buy a car if you can get one whenever you need or want it?
15 You want to go downtown, you flip open your smartphone and call for an autonomous taxi. The vehicle drops you off at your destination, then goes on to its next job. There would be less need for huge parking lots and parking garages. There
20 would be fewer emissions as people waste less time cruising around looking for a parking space. People who are unable to drive (because of age, disability, or because they are drunk) could still get from one place to another. Self-driving cars
25 would be a new form of public transportation. The way cities are designed would change.

There are still problems to be solved. Who is responsible when an autonomous vehicle is involved in an accident? Will people overcome
30 their fear of losing control over their cars? What about the transition period when human and non-human drivers share the same roads? It is only a question of time until these issues have been settled. The future is coming, and Google
35 wants to get there first.

► LP 15 Connecting your thoughts (sentence structure)

1 **BASIC** Your partner has given you this text to proofread. Rewrite it to improve the style without leaving out any information.

Frank McCourt was born in Brooklyn, New York in 1930, which was the first year of the Great Depression. Both of his parents were immigrants from Ireland. They had come to America like millions of other Irish men and women who were looking for a better life. But they didn't find a better life, they only found poverty and misery. The McCourts, who were disappointed with life in America, decided to move back to Ireland. But their new life in Limerick, which was the hometown of Frank's mother, was no better than their life in Brooklyn. Young Frank had to leave school to support his family. He did odd jobs to earn a few pounds. After he had saved enough money for a ticket to New York, he left Ireland for good and didn't even tell his family.

Texts that contain unnecessary words or that connect ideas too loosely don't read well. A few simple techniques can help you make your sentences more compact and connected:

Loose connection		Stronger connection
Relative clause: *Frank McCourt was born in Brooklyn, New York in 1930, which was the first year of the Great Depression.*	→	**Apposition:** *Frank McCourt was born in Brooklyn, New York in 1930, the first year of the Great Depression.*
Relative clause: *They had come to America like millions of other Irish men and women who were looking for a better life.*	→	**Participle construction:** *They had come to America like millions of other Irish men and women looking for a better life.*
Compound sentence: *But they didn't find a better life, they only found poverty and misery.* *After he had saved enough money for a ticket to New York, he left Ireland for good and didn't even tell his family.*	→	**Gerund construction:** *But instead of finding a better life, they only found poverty and misery.* *After saving enough money for a ticket to New York, he left Ireland for good without even telling his family.*

Participle phrases can also be used instead of adverbial clauses with a variety of meanings:

Example	Function of participle construction
Arriving in New York, he looked for a cheap room.	Time (simultaneous action)
Having served in the Army during the Korean War, Frank was offered the chance to go to college.	Time (antecedent action)
Wanting to improve his status, he got a degree in English from NYU.	Reason
McCourt taught in New York schools for thirty years, never forgetting the bitter poverty he had experienced in Ireland.	Accompanying circumstance

2 Rewrite the final paragraph of the text on Frank McCourt, using participle phrases in suitable places to improve the style.

After he had retired from teaching, McCourt began writing his memoires. They appeared in fictionalized form in 1996 as Angela's Ashes. The novel was a worldwide success and also won its author a Pulitzer Prize. McCourt looks back on his childhood in Limerick with irony and wit, and he describes how hard life was for poor Irish families in the 1930s and 40s. McCourt was amused at the unexpected success of his book and said that it was the first time in history that a man had become rich by writing about being poor.

Focus on Vocabulary

▶ LP 16 Avoiding Germanisms

1 **BASIC** Each of the following sentences contains a 'typically German' mistake in red. Copy the sentences and correct the mistakes:

1 The plot of the film is typical for romantic comedies.
2 Jackie stepped into the corridor to phone with her lawyer.
3 Young people often use the internet to watch videos or hear music.
4 Music critics wondered when the single 'Thrift Shop' by a little-known rapper duo stormed the US charts in 2013.
5 We can meet us later in the city centre.
6 Some schools have introduced programmes to prevent cybermobbing.

German and English have much in common. This is often a help, but sometimes it is a source of confusion. The table below lists some common pitfalls:

	Source of confusion	Examples
a	similar word, different meaning	aktuell ≠ actual; eventuell ≠ eventual; Meinung ≠ meaning; spenden ≠ spend; sich wundern ≠ wonder
b	similar expression, different preposition	married **to** sb. = verheiratet **mit** jdm.; contact **with** sb. = Kontakt **zu** jdm.; example **of** sth. = Beispiel **für** etwas; typical of sb. = typisch **für** jdn.; do sth. **about** sth. = etwas **gegen** etwas tun
c	word-for-word translation of German phrase	~~hold~~/make a speech; ~~with 29 years~~/at the age of 29; on the one ~~side~~/hand; ~~make~~/take a photo; ~~hear~~/listen to music
d	verb used with/without a preposition	phone sb. = mit jdm. telefonieren; surf the internet = im Internet surfen; discuss sth. = über etwas diskutieren; comment on sth. = etwas kommentieren; discriminate against sb. = jdn. diskriminieren
e	Denglish used instead of English	~~beamer~~ (projector); ~~mobbing~~ (bullying); ~~handy~~ (mobile/cellphone); ~~boxes~~ (loudspeakers)
f	reflexive in German, non-reflexive in English	meet = sich treffen; identify with sb. = sich mit jdm. identifizieren; concentrate on sth. = sich auf etwas konzentrieren; feel = sich fühlen

2 For each of the following sentences, decide which word is missing (if any). If you aren't sure, the letter in brackets will tell you where to look in the table.

1 People write letters to the editor when they want to express their … (a)
2 The press secretary refused to comment … the minister's decision. (d)
3 In a speech that he … on March 4, Obama called for a new initiative on gun control. (c)
4 Jared is the only character in the novel that readers could possibly identify … with. (f)
5 Some teens spend far too much time surfing … the internet. (d)
6 The author names three examples … the abuse of power by the present government. (b)
7 It's high time for the town council to do something … this problem. (b)
8 To show the DVD in our classroom, we need a … and a pair of … as well as a laptop. (e)

▶ LP 17 Spelling

1 `BASIC` Copy the words below, adding the missing letters. Careful: sometimes no letters are missing!

1 int■rested
2 nec■essary
3 happ■ly
4 chara■ter

5 mis■understanding
6 d■scribe
7 public■ly
8 refer■ing

9 standar■
10 politic■an
11 av■rage
12 assist■nt

13 wel■fare
14 consc■ous
15 desp■rate■
16 non-viol■nce

> Unfortunately, there are very few rules for English spelling. The best strategy is to keep track of the words that you frequently misspell and practise writing them, for example before exams.

2 The following text is a student's essay on a British novel. There are ten spelling mistakes. Correct them:

Never Let Me Go by Kazuo Ishiguro is one of the best novels I have ever read. The autor tells the story from the point of view of Cathy, a young women, who reflects on her live as a student at a boarding school called Hailsham, and later as a so-called 'carer'. At first the reader thinks this is
5 just an other story about adolesence, but as the novel progresses, we slowly realize that there is something special about the young people at Hailsham: as human as they appear to the reader, they are really clones who must donate their organs to others when they have reached maturity. Although they seem to know this, they don't really understand
10 their situation, and each of them clings to the hope that somehow they will be allowd to live a bit longer then the others. The novel has also been adapted for the screen, and although I usualy avoid films based on books I love, I have to admit that this one is outstanding and succedes brillantly in capturing the spirit of the novel.

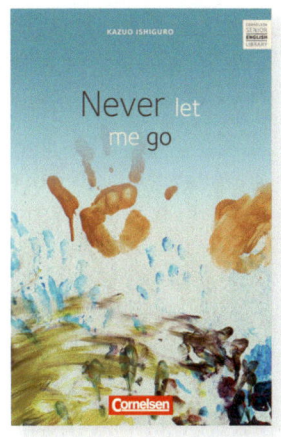

▶ LP 18 Writing about texts

There are many special expressions that you need when you write essays in German. The same is true of English. Knowing these phrases makes it easier for you to express yourself clearly.

1 `BASIC` The table below contains German and English phrases for text analysis. Both lists are in alphabetical order. Copy the table, matching the German phrases and their English equivalents:

German	English
1 angesichts …	a according to …
2 auf den ersten Blick	b as a rule
3 bei näherer Betrachtung	c as for … / as far as … is concerned
4 in Bezug auf …	d at first sight
5 dabei (d.h., während man etwas tut)	e focus on …
6 im Allgemeinen	f in connection with …
7 im Gegensatz zu …	g in contrast to …

German	English
8 im Großen und Ganzen	h in general
9 im Zusammenhang mit …	i in the process
10 in der Regel	j in view of …
11 laut …	k on closer examination
12 seitens …	l on the part of …
13 was … betrifft	m on the whole
13 … auf den Punkt bringen	n put … in a nutshell
15 … in den Mittelpunkt stellen	o with regard to …

2 Translate the following sentences into English with the help of your table:

1 Auf den ersten Blick hält man den Autor für einen Befürworter[1] der amerikanischen Umweltpolitik[2].
2 Bei näherer Betrachtung erkennt der Leser, dass er viele Dinge in den USA kritisch betrachtet.
3 Der Autor stellt die Auswirkungen der globalen Erwärmung in den Mittelpunkt.
4 Der Autor schildert die Folgen des Fracking in den USA. Dabei macht er deutlich, dass er diese Technik ablehnt.
5 Angesichts der Umweltbelastung[3] kann der Leser ihm nur zustimmen.
6 Im Gegensatz zu den Amerikanern, die Fracking im Großen und Ganzen akzeptieren, sind die Deutschen skeptisch eingestellt[4].
7 Im letzten Absatz bringt der Autor das ganze Dilemma auf den Punkt.

▶ LP 19 Collocations

Verbs and nouns

1 **BASIC** Choose the right verb for each of the sentences below:

1 Young people today sometimes find it hard to get/make a living in a tight job market.
2 Sam's teachers urged him to give/pay more attention to his school work.
3 The girls apologized to their victim, saying that they hadn't meant to do/make any harm.
4 The journalist calls/attracts attention to the problems in the region.
5 We think our school should make/set a good example by banning plastic tableware from the canteen.
6 The storm made/did considerable damage on its way northward.

> In English as well as in German, certain nouns are used together with certain verbs, e.g. you can only *take* (not ~~make~~) a *photo* in English. These 'natural pairs' are called collocations. Knowing the most common ones will help you avoid mistakes. The table below contains a selection of verb-noun collocations:

call attention (to sth.)	do damage	meet expectations	set an example
change your mind	exert influence (on sb.)	pay attention (to sb.)	take measures
commit a crime	make a living	put pressure on sb.	take offence (at sth.)
do justice to sth.	make history	put sth. to a vote	take a photo (of sb./sth.)
do good/harm	make an impression	reach an agreement	tell the truth/a lie

2 Complete the following sentences with the missing verb. All collocations are from the table above:

1 Did the hotel … your expectations?
2 The only way we'll ever … an agreement is to … the matter to a vote.
3 Yesterday, history was … as government officials and rebel leaders met for direct talks.
4 As a member of the Board of Overseers she still … considerable influence on University policy.
5 It is important to … a good impression when you go for a job interview.
6 To my mind the film doesn't … justice to the novel.
7 The management … pressure on the workers to accept a pay cut.
8 The police agreed that further measures should be … to stop young people from … crimes.

[1] **Befürworter** supporter   [2] **Umweltpolitik** environment policy   [3] **Umweltbelastung** negative environmental impact
[4] **skeptisch eingestellt** sceptical

Adjectives and nouns

3 **BASIC** The grey boxes on the right contain adjectives and nouns that form collocations. Form matching pairs and use them to complete the sentences:

bright	*air*
equal	*damage*
fresh	*feelings*
heavy	*idea*
high	*opinion*
human	*parents*
negative	*publicity*
strict (2x)	*rights (2x)*
strong	*rules*

1 Let's step outside and get some … …
2 The firm finally agreed to the protesters' demands to avoid further … …
3 The Declaration of Independence names 'life, liberty and the pursuit of happiness' as basic … …
4 Listen, everybody! I just had a … …
5 The hurricane caused … … all along the coast.
6 African Americans have fought a long battle for … …
7 I can't believe how … Tamira's … are.
8 Don't make jokes about veggie burgers – Katrina has very … … about animal rights.
9 This boarding school has very … …, and all students are expected to obey them.
10 I wasn't surprised when Steve was chosen for the scholarship – I've always had a … … of his character.

> Some adjectives 'belong together' with certain nouns, forming a new 'compound noun': *a human being, fair play, real life*. Others are frequently used together and form a collocation (*hard work, poor health*). Knowing common adjective-noun collocations will help you avoid mistakes and express yourself more idiomatically.

4 What adjective(s) could you use to describe each of the following nouns? Write down your ideas first, then check them with the help of a monolingual dictionary (look at the usage examples):

1 burden	3 example	5 rise	7 topic	9 price
2 conscience	4 gesture	6 treatment	8 argument	10 working conditions

5 Use five of your collocations in sentences that illustrate their meaning, e.g. *In Germany, fracking is a very controversial topic*.

Prepositions

6 **BASIC** Choose the correct preposition for each of the numbered gaps in the following sentences:

I agree (1) the author that it is high time to do something (2) the problem of toxic waste. We can't just turn our backs (3) the problem or wait (4) industry to take the initiative. Everyone who is worried (5) the future of life (6) this planet should get involved (7) a campaign (8) toxic waste. Photos (9) young children playing on heaps of toxic rubbish in India or other countries can easily be found (10) the internet or (11) newspapers and magazines. No one can look (12) such photos without feeling their own responsibility (13) the present situation.

> Many common expressions in English include a preposition. You can't learn them all, but the more you know, the fewer mistakes you will make. If you aren't certain which preposition to use with a certain word, look at the example sentences under the corresponding headword in a monolingual dictionary.

7 Use a dictionary to find out which preposition(s) can be used with each of the following words:

1 a lack … something	6 appeal … something	11 remind someone … something
2 a novel written … someone	7 be critical … something	12 struggle … a goal
3 accuse someone … something	8 blame someone … something	13 sympathize … someone
4 allude … something	9 contribute … something	14 take a look … something
5 an attempt … something	10 good … sth.	15 thank someone … something

▶ LP 20 Word formation

Prefixes

1 **BASIC** In the table below, match the prefixes to the correct meanings.

Meaning	Prefix(es)
1 against sth.	a multi-
2 for sth., in favour of sth.	b pseudo-
3 having two (sides, aspects, etc.)	c re-
4 having only one	d pre-
5 having or connected with several	e anti- counter-
6 not	neo-
7 no longer	f semi-
8 done badly or wrongly	g ex-
9 one of two	h pro-

Meaning	Prefix(es)
10 new	i non- dis-
11 happening before sth.	j mono-
12 happening after sth.	k co-
13 again, for the second time	l bi-
14 not really	m post-
15 referring to or done by yourself	n ultra-
16 only half, not completely	o mis-
17 extremely	p self-

Adding a prefix to an existing word changes the meaning without influencing the grammatical class: *un + able → unable*. Knowing the meaning of prefixes can help you to understand words you have never seen before.
Some of the prefixes (especially anti-, non-, self-, neo- and pseudo-) are often separated from their root word with a hyphen: anti-aircraft, neo-Colonial, etc.). But as there are no fixed rules for English spelling, it is best to check your dictionary to be sure.

2 Use a prefix from the list above to create an expression that matches each of the following definitions. Example: strong belief in your own abilities: *self-confidence*

1 a film that presents war in a negative light
2 a measure that produces the opposite of the intended effect
3 a former husband
4 one of the two captains of a team
5 a theory that pretends to be scientific but isn't
6 discover sth. for the second time, e.g. in later life
7 a person who is not a resident of the country they are staying in
8 interpret sth. the wrong way
9 an organization that operates in several countries
10 a worker who has some qualifications but fewer than a skilled worker
11 Germany after the war
12 having two poles

Suffixes

3 **BASIC** Copy the table below and sort the words on the right into groups. Underline the suffixes.

apparition · certify · complicity · egalitarian · enactment · furious · hypothesize · identical · laudable · marital · notification · obligatory · supportive

Nouns	Verbs	Adjectives

Like German, English can form a new word by adding a suffix to an existing root: *present* + *-able* →
presentable. Since the suffix determines whether the word is a noun, verb or adjective, recognizing
common suffixes can help you figure out the meanings of unfamiliar words. You probably haven't seen
any of the words in the box above before, but the suffixes give you information about what they mean.

4 Drawing on your knowledge of English as well as other languages, make an
intelligent guess as to the meaning of each word. When you have finished,
check your answers using a dictionary.

Word families

5 BASIC   The table below contains words related to each other. Copy the table and fill in the blanks, using a
dictionary if necessary. Make sure you know the meanings of all the words:

Verb	Noun	Adjective	Noun
act	(1)	active	activity
create	creation	(2)	creativity
depend (on)	(3)	dependent/dependable	dependability
rely (on)	reliance	reliable	(4)
select	selection	(5)	selectivity
compare	comparison	(6)	comparability
tolerate	(7)	tolerable	tolerability
adapt (to)	adaptation	adaptable	(8)
criticize	(9)	critical	...
destroy	(10)	destructive	destructiveness

6 Use words from the table to rewrite the underlined parts of the following sentences. You may have to
change the word order or add words in some cases:

Example: Meteorologists underestimated how destructive Hurricane Ivor would be.
      → *Meteorologists underestimated the destructiveness of Hurricane Ivor.*

1 We've had enough of speech-making; now is the time to act.
2 The author claims that classical music and popular music can't be
   compared.
3 All children have a natural creativity.
4 Gerald quit his job in India because he could not tolerate his working
   conditions.
5 Our firm expects all employees to be reliable.
6 The fact that our country is dependent on foreign oil and gas is a
   serious issue.
7 While doing her gap year in Uganda, Shirin demonstrated how well
   she can adapt.
8 The so-called Ivy League universities in the US are said to select their
   students very carefully.

Princeton,
an Ivy League university

Everyday English

EE 1 Eating in and out 268
Fact File:
Eating out – American style . . . 268
EE 2 Planning a trip using
the internet 269

EE 3 Dealing with medical
emergencies 270
Fact File:
Getting medical assistance. . . . 270

EE 4 Making phone calls 271
EE 5 Watch your valuables! 272

Download the suggested answers to the tasks here:
 Webcode context-32

▶ EE 1 Eating in and out

Eating customs often vary from culture to culture and knowing a few basics can come in handy while abroad.

1 In what situation might someone use each of the following expressions?

1 Thanks, I'm fine.
2 Just help yourself.
3 It's delicious, but I'm full.
4 Could you pass the …, please?
5 This has been a wonderful meal!
6 Could I have some more, please?

You can find your role cards here:
 Webcode context-33

2 ROLE-PLAY Use the phrases from part **1** and the role cards to act out a short dialogue.

■ **FACT FILE**

Eating out: American style

In sit-down restaurants in the United States where you are served at your table, there are a few customs that you should be aware of that are different from those in Europe:

- 'Please wait to be seated' is posted near the entrance in many restaurants. You are expected to wait to be taken to a table (even if the restaurant is completely empty!). Someone (a host or hostess) will probably ask how many are in your 'party' (e.g.: 'Just the two of you?' or 'How many are in your group?'), and either take you to a table or ask for your name so that they can call you when your table is ready.
- 'Designing your own meal' with your choice of meat and vegetable from the menu is not uncommon in the USA. A typical dish could be, for example, a sirloin steak with a choice of vegetable or side-salad and potatoes cooked in a specific way. Examine the menu and make your selection so that you are ready to order when the server arrives.
- 'Would you like a refill?' is a typical phrase in restaurants in the USA. Most restaurants offer free refills of at least coffee and soft drinks. The server exchanges your empty glass for a full one or refills your glass at your table. Tap water (usually with ice cubes) is provided for free.
- A 'service charge' is usually not included on the bill. Servers are not well paid in most regions of the USA and a tip of 15–20% is expected. You can either leave a cash tip on the table or, if paying with a credit card, there will be a place on the bill where you can add a tip to the total.

■ TIP

Soft drinks are called different things in different parts of the USA. As a general rule:
On the East and West Coasts: **soda**
In the Midwest: **pop**
In the South: **coke** (even for soft drinks that are not cola)

In groups of 4–5, write and act out a short theatrical scene that takes place in a US restaurant. Use the information above and the vocabulary below to help you.

Some useful terms			
main dish entrée ['ɒntreɪ] (AE)	*Hauptgericht*	menu ['menjuː]	*Speisekarte*
starter (BE) appetizer (AE)	*Vorspeise*	four-course dinner / meal	*Vier-Gang-Menü*
side dish, side order	*Beilage*	tip	*Trinkgeld*
dessert [dɪˈzɜːt] sweet (BE), pudding ['pʊdɪŋ] (BE) afters (BE, *infml*)	*Nachspeise*	VAT (BE) sales tax (AE)	*Mehrwertsteuer*
bill; check (AE)	*Rechnung*	tap water	*Leitungswasser*

■ TROUBLE SPOT
Ger. *Menü* ≠ Eng. **menu**

■ TROUBLE SPOT
entrée (BE) ≠ **entrée** (AE)

▶ EE 2 Planning a trip using the internet

The internet is a handy tool for making travel plans. You can book travel arrangements and hotel accommodation, find out information about museums and other places of interest, order food and make restaurant reservations, as well as even reserve concert, theatre or movie tickets.
Imagine your class is planning a week-long trip to London. You will be in the city from Monday to Friday. Form three groups (A, B, C). Each group has its own planning task.

Group A: Getting around in London

Explore the options for public transport during your stay. London offers a variety of tickets with different prices and conditions. It might be helpful to know how many students there are in your class and their ages.

- Split your group into 3–4 smaller groups. Each of the mini-groups explores one option and presents it to the rest of the class.
- Consult relevant websites to find out what options are available, what conditions are attached to their use, and how much they would cost. Calculate the total cost for the group.

Group B: A day trip to Greenwich

While in London, your class wants to take a day trip to Greenwich. How will you get there? The closest station to your hotel is Bayswater Tube Station.

- Divide your group into 3 mini-groups. Each mini-group researches a different way of getting to Greenwich.
  Mini-group 1: Docklands Light Railway
  Mini-group 2: Thames Riverboat
  Mini-group 3: Greenwich Foot Tunnel
  Take into account what interesting sights different travel options might offer along the way.
- What is the total price for the group (not including the cost of any Tube travel)?

Group C: The Royal Museums Greenwich

The Royal Museums Greenwich (RMG) is a complex of buildings and sites of historical, architectural and scientific interest.

- What does the RMG consist of? Use the internet to explore the various possibilities.
- Divide your group into 3 mini-groups. Each mini-group puts together a different suggestion for a visit to the RMG.
- What can you see and do? When and where? How much does it cost for your group?
- Are there adequate food options available there for a group of your size?

Some useful terms			
peak (hours, etc.)	*Spitzenzeiten*	fare	*Fahrpreis*
entry (to a building, etc.)	*Zutritt*	swipe card	*Magnetstreifenkarte*
opening hours	*Öffnungszeiten*	vending machine	*(Verkaufs-)Automat*
admission (fee)	*Eintritt(spreis)*	destination	*(Reise-)Ziel*
exhibition	*Ausstellung*	venue	*(Veranstaltungs-)Ort*
surcharge	*Aufschlag*	closing time	*Schließzeit*
concession/discount	*Ermäßigung*	pay-as-you-go credit	*Prepaid-Guthaben*

 FACT FILE

Greenwich [ˈɡrenɪtʃ], a district of South East London, is on 0° Longitude *(Prime or Greenwich Meridian)* and sets the global time standard *(Greenwich Mean Time)*.

► EE 3 Dealing with medical emergencies CD3 08

A medical emergency can happen anywhere. The cause can be an accident or a sudden illness. Before you go abroad, make sure you have health insurance coverage[1] for your country of destination. Travel medical insurance[2] is inexpensive and covers all medical expenses during a brief foreign stay.

> MY GOODNESS, MR. GRTPTZSK – HOW LONG HAS IT BEEN SINCE YOU HAD A VOWEL MOVEMENT?

■ FACT FILE

Getting medical assistance
In the event of an emergency, call 999 (UK), 911 (USA) or 000 (Australia). From mobile phones, the number 112 will also connect you with the emergency services in many countries.

5 **Hospital:** If you or someone else needs medical help, consult a physician / doctor or go to the outpatient clinic[3] of the nearest hospital, where you can be treated without being admitted to the hospital[4].

Pharmacy: In the UK and the US, shops that sell medicine are called pharmacies, drugstores (US) or chemist's (UK). They offer a wider range of products than a German *Apotheke*, including

10 health and beauty products, and sometimes travel essentials.

Prescriptions: Medicine that has been prescribed by a doctor is dispensed at the pharmacy counter within the shop. In the US, you are given the exact dosage prescribed by the doctor. If, for example, your prescription says three capsules daily for five days, you will be given 15 capsules in a

15 small bottle, not the original package.

■ TROUBLE SPOT

ärztliches Rezept = **prescription**
Kochrezept = **recipe** ['resəpi]

A group of students in the eighth class at your school are about to go on their first exchange to the UK. Prepare an informative and funny two-minute talk for them in English on medical assistance abroad.

1 In the event that you need medical help, it is important that you understand the doctor's questions and can give precise answers. Test your knowledge by matching the English words to their German equivalents.

1 abdomen	11 have a temperature	a allergisch	k Schnittwunde
2 allergic	12 headache	b Bauch, Unterleib	l Schürfwunde
3 bowel movement	13 nausea ['nɔːziə]	c Durchfall	m Schwindel
4 bruise [bruːz]	14 numb	d Fieber haben	n sich übergeben
5 congested	15 scrape	e Halsschmerzen	o Stuhlgang
6 constipated	16 shiver	f Husten	p taub
7 cough [kɒf]	17 sore throat	g Impfung	q Übelkeit
8 cut	18 stomach ache [eɪk]	h Kopfschmerzen	r verschnupft
9 diarrhoea [ˌdaɪəˈrɪə]	19 vaccination	i Magenschmerzen	s verstopft
10 dizziness	20 vomit	j Prellung	t zittern

2 Sabine is staying with her host family in the USA. She isn't feeling well and her host parents take her to the doctor. Listen to the dialogue and answer the questions.
1 How does Sabine describe her symptoms?
2 What information does Dr Felter want from her?
3 What does Dr Felter give her?

Listen to the audio file on the CD or download it here:
 Webcode context-37

3 ROLE-PLAY **Partner A** is cycling near Bristol with his or her British host-brother, Toby. All of a sudden, Toby hits a hole in the road and falls off his bike. He is badly hurt. Phone for help! **Partner B** will be the person taking calls for emergency services in the Bristol area. Use the role cards.

You can find your role cards here:
 Webcode context-38

---

[1] **health insurance coverage** *Krankenversicherungsschutz*   [2] **travel medical insurance** *Auslandskrankenversicherung*
[3] **outpatient clinic** *Ambulanz*   [4] **admit sb. to the hospital** *jdn. stationär aufnehmen*

▶ EE 4 Making phone calls

Talking on the telephone has become less common in the age of text messages, but there are still situations in which it is unavoidable. The box below lists example phrases that can be used when talking on the phone.

1 Match the phrases from the box below to the following typical situations:

1 You phone a number and say who you are.
2 You explain why you are calling.
3 You answer the phone.
4 You are not the intended recipient of the call.
5 You ask for clarification.
6 You want to end the conversation and hang up.

a	Hello. My name is Lisa Weber. I'm calling from Cologne in Germany.	k	I think you've dialed the wrong number.
b	The reason I'm calling is …	l	I'm calling about the advert you posted …
c	I'm sorry, I didn't catch that. Could you repeat your name please?	m	Thank you for returning my call / Thanks for getting back to me. *(infml)*
d	May I ask why you are calling?	n	Good afternoon. Caroline Schlegel speaking.
e	Can I take a message?	o	Could you spell that, please?
f	It was nice talking with you.	p	I have a problem, could you connect me with Customer Services, please?
g	Good morning. This is Max Kunze in Dresden, Germany.	q	Robert Peters here. What can I do for you?
h	I'm afraid she isn't here. Would you like her to call you back?	r	Sorry, the line is busy. Would you like to speak to someone else?
i	I'd like to speak to …	s	Mr Adams tried to reach me while I was out. I'm returning his call.
j	May I ask who's calling, please?	t	Thank you for your call.

2 ROLE-PLAY Working together with a partner, use the information on the role cards to carry out a conversation on the phone.

You can find your role cards here:

Webcode context-39

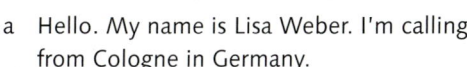

Some useful terms	
line	*Leitung*
engaged (BE), busy (AE)	*besetzt*
dial a number	*eine Nummer wählen*
answer the phone	*einen Anruf entgegennehmen*
return sb.'s call, get back to sb.	*jdn. zurückrufen*
hold	*in der Leitung bleiben*
put sb. through (to sb.)	*jdn. (zu jdm.) durchstellen*
hang up	*auflegen*

HELLO!
THIS IS LIBERTY SPEAKING——

▶ EE 5 Watch your valuables!

When staying abroad, whether on holiday or as part of an exchange programme, you will need money. There are different ways of taking money abroad.

1 Match the lettered boxes to their corresponding method of taking or accessing money abroad.

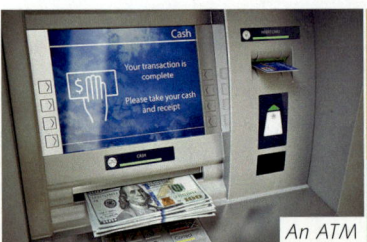

An ATM

Money Management Methods:
1 a bank card / debit card (AE)
2 a credit card
3 traveller's cheques
4 cash

A
- must be exchanged for local currency
- no way of preventing a thief from using it

B
- equivalent to the German 'ec-Karte' or Girocard
- can be used to withdraw cash at an ATM (more commonly called a cash machine or 'hole in the wall' in the UK) or to pay for goods and services in many countries

C
- can be used to pay bills in many hotels and restaurants without a PIN
- can sometimes be used with the PIN to withdraw cash from an ATM
- can be cancelled if lost or stolen

D
- must be bought before you leave home
- can be cashed in any bank during opening hours

Plastic money is very practical, but use caution:
- Before you travel, check whether your bank at home has a partnership with a bank where you're staying abroad. It might be cheaper for you to use that bank to withdraw cash.
- In many countries, ATMs are not inside banks, but on the walls outside. For safety reasons, try to use an ATM in a well-lit area or inside the bank building.
- Make sure nobody can see the number keys while you are entering your PIN.
- Be aware that there will probably be a fee every time you withdraw cash from a foreign ATM.

If your card is lost or stolen, take immediate action:
- Make sure you know how to reach your bank and/or credit card company in case you need to block or cancel your card. (The phone number can change depending on where you are travelling.)
- Phone and have the card blocked as soon as you realize your card is lost or stolen.
- Report the theft to the local police.

2 ROLE-PLAY Oh, no! You have been robbed! Report the theft to the local police. Use role cards and the vocabulary in the box below for your dialogue.

You can find your role cards here:
🔘 **Webcode** context-40

Some useful terms			
valuables	*Wertsachen*	bank card, debit card	*ec-Karte; Girocard*
purse / wallet	*Geldbörse, Portemonnaie*	have your card blocked / cancelled	*deine Karte sperren lassen*
cash	*Bargeld*	suspicious [səˈspɪʃəs] behaviour	*auffälliges Verhalten*
pickpocket	*Taschendieb/in*	report a crime, etc. (to the police)	*eine Straftat usw. anzeigen*

■ TROUBLE SPOT
rob sb. = steal sth. from sb.

Communicating across Cultures

CC1 Cultural awareness 273
CC2 The language of politeness . . . 274
CC3 Polite behaviour 275

CC4 Meeting and greeting 275
CC5 Making small talk 276
CC6 Talking about sensitive issues . 276
     Fact File: Political correctness . 277

CC7 Making polite complaints 277

Download the suggested answers to the tasks here:
 Webcode context-41

▶ CC1 Cultural awareness

Like a fish out of water: A fish doesn't know what water is – until the water suddenly isn't there anymore. Likewise, we often take the culture we grow up with for granted – customs, body language, how people interact in everyday situations – and don't really notice it while it surrounds us. As a result, experiencing different cultures can open our eyes to aspects of our own culture and also give us insight into ways other people behave.

1 Put yourself in each of the following situations and choose the reaction that comes the closest to your own.

  1 A crowded cafeteria at lunchtime. You have been waiting patiently for the last ten minutes. Someone comes into the room, spots a gap near the front of the queue and jumps in.
    a You look away and say nothing.
    b You grumble to your neighbour, 'So selfish!'
    c You shout out loud, 'Hey you! Go to the back of the queue!'
  2 While waiting at the bus stop, you see an exchange student who is in one of your courses. He comes over to chat and stops about thirty centimetres in front of you (try it out with a partner, using a ruler to measure the distance between the tips of your noses).
    a You take a step backward.
    b You turn a bit to the side to avoid facing the other student directly.
    c You stand your ground and look the other person directly in the eye.
  3 You get a note from a guidance counselor asking you to come to her office after school. When you arrive, the door is half open; the counselor is working at her desk.
    a You walk in, say hello and sit down opposite her.
    b You stand in the doorway and say, 'You wanted to see me.'
    c You knock lightly on the door and say, 'Excuse me, may I interrupt you?'

2 In groups of not more than three, compare your reactions to the situations in exercise **1** and your reasons for choosing them. Discuss the following points:
  ▪ How do you feel about (not) playing by the rules?
  ▪ How close is too close – when do you feel that someone is invading your personal space?
  ▪ What does eye contact signify?
  ▪ What does an open (or closed) door mean?
Compare your views and decide which forms of behaviour you think are typical in your society.

▶ CC 2 The language of politeness

1 People don't always say what they really mean; sometimes they even say the opposite:

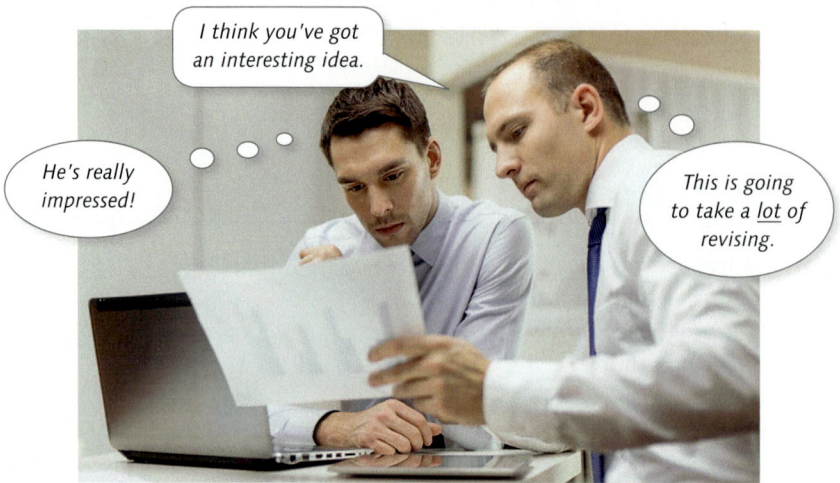

To a certain degree, understatement and exaggeration are part of national culture. Americans tend to be highly enthusiastic ('Fantastic!' – 'I'd love to!' – 'I'm dying to meet him!'), whereas the British are more reserved in their way of expressing themselves ('I'm afraid we've got a bit of a problem.'). These are, of course, just generalizations, as each person has their own style.

In conversations, always try to be friendly and polite, but remember that polite phrases cannot always be taken literally. The list on the left in the table below shows some polite phrases you might hear, especially in the UK. First, decide what you think they mean, then choose the 'translation' from the list on the right.

1 There's room for improvement.	a I'm just being polite.
2 I wouldn't mind.	b I'm very annoyed.
3 Very original work.	c I expect you to read it.
4 You must come over for dinner.	d I'd love to.
5 I was a bit disappointed that …	e That's really good.
6 You might want to have a look at it.	f I expect you to apologize.
7 I'm sure it was my mistake.	g Hopeless stuff.

2 The table below contains polite phrases that can be used in everyday situations. Match them, then use one or two of the matching pairs to write a short dialogue (with a partner, if you prefer):

1 Would you mind if I borrowed one of these? I can't find mine.	a Great idea! I'd love to!
	b Sure, come in and have a seat.
2 Sorry, I didn't know …	c Certainly. Here you are.
3 Thanks a lot!	d I'll have to think about that.
4 Is it all right with you if I …?	e Sure, help yourself.
5 Could I bother you for a minute?	f That's all right. Don't worry about it.
6 Would it be possible for me to …?	g You're very welcome.
7 We were wondering if you would be interested in …	h Of course. Feel free.
8 Could I get a …, please?	

▶ CC3 Polite behaviour

Leon is an exchange student in the USA. Read the following descriptions of everyday situations and decide whether he breaks any rules of polite behaviour. Then discuss your reactions in a group. Have you experienced similar situations? Why do you feel that certain behaviour is polite or impolite?

Compare your views with additional comments here:
Webcode context-42

1 Leon meets his host parents and host brother, Matt, for the first time. He offers them his hand in greeting.
2 Leon calls his host parents 'Frank' and 'Brenda'.
3 At his American home, Leon always keeps his bedroom door shut.
4 Leon and Matt are watching TV when Matt's grandparents enter the room. Leon stays seated.
5 It's dinner time and Leon is very hungry. He starts eating as soon as he has something on his plate.
6 Leon can't follow the conversation at the dinner table, so he starts playing games on his smartphone.

▶ CC4 Meeting and greeting

1 The phrases below can be used in different social situations: when you meet someone for the first time, when you meet a friend on the street, or when you want to end a conversation. Copy the table below and put the phrases from the list in the correct column (some can be used more than once).

1 Fine thanks. And you?
2 Hi, how's it going? (infml)
3 Hi, nice to meet you. (infml)
4 How are things going? (infml)
5 How do you do? (fml)
6 Sorry, I've got to run. (infml)
7 I'd like you to meet XY.
8 It's been wonderful talking to you.
9 Not too bad. What about you? (infml)
10 (I'm very) Pleased to meet you.
11 Thanks, and the same to you!
12 See you later. (infml)
13 Bye now. Take care! (infml)
14 Have a good time!

Meeting someone for the first time	Meeting someone you know	Saying goodbye

2 Select an appropriate response from your table for each of the following situations:
1 You work for an organization that employs mostly young people. Your supervisor brings a new colleague over to meet you and says: 'Hi Rebecca, this is James, our new trainee.' You say:
2 You see a co-worker in the hallway. She says: 'Hi, how are things going?' You say:
3 Going back to your office, you see your supervisor talking to an older woman. He calls you over and says: 'Rebecca, I'd like you to meet our regional coordinator, Deirdre O'Connor.' You say:
4 After Ms O'Connor has asked you a couple of questions about your job, you want to end the conversation and go back to work. You say:
5 You drive a friend to the train station. As he gets out of the car, he says: 'See you later!' You say:
6 You're a bit late for work when you run into an old friend. When she starts telling you all about her new boyfriend, you make it clear that you're in a hurry and say:
7 On the last day of work before the holidays, a co-worker waves to you as you are leaving and calls out: 'Have a good break!' You say:

> ■ TIP
>
> - 'How do you do?' isn't really a question; it is just a very formal way of saying 'Nice to meet you'.
> - When someone asks 'How are you?', they usually don't want a medical update. Just say 'Fine, thanks' or 'Not too bad, thanks'.

▶ CC5 Making small talk 🎧 CD3 09

Small talk is an art. That means that some people are, by nature, better at it than others. However, everybody can work on their skills and practise developing them.

1 Listen to two short conversations and describe the differences between them. Why is one more successful than the other?

> Listen to the audio file on the CD or download it here:
> 🔊 **Webcode** context-43

2 The list below contains tips for making small talk. In each tip, one or more phrases is missing. Complete the tips with phrases from the box below right.
   1 Stand roughly at arm's length from your partner and … while you are talking.
   2 Choose a topic that involves something you and your partner … (e.g. social or regional background, personal experiences, present situation, the weather, etc.).
   3 Don't ask any questions that you wouldn't …
   4 Avoid … ('Do you like sport?'); use … instead ('What's your favourite sport?').
   5 Give your partner the opportunity to talk about him- or herself before you make a comment or …
   6 Encourage your partner to … by interjecting remarks such as 'That's really interesting!' or 'Wow! That must have been awesome!'.

   a change the subject
   b keep talking
   c have in common
   d end the conversation
   e coming to a natural end
   f open questions
   g look them in the eye
   h want to answer
   i 'yes-or-no' questions

   7 Pay attention to the silences; they may be a sign that your conversation is …
   8 Phrases like 'It's been great talking to you' or 'We'll have to continue this conversation some other time' can help you to … elegantly.

3 ROLE-PLAY You meet someone new at a youth hostel in Germany. Use the role cards to guide your conversation with a partner.

> You can find your role cards here:
> **Webcode** context-44

4 Choose a new partner and practise making small talk without the help of role cards. Try to keep your conversation going for at least two minutes.

▶ CC6 Talking about sensitive issues 🎧 CD3 10

Which topics are considered sensitive and which are absolutely taboo varies from culture to culture. A good indicator is humour: which topics do people make jokes about? Which do they seem to avoid? (Watching comedy shows on TV can tell you a lot about social norms.)

1 Imagine you are going to the USA for a year. Rank the ten topics below on a scale from 1 (harmless) to 10 (taboo) as discussion topics. Compare lists with your partner or in a group and discuss your reasons.

> *food preferences • sports • patriotism • gun control • religion and church-going • parents' jobs • politics • race relations • career goals • the United States' role in the world*

2 Emma, a German exchange student in Ohio, is asked by her American social studies teacher about her impressions of life in the USA. Listen to two different versions of the story and make notes on the differences. How is the tone of the conversation affected by the way Emma responds?

> Listen to the audio file on the CD or download it here:
> **Webcode** context-45

■ FACT FILE

Political correctness

In the mid-20th century in the USA, political correctness became an important topic when minority groups criticized how people spoke about them as
5 a form of discrimination. Other groups soon followed suit.
Racial minorities: During the Civil Rights Movement, African Americans rejected names such as 'negro' or 'colored' that identified them on the basis of skin
10 colour. They preferred the term 'African American', which was similar to traditional terms such as 'Irish American' or 'Italian American'. (Note: Today, it is also acceptable to use the adjective 'black'.) American Indians often want to be called 'Native
15 Americans' or 'First Nations Peoples', and the indigenous peoples of Canada and Alaska prefer to be called 'Inuit' or 'Alaska Natives' instead of 'Eskimos'.
Gender: There are various job titles in English that
20 refer only to the male (or, less often, to the female)

gender: postman (*AE:* mailman), salesman, actress, stewardess, etc. Such terms have generally been replaced by gender-neutral ones: 'the chair' (instead of 'chairman/chairwoman'), postal carrier (*AE:* mail carrier), salesperson, flight attendant, etc. 25
Health: Certain terms used to refer to health issues are sometimes regarded as discriminatory, as they can suggest that there is something inherently wrong with people. People who are physically handicapped should be referred to as 'physically disabled' 30 and mentally challenged people have 'special needs', 'learning disabilities' or are 'intellectually impaired'.
Other politically correct terms would be, for example, 'vision impaired' for the blind or 'hearing 35 impaired' for the deaf.

Think of other politically correct terms that are used in German. Can you find the English equivalents?

▶ CC 7 **Making polite complaints** 🎧 **CD3** 11, 12 and 13

Travelling abroad is always complicated, and mix-ups and misunderstandings can easily happen. The important thing is to stay calm and, if necessary, get competent help as quickly as possible.

1 Michaela Börner from Düsseldorf is spending a year abroad in North Carolina. When she arrives at the airport in Charlotte, her host family is waiting for her. Listen to the dialogue. What phrases do they use to greet each other? What questions have to be resolved before they can communicate easily?

2 At the baggage claim, Michaela and her host family wait for Michaela's suitcase. Listen to the sound file and identify the English words for the following terms:

1 Förderband 2 Gepäckstück 3 Haupthalle 4 Schalter 5 zurückbekommen

> *Listen to the audio files on the CD or download the audio files that correspond to exercises **1**, **2** and **3** here:*
> **Webcode** context-46

3 Michaela and her host family go to the baggage services office. Listen to the sound file. Write down the English equivalents of the following expressions:

1 Kann ich Ihnen behilflich sein?   5 Sie dürfen sich jederzeit an uns wenden.
2 Darf ich bitte …?   6 Wäre es vielleicht möglich, dass unser Gast …
3 Ist das so richtig?   7 Sie waren sehr hilfreich.
4 Ihr Ärger ist verständlich.   8 Gern geschehen.

4 When you encounter a situation for the first time, you may be confronted with vocabulary you haven't heard before. Here is a short list of words that Michaela had trouble understanding. Just as Amanda would have tried to help Michaela, try explaining in English what the following terms mean.

1 baggage receipt   2 written confirmation   3 toll-free number   4 reimbursement

5 ROLE-PLAY Waiting at the airport baggage claim, you see your suitcase coming down the belt. Read the role card and act out the scene with your partner.

> *You can find your role cards here:*
> **Webcode** context-47

Language Awareness

LA1 Varieties of English 279

LA2 Communication problems and compensation strategies 280

LA3 Similarities and differences of languages 281

LA4 Influencing through language 282

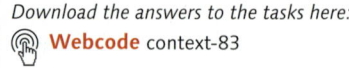

Download the answers to the tasks here:
Webcode context-83

What is language awareness?

*In order to improve your language skills it is not enough to be more or less fluent in writing and speaking English, but you also need to be aware of how **language as a system** is structured, how it works in different contexts and can be used unknowingly or intentionally to have a certain **effect on other people**. For some specific areas and usages of English you must therefore adopt a kind of meta-position and be able to observe English as a language in general, compare it to your **mother tongue** and possibly other languages but also evaluate your own individual use of it in order to not only avoid mistakes but also be as successful as possible in written and spoken communication. In that way you are also protected from verbal manipulation by others.*

*The ALA (= Association for Language Awareness) defined language awareness as **'explicit knowledge about language, and conscious perception and sensitivity in language learning, language teaching and language use'** (2012).*

*The knowledge you gain in the field of language awareness contains aspects of grammar, but is definitely much more than learning about the rules. It is not achieved for its own sake or in order to be tested but it is supposed to support **further language learning** and should result in using it actively in any form of your own language production.*

In some cases it might prove interesting and probably also fun to learn about pecularities of languages, how they developed and influenced each other and how language in general affects human lives. Thus, language awareness might even have a positive feedback on your knowledge of your mother tongue and on cultural stereotypes.

*In the preceding chapters of the book you may have worked on **language awareness tasks** (cf. e.g. p. 154) which follow the same principle. They direct you to focus on a language phenomenon used in the text (e.g. direct and indirect speech). In a next step you are supposed to analyse this form and its specific function in the text and for the readers. Doing this you become aware of these phenomenons (again) and make them available for your own language production in similar texts and contexts.*

*In the margin of some texts you can find so-called **language awareness boxes** (e.g. on p. 154) which are meant to draw your attention to further phenomena of the English language. They refer you to this part which provides more explanations but also additional exercises so that you can directly put newly acquired knowledge to use.*

▶ LA1 Varieties of English

"ACTUALLY, THAT MEANS ENGLISH AS A SECOND LANGUAGE...THE ELEPHANT SINGLES LOUNGE IS ACROSS THE STREET!"

Today, English is spoken by around 980 million speakers worldwide. For about 370 million of them, English is their first language, i.e. they are **native speakers**, while the rest use it as a second or a foreign language. English is also the modern **lingua franca**: it is used as a means of communication by non-native speakers of English who do not share any other common language. Thus, English is far more than one uniform language. It comprises a lot of varieties, which you can distinguish according to certain linguistic features in the fields of spelling, pronunciation, vocabulary and grammar. These distinguishable features can be linked to areas, social aspects, time or a combination of all these, resulting in **regional varieties, social varieties and varieties of discourse**.

Regional varieties or **dialects** reflect where the speaker is from and where they live. Apart from British English there are other regional varieties such as American, South African or Australian English. They owe their existence to the spread of the British Empire and the consequent colonialization of countries around the globe. Within these varieties other forms like Irish or Scottish English or the Southern versions of American English can be distinguished. These varieties sometimes absorbed grammatical or lexical elements from the native languages of invaded nations or trade partners.

Social variation refers to the fact that different social groups tend to use different words or grammatical structures or pronounce some words differently. A sociolect (also referred to as **vernacular**) can convey an atmosphere of status or lack thereof, but also reinforces the peer feeling and unites human beings in a linguistic group.

Varieties of discourse refer to the differences in vocabulary or structures depending on the context people are speaking in. Are they speaking or writing? Which type of text are they using and who are they addressing?

While all naturally occurring varieties are considered to show the same degree of **complexity**, globalization and its need for an easy common language has led some people to suggest using a simpler form of English (e.g. **'Globish'**) that has a restricted vocabulary and simplified grammar.

PRACTICE

1 Discuss with a partner why the following sentences may have totally different meanings or may be even offending, depending on whether they are used in an American or in a British context. You may want to use a dictionary.

a I'm mad about my flat.
b I have knocked her up.
c Let's meet on first floor.
d Can I have the bill, please?
e Was that a sleeping policeman I ran over?
f Can I borrow your pants?
g It says exactly a pint.
h I have run out on gas.
i He is a really homely person.
j She is anxious to meet her in-laws.
k You should walk on the pavement.
l Join us in a game of hockey!
m I love football.

2 Many English words are loanwords, i.e. they originally come from other languages. Some of them took the direct way into English, some of them found their way via some intermediate languages. Look at the following list: what languages may these words originally come from? Check your results with a partner. Your teacher will give you the solutions.

algebra · amok · apartheid · avatar · balcony · ballet · blitzkrieg · bungalow · canoe · chair · checkmate · chocolate · court · cummerbund · delicatessen · entrepreneur · excavate · fictitious · jungle · ketchup · kindergarten · lilac · penguin · shampoo · skipper · skirt · slaughter · street · they · schlep sth. around · tobacco · typhoon · ultimate · vanilla · wunderkind · yoghurt · zero

▶ LA2 Communication problems and compensation strategies

If you speak or write something, there is always the **possibility of misunderstandings** or even misinterpretations, even more so if the language you use is not your mother tongue and doesn't come to you so easily.

Once you've realized that something has gone wrong in communication, the best thing to do is to stay calm and polite and make up for the misunderstanding. You should try to help everybody to overcome the difficulties with the help of so-called **compensation strategies** such as asking back politely, explaining again what you wanted to say and using other (perhaps simpler) phrases.

Of course, you should try and think ahead. If you have the opportunity to plan your contribution in advance (e.g. in presentations), think about possible misunderstandings beforehand and try to prevent them. Whenever you don't know the English equivalent for something you want to say you can use paraphrases, e.g. by using relative clauses (e.g. 'A parachute is a device with which you can jump from a plane.'). Or you can use synonyms (e.g. small/tiny/little) or antonyms (e.g. tiny – gigantic, fast – slow) to describe what something means.

In the course of learning English you will have developed a set of such compensation strategies that suit your individual **learner biography**. By choosing strategies that meet your needs you turn into **an individual and independent learner**. These methods do not only include language material, but also **language learning skills** in general, such as possible arrangements for word material to include new words or enlarge your vocabulary and range of words, e.g. tables, mind maps or other forms of visualization as well as assessment and feedback strategies to evaluate your language proficiency and to detect and, eventually, to avoid mistakes.

PRACTICE

Look at the following semantic or word fields. Arrange them in a way that illustrates their different meanings, e.g. in a line from weakest to strongest or a mind map. You might group synonyms together or perhaps antonyms or words that express the same idea but can only be used in different contexts. Find a partner and present your results to each other. Discuss and explain differences and add more words if you can.

Size	big · giant · gigantic · grand · huge · humongous · immense · large · little · majestic · medium · microscopic · miniscule · normal · petite · small · tiny · wee
Emotion	adoration · affection · aversion · compassion · devotion · disgust · envy · fondness · friendship · hatred · idolization · indifference · loathing · love · reference · sympathy · trust · worship
Appearance	agreeable · attractive · awkward · beautiful · cute · dazzling · disgusting · dull · good-looking · handsome · neat · nice · ordinary · pleasant · pretty · ravishing · stunning · ugly

▶ LA3 Similarities and differences of languages

While learning English you may have come across a number of aspects in which your mother tongue and English resemble each other. Such similarities facilitate learning a new English phrase or construction. If you know any other languages apart from English, you may have noticed that they have a different system or grammar which sometimes interferes or clashes with that of your native language and results in mistakes or misunderstandings, or there may be aspects that you find hard to grasp or keep in mind. There are, for instance, languages in which nouns do not only have a singular and a plural form, but also a third form referring to exactly two things or people.

In the field of vocabulary there may be interference as a result of **false friends**, i.e. words or phrases occurring in two languages that look similar or appear to be identical but that have completely different meanings. There are also constructions in English, e.g. the progressive form, that may not exist in your mother tongue, making them difficult for you to learn. Awareness of such similarities and differences will help you to speak and write better English. It may even help you to understand the system of your first language better.

PRACTICE

1 Look at the following pairs of words, one of them being a word you may be familiar with from German, the other with a slight difference but having a different meaning. Use a dictionary if necessary and find out which one is the false friend or is, at least, not a direct translation.

motif – motive	artist – artiste	critic – critique	receipt – recipe
model – modal	heroin – heroine	physicist – physician	personell – personal

2 In English, unlike in German, consent or dissent are often expressed indirectly, so you shouldn't simply answer by saying 'Yes' or 'No'. Use at least a so-called short answer ('Yes, I do', 'No, I haven't', 'No, you wouldn't' etc.), sometimes followed by a question tag ('No, you wouldn't, would you?').

·····▶

In the following game, you are not allowed to use the two words *yes* and *no*. Form groups of four and take turns in asking each other questions on any of the following topics:

- weekend activities
- hobbies and pastimes
- favourite music, books, forms of art etc.
- general likes and dislikes

■ LANGUAGE HELP

- You are certainly right that …
- You are absolutely correct in saying that …
- I am not quite sure about that …
- As far as I am concerned I have to say that …
- That is an interesting/fascinating/… question.
- I can't quite follow you here.
- I have never thought about it in that way, but …
- You are right to a certain extent, however …
- Sorry, could you repeat your question …
- Never ever would I do that …
- I am afraid I can't accept that …

Whenever one of you answers by saying 'Yes' or 'No', their name gets ticked in a list. The game is finished when one of you has five ticks. The student with the fewest ticks has won. **▶ LANGUAGE HELP**

▶ LA4 Influencing through language

The primary purpose of language is to pass information from one person to another. But language can do much more. Often, language is used in order to reach a certain aim. You may ask people to do you a favour, you try to convince them of an idea, you persuade them to vote for you – all this by using language in a particular way. English has some phrases that beautifully reflect this function of language. For instance, when you first meet somebody you fancy, you 'chat them up', hoping that the other person will fall in love with you.

If you know a language and the way it works, you can use it effectively in order to achieve a certain aim or reach a target group or audience. You can change your style and register and use different words or constructions in order to get your message across more successfully. Reversely, knowing about the way language works can also help you not being 'talked into anything', in other words it can protect you from being manipulated.

PRACTICE

1 In the box of phrases below, find groups of three with roughly the same meaning. For each phrase, decide whether it is formal, neutral or informal and enter it in a copy of the table. Check the meaning of the phrases in a dictionary if necessary.

> escape (v) • without money • continue • use the toilet • I would be grateful if you made a little less noise. • He went insane. • I am down with influenza. • I'm gonna ask for help. • I have a rotten cold. • yuck • be out of funds • My friend is very tired. • Please be quiet. • I have recently caught a cold. • need to pee • He went bananas and totally lost it. • nauseating • I could do with some help. • My mate is bloody knackered. • get out • go on • come off • He went mad. • I require some assistance. • powder one's nose • proceed (v) • Shut up. • My companion seems to be a bit unenergetic at the moment. • disgusting • flat broke

Informal	neutral	formal

Together with a partner check your solutions and discuss situations where you would use the various phrases. Describe the situations to each other, e.g. where you are and who you are talking to.

2 Take turns in performing the following role plays.
You have accidentally bumped into somebody. How do you respond to the situation if it is
– a little boy or girl who seems to be quite shocked or even hurt,
– a peer who you had a serious fight with in a ballgame in the PE lesson at school yesterday,
– your school principal,
– a handicapped or elderly person.

Make sure that you always stay respectful. You could use some of the following phrases. Remember that you can also introduce irony where you consider it useful and suitable.

> Sorry 'bout that. • I didn't mean to hurt you. • My fault. • Oh my goodness, I apologize. • I sincerely apologize. • Oh, it's you again. • Do you need any assistance? • I owe you an apology. • My fault bro. • I take full responsibility. • My bad. • I'm sorry for any problems I have caused. • Well, that figures. • Can I help you? • I hope you can forgive me. • I'm honestly sorry. • I would like to apologize. • Whoops, sorry. • Oh, come on, don't be pathetic.

Skills File

Language learning and study skills

SF1 Dealing with unknown or new words **P** 284

SF2 Using a dictionary and a grammar book **P** 286

SF3 Doing research **P** 287

SF4 Doing project work 288

SF5 Structuring information and ideas: visual aids and outlines **P** 289

SF6 Paraphrasing **P** 290

SF7 Working with closed test formats 291

SF8 Learning languages with electronic devices 292

SF9 Assessing yourself and giving feedback 293

SF10 Finding and developing your individual language learning skills 294

Text skills

SF11 Analysing pictures **P** 295

SF12 Analysing charts and graphs **P** 296

SF13 Analysing cartoons **P** 296

SF14 Reading strategies **P** 298

SF15 Marking up a text / Making and taking notes 301

SF16 Identifying text types (non-fiction) 302

SF17 Analysing stylistic devices . . . 305

SF18 Analysing non-fiction 305

SF19 Analysing narrative prose. . . . 306

SF20 Analysing drama 308

SF21 Analysing poetry 309

Listening and viewing skills

SF22 Listening 312

SF23 Analysing a film 313

Speaking skills (monologues and dialogues)

SF24 Giving a presentation 315

SF25 Giving a speech **P** 317

SF26 Taking part in an interview **P** . 319

SF27 Having a discussion 319

SF28 Having a debate 321

Writing skills

SF29 Writing a formal letter or email. 323

SF30 Writing an application **P** 324

SF31 Writing a summary **P** 326

SF32 Writing a review **P** 327

SF33 Writing a report **P** 330

SF34 Argumentative writing. 331

SF35 Writing a character profile . . . 333

SF36 Writing a text analysis **P** 335

SF37 Doing a creative writing task. 336

SF38 Writing a well-structured text. 337

SF39 Quoting a text **P** 338

SF40 Proofreading **P** 340

Mediation skills

SF41 Mediation of written and oral texts **P** 341

P A task allows you to practise the skill.

> *Download the suggested answers to the Skills File PRACTICE tasks here:*
> **Webcode** context-84

Language learning and study skills

▶ SF1 Dealing with unknown or new words

READING, LISTENING AND MEDIATING ENGLISH INTO GERMAN

When you read or listen to texts, you usually won't understand every single word. Luckily, in many cases, you won't need to because you can understand texts without knowing each individual word. However, if the meaning of a word is essential to a sentence, there are some techniques that can help you work it out.

Look at the highlighted words in the text on the left and, on the right, read what strategies to use to work out their meaning.

In order to remain competitive, the industrial nations have to raise their productivity, encourage innovation and lower their production costs.

To reduce costs and to maximize profits, multinational companies often relocate facilities to other countries (= outsourcing) to profit from lower wages they pay their workers and from less restrictive laws. The problem is that it diminishes work prospects for workers here.

- *competitive:* think of words from the same word family (*competition / (to) compete / competitor*)
- *encourage:* identify parts of the word that you know (*courage → give someone courage*)
- *maximize:* think of similar words in other languages (German *maximieren*) but watch out for false friends (*prospects = Aussichten,* not: *Prospekte*)
- *multinational:* identify suffixes or prefixes (*multi = many → multinational = belonging to many nations*)
- *wages:* use the context of the word ('pay their workers')

Using different strategies, try to infer the meaning of the underlined words:

One of the Queen's underlined recurrent royal responsibilities was to open Parliament, an obligation she had never previously found particularly burdensome and actually rather enjoyed: to be driven down the Mall on a bright autumn morning even after fifty years was something of a treat. But not any more.

From: Alan Bennett, *The Uncommon Reader*, 2008, p. 32 (cf. *Context* p. 58, ll. 1–4)

SPEAKING, WRITING AND MEDIATING GERMAN INTO ENGLISH

When you want to express a certain concept in English when talking, writing or mediating and you don't know the word, you can paraphrase it. (▶ SF 6: Paraphrasing)

LEARNING NEW WORDS

Learning vocabulary is a lifelong activity – even in your own language you never stop learning new words. There are different methods for expanding your vocabulary. Try out a variety of methods until you find the one that works best for you.

Step 1: Identify words that could be useful to you. These might be:
- words that are related to the topic you are dealing with (e.g. Shakespeare's dramas)
- words that help you talk or write about texts or topics in class
- words that go together with other words (collocations) or that belong to a word family that you already know
- words that belong to a neutral *register (words that are either very formal or very informal can only be used in limited situations).

Step 2: Arrange your words in a suitable form. This could be a mind map or a list – or you might want to use index cards. Indicate the meaning of your words by:
- giving synonyms (e.g. *dogma* = *belief / principle*)
- giving antonyms (e.g. *upheaval* ≠ *stability*)
- making sketches/drawings
- giving examples (e.g. the arts = *art, music, literature, etc.*)
- giving the German equivalent (e.g. *achievement* = *Errungenschaft*).

If possible, write down words in contexts or collocations; this will help you to use them in a sentence (e.g. *be torn between, remember sb. for sth.*).

The Elizabethan Age is often remembered as a Golden Age for its many achievements in the arts. However, England was struggling for peace and stability at home – religious, social, political and economic developments challenged society.
People were torn between a traditional world view and a more modern one; they generally accepted the Earth as the centre of the cosmos and the Church as the centre of life on Earth, but were keen to discover new truths beyond the old dogmas. Shakespeare's drama reflects this upheaval.

Step 3: Use your new vocabulary as soon and as often as possible, e.g. include it in a short text, prepare a one-minute speech, study your index cards, etc.

Step 4: Revise your vocabulary regularly; first in short intervals, then in longer ones.

> **▬ TIP**
>
> Be active when learning new words: do not just write them down, say them out loud as well. Sometimes movements, e.g. walking around while learning or giving them a rhythm or tune, can also be helpful.

▶ SF 2 Using a dictionary and a grammar book

USING A BILINGUAL DICTIONARY

Here you can look up translations of words. For example if you do not know the English word for *Ruf* you can look it up in the German-English section or type it into your digital dictionary.

- The running heads at the top of each page help you find the right page quickly (top left-hand corner: first entry on page, top right-hand corner: last entry at bottom of page).
- In the example on the right, *Ruf* is the head-word: the different translations are listed, numbers or letters in boxes indicate the different meanings.
- The notes in *italics* help you to find the particular meaning you are looking for.
- Examples and collocations are found below the headword.

> **Ruf**
> **1** *auch übertragen* call /kɔːl/; *lauter* shout
> /ʃaʊt/: *der Ruf nach schärferen Gesetzen* the
> **call for** tougher laws
> **2** ≈ *Ansehen* reputation /ˌrepjuˈteɪʃn/

From: *Schulwörterbuch English G 21*

USING A MONOLINGUAL DICTIONARY

Sometimes a monolingual dictionary can prove more helpful than a bilingual dictionary because it doesn't only give equivalents of words in another language, but definitions and example sentences. In this way, an English-English dictionary will help you to find the words that fit best to express exactly what you want to say. If you don't understand an English word of Latin or Greek origin, a monolingual dictionary will usually be more helpful than a bilingual one because the bilingual one will often give you a translation that is similar to the English word, e.g. *cosmopolitan = Kosmopolit*.

- In order to choose the right meaning from those given, always read the whole entry.
- The information on usage and style helps you to avoid using the wrong *register.
- Looking at the examples of common collocations and idioms can help you avoid false friends.
- Many dictionaries provide more specific information on typical error areas.

> **TIP**
>
> - To find the pronunciation of an English word, check the English-German section of your dictionary or listen to the soundfile in a digital dictionary.
> - In the English-German section you will also find references to irregular verb forms, irregular plural forms, etc.
> - Always read the additional information next to your headword (above: in *italics*). This will prevent you from using the wrong translation.

> **grim** /grɪm/ *adj.* (**grim·mer**, **grim·mest**) **1** looking or
> sounding very serious: *a grim face/look/smile* ◊ *She*
> *looked grim.* ◊ *with a look of grim determination on his*
> *face* ◊ *grim-faced policemen* **2** unpleasant and depress-
> ing: *grim news* ◊ *We face the grim prospect of still higher*
> *unemployment.* ◊ *The outlook is pretty grim.* ◊ *Things are*
> *looking grim for workers in the building industry.* **3** (of a
> place or building) not attractive; depressing: *The house*
> *looked grim and dreary in the rain.* ◊ *the grim walls of the*
> *prison* **4** [not before noun] (*BrE*) *informal*) ill/sick: *I feel*
> *grim this morning.* **5** [not usually before noun] (*BrE*, *in-*
> *formal*) of very low quality: *Their performance was fairly*
> *grim, I'm afraid!* ▶ **grim·ly** *adv.*: *'It won't be easy,' he said*
> *grimly.* ◊ *grimly determined* **grim·ness** *noun* [U]

From: *Oxford Advanced Learner's Dictionary*

PRACTICE

Translate the following sentences:
1 *Genetisch veränderte Lebensmittel haben in vielen europäischen Ländern einen eher schlechten Ruf.*
2 *Es gibt auch noch den Ruf nach mehr Beschrän-kungen für den freien Markt.*
3 *Sein Rufen schien niemand zu bemerken.*

USING A GRAMMAR BOOK

A grammar book is useful for correcting mistakes and improving your grammar. You should consult it when you come across a grammar problem while writing a text (e.g. if you are not sure whether or not to use a gerund) or when you realize that you keep making mistakes in certain fields of grammar. To identify these areas, analyse the feedback you receive from your teacher on your tests or homework.

Step 1: Find your grammatical problem area (e.g. word order or tenses) in the contents page or in the index pages at the back of the book. Read the relevant entry (both rules and examples).

Step 2: In order to avoid mistakes in the future, use your grammar book in different ways, e.g.:
- Copy problematic grammar rules onto index cards and use them to revise your grammar points. (Use the same colours for similar aspects or leave space on the cards for examples you add later, etc.)
- Create a poster with your own typical grammar traps.
- Look for the grammar point in question in texts you are working with or in your own texts.
- Do some exercises on the topic.
- Say the rule and some example sentences out loud, perhaps using your grammar card.

PRACTICE

In your latest test the sentences below have been marked as wrong. Say what grammar topic you will look up in your grammar book, then correct the mistakes.
1 *They never went to England before.*
2 *They have known each other since six years.*
3 *If they would be older, they would do it.*
4 *Alicia feels not comfortable.*
5 *She asked me if I am happy.*
6 *They were all the time there.*

▶ SF3 Doing research

For projects, presentations or other school work you usually have to research individual aspects and find specific information. For this you can use the internet, but also other sources of information. Here are some ways to make your research more effective.

THE PREPARATION STAGE
Step 1: Clarify what your topic is, then brainstorm it. Decide what information you need so that you can structure your research accordingly.

Step 2: Plan your research:
- Decide which sources are helpful for your research: the internet, textbooks, encyclopaedias, newspapers or magazines, experts or contemporary witnesses?
- Concentrate on English language sources. Using German information and translating it into English will take a long time and often leads to unidiomatic English.
- Make a list of keywords that you want to check.

THE RESEARCH STAGE
Step 1: Check your sources: Older publications may contain outdated information; information published by individuals, interest groups or companies may be biased (i.e. have a tendency to be in favour of this group or company). Check for cross-references and do not just rely on one source.

Step 2: Make notes on the information you find. (▶ SF 15: Marking up a text / Making and taking notes)
- Using index cards might make it easier to organize the information later.
- Copy the exact wording and note down the source (▶ SF 39: Quoting a text), as it normally needs to be given in a bibliography (an alphabetical list of sources used) at the end of your presentation or project work.

·····▶

■ TIP

When doing research on the internet, the following tips may help you to find useful information:

How can you determine whether a website provides reliable information?	Domain names ending with *.gov* or *.edu* indicate that the information is likely to be accurate, as it is usually an official website. Sites of scientific institutions are also usually reliable.
	Personal blogs or home pages often just give statements by individuals – they tend to be biased.
How can you limit the number of hits so that you will find useful information more quickly?	Brainstorm which keywords would most likely appear in the perfect article to answer your search question. Combine them to get the most exact results. Typing in 5–7 keywords is better than just two or three. The more specific the word(s), the better.
How can you find the original source of a quote?	Enter the full quote or parts of it, using quotation marks. This way you will only find websites with that exact quote. From these, you will normally be able to find the original source of a quote.

PRACTICE

'German vs. British political system – similarities and differences'. Use the internet and/or printed works to find out about the German political system and compare it to your findings from Chapter 3, p. 60.

▶ SF 4 Doing project work

A project is a complex task usually done in a group, involving several hours of work and often resulting in a written or oral product, e.g. a wall display or a presentation. Project work typically proceeds along the following stages:

Step 1: Plan your work:
- Agree on a topic or look closely at the topic assigned to you.
- Decide what has to be done and how to present your results (e.g. a display, a presentation, a web page, a class magazine).
- Discuss how everybody can contribute best to the project and assign the tasks accordingly.
- Agree on a schedule, including regular group meetings at which all group members give status reports, present their results so far and discuss problems.

Step 2: Research your topic. (▶ SF 3: Doing research)

Step 3: Organize your findings (▶ SF 5: Structuring information and ideas) and start preparing your final result, i.e. your presentation (▶ SF 24: Giving a presentation) and/or any kind of written material (e.g. a wall display, a written text to be handed in, your web page, etc. (▶ SF 5: Structuring information and ideas). Bear in mind any specifications you were given by your teacher (e.g. length of presentation or text, etc.).

Step 4: Check your written and visual material. Is it well organized and clear? Is the English correct? (▶ SF 40: Proofreading) Give your product to someone else in your group to check it again.

Step 5: Present your results. (▶ SF 24: Giving a presentation)

Step 6: After your presentation, assess your work. With your group, discuss what went well and what you could do better next time or ask your audience or teacher for feedback.

▶SF5 Structuring information and ideas: visual aids and outlines

Structuring is both an analytical and a productive skill:

- *Finding the structure in a given text and giving this structure a visual representation help you to understand the text*

- *Outlining your ideas in a clear and logical way enables you to produce and present a coherent and convincing text.*

ANALYZING THE STRUCTURE OF A TEXT AND MAKING VISUAL AIDS

Visual aids can have three purposes:

- *to help you get a clearer picture of the content of a text*
- *to structure information before writing a text*
  (▶SF5: Structuring information and ideas)
- *to present information to accompany a presentation*
  (▶SF24: Giving a presentation).

Some typical examples of visual aids are

- *timelines: order of events, dates*
- *flow charts: cause and effect*
- *pie charts: percentages, amounts*
  (▶SF12: Analysing charts and graphs)
- *clusters/mind maps: structured ideas.*

The following instructions explain how to make a flow chart after reading a text:

Step 1: Read the text and highlight the most important information. (▶SF15: Marking up a text/Making and taking notes)

> The reduction of oxygen-giving forests, especially the tropical rainforests, is one component of the climate change that scientists have been observing over the past few decades. This global warming appears to be causing the polar ice caps to melt, which could lead to the flooding of many coastal regions. At the same time as we rob the earth of its natural resources, we pollute the air and water with the waste products of those resources. Some of the emissions our technology produces are to blame for the greenhouse effect, which further contributes to the global warming phenomenon.
>
> 5
>
> 10

Step 2: Work out how the different aspects are connected.

- *reduction of forests: leads to climate change/global warming*
- *climate change/global warming: leads to melting of the polar ice caps*
- *melting of the polar ice caps: can cause floods*
- *pollution of air and water through waste: emissions cause greenhouse effect*

Step 3: Show the connection with arrows or other symbols.

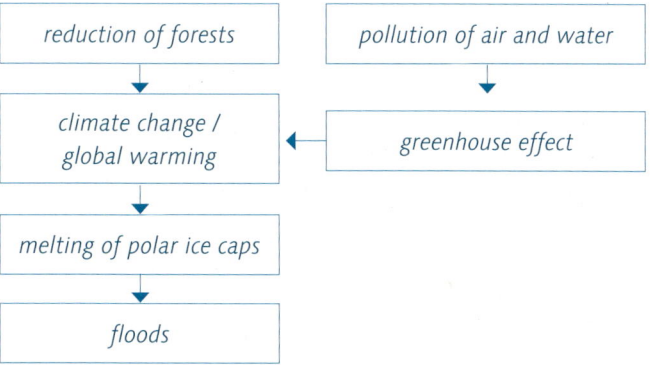

■ TIP

Use single terms or short phrases if possible; otherwise your chart will look too full and be visually confusing.

PRACTICE

Read ll.29–66 of the Fact File on p.64. Make a visual aid that presents the information on the Commonwealth in a suitable way.

STRUCTURING IDEAS AND OUTLINING YOUR TEXT

Structuring ideas is an important step after collecting information and before preparing a text (which may be written or spoken). Arranging your arguments in a logical order is a prerequisite to an effective text. (► SF 38: Writing a well-structured text)

Step 1: When you have collected your ideas, decide on an order in which to present them:
Most texts you produce will follow the general structure **1. Introduction → 2. Main part / Body → 3. Conclusion**. Decide on the order in which to present your ideas in the main part. Often the text-type you are being asked to produce will demand a specific structure (► SF 16: Identifying text types). For example, if you are asked to discuss a statement you will probably divide up your ideas into pro- and con-arguments (► SF 34: Argumentative writing). Other possibilities are a chronological order or *problem → cause → solution*. It may be helpful to use a flow-chart (► SF 5: Structuring information and ideas) at this stage.

Step 2: Make an **outline** of your text (cf. the box on the right).
All 'main ideas' are of equal importance, as are the 'important facts', etc.

Step 3: Add the ideas you have collected to your outline. Use keywords.

Step 4: Before you start producing the final text or notes, review your outline. Make sure you have found the most appropriate place for each piece of information. (► SF 38: Writing a well-structured text)

> **OUTLINE**
> **1. Introduction**
> **2. Main part / Body**
>   I. Main idea 1
>   A. Important fact
>   1. Supporting fact
>   2. Supporting fact
>   a. Example or detail
>   b. Example or detail
>   B. Important fact
>   …
>   II. Main idea 2
>   …
> **3. Conclusion**

► SF 6 Paraphrasing

Paraphrasing is useful when you don't know the exact word or phrase in a conversation, when writing a text or mediating into English. There are different techniques for paraphrasing:

Paraphrasing technique	Example
Antonym Antonyms denote the opposite of the original word.	*Reichtum:* 'the opposite of poverty'
Comparison Comparisons help you illustrate what you mean by creating images.	*Handschuh:* 'It's like a hat for your hand.'
Definition or explanation (often using relative clauses) With definitions or explanations, relative clauses help you add detail to general terms (e.g. 'a person', 'a machine').	*Freiwillige/r:* 'a person who offers to do something but doesn't ask for money in return' *Navigationsgerät:* 'a machine that tells you how to get to your destination; often in a car'

PRACTICE

Paraphrase the German words and phrases using the strategies in brackets:

Krankenschwester (definition/explanation)	*Dach* (comparison)
unangenehm (antonym)	*langweilig* (antonym)
Herbergsvater (definition/explanation)	*Garage* (comparison)

▶SF7 Working with closed test formats

In both lessons and written examinations you will come across test formats that don't ask you to write complete texts or answers to questions:

- *In **half-open formats** you write keywords only, e.g. when taking notes, completing tables or finishing sentences.*
- *In **closed test formats**, you don't write at all, but just indicate which of the given solutions is correct or which items go together. The most common forms are multiple-choice tasks, true/false statements, matching tasks and gapped texts (see below).*

Before an exam, ask your teacher which closed test formats you might expect.

The following strategies will help you deal with closed test formats.

Step 1: Preparing for the test

- Read the **instructions** carefully and work out what information you have to look for. It might help to underline keywords in the task.
- Try to **imagine** the situation of the text and anticipate what you might read or hear.

Step 2: Doing the test

- Focus on the **information that is necessary** to complete your task. Take notes. (▶SF 15: Marking up a text / Making and taking notes)
- In **listening tasks**, complete as much as possible during the first listening. Use the second listening to add the missing information or to correct what you have done before. (▶SF 22: Listening)
- Keep an eye on the time while working on **reading tasks**. Tasks that require you to read for gist only allow you a short time to skim the texts (▶SF 14: Reading strategies). First work on the questions you are sure about, then go back to those you're struggling with.
- Never leave an **item unanswered**. If you do not know the answer, make a sensible guess – your chances of getting the credit for it are 25% in a multiple-choice task with four options!

Here are some specific tips for the different types of closed test formats:

Multiple-choice task (i.e. choosing the correct answer from multiple given options; cf. p. 158 above, task 1)
- Read the given options carefully – they may contain traps: They may use keywords from the text, but e.g. say the exact opposite of what is said in the text!
- If you are unsure which of the options is correct, go through them one by one and ask yourself why they might be incorrect.

True/false statements (i.e. classifying each given statement as 'true' or 'false'; cf. p. 107, task 2)
- In the case of false statements, you will typically find the opposite information in the text.
- In a half-open version of this format, you may be asked to give evidence for why you think an answer is right or wrong or to correct it.

Matching task (i.e. matching items from two lists, e.g. paragraphs with headings; cf. p. 15, task 1c)
- Don't match items just because they contain words or phrases that are similar. Instead, paraphrase the items and match those with a similar meaning.

Gapped text (i.e. identifying passages that have been left out of a text; cf. p. 80, task 1)
- Watch out for words that link sentences/ideas such as connectors (e.g. *therefore, moreover*), pronouns (e.g. *she, there, this*) or connected vocabulary (e.g. *bird – eagle, sparrow*) and pay attention to the sequence of time in the text. They may provide useful hints.
- After completing the text make sure that the grammar fits and the line of thought works (e.g. *cause and effect*).

▶ SF 8 Learning languages with electronic devices

You probably use various electronic devices and digital media in different spheres of life already – maybe even to improve your English. The following will give you some ideas on how to do so sensibly and on how to make the most of the digital media you use.

When using digital devices, you should always ask yourself whether they provide the special help and support you need. Don't expect them to do the trick and miraculously expand your language skills: learning a foreign language needs time and effort, whether it's done with or without electronic devices.

When using electronic devices to improve your language skills, you can make use of their benefits to different degrees:

LEVEL 1   You simply use an electronic device instead of using a printed text or writing things by hand. The device may be the medium at hand, which is comfortable to use and possibly also more fun, but there is no extra value in it.

LEVEL 2   You use an electronic device because it offers extra (support) functions, e.g.:

- You watch an American series online because it is not dubbed and you get a lot of language input through the original version.
- You use an electronic dictionary rather than a printed one because it is faster and you can also listen to the pronunciation.
- You rehearse your English presentation and record it digitally because then you can check it or get others to assess it.
- You type your homework out on your computer, not only because it's easier to read a printed text than your handwriting, but also because it can be revised much more comfortably. Plus, you can use the spellcheck function.
- You learn your new vocab via an app. It keeps track of the words you want to learn and presents them to you again and again until you've memorized them – and there is no cheating!
- You revise grammar via an app that offers you special exercises for your individual weak spots.
- You decide in favour of an electronic presentation, not only because it is likely to impress the audience, but also because this is the only way you can link your presentation with other media and present sources of information from the internet.
- It is only you who can make use of the extra functions an electronic device offers. If you decide to ignore the spell checker or the recommendations of your app, they cannot help you!

LEVEL 3   You use digital devices for a completely different working and learning process. For example, if you work on a project as a team and you cannot meet regularly, you can save it in the cloud and give each team member access to the documents. Thus, you can all work on your product at different times and in different places. You can use chat-functions to add remarks and ideas for improvement or you can revise your product in a correction circle. And finally, nothing gets lost, because it's safely stored online.

▶ SF9 Assessing yourself and giving feedback

Feedback from others helps you to evaluate your own skills and products more objectively. It is always easier to assess somebody else's work than your own. Furthermore, giving others feedback not only improves your evaluation skills – something that you will find useful in other fields of life too – but also teaches you alternative ways of dealing with and solving a task.

ASSESSING YOURSELF

Assessing yourself is difficult because it involves having to find and then applying an objective benchmark. You should try and compare your results, your texts, presentations etc. with a set of rules, a good example text or any other model or pattern that helps you to identify your strong points as well as your weaker spots or mistakes. See, for instance, the Common European Framework of Reference for Languages or marking schemes that your teacher uses and that are mandatory for your final (*Abitur*) exams.

It may be also be helpful to prepare a list of your 'favourite' mistakes or to decide on a particular aspect of the task in question that you want to check and improve on. That way you avoid looking at your product in a very generalizing way and ending up with the impression that it is neither very good nor very bad.

ASSESSING THE WORK OF OTHERS AND GIVING FEEDBACK

If you want to give feedback to others, a feedback sheet or a checklist will be helpful. You may also ask your partner whether there are any aspects they want you to pay particular attention to. The more detailed and focused your feedback is, the better, even more so, if you not only criticize, but also suggest a way to correct a mistake or improve a weakness. Always start with the positive aspects – do not only refer to mistakes, but point out strong elements or passages.

There are some golden rules of feedback:

- Be specific. Don't just say 'You did a good job', but tell your partner exactly in what respect.

- Describe, don't evaluate. Don't say that something was 'nice', not even that it was 'splendid', but 'You linked your arguments with connectors and supported each of them with evidence or aspects from your personal experience.'

- Focus on the product, not on the person. Instead of 'You are not being logical', say 'Your line of arguments is not very logical in paragraphs two and three, where you write …'

- Be friendly and appreciative, but clear. 'That was okay, I quite liked it' doesn't help your partner; instead, you say 'In general I can see improvement in a lot of fields like line of arguments, good linking words, convincing examples; but you still don't check on your spelling. Sometimes it's really hard to understand what you mean.'

Receiving feedback isn't always very easy either. You may tend to defend your product or yourself, because you feel attacked by what the other person is saying. Try to listen quietly, because feedback is not about being right or wrong, but about supporting each other in a process of possible improvement.

It is not absolutely necessary to write anything down when giving or receiving feedback. On the other hand, it may be very useful indeed to keep and compare notes or look at several revised pieces of work. You may notice patterns of frequent mistakes or even see a learning curve where things have changed for the better.

▶ SF 10   Finding and developing your individual language learning skills

You have used some of the skills and strategies presented in the Skills File since you started learning English. In the years to come you will need to customize them for yourself in order to support your language learning process at school and beyond, for learning English or any other foreign language. There are three important steps to take – and you should be honest with yourself:

Step 1:   **Where am I?**

Here you have to take stock and review your language skills and learning process. In order to do so, you should reflect on yourself, look at your results and achievements in English, consider the results of self- and peer evaluation that you have done or been given, and maybe even ask your teacher where you stand with learning English. Do you know how to actively learn English and improve on your results? Or have you just passively gone with the flow?

Step 2:   **Where would I like to be?**

Would you e.g. simply want to avoid some of your pet mistakes, to be better at speaking or to receive a better mark for your essay? Do you wish to be well-prepared for the next written test, to hand in a fitting application for a job, scholarship or exchange year or do you simply want to survive the Abitur in English? Set yourself reachable goals.

Step 3:   **What are the next steps?**

Now that you've decided what you'd like to achieve, you will have to consider when and how to do so. What are the precise methods and strategies you can use in order to reach these goals? What can you do? And within what period of time?

- If you have to enlarge your vocabulary, what is your strategy (e.g. using an electronic app or rather reading and writing more texts)?
- If you have problems with mediation, is it because you have difficulties getting ideas into English or rather because you don't know enough about English text types like email, formal letter, leaflet etc.? Should you rather practice explaining things in English or applying the correct text features?
- If you are not very successful in presentations, is it due to a lack of communicative skills or are you unsure about the choice of content to present? Should you e.g. practice how to identify relevant content or how to get it across in front of an audience

Text skills

▶ SF 11 Analysing pictures

There are different types of pictures: photos, posters, paintings, drawings, or sketches. Often they are combined with written text, either as a title or a caption.

John Gast, *American Progress*, 1872

in the top right-hand corner

in the background

in the centre

in the bottom left-hand corner

in the foreground

Step 1: Basic information

- State your first impression of the picture.
- Read the title or caption and identify the general topic.
- Check when (and where) the picture was created or published.

- *title: 'American Progress'*
- *general topic: American settlers moving west / conquering the continent*
- *artist, date: John Gast, 1872*

■ LANGUAGE HELP

- This picture/painting/photo/poster/drawing/sketch … shows / provides proof of / gives information on / introduces the topic of / conveys the impression that / depicts / portrays/ illustrates / is about/ …
- In the picture, … can be seen.

Step 2: Description
Choose one of these approaches:

- Start with the main subject, i.e. a dominant object, describe it in detail, then describe the background (useful for a picture with one dominant image).
  OR
- Start at the left of the picture and work across to the right or vice versa (useful for pictures with a lot of activity).
  OR
- Start at the top of the picture and work down to the bottom or vice versa (useful for pictures where the interest tails off towards the top or bottom).

- *dominant figure in the middle of the painting: woman, made to appear like a goddess or angel, holding a book in her left hand, moving towards the left of the picture, …*
- *painting shows landscape with a lot of detail*
- *right-hand side: bright, especially at the top; background: ships and railway lines*
- *in the bottom right-hand corner: farmers and a horse-drawn coach*
- *left-hand side: considerably darker / more threatening: clouds, ragged mountains, wild landscape*
- *bottom-left corner: Native Americans*
- *…*

·····▶

Step 3: Analysis and interpretation

Draw conclusions about what the picture is meant to convey, whether it does this effectively and how it achieves its effect. You can look at …

- the technique, colours
- the effect on the viewer
- who is addressed and why
- the artist's/photographer's intention/ message.

- *right half of the painting (i.e. east) represents the American east (where the first settlers landed and lived); left half of the painting represents the 'wild west'*
- *colours and light: the east appears warm/bright; the west seems to be threatening and dark ('wild' west)*
- *all objects/people (trains, coaches, people, dominant figure) move from right to left → westward movement of American settlers → picture illustrates the idea of 'Manifest Destiny', which was …*
- *dominant figure: could represent culture, learning and progress (cf. the title); her angelic impression underlines the importance and positive connotation the artist places on those aspects*

■ **LANGUAGE HELP**

- The artist's/photographer's use of … creates … / conveys the impression of …
- By … the picture effectively illustrates …
- The dominance of … / The way the light/ shadow … directs the viewer's attention to …

- As the foreground/ background is …, the impression given is that …
- … is a symbol of … / … helps to create an atmosphere of / which …
- This has the effect that …

Step 4: Evaluation

Evaluate the picture by analysing how or how well it achieves an effect and by describing its effect on you.

- *painting clearly/effectively illustrates the idea that American people were chosen by God to conquer the American continent*

PRACTICE

Analyse one of the pictures on p. 94.

▶ SF 12 Analysing charts and graphs

Charts and graphs present complex information visually. There are different types, e.g. pie charts, bar charts, line graphs or tables.

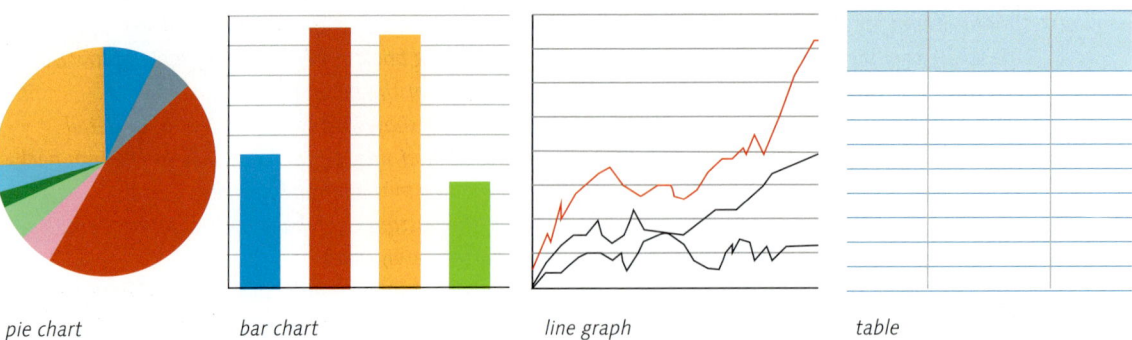

pie chart
('Tortendiagramm')

bar chart
('Säulendiagramm')

line graph
('Kurvendiagramm')

table
('Tabelle')

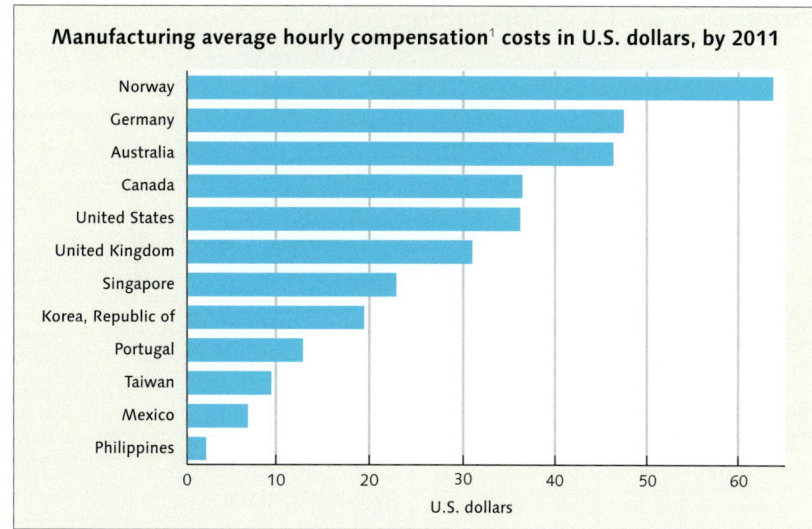

Manufacturing average hourly compensation[1] costs in U.S. dollars, by 2011

From: the website of the U.S. Department of Labor

When analysing charts and graphs like the one on the right, follow these three steps:

Step 1: Identify the type of chart or graph you are dealing with. Analyse the source:
- Is the source reliable?
- Is the data up to date?

- *bar chart*

- *source: U.S. Dept. of Labor: reliable*
- *data from 2011: not exactly up to date*

Step 2: Describe the graph/chart:
- What is it about and what information does it give?

- *shows the differences in the hourly wage of workers in manufacturing in different countries in 2011*
- *gives the hourly compensation in $ (absolute numbers)*
- *compares data from 2011*

- Does it show a development or does it compare different items at one point in time?
- Does it use absolute figures or percentages?

- *at the top of the ranking: countries with the highest hourly compensation (Norway: first, Philippines: last)*
- *countries at the bottom: hourly compensation is less than a sixth of the countries at the top*

■ LANGUAGE HELP

- The bar chart/pie chart/line graph/table … shows the different/compares the size/number of …/ deals with/is about …/contrasts … with …
- It shows … in contrast to…
- It is taken from/It contains data from …/It was published in …

Bar chart:
- The bars are arranged horizontally/vertically.
- There are big/vast/surprising differences between …
- At the top/bottom of the ranking comes…
- … is first/last in rank
- … has the largest/second largest …

Pie chart:
- The chart is divided into … segments, which show/ represent …
- The smallest/biggest segment/The segments representing … and … constitute the majority …/ A huge majority/minority is …

Line graph:
- The graph shows the relationship between … and …
- … is twice/three times as high as …/… There are more than/nearly twice as many … as there are …
- increase/decrease/reach a high point/rise/fall/ drop/grow steadily

·····▶

---

[1]**compensation** wage

Step 3: Draw conclusions from the chart/graph.

- *vast differences in the hourly wage → huge differences in the production costs of the goods → outsourcing of time-consuming jobs to countries with a lower hourly wage*

Look at the table on the right and decide whether the figures would best be shown in a pie chart, a bar chart or a line graph and why. Use a computer to design the chart.

Find a tool to create info-graphics here:

Webcode context-57

The world's most livable cities		
Rank	City	Score
1	Vienna/Austria	99.1
2	Melbourne/Australia	98.4
3	Osaka/Japan	97.7
4	Calgary/Canada	97.5
5	Sydney/Australia	97.4
6	Vancouver/Canada	97.3
7	Toronto/Canada	97.2
8	Tokyo/Japan	97.2
9	Copenhagen/Denmark	96.8
10	Adelaide/Australia	96.6

From: *The Economist Intelligence Unit Limited 2018*

▶ SF 13 Analysing cartoons

The following steps will help you to describe and analyse a cartoon systematically.

Step 1: Basic information

- What is your first impression of the cartoon?
  first impression: humorous, eye-catching, cartoon exaggerates a common school situation to illustrate a serious topic
- What is the cartoon about?
- What is its topic?
  topic: genetic engineering and its uncontrollable consequences
- (Where/when was it published?)

GENETIC ENGINEERING 101

'Okay – is there anybody ELSE whose homework ate their dog?'

Step 2: Description

- Describe the cartoon systematically.
  - *classroom with students who all have brought colourful fantasy animals / monsters with them*
  - *in the background: blackboard with writing 'Genetic Engineering 101' (= name of the class); in front of the class: teacher looking angry*
  - *one student: putting up his hand, looking at his dinosaur-like animal*
  - *caption: the teacher's words*
- What people, events or trends does the cartoon refer to? Mention any labels, speech bubbles or captions. (▶ SF 11: Analysing pictures)

Step 3: Analysis

The following questions may help you when analysing a cartoon:

- Are the figures or issues presented in a positive or negative light? How is this impression achieved?
- Does the cartoon make use of *symbols or *irony? Explain their use.
- Does the cartoon depict well-known persons? Who are they and what is their role in connection with the topic of the cartoon?
- What point is the cartoonist trying to make? What means are used to get the message across?
  - *cartoonist reverses a common classroom cliché: a common excuse for students who don't have their homework is that their dog ate their homework; here, the homework (i.e. the genetically engin-eered animal) has eaten the dog*
  - *illustrations of the fantasy animals: exaggerated, eye-catching, funny shapes and colours*
  - *cartoon = criticism of uncontrollability of genetic engineering; even experts (here: the teacher) are unable to control the risks*

Step 4: Evaluation

Is the cartoon effective or not? Give reasons, using your background knowledge about the topic.

*The cartoon criticizes the dangers of scientific research and genetic engineering effectively. To get its message across, it uses a funny twist by turning a well-known *cliché upside-down. By choosing a seem-ingly harmless setting to illustrate the devastating consequences of genetic engineering, the cartoonist criticizes it in a forceful way.*

'I'd like to change my major from electrical engineering to English or something.'

DEAN OF STUDENTS

PRACTICE

Describe and analyse the cartoon on the left.

▶ SF 14 Reading strategies

When working with longer texts, there are different ways of reading. Which strategy you need to apply depends on what you want to do with your text: look for the main ideas or specific information, read for pleasure or analyse it. You also need to have a strategy to deal with unknown words (▶ SF 1: Dealing with unknown words).

SKIMMING

Skimming (or reading for gist) means going through a text quickly to identify its main ideas. This technique is helpful when there is lots of material to be taken in and only a limited amount of time, e.g. when you are doing research on a certain subject and you have to find out which texts could be relevant for your topic.

Step 1: Look at illustrations, pictures, keywords, headings or subheadings to get an idea of the content of the given text.

Step 2: Don't read every sentence. Let your eyes run over the whole text and look for words or phrases that contain useful information.

Step 3: Read the first and the last sentence of each paragraph – one of them usually states the main idea of that paragraph and the very last sentence of the text often contains a summary.

Step 4: Summarize the text. If you are able to do this without a problem, your skimming was probably successful.

SCANNING

Scanning means looking out for for specific information. You can use this technique when you want to find answers to a particular question or to compare particular aspects in different texts.

Step 1: Think of keywords or phrases that might be useful to search for when looking for the information you need.

Step 2: Move your eyes quickly down the page. Stop when you find a keyword or phrase and read the part where you found it. Then continue scanning the text.

EXTENSIVE READING

Extensive reading means reading for pleasure, e.g. when reading a novel. You read at your own speed and concentrate on what's happening (the events of the plot) without looking up unknown words.

CLOSE READING

Close reading is necessary when analysing a text (▶ SF 17–21). You will need to understand not only what is being said in the text, but also how it is being said. To do that, you will have to read the text more than once and make sure you understand every word.

PRACTICE
1 Skim the text 'The need for a new label' (p. 129) and note down what the text is about in a few words.
2 Scan the third paragraph of 'India then and now' (p. 76) for facts and figures showing which challenges India has to face.

▶ SF 15 Marking up a text / Making and taking notes

When working with photocopied texts or printouts, you can mark up important information so that you can find it more easily when you are working with the text again, e. g. when you are writing about it or preparing for a test.

> **TIP**
>
> When working with a borrowed book, put a transparency on the page and mark important information on it.

MARKING UP A TEXT

Step 1: As you read the text, bear in mind what information you are looking for. You may want to read the task/question again.

Step 2: When you find the relevant information in your text, mark it by underlining, highlighting or circling the relevant words or passages. Only mark keywords.

> **TIP**
>
> 1. Use different colours for different tasks.
> 2. Also mark words which show that a different opinion or a contrast is being introduced to help you understand the logical structure of the text.

Step 3: Finally, add headings or keywords in the margin or summarize passages with short phrases or sentences.

Tasks: **a** Point out what recruiters do and how they work.
b Collect tips on how to write a CV to arouse a recruiter's interest.

How to please recruiters
Clare Whitmell

A recruiter can be your short cut into a new job. With a good understanding of industry trends – and insider knowledge of that particular employer's preferences and needs – a recruiter will be briefed to find exactly the right candidate with a specific set of skills, experience and qualities. To even be considered for the role, you need to make sure that your CV hits the right notes with them. ⁵

Recruiters can be generalists working in a number of sectors or headhunters specialising in one, but there are a few pet hates they all share. Avoid these and you'll be giving yourself a better chance of getting into the yes pile each time. [...] ¹⁰

Zena Everett, director and career coach at Second Careers and career guru at Mumsnet, has researched how headhunters, recruiters, employers and HR professionals screen CVs. She found that they all – without exception – looked first at the most recent work experience and job title. These must be relevant for the CV to get a second look in a competitive job market. ¹⁵–²⁰

For recruiters to put you forward to an employer, they need to see that your background matches the role. A simple way to ensure that you're giving your CV the best possible chance is to search the job description for key criteria, then make sure you include relevant details on your CV that show you're a good match. ²⁵

recruiters' knowledge

recruiters' tasks

recruiters' areas of work

Show that your most recent work experience is relevant for the job.

Show that you fulfil the most important criteria for the new job.

From: 'What makes a recruiter hate your CV?', *The Guardian*, 8 April 2014

MAKING AND TAKING NOTES

In cases where you cannot mark up a text (either because you are not working with your own book or because you are listening to an audio file), you can first *take notes* (i.e. extract important information from the text), then *make notes* (i.e. organize your ideas). Making notes will also help you structure your own ideas, e.g. after brainstorming or when preparing for a speaking task (▶ SF 5: Structuring information and ideas; ▶ SF 24–28).

▶ SF 16 Identifying text types (non-fiction)

In class you often have to analyse texts. The first step of the analysis is to identify the text type you are dealing with.

Texts can be classified into two main categories:

Fictional texts (i.e. literary texts, *Dichtung*, ▶SF 19–21)	Non-fictional texts (i.e. *Sachtexte*, ▶SF 18)
• The text describes a world that was created in the mind of its *author. • Its *setting, *characters and events may or may not seem realistic.	• The text talks about the real world. • It was written to convey information, convince the reader or criticize something.

Knowing what type of non-fictional text you're dealing with and what characteristic features this text type has will help you to anticipate what kind of information might be given and how it might be presented. Follow these steps:

Step 1: Skim the text (▶SF 14: Reading strategies) and try to get a general idea of its content:
- Sum up in one or two sentences what the text is about.
- If possible, find out when and where it was published (newspaper, book, journal, internet).

Step 2: Examine the text more closely. Look at:
- its content and purpose: Is the text meant to inform, persuade, entertain, …?
- its *style and *tone: Is the language formal or informal, simple or complex?

Step 3: Identify the text type. The following table will help you.

Non-fictional texts	
Text type and examples	**Contents and purpose**
Expository texts: *feature story, *news story, summary, etc.	• contain comprehensive and detailed information • are intended to be objective and factual • give no personal opinion • describe a situation, scientific findings, historic occurrences
Descriptive texts: travel book, biography, etc.	• describe actual places, objects, events or people based on the writer's observations and impressions • are intended to create a vivid picture in the reader's mind • tend to give a lot of detail
Argumentative texts: *editorial, *column, *letter to the editor, *review, *speech, *comment, etc.	• discuss problems and controversial ideas • evaluate a topic by giving reasons and stating the pros and cons of an issue • show a clear line of argument • tend to use expert opinions, statistics, quotations and technical/scientific language • aim to convince the reader
Persuasive texts: *speech, advertisement, etc.	• use stylistic devices • often use imperatives as an appeal to do something specific • try to persuade or convince the reader/listener
Instructive texts: manual, brochure, etc.	• are intended to instruct the readers, tell them what to do or how to do it • use imperatives and passive constructions (▶LP 7: The passive)

▶ SF 17 Analysing stylistic devices

When you listen to or read texts, you will normally notice that they have some kind of effect on you – you might strongly agree or disagree or you might feel amused, entertained, informed or perhaps irritated. This effect is created through the way the text is written, and especially by the *stylistic devices used. So when analysing texts, you should try to find out how certain effects are created. Stylistic devices may relate to sound (e.g. *alliteration), structure (e.g. *repetition, *parallelism) or meaning (e.g. *imagery).

Step 1: When reading the text pay attention to the effects that certain passages have on you.

Step 2: Study the passages in question to find the stylistic devices that create these effects. In the table below there are some examples.

Step 3: Consider why these effects may have been intended in this context. (▶ SF 36: Writing a text analysis)

> ■ TIP
>
> If you cannot pinpoint any specific effects while listening or reading, you can try it the other way round: Study the text for the most common stylistic devices (cf. the table below) and see if you can find a reason why the author may have used them.

Example	Effect	Stylistic device
'The most restless, the most adventurous, the most innovative, the most industrious of people [...].' From: William J. Clinton, 'Commencement Address at Portland State University', 13 June 1998; *cf. Context*, p. 110, ll. 14ff.	• reader/listener may feel overwhelmed, impressed by positive qualities	• *enumeration of superlatives
'What do the changes mean? They can either strengthen and unite us, or they can weaken and divide us.' From: William J. Clinton, 'Commencement Address at Portland State University', 13 June 1998; *cf. Context*, p. 110, ll. 27ff.	• reader/listener may feel drawn into the argumentation by being asked a direct question • reader/listener feels a little under pressure, even manipulated to answer the question in a specific way	• *rhetorical question • *contrast of two possible answers: one with strongly positive, the other with strongly negative *connotations
'Eighty-five percent said they felt they belonged to Britain. More than half (55%) said their national identity was important, compared with 44% of the general population. Religious identity is extremely or very important to 94%, and more than half pray at least five times a day or engage in worship of some kind.' From: Harriet Sherwood, 'Muslims place greater importance on national identity, finds study', *The Guardian*, 21 March 2018; *cf. Context*, p. 69, ll. 4ff.	• reader may feel convinced by factual information/objective numbers	• statistical data • reliable sources *(The Guardian)*
'Many Indians despair over the divisiveness[1] of caste and would prefer to wish it away. However, the hold of the Indian way of life is also a bulwark[2] against the onslaught[3] of the global culture [...].' From: Gurcharan Das, *India Unbound*, 2001; *cf. Context*, p. 72, ll. 14ff.	• reader may have difficulty understanding individual words, may find this irritating	• *register, sophisticated/academic choice of words ('divisiveness', 'hold', 'bulwark', 'onslaught')

[1] **divisiveness** force that splits people into different groups   [2] **bulwark** *(fml)* thing that protects sth.   [3] **onslaught** strong attack

From the beginning of a survey: 'Welcome to our most recent piece of research, an exploration into the career aspirations of 14–19 year olds at one of the most crucial decision making cross roads in their lives. The 3,154 young people we surveyed are making decisions now that will shape their futures. But do they have all the information they need to make informed choices that will give them the best chance of thriving in the workplaces of today and tomorrow?' From: https://www.economicmodelling.co.uk/wp-content/uploads/CG_Great-Expectations_Online-FINAL.pdf. ©2015 The City and Guilds of London Institute. All rights reserved. Cf. *Context*, p. 169	• reader may feel directly addressed and involved, connected to the writer	• direct address of reader without introduction • imitation of spoken language, of personal interaction • use of personal pronoun 'we', 'you'.
'For me, school had been a Darwinian exercise. A daily gauntlet[4] of ridicule, abuse, and isolation.' From: Ernest Cline, *Ready Player One*, 2012, p. 31; cf. *Context*, p. 188, ll. 21ff.	• reader will be able to picture the situation very clearly	• *images/*metaphors ('Darwinian exercise', 'gauntlet of ridicule') • incomplete sentence
'War is as old as Europe. Our continent bears the scars of spears and swords, canons and guns, trenches[5] and tanks[6], and more.' From: Herman Van Rompuy, 'From war to peace', 10 December 2012; cf. *Context*, p. 122	• reader gets a lively idea of the wounds inflicted on Europe through war • list of nouns draws reader's attention to the numerous weapons which caused the injuries	• *personification of an object ('continent bears the scars') • alliterations ('spears and swords', 'trenches and tanks')
'I fear the day technology will surpass our human interaction. The world will have a generation of idiots.' (Anonymous)	• reader may be taken aback by this provocative statement • the reader's interest will be aroused	• *exaggeration (to stress a point)

When analysing the effects created by a text, make sure you also pay attention to its *tone (i.e. the way a writer treats his/her topic). The tone may be formal, intimate, playful, ironic, humorous, etc.)	**■ LANGUAGE HELP** | The author	uses employs makes use of	a metaphor a simile enumeration irony personification	to illustrate … to show … to emphasize … to underline … to draw the reader's attention to …	

---

[4] **gauntlet** fight with a lot of people attacking you   [5] **trench** *Schützengraben*   [6] **tank** *Panzer*

▶ SF 18 Analysing non-fiction

When analysing a non-fictional text you have to say more than just what it is about. You have to find out what type of text it is, for example a *feature story, an *editorial or a *comment (▶ SF 16: Identifying text types). By looking at how its content, its structure and its language interact you can find out what its function and its message might be.

Here is an excerpt from a newspaper article written by a young British woman. Analyse the way she presents her own experiences as a non-white woman in Great Britain.

Step 1: Read the text and decide what type of text it is. Collect extracts that help you analyse the text, e.g. its line of argument, *stylistic devices, choice of words, etc. (cf. the highlighted passages). (▶ SF 17: Analysing stylistic devices)

... It's not that I'm embarrassed about my ethnic background. I don't think about it much, though it's good for jokes ('I'm half Iranian, half American – so basically, I hate myself'). But some people seem to want me to think about it. 'Why don't you visit Bombay?' they enthuse. 'You'd love it.' They may be right, but have yet to explain to me why I'd love it more than Tokyo, or Guatemala, or any of the other places I haven't yet been. It's an odd misconception that you should somehow feel connected to a far-flung country because your ancestors lived there centuries ago, even if your entire life has been spent morris dancing[1] in Loughborough.

5

10

From: Ariane Sherine, 'It may not be racist, but …', *The Guardian*, 3 March 2010

Step 2: Organize your findings. Make sure all examples e.g. for stylistic devices go together.

- *line of argument: does not think much about her background (l. 1), people seem to think she ought to care about it (ll. 3–4), she thinks her parents' country of origin is just as relevant for her as any other country (ll. 5–7)*
- **humour: joke (ll. 2–3), compares her parents' country of origin with other countries she does not know (ll. 5–7)*
- *choice of words: 'odd misconception' (l. 7), 'far-flung country' (l. 8), 'ancestors' (l. 9), 'morris dancing' (l. 10): humorous*
- **stylistic devices: *exaggeration 'centuries ago' (l. 9), quotations (ll. 4–5)*

Step 3: Analyse the effect that is created by the stylistic devices that you have identified.

- **humour, choice of words: give the text a light-hearted tone*
- *quotations: help the reader imagine the specific situation, make the text more lively*
- **exaggeration: shows how absurd she finds other people's ideas*
- *light-hearted tone: she's not seriously offended*

Step 4: Examine the connection between the effect identified in **Step 3** and the author's line of argument.

- *readers ought to realize how ridiculous it is to keep identifying the descendants of immigrants with their parents' country of origin, to not accept them as fellow-citizens*
- *no acid criticism, no fierce accusation of racism, but a fairly lighthearted account of people's everyday misconceptions*

[1] **morris dance** *(v)* do a traditional English dance

When working on **Step 1** do not only follow the chronology of the text and wait until something catches your eye. Make sure you examine the text systematically by checking its use of stylistic devices, its choice of words, etc.

- The author uses vivid/collo-quial/objective/emotive … language.
- The sentences are long-winded/paratactical/simple/complex/ …
- The author's tone is friendly/humorous/critical/optimistic/sarcastic …

- His/her choice of words under-lines …
- The stylistic devices used sup-port/emphasize/underline …
- The reader can easily picture the situation/follow her/his train of thought/line of argument …

▶ SF 19 Analysing narrative prose

When you have to analyse a *short story, a *novel or any other *narrative text you are usually asked to pay attention to one or two specific aspects. The most common aspects for a text analysis are:

Aspect	Example
Character constellations or relationships (▶ SF 35: Writing a character profile) • Who is in the story? • What relationships do the *characters have to each other? Are they dependent on each other/equals, etc.? • Do they belong to similar/different groups (social/ethnic, etc.)? • Do they serve as foils for each other, i.e. do they contrast with another character to highlight particular qualities of the other character? • How does the author characterize them, *directly or *indirectly? • Are the characters *round or *flat?	High-school student Mitch is a reporter for the school magazine and on his way to his first interview with his former PE-teacher McNulty: I parked my mom's Ford Focus by the gym, eased out of the front seat, and looked around. When I spotted McNulty loading tackling sleds[1] into a school van, I tensed. To him, I'd always be a fat loser and nothing more. But a reporter has to have the courage to approach people, ask them questions [...]. From: Carl Deuker, *Payback Time*, 2010, p. 22; cf. *Context*, p. 174, ll. 1ff. • *reporter and coach share a history* • *reporter feels inferior; tries to overcome his fear* • *…*
The *narrator or the narrative perspective • Who is telling the story and to whom? Is it a *first-person narrator, a *third-person narrator or an *omniscient narrator? • How much does the narrator know or not know? What are the limiting factors? Does the narrator have a *limited or an *unlimited point of view?	Some nights I lie next to Tony, here in America where I live like a worm avoiding the sunlight, and I wonder if he knows. And is it only because it was his brother that he does not sense that another man's body has come between us. From: Shauna Singh Baldwin, 'English Lessons', *English Lessons and Other Stories*, 1996; cf. *Context*, p. 91, ll. 46ff. • *first person narrator (*protagonist), probably female, might be an immigrant* • *tells the reader a secret that apparently the husband does not know; but since the narrator cannot know the husband's thoughts, neither he/she nor the reader know for sure* • *…*

[1] **tackling sled** *Angriffsschlitten (schweres Trainingsgerät im American Football)*

The *plot

- How are the events connected by cause and effect to form a plot?
- How does the author attract or keep the reader's attention by creating *tension or *suspense?
- Is there a *climax and/or a *turning point?
- Does the story have an ending or a conclusion? Or is there an *open ending/a *denouement?

Dan, a high-school student whose parents have recently lost their jobs, is approached by another student, who tries to recruit him for a protest march:

> I felt myself tense. All my friends, plus a couple of kids at the sign-up table, were watching and listening. 'Why do you ask?' 'Seems like a good time,' he said. Had he heard that we'd lost our home? Did he think that would make me more sympathetic to his cause? 'Why's that?' I gave him a hard look.

From: Todd Strasser, *No Place*, 2014, S. 8

- *tension between characters is building up*
- *suspense: reader does not know if the secret is going to be discovered*
- …

The *setting and the *atmosphere

- Where and when does the action take place?
- Are there any people? How do they react to the setting?
- How does the setting influence the atmosphere? (E.g. sunny spring days usually create an optimistic atmosphere, a crowded place may create a tense or exciting atmosphere, etc.)
- Are you told directly or do you have to draw your own conclusions?

Her Majesty the Queen is on her way to open Parliament:

> One of the Queen's recurrent royal responsibilities was to open Parliament, an obligation she had never previously found particularly burdensome[1] and actually rather enjoyed; to be driven down the Mall[2] on a bright autumn morning even after fifty years was something of a treat.

From: Alan Bennett, *The Uncommon Reader*, 2008, p. 32; cf. Context, p. 58, ll. 1ff.

- *autumn, sunny*
- *the Queen: about to do a job she enjoys*
- *positive atmosphere (to be concluded from the setting)*
- …

LANGUAGE HELP

- The relationship between the characters is strongly influenced by … Their power struggle reveals itself when … Their lack of communication shows …
- X's behaviour when … reveals that …
- The description underlines/emphasizes …/conveys the impression that …
- The image suggests …
- By using words like … the author stresses …

- The overall effect is … It can be portrayed as …
- The perspective is biased/one-sided …
- As the first-person narrator has a limited perspective, the reader must … The author chose an omniscient narrator because …
- The story has an open ending, so …
- In the end the conflict is solved when …

---

[1] **burdensome** implying hard work   [2] **the Mall** road leading to Buckingham Palace

▶ SF 20 Analysing drama

A *drama or *play is a script in which a *playwright presents what *characters say and what they do. A drama is written to be performed on stage, so when you read a play, you will enjoy it more if you imagine what it would look and sound like on stage.

When analysing drama, typical aspects to look at are:

Aspect	Examples and explanations
Structure • Is the play divided up into ***acts** and ***scenes** or is there a different structure? • What function do these divisions have in the play? • Do they correspond to action, time, place or a combination of these?	• Shakespeare's plays used to be performed without intermissions – **rhyming couplets* would indicate the end of one scene. Nowadays his plays are conventionally edited to have four or five acts and scene divisions, which usually mark a change in the set of characters on stage. • Most modern plays have two or three acts. Some (e.g. *Artefacts*, cf. pp. 66f.) have no act division at all and are meant to be performed without a break. Still, *Artefacts* is divided into three parts, which are set in the two different countries. *Clybourne Park* (cf. pp. 175f.) has two acts, separated by a time gap of 50 years.
The construction of action • Does the script contain ***stage directions**? If so, what information do they provide? • How does the **action** unfold through the **dialogue**? • Are there ***monologues**? What function do they have? • What kind of **language** is used?	• In *Clybourne Park* (cf. pp. 105f.) there are some stage directions. They describe how actors should speak certain lines or move (e.g. 'chuckles with amazement, shakes his head', p. 106, ll. 109f.), but there are very few descriptions of settings or actions except at the beginnings of each of the two acts. • Dramatic dialogue has to be very carefully constructed (and yet sound realistic) so that it never gets boring and gives enough clues about what is actually happening. • Monologues usually serve to show a character's thoughts to the audience, but not to the other characters, i.e. they are not part of the interaction. Shakespeare often made use of them to give the audience more insight into a character's mind. • In the extract from *Macbeth* (cf. pp. 39f.) Lady Macbeth uses aggressive language, calling her husband a coward when he hesitates to commit the murder as planned. His question 'If we should fail?' shows his hesitation, whereas her answer 'We fail!' shows her determination to succeed (cf. p. 39, ll. 36f.). This interchange actually drives the action forward because it serves to persuade Macbeth to act as planned. • In *Artefacts*, Kelly's informal language (cf. pp. 66f.) serves to characterize her as a modern British teenager and makes the dialogue more realistic, e.g. 'Yeah, all right then, tell me what I think.' (ll. 69)

Characters

(▶ SF 35: Writing a character profile)

- Who are the *characters?
- What information do we get about them and what issues do they have to deal with in the play?
- Do they develop over the course of the play?

- Do they stand for a particular idea or are they part of the play's message?

- Normally it's not the playwright who tells us directly about the characters, but as in real life we get an idea of them through the way they act or talk about themselves, their lives or about others. *Monologues in particular can give the audience an insight into a character's motivations, feelings or problems.
- Macbeth (cf. pp. 39f.) develops from a man reluctant to kill into a ruthless murderer. In *Artefacts* (cf. pp. 66f.) Kelly first refuses to go to Iraq, but later we see that she has actually gone there.
- In *Clybourne Park* (cf. pp. 105f.), the members of the white community who oppose black neighbours represent racist ideas. Lady Macbeth (cf. pp. 39f.) represents ruthless ambition as she is even willing to commit murder to achieve the ultimate success she wants.

Audience

- What does the audience know or see that the characters don't know or see?
- What is left to the audience's imagination?

- In Shakespeare's *Romeo and Juliet*, Romeo has heard that Juliet is dead and kills himself. The audience however knows that she only looks dead – an example of *dramatic irony.
- Sometimes characters speak of actions that do not actually happen on stage, even though they are important for the plot.

■ LANGUAGE HELP

- The play is divided into … acts and … scenes / The development of the action corresponds with the play's division into acts/scenes …
- The overall theme of the play is …
- In the play the conflicts develop between …
- The audience is drawn into the plot by … / The action is supposed to please/shock/enrage/fascinate the audience …
- The … act ends in a cliffhanger / In the end the conflict is solved …

- The stage directions draw a concise picture of the scenery / There are almost no stage directions, so … / The play works with almost no props / a bare stage …
- Even though X appears as a friendly character at first, he later shows … / … stands for / represents …
- The social differences between the characters can be seen in the language they use … / The characters speak in blank verse …

The Globe Theatre, London

■ TIP

play = Theaterstück
drama = Drama (i.e. text form), e.g. *modern drama* or *Elizabethan drama* (i.e. the plays produced during the time when Queen Elizabeth I reigned)
playwright, dramatist = Stückeschreiber/in, Dramatiker/in
character = Figur
actor, actress = Schauspieler/in

▶ SF 21 Analysing poetry

*When you are asked to analyse a poem, you should not only look at its poetic features such as its form, its
*rhythm or its language, you must also look at its content and link this to the poem's form. Only then will you
be able to fully understand what the poem conveys.*

Here is a poem by Gavin Ewart, followed by a step-by-step guide.

Ending *Gavin Ewart*

The love we thought would never stop
  now cools like a congealing[1] chop[2].
The kisses that were hot as curry
  are bird-pecks[3] taken in a hurry.
The hands that held electric charges   5
  now lie inert[4] as four moored barges[5].
  The feet that ran to meet a date
  are running slow and running late.
The eyes that shone and seldom shut
    are victims of a power cut.   10
The parts that then transmitted joy
  are now reserved and cold and coy[6].
  Romance, expected once to stay,
  has left a note saying gone away.

From: *The Collected Ewart*, 1982

Step 1: Read the poem two or three times, then summarize it in one or two sentences. Consider	• *two people in a relationship that has lasted for some time*
• the poem's title, *setting and *theme	• *title: ending of a relationship*
• the *speaker and the addressee	• *couple: one person is speaker, one is addressee*
• the link between the title and the poem's content.	• *contrast: what the relationship was like before and what it is like now*
Step 2: Look at the poem's structure (*stanzas, *rhythm, *rhyme scheme, *metre). (It may help to read the poem out loud to get a feeling for the way it sounds.)	
• Is it built regularly or are there interruptions in the rhythm or rhyme scheme?	• *seven couplets*
• Is there a *refrain?	• *each couplet rhymes (aa,bb, cc, etc.) → regular pattern, conventional*
• Is it a *sonnet?	• *regular metre, regular rhyme scheme*

---

[1]**congeal** *(here)* become unpleasantly dry   [2]**chop** thick slice of meat with a bone attached to it   [3]**peck** quick kiss / bird's bite
[4]**inert** unable to move   [5]**moored barge** *(here)* small boat that has been fixed to land   [6]**coy** not willing to give away much about yourself

Step 3: Examine the poem's language more closely. Look for

- *imagery, e.g. *simile, *metaphor, *analogy, *personification
- sound effects, e.g. *alliteration, *assonance, *onomatopoeia
- *contrasts, *repetitions and specific sentence structures (simple/complex sentence, *enjambement)
- mythological/literary/social/historical references
- *symbols.

contrast between past and present, e.g. 'love that never ends' (l. 1) ⟷ 'congealing chop' (l. 2)
changes are conveyed through descriptions of body parts: hand (l. 5), feet (l. 7), eyes (l. 9), parts (l. 11)
vivid images for love in the past, e.g. 'hot curry' (l. 3), 'electric charges' (l. 5)
images of disconnectedness/cold/passiveness of love today, e.g. 'lie inert as four moored barges' (l. 6), 'power cut' (l. 10)
personification: 'romance' (l. 13)
short and simple sentences
down-to-earth metaphors

Step 4: Describe the poem's effect and analyse how it is achieved by connecting your findings on its form to its content.

clear and regular structure → monotony, conventionality
clear and precise images → easy to understand, common problem
→ lack of drama
…

■ LANGUAGE HELP

- The poem by … deals with/is about … In the poem … describes/reflects on … The poet addresses the topic of …
- The title reminds the reader of …/refers to …
- The poem is made up of …/consists of … verses/stanzas.
- The rhyme scheme is …/There is no consistent rhyme scheme. The word … rhymes with … The use of … creates a certain rhythm.
- Line … runs into line …, which emphasizes …

- The poet employs specific images, such as metaphors or similes, in order to …
- The diction/register is simple/colloquial/formal, which intensifies the feeling of …
- The most prominent stylistic device used in the poem is …, which serves to …
- All in all, … The overall effect is … The poem aims to show/illustrate/convey/express the idea that … The overall message of the poem is …

Listening and viewing skills

▶ SF 22 Listening

When you have to deal with a listening task at school, you are normally first given time to read the questions you will have to answer. These questions may be closed such as multiple choice (▶ SF 7: Working with closed test formats) but they can also be more open. After reading the tasks you are usually allowed to listen to the audio file twice.

> **■ TIP**
>
> In contrast to listening at school, you will not normally have the opportunity to listen to something twice in real-life situations, e.g. to a train announcement. You then need to be able to identify relevant information right away – or you may ask people for clarification who have listened to the same thing. In a conversation, you may ask the speaker to repeat what they have said.

LISTENING FOR GIST

Listening for gist is what you do to find out what the main topic of a spoken text is, e.g. when you want to see if an audio file is relevant for you.

Step 1: Before listening for gist, collect information on the following if possible:
- the text type (e.g. newscast, lecture, panel discussion, interview) and its addressee
- the situation and *setting
- the number of speakers and their role in the audio file. For example, will there be conflicting points of view?
- the topic dealt with in the audio file and what points of view or concepts you are likely to encounter.

Step 2: When listening for gist,
- do not try to understand every detail that is said
- watch out for 'signpost expressions' that show somebody's train of thought, e.g. *the biggest issue is …, the most important argument is, on the one hand …*
- listen carefully to a speaker's intonation; it may help you identify their attitudes or intentions.

Step 3: Summarize the text so as to prove that you can identify its topic.

LISTENING FOR DETAIL

You listen for detail if you need specific information, e.g. tips given for a specific problem.

Step 1: Before listening for detail,
- remember what you know about the text (its speaker, addressee, situation, setting and/or topic) and try to anticipate what might be said in the text
- collect keywords that are relevant to your question, e.g. names, dates or numbers
- prepare your notepad so that you can take notes quickly. (▶ SF 15: Marking up a text / Making and taking notes)

Step 2: When listening for detail,
- watch out for the keywords you collected
- take notes, using abbreviations and symbols.

▶ SF 23 Analysing a film

Watching a film can make you laugh or cry, feel angry or scared. Those reactions are not only caused by the story the film tells but also by the way it tells its story. Just like written texts can provoke a reaction in their readers through the choice of words and *stylistic devices, films can achieve a certain response in the viewer through, for example, their camera work, editing and sound.

BEFORE VIEWING

Step 1:   Find out what kind of film you are going to watch and try to get an idea of what to expect by looking at available information on the film (e.g. film posters, reviews, DVD covers, magazine information). What genre does it belong to (feature film, documentary, video clip, commercial, etc.)?

WHILE VIEWING

Step 1:   Watch one or more scenes and make notes on how the characters act, what the *setting is like or what information is presented. You may also add some observations on cinematic devices such as camera angle, sound and light. A **viewing log** can help you structure your notes. Here is one example for the first scene of *Never Let Me Go* (you may choose other categories to serve your own purposes):

Scene	What?	Where?	Who?	Camera	Sound	Light	Effect
1	a patient (Tommy) is being prepared for a surgery	hospital: operating room	carer (Kathy) and patient	close-up of Kathy, over-the-shoulder shot towards Tommy → Kathy's point of view	only voice-over of Kathy, no other sound	operating room is illuminated, no addi-tional light	very emotional
…	…	…	…	…	…	…	…

Step 2:   Watch the specific scenes once more and have a closer look at the cinematic devices used and the effect they achieve. Add your observations to your viewing log. The table below may help you.

Camera angle/movement or sound	Example	Possible effect
The camera seems to be looking through the eyes of the character or is looking directly over his or her shoulder (**over-the-shoulder shot**). One character's face is shown in **close-up** (cf. the picture on the right), while the other characters are presented through **long** or **medium shots**.		The character's emotions are revealed and you identify with that character.
A character is shown through a **low-angle shot**.		The character appears bigger. He or she seems to be dominant, i.e. to have power over the other characters in this scene.

•••••▶

A character is shown through a **high-angle shot**.		The character appears smaller. He or she seems to be inferior, i.e. to have less power than the other characters in this scene.
Two or more characters are shown through **eye-level shots**.		The characters appear to be on the same level.
The scene is rather dark. People and objects cannot be clearly distinguished. The **soundtrack** is eery or moves towards a *climax.		The viewer may feel tense or scared.
There are short **shots** and lots of **cuts**. *Flashbacks (showing past events) or **flash-forwards** (showing future events) are used.		The *action is fast-paced and exciting.
The camera takes a steady position.		The action appears slower.
The music is uplifting, pleasant or catchy.		The viewer feels relaxed and in a good mood.

■ LANGUAGE HELP

- The film is about … / shows … / tells the story of …
- The music intensifies/fades as … / creates/builds tension/suspense/joy/…
- The actor's body language and facial expressions add to the feeling of …
- In this scene the music and lyrics / the props support the plot / underline the feeling of …

- The soundtrack/lighting/editing establishes/reinforces the mood of the scene.
- The camera movement creates a feeling of …
- The camerawork/soundtrack helps to … / underlines/emphasizes …
- The close-ups reveal his/her emotional state.
- The props in her room characterize her as a … person.

▶ DVD   **PRACTICE**

You are going to watch an extract from *The Hunger Games*, a 2012 science fiction film. It depicts a dystopian state in which every year a group of teenagers, the 'tributes', are forced to take part in a televised event and fight each other to the death until only the victor remains alive. In the extract you are going to watch the protagonist Katniss is being chased by other tributes.

1 Watch the extract and use a viewing log to structure your observations. Work with a partner to complete your notes.

2 The extract is full of contrasts: the wild forest vs. the television headquarters, Katniss on her own vs. the group of other tributes, the wild chase vs. a moment of rest when the other tributes let Katniss be for some time. Choose one of the contrasts, watch the extract again and examine the cinematic devices used to create this contrast.

Speaking skills (monologues and dialogues)

▶ SF 24 Giving a presentation

Informing an audience about a topic is an important skill to master and one that will be useful not only in school (classroom presentations, etc.) but also in later life (university, work, etc.). To give a successful presentation the following steps may be a helpful guide.

PLANNING A PRESENTATION

Step 1: Find out about the general framework for your talk, e.g.
- its topic
- the time limit for your presentation
- your audience and their background knowledge of the topic
- the kind of equipment available (smartboard, blackboard, flip chart, digital/video projector, laptop).

Step 2: Research your subject and make notes in English. (▶ SF 15: Marking up a text / Making and taking notes; ▶ SF 3: Doing research)
- If you are working in a team, decide who is going to work on which aspect.
- Use different sources so that you cover all relevant aspects and your information is reliable.

PREPARING A PRESENTATION

Step 1: Decide what information you need and work out a structure for it. (▶ SF 5: Structuring information and ideas)

Step 2: Think of ways to make your talk interesting and easy to understand for your audience:
- Plan the beginning of your presentation carefully: refer to interesting facts or give anecdotes which lead to the topic of your presentation.
- Remember the KISS-rule: **K**eep **i**t **s**hort and **s**imple!
- Keep your audience's attention by naming interesting or funny details or examples.
- Check whether there are words or phrases that need to be explained to the audience so that they can follow your presentation.
- If suitable, prepare charts, visuals, diagrams, etc. to present facts and figures visually. (▶ SF 5: Structuring information and ideas)

Step 3: Prepare a handout or poster or use a presentation programme to accompany your presentation:
- Design them so that your audience to follow your presentation.
- Proofread your material. (▶ SF 40: Proofreading)
- Before the actual presentation, make sure that any electronic media you want to use are working and that you can handle them.

Find a tool to make your poster here:
🔘 **Webcode** context-50

TIP

When preparing a **poster** or **wall display**:
- Give it a clear structure or line of thought that guides the reader through the various sections of the poster.
- Make it visually attractive and informative.
- Present complex information visually, e.g. through diagrams.
- Keep a good balance between visuals and written information.
- Make sure that the writing can be read from the back of the room.
- Use bullet-points, short sentences or key-words and try to avoid any redundancies.
- Indicate the sources you used.

When preparing a **handout**:
- Decide if you want to distribute it before the presentation so that it helps your audience to follow your talk (in that case it might make sense to leave room for notes) or if you want to hand it out after the presentation to remind your audience of the main points (in that case tell them that a handout will be distributed at the end).
- Give it a clear structure.
- Present the most important information, key quotations, diagrams and/or charts on it.
- Use bullet-points, short sentences or key-words and try to avoid any redundancies.
- Indicate the sources you used.

·····▶

Step 4: If you are giving your presentation in a team
- decide who is going to present which parts
- check that the different parts add up to a coherent presentation
- make sure that everybody takes part in the presentation.

Step 5: Prepare notes that will guide you through your presentation and help you to speak freely without reading from the page. (▶ SF 15: Marking up a text / Making and taking notes)

> ### ■ TIP
> Write keywords or notes on index cards, number the cards and use only them during your presentation.

Step 6: Practise your presentation:
- Look up the pronunciation of difficult words in a dictionary.
- Practise your presentation in front of friends or a mirror or record it, e.g. using a smartphone. If you are doing a team presentation, practise as a team.
- Make sure you don't exceed your time limit.

DOING A PRESENTATION

Step 1: Give your presentation:
- Wait until the audience are quiet, then greet them and give an overview of your presentation.

> ### ■ LANGUAGE HELP
> 'Hello everybody. My talk today is going to be on … First I will give you a general idea of … After that I will tell you more about … At the end of the talk I will explain why … and give you some examples.'

- Speak clearly, loudly and not too fast. Make suitable pauses.
- Speak freely and don't read out complete sentences.
- Avoid extremely long sentences and too many figures or new words. Remember that your audience can only listen to your presentation once.
- Refer to your poster, wall display or handout if appropriate, but don't read it out word for word.
- Try to maintain eye-contact with your classmates.
- If you use new or difficult words, help your audience by writing them on the board and explaining them.

> ### ■ TROUBLE SPOT
> **word by word** = one word at a time, one word after the other
> **word for word** = in exactly the same words

Step 2: Round off your presentation by
- summarizing the most important aspects
- thanking your audience for their attention
- asking them if they have any questions.

> ### ■ LANGUAGE HELP
> 'So, as I have pointed out, … It is important to keep in mind that … That was my presentation on … Thank you for listening. I hope you enjoyed my/our presentation. Do you have any questions?'

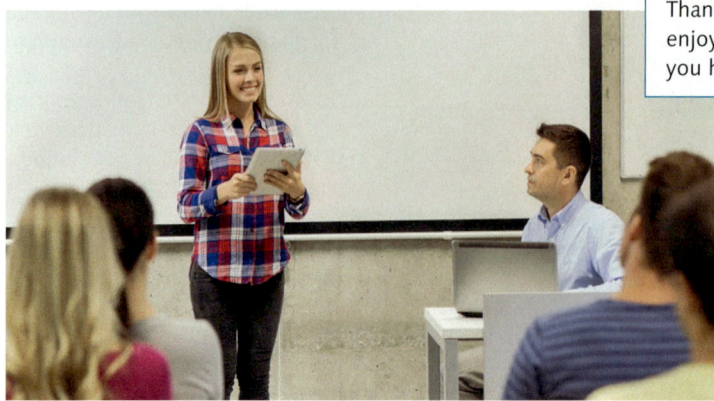

▶ SF 25 Giving a speech

When you give a speech you want to reach your audience and persuade them of your point of view on a topic. In order to achieve this goal, you need two things: firstly, a well-structured text with carefully chosen words and *stylistic means and secondly, an effective way of delivering it.

PLANNING A SPEECH

Step 1: Find out about the general framework for your speech, e.g.
- its topic
- the time available

- the purpose of your speech: do you want it to inspire people / lead to a specific action / …?
- your audience and their background knowledge / attitudes.

- *task: convince your student body council that your school should become more environmentally friendly*
- *purpose: lead to action*

- *audience: some students have talked about it in class; some might be tackling the issue already*

Step 2: Brainstorm and/or research your topic: collect any ideas, stories or arguments that fit your topic and form your own opinion on it. Make notes (▶ SF 15: Marking up a text / Making and taking notes).

- *things you can do every day, e.g. separate rubbish, turn off lights, don't use paper cups for your coffee, …*
- *may be inconvenient at first, but will become normal*

PREPARING A SPEECH

Step 1: From your ideas choose essential points that are relevant to your topic and the message you wish to get across to your audience. Make notes and organize them
- by structuring them into introduction/ body/conclusion (▶ SF 5: Structuring information and ideas)
- by choosing the best two to five ideas for the body of your speech and putting them in a suitable order (▶ SF 5: Structuring information and ideas).

- *introduction: watching* The Day after Tomorrow *made me depressed – how can I make a change?*
- *body: little things done by normal people can make a change; it's no use blaming politicians for not acting; …*
- *conclusion: be the change!*

Step 2: Unless you are a highly experienced speaker, write out your complete speech:
- Choose the correct *register for your specific audience, e.g. scientific, colloquial, … (▶ LP 11: Using the right register)

- Use your own experience.

- Use clear and short sentences. Make logical connections clear by using linking words (▶ SF 38: Writing a well-structured text).

- *register: colloquial, e.g. 'Look at this school. We are a huge number of people. Think about the mountain of rubbish we produce every day. Is it really necessary?'*

- *personal experience: 'We throw away a lot of different things at school: paper, Kleenex, sweet wrappers, broken pens.'*
- *short sentences: 'So, take a stand. Ask the school for separate bins for paper, plastic and other rubbish.'*

·····▶

- Be persuasive: use *stylistic devices to convince your audience, e.g. *contrasts, *rhetorical questions, *enumerations, *alliterations, direct address of audience …

- *contrast: 'A small act – like closing the window before you leave – can have a big effect.'*

Step 3: Write introduction and conclusion:
- Write a conclusion: sum up the main points, give a final effective example supporting your message, further food for thought or an appeal for action.
- When you have prepared most of your speech, think of a good introduction, e.g. a true story, a quotation, a rhetorical question, an interesting statistic, a joke.

- *conclusion: 'You could argue that some students might not be interested in environmentally friendly behaviour and I have to agree. That is why I need your support. Set an example. Do the right thing. Help our school become active in our fight for a healthier planet.'*
- *introduction: 'Last Saturday I watched the film The Day after Tomorrow and felt really depressed. I don't want my world to be flooded or frozen over. I want to be able to live in a beautiful, clean world. So if I want that, what can I do to make a change?'*

Step 4: Prepare the presentation of your speech:
- Print out your speech in a format that is easy to read out from (fonts and margins not too small). If you know your speech by heart write keywords or notes on index cards.
- Mark passages and words that you want to emphasize.

Step 5: Practise your speech by reading or saying it out loud (check the pronunciation of difficult words if necessary). Even if you read it, try to make it sound as if you were delivering it freely. Practise it in front of friends or a mirror or record it, e.g. using a smartphone. Make sure you don't exceed your time limit.

> ■ **TIP**
>
> Write keywords or notes on index cards, number the cards and use only them during your presentation.

GIVING A SPEECH

Giving a speech is not like reading something out (even if you have written it down). Try to speak as freely as possible and maintain the attention of your audience.

- Wait until the audience are quiet, then greet them and state your topic.
- Speak clearly, loudly and not too fast. Pause in suitable places.
- Use facial expressions and gestures to emphasize important points.
- Try to maintain eye-contact with your listeners.
- Thank your audience for their attention.

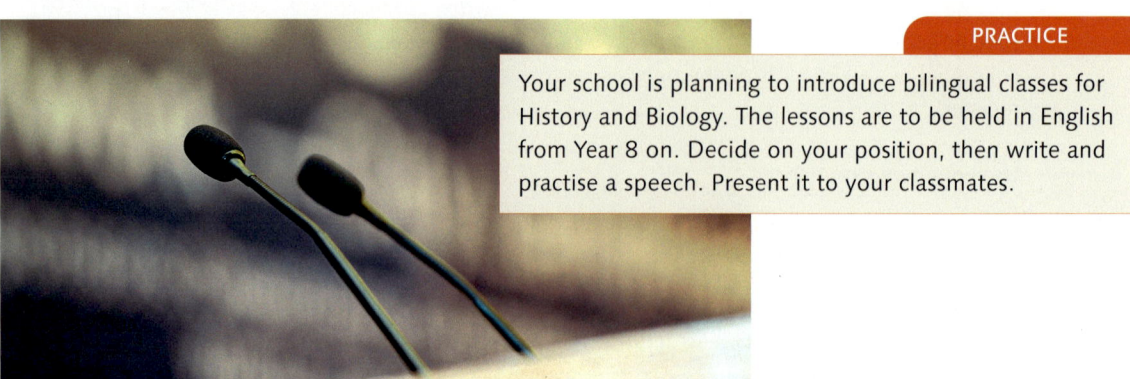

PRACTICE

Your school is planning to introduce bilingual classes for History and Biology. The lessons are to be held in English from Year 8 on. Decide on your position, then write and practise a speech. Present it to your classmates.

▶ SF 26 Taking part in an interview

In lesson situations but also when applying for a job you may be asked to take part in interviews, either asking or answering questions. It is essential to prepare for an interview and to follow some general guidelines.

PREPARING FOR AN INTERVIEW
- On the basis of your role card or the task given prepare questions you are going to ask (as interviewer) or think of possible answers to questions you might be asked (as interviewee).
- For **job interviews,** you need to be prepared to say why you might be suitable for the offered position. Do research on the company you are applying for and prepare some questions you might want to ask. It might be useful to rehearse a job interview with a friend or parent.

MASTERING THE INTERVIEW
- Speak loud enough and clearly. Be aware of your non-verbal communication: Try to maintain eye-contact with the interviewer/interviewee and smile when saying hello at the beginning or thanking your interviewer/interviewee at the end. (▶ CC 4: Meeting and greeting)
- As an **interviewer**: Start off by using your prepared questions, but be flexible – phrase new questions if some interesting aspect is touched on or rephrase a question if you feel that it was not answered fully.
- As an **interviewee**: Take your time to think about your answers rather than blurting out a reply that does not show you in a good light. Do not simply answer questions with *yes* or *no*, but use your answers to show your qualifications or to express your thoughts. If you have not understood a question fully, ask the interviewer to clarify it.

■ LANGUAGE HELP

Interviewer
- Nice to meet you./Thank you for coming.
- To start off, would you like to say something about …?/First, let me ask you …/My next question would be   /If you think so, then why didn't you …/Let's get back to my original question …
- You just said …, how does that relate to …?
- Thank you very much for taking part in this interview.

Interviewee
- Nice to meet you too./Thank you for inviting me today./I am fine, thank you.
- I am not sure I have understood your question correctly./Sorry, could you rephrase that?/ I'm glad you asked that question because …/… is very important to me, as …/A good example of the aspect you mention is …/Let me explain that in some more detail.
- Thank you for the chance to speak to you.

PRACTICE

You want to find out your fellow students' priorities for their future lives – earning a lot of money or following their dreams? Choose someone from your class and prepare and conduct an interview with them.

▶ SF 27 Having a discussion

In a (classroom) discussion you exchange ideas and opinions with others. Discussions may be spontaneous or they may be more formal, e.g. in panel discussions or debates (▶ SF 28: Having a debate). If possible, you should prepare for the discussion so that you have your arguments and useful words and phrases ready.

THE PREPARATION STAGE
Step 1: Research the topic and make notes (▶ SF 3: Doing research, ▶ SF 15: Marking up a text / Making and taking notes). Form an opinion on it and note down arguments. In a role-play you may have to take a position which is not really your own, so make sure that your arguments are in line with *your role*. Think of counter-arguments and of ways to reject them.

Step 2: Structure your notes (▶ SF 5: Structuring information and ideas) and arrange them in a way that helps you to have the relevant facts ready during the discussion.

Step 3: Prepare an initial statement on the topic; this will ease your way into the discussion. If you are assigned a specific role, be prepared to introduce yourself.

THE DISCUSSION STAGE

Step 1: State your point of view on the topic, e.g. give your prepared statement.

Step 2: Listen to what others say and refer back to their statements, e.g. by saying which of their arguments do not convince you and why. You might also counter an argument by asking a provocative question. Remember to bring in the facts you collected to support your view.

■ LANGUAGE HELP

Stating your opinion	Agreeing	Disagreeing
• In my opinion/view … • As far as I'm concerned … • Well, I'd say … • It's a fact that … • The way I see it, … • Personally, I think … • If you ask me … • It seems to me that … • I think/feel/reckon/believe … • First of all …/To start with I'd like to point out that … • There can be no doubt that … • Nobody will deny that … • I'm absolutely convinced that …	• I quite agree. • I couldn't agree with you more. • Quite!/Exactly!/Precisely! • Certainly!/Definitely! • You're quite right. • I agree entirely/completely. • That's just how I see it/feel about it. • You've got a good point there. • That's exactly how I see it. • Yes, indeed.	**Polite disagreement:** • I'm afraid I don't quite agree there. • I'm not so sure, really. • Do you really think so? • Well, that's one way of looking at it, but … • I'm not convinced that … • Well, I have my doubts about that. **Strong disagreement:** • I doubt that very much. • That doesn't convince me at all. • I don't agree with you at all. • I disagree entirely. • It's not as simple as that.
Asking for clarification	**Signalling that you would like to say something**	**Adding a point**
• I'm sorry, but I don't understand/know what you mean by … • Could you give an example/explain that, please? • Can you prove that?/I would be very interested in some data/examples that prove your statement.	• May I interrupt?/Excuse me, I would like to add to that. • An important aspect is missing here, namely … • That illustrates perfectly what … • Can I just say/explain that …? • I would just like to jump in here, to clarify that … • I hope you don't mind me interrupting, but it is important to stress …	• Another thing is … • What's more, … • On top of that, … • We must also consider … • I would like to add to that … • Have you ever considered/thought about …
Buying time		
• Well, that is an interesting point./I see what you mean. • I think the question we were discussing was …	• You have given your opinion, however … • Why don't we see what X has to say about that?	

Step 3: At the end of the discussion, summarize your point of view or your main arguments.

■ LANGUAGE HELP

- I have shown that …/It has become clear that …
- Let me just state again that it is vital to …/The most important argument is …/At the end of the day you can't deny that …
- If we don't … then…/In spite of everything we have heard from the other side …

Step 4 *(optional)*: If a chairperson has moderated the discussion, he/she may summarize the main line of the discussion and round it off.

■ LANGUAGE HELP

- We have seen/heard that …/The majority on the panel/in the audience thinks that …/Some are in favour of …, others against it, but in general you can say that …

- The general trend seems to be …/On the one hand, … On the other hand, …
- All in all this discussion has shown …

▶ SF 28 Having a debate

A debate is a formal discussion of a 'motion' (proposal) that ends in a vote. Similar to a discussion, the aim of a debate is to present arguments as convincingly as possible, so participants need well-prepared arguments as well as rhetorical skills. There is often a particular set of rules for the debate, which participants have to agree on before holding the debate. The following steps outline how you could go about holding a formal debate.

Step 1: Organizing a debate

The 'motion' (i.e. a controversial topic) is the starting point for a debate. Often it is provided by the teacher, but in other cases, your class may be asked to suggest a number of motions and then agree on one of them. The motion is then phrased in a formalized way:

- 'This house proposes that *(… students should be allowed to use smart phones during lessons)*.'
- 'This house would *(… abolish the death penalty world-wide).'*
- 'This house believes that *(… minimum wages are a threat to the German economy)*.'

The class is then divided into two groups, one for and one against the motion.
Usually a chairperson and a timekeeper are chosen and a time-limit for each speaker is specified (often 3–6 minutes per speaker).

Step 2: Preparing the debate

- In your group (either for or against the motion) research the topic, collect and note down arguments for your side. Your personal opinion on the motion is not relevant here – you must argue for your team. List and rank the arguments that you have for your team in order of importance.
- Write your arguments on index-cards so that you have them ready during the debate.
- Think of arguments for the opposing view and ways to reject them.
- Choose speakers for your side. The other students are the audience, called the 'floor'.

Step 3: Holding the debate

A debate follows a clear structure. The 'chair' will make sure that the rules are followed and that time-limits are respected.

....▶

Team in favour of the motion	Team opposing the motion

FIRST PROPOSAL: The first speaker proposes the motion (= argues in favour of the motion) and gives some main arguments.

> **LANGUAGE HELP**
> - This house firmly believes that …
> - Not only is … but also …

FIRST OPPOSITION: The first speaker of this team opposes the motion (= argues against the motion).

> **LANGUAGE HELP**
> - We strongly advise against following the proposed motion because …
> - The most obvious reason for this is that …

SECOND PROPOSAL: The second speaker of the affirmative team presents further arguments in favour of the motion. He/she also responds to the aspects mentioned by the first speaker of the opposing team, outlining where the positions conflict.

> **LANGUAGE HELP**
> - The opposing team has tried to create the impression that …
> - However, we can prove that …
> - It is therefore evident that …

SECOND OPPOSITION: The second speaker of the opposing team presents further arguments against the motion and/or restates the position of his/her team. The main task here is to defeat the arguments presented by the team in favour of the motion.

> **LANGUAGE HELP**
> - Again it needs to be stated that by following the arguments, …
> - … would lead to / cause …

A short recess may be taken here to prepare for the following 'rebuttals'.

FIRST REBUTTAL: The team against the motion defends their arguments and tries to rebut the arguments of the affirmative team.

SECOND REBUTTAL: The affirmative team supports their point of view and tries to rebut the arguments of the opposing team.

THIRD REBUTTAL: The opposing team give their closing statements.

FOURTH REBUTTAL: The affirmative team give their closing statements.

Rules for the debate:
- Speakers may not interrupt each other at any point.
- Speakers must wait their turn.
- The time-limits as given by the chair must be respected.
- Speakers must remain polite and respectful of the other team.
- Statements must be backed up by giving examples or proof, by referring to research, experience, etc.

Step 4: Concluding the debate
- The 'floor' (i.e. the audience) may ask questions and/or present their ideas on the topic.
- The 'house' (i.e. everyone present) may take a vote on the motion by a show of hands, not based on what they personally agree or disagree with, but on who made the better case by presenting the best arguments and speaking most convincingly.
- Members of the two debating teams may get some feedback from their classmates.

Writing skills

▶ SF 29 Writing a formal letter or email

When applying for a place at university, asking for information from a company or organization, etc., your email or letter should follow certain formal rules.

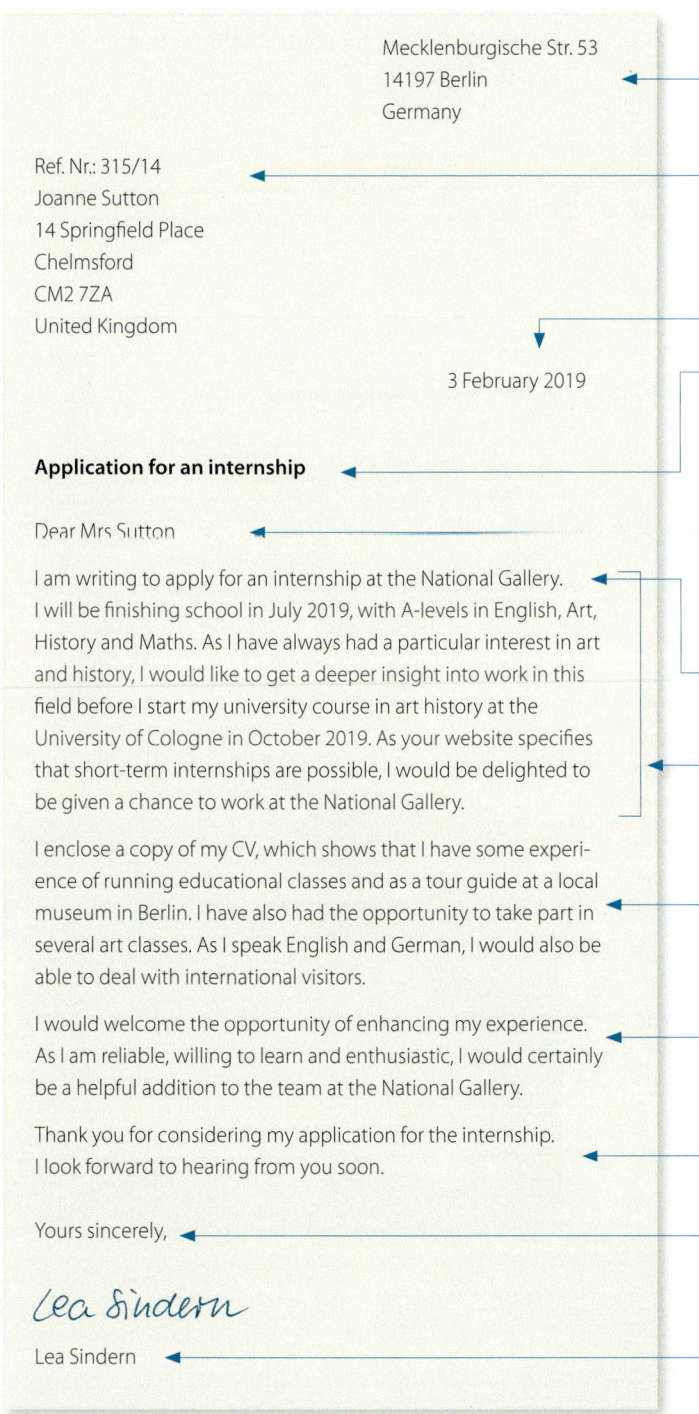

Mecklenburgische Str. 53
14197 Berlin
Germany

Ref. Nr.: 315/14
Joanne Sutton
14 Springfield Place
Chelmsford
CM2 7ZA
United Kingdom

3 February 2019

Application for an internship

Dear Mrs Sutton

I am writing to apply for an internship at the National Gallery. I will be finishing school in July 2019, with A-levels in English, Art, History and Maths. As I have always had a particular interest in art and history, I would like to get a deeper insight into work in this field before I start my university course in art history at the University of Cologne in October 2019. As your website specifies that short-term internships are possible, I would be delighted to be given a chance to work at the National Gallery.

I enclose a copy of my CV, which shows that I have some experience of running educational classes and as a tour guide at a local museum in Berlin. I have also had the opportunity to take part in several art classes. As I speak English and German, I would also be able to deal with international visitors.

I would welcome the opportunity of enhancing my experience. As I am reliable, willing to learn and enthusiastic, I would certainly be a helpful addition to the team at the National Gallery.

Thank you for considering my application for the internship. I look forward to hearing from you soon.

Yours sincerely,

Lea Sindern

Lea Sindern

Write your address (without your name) in the top right corner of your **letter**. Don't use typical German letters like *ä, ö, ü* or *ß*.

Write the address of the person or company you are writing to on the left. If you have a reference number, write it above the recipient's address.

Write the date on the right.

Show what the letter is about in a heading.

Start your letter with *Dear Madam or Sir* if you don't know the recipient's name, otherwise write *Dear Mr/Mrs/Ms …* In BE, there is usually no comma after the greeting; in AE a colon after the greeting is used in formal letters.

Always start with a capital letter (e.g. *With great interest, I read …*).

State the reason you are writing in the opening paragraph.

Add more detailed information in the following paragraphs (reasons for applying, qualifications, why you are the right person for the position etc.).

Use long forms (*I am / We are / I would*) rather than short forms (*I'm / We're / I'd*) and abbreviations.

If you are asking for information or a favour, thank the recipient in advance.

Finish your letter with *Yours faithfully* if you don't know the recipient's name, otherwise write *Yours sincerely* (AE: *Sincerely, Sincerely yours* or *Yours truly*).

Type your name at the end of the letter, leaving space for a handwritten signature.

·····▶

When writing a **formal email**

- you don't need to include the recipient's address or the date in the body of your email, as they appear automatically in the header
- open and close your mail the same way you would when writing a formal letter
- do not use emoticons, smileys, etc.
- type your name and contact details at the bottom.

A **letter to the editor** follows most of the conventions of a formal letter or email. Note the following, however:

- Nowadays, letters to the editor are very often sent by email. Watch out for contact information on the magazine's or paper's website.
- Your letter should be brief.
- Start like this: *Sir or Madam* (i.e. leave out *Dear*).
- Omit the closing remarks (*Yours faithfully/sincerely*).
- Don't forget to give your name, address and phone number.

▶ SF 30 Writing an application

If you want to apply for a holiday job or a position in a company (e.g. an internship), you should send them a cover letter and a CV (curriculum vitae).

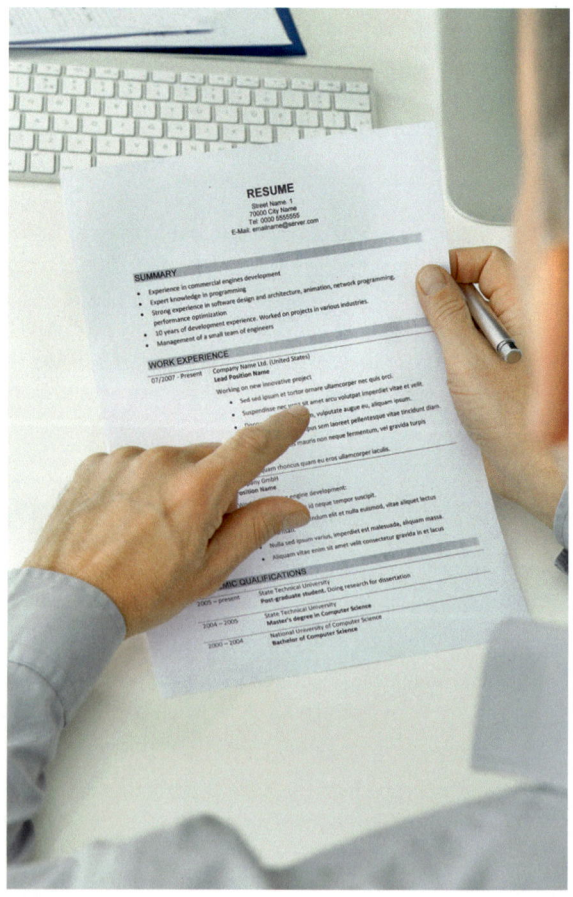

THE COVER LETTER

The cover letter for an application (cf. p. 323) follows the rules of a formal letter (▶ SF 29). Since you are presenting yourself, it is important to avoid mistakes and to use formal language (▶ LP 11: Using the right register). State in what ways you are suited for the position you are applying for. Show that you have collected information about the company you are writing to and that you have a real interest in the position advertised. Mention what documents you are enclosing. At the end of the letter, express hope for a reply or an invitation to an interview.

THE CV (*AE*: résumé ['rezəmeɪ])

Your CV (cf. p. 325) gives information about you, about your education, qualifications, etc. to the person you are applying to. A CV should be clear and effective – remember the KISS rule ('Keep it short and simple'). Use a clear and easy-to-read font, highlight particularly relevant information, and don't forget to check your CV for spelling mistakes.

CURRICULUM VITAE
Lukas Meister

Mecklenburgische Str. 53, 14197 Berlin, Germany
Telephone: +49(0)201 000 8xxx Mobile: +49 178 000 4xxx
Email: Lukasmeister@mail.de

Give your personal details: name, contact details, nationality, etc.

Personal statement
I have always enjoyed working with visual media, i.e. films, photographs, etc. and with computers. Being creative, I enjoy developing ideas to solve problems.
English is my favourite subject at school and I expect to improve my language skills further and to become a more independent person by spending time in the UK.

Add a personal statement explaining why you are suitable for the specific place or job.

Education
2013–date   Secondary School: Alfred-Krupp-Schule, Berlin
2009–2013   Primary/Elementary School Gartenstrasse, Essen

Show the stages of your education so far (schools, exams, etc.).

Qualifications/skills
IT skills   Excellent knowledge of MS Word, PowerPoint, Excel, web design, photoshop
Language skills   German native speaker; good written and spoken English, basic French
Technology   Winner of the gold medal 2014 for 'school inventors' in the 'Junior Ingenieur Akademie' (school engineering course)

List your qualifications and present your key skills, especially those the employer is looking for.

Work experience
May 2017   Placement: two weeks at local IT company, organized by my school

Give information on any work experience.

Hobbies and interests
Member of school drama club, member of school computer club, member of after-school basketball club. I enjoy listening to and playing music and making films.

Write something about your hobbies or interests.

References
Available on request

Note down that references are available on request.

Read the job advert on the right. Then write an application, consisting of a cover letter and your curriculum vitae, for the position of management assistant. (You may also make up a person applying for the job.)

SELLIT
International advertising company based in Nottingham, UK, is looking for a Management Assistant (entry level) for office-based work.
Requirements:
• degree in International Management
• good IT-skills
• fluent English (spoken and written)
• long-term availability.

CONTACT:
Sellit
Peter Miller
pmiller@sellit.co.uk
12 Springfield Road
Nottingham
NG1 5ZA
Great Britain

▶ SF 31 Writing a summary

When you work with written or spoken texts, you are often asked to summarize the text or certain aspects of it. To do this, you need a proper overview of the text, its content and its message. Then you have to decide what to include in your summary and what to leave out. The following steps and rules can guide you.

PLANNING YOUR SUMMARY

Step 1: Listen to or read the text carefully. Either make notes or mark the most important words and phrases (▶ SF 15: Marking up a text / Making and taking notes). Find out which text type you are dealing with (▶ SF 16: Identifying text types).

Step 2: Listen to or read the text again and try to answer the '5 Ws' (*Who? What? Where? When? Why?* Perhaps also *What is the consequence?*). To get a better understanding of the text, you may also want to use the reading strategies explained in ▶ SF 14: Reading strategies.

Step 3: Decide which passages of the text (marked green in the example below, cf. *Context* pp. 134ff.) contain essential information that needs to be part of your summary and which passages can be left out. Take your time to check which parts of the text contain examples, numbers, comparisons, quotes, *imagery, direct speech, etc. – these parts do not belong in a summary.

Linguistic diplomacy: the Eurovision Song Contest *R.L.G.*

Where?/What?	Last Saturday saw Denmark win the Eurovision Song Contest, the country's third win in the contest's history. A prototypically apple-cheeked[1] blonde took the trophy for her
Who?	country, but she did so with the rather un-Danish name of Emmelie de Forest and the
What?	equally un-Danish title, 'Only Teardrops'.

The contest has always been about more than music. Every year comes a slew[2] of artic- (5)

What/Why? les about the political nature of the voting. Countries that share ethnic or political friend-
(Examples) ships routinely give each other high marks: Greece and Cyprus typically give each other the maximum of 12 points while stiffing[3] Turkey with *nul points*[4], for example. Estonia and Latvia this year gave Russia 12 points, no doubt because those countries' large Russian populations voted for their neighbour. (10)

What? Language, of course, plays a role in this as well. 'Ethnicity'[5] in Europe is often linguis-tic: an ethnic Russian is not apparent on the streets of Riga until he opens his mouth.
Why? Linguistic neighbours will tend to be generous to one another. Finland and Estonia are
(Examples/ friendly not only because they are nearby but because their Finno-Ugric languages resem-
numbers) ble each other, while being utterly unrelated to their neigbours'. (Hungarian is also (15)
Finno-Ugric.) Each country can give 12 points to only one other country, and this year Denmark and Sweden gave their 12's to Norway, Norway its 12 to Sweden, as befits[6] the Scandinavian language continuum.

But the Scandinavians share something else besides apple-cheeked blondes and North
What? Germanic languages: their tendency to sing in English. In that, they are like most coun- (20)
tries nowadays. But some interesting variation clouds the picture.

From: 'English atop the Eurovision pile, yet again', *The Economist*, 20 May 2013

---

[1] **apple-cheeked** having cheeks (= *Wangen*) the colour of apples   [2] **slew** *(ifml)* large number
[3] **stiff sb. with sth.** *(here)* reject/ mildly insult sb.   [4] **nul points** [nyl pwɛ] *(French)* nil (= no) points
[5] **ethnicity** fact of belonging to a particular race   [6] **befit sb.** *(fml)* be suitable for sb.

WRITING YOUR SUMMARY

Step 1: Write your summary in your own words.

1 Write an introductory phrase, mentioning the essential aspects, such as the title, *author, topic, main message and source of the text. (▸ LP 18: Writing about texts)

> ■ **LANGUAGE HELP**
> - The story/text is about …
> - The text deals with …
> - In the text the reader gets to know …
> - The topic of the text is …
> - The article shows …

The article 'Linguistic diplomacy: the Eurovision Song Contest', written by an author abbreviated as R.L.G. and published in The Economist on 20 May 2013, investigates the languages of songs entered for the Eurovision Song Contest and points out that English has had a leading role over the years.

2 Use the present tense (▸ LP 3: Simple present and present perfect). Don't copy the original text – use your own words. Use linking words to connect your ideas (▸ SF 38: Writing a well-structured text).

In the article, the author takes Denmark's win of the last ESC as a starting point to look into different influencing factors of the voting.
After mentioning political reasons, i.e. neighbouring or politically close countries, the writer moves on to the main topic: the chosen languages of the songs being entered. Countries seem to give more points to songs from countries sharing the same language. Using the starting point of Denmark's win again, the writer focuses on the dominance of English …

3 Round off your text by restating the main message or *action.

All in all, the text focuses on … and invites the reader to make up their mind whether …

Step 2: Check your summary. Does it contain the most important facts and ideas from the original text? Have you left out examples, unnecessary details, etc.? Have you checked the spelling, punctuation, tenses, etc.? (▸ SF 40: Proofreading, ▸ LP 12: Spelling)

> **PRACTICE**
>
> Summarize the extract from Alan Bennett's *The Uncommon Reader* (pp. 58f.) in no more than 200 words.

▸ SF 32 Writing a review

When writing a review, you provide information on a book, play or film you have read or watched, as well as expressing your opinion about it. Reviews are meant to either recommend the work in question or to discourage people from reading or seeing it.

PREPARING YOUR REVIEW

Step 1: Read the book or watch the film/play you want to write about, making notes of interesting, very good or very bad aspects. It may be useful to consider typical elements of the text-type in question (▸ SF 16: Identifying text types).

Step 2: Add to your notes, writing down important information about the book or the film. Structure your ideas (▸ SF 5). The grid on the next page will help you to identify the relevant aspects, but you could also use a mind map to structure your ideas.

·····▶

Header Title Running time Your rating Year Director's name	*2012* *157 minutes* **** (out of five) (= okay)* *2009* *Roland Emmerich*
Introduction Basic information: type of movie/book, characters	• *disaster film / science fiction action film* • *science fiction writer Jackson Curtis tries to rescue his two children and his ex-wife from a geological and meteorological super-disaster*
Main part Short summary of the plot (Be careful: perhaps your readers don't want to be told the ending before they have read the book or watched the film themselves.) Cast/characters	• *2009: scientist discovers that the temperature of the Earth is rising unexpectedly; international leaders plan to save a certain number of people on Arks* • *2012: Jackson Curtis (John Cusack), a divorced writer of science fiction, takes children Noah (Liam James) and Lily (Morgan Lily) camping in Yellowstone National Park, hears fears about the end of the world by Charlie Frost (Woody Harrelson)* • *they return home; earthquakes are everywhere; Jackson rents plane for his children and ex-wife; they leave LA before California is destroyed* • *family tries to get to the Arks; the President of the US dies in a tsunami* • *Jackson and his family reach the Arks and manage to get on board*
Comments Your opinion, e.g. on *plot, *actors, *characters, *dialogues, special effects, the 'message', etc.	• *great special effects in the depiction of the catastrophe, impressive when famous buildings collapse* • *dramatic music/great sound* • *the film is fun to watch if you like action films* • *John Cusack convincing as Jackson Curtis: not the typical action hero, but likeable and a bit quirky – good contrast to the action scenes* *BUT:* • *parts of the film are not logical, i.e. characters use mobile phones while the earth is exploding around them* • *film has some quite scary parts* • *film is far too long* • *all in all, film seems to be a bit far-fetched*
Conclusion Summary of your opinion, recommendation/target group	• *quite good science fiction disaster film with great action scenes* • *too long and partly exaggerated* • *only suitable for lovers of action/disaster movies – don't expect too much!*

 FANTASY ACTION HORROR ROMANCE SCI-FI MUSICAL

WRITING YOUR REVIEW

• Start with a catchy title and a **header** which contains basic facts. • Use the present tense. • Avoid imprecise words like *good, really bad*, etc. • Start with an **introductory paragraph** with basic information.	*A film review:* **2012:** *not quite the perfect disaster* *2009 running time: 157 minutes rating: *** (okay)* *The science fiction disaster film 2012, directed by Roland Emmerich, is an action-packed and generally enjoyable film, which has some riveting images and lots of gripping scenes, but which is also rather far-fetched in many places …*
• In the **main part** first give a short summary of the plot without giving away the end of the film/book.	*After a scientist …* *After having obtained a map from Charlie, who dies while reporting about the events, the family tries to get to the Arks, …*
• Then **comment** on the positive or negative aspects of the book/film/play.	*The special effects in 2012 are definitely worth seeing: images of the earth being destroyed are powerful and often scary. The special effects are sometimes truly breath-taking …* *… all this is underlined by a dramatic score. So for all lovers of action films, 2012 definitely is fun to watch. It even has some good acting: John Cusack shines in his role as …*
• Finish your review by **summarizing** the main aspects and by giving a **recommendation** whether the book/film is worth watching/reading. • Use linking words to connect your ideas. (▶SF 38: Writing a well-structured text; ▶LP 12: Linking words and phrases; ▶LP 15: Connecting your thoughts)	*But is the film a real masterpiece? Unfortunately not. It is irritating for the viewers that …* *… And last but not least, the film might be considered just a bit too scary for the faint-hearted!* *All in all, it might have been a good idea to tone the film down a little.* *So here is my final verdict. Is 2012 a perfect film or is it a disaster? It is neither one nor the other but it is a perfect disaster film, and lovers of action films and disaster are going to get their money's worth – and perhaps even more than they bargained for. However, if you are looking for a scientifically correct, logical plot and deeper insights into life, I recommend finding a different film for your Saturday night.*
• Proofread your text. (▶SF 40: Proofreading; ▶LP 17: Spelling)	

PRACTICE

Choose a film that you enjoyed watching in the past six months. Write a short review, focusing on the film's strengths and – if you found any – weaknesses and recommending it to your classmates.

ANIMATION

DRAMA

HISTORY

▶ SF 33 Writing a report

Reports offer factual information about a recent event. The information is given in a chronological order and the language used is objective and formal.

The following instructions will guide you through the steps of writing a report. Your task is to write a report on a family dispute that caused extreme reactions on the parents' side.

Steps	Example
Step 1: Gather as much information about the event as possible. Try to answer the '5 Ws' (who? where? what? when? why? and if possible: what are the consequences?). If your report is based on a fictitious event (e.g. from a novel or play) you might need to add missing details such as last names, place names or dates.	(The story deals with the experiences of second-generation Indian immigrants in London. The narrator, Karim, is visiting his cousin, Jamila. Jamila and her father, Anwar, are fighting.) 'What's going on here?' I asked her. 'Look at him, Karim, he hasn't eaten or drunk anything for eight days! He'll die, Karim, if he doesn't eat anything won't he!' 'Yes, you'll cop it[1], boss, if you don't eat your grub[2] like everyone else.' 'I won't eat. I will die. If Gandhi could shove out the English from India 5 by not eating, I can get my family to obey me by exactly the same.' 'What do you want her to do?' 'To marry the boy I have selected with my brother.' 'But it's old-fashioned, Uncle, out of date,' I explained. 'No one does that kind of thing now. They just marry the person they're 10 into, if they bother to get married at all.' This homily[3] on contemporary morals didn't exactly blow his mind[4]. 'That is not our way, boy. Our way is firm. She must do what I say or I will die. She will kill me.' From: Hanif Kureishi, *The Buddha of Suburbia*, 1990, pp. 59–60
Step 2: Put the information in chronological order. If necessary, add further details.	• *London* • *family of Indian origin* • *domestic dispute* • *daughter's refusal to agree to arranged marriage* • *day eight of father's hunger strike* • *…*

Step 3: Write your report:
- Use the simple past. (▶ LP 4: Present perfect and simple past)
- Start off with a summarizing sentence.
- If you write a longer report, divide it into paragraphs. (▶ SF 38: Writing a well-structured text)
- Use linking words to connect your ideas. (▶ SF 38: Writing a well-structured text)
- Make your report sound formal and matter-of-fact by using objective language and the passive voice where possible. (▶ LP 7: The passive; ▶ LP 11: Using the right register)
- Don't state personal thoughts, feelings or opinions. Try to focus on the facts, even if you use quotes from witnesses.

Step 4: Proofread yout text. (▶ SF 40; ▶ LP 17: Spelling)

---

[1] **cop it** *(BE, infml)* die   [2] **grub** *(infml)* food   [3] **homily** *(fml)* talk that gives advice on how to live
[4] **blow sb.'s mind** *(infml)* produce a strong feeling in sb.

■ LANGUAGE HELP

- On … an incident/occurrence of … was reported to …
- … domestic disputes such as …/another case of …
- It is believed/assumed that …
- … confirmed/claimed/revealed that …
- People are concerned about …/that …
- … took it to extremes when …/The intervention by … has not been successful …
- neighbours / a relative

PRACTICE

Look at the examples given for **Step 2**. Add further details from the text or invent them. Then put them in a suitable order and write your report. You may start like this: *Last night a middle-aged man of Indian origin was brought to St George's Hospital after having nearly starved himself in a hunger strike.*

▶ SF 34 Argumentative writing

When writing an argumentative text, you have to structure your text clearly and argue in a logical manner.

THE PLANNING STAGE

The starting point for an argumentative text can be a statement, a text you have read or a thesis you have been given, for example:

- 'For learners of English at German schools, Shakespeare's plays are incomprehensible, outdated and simply irrelevant. Therefore, his plays ought to be deleted from the curriculum of English classes.' Discuss.

> In a written **discussion** (*Operator: discuss*) you give arguments for and against something and come to a justified conclusion. In a **comment** (*Operator: comment on/write a comment*) you want to convince the reader of your own opinion on an issue. You have to give arguments to support it and may even introduce counter-arguments which you refute to make your own arguments even stronger.

Step 1: Brainstorm your topic and make notes.

Step 2: Collect pro and con arguments.

Pro: *Shakespeare's plays ought to be deleted from the curriculum of English classes.*	**Con:** *Shakespeare's plays should not be deleted from the curriculum of English classes.*
• *Students struggle with the language and ideas of the Elizabethan Age and therefore don't enjoy studying Shakespeare's works.* • *Students would benefit more from reading about events, characters and stories that are relevant to their own daily lives.* • *…*	• *Shakespeare's works are a vital part of English culture – learning about him and his works is part of general knowledge.* • *The topics and conflicts dealt with in Shakespeare's works are universal and can easily be transferred to a modern world (cf. the numerous modern versions of his plays).* • *…*

·····▶

Step 3: Arrange your arguments in a logical way, following either of these two patterns:

Pattern A	**Pattern B**
Present the arguments for and against in separate paragraphs:	Answer each argument immediately with its counter-argument:
1. Introduction	1. Introduction
2. Arguments pro	2. Argument 1 ▸ counter-argument 1
3. Arguments con	3. Argument 2 ▸ counter-argument 2
4. Conclusion	4. Argument 3 ▸ counter-argument 3
	5. Conclusion

It is usually a good idea to finish with the argument that supports your position most strongly because this is the one the reader will remember most. Sometimes, however, it may be helpful not to postpone your strongest argument until the very end, because you want to catch the reader's attention.

- *my position: con*, i.e. Shakespeare's works should not be deleted from the curriculum
- *line of argument*: pattern B (argument → counter-argument)
- *argument 1*: Most students find Shakespeare's texts difficult to read.
  → *counter-argument 1*: Shakespeare's texts are a vital part of English culture and are often referred to in everyday speech, so understanding them will eventually help students in everyday situations.
- *argument 2*: Shakespeare's texts are set in a remote past, so students can't profit from them in their everyday lives. → *counter-argument 2*: Once students have understood a text from Shakespeare's plays, they will realize that the themes dealt with depict universal conflicts which can easily be transferred to modern life.
- …

THE WRITING STAGE

Step 1: Write your introduction. Refer to the topic. In a comment, you can give your point of view here.

Young people today are confronted with a world that is becoming more and more complex and which offers new technology, new information and new forms of literature. Classic literature, notably the plays by William Shakespeare, no longer seem to be relevant to some people today. So they claim that Shakespeare's plays ought to be taken off the curriculum for English classes.

Step 2: Present your line of argument, following either pattern A or B (see above). Use linking words (▸ SF 38: Writing a well-structured text; ▸ LP 14: Using linking words and phrases; ▸ LP 15: Connecting your thoughts)

Many students claim that reading Shakespeare's plays is a challenge and not worth the effort: they argue that not only his language but also the ideas from his times are incomprehensible to young people in the 21st century.
However, Shakespeare's plays are a vital part of English culture – quotations from his plays have found their way into everyday English, into sayings and proverbs. Knowing about Shakespeare's works provides an important background for understanding the heritage of modern language and modern texts.
When I was first made to read Romeo and Juliet *in school, I also struggled with Shakespeare's language and ideas and initially only saw the story in its historic context. But once I had fully understood …*

■ TIP

Your arguments will appear more convincing if you
1. quote authorities, experts or statistics; present facts
2. refer to your personal experience whenever possible

Step 3: Write a conclusion. Round off your text by stating your thesis once again, but do not give new information and do not use the same phrases that you used in the introduction.

In conclusion, it seems clear that taking Shakespeare's plays off the curriculum for English classes would mean that students would be denied the chance of getting to know …

Those precious works of English literature should therefore remain a compulsory part of the curriculum for English classes.

Step 4: Proofread your text. (▶ SF 40)

▶ SF 35 Writing a character profile

*Characters in fictional texts are presented through descriptions by the *narrator or other characters (*direct characterization) and through their appearance, language, attitude, behaviour, relationships to other characters and their thoughts and actions (*indirect characterization).

> ■ TIP
>
> When writing a character profile, do not describe *what* the character does, but explain *why* he/she says or does what he/she does.

Read the excerpt from the *novel *Payback Time* on pp. 174f. and describe Coach McNulty's character.

Step 1: Collect relevant passages in the text and make notes on

- general information we get about the character (outward appearance, social background, etc.)

  - 'He took a seat behind a neatly organized desk.' (l. 9)

- what the narrator or other characters say about the character you are dealing with

  - (Mitch:) 'To him I'd always be a big fat loser and nothing more.' (l. 3)

  - 'But McNulty's eyes were scary. I squirmed[1] as he stared at me, feeling like a snot-nosed preschooler who'd been caught marking a wall with crayons[2].' (l. 44)

- what the character says about him-/herself

  - ' "I do not intend to spend my life coaching high school." ' (l. 57)

- what the character says and does.

  - ' "What's funny?" McNulty said, his blue-gray eyes glittering like shiny stones.' (l. 18)

  - ' "No, no, no," McNulty said, pointing the pencil at me again. 'No questions – not today, not ever.' (l. 34)

  - ' "You write down or tape what I tell you. When I'm done, jazz it up[3] whatever you want, but never make me, my coaches, or my players look bad. Understand?" ' (l. 35)

  - ' "Understood?" he said again, a threat in his voice.' (l. 46)

  - ' "Every sports story needs pictures. Either you've got to take them yourself, or you've got to get a photographer. Didn't you know that?" ' (l. 63)

All quoted passages from: Carl Deuker, *Payback Time*, 2010, pp. 22–25

---

[1] **squirm** *sich winden*   [2] **crayon** *Buntstift*   [3] **jazz sth. up** *(infml)* make sth. more interesting or attractive

Step 2: From your notes draw conclusions about the character.
Always note down examples from the text to give evidence on what you have concluded.

- *according to Mitch: judges people by their outward appearance and athletic ability, not their character → superficial, biased*
- *neatly organized desk → disciplined, conscientious*
- *controls what is being done and said → hungry for power superior, patronizing*
- *uses intimidation to achieve his aims → ruthless, cold*
- *makes others feel stupid → patronizing, condescending*

■ LANGUAGE HELP

- X appears to be … is portrayed as … This behaviour shows/indicates … Evidence for this can be found in lines … The way she/he talks implies that …
- Her/his dress sense shows … This proves that … X is a person who can be considered courageous/optimistic/trustworthy/unreliable/disloyal/…

Step 3: Write up your text.
- Structure your text (▸ SF 5) into
  - introduction (should include names, general information, the role the character plays in the story, etc.)

  - main part (should include details about the character, e.g. character traits, ambitions, aims, problems, inner conflicts, etc.)

  - conclusion (should summarize why the character acts/reacts she way he/she does).

- Use the present tense. (▸ LP 3: Simple present and present perfect)

- Use linking words to connect your ideas. (▸ SF 38: Writing a well-structured text; ▸ LP 14: Linking words and phrases)

- Support your findings using quotes from the text. (▸ SF 39: Quoting a text)

- *Coach McNulty is a PE teacher and high school football coach who considers himself destined for greater things and therefore openly displays his superiority and power.*
- *…*

- *McNulty is very ambitious and does not 'intend to spend [his] life coaching high school football' (l. 57).*
- *To make sure he can achieve that goal he is willing to use threats ('Understood?', l. 46)*
- *He is very condescending towards the reporter.*
- *…*

- *In summary, one can say that Coach McNulty's ruthless ambition, his condescension and his patronizing manner reveal him to be an unfeeling, cold-hearted character and not a stereotypical friendly high school coach and teacher.*

Step 4: Proofread yout text. (▸ SF 40; ▸ LP 17: Spelling)

▶ SF 36 Writing a text analysis

Text analyses can be done with different types of texts, *fictional or *non-fictional texts. The aspects you analyse may differ from text type to text type (see the entries in the Skills File to find out which information is relevant for each text type, ▶ SF 18–21), but the process of analysing texts is usually the same for all of them.

PREPARING YOUR TEXT ANALYSIS

Step 1: Read the task carefully to make sure you know exactly what you are asked to do (cf. 'Verbs for tasks', pp. 384f.). Sometimes you will be given a specific aspect to analyse, sometimes you will be free to select aspects yourself. The following are some suggestions for questions you might ask yourself:
- Which *stylistic devices are used? To what effect? (▶ SF 17: Analysing stylistic devices)
- Which noteworthy words and phrases are used? To what effect?
- How does the structure of the text add to its general meaning / line of argument?
- How is the reader influenced by the text? To what effect?
- What information is being withheld? Why / To what effect?
- In what way does this text differ from other texts of the same type? (▶ SF 16: Identifying text types)
- …

Step 2: Read the text carefully and make sure you understand it properly. Use a dictionary where necessary (▶ SF 2). Make notes on features or aspects of the text that strike you as relevant to your analysis (▶ SF 15: Marking up a text / Making and taking notes). Remember to note down references from the text that support your analysis (▶ SF 39: Quoting a text).

Step 3: Structure your ideas (▶ SF 5). Do not follow the text chronologically, but structure your ideas according to the different aspects you are analysing.

WRITING YOUR TEXT ANALYSIS

Step 1: Write an introductory sentence in which you give the source and author of the text, the topic and a first general idea to answer your question. Write only one short paragraph, e.g.
In his speech given at Portland State University on 13 June 1998, President Bill Clinton focuses his speech around the topic of ethnic diversity in the US and stresses its positive aspects and the opportunities it offers, using various stylistic devices to bring his message home. (Cf. pp. 110f.)
Use the present tense. (▶ LP 18: Writing about texts)

Step 2: Write the main part of your text:
- Present your findings to support the central idea you stated in the introduction.
- Use different paragraphs for different ideas and introduce these paragraphs with topic sentences to guide the reader. Use linking words. (▶ SF 38: Writing a well-structured text)
- Remember to provide evidence from the text, i.e. to use quotations. (▶ SF 38: Quoting a text)

Step 3: Write a short conclusion:
- Refer to your introduction and write a concluding sentence in which you restate your first general idea or your main findings.
- Do NOT add new aspects at this point!
- Do NOT give your personal opinion or an evaluation!

Step 4: Proofread yout text. (▶ SF 40; ▶ LP 17: Spelling)

> **PRACTICE**
>
> Read the text 'Linguistic diplomacy: the Eurovision Song Contest' (pp. 134f.). Write an outline (▶ SF 5) for the following task: 'Analyse the different means the author of this article uses to get the reader's attention.'

▶ SF 37 Doing a creative writing task

Most creative writing tasks ask you to create a text using an existing piece of writing as a starting point.

NON-FICTIONAL TEXTS

Your creative task may take a *non-fictional text (such as a *speech or newspaper *article) as a starting point. In this case you usually have to assume a certain perspective and evaluate a situation through the eyes of a fictitious *character. You might, for example, be asked to read an article on a climate conference and then write an article from the perspective of a reporter who attended the conference. (▶ SF 18: Analysing non-fiction, ▶ SF 34: Argumentative writing).

FICTIONAL TEXTS

When dealing with *fictional texts a common creative task might be to write an ending to a story or to rewrite the story from a *character's point of view, i.e. to change perspective.

Continuation of a story

Step 1: Brainstorm ideas. Look at the *setting, events, dates, characters and their relationships in the original text and watch out for hints as to how the story might continue.

Step 2: Compare your ideas to the original text to make sure they don't contradict the reality depicted in the story.

Step 3: Identify the narrative perspective of the original text (e.g. *first-person or *third-person narrator) and consider what limitations that specific perspective might have or not have.

Step 4: Write your continuation. Try to imitate the style and language used in the original.

Change of perspective

A change of perspective means that you take over the role of one of the characters in the story from whose perspective the story is *not* told. You retell its events from your point of view e.g. in a diary entry, a letter or an interior monologue.

Step 1: Brainstorm ideas. Pay attention to the relationships your character is involved in and to specific features such as his/her social status, age or special character traits.

Step 2: Ask yourself what your character might think and feel in a specific situation and also what your character knows and doesn't know.

Step 3: Write your text in a way that is appropriate to your character. Age, social status and other features usually determine how you speak or write.

Step 4: Pay attention to the *text type you're using. For example if you write a letter, you must address the addressee and sign it; if you write a dialogue, you should use typical elements of spoken language; if you write a diary entry you should focus on thoughts and feelings.

> ■ TIP
> - Do not stray too far from the original text because your text may become illogical or far-fetched.
> - Do not invent things that contradict the events of the original story.

▶ SF 38 Writing a well-structured text

A well-structured text makes it easy for your reader to follow your line of thought and to understand your text. The structure you use will depend on the kind of text you are writing. For instance, if you are telling a story or writing a report (▶ SF 33: Writing a report), you might want to relate the events in a chronological order. However, there are some rules which apply to all kinds of texts.

Step 1:   Collect ideas. Make an outline for your text and structure your ideas accordingly. (▶ SF 5: Structuring information and ideas)

Step 2:   Write your text:
- Begin a new paragraph for each new event, point, argument or idea.
- Structure your text visually, for example by leaving spaces between your paragraphs.
- Make the first sentence in each paragraph a **topic sentence**, i.e. a sentence that states what the paragraph will be about.
- Use **linking words** to make the connections between individual ideas clear (▶ LP 14: Linking words and phrases; ▶ LP 15: Connecting your thoughts).

Step 3:   Proofread your text. (▶ SF 40: Proofreading; ▶ LP 17: Spelling)

■ LANGUAGE HELP

Linking words

Enumeration/ Structure	first, second, third; firstly, secondly, …; to begin/start with …, in the first place …; next, then; finally, last (but not least), lastly, to conclude
Addition	furthermore, moreover, in addition (to that), above all, what is more …
Comparison	equally, likewise, similarly, in the same way …
Summary/Conclusion	then, all in all, to conclude, to sum up, in summary/conclusion …
Exemplification	namely, for instance / for example (e.g.), that is to say …
Reasoning	that is why … because …, one reason for this is that …
Result	consequently, as a consequence, therefore, thus, after all, as a result, this leads to / results in …
Reformulation	or rather, to put it another way, in other words …
Alternatively	on the one hand … on the other hand …, either … or, neither … nor …
Contrast	on the contrary, in contrast to, opposite to, unlike …
Concession	however, nevertheless, still, though, in spite of that, despite that, …

▶ SF 39 Quoting a text

*Quoting is used when you want to support your own statements (e.g. in an analysis) by giving evidence from other texts or the text you are working on. You can either paraphrase / **quote indirectly** (i.e. use your own words to express ideas from a text, ▶ SF 6) or you can use a **direct quote** (i.e. use the exact words of the text).*

Here are some rules for quoting properly:

- With a direct quote, repeat exactly what the author wrote – this also refers to spelling, punctuation, etc.
- Use quotation marks to show where the direct quote begins and ends: A direct quote must be clearly indicated as someone else's thoughts to avoid giving the impression of plagiarism. Remember that in English, quotation marks start and end above the line ('…').
- Always give the exact **source** of your quotation: line or verse numbers and – when dealing with longer texts – page numbers). If you are quoting from more than one text, indicate the author and year of publication. Remember these **abbreviations**: *p./l.* is used for one page/line (e.g. 'p. 4'); *pp./ll.* for more than one page/line (e.g. 'pp. 11–14'); *f./ff.* after the number of a page/line means 'and the following page(s)/ line(s)'.
- Especially when working on projects, you may have to quote from more than one text. In this case you need to indicate in a **bibliography** which texts you have used. For each text, provide the author, title, place and date of publication, publisher or URL.

Strategy	Example
Indirect quotes If you use an indirect quote (i.e. you paraphrase or summarize ideas from a text in your own words) you do not use quotation marks, but indicate that you are referring to somebody else's ideas by using *cf.* (= German *vgl.*) and the page number and/or line.	*Franklin D. Roosevelt suggests in his speech that people who are threatened by poverty are easy prey for dictators (cf. p. 164, ll. 2f.).*
Direct quotes: complete sentences When quoting complete sentences make sure that you explain them, refer to or comment on them, so as to avoid disconnected quotations. Using quotes without further comment may give the impression that you have no ideas of your own! Use a colon (:) to separate the quotation from your introductory phrase or sentence.	*Clinton is convinced that immigration has benefitted the USA: 'More than any other nation on Earth, America has constantly drawn strength and spirit from wave after wave of immigrants.' (p. 110, ll. 12–13)*
Direct quotes: words or phrases If you want to refer to individual words from the text (e.g. in an analysis), you can incorporate words/phrases into your own sentence. Be careful: Work the quotations into your sentences as smoothly as possible so that they fit syntactically.	• *In the prologue to Romeo and Juliet, the unhappy ending of the play is already foreshadowed by the phrase 'starcrossed lovers' (Prologue, v. 6).* • *In his article, Eliot A. Cohen admits that Trump 'inherited a mess' (Context, p. 115, l. 1) and that these were circumstances that 'would have caused severe headaches' (Context, p. 115, l. 9) for any president.*
Direct quotes: poems or plays in verse With texts written in verse, indicate the end of lines with a slash (/). When quoting from plays, provide the act, scene and verse, i.e. II/2/6 = act II, scene 2, verse 6.	*In Aoife Mannix's poem 'Keeping the accent' the speaker experiences that her accent is seen as something positive: 'Then he tells me my accent is so cute, / he is going to give me one of the drinks for free' (p. 133, ll. 5f.).*

Deleting from or adding to a direct quote If you want to leave out part of a quote indicate this by using square brackets […]. If you need to add to a quote, for example to make it fit into your sentence syntactically or logically, indicate this by adding words in square brackets, too. Make sure that you don't change the meaning of the quote and that it is still syntactically correct.	• *'Once a child starts to excel at something […] he or she gets praise, admiration, and satisfaction.' (p. 18, ll. 30–32.)* • *Mitch says that 'Mr. Dewey had warned [them] about people like McNulty'. (p. 175, l. 38)*
Direct quotes: texts containing quotation mark When quoting a passage that includes quotation marks (e.g. in direct speech), use two different kinds of quotation marks, i.e. '…' and "…".	*In Genesis, the first book of the Bible, it says: 'And God said, "Let there be light" and there was light' (Genesis 1.6).*

◼ TIP

Check your assignment before using quotes – when answering comprehension questions, you are often asked to express ideas from the text in your own words and are therefore not supposed to quote.

PRACTICE

In the following extract from an essay on why people emigrated to the US, certain passages have been underlined. Quote them to complete the sentences given below the text. Add line references.

Political and Economic Freedom   *Milton and Rose Friedman*

Ever since the first settlement of Europeans in the New World – at Jamestown in 1607 and at Plymouth in 1620 – America has been a magnet for people <u>seeking adventure, fleeing from a tyranny, or simply trying to make a better life for themselves and their children.</u>

<u>An initial trickle[1]</u> swelled after the American Revolution and the establishment of the United States of America and became <u>a flood</u> in the nineteenth century, when millions of people streamed across the Atlantic, and a smaller number across the Pacific, driven by misery and tyranny, and attracted by the promise of freedom and affluence[2]. 5

When they arrived, they did not find streets paved with gold; they did not find an easy life. <u>They did find freedom and an opportunity to make the most of their talents.</u> Through hard work, ingenuity[3], thrift[4], and luck, most of them succeeded in realizing enough of their hopes and dreams to encourage friends and relatives to join them. 10

From: *Free to Choose*, New York 1980

1   The text states that the people who came to the US did this for a variety of reasons, as there were people …
2   The text describes the rising number of immigrants as … after the American Revolution and as … during the nineteenth century.
3   Even though the immigrants couldn't expect to become rich without effort, they did get the chance to fulfil their dreams if they were willing and able to work hard: …

---

[1]**trickle** *Rinnsal*   [2]**affluence** wealth   [3]**ingenuity** ability to find solutions to problems   [4]**thrift** careful spending of money

▶ SF 40 Proofreading

Whenever you write a text, it is important to check the correctness and the style of the English you have used. Ideally ask someone else to read it through. Others will often see more because they are not as involved with the text as you are. If possible, read your text out loud. This will help you spot if you have accidently left out any words.

Step 1: Checking structure

- Check that you have included an introduction and a conclusion. (▶ SF 5: Structuring information and ideas)
- Check that you have followed all the rules for a sensible text structure, e.g. topic sentences, paragraphs, etc. (▶ SF 38: Writing a well-structured text)
- Make sure that your paragraphs include more than one sentence but still focus on one basic thought, argument or idea.

Step 2: Checking style

- Look at your sentences. If your text consists of lots of unconnected main clauses only, then add linking words to express logical connections between your ideas and thus make your text more readable. (▶ SF 38: Writing a well-structured text)
- Make sure you used the right collocations. (▶ LP 19: Collocations) If in doubt, look them up in a dictionary. (▶ SF 2: Using a dictionary and a grammar book)
- Check for repetitions. Substitute words you have used repeatedly with synonyms.

- *He is a very conscientious person. He goes to work even when he feels sick. People know that when he is not at work, something serious must have happened. →*
  He is a very conscientious person who goes to work even when he feels sick. That is why people know that when he is not at work, something serious must have happened.
- *Social networks can hurt people's privacy. →*
  Social networks can violate people's privacy.

- *Not everybody can achieve the American Dream but there are some people who work hard and achieve it in the end. →*
  Not everybody can achieve the American Dream but there are some people who work hard and reach it in the end.

Step 3: Checking correctness

- Keep a checklist of mistakes you have regularly made in the past, e.g. correct tenses in the *if*-clause, the use of adverbs, etc. Look specifically for these mistakes when reading your text.
- Check spelling and punctuation. (▶ LP 17: Spelling) If possible take advantage of your computer's spell-checker, but always double-check its suggestions rather than accepting them blindly.

- **She is terrible upset about her husband's death. →*
  She is terribly upset about her husband's death.

> **■ TIP**
>
> Try to think in English when you write because otherwise phrases or sentence patterns sometimes sound more German than English.

The following is the beginning of a student's text analysis. It includes nine mistakes (both grammatical and stylistic errors). Find all the mistakes and correct them.

In the short story 'No speak English' from Sandra Cisnero the main character which is called Mamacita, is a beautiful woman. Actually she never leave her apartment, instead the narrator basically speculates about why she behaves in this way. He only knows that she is married and has one kid and he only knows that she speaks only eight words of English. The narrator thinks that she doesn't like English. She always listens to the Spanish radio shows. The husband wants that she integrates into US-American society but she misses her real home, Mexico, too much.

Mediation skills

▶ SF 41 Mediation of written and oral texts

Not everybody speaks and understands both German and English. So you may sometimes find yourself in a situation where you have to help people understand each other – where you have to mediate between speakers of German and English or where you have to explain what is written in texts in the other language. A mediation is not *a translation, i.e. you do* not *translate a text word for word.*

Your English-speaking e-pal is leaving school next year but is finding it difficult to decide on his career plans. You have just read the article below and want to send him an email giving some advice on how to proceed.

> # So findest du deinen Traumberuf
>
> Die Entscheidung für den späteren Beruf fällt vielen Jugendlichen schwer – schließlich haben die wenigsten von ihnen Kontakt zur Berufswelt. Welcher Beruf könnte für mich der richtige sein? Und welchen Weg soll ich nach dem Schulabschluss einschlagen? Eine Ausbildung machen, um möglichst bald einiges Geld zu verdienen? Oder lieber studieren, auch wenn man dafür mehrere Jahre seines Lebens investieren muss? Die richtige Wahl zu treffen ist nicht leicht, und es steht viel auf dem Spiel. 5
>
> Als Erstes solltest du versuchen herauszufinden, was dir liegt: Arbeitest du lieber mit Menschen oder mit Maschinen? Fühlst du dich in einem sauberen, angenehm temperierten Raum oder im Freien am wohlsten? Bist du gern mitten im Trubel oder liebst du klare, geordnete Abläufe? Selbstfindungstests im Internet oder bei der Bundesagentur für Arbeit 10 können dir helfen, deine Stärken und Interessen rechtzeitig zu erkennen.
>
> Wichtig ist auch, auf Termine zu achten. Willst du dich um einen Ausbildungsplatz bewerben, musst du dich bereits im Jahr vor deinem Abschlussjahr darum kümmern. Ähnliches gilt auch für das Studium: Auch hier sollte man sich rechtzeitig informieren, um alle Bewerbungsunterlagen fristgerecht zur Hand zu haben. Wenn du einen Studiengang mit 15 Numerus Clausus oder mit einer eng begrenzten Zahl von Studienplätzen gewählt hast, ist es sinnvoll, auch einen Plan B in der Tasche zu haben, falls du beim ersten Anlauf leer ausgehst.

How to proceed	Example
Step 1: Select the relevant information from the text, bearing in mind what specific information your partner needs. Remember: the mediated text will usually be much shorter than the original because you select only the information you need.	• *first find out what you enjoy doing* • *get some help from online-tests or the 'Bundesagentur für Arbeit'* • *start early*
Step 2: Analyse the communicative situation: • Who are you talking or writing to? What is the appropriate *style and *register? (▶ LP 11: Using the right register) • What text type are you expected to produce (an informal letter or email, an article for a school magazine? (▶ SF 29: Writing a formal letter or email; ▶ SF 33: Writing a report) • Will you be speaking or writing? (Speaking allows you to use gestures and other non-verbal means of communication.)	• *Your friend needs to know the basic steps he can take to decide on his career.* • *a friend → informal language* (If you were e.g. giving a speech at a symposium on young people's career choices you would use a formal style.) • *an email* • *written text*
Step 3: Structure the relevant information, then phrase it in the target language. (▶ LP 12: Avoiding German-sounding sentence-patterns) Watch out for aspects that are specific to one culture and explain them in more detail. (▶ LP 12: Avoiding Germanisms) If you don't know words in the other language, paraphrase them. (▶ SF 6: Paraphrasing)	*The article I have read gives you some advice:* • *The first step is to find out what you enjoy and what you are good at. You can use online-tests or you can get help at the Job Centre.* • *It's important to start early – here in Germany you have to apply well before for trainee programmes or places at university.* • *'Bundesagentur für Arbeit': Job Centre / a state institution that helps people find jobs*

PRACTICE

A 'career's night' is being held at your school for your entire year group. You are asked to give a short talk in German about what careers young people tend to choose and why. Using the text 'Teenagers' career aspirations' (pp. 169f.), prepare a script for your speech (▶ SF 25 Giving a speech).

Exam Practice

EP 1 How to do exams in general **P** 343
EP 2 Working with texts **P** 344
    EP 2.1 *Anforderungsbereich I*: comprehension 345
    EP 2.2 *Anforderungsbereich II*:
           analysis/interpretation 345
    EP 2.3 *Anforderungsbereich III*: beyond the text 346

EP 3 Mediation **P** 352
EP 4 Listening and viewing **P** 354
EP 5 Speaking 356
EP 6 Closed test formats 359

P A task allows you to practise this skill.

> *Download the suggested answers to the PRACTICE tasks here:*
> **Webcode** context-49

▶ EP 1 How to do exams in general

You are likely to come across many different tests and exams for English at school, for your *Abitur* or after school. Before sitting an exam, you should therefore familiarize yourself with its specific format. However, there are certain general tips that might help you to be successful. In this *Exam Practice* you will find guidance for both written and oral test formats.

BEFORE THE EXAM
Start early and organize your work.

Collecting information
- Make sure you know how to use aids that are allowed in the exam, e.g. dictionaries. (▶ SF 2. Using a dictionary and a grammar book)
- Find out details of the exam situation. Who will be present? Where will it take place? How long will you have? (Especially for oral exams:) Will you be given preparation time? (▶ EP 5)
- Try to get hold of old test papers to see what they require.
- Make sure you understand what the different tasks require from you (cf. 'Verbs for tasks', pp. 384–385).
- Learn about the evaluation criteria of the exam – this will help you to focus on the relevant aspects.

Practising
- Go over old tests or homework tasks to identify your problem areas and learn from your mistakes.
- Don't practise what you already know but focus on your weak areas. (▶ LP 1–20)
- Practise the specific type of exam you will be sitting. If you have to pass an oral exam, practise with a partner. If you have to write a comment, write comments or different parts of a comment.

IN THE EXAM
- Be on time for the exam.
- Read the instructions of the test carefully, they provide crucial information. Make sure you understand what you are supposed to do – it may help to highlight the instructions.
- If you are allowed to choose between different tasks, read all alternatives before deciding which one you want to do.
- If you notice that you are becoming nervous, take a quick break before continuing.
- Use your time efficiently, e.g. leave enough time for checking your work.

.....▶

A teacher has added this comment to a student's text:

The argumentation of your comment is convincing. You might put forward some more arguments though and back up all your findings with passages from the text. The overall structure of your text is well-chosen, but try to connect the paragraphs more effectively. Linking words and special phrases may help you to do so. Your style of writing is your strength: you write fluently and right to the point. You have expanded your vocabulary successfully and most passages are idiomatic. There are hardly any mistakes, but you should revise conditional sentences.

1 Look at the following list of criteria and say whether the student's text fulfilled them very well or just satisfactorily or whether it needs improvement in that area.

Criteria		
▪ Content: quality	▪ Content: quantity	▪ Structure
▪ Use of quotes	▪ Linking words	▪ Useful phrases for interpretation
▪ Vocabulary: general flexibility	▪ Ability of expression	▪ Grammar

2 Look at the sections Skills File (pp. 284–342) and Language Practice (pp. 246–267) and identify relevant sections that could help the student to improve his/her weak areas.

3 Now collect your own 3–5 weak areas and identify the relevant sections in Skills File and/or Language Practice. Develop an action plan to work on your weak areas.

▶ EP 2 Working with texts

In most of your exams you will be faced with one or more texts, which you have to respond to (▶ SF 11–13, ▶ SF 16–21). These may include:
- *fictional texts (e.g. *short stories, *poems; extracts from *novels, *dramas or *film scripts)
- *non-fictional texts (e.g. articles, *speeches)
- visuals (e.g. *cartoons, pictures, films, advertisements, leaflets).

You may be given a single written text or a written text combined with another text or a visual. You will be expected to work on different tasks. For instance, you may be asked to analyse a short story or to mediate a newspaper article. In order to be successful you will need to apply different skills, e.g.:
- skimming, scanning (▶ SF 14: Reading strategies)
- underlining or highlighting important sections (▶ SF 15: Marking up a text / Making and taking notes)
- making notes in the margin (▶ SF 15: Marking up a text / Making and taking notes)
- making notes on a separate piece of paper, e.g. mind maps, outlines, drawings (▶ SF 5: Structuring information and ideas: visual aids and outlines)
- writing a well-structured text (▶ SF 38).

Find a mindmapping tool here:
🖐 **Webcode** context-53

In general, when dealing with a text you will be asked to consider the following three aspects:

Anforderungsbereich I	*Anforderungsbereich II*	*Anforderungsbereich III*
comprehension (focus on content) ▶ EP 2.1	analysis/interpretation (focus on form and function) ▶ EP 2.2	composition (focus on evaluation and re-creation) ▶ EP 2.3

In an exam, you may be given tasks that clearly relate to one of these three aspects, or there might be complex tasks that combine two or all three of them.

▶ EP 2.1 *Anforderungsbereich I*: comprehension

This type of task focuses on the content of a text and is intended to check whether you have understood the information. Comprehension tasks can be quite open, i.e. they require you to write a free text, as in summary writing (▶ SF 31) or answering comprehension questions. They can also occur in the form of closed test formats, e.g. multiple choice or true/false exercises (▶ SF 7: Working with closed test formats; ▶ EP 6).

TYPICAL INSTRUCTIONS FOR *ANFORDERUNGSBEREICH I* (OPEN TASKS)

Here are some instructions that are frequently used for *Anforderungsbereich I*. To see the complete list of instructions, have a look at pp. 384–385 ('Verbs for tasks').

Instruction	Example	What you are expected to do	Tips
outline ['– –] *umreißen, skizzieren*	**Outline** the writer's views on …	*Give the main features, structure or general principles of a topic, omitting minor details.*	Structure your answer using main and subordinate points.
state *darlegen*	**State** the author's opinion on the main character's decision.	*Specify something clearly.*	Be precise and brief.
summarize (*also:* **give/write a summary of; sum up**) *zusammenfassen*	**Summarize** the incident in the church in no more than four sentences.	*Give a concise account of the main points of something.*	Be concise; leave out details and examples.

To practise *Anforderungsbereich I*, have a look at **Practice I** (p. 349) or **Practice II** (p. 350).

▶ EP 2.2 *Anforderungsbereich II*: analysis/interpretation

In this part of the exam, you 'read between the lines' of a text. You might examine why an author gives the text a certain form, why he/she characterizes the figures in a drama in a certain way, etc. To do exactly what you are asked to do, make sure you understand the instructions (cf. 'Verbs for tasks', p. 384). Also, provide a suitable structure for your findings (▶ SF 5: Structuring information and ideas).

TYPICAL INSTRUCTIONS FOR *ANFORDERUNGSBEREICH II*

Here are some instructions that are frequently used for *Anforderungsbereich II*. To see the complete list of instructions, have a look at pp. 384–385 ('Verbs for tasks').

Instruction	Example	What you are expected to do	Tips
analyse (*BE*), **analyze** (*AE*) ['ænəlaɪz]/ **examine** [ɪɡ'zæmɪn] *analysieren, untersuchen*	**Analyse** the main elements of the poster. **Examine** the writer's attitude towards the protagonist.	*Describe and explain certain aspects and/or features of the text in detail.*	Do not just list e.g. stylistic devices the author uses, but always connect them to the effect they are used to create.
explain *erklären*	**Explain** the main character's reaction to her mother in the first scene.	*Describe and define in detail.*	Do not just describe something, but give reasons why it is the way it is.

Authors always write their texts to achieve an effect – they may want to persuade or inform the readers, they may try to arouse compassion or contempt for a character in their story, etc. When analysing a text, you need to examine which means the author has used to create a specific effect (▶ SF 17: Analysing stylistic devices; ▶ SF 18: Analysing non-fiction; ▶ SF 19–21: Analysing fiction). The table below gives some examples.

Category	Some typical means	Possible effects
techniques of persuasion	quote from or use of statistics from reliable sources and experts	creates credibility
	example from everyday life	makes an argument more comprehensible and concrete
	direct address of reader	makes the reader sympathize with a concept or adopt the writer's view
use of language	use of *images (e.g. *metaphor, *symbol, *simile, *personification)	helps to evoke a graphic, vivid picture in the reader's mind
	use of *stylistic devices such as *anaphora, *alliteration or *repetition	stresses a certain aspect
	use of *irony, *sarcasm	creates humour, emphazises a point or message
	use of technical jargon	creates credibility, makes the writer appear more expert
narrative techniques	use of a *first-person narrator	helps the reader to identify with the narrator, to understand his or her attitude

To practise *Anforderungsbereich II*, have a look at **Practice I** (p. 349) or **Practice II** (p. 350).

▶ EP 2.3 *Anforderungsbereich III*: beyond the text

Part III of the exam requires you to produce a text. It may be based on a text or on visuals (e.g. cartoons or photos) or it may take just a topic as a starting point. It may be called *comment, composition, creative writing* or *writing*.
In some exams you will be asked to write a certain type of text. The task may also give you aspects that need to be (or may be) taken into consideration. The following table gives you an idea about the most common text types, their purpose, content/structure and specific language.

Text type	Purpose	Content/Structure	Language
*feature story/ article	• inform sb. • entertain sb. • provide background information	• catchy headline • first paragraph must arouse reader's interest (example, anecdote) • use of anecdotes, examples, quotes • personal angle	• less formal language, some slang may be used
report (▶ SF 33: Writing a report)	• inform sb. • provide background information • influence sb.	• catchy headline • clear paragraphs • from general aspects to detail	• less formal language, some slang may be used

*comment (▶SF 34: Argumentative writing)	• pass judgment on an issue • express and support your opinion	• introduction: outline of topic and attitude • body: arguments for personal position, refutation of counter-arguments • conclusion: summary of personal position • use of examples to illustrate arguments	• formal/neutral language
argumentative essay/ discussion (▶SF 34: Argumentative writing)	• weigh up both sides of an issue remaining fairly neutral	• introduction: outline of topic • body: pros and cons of the issue • conclusion: summary of arguments, statement of personal opinion • use of examples to illustrate arguments	• formal/neutral language
(written) interview (▶SF 37: Doing a creative writing task; ▶SF 26: Taking part in an interview)	• present a topic/a person's views • portray a celebrity	• introduction: basic facts on interviewee • official welcome of inter-viewee • body: interviewee's answers to questions (which should be polite, may be provoca-tive) • concluding statement or question; words of goodbye and expression of gratitude	• imitation of spoken language • polite language
*letter (e.g. letter to the editor, cover letter for an appli-cation, personal letter) email (▶SF 34: Writing a formal letter or email)	• various, e.g. apply for a job, tell reader about a topic, express your opinion	• content varies according to addressee and purpose • structural elements: letterhead, greeting, body, signature	• varies according to addressee and purpose
review (▶SF 32: Writing a review)	• describe something you have read or experienced (book, film, etc.) and ex-press your opinion on it • make recommen-dations	• introduction – body (brief summary, evaluation) – conclusion	• varies according to type of magazine or newspaper • use of words that describe the film, book, etc. and your opinion in a differentiated way (adjectives, adverbs; words with positive or negative connotations)

| *speech script (▶ SF 25: Giving a speech) | • various, e.g. move/ convince/inform/ entertain sb. | • introduction: welcome audience; outline topic and intention of speech
• body: well-structured arguments backed up with evidence/examples
• conclusion: summary, appeal to listeners, expression of gratitude | • varies according to context, i.e. audience, speaker, occasion
• stylistic devices |

Your task may also be creative writing (▶ SF 37: Doing a creative writing task), i.e. you may be asked to add something to an already existing text (mostly fictional) or to change it. You might change the *point of view of a text, add an ending to a story (or write a different one), add a part to the text or fill a gap in it (e.g. an *interior monologue). Remember that your writing must match the language style of the original.

You may also come across 'free' creative writing tasks. They are not based on or linked to a certain text but require you to apply your knowledge and skills – as for example when writing a poem on a given topic.

TYPICAL INSTRUCTIONS FOR *ANFORDERUNGSBEREICH III*

If you are not given a certain text type to write, you may find one of the tasks listed in the table below. See pp. 384–385 for a complete list of instructions ('Verbs for tasks').

Instruction	Example	What you are expected to do	Tips
comment on ['kɒment] *kommentieren, Stellung nehmen zu*	**Comment on** the speaker's belief that …	*State clearly your opinions on the topic in question and support your views with evidence.*	Say exactly what you think and why.
discuss *diskutieren, erörtern*	**Discuss** how education influences attitudes towards immigration.	*Investigate or examine by argument; give reasons for and against.*	Structure your ideas clearly. Weigh up both sides of an issue and support your final position with arguments.
justify *begründen, rechtfertigen*	**Justify** your answer.	*Show adequate grounds for decisions or conclusions.*	If possible and suitable, use statistics or research results as support.

In all your writing tasks make sure to apply general writing skills such as structuring a text or linking ideas (▶ SF 5: Structuring information and ideas; ▶ SF 38: Writing a well-structured text).
To practise *Anforderungsbereich III*, have a look at **Practice I** (p. 349) or **Practice II** (p. 350).

Working with a non-fictional text: *Anforderungsbereich I, II and III*

A great honour   *Ewen MacAskill*

NSA whistleblower Edward Snowden said he was humbled and honoured after Glasgow University students voted overwhelmingly for him to serve as their rector for the next three years. In a statement to the Guardian, Snowden described it as bold and historic decision in support of academic freedom. 'In a world where so many of our developing thoughts and queries and plans must be entrusted to the open internet, mass surveillance is not simply a matter of privacy, but of academic freedom and human liberty,' Snowden said. The vote is purely symbolic as Snowden is unlikely to be in a position to become a working rector, able to represent students at meetings of the university's administrators. He is wanted by the US for leaking tens of thousands of documents to journalists and has been granted temporary asylum in Russia. The result of the online election was announced to candidates and their supporters shortly after polls closed at 5pm on Tuesday. Snowden was nominated by a group of students at the university who said they had received his approval through his lawyer. He defeated the former champion cyclist Graeme Obree, the author Alan Bissett and the Rev Kelvin Holdsworth, who also stood for the post. Chris Cassells, Snowden's spokesman for the rectorial election campaign, said: 'We are delighted to see Edward Snowden elected as the new rector of the University of Glasgow. We have a proud and virtuous tradition of making significant statements through our rectors and today we have once more championed this idea by proving to the world that we are not apathetic to important issues such as democratic rights.' [...] Charles Kennedy, the outgoing rector and former Lib Dem leader, said: 'It has been a pleasure and a privilege to serve the students of the University of Glasgow for the past six years. The post of rector is an important one, and I would like to wish my successor all the very best for his term of office.'

Snowden, in his statement, said: 'I am humbled by and grateful to the students of Glasgow University for this historic statement in defence of our shared values. We are reminded by this bold decision that the foundation of all learning is daring: the courage to investigate, to experiment, to inquire.' He added: 'If we do not contest the violation of the fundamental right of free people to be left unmolested in their thoughts, associations, and communications – to be free from suspicion without cause – we will have lost the foundation of our thinking society. The defence of this fundamental freedom is the challenge of our generation, a work that requires constructing new controls and protections to limit the extraordinary powers of states over the domain of human communication. This election shows that the students of Glasgow University intend to lead the way, and it is my great honour to serve as their rector.'

From: 'Edward Snowden "humbled" by his election as Glasgow University rector', *The Guardian*, 18 February 2014

(Line numbers in margin: 5, 10, 15, 20, 25)

---

¹ **whistleblower** *Enthüller/in*
² **rector** *(BE)* head of a university or college
³ **bold** *(here)* brave
⁸ **leak sth.** *(here)* reveal sth.

¹³ **Rev Kelvin Holdsworth** clergyman of the Scottish Episcopal Church in Glasgow
¹⁷ **Lib Dem** (= The Liberal Democrats) a socially liberal political party in the United Kingdom

²¹ **humble sb.** *jdn. mit Demut erfüllen*
²³ **daring** ready to do dangerous or unusual things, brave
²⁴ **unmolested** not disturbed by anybody

1 Possible task for *Anforderungsbereich I*

Summarize what the article tells you about Snowden's election and his personal reaction to it.
(▶ SF 31: Writing a summary)

2 Possible task for *Anforderungsbereich II*

Examine how MacAskill expresses his indirect support for Snowden's actions. Consider his line of argument, his techniques of persuasion and his use of language.
(▶ SF 18: Analysing non-fiction)

> ◼ TIP
>
> Reread EE 2.2, then collect ideas and structure them before starting to write.
> (▶ SF 5: Structuring information and ideas)

3 Possible tasks for *Anforderungsbereich III*

Before working on the tasks you might want to do some research on the controversy around Edward Snowden.

a Some people have called Snowden a traitor because he leaked confidential information from the NSA. Discuss this view. ▶ LANGUAGE HELP (▶ SF 34: Argumentative writing)

b Write an interview with an American politician who considers Snowden a hero who opened the world's eyes to mass surveillance. ▶ LANGUAGE HELP (▶ SF 37: Doing a creative writing task)

c Imagine you are a student at Glasgow University before Snowden's election as rector. You have been asked to give a speech in front of undecided fellow students convincing them (not) to vote for him. Write a speech.
▶ LANGUAGE HELP (▶ SF 25: Giving a speech)

LANGUAGE HELP

- endanger national security
- destabilize international relationships
- commit a crime
- cause unpredictable political turmoil
- be on an ego-trip
- brave hero
- support freedom of speech
- fundamental democratic right
- trigger a much needed debate
- defense of democratic values
- principles of the American Dream
- international peacekeeping

Working with a fictional text: *Anforderungsbereich I, II and III*

PRACTICE II

In the novel *The Uncommon Reader* Queen Elizabeth II discovers a travelling library outside of Buckingham Palace. She starts to borrow books regularly and slowly, her character begins to change. In this excerpt she is talking to her equerry after performing a ceremony.

The monarch's truly human side *Alan Bennett*

'Less spontaneous this morning, ma'am,' one of the bolder equerries ventured to say.

'Was I?' said the Queen, who would once have been most put out at even this mildest of criticisms, though these days it scarcely impinged. 'I think I know why it is. You see, Gerald, as they kneel one looks down on
5 the tops of people's heads a good deal and from that perspective even the most unsympathetic personality seems touching: the beginnings of a bald patch, the hair growing over the collar. One's feelings are almost maternal.'

The equerry, with whom she'd never shared such confidences before and who ought to have been flattered, simply felt awkward and embarrassed. This was a truly human side to the monarch of which he'd never been
10 previously aware and which (unlike its counterfeit versions) he did not altogether welcome. And whereas the Queen herself thought that such feelings probably arose out of her reading books, the young man felt it might be that she was beginning to show her age. Thus it was that the dawn of sensibility was mistaken for the onset of senility.

Immune to embarrassment herself, as she was to any that she might cause, the Queen would once not have
15 noticed the young man's confusion. But observing it now she resolved in the future to share her thoughts less promiscuously, which was a pity in a way as it was what many in the nation longed for. Instead she determined to restrict her confidences to her notebooks, where they could do no harm.

The Queen had never been demonstrative; it was not in her upbringing; but more and more these days, particularly in the period following Princess Diana's death, she was being required to go public about feel-
20 ings she would have preferred to keep to herself. At that time, though, she had not yet begun to read, and it was only now that she understood that her predicament was not unique and that she shared it, among others, with Cordelia. She wrote in her notebook: 'Though I do not always understand Shakespeare, Cordelia's "I cannot heave my heart into my mouth" is a sentiment I can readily endorse. Her predicament is mine.'

From: *The Uncommon Reader*, 2007, pp. 80–81

² **equerry** [–'– –] male officer who acts as an assistant to the royal family
venture to do sth. *etwas zu tun wagen*
⁴ **scarcely** almost not
impinge have a noticeable effect
⁶ **bald patch** area on top of the head without hair
collar *Kragen*
⁷ **maternal** *mütterlich*

⁸ **be flattered** *sich geschmeichelt fühlen*
⁹ **awkward** uncomfortable
¹⁰ **counterfeit** fake
¹¹ **arise out of sth.** happen as a result of sth.
¹² **dawn of sensibility** *Anflug von Empfindsamkeit*
onset beginning
¹⁶ **promiscuously** *(here)* with lots of people
¹⁷ **harm** damage, injury

¹⁸ **be demonstrative** show your feelings in public
upbringing education
¹⁹ **Princess Diana** (1961–1997) first wife of the Queen's son Charles
²¹ **predicament** situation where it is hard to know what to do
²² **Cordelia** character from William Shakespeare's drama *King Lear*
²³ **endorse sth.** say publicly that you support sth.

1 Possible task for *Anforderungsbereich* I

Briefly describe the situation as well as the monarch's and Gerald's attitudes and feelings.

2 Possible task for *Anforderungsbereich* II

Examine how the author employs narrative perspective to show the differences between the behaviour and views of the Queen and the equerry. (▶ SF 19: Analysing narrative prose)

Step 1: Put a transparency over the text and mark relevant passages revealing information on
　　1　the Queen's behaviour and how she explains it
　　2　the equerry's observations and how he explains them.

Step 2: Determine the narrative perspective and examine how it influences the reader's perception of both characters. What effect does it have on the presentation of both characters' behaviour and views?

Step 3: Add your observations to the structure below to create an outline. (▶ SF 5: Structuring information and ideas)
Don't forget to use quotes and to indicate the lines. (▶ SF 39: Quoting a text)

Paragraph 1: *narrative perspective*
　　　　　　…

Paragraph 2: the Queen's behaviour and her self-image
　　　　　　2.1. Her behaviour　　　　*2.2. How she explains it*
　　　　　　…　　　　　　　　　　　…

Paragraph 3: the equerry's view
　　　　　　3.1. The equerry's observations　*3.2. How he explains them*
　　　　　　…　　　　　　　　　　　…

Step 4: Add suitable notes for introduction and conclusion, then write a coherent text.
(▶ SF 38: Writing a well-structured text)

Introduction
- *an 'uncommon' picture of the British monarch*
- *Queen's new hobby → effect on her behaviour → effect on her subjects / the equerry*

Conclusion
- *omniscient third-person-narrator → two perspectives (Queen, equerry)*
　…

3 Possible tasks for *Anforderungsbereich* III

a Discuss whether the British monarch is supposed to 'go public about feelings' (l. 19) considering his/her duties and function. (▶ SF 34: Argumentative writing)

b The Queen takes Cordelia's utterance as a starting point for her notebook entry (ll. 22f.). Finish her entry reflecting on her latest experience and self-image. (▶ SF 37: Doing a creative writing task)

▶ EP 3 Mediation

Mediating basically means to summarize information (from a written or oral text) in another language. (▶ SF 41: Mediation of written and oral texts). Note that a mediation is *not* a translation; i.e. you do *not* translate a text word for word.

Your task is normally embedded in some kind of context, so you have to consider the situation and your relationship to the addressee to find out what information to select from the original text and in what form to put it. *Form* here can refer to a specific *text type but also to a suitable *register.

To get the maximum number of points in your exam, it is helpful to know which criteria your teacher will apply when assessing your exam:

- **content:** selection of relevant aspects for the situation given (answers given to all the addressee's questions, but no superfluous information)
- **form:** choice of suitable text type and ability to apply its rules
- **appropriateness** of *style and *register for the given situation
- **powers of expression:** ability to deal with unknown words / technical terms or culture-specific concepts; lexical and syntactical flexibility, etc.
- **grammar:** amount and types of mistakes.

> ■ TIP
>
> Be aware of (cultural) misunderstandings, German idioms and false friends.
> (▶ CC 1–7) Do not translate word for word because cultural peculiarities often do not have a translation. Paraphrase.
> (▶ SF 6: Paraphrasing)

PRACTICE

Your British friend is coming to visit you. She has heard that a new Primark shop has just opened in your town and cannot wait to go there during her stay with you. You come across the article below.

Erschütternder Hilferuf in Kleid von Primark eingenäht

In westlichen Kleiderläden verführen bunte, billige Klamotten zum Kauf. Die Arbeitsbedingungen der Näherinnen in den indischen Textilfabriken sind dabei meist ganz weit weg. Nicht so für eine britische Primark-Kundin: Denn jemand hatte eine Botschaft in ihr Kleid genäht. Die britische Primark-Kundin Rebecca Gallagher hat überraschend erfahren, unter welchen Bedingungen ihr Kleid offenbar
5   hergestellt wurde, berichtet die „South Wales Evening Post online". Sie habe in ihrem zwölf Euro teuren Sommerkleid von Primark ein Etikett mit einer Nachricht gefunden. „Forced to work for exhausting hours", zu Deutsch etwa „gezwungen, stundenlang bis zur Erschöpfung zu arbeiten", sei handschriftlich auf dem Etikett gestanden, das jemand mit der Hand zwischen die anderen genäht hatte. Es sei ihr
10   aufgefallen, als sie nach der Waschanleitung geschaut habe, erzählte die 25-Jährige der Zeitung. Daraufhin habe sie gelobt, das Kleid nie wieder anzuziehen. Sie fühle sich schuldig und habe Angst, dass eine übermüdete Arbeiterin sich dafür in einem Sweatshop irgendwo in einem fernen Land quälen musste. „Um ehrlich zu sein, habe ich noch nie darüber nachgedacht, wie die Kleider hergestellt werden", sagte sie. „Aber das hat mich jetzt zum Nachdenken darüber gebracht, woher wir unsere
15   billigen Klamotten bekommen." Ein Primark-Sprecher sagte der Zeitung, ihm seien keine weiteren Vorfälle dieser Art bekannt. Trotzdem bat er um Rückgabe: „Wir wären der Kundin dankbar, wenn sie das Kleid an uns übergeben würde, damit wir untersuchen können, wie das Schildchen an das Kleid gelangte und ob dieser Sache weiter nachgegangen werden muss."

Vor mehr als einem Jahr stürzte das Rana Plaza in Bangladesch ein. Beim schwersten Unglück in
20   der Textilindustrie starben mehr als 1130 Menschen, mehr als 2500 wurden teils schwer verletzt.

Die Arbeitsbedingungen der Näherinnen, die dort zu Dumpinglöhnen Hosen, T-Shirts und Kleider für westliche Kunden herstellen, gerieten in die Kritik. Zu den Unternehmen, die in einer der Fabriken in dem Gebäude produzieren ließen, gehörte auch das irische Unternehmen Primark.

From: *Focus*, 25 June 2014

Possible mediation task

After reading the article, you are concerned about buying new clothes. Write an email to your friend (in English) in which you tell her what you have found out about working conditions in Asian textile factories.

Step 1: Look at the following pieces of information from the text and say whether you would include them in your email or not.

1 A British customer found a message sewn into her Primark dress saying 'forced to work for exhausting hours'.
2 The customer is 25-year-old Rebecca Gallagher.
3 She found the message when looking for the washing instructions.
4 The shopper feels guilty because of the exploitation of workers in clothes factories.
5 Primark asked the young woman to return the dress to find out how the label got there.
6 In 2013, more than 1130 people were killed when a factory which produced clothes for western companies collapsed in Bangladesh.

Step 2: Collect more information from the text that you consider relevant for your email, then structure your ideas. (▶ SF 5: Structuring information and ideas)

Step 3: Read the following model answer, which is not at all perfect. Say what might be improved.

> Hi there,
>
> I have a serious problem. Primark forces children to produce cheap clothes. I read that in an article in some newspaper. A woman discovered a label sewn in her Primark dress saying 'forced to work for exhausting hours'. She only paid €12 for the dress. There was also an accident in one of those sweatshops abroad. It's horrible, isn't it? I suggest we don't go there.
>
> Hope to hear from you soon!

Step 4: Write your email, bearing in mind the following points:

- form: email (fairly informal)
- addressee: a friend from the UK you do not know that well (→ don't be too informal!)
- situation: your friend wants to go to the new Primark shop, but you have found out about sweatshops and want to dissuade her.
  - Don't get right to the point: make polite small talk first, maybe tell her how happy you are about the visit.
  - Try to voice your doubts about the idea without offending your friend. You might suggest some kind of compromise.

▶ EP 4 Listening and viewing

Your exam task may be based on a short audio (e.g. an interview, a speech) or video (e.g. an interview, a documentary, an extract from a film) of about four minutes.

To prepare for this exam, use every opportuvnity you get to listen to spoken English. For instance, listen to BBC radio or watch your favourite British or American TV show on DVD or online in English. Start with English subtitles and switch them off when you feel ready. If possible, listen to a wide variety of speakers (different accents, different speeds, various topics).

In listening tasks, you will often only be asked to answer questions on *Anforderungsbereich I*, i.e. text comprehension (▶ EE 2.1), and they are often closed test formats such as multiple choice (▶ SF 7: Working with closed test formats; ▶ SF 22: Listening). Viewing tasks, but also some listening tasks, go beyond simple understanding and require you to analyse the film clip or audio, so make sure you are familiar with aspects to examine. (▶ SF 23: Analysing a film)

There is usually a standard exam procedure when it comes to listening or viewing:

Step 1: You get some time to read the instructions and further information and vocabulary, if provided. The questions will normally come in the same order as the information in the recording.

Step 2: First listening/viewing: you are allowed to write while listening/viewing, so start working on your tasks right away. Try to complete as much as possible.

Step 3: Time to work on the tasks: fill in missing information and/or read through the tasks again. Mark things you are not sure about and any gaps that are still there.

Step 4: Second listening/viewing: try to fill any gaps that might be left and check the answers you've already noted down.

Step 5: Time to complete your tasks and check your answers.

In a viewing activity your teacher might show you the video a third time.

TIP

Before listening/viewing:
- Read the instructions carefully and make sure you know what you have to focus on.
- Try to make predictions about the audio/video and the answers to the questions.

While listening/viewing:
- Read all answers, even if you are sure that you have found the correct one. The differences between the right and the wrong answers are often subtle or tricky.
- If you need to take notes, only jot down keywords or short phrases.
- If your task requires you to write a text, try to note down particular phrases from the audio/video and use them as quotes in your text.

After viewing/listening:
- Don't leave an item unanswered. If you don't know the answer, make an educated guess – you still stand a good chance of getting the credit for it (e.g. 25% in a multiple choice item with four options!)
- If you are asked to write a text, …
  - don't forget to use all the background information from the instructions.
  - back up your findings with concrete evidence, i.e. refer to relevant phrases or expressions used by a speaker/actor or describe special (cinematic) moments.

Listening   (▶ SF 22: Listening)

Former First Lady Hillary Rodham Clinton was US Secretary of State from 2008 to 2012. You are going to listen to an extract from an interview with her broadcast in 2014, in which she speaks about the challenges as a female Secretary of State and women's issues in general.

🎧 **CD3** 14

perseverance *Beharrlichkeit*
hostility *Feindseligkeit*
private capacity private life
inconsequential unimportant
**break through the highest glass
 ceiling** *die letzte Hürde nehmen*
renowned famous
assertive *durchsetzungsfähig*

1 Choose the correct answers. Sometimes more than one answer is correct.

  a On women as US Secretary of State:

    1 When Clinton came to office, three women had done the job of US Secretary of State before.

    2 Having a female Secretary of State has changed the way people perceive women considerably.

    3 In countries like the UK, a female US Secretary of State is nothing special.

    4 Hillary Clinton never got used to being the only woman in the room on meetings in some foreign countries.

  b To Clinton, making women and girls an important element of US foreign states policy is …

    1 a necessity   3 both a luxury and a necessity
    2 a luxury   4 neither a luxury nor a necessity.

  c During her fight for women's rights she was often faced with …

    1 hostility

    2 interest

    3 people rolling their eyes at her

    4 people who considered this topic an unimportant hobby horse of hers.

2 List three brutal actions that girls are confronted with in a lot of countries according to Clinton.

3 List two fields of life in which women still face challenges in Western civilization.

4 List two ways in which women break the law in Saudi Arabia.

5 How does Clinton decide if and how to speak out in cases where women are treated badly?

Viewing   (▶ SF 23: Analysing a film)

Margaret Thatcher was the first female British Prime Minister (1979–1990). Her nickname 'the Iron Lady' was coined because of her tough opposition towards the Soviet Union and socialism as such in the Cold War era. The scene from the film *The Iron Lady* (2011) that you are going to watch shows her with the members of her Cabinet discussing a new tax.

▶ **DVD**

council estate *(here)
(oft sehr armer) Wohnort*
resent sth. (strongly) dislike sth.
slacker *(infml) Faulenzer/in*
sovereignty *Souveränität*
concession *Zugeständnis*
beret type of French hat

1 Possible task for *Anforderungsbereich I*
Briefly sum up the content of the scene.

2 Possible tasks for *Anforderungsbereich II*

  a Examine Margaret Thatcher's character as presented in this scene. Focus on her attitudes and her behaviour towards the members of the Cabinet present. (▶ SF 35: Writing a character profile)

  b Analyse the cinematic devices employed to create this picture of Thatcher. (▶ SF 23: Analysing a film)

3 Possible tasks for *Anforderungsbereich III*

  a Assess Margaret Thatcher's leadership qualities as shown in this scene.

  b After the meeting, two Cabinet members talk about the incident, commenting on Thatcher's leadership qualities. Write their dialogue. (▶ SF 23: Doing a creative writing task)

▶ EP5 Speaking

Many exams nowadays are exclusively communication exams or they may include a part in which you have to prove your communicative capacity. Preparing for and successfully passing a speaking exam is different from a written exam because you need to use different skills and strategies. (▶ SF24 – SF28)

Usually, oral exams consist of two parts which are thematically linked, a monologue and a dialogue:

Monologue	Dialogue
In this part, you are asked to give a presentation based on e.g. a diagram, statistics, picture, cartoon, quote or short text.	In the second part, you are asked to interact with a partner or a group of students in a role-play or a discussion. It may be based on the material you have worked on for the monologue. Your fellow students have probably dealt with similar material.

To prepare for your exam, ask your teacher about the specific conditions of your exam, e.g.
- What kind of prompts can you expect (i.e. cartoons, pictures, quotes, etc.)?
- Will you be given time to prepare only the monologue or both parts?
- If there is preparation time for the dialogue, will it be at the very beginning or shortly before the dialogue?
- How long will the preparation time be?
- How long will both parts of the exam be?
- How many people will take part in the dialogue?
- Will the participants in the dialogue be other students or teachers?

To get the maximum number of points in your exam, it is helpful to know which criteria you teacher will apply when assessing your exam:
- **communicative strategies** (structure, eye contact, interaction with partners, etc.)
- **pronunciation** (clarity, fluency, intonation, accuracy)
- **powers of expression** (choice of words, ability to deal with unknown words/technical terms, flexibility, etc.)
- **grammar:** amount and types of mistakes
- **content:** quality and meaningfulness of statements/arguments, etc.

■ TIP

Before the exam:
- Practise monologues by describing a picture to a fellow student. (▶ SF24: Giving a presentation)
- Learn phrases which you can use during presentations, speeches or discussions (cf. the table on p.357).
- Study your classroom material and look for controversial issues which could be discussed, then collect arguments for and against them.
- Watch (current) political debates online to get an idea of the culture of reflection and debate.

In the exam:
- If there is a preparation time, use it to arrange your material so that you can use it effectively. Structure your ideas clearly. Use clear handwriting. Use abbreviations, keywords, etc. (▶ SF5: Structuring information and ideas)
- You may have to adopt a role or defend a position which you don't like. Try to disregard your personal opinion, stick to the facts and give evidence if possible.
- In the dialogue part, take your time to react but do not hesitate too long. (▶ SF27: Having a discussion)
- Ask for clarification of crucial points. Be provocative and polite at the same time; avoid attacks or insults.
- Don't be too emotional.
- Use appropriate body language and facial expressions.
- Choose the right moment to sum up your points and introduce a new aspect.

Stages of conversation

Every communicative situation consists of different stages. If you know about these stages and useful expressions to use, you can keep a conversation going and make it successful:

Stage of conversation	Explanation	Phrases
starting a conversation	You either introduce the situation or explain the topic.	Well, our topic seems to be very controversial … Why don't we … first? Recently, I heard that somebody …
expressing one's opinion	You elaborate the arguments concerning the topic.	I'm convinced that … It seems to me that … To me …
involving a partner	You invite a partner who so far hasn't contributed much to the conversation.	What do you think about …? Is there anything you'd like to add? How about you? Would you agree with that?
contradicting	You politely express that you have an opposing opinion.	That's not the way I see it. That is true to a certain extent but …
interrupting	You try to find your way into the conversation without cutting the other person short.	Sorry to interrupt you but … May I interrupt you for a moment, please?
asking for clarification	You are not sure that you have understood your partner correctly.	Excuse me, I didn't quite catch your point about … Do you mean …? Sorry, could you say that again, please?
gaining time to think	You need time to think or work on your own argumentation.	Well, that's a good point, but I think … Well, now, let me see … It's difficult to say exactly, but … If I understood the question correctly, … I don't know whether this is what you meant, but …
summing up	You bring the conversation to an end, e.g. by mentioning the most important aspects or giving a view into the future or establishing a compromise.	So, to sum up … In brief … To cut a long story short …

·····▶

1 Monologue: preparing and giving a presentation (▶SF 24: Giving a presentation)
   a Work with a partner. Each of you choose one of the cartoons below, then prepare a presentation in which you comment on it.
   b First partner A presents his/her cartoon, then Partner B.

'THIS DESIGNER BABY IS NO LONGER FASHIONABLE'

2 Dialogue: discussing a topic (▶SF 27: Having a discussion)
   You are going to have a discussion on the benefits and dangers of scientific progress.
   a Work with a partner. Read the role cards below, then decide who is going to take which role.

Partner A	Partner B
Your little brother had leukemia and the doctors were able to treat it with a bone marrow transplant[1]. You are glad about scientific progress and the possibility that it might one day help to prevent leukemia.	You suffer from strong allergic reactions to certain foods and you suspect it's because you might have eaten genetically modified soy[2]. You are afraid of fast progress in science because you fear that its side effects cause more harm than good.

   b Collect arguments for your position. Also collect counter-arguments and think of possible ways to refute them. You might tackle the following issues: pre-implantation genetic diagnosis, designer babies, genetically modified food, genetic engineering in health care, stem cell research, etc.
   c Discuss the topic for about 10–15 minutes. Begin by introducing yourself and your general standpoint. You can take your cartoon as a starting point for the debate.

---

[1] **bone marrow transplant** *Rückenmarksspende*   [2] **soy** *Soja*

▶ EP6 Closed test formats

In many exams in and after school there are special forms of tests that are called 'closed test formats' (▶SF7: Working with closed test formats). In closed test formats, you don't write at all, but just indicate which of the given solutions is correct or which items go together.

Closed test **formats** include:
- multiple choice tests with one or more correct answer/s
- true/false statements
- matching: matching questions, statements or headings to different texts or sections of a text
- gapped text: locating and replacing missing segments of a text

Before an exam, ask your teacher which closed test formats you might expect.

Closed test formats tend to occur mostly in listening and reading comprehension tasks (▶EP2.1, EP4). In language tests such as TOEFL, Cambridge Certificate and TELC they may also be used for grammar or vocabulary.

To be successful in a closed test format, the following **skills** may be helpful:
- strategies of dealing with unknown words (▶SF1: Dealing with unknown or new words)
- the ability to identify different *text types and to know what to expect from them. For example, if you follow a discussion, you can expect the speakers to have different opinions on a topic.
- knowledge about typical text structures and the use of linking words, which may indicate e.g. a contrast, an addition, a conclusion (▶SF5: Structuring information and ideas; ▶SF38: Writing a well-structured text).

If you are taking part in a test for a language certificate such as TOEFL, you should try to get information from this organization. Look for sample questions to get a better idea of what to expect in the exam. Since some of these tests are computer-based, you should get some computer practice in how to handle them.

■ TIP

- Read the instructions carefully and make sure you know what you have to focus on.
- Try to make predictions about the listening/reading text and about the answers to the questions.
- Read all answers, even if you are sure that you have found the correct one. The differences between the right and the wrong answers are often subtle or tricky.
- Fill in answers to questions that you are sure about straight away. If you are unsure, leave the item aside and come back to it later.
- Don't skip questions you cannot answer. Make educated guesses – you still stand a good chance of getting the credit for a question (e.g. 25% in a multiple choice item with four options!).

Glossary

When looking for a term in the Glossary, go to the alphabetical list of terms on p. 376 to find its exact page. An asterisk (*) before a term indicates that it is explained in the Glossary.

Literary texts

▶ Fiction

A fictional text is an imaginative work in which an author ['ɔːθə] creates his or her own world and/or presents an invented story. The reader is expected to accept this world or story as existing or true (this is called suspension of disbelief). Fiction can take different forms. The main types are *narrative prose (e.g. *novels, *short stories) and *drama.

Fiction usually comprises a variety of elements, such as *characters, *action and plot, *setting and *atmosphere. The *mode [məʊd] of presentation (scenic or panoramic) and the *point of view adopted (first-person or third-person, limited or unlimited, *reliable or *unreliable *narrator) play a central role in how the reader reacts to the story.

A literary text is often structured and held together by a specific theme [θiːm] or a so-called motif [məʊ'tiːf], which may be a recurring image or a specific phrase or sentence.

▶ Narrative prose

A narrative ['nærətɪv] prose text is a *fictional text which is told by a *narrator and is written in prose [prəʊz], i.e. writing that is formed by sentences in a continuous flow and is broken up only by paragraphs (cf. verse [vɜːs], which is used in poetry and refers to a single line of a poem, or a *stanza). Typical examples of narrative prose are *novels and *short stories. Fiction can further be subdivided by aspects of content (e.g. *coming-of-age stories or *fables).

novel ['nɒvl] *Roman* ■ TROUBLE SPOT **novel** = Roman Not: ~~Novelle~~	A novel is a long and complex fictional narrative text often divided into chapters. The storyline and structure of a novel are normally more complicated than those of shorter fictional works and, accordingly, there may be greater variety and a more detailed development of *characters and *setting (i.e. the time and the place). In every novel the author must decide from which *point of view the story will be told. In some cases there is more than one *narrator. No other art form can recreate life on the same scale as the novel with its almost unlimited possibilities.
short story [ˌʃɔːt'stɔːri] *Kurzgeschichte*	There is no generally accepted definition of the short story that clearly separates it from other narrative texts like the *novel. However, there are some elements that can be regarded as characteristic. Most short stories can be read at one sitting and concentrate on one *character, situation, dilemma or problem. In a short story the characters, the situation, etc. are not fully developed (unlike in a novel); the focus is on one single aspect which undergoes a change in the course of the story. There are different types of short stories, e.g. the *coming-of-age story or the slice of life story (which shows just one particular aspect of everyday life).
microfiction, **flash fiction** *Kürzestgeschichte*	Microfiction (or flash fiction) is an extremely short fictional text. It refers to a new literary genre ['ʒɒ̃rə, 'ʒɒnrə] that originates from the *short story. Although there is no general agreement regarding its length, microfiction is much shorter than a short story and usually does not exceed one thousand words.

fable *Fabel*	A fable is a short narrative text in which animals represent human types or act like human beings. Fables are usually didactic since they intend to teach a moral lesson, make a satirical comment or illustrate some general truth. A moral may be understood from the text or there may be a moral (epilogue ['epɪlɒg]) at the end, which in modern fables is often *ironic.
coming-of-age story *Entwicklungsroman,* *Initiationsgeschichte*	A coming-of-age story is a *short story or *novel in which the process of growing up is portrayed. Usually the *protagonist is a child / an adolescent undergoing an experience which changes his/her outlook on life and marks an important stage in his/her development towards adulthood. It is also called story of initiation.
frame story *Rahmenhandlung*	A frame story is a *novel or *short story which contains one or more quite independent stories within it. The main story provides the frame for the other stories. Often the main story consists of a *character in one *setting recounting another story in another setting.

▶ Poetry

A poem is a piece of creative writing structured by lines and rhythm ['rɪðəm] (i.e. the arrangement of stressed and unstressed syllables in a line). The lines of a poem are often arranged into groups called stanzas ['stænzəs]. Phrases or lines repeated at intervals throughout a poem form the refrain [rɪ'freɪn]. To emphasize the structure and to create certain effects, traditional poets frequently make use of *rhyme. Modern poetry often uses free verse [ˌfriː 'vɜːs], which makes little use of rhyme. The poetry comes from *repetition, *imagery and the arrangement of words and stresses in the poem. Poems are often lyrical ['lɪrɪkl] (i.e. they express personal thoughts and feelings), but they can also be narrative (i.e. they tell a story). The speaker is the voice in which a poem is spoken, especially when the personal pronoun *I* is used. This speaker is not always identical with the voice of the poet.

sonnet ['sɒnɪt] *Sonett*	A sonnet is a special form of a poem that consists of 14 lines. Sonnets became popular in England in the 17th century and were mostly used for love poetry, but later they came to embrace a wide number of themes. There are various types of sonnets with different structures and forms. Shakespeare's sonnets comprise three quatrains ['kwɒtreɪns] (i.e. four lines with a shared rhyme scheme) and a couplet ['kʌplət] (i.e. two successive lines which rhyme). The couplet has a rhyme scheme that differs from the rest of the sonnet and it is used to sum up the theme or thought. The couplet is usually accompanied by the volta ['vɒltə], i.e. the turning point in a sonnet, which can be identified by words like *but*, *yet* or *and yet*. *Example:* William Shakespeare, 'Sonnet 116'; cf. *Context*, p. 48
shape poem, concrete poem ['kɒŋkriːt] *konkrete Poesie*	A shape poem (also called a concrete poem) is a poem in which the printed words form a shape or picture. The shape usually reflects the theme or contents of the poem.
rhyme [raɪm] *Reim*	Rhyme is the similarity of sounds between certain words (especially stressed syllables), usually at the end of lines. When identifying the rhyme scheme ['raɪm skiːm] (i.e. which words at the end of the lines rhyme), it is usual to use small letters to indicate that words share a rhyme. If e.g. the words *abide*, *thee*, *wide* and *see* occur respectively at the end of four successive lines, the rhyme scheme is written as **a b a b** (this pattern is called alternate rhyme [ɔːl'tɜːnət]). If *abide*, *wide*, *thee*, and *see* occur respectively at the end of four successive lines, the rhyme scheme is written **a a b b** (this pattern is called rhyming couplets). Other letters are then used for other rhymes.

·····▶

| metre ['miːtə] Metrum, Versmaß | Metre is the regular rhythm of the words in a poem. Traditionally, this is achieved by the arrangement of stressed and unstressed syllables in the line of a poem. The most common metre in English is the iambic pentameter [aɪˈæmbɪk penˈtæmɪtə], which consists of a line of five feet (each foot consists of an unstressed syllable followed by a stressed syllable). | *Example:*

 O *no*! It *is* an *ev*-er *fix*-ed *mark*

 From: William Shakespeare, 'Sonnet 116'; cf.*Context*, p.48

 The syllables **in bold** are stressed. |

▶ Drama

A drama or play is written to be performed by actors or actresses in a theatre, in a film, on TV or on the radio. The author of a play is called a playwright ['pleɪraɪt] or dramatist ['dræmətɪst] while a scriptwriter creates scripts for films and television. Plays are usually divided into several acts (in classical drama, there were usually five acts, but modern plays normally consist of three and sometimes of only one act). An act may be subdivided into scenes.

A scene [siːn] is a smaller unit of action in which there is no change of place or break in time. The actors take on roles of *characters, perform the *action and express themselves in the form of dialogues, monologues or soliloquies. While a dialogue ['daɪəlɒg] involves at least two actors engaged in a conversation, the monologue ['mɒnəlɒg] is a lengthy speech by just one character in the company of others. The soliloquy [səˈlɪləkwi] differs from the monologue as it is spoken by one person who is alone on stage. It can give the audience more knowledge of events or individuals than the other characters and actions can take on different meanings for the audience than for the other characters of the play (this literary device is called dramatic irony). The actors' way of speaking, their appearance and their movements, as well as the *setting, the arrangement of props (i.e. all kinds of objects used by actors on stage or in a film), the sound and lighting, etc. are often given in the stage directions – this helps an acting company perform a play.

tragedy ['trædʒədi] Tragödie, Trauerspiel	A tragedy is a type of *drama in which the *protagonist passes through a series of misfortunes towards his or her downfall. Usually the downfall is brought about partly by the protagonist's own fault, e.g. through too much pride, weakness, uncertainty, etc. *Example:* William Shakespeare, *Macbeth*; cf.*Context*, pp.39f.
comedy ['kɒmədi] Komödie, Lustspiel	A comedy is a type of *drama which deals with a light topic or a more serious one in an amusing way. A comedy always has a happy ending. *Example:* William Shakespeare, *The Taming of the Shrew*; cf.*Context*, pp.45f.
feature film ['fiːtʃə] Spielfilm	A feature film is a full-length film that has a story and *characters, who are played by actors. A feature film is based on a film script, which the director then turns into a film. Important elements in a film are the dialogue, the use of camera techniques and the acting.
TV/radio series ['sɪəriːz] Fernseh-/Radioserie	A series is a regular programme on TV or radio about the lives and problems of a *character or, more usually, a group of characters. A series may centre on a couple or family life or a leading character's career, and some involve magic and/or fantasy. Each programme is self-contained, i.e. it deals with a particular issue or storyline which is concluded at the end of the programme. The lives of the characters evolve slowly over the course of a series. *Example: Downton Abbey*; cf.*Context*, p.73

sitcom *Sitcom*	A sitcom (= *situation comedy*) is a comic TV/radio *series which usually centres around a *character or group of characters. They are often stereotypes as they do not evolve over the series. It may be filmed in front of a live audience or have canned laughter added to make the audience aware of or to reinforce the funny lines.
soap (opera) *'Seifenoper'*	A soap (= *soap opera*) is a regular TV or radio programme about the everyday lives of a group of people. The storyline of a soap, unlike that of a normal TV/radio *series, develops from programme to programme and may often end with a cliffhanger ['klɪfhæŋə] (i.e. an exciting situation that makes you want to know what will happen next) to encourage the audience to tune in to the next episode.

▶ Narrator

The narrator [nəˈreɪtə] is the voice or *character who tells the story and is part of the fictional world created by the author. There are three types of narrator:

first-person narrator *Ich-Erzähler*	The narrator is a *character in the story and refers to him- or herself as *I*. The reader must take care when reading the text, as only one person's point of view is given. *Example:* I'd attended school in the real world up until the sixth grade. It hadn't been a very pleasant experience. From: Ernest Cline, *Ready Player One*, 2012, p. 30; cf. *Context*, p. 188, ll. 1–2
third-person narrator *personaler/auktorialer Erzähler*	The narrator is not a *character in the story and refers to the characters as *he, she* or *they* or by their names. *Example:* It was with some relief that she got back into the coach and reached behind the cushion for her book. It was not there. Steadfastly waving as they rumbled along, she surreptitiously felt behind the other cushions. From: Alan Bennett, *The Uncommon Reader*, 2008, p. 34; cf. *Context*, p. 58, ll. 34–36 In this example, the narrator is a third-person narrator as he or she is not part of the fictional world and refers to the *protagonist by using the personal pronoun *she* (= the Queen). This excerpt is, however, told from the Queen's point of view (i.e. there is a *limited point of view) as the readers experience the story from her perspective. They are informed about her feelings and are also puzzled about the disappearance of her book.
omniscient narrator [ɒmˈnɪsɪənt] *allwissender Erzähler*	The narrator has an *unlimited point of view, i.e. he or she can move freely in place and time and enter the minds of the *characters at will.

▶ Point of view

The point of view is the perspective from which *characters, events, etc. are presented in a *fictional story. This has an important effect on the reader: for example, we tend to respond more sympathetically to a character whose mind we enter, as we experience for ourselves what he or she goes through. A fictional work can have several points of view (depending on the *narrator):

·····▶

limited point of view	A *first-person narrator can have a limited point of view: a *character in fictional work does not know everything that occurs, therefore he or she imposes his or her understanding and interpretation on the action.
	A *third-person narrator can have a limited point of view: the *narrator looks at the events and characters from the perspective of one of the *characters or from the outside (as an observer narrator) and so does not have access to the thoughts and feelings of all the characters.
unlimited point of view	A third-person narrator can have an unlimited point of view: the narrator can move freely in place and time and enter the minds of the *characters at will (here we speak of an omniscient narrator [ɒmˈnɪsɪənt]).

Often, the point of view changes to make for more interesting reading. A reader must ask him- or herself how reliable a narrator is. Often one cannot take everything in a fictional work at face value:

| reliable narrator [rɪˈlaɪəbl] | The reader may take everything the *narrator tells at face value. |
| unreliable narrator [ˌʌnrɪˈlaɪəbl] | The reader must find out just how much of what the *narrator says can be accepted. *First-person narrators are usually unreliable as they give only one perspective on the action and the *characters. |

▶ Mode of presentation

The way a writer narrates events is known as mode of presentation. There are two modes of presentation, and usually a combination of both is used in a narrative text:

| scenic presentation | If the author shows an event in detail as it occurs, using dialogue, depicting thoughts and emotions, describing a scene, etc., he or she uses scenic presentation (also known as showing).
Example: |

> When they arrived at the palace she had a word with Grant, the young footman in charge, who said that while ma'am had been in the Lords the sniffer dogs had been round and security had confiscated[1] the book. He thought it had probably been exploded.
> 'Exploded?' said the Queen. 'But it was Anita Brookner.'[2]
> The young man, who seemed remarkably undeferential[3], said security may have thought it was a device.
> The Queen said: 'Yes. That is exactly what it is. A book is a device to ignite[4] the imagination.'
>
> ---
> [1]**confiscate sth.** take sth. away [2]**Anita Brookner** (1928–2016) British novelist and art historian [3]**undeferential** showing no respect [4]**ignite sth.** *etwas entzünden*

5

From: Alan Bennett, *The Uncommon Reader*, 2008, p. 34

| interior monologue [ɪnˈtɪərɪə ˈmɒnəlɒg] *innerer Monolog* | This is a particular kind of *scenic presentation in which the author depicts the thoughts and feelings passing through a *character's mind. Often an interior monologue does not follow a chronological [ˌkrɒnəˈlɒdʒɪkl] order, since when people think, their thoughts jump from one subject to another. Interior monologues are normally narrated in the present tense. However, it is more common to find reported thought, in which the thoughts are presented as reported speech (i.e. in the past tense). |

panoramic presentation	If the author tells the story as a condensed series of events, summarizing in a few sentences what happens over a longer period of time (e.g. an hour, a week, months), he or she uses panoramic presentation (also known as 'telling'). *Example:*

> For me, school had been a Darwinian exercise. A daily gauntlet[1] of ridicule, abuse, and isolation. By the time I entered sixth grade, I was beginning to wonder if I'd be able to maintain my sanity[2] until graduation, still six long years away.
>
> ---
> [1] **(run a) gauntlet** ['gɔːntlət] deal with a lot of people criticizing or attacking you
> [2] **sanity** ['sænəti] mental health

From: Ernest Cline, *Ready Player One*, 2012, p. 31; cf. *Context*, p. 188, ll. 21–23

▶ Characters

Characters ['kærəktəz] are the people in a fictional text. They are usually presented through their actions, speech and thoughts as well as by description. The main character in a story is called the protagonist [prə'tægənɪst]. There are generally speaking two types of characters in *fictional works:

round character	A round character may be similar to real individuals and have several traits and behave in a way that is life-like. A round character usually changes in the course of a story. The main character in a story, the protagonist, is almost always a round character.
flat character	A flat character has only a limited number of traits or represents only a single quality. A crude representation of a character which is meant to be laughed at is called a caricature.

> **■ TROUBLE SPOT**
>
> When talking about the characters in a fictional text, do not use the words *people* or *person*.

▶ Characterization

Characterization [ˌkærəktəraɪ'zeɪʃn] is the way in which the author presents his or her characters. We usually distinguish between two kinds of characterization, which are often combined by authors in their presentation of the characters.

direct [də'rekt, dɪ'-, daɪ'-] or **explicit characterization**	The reader is told about a character's personality directly by a) the *narrator, b) another character or c) the character him- or herself.	*Example:*

> But McNulty's eyes were scary.
>
> From: Carl Deuker, *Payback Time*, 2010, p. 24; cf. p. 175, l. 44

indirect [ˌɪndə'rekt, ˌɪndaɪ'rekt] or **implicit characterization**	The reader is expected to draw conclusions about a character by studying his or her behaviour, opinions, choice of words and/or way of talking. *Example:*

> I cleared my throat. 'How about we get started? I've got some questions. First –' 'No, no, no,' McNulty said, pointing the pencil at me again. 'No questions – not today, not ever. This job

·····▶

takes forever and pays peanuts. Here's how it works. You write down or tape what I tell you. When I'm done, jazz[1] it up whatever you want, but never make me, my coaches, or my players look bad. Understand?'

[1]**jazz sth. up** (*infml*) make sth. more interesting or attractive

From: Carl Deuker, *Payback Time*, 2010, p. 24; cf. *Context*, p. 174, ll. 33–37

■ TROUBLE SPOT

An author *characterizes* somebody, i.e. invents the traits of a character. A reader *describes the character* of somebody when talking about his or her traits.

■ LANGUAGE HELP

- main/central/major character/figure
- minor/secondary character/figure
- hero/heroine

▶ Action

Action ['ækʃn] is everything that happens in a *fictional story. Action may be on two levels:

external action [ɪk'stɜːnl]	The author describes what the *characters do and the events that take place. *Example:* [...] she got back into the coach and reached behind the cushion for her book. It was not there. Steadfastly waving as they rumbled along, she surreptitiously[1] felt behind the other cushions. [1]**surreptitious** subtle From: Alan Bennett, *The Uncommon Reader*, 2008, p. 34
internal action	The author describes what is going on in the minds of the *characters, i.e. the reader is shown the thoughts of the characters. *Example:* She was dreading the two hours the whole thing was due to take, though fortunately they were in the coach, not the open carriage, so she could take along her book. From: Alan Bennett, *The Uncommon Reader*, 2008, p. 32

▶ Plot

Plot [plɒt] refers to the structure of events in a *fictional story. The story is usually told through cause and effect. The English novelist E.M. Forster described plot in these terms: '"The king died and then the queen died" is a story. "The king died and then the queen died of grief", is a plot.' (*Aspects of the Novel*, 1927). The plot usually develops in a number of stages:

1. **exposition** [ˌekspə'zɪʃn]	The *characters, theme, *setting, etc. are introduced.
2. **rising action**	A conflict ['kɒnflɪkt] is developed (i.e. the struggle or opposition between different forces, characters, etc.).
3. **climax** ['klaɪmæks]	The conflict reaches its highest point.
4. **turning point**	There is a change in the conflict or *suspense.
5. **falling action**	The *suspense is reduced.

6. **denouement** [deɪ'nuːmõ] (also known as the **solution** [sə'luːʃn])	Some resolution of the conflict is achieved.
which may also be: **surprise ending**	The reader's expectations concerning the course of the story are not fulfilled but instead an unexpected solution of the conflict is presented.
or instead: **open ending**	The conflict is not fully resolved and the reader is left wondering what might happen next.

A plot will have some element of *suspense and *tension. In order to create suspense or to make a story more exciting, authors also make use of flashbacks and foreshadowing:

suspense [sə'spens] *Spannung*	Suspense is created when the reader does not know the outcome of a conflict or of the action.
tension ['tenʃn] *(An)spannung*	Tension is the feeling evoked in the reader when a story/drama is full of *suspense, i.e. the reader is curious about what will happen.
flashback ['flæʃbæk] *Rückblende*	Authors do not always tell their stories strictly chronologically [ˌkrɒnə'lɒdʒɪkli]. In some stories the authors make use of flashbacks, i.e. the *narrator goes back into the past to describe a scene that has relevance to the plot.
foreshadowing [fɔː'ʃædəʊɪŋ] *Vorwegnahme*	Foreshadowing (also called anticipation) is the technique of hinting at later events in a *fictional text so that the reader is prepared for them or can anticipate them. *Example:* In William Shakespeare's *Macbeth*, the three witches allow the audience to believe that Macbeth will become king.

■ TROUBLE SPOT

happy ending
Not = ~~happy end~~

■ LANGUAGE HELP

- open/surprise/unexpected/happy/sad/tragic ending
- centre around sth.
- a conflict between … and …

▶ **Atmosphere**

Atmosphere ['ætməsfɪə] is the feeling or mood created by an author in his or her work. The *setting, use of language and *characterization all contribute to the atmosphere of a work.	*Example:*
	One of the Queen's recurrent royal responsibilities was to open Parliament, an obligation she had never previously found particularly burdensome[1] and actually rather enjoyed: to be driven down the Mall[2] on a bright autumn morning even after fifty years was something of a treat.
	[1]**burdensome** implying hard work [2]**the Mall** road leading to Buckingham Palace

From: Alan Bennett, *The Uncommon Reader*, 2008, p. 32; cf. *Context*, p. 58, ll. 1–4

Here the description of the Queen's drive down the Mall together with the bright autumn morning creates a positive atmosphere.

▶ Setting

Setting is the time and place in which a literary work takes place. The setting can have symbolic overtones; it may serve to reveal something about the characters and also contribute to the *atmosphere of the story. *Example:* The extract quoted above from the novel *The Uncommon Reader* by Alan Bennett (cf. Context p. 58, ll. 1–4) is set in contemporary Britain on a sunny autumn morning. The season contributes to the positive and light-hearted atmosphere of the story.

Non-fictional texts

▶ Non-fiction

A non-fictional [ˌnɒn ˈfɪkʃənl] text (e.g. *news story, *advertisement, *speech, *letter, etc.) normally refers to the real world whereas a *literary text creates its own fictional world. Non-fictional texts may serve a variety of practical purposes, e.g. to inform, persuade, express personal opinions, criticize, etc. There is a variety of non-fictional text types:

news story, news(paper) article *Zeitungs-bericht*	The terms *news story, news(paper) article*, *news item* and *news report* can be used inter-changeably to refer to reports of recent events of general interest or to a specific topic that appear in print or digitally. They can be of any length. In theory, they are meant to be objective and unbiased presentations of the facts, providing answers to the five w's, i.e. the questions *who?, what?, when?, where?* and *why?* and often quoting sources or people as support. In practice, however, totally impartial reporting is impossible. The choice of words, the *style and *tone, the choice of detail and examples, the emphasis [ˈemfəsɪs] given to certain aspects of the story, the position of the article in the paper and on the page, the headline and layout all contribute to influence the reader. There are two common formulas used in news stories: a) The pyramid, in which the most important item or element in the story is reported first and then the rest of the information is offered in descending order of importance. b) The Wall Street Journal formula, in which the news story starts with a particular (usually personal) example to attract the reader's attention before the topic is discussed. It differs from a *feature story in that the latter puts more emphasis on the personal account in order to illustrate a topic, while the former uses the personal account merely to attract the attention of the reader.
feature story [ˈfiːtʃə] *Zeitungs-reportage*	A feature story deals with a topic by concentrating on a particular person or on particular people. It often takes an individual case as its starting point to discuss the different aspects of the topic on a personal level and leaves the reader to draw more general conclusions from this individual case. The writer of a feature story makes use of direct quotes from the people involved in the story and relies on first-hand reporting, i.e. the journalist writes mostly about things and people he or she has actually encountered. A feature story often opens with the description of an event or a person in order to attract the reader's attention.
editorial [ˌedɪˈtɔːriəl] *Leitartikel*	An editorial (in British English also known as a *leading article* or *leader*) is an article that expresses the opinion of the newspaper's editor or editorial team about an item of news or a political or social issue, etc. In American usage an editorial can also be a comment [ˈkɒment] on radio or television that expresses the opinion of the station or network. Unlike *columns, editorials are not supposed to be personal and do not appear with a byline, i.e. with a line that gives the writer's name.

column ['kɒləm] *Kolumne*	a) *Column* is the term used for any of the vertical sections into which the printed page of a newspaper is divided. b) *Column* is the term used for a regular item in a newspaper or magazine which either deals with a particular subject (e.g. gardening, gossip, financial, agony column) or is written by a particular writer (called a columnist). Columnists often write highly personal essays on topics of their choosing. Unlike *editorials, columns appear with a byline, i.e. with a line that gives the writer's name.
speech *Rede,* *Ansprache*	A speech is an address delivered to an audience. A speaker may try to establish contact with his or her listeners in various ways: by flattering them, addressing them directly (direct address) or using the first person plural (e.g. *we, our*) to involve them in what he or she is saying. A speaker may appeal to shared experiences and values, e.g. by quoting from or alluding to sources such as the Bible or history. A speaker often uses *stylistic devices to heighten the impact of what he or she is saying. Contrast ['kɒntrɑːst] may be used to highlight differences between the speaker and his or her opponents. *Repetition and *alliteration often help the audience follow the speech and remember key ideas and phrases. *Example:* '9/11 – A game changer'; cf. *Context* pp. 196f.
essay *Essay*	An essay is a text form in which the writer expresses his or her personal views on some topic. Essays can vary widely in length, subject matter and *tone, some being serious and others light-hearted and entertaining.
letter *Brief*	There are many types of letters. They can be personal or business-oriented, depending on the relationship between the sender and receiver, the occasion and the purpose of the letter. Letters are a very flexible text form and comprise thank-you notes, emails, covering letters (in American English, *cover letters*), letters of complaint, *letters to the editor, etc. The beginnings and endings of letters follow certain conventions. Usually, letters consist of the following parts: **1** the address of the sender (and in the case of a business letter, the address of the recipient), **2** the date, **3** the salutation (e.g. *Dear Mark*), **4** the body of the letter, i.e. the information the sender wants to convey, **5** a conventional phrase to close the letter (e.g. *Yours faithfully, Yours sincerely, Love*) and **6** the signature. *Example:* the letter from Chetan Bhagat to Gandhi; cf. *Context* pp. 81f.
letter to the editor *Leserbrief*	A letter to the editor is a letter in which a reader expresses his or her opinion concerning an article in a newspaper/magazine or a problem which is of public interest. The letter may criticize or support an article, or state a personal opinion concerning a topic which is being discussed in public or attract the attention of other readers to a topic that has been ignored or is worthy of attention.
biography [baɪ'ɒɡrəfi] *Biografie*	A biography is a book or text written by one person about the life of another person. If the person writes his or her own life story, this is referred to as an autobiography [ˌɔːtəbaɪ'ɒɡrəfi]. Usually the biography belongs to the genre of *non-fiction as it portrays the life of a person that really exists/existed. However, there are also *fictional biographies, where the author invents a *character and his life story (e.g. *Robinson Crusoe*).
blurb [blɜːb] *Umschlagtext,* *Klappentext*	A blurb is the short promotional text on the back cover of a book or a DVD case.
advertisement [əd'vɜːtɪsmənt] *Werbung, An-* *zeige, Annonce*	An advertisement (informally also called an *advert* or *ad*) is a text which attempts to persuade people to do something (e.g. buy a particular product or contribute money to a cause). It normally consists of pictures and text (called *copy*) and is designed to catch the attention of the reader through its layout.

·····▶

Common elements of advertisements are *wordplay in the title or headings and *humour to win the sympathy of the reader. Advertisers often use the AIDA formula (**A**ttention, **I**nterest, **D**esire, **A**ction) in their advertisements. Newspaper or magazine advertisements dealing with job offers, buying, selling or renting something, etc. are called *small* or *classified ads.* Advertisements on the radio or on television are known as *commercials*.

blog [blɒg] *Blog*	A blog is a regularly updated website containing 'blog posts' or 'blog entries' that publish information or discussions on current issues or topics. These blog posts normally appear in reverse chronological order on the website. On most blogs, readers can leave comments and interact with other users. Originally blogs were created by an individual or a small group of people and consisted of informal, diary-style entries. The growing popularity of blogs has led to the appearance of more professional blogs, which are written by larger numbers of authors and supported by newspapers, companies, universities and similar institutions with branding, advertising, educational or informative functions.
cartoon *Karikatur,* *Cartoon*	A cartoon is an amusing drawing in a newspaper or magazine that deals with human nature or a current political or social issue. Complex issues are reduced to memorable pictures. Cartoons often include captions or speech bubbles. Techniques employed by cartoonists include caricature ['kærɪkətʃʊə], *exaggeration, *wordplay and the use of *symbols. Cartoons usually presuppose that the reader has background knowledge of the political, social and cultural issues being dealt with, which often makes them difficult for the non-native reader to understand. *Example:* 'Being five. A boy and his blog'; cf. *Context*, p.182

Style and Language

 ## Style

Style [staɪl] is the way in which a text is written. In order to examine the style of a text it is necessary to examine aspects such as the *register, the *diction and the *tone of the text, as well as the grammar and the sentence structures used in the text.

tone [təʊn] *Ton(fall)*	Tone is the way in which a writer treats his or her topic, thereby reflecting his or her emotional attitude towards that topic and also towards the reader. The tone can be formal, intimate, solemn, playful, serious, ironic (cf. *irony), humorous (cf. *humour), angry, etc.
humour ['hju:mə] *Humor*	Humour is based on the human ability to see and laugh at the strangeness of a *character, an action or comment, etc. because it is unexpected or unsuitable in a particular situation. At one end of the spectrum, humour is gentle, understanding and tolerant and makes the reader smile at human weaknesses; at the other end, it is divisive, bitter or sarcastic, evoking contempt and moral indignation at human vices and corruption. *Example:* ... [The Queen] had got quite good at reading and waving, the trick being to keep the book below the level of the window and to keep focused on it and not on the crowds. From: Alan Bennett, *The Uncommon Reader*, 2008, p.32; cf. *Context*, p.58, ll.7–9 Here the Queen's well-known behaviour of waving at the crowd is ridiculed by the fact that she is reading a book at the same time.

diction *Diktion,* *Ausdruck,* *Wortwahl*	Diction is the words a writer chooses for his or her text. Diction is very important as words influence the reader or listener. In many argumentative texts, for example, the writer will use words that have a positive connotation [ˌkɒnəˈteɪʃn] (i.e. the associations a word has beyond its literal or dictionary meaning) to support his or her arguments, or words with negative connotations to attack those he or she opposes. The choice of words often reveals the writer's attitudes. A writer can also use emotive language (i.e. words and expressions with particular connotations that appeal to the reader's or listener's emotions) and so influence him or her to react in a particular way. When the writer makes use of the literal and limited meaning of a word, regardless of the ideas and emotions it might connote, this is called denotation [ˌdiːnəʊˈteɪʃn].
register [ˈredʒɪstə] *Sprachebene,* *Stilebene*	Register is the level of language (the choice of words, grammar, etc.) used in a particular situation. The register in a text may be formal, neutral or informal.

Formal style consists of difficult vocabulary, often of Latin origin, and complex sentence structure; it is usually only used for serious purposes, e.g. essays or academic publications, or in official situations, and would not be appropriate in normal everyday conversation.
Example:

> A new widely-debated approach is gene pharming. Pharma crops are genetically modified plants like maize that produce much-needed medicines.

From: 'Science – motor of progress?', cf. Context, p. 140, ll. 22–24

The writer uses difficult words and grammar so that the reader must examine the sentence closely to understand what the writer is saying.

Neutral style falls between *formal and *informal style and is the style generally used by educated people; it is used in *feature stories, *news stories, etc.
Example:

> [P]eople's 'likes' and 'dislikes' are carefully stored, along with a great number of other details gathered about the users, to be exploited by businesses or political organizations.

From: 'Living interactive lives', cf. Context, p. 184, ll. 6–9

The writer uses straightforward sentences and words that are neither formal nor informal.

Informal style is characterized by fairly simple, often incomplete sentences, short forms (e.g. *can't, you'll*), phrasal verbs and colloquial words, often of Germanic origin; it is used between friends or in a relaxed or informal situation.
Example:

> That waitress sized us up in two seconds. We're black, and 'black people don't tip' so she wasn't gonna waste her time; someone like that, nothing you can do to change their mind.

From: Paul Haggis, Crash, 2004, p. 8, cf. Context, p. 23, ll. 16–19

The short forms like 'we're', 'wasn't' or gonna, the use of simple words like 'do', 'go' and phrases like *to* 'size sb'. *up* indicate that the characters are using informal style.
Informal style may include the use of slang and/or taboo words: Slang is very informal language, mainly used in dialogue between people of the same age or from a similar background, etc.
Taboo words [təˈbuː] are generally considered obscene, vulgar or shocking and are used only if the writer is trying to make a particular point or shock his or her reader.

•••••▶

Glossary

layout *Layout,* *Aufbau*	The way elements are arranged on a printed page is known as the layout. The layout includes elements such as the type and size of letters, the use of **bold** or *italic* typeface, <u>underlining</u>, headings and sub-headings, bullets (i.e. dots or other symbols used at the beginning of a text passage), the size and number of *columns, the length of paragraphs, the colour and the placement of illustrations. The layout determines whether a text attracts the attention of the reader and is pleasant to read, and it helps writers to structure their texts and to emphasize certain words, phrases or passages. The layout is particularly important when considering newspaper articles, *advertisements and brochures.
thesis ['θiːsɪs] *These*	An idea or a view that an author of an argumentative text presents and discusses in a formal way.
antithesis [æn'tɪθəsɪs] *Antithese*	An antithesis is an idea that is the opposite of an idea (thesis) already put forward by a writer. Often the writer will put forward the antithesis in order to stress his own thesis.

▶ Stylistic devices

Stylistic devices [staɪ'lɪstɪk dɪ'vaɪsɪs] (also called *rhetorical devices* [rɪ'tɒrɪkl dɪ'vaɪsɪs]) are methods and techniques used to produce a particular effect. Stylistic devices may e.g. relate to sound (e.g. *alliteration), structure (e.g. *repetition, *parallelism) or *imagery.

> ■ **LANGUAGE HELP**
>
> *The author uses alliteration/contrast/exaggeration/ repetition … (uncountable nouns)*
> *In line 5 there is a metaphor/allusion/symbol/rhetorical question/pun (countable nouns)*

Imagery

metaphor ['metəfə, 'metəfɔː] *Metapher*	A metaphor is a comparison between two things which are basically quite unlike one another without using the words *as* or *like* (cf.*simile).	*Example:* There's daggers in men's smiles. <div align="right">From: William Shakespeare, *Macbeth*</div>
personification [pə,sɒnɪfɪ'keɪʃn] *Personifikation*	Personification is the technique of representing animals or objects as if they were human beings or possessed human qualities. *Example:* Love's not Time's fool, though rosy lips and cheeks / Within his bending[1] sickle's[2] compass[3] come: / Love alters not with his brief hours and weeks, / But bears[4] it out even to the edge[5] of doom. [1]**bending** curved [2]**sickle** *Sichel* [3]**compass** *Reichweite* [4]**bear out sth.** endure sth. [5]**edge of doom** end of time From: William Shakespeare, 'Sonnet 116', cf. *Context*, p. 48 Here, both love and time are personified. Love in particular is described as a person with the appearance of 'rosy lips and cheeks'.	
simile ['sɪməli] *Vergleich*	Like a *metaphor, a simile is a type of comparison. But while metaphors say that something *is* something else, a simile says that something *is like* something else and uses the words *like* or *as* to draw the comparison.	*Example:* My mistress eyes are nothing like the sun. <div align="right">From: William Shakespeare, 'Sonnet 18'</div>

symbol ['sɪmbl] *Symbol*	A symbol is a thing, word or phrase signifying something concrete that stands not only for itself but also for a certain abstract idea. As in the case of a *metaphor or a *simile the meaning of a symbol goes beyond the literal. *Example:* A red rose is often a symbol of love.

> ■ TROUBLE SPOT
> **symbol of sth.**
> Not: ~~symbol for sth.~~

Sound

alliteration [ə‚lɪtə'reɪʃn] *Alliteration*	Alliteration is the repetition of a sound, normally a consonant, at the beginning of neighbouring words or of stressed syllables within such words, to produce a usually rhythmic, but sometimes also comic effect. *Example:* Around the rugged rock the ragged rascal ran.

assonance ['æsənəns] *Assonanz*	Assonance is the repetition of the same or similar vowel sounds within stressed syllables of neighbouring words.	*Example:* Beside the lake, beneath the trees, Fluttering and dancing in the breeze. From: William Wordsworth, 'I wandered lonely as a cloud'
onomatopoeia [‚ɒnə‚mætə'piːə] *Lautmalerei*	Onomatopoeia is the use of a word which imitates the sounds it refers to, e.g. *buzz* or *hum*. In a group of words or a phrase it may evoke a particular feeling, mood, sound or movement.	*Example:* Only the stuttering rifles' rapid rattle. From: Wilfred Owen, 'Anthem for doomed youth' The repetition of 't's and 'r's sounds like the shooting of rifles, which the words describe.

Structure

accumulation [ə‚kjuːmjə'leɪʃn] *Akkumulation, Ansammlung*	Accumulation is a listing of words and expressions with similar meaning. Thus, the words are emphasized or become more descriptive. *Example:* Then shall our names / Familiar in his mouth as household words / Harry the King, Bedford and Exeter / Warwick and Talbot, Salisbury and Gloucester, / Be in their flowing cups freshly remembered. From: William Shakespeare, *Henry V* This excerpt displays an accumulation of several addresses for 'King Harry'.
analogy [ə'nælədʒi] *Analogie*	Analogy is the comparison of two things which are similar in several aspects. By comparing an object, situation or person to something familiar, the explanation becomes easier to understand. *Example:* What's in a name? That which we call a rose. / By any other word would smell as sweet. / So Romeo would, were he not Romeo called. From: William Shakespeare, *Romeo and Juliet* Juliet states that just like a rose that will always keep its sweet smell whichever name it is called, Romeo will stay the same even if he changes his name.

anaphora [ə'næfərə] Anapher	Anaphora is a form of *parallelism which repeats the same word or group of words at the beginning of successive clauses.	*Example:* Come in, I say. Come in and eat with us. From: Imtiaz Dharker, 'The right word', *The Terrorist at My Table*, 2006, p. 25
enjambement [ɪn'dʒæmbmənt] Enjambement	Enjambement describes incomplete syntax at the end of the line where the meaning runs over to the next line without any punctuation at the end. An enjambement is also called *run-on line*.	*Example:* The child steps in And carefully, at my door, Takes off his shoes. From: Imtiaz Dharker, 'The right word', *The Terrorist at My Table*, 2006, p. 26
enumeration Aufzählung	Enumeration is the listing of words, phrases or ideas. In instructive or argumentative texts the list of enumerated elements can be given numbers or bullet points so the reader can see each new element clearly.	*Example:* go, my son, multiply, divide, conquer. From: Philip Levine, 'Corporate Head'; cf. *Context*, p. 173
parallelism ['pærəlelɪzəm] Parallelismus	Parallelism is the deliberate repetition of similar or identical words, phrases, sentence constructions, etc. in the same or neighbouring sentences. Parallelism draws the attention of the reader to certain ideas that the writer may consider important. It may be used to show that the elements are of similar importance, or it may be used in a climactic sequence, with the most important element listed at the end.	*Example:* Which alters[1] when it alteration finds, Or bends with the remover to remove[2]. [1] **alter** change [2] **remover** person who goes away From: William Shakespeare, 'Sonnet 116', cf. *Context*, p. 48, ll. 3–4
repetition Wiederholung	Repetition is the deliberate use of a word or phrase more than once in a sentence or a text to create a sense of pattern or form, or to emphasize certain elements for the reader or listener.	

Miscellaneous

allusion [ə'luːʒn] Allusion, Anspielung	Allusion is the direct or indirect reference to something or somebody the reader or listener is supposed to recognize and respond to. An allusion may be to a work of literature, a historical event, a religious text like the Bible, etc. *Example:* 'This place is like the garden of Eden'. This allusion refers to the 'garden of God', i.e. paradise, which appears in the Bible.
cliché ['kliːʃeɪ]	A cliché denotes the fact that an expression has been overused to the extent that the original meaning has been lost. It may also refer to predictable events or actions.

exaggeration [ɪɡ,zædʒə'reɪʃn] *Übertreibung*	Exaggeration is the use of a strong overstatement. It may be used to create either a serious or comic effect. A single phrase containing an exaggeration is called hyperbole [hʌɪ'pɔːbəli]. (cf. also *understatement)	*Example:* I fear the day technology will surpass our human interaction. The world will have a generation of idiots.
irony ['aɪrəni] *Ironie*	Irony is the term used when a person makes fun of somebody or something without openly doing so. A person using irony may use certain words and actually mean the opposite of what those words normally mean. Also, a person may appear to support someone or something while at the same time making it clear (e.g. by his or her tone of voice) that he or she is actually criticizing or revealing the contradictions in the other person's behaviour. A text which uses irony to ridicule or make fun of an institution, person, set of beliefs, etc. is called a satire ['sætaɪə].	
juxtaposition [,dʒʌkstəpə'zɪʃn] *Gegenüberstellung*	Juxtaposition is a very strong contrast ['kɒntrɑːst] of opposing ideas, arguments, views, mostly introduced by words like *but*, *however* or *nevertheless*.	
rhetorical question *rhetorische Frage*	A rhetorical question is a question to which the answer seems obvious and is therefore not necessary. Such questions push the reader or listener to a certain conclusion. As such they are popular in political *speeches, etc. when a person is trying to influence others.	*Example:* What do the changes mean? They can either strengthen and unite us, or they can weaken and divide us. From: William J. Clinton, 'Commencement Address at Portland State University'; cf. *Context*, p. 110, ll. 27–28 Here the rhetorical question is used to draw the reader/listener into the argument by posing a direct question. The reader/listener might feel a little under pressure, even manipulated to answer the question in a specific way.
understatement *Untertreibung*	Understatement is a statement in which the true magnitude of an idea, event or fact is minimized, so that something is deliberately presented as being much less important, valuable, etc. than it really is. Understatement is often used for *ironic effect, e.g. saying 'It is a bit cold today', when the temperature is 10 degrees below freezing. (cf. also *exaggeration)	
wordplay or **pun** [pʌn] *Wortspiel*	Wordplay (also called pun) is the use of a word which may be understood in two different ways or which may be put into a different context to alter the meaning. *Example:* The magician got so mad that he pulled his hair out. Here, the word *hair* alludes to *hare* (= *Hase*), an animal commonly associated with magicians.	

Glossary

Alphabetical list of words in the Glossary

Words in **bold** print have their own entries in the Glossary; words in blue print do not have their own entry and appear as part of another entry.

accumulation 373
act 362
action 366
actor/actress 362
ad 369
advert 369
advertisement 369
alliteration 373
allusion 374
alternate rhyme 371
analogy 373
anaphora 374
anticipation 367
antithesis 372
article 369
assonance 373
atmosphere 367
author 360
autobiography 368
biography 368
blog 370
blurb 369
byline 369
caricature 370
cartoon 370
character 365
characterization 365
classified ads 370
cliché 374
cliffhanger 363
climax 366
column 369
comedy 362
coming-of-age story 361
comment 369
commercial 370
concrete poem 361
conflict 366
connotation 371
contrast 369
couplet 361
denotation 371
denouement 367
dialogue 362
diction 371
direct address 369

direct characterization 365
drama/dramatic text 362
dramatic irony 362
dramatist 362
editorial 369
emotive language 371
emphasis 368
enjambement 374
enumeration 374
epilogue 361
essay 369
exaggeration 375
explicit characterization 365
exposition 366
external action 366
fable 361
falling action 366
feature film 362
feature story 368
fictional text/fiction 360
first-person narrator 363
flashback 367
flash fiction 360
flat character 365
foot 362
foreshadowing 367
formal style 371
frame story 361
free verse 361
genre 360
humour 370
hyperbole 375
iambic pentameter 362
image/imagery 372
implicit characterization 365
indirect characterization 365
informal style 371
interior monologue 364
internal action 366
ironic/irony 375
juxtaposition 375
layout 372
leader 369
leading article 369
letter 369
letter to the editor 369
limited point of view 364
line 361
literary text 360
lyrical (poem) 361

metaphor 372
metre 362
microfiction 360
mode of presentation 364
monologue 362
motif 360
narrative (prose) 360
narrator 363
news(paper) article 368
neutral style 371
news item 368
news report 368
news story 368
non-fiction/non-fictional text 368
novel 360
omniscient narrator 363
onomatopoeia 373
open ending 367
panoramic presentation 365
parallelism 374
personification 372
play 362
playwright 362
plot 366
poem/poetry 361
point of view 363
props 362
prose 360
protagonist 365
pun 375
quatrain 361
refrain 361
register 371
reliable narrator 364
repetition 374
reported thought 364
resolution 367
rhetorical device 372
rhetorical question 375
rhyme 361
rhyme scheme 361
rhyming couplet 361
rhythm 361
rising action 366
round character 365
run-on line 374

satire 375
scene 362
scenic presentation 364
script 362
scriptwriter 362
setting 368
shape poem 361
short story 360
showing 364
simile 372
sitcom 363
slang 371
soap (opera) 363
soliloquy 362
solution 367
sonnet 361
speaker 361
speech 369
stage directions 362
stanza 361
story of initiation 361
style 370
stylistic devices 372
surprise ending 367
suspense 367
suspension of disbelief 360
symbol/symbolic 373
taboo words 371
telling 365
tension 367
text type 368
theme 360
thesis 372
third-person narrator 363
tone 370
tragedy 362
turning point 366
tv/radio series 362
understatement 375
unlimited point of view 364
unreliable narrator 364
verse 360
volta 361
wordplay 375

Historical Documents

Excerpts from the Magna Carta (1215)

Until King John (king from 1199–1216) was forced by his barons to sign a document called the Magna Carta ('great charter'), the will of the king had been law. The Magna Carta was the first step on the long road which led to the constitutional principle that the 'Law is King'. Six of its 63 articles are printed here.

(12) No scutage or aid shall be imposed in our kingdom, unless by the general council of our kingdom; except for ransoming our person, making our eldest son a knight and once for marrying our eldest daughter; and for these there shall be paid no more than a reasonable aid. [...]

5 (14) And for holding the general council of the kingdom concerning the assessment of aids, except in the three cases aforesaid, and for the assessing of scutage, we shall cause to be summoned the archbishops, bishops, abbots, earls, and greater barons of the realm, separately by our letters. [...]

(20) A freeman shall not be amerced for a small offence, except in accordance with
10 the degree of the offence and for a grave offence he shall be amerced according to its gravity, without imperilling his status; and a merchant similarly without imperilling his stock-in-trade; and similarly a villain shall be amerced always without loss of wainage – if their liability is to us. And none of the aforesaid amercements shall be imposed except by the sworn evidence of worthy men of the
15 neighbourhood.

(38) In future no official shall put anyone to trial merely on his own testimony, without reliable witness produced for this purpose.

(39) No freeman shall be taken or imprisoned, or deprived of his freehold, or outlawed, or banished, or in any way destroyed, nor will we take or order action
20 against him, unless by the lawful judgment of his peers, or by the law of the land.

(40) We will sell to no man, we will not deny to any man, either justice or right.

1 **scutage** ['skjuːtɪdʒ] (in feudal times) money paid by a knight instead of doing military service, or by a landowner instead of personal service
6 **aforesaid** [– '– –] mentioned before
7 **summon sb.** (fml) order sb. to come to you
9 **freeman** ['– –] (in feudal times) a citizen
amerce sb. [ə'mɜːs] make sb. pay a fine
in accordance with sb./sth. *in Übereinstimmung mit jdm./etwas*
11 **imperil sth.** [– '– –] endanger sth.
12 **stock-in-trade** goods kept on sale by a merchant
villain ['vɪlən] (hier) Leibeigene/r
13 **wainage** (old use) profit or produce from the cultivation of land
if their liability is to us if the offence they committed was against us
14 **sworn evidence** *Aussage unter Eid*
16 **official** (n) person in a position of authority
18 **freehold** ['– –] ownership of land

Excerpts from the Bill of Rights (1689)

When James II (king from 1685–1688) tried to restore Catholicism to Britain, he met with resistance from all sides. Parliament forced James into exile in the 'Glorious Revolution' of 1688. Prince William of Orange and his wife, Princess Mary, were offered the throne on the condition that they accepted the 'Bill of Rights'. Thus Britain's constitutional monarchy was established. From then on, the British monarch ruled not by the grace of God, but by the grace of Parliament.

The said Lords Spiritual and Temporal, and Commons [...] do declare:

(1) That the pretended power of suspending of laws, or the execution of laws, by regal authority, without consent of Parliament, is illegal.

(2) That the pretended power of dispensing with laws or the execution by laws by
5 regal authority as it has been assumed and exercised of late is illegal.

(4) That levying money for or to the use of the Crown by pretence of prerogative, without grant of Parliament, for longer time or in other manner than the same is or shall be granted, is illegal.

1 **said** (adj; fml) mentioned before
Lords Spiritual archbishops and bishops
Lords Temporal ['temporal] lords who are concerned with worldly affairs, rather than with spiritual things; together with the Lords Spiritual they constitute the House of Lords
Commons House of Commons consisting of representatives of counties and towns
5 **of late** in recent times
6 **by pretence of prerogative** ['prɪ'tens, prɪrɒgətɪv] by claiming that the king has the right to do sth.

9 **commitment** (old use) =
committal act of sending sb. to
prison
15 **impeach sth.** (here) prevent sth.
16 **bail** Kaution
impose a fine demand money
as punishment
18 **redress of grievances** (fml)
correction of sth. considered
unfair

(5) That it is the right of the subject to petition the King, and all commitments and prosecutions for such petitioning are illegal.

(6) That the raising or keeping a standing army within the kingdom in time of peace, unless it be with the consent of Parliament, is against law.

(8) That elections of members of Parliament ought to be free.

(9) That the freedom of speech, and debates and proceedings in Parliament, ought not to be impeached or questioned in any court or place out of Parliament.

(10) That excessive bail ought not to be required nor excessive fines imposed; nor cruel and unusual punishment inflicted.

(13) And that for redress of all grievances, and for the amending, strengthening, and preserving of the laws, Parliament ought to be held frequently.

Excerpts from the Declaration of Independence (1776)

Unhappiness with British rule had been on the rise in the American colonies during the 1760s. In 1775, open fighting broke out between British troops and American colonists – the beginning of the Revolutionary War. When Congress adopted the Declaration of Independence on 4 July, 1776, this ended more than a century and a half of colonial dependency, even though the war was to go on until 1783.

3 **assume sth.** etwas übernehmen
station (old-fashioned or fml)
status
5 **impel sb. to sth.** [–'–] force sb.
to do sth.
8 **endow sb. with sth.** [ɪn'daʊ]
(fml) give sb. sth.
unalienable (old use)
= **inalienable** [ɪn'eɪliənəbl] (fml)
that cannot be taken away
9 **pursuit of sth.** (fml) act of trying
to achieve sth.
10 **consent** [–'–] (n) agreement

When in the Course of human events, it becomes necessary for one people to dissolve the political bands which have connected them with another, and to assume among the powers of the earth, the separate and equal station to which the Laws of Nature and of Nature's God entitle them, a decent respect to the opinions of mankind requires that they should declare the causes which impel them to the separation.

We hold these truths to be self-evident, that all men are created equal, that they are endowed by their Creator with certain unalienable Rights, that among these are Life, Liberty and the pursuit of Happiness. That to secure these rights, Governments are instituted among Men, deriving their just powers from the consent of the governed. That whenever any Form of Government becomes destructive of these ends, it is the Right of the People to alter or to abolish it, and to institute new Government, laying its foundation on such principles and organizing its powers in such form, as to them shall seem most likely to effect their Safety and Happiness.

The Bill of Rights (1791)

At the time the Constitution of the USA was discussed and ratified, critics felt it did not sufficiently protect individuals against abuse of their civil liberties and rights by the federal government. Therefore, ten amendments to the Constitution known as the Bill of Rights were proposed by Congress and passed in 1791.

1 **respecting** concerning
2 **the free exercise thereof**
deren freie Ausübung
abridge sth. limit sth.
4 **redress of grievances** (fml)
correction of sth. considered
unfair

First Amendment Congress shall make no law respecting an establishment of religion, or prohibiting the free exercise thereof; or abridging the freedom of speech, or of the press; or the right of the people peaceably to assemble, and to petition the government for a redress of grievances.

5 **Second Amendment** A well-regulated militia, being necessary to the security of a free state, the right of the people to keep and bear arms shall not be infringed.

Third Amendment No soldier shall, in time of peace be quartered in any house, without the consent of the owner, nor in time of war, but in a manner to be prescribed by law.

10 **Fourth Amendment** The right of the people to be secure in their persons, houses, papers, and effects, against unreasonable searches and seizures, shall not be violated, and no warrants shall issue, but upon probable cause, supported by oath or affirmation, and particularly describing the place to be searched, and the persons or things to be seized.

15 **Fifth Amendment** No person shall be held to answer for a capital, or otherwise infamous crime, unless on a presentment or indictment of a grand jury, except in cases arising in the land or naval forces, or in the militia, when in actual service in time of war or public danger; nor shall any person be subject for the same offense to be twice put in jeopardy of life or limb; nor shall be compelled in any criminal

20 case to be a witness against himself, nor be deprived of life, liberty, or property, without due process of law; nor shall private property be taken for public use, without just compensation.

Sixth Amendment In all criminal prosecutions, the accused shall enjoy the right to a speedy and public trial, by an impartial jury of the state and district wherein

25 the crime shall have been committed, which district shall have been previously ascertained by law, and to be informed of the nature and cause of the accusation; to be confronted with the witnesses against him; to have compulsory process for obtaining witnesses in his favor, and to have the assistance of counsel for his defence.

30 **Seventh Amendment** In suits at common law, where the value in controversy shall exceed twenty dollars, the right of trial by jury shall be preserved, and no fact tried by a jury, shall be otherwise re-examined in any court of the United States, than according to the rules of the common law.

Eighth Amendment Excessive bail shall not be required, nor excessive fines

35 imposed, nor cruel and unusual punishments inflicted.

Ninth Amendment The enumeration in the Constitution, of certain rights, shall not be construed to deny or disparage others retained by the people.

Tenth Amendment The powers not delegated to the United States by the Constitution, nor prohibited by it to the states, are reserved to the states respectively,

40 or to the people.

Preamble to the Charter of the United Nations (1945)

Drafted immediately after the Second World War, the Charter of the United Nations set out to formulate the aims of this new organization.

WE, THE PEOPLES OF THE UNITED NATIONS, DETERMINED,

to save succeeding generations from the scourge of war, which twice in our lifetime has brought untold sorrow to mankind, and

to reaffirm faith in fundamental human rights, in the dignity and worth of the

5 human person, in the equal rights of men and women and of nations large and small, and

---

**Glossary (right column):**

6 **infringe sth.** *(fml)* etwas verletzen

8 **but** except

11 **effects** *(pl; fml)* personal property
seizure ['siːʒə] Beschlagnahme

12 **warrant** Durchsuchungs- oder Haftbefehl

13 **affirmation** [ˌæfəˈmeɪʃn] eidesstattliche Erklärung

15 **hold sb. to answer for sth.** accuse sb. of sth. (in a court of law)

16 **infamous** ['ɪnfəməs] evil, shameful
presentment [– '– –] formelle Anschuldigung
indictment [ɪnˈdaɪtmənt] Anklage
grand jury *(AE)* panel of 12 or 23 citizens who investigate accusations and officially charge criminals to be tried before a jury if there is sufficient evidence

19 **in jeopardy of life and limb** ['dʒepədi] in Gefahr für Leib und Leben

21 **due process of law** proper legal procedures

26 **ascertain sth.** [ˌæsəˈteɪn] *(fml)* determine sth.

28 **obtain sb.** (hier) jdn. vorladen
counsel lawyer giving legal advice

30 **common law** unwritten law based on custom, usage and former decisions of courts of law

31 **trial by jury** Verfahren vor Geschworenen

32 **try sth.** examine and decide sth. in a court of law

34 **bail** Kaution

37 **construe sth.** [– '–] interpret sth.
disparage a right [dɪsˈpærɪdʒ] ein Recht schmälern

2 **scourge** [skɜːdʒ] *(fig)* person or thing that causes suffering

4 **reaffirm sth.** etwas erneut bekräftigen

7 **obligation** *Verpflichtung*
10 **end** aim, purpose
14 **ensure sth.** *(BE) = (AE)* **insure sth.** guarantee sth.
18 **resolve** [rɪ'zɒlv] decide firmly

to establish conditions under which justice and respect for the obligations arising from treaties and other sources of international law can be maintained, and

to promote social progress and better standards of life in larger freedom,

AND FOR THESE ENDS   10

to practise tolerance and live together in peace with one another as good neighbours, and

to unite our strength to maintain international peace and security, and

to ensure, by the acceptance of principles and the institution of methods, that armed force shall not be used, save in the common interest, and   15

to employ international machinery for the promotion of the economic and social advancement of all peoples,

HAVE RESOLVED TO COMBINE OUR EFFORTS TO ACCOMPLISH THIS AIM.

Preamble to the Universal Declaration of Human Rights (1948)

The Universal Declaration of Human Rights, which was adopted by the General Assembly of the United Nations on 10 December, 1948, outlines a basic view of human rights, but it is not a legally binding document.

1 **whereas** because of the fact that
inalienable [in'eɪliənəbl] *(fml)* that cannot be taken away from you
4 **disregard** *(n) Missachtung*
contempt feeling that sb./sth. is without value and deserves no respect
5 **outrage sb.** make sb. very shocked and angry
advent of sth./sb. ['––] coming of sth./sb. (an important event, person, technology, etc.)
9 **compel sb. to do sth.** [– '–] *(fml)* force sb. to do sth.
have recourse to sth. *Zuflucht zu etwas nehmen*
as a last resort [rɪ'zɔːt] *als letzten Ausweg*
14 **reaffirm sth.** *etwas erneut bekräftigen*
18 **pledge yourself to sth.** formally promise to do sth..

Whereas recognition of the inherent dignity and of the equal and inalienable rights of all members of the human family is the foundation of freedom, justice and peace in the world,

Whereas disregard and contempt for human rights have resulted in barbarous acts which have outraged the conscience of mankind, and the advent of a world in   5
which human beings shall enjoy freedom of speech and belief and freedom from fear and want has been proclaimed as the highest aspiration of the common people,

Whereas it is essential, if man is not to be compelled to have recourse, as a last resort, to rebellion against tyranny and oppression, that human rights should be   10
protected by the rule of law,

Whereas it is essential to promote the development of friendly relations between nations,

Whereas the peoples of the United Nations have in the Charter reaffirmed their faith in fundamental human rights, in the dignity and worth of the human person   15
and in the equal rights of men and women and have determined to promote social progress and better standards of life in larger freedom,

Whereas Member States have pledged themselves to achieve, in co-operation with the United Nations, the promotion of universal respect for and observance of human rights and fundamental freedoms,   20

Whereas a common understanding of these rights and freedoms is of the greatest importance for the full realization of this pledge,

Now, therefore, the GENERAL ASSEMBLY proclaims this UNIVERSAL DECLARATION OF HUMAN RIGHTS as a common standard of achievement for all peoples and all nations, to the end that every individual and every organ of society,   25
keeping this Declaration constantly in mind, shall strive by teaching and education to promote respect for these rights and freedoms and by progressive measures, national and international, to secure their universal and effective recognition

and observance, both among the peoples of Member States themselves and among the peoples of territories under their jurisdiction.

30 **jurisdiction** *Zuständigkeit, Gerichtsbarkeit*

30

Preamble to the Treaty of Rome (1957)

The European Economic Community (EEC), the precursor to today's much larger European Union, was established on 27 March, 1957, when the six founding members – France, West Germany, Italy, Belgium, the Netherlands and Luxembourg – signed the Treaty of Rome, which is also called the Treaty Establishing the European Community.

His Majesty the King of the Belgians, The President of the Federal Republic of Germany, The President of the French Republic, The President of the Italian Republic, Her Royal Highness the Grand Duchess of Luxembourg, Her Majesty the Queen of the Netherlands,

5 DETERMINED to lay the foundations of an ever closer union among the peoples of Europe,

RESOLVED to ensure the economic and social progress of their countries by common action to eliminate the barriers which divide Europe,

AFFIRMING as the essential objective of their efforts the constant improve-
10 ments of the living and working conditions of their peoples,

RECOGNIZING that the removal of existing obstacles calls for concerted action in order to guarantee steady expansion, balanced trade and fair competition,

ANXIOUS to strengthen the unity of their economies and to ensure their harmonious development by reducing the differences existing between the various
15 regions and the backwardness of the less favoured regions,

DESIRING to contribute, by means of a common commercial policy, to the progressive abolition of restrictions on international trade,

INTENDING to confirm the solidarity which binds Europe and the overseas countries and desiring to ensure the development of their prosperity, in accord-
20 ance with the principles of the Charter of the United Nations,

RESOLVED by thus pooling their resources to preserve and strengthen peace and liberty, and calling upon the other peoples of Europe who share their ideal to join in their efforts,

HAVE DECIDED to create a EUROPEAN COMMUNITY ...

5 **determined** [dɪˈtɜːmɪnd] *(adj)* having made a firm decision to do sth.
7 **resolved** [rɪˈzɒlvd] *(adj) (fml)* having made a firm decision to do sth.
11 **concerted** [– ˈ– –] *(adj)* gemeinsam, gemeinschaftlich
13 **anxious to do sth.** [ˈæŋkʃəs] wanting to do sth. very much
15 **backwardness** state of having made less progress than normal
17 **abolition** [ˌæbəˈlɪʃn] *Abschaffung*
21 **pool sth.** collect sth. (money, information, etc.) from different people or groups so that it can be used by all of them
resource supply of sth. that a country, an organization or a person has and can use, esp. to increase their wealth

Charts

The British System of Government

Monarch

official head of state (mostly representative functions), signs bills passed by Parliament thereby making them law

officially appoints

The Government

Prime Minister
head of the government
leader of the strongest party in the House of Commons

Cabinet
about 20 of the most important Ministers
(heads of government departments)

officially appoints
(on the recommen-
dation of the PM)

Parliament

House of Lords
ca. 700 members (life peers, 26 Anglican bishops, and 92 hereditary peers)
scrutinizes bills passed by the House of Commons

House of Commons
650 MPs from constituencies
makes laws
elected for each constituency in a first-past-the-post system, elections are held at least every five years

is accountable to

elects

Electorate
all men and women over the age of 18

The US System of Government

System of Checks and Balances

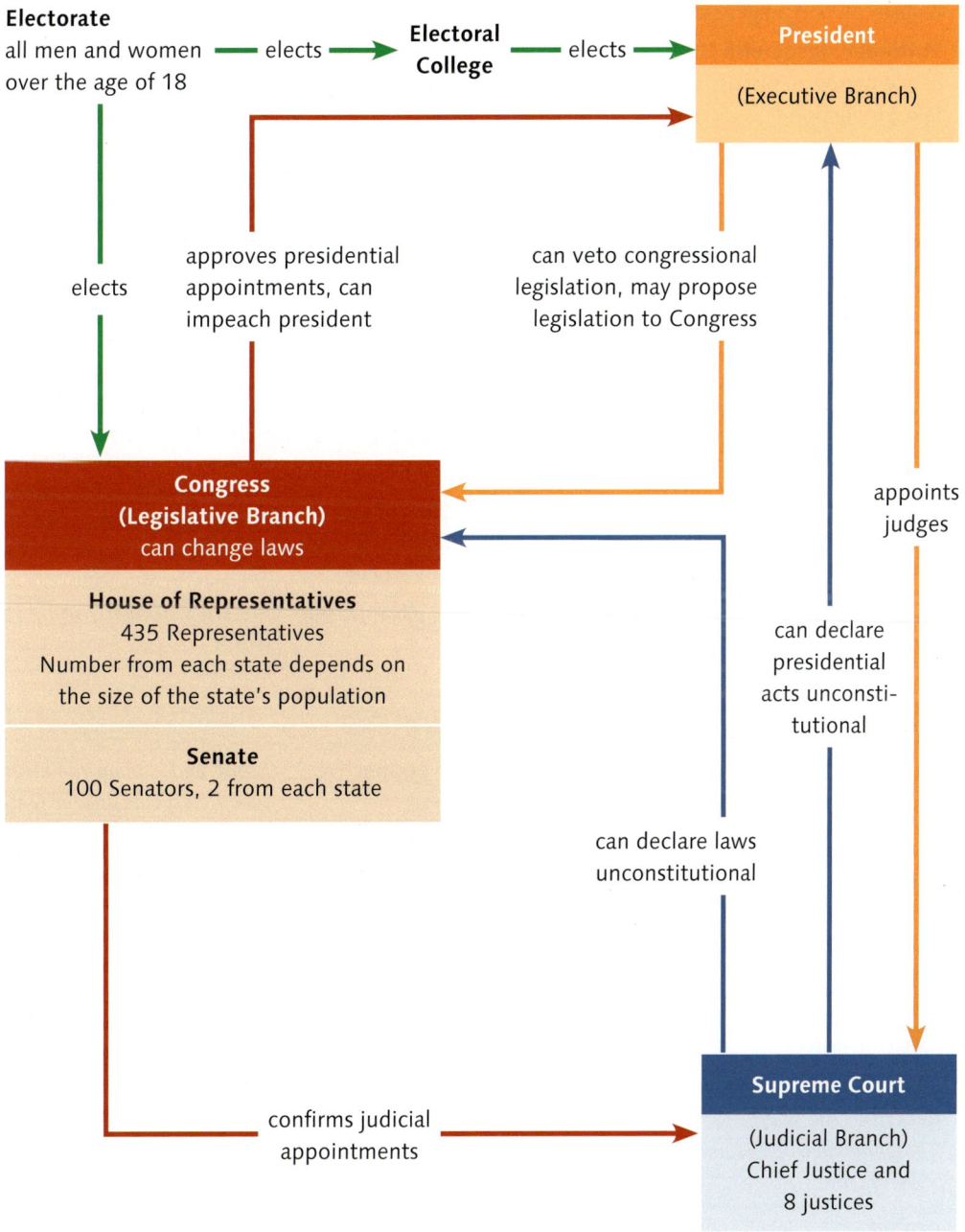

Electorate
all men and women
over the age of 18

elects → **Electoral College** → elects → **President** *(Executive Branch)*

elects

approves presidential
appointments, can
impeach president

can veto congressional
legislation, may propose
legislation to Congress

appoints
judges

Congress
(Legislative Branch)
can change laws

House of Representatives
435 Representatives
Number from each state depends on
the size of the state's population

Senate
100 Senators, 2 from each state

can declare
presidential
acts unconsti-
tutional

can declare laws
unconstitutional

confirms judicial
appointments

Supreme Court
(Judicial Branch)
Chief Justice and
8 justices

Verbs for Tasks ('Operatoren')

Context uses the same special vocabulary ('Operatoren') for tasks that is used in standard tests, including the 'Abitur'. Be sure you understand what's required of you when you come across one of the verbs below.

'Anforderungsbereich I' COMPREHENSION
refers to text comprehension and definition.

'Anforderungsbereich II' ANALYSIS
focuses on text analysis and comparison, and stylistic devices.

'Anforderungsbereich III' BEYOND THE TEXT
concentrates on discussion, comment, evaluation and text production.

> *Find a further list of verbs for tasks, this one ordered by skills (writing, mediation, listening, speaking), here:*
> **Webcode** context-58

The instructions say	Example	What you are expected to do
'Anforderungsbereich I' COMPREHENSION		
describe *beschreiben*	**Describe** the photo.	*Give an accurate account of sth. in your own words.*
give an account of *berichten über*	**Give an account of …** (as described in …).	*Outline the information required.* *Give the main features, structure or general principles of a topic in your own words omitting minor details.* *Do not include your own opinion or interpretation.*
outline ['– –] *umreißen, skizzieren*	**Outline** the information the narrator/author provides on …	
summarize / sum up *zusammenfassen*	**Summarize** the content of the article. **Sum up** the main points of the German newspaper article.	
state *darlegen*	**State** the information given by the author …	*Present sth. clearly using your own words.*
'Anforderungsbereich II' ANALYSIS		
analyse *(BE)*, **analyze** *(AE)* ['ænəlaɪz] *analysieren*	**Analyse** the narrative perspective in the given excerpt.	*Name and explain the meaning of specific aspects and/or features of the text and their effects on the reader/ audience.*
examine [ɪgˈzæmɪn] *untersuchen*	**Examine** the problems the protagonist faces …	
compare / contrast [kənˈtrɑːst] *vergleichen, kontrastieren, gegenüberstellen*	**Compare** the cartoon with the main point(s) of the text. **Contrast** the author's concept of multiculturalism with concepts you have encountered in class.	*Point out similarities and differences.*
describe (the way) *beschreiben (die Art und Weise, wie …)*	**Describe** the way the playwright creates an atmosphere of suspense.	*Give an accurate account of sth. in your own words.*
explain *erklären*	**Explain** the diagram.	*Describe in detail and give reasons for / refer to causes/effects.*

relate (to) *in Verbindung bringen (mit), in Zusammenhang bringen (mit)*	**Relate** the photo **to** the overall situation in the USA.	*Establish a connection between two things.*
show (how) *erläutern, veranschaulichen (wie)*	**Show** how the boy is characterized in this excerpt.	*Point out and illustrate sth.*

'Anforderungsbereich I/II' MEDIATION		
outline / give an account of / sum up	**Outline** the information from Text B that refers to …	*Give the relevant information on the topic. Use paraphrases.*

'Anforderungsbereich III' BEYOND THE TEXT		
assess [ə'ses] **/ evaluate** [ɪ'væljueɪt] *auswerten, beurteilen, bewerten, einschätzen*	**Assess** whether the statement applies to the short story as well. **Evaluate** the author's view of the impact Obama's speech had on his audience.	*Decide on the value or the state of something and give reasons for your decision.*
comment on ['kɒment] *kommentieren, Stellung nehmen zu*	**Comment on** the future of multiculturalism in the USA.	*Based on arguments express your personal view on a problem / certain behaviour, attitudes or viewpoints.*
convince *überzeugen*	In a formal letter, **convince** the head of your school that the introduction of bilingual classes would be beneficial.	*Present arguments so that the addressee will support your view.*
discuss *diskutieren, erörtern*	**Discuss** advantages and disadvantages of introducing full-body scanners at airports.	*Examine / Analyse, give reasons for and against and come to a justified conclusion. Present arguments with supporting evidence and conclude with your personal view.*
interpret [ɪn'tɜːprɪt] *interpretieren, deuten, auswerten*	**Interpret** the drawing.	*Establish the meaning of something in a wider context and give your own view.*
justify *begründen, rechtfertigen*	**Justify** the protagonist's behaviour in light of …	*Show adequate grounds for decisions or conclusions.*
reflect on *nachdenken über*	Referring to a character from literature or film, **reflect on** the influence of … on this person's life.	*Consider / Contemplate / Think carefully and deeply about a problem / certain behaviour, attitudes or viewpoints.*
verify *überprüfen, verifizieren*	**Verify** the author's thesis …	*Analyse and show that something is true.*

Acknowledgements

Texts

° = Der Text wurde aus didaktischen Gründen bearbeitet.

pp. 18–19: *Successful children*. Excerpt(s) from BATTLE HYMN OF THE TIGER MOTHER by Amy Chua, copyright © 2011 by Amy Chua. Used by permission of Penguin Press, an imprint of Penguin Publishing Group, a division of Penguin Random House LLC. All rights reserved; **p. 21:** *Growing up queer in 2018*. Out Front Magazine / Arianna Balderrama https://www.outfrontmagazine.com/inthemag /growing-queer-2018/, 12 January 2018 / 24 January 2019; **p. 23:** *Stereotypes in Los Angeles*. Crash. Draft with final revisions, 2004, p. 8–10, 29–32 Blackfriar's Bridge & The Harris Company / Paul Haggis; **p. 27:** *Quote by Banksy*. From: Banksy, Wall and Piece, Random House UK Ltd., 2014; **p. 28:** *Quote by Boyan Slat*. Reprinted with permission of Pacific Standard © 2018; **p. 28:** *Quote by Malala Yousafzai:* From: United Nations Education Speech, 2013; **pp. 29–30:** *Volunteering in Germany*. https://www. stern.de/panorama/herzschlag/soziales-engagement-in-deutschland-ist-beliebt-3842336.html, 29 November 2014 / 22 January 2019 © Alexandra Mankarios; **p. 48:** *Marital Sonnet 4*. By kind permission of the Estate of James Simmons c/o The Gallery Press, Loughcrew, Oldcastle, County Meath, Ireland from Poems, 1956–1986 (1986); **p. 52 (u. p. 374):** Text from The Terrorist at My Table (Bloodaxe, 2006), © Imtiaz Dharker 2006, used by permission of the author and the publisher. http://www.imtiazdharker.com/poems_7-the-right-word; **pp. 58–59 (u. p. 285, p. 307, p. 350, p. 363, p. 366, p. 367, p. 370):** *Dangerous books*. From Alan Bennett: The Uncommon Reader. Faber & Faber Ltd., London 2008, pp. 32–35; **pp. 66–67:** *Between two cultures*. From Mike Bartlett: Artefacts. Published by Methuen Drama 2008 © 2008 by Mike Bartlett; **p. 69:** *A closer look at Britain's Muslims*. From: Harriet Sherwood: Muslims place greater importance on national identity, finds UK study. Copyright Guardian News & Media Ltd 2018; **pp. 70–71** *Trying to understand the Brexit vote*. Catherine Hickley / Die Zeit. https://www.zeit.de/wirtschaft/2017-02/brexit-remain-grossbritan nien-deutschland-3, 20 February 2017 / 24 January 2019; **pp. 79–80:** ° = *The British Empire from an Indian perspective*. Excerpt(s) from INDIA UNBOUND by Gurcharan Das, copyright © 2000 by Gurcharan Das. Used by permission of Alfred A. Knopf, an imprint of the Knopf Doubleday Publishing Group, a division of Penguin Random House LLC. All rights reserved; **pp. 81–83:** *Gandhi remembered*. © Chetan Bhagat; **p. 88:** *Interview*. From: Carolin Roder, Sandra Kurz, Maxim Derenko / Campus Künzelsau – Reinhold-Würth-Hochschule; **p. 88:** *Indian truck art*. http://www.projecthornplease.com/about/, 2012 © Shantanu Suman; **p. 89:** *A taste of the Indian diaspora*. http://www.bbc.co.uk/food/0/25745902, 20 January 2014, © BBC Worldwide / Michelle Warwicker; **pp. 90–92:** *English lessons*. Originally published in English Lessons and Other Stories © 1996 by Shauna Singh Baldwin. Reprinted by permission of Goose Lane Editions; **p. 98:** *Unlike other nations*. From David Kamp: Rethinking the American Dream. quoted in: https://www.vanityfair.com/culture/ 2009/04/american-dream200904, 5 March 2009 / 24 January 2019; **p. 99:** ° = *Reinventing the American dream*. From: http://archive.naplesnews.com/opinion/perspec tives/guest-column--the-american-dream-revisited-ep-387952910-342446451.html, 8 August 2012 / 24 January 2019 © June Sochen; **pp. 105–106:** *The new neighbours*. From Clybourne Park, 2010 – Act One © Bruce Norris; **pp. 108–109:** *Integration or frustration?* From: https://news.harvard.edu/gazette/story/2018/03/harvard-professor-reflects-on-the-kerner-report-50-years-on/, 21 March 2018 / 24 January 2019 © Harvard Gazette / Stephanie Mitchell; **pp. 110–111:** *The changing face of America*. From: William J. Clinton. 'Commencement Address at Portland State University', 13 June 1998; **pp. 115–116:** *The end of the American era?* https://www. theatlantic.com/magazine/archive/2017/10/is-trump-ending-the-american-era/537888/, October 2017 / 24 January 2019, © 2017 The Atlantic Media Co., as first published in The Atlantic Magazine. All rights reserved. Distributed by Tribune Content Agency; **pp. 124–125:** *Europe's lost generation*. https://www.telegraph.co.uk/ news/2018/09/13/future-europe-can-eu-save-lost-gene ration-left-fighting-life/, 13 September 2018 / 1 February 2019; **p. 126:** *Hunting for personnel*. https://www.stutt garter-nachrichten.de/inhalt.weil-krankenpfleger-fehlen-ol-im-op-kliniken-suchen-in-spanien-fehlendes-personal. ec1ddd77-3af7-46ea-b96a-d40240859576.html, 12 October 2012 / 1 February 2019 © Stuttgarter Zeitung / Sascha Schmierer; **p. 129:** *The need for a new label*. https:// www.theguardian.com/commentisfree/2011/may/01/ lucy-siegle-human-cost-consumerism, 1 May 2011 / 1 February 2019, Copyright Guardian News & Media Ltd 2018; **pp. 130–131:** *The return of the nation state*. https:// www.theguardian.com/commentisfree/2018/sep/26/ donald-trump-globalisation-nation-state, 26 September 2018 / 1 February 2019, Copyright Guardian News & Media Ltd 2018; **p. 133:** *Keeping the accent*. From: Aoife Mannix: The elephant in the corner: new & selected poems (Luton: tall-lighthouse, 2005, p. 54) Copyright Aoife Mannix, 2005; **pp. 134–135:** *Linguistic diplomacy: the Eurovision Song Contest*. © The Economist Group Limited, London (2013); **p. 142:** From: Laura Roberts : *A saviour sibling* © Telegraph Media Group Limited 2010; **pp. 144–145:** *You are mine to kill*. From: Nick Dear: Frankenstein. Faber & Faber Ltd., London 2001; **p. 147:** Patricia Piccinini. Caption: *The Long Awaited, 2008* silicone, fibreglass, human hair, plywood, leather, clothing 152 x 80 x 92 cm high. Courtesy of the artist, Tolarno Galleries, Melbourne, Roslyn Oxley9 Gallery, Sydney, and Hosfelt Gallery, San Francisco; Essay (excerpt) from: patricia piccinini.net/writing/41/232/29#, 23 January 2019; **pp. 148–149:** *Animals with bonus features*. © 2010 New Scientist Ltd. All rights reserved. Distributed by Tribune Content Agency; **pp. 151–154:** *Can this woman cure ageing with gene therapy?* https://www.theguardian.com/science/ 2016/jul/24/elizabeth-parrish-gene-therapy-ageing, 24 July 2016 / 24 January 2019. Copyright Guardian News & Media Ltd 2018; **p. 156:** *The future of energy in Germany*. www.agora-energiewende.de https://www.agora-energie wende.de/die-energiewende/einfuehrung/, 2014 / 24 January 2019; **p. 164:** *The second Bill of Rights*. Franklin D.

Roosevelt https://fdrlibrary.org/address-text 4 February 2019; **pp. 165–166:** *More work, fewer workers.* Courtesy of CNBC https://sg.finance.yahoo.com/news/real-reason-disappearing-jobs-isnt-170208224.html?guccounter=1, 21 November 2015 / 4 February 2019, Courtesy of CNBC; **p. 167:** *Income inequality and guaranteed income.* https://www.pbs.org/newshour/nation/will-guaranteed-income-ever-come-america, 7 April 2014 / 29 January 2019 © Felix Oberholzer-Gee; **pp. 169–170:** *Teenagers' career aspirations.* From: https://www.economicmodelling.co.uk/wp-content/uploads/CG_Great-Expectations_Online-FINAL.pdf. © 2015 The City and Guilds of London Institute. All rights reserved. **p. 172:** *Do you love your job?* https://www.zeit.de/2013/44/glueck-arbeit-zufriedenheit-essay, 24 October 2013 / 29 January 2019 © ZEIT online / Uwe Jean Heuser; **p. 173:** *Corporate Head.* Philip Levine: New Selected Poems, Knopf: 1991; **pp. 174–175:** *Mitch's first glimpses of the world of work.* Cover and text excerpt from PAYBACK TIME by Carl Deuker. Copyright (c) 2010 by Carl Deuker. Reprinted by permission of Houghton Mifflin; **pp. 176–177:** *Ten things not to say in a job interview.* Copyright Guardian News & Media Ltd 2018; **pp. 177–178:** *Help wanted in Paradise.* Copyright Guardian News & Media Ltd 2018; **pp. 188–189:** *Online learning in 2044.* From: Ernest Cline. Ready Player One. Penguin Books 2012; **pp. 190, 304, 363, 365:** Cline, Ernest: Ready Player One. Penguin Books 2012; **pp. 192–193:** Gerhard Witossek, „Digitale Medien im Lehr- und Lernprozess", http://www.muc.kobis.de/index.php?id=schule, October 2014 / 24 January 2019; **pp. 196–197:** *9/11 a game changer.* Barack Obama: Barack Obama: Remarks by the President on Review of Signals Intelligence, 2014. http://www.whitehouse.gov/the-press-office/2014/01/17//remarks-president-review-signals-intelligence, 17 January 2014 / 23 January 2019; **pp. 198–199:** *The future of fake news: don't believe everything you read, see or hear.* https://www.theguardian.com/technology/2017/jul/26/fake-news-obama-video-trump-face2face-doctored-content, 26 July 2017 / 24 January 2019. Copyright Guardian News & Media Ltd 2018; **pp. 206–207:** *Living in London, New York, Rio de Janeiro.* https://www.theguardian.com/cities/series/cities-debate, 29 January 2014 / 20 February 2019; Copyright Guardian News & Media Ltd 2018; **p. 211:** *Urban decay, urban renewal.* From: Format, 7.8.2013. Alexandra Rotter: „Auch in Europa gibt es Städte, die verwaisen, vergreisen und verarmen". https://www.trend.at/service/die-redaktion-empfiehlt/auch-europa-staedte-363654; **p. 214:** Excerpt(s) from THE END OF THE SUBURBS: WHERE THE AMERICAN DREAM IS MOVING by Leigh Gallagher, © 2013 by Leigh Gallagher. Used by permission of Portfolio, an imprint of Penguin Publishing Group, a division of Penguin Random House LLC. All rights reserved. http://ideas.time.com/2013/07/31/the-end-of-the-suburbs/, 31 July 2013 / 20 February 2019; **pp. 216–217:** *A suburban street.* John Lanchester: Capital. Faber & Faber London, 2012, pp. 1–7; **p. 218:** *Country living.* From: Patricia Neely-Dorsey. Reflections of a Mississippi Magnolia – A life in Poems, 2008; **pp. 219–220:** *Small-town stories.* From: Garrison Keillor: Dennis Kitchen, Our Smallest Towns, intr. by Garrison Keillor, Chronicle Books, San Francisco, 1995, pp. 9–11; **pp. 233 (u. 306):** Shauna Singh Baldwin: 'English Lessons', English Lessons and Other Stories, Fredericton, NB: Goose Lane Editions, 1996, pp. 129–134; **p. 233:** *Remember that your future position* [...] Quote from: Arthur Miller: Death of a Salesman, 1949; **p. 233:** *It is a fabulous country* [...] Quote from: Thomas Wolfe: Of Time and the River, 1935; **p. 235:** *The End of an American era?* From: Eliot A. Cohen: How Trump is Ending the American Era © 2017 The Atlantic Media Co., as first published in The Atlantic Magazine. All rights reserved. Distributed by Tribune Content Agency; **p. 284:** Oxford Advanced Learner's Dictionary; **p. 286:** Oxford Advanced Learners Dictionary © Oxford University Press / Albert Sydney Hornby; **p. 301:** *How to please recruiters.* https://www.theguardian.com/careers/careers-blog/recruiter-hate-cv-new-job-application, 8 April 2014 / 1 February 2019. Copyright Guardian News & Media Ltd 2018; **p. 303:** Das, Gurcharan: Indian Unbound, Knopf: 2000; **p. 305:** Ariane Sherine: It may not be racist, but it's a question I'm tired of hearing. Copyright Guardian News & Media Ltd 2018; **pp. 306, 333, 365:** Deuker, Carl: Payback Time. Graphia 2010; **p. 307:** *I felt myself tense.* From: Todd Strasser, No Place, 2014, p. 8; **p. 310:** Gavin Ewart: *Ending,* from 'The Collected Ewart', Century News Edition 1982; **p. 326:** *Linguistic diplomacy: the Eurovision Song Contest.* R.L.G. From: The Economist, 20 May 2013; Economist / R.L.G.; **p. 330:** *What's going on here?* From Hanif Kureishi: The Buddha of Suburbia. Faber & Faber, 1990; **p. 339:** *Political and Economic Freedom.* Excerpt from FREE TO CHOOSE. A PERSONAL STATEMENT by Milton and Rose Friedman. Copyright © 1980 by Milton Friedman and Rose D. Friedman. Reprinted by permission of Houghton Mifflin Harcourt Publishing Company. All rights reserved; **p. 349:** *A great honour.* PA Group Limited / Ewan MacAskill; **pp. 352–353:** Anna Schmid: *Erschütternder Hilferuf in Kleid von Primark eingenäht.* Aus: FOCUS Online vom 25.06.2014. https://www.focus.de/kultur/mode/zwischen-die-etiketten-genaeht-frau-findet-hilfeschrei-einer-naeherin-im-primark-kleid_id_3942759.html

Cover

Getty Images / Pawel Libera

Illustrations / Graphics

Roland Beier (p. 313; p. 314); **Andreas Fischer** (p. 142 scientist, p. 142 embryo, p. 142 toddler, p. 142 woman)

Photos

action press (p. 15 Severn Suzuki: Vesa Moilanen / Lehtikuva; p. 27 top: Adam Gray; p. 85 bottom: Everett Collection / © The Revolutionary Optimists Productions 2017; p. 103 bottom: EXTRAPRESS; p. 122 bottom: News Pictures / face to face; p. 136 top: NOWOTNY, GEORG, bottom: NOWOTNY, GEORG); **akg-images** (p. 76 bottom: GandhiServe e.K.; p. 94 A: Joseph Martin; p. 104 top: Jasper Johns / © VG Bild-Kunst, Bonn 2019, Jasper Johns, Flag, Detail, 1955, bottom: Jasper Johns / © VG Bild-Kunst, Bonn 2019, Jasper Johns, Flag, Detail, 1955; p. 122 top; p. 295 left: Universal Images Group / Universal History Archive); **Andertoons** (p. 161 D: Mark Anderson; p. 163:

Acknowledgements

Mark Anderson); **ApolloMedia Film** (p. 23: A. Schwarz); **beingfivecomics** (p. 182 bottom: George Sfarnas); **bpk** (p. 211 top); **Bridgeman Images** (p. 28 centre: History/Russell Watkins; p. 34 Shakespeare (M): © Look and Learn English School, (19th century); p. 38: © Look and Learn English School, (20th century); p. 60 bottom: SZ Photo; p. 76 top: Granger; p. 84 bottom: Everett Collection; p. 94 B: Signing the Declaration of Independence, July 4th, 1776 engraved and pub. by Nathaniel Currier (1813–88) (colour litho), Trumbull, John (1756–1843) (after)/Library of Congress, Washington D.C., USA/Bridgeman Images; p. 98 top: Granger; p. 145 top: Tristram Kenton; p. 164: Everett Collection; p. 218: Photo© Christie's Images/© Heirs of Josephine N. Hopper/ VAGA at ARS, NY/ ©VG Bild-Kunst, Bonn 2019); **Cagle Cartoons** (p. 101: Cameron Cardow; p. 197: Nate Beeler); **Cartoon Bank** (p. 96: Peter Steiner); **Cartoonstock** (p. 53: Delgado; p. 72: Trevor White; Roy; p. 120: Karsten Schley; p. 140: S. Harris; p. 145 bottom: Grizelda; p. 146: Vahan Shirvanian; p. 158 bottom: Grizelda; p. 161 E: Bill Abbott; p. 191: John Martin; p. 193 bottom: Royston Robertson; p. 201: Harley Schwadron; p. 204: Mike Baldwin; p. 270: Rex May Baloo; p. 276: Royston Robertson; p. 279: Brian Fray; p. 299; p. 358 right: Grizelda; p. 358 left: Jackson Graham); **City & Guilds:** p. 169 (Grafik); **ClipDealer GmbH** (p. 273: Sergej Khackimullin; p. 301: Markus Gann); **www.colourbox.de** (p. 93 flags: Ruskpp; p. 117: Sigrid Olsson; p. 172: Colourbox. com; p. 247 top: Pressmaster); **Courtesy of the artist and Tolarno and Roslyn Oxley9 Galleries** (p. 147: Patricia Piccinini); **culture-images GmbH** (p. 32 top: Lebrecht/Lebrecht Music & Arts); **David Datuna** (p. 187 top and bottom); **ddp images** (p. 18: interTOPICS/Lynn Goldsmith; p. 82: ddp USA/Hindustan Times; p. 115: ddp images); **dpa Picture-Alliance** (p. 15 Christopher Reeve: Süddeutsche Zeitung Photo; p. 58 bottom; p. 65: CPA Media/CPA Media Co.; p. 83: Heritage-Images; p. 84 top: AP Photo; p. 88 centre: Robert Harding World Imagery/Robert Harding; p. 95 E: Everett Collection; p. 109: AP Photo; p. 123 A: Zentralbild/Dieter Palm, B: B1861_Lehtikuva_Oy/picture-alliance/B1861_Lehtikuva_ Oy, C: AP/ASSOCIATED PR, D: AP/ASSOCIATED PR, E: ANSA/dpaweb, F: AP/ASSOCIATED PR; p. 168: KEYSTONE/ picture-alliance/KEYSTONE); **F1online** (p. 14 B: F1online/ vAGE/VWPics/Paulo Amorim); **fotogloria** (p. 153 bottom: Pere Arnaldo/GranAngular); **GlowImages** (p. 138 A: Image Source); **Shawn Gruver** (p. 173 left); **Houghton Mifflin Harcourt Publishing Company** (p. 174: Cover from PAYBACK TIME by Carl Deuker. Copyright © 2010 by Carl Deuker. Reprinted by permission of Houghton Mifflin Harcourt Publishing Company. All rights reserved.); **IFLA (International Federation of Library Associations and Institutions)** (p. 199: Creative Commons Attribution 4.0 International (CC BY 4.0)); **Image Source** (p. 251: Ashley Corbin-Teich); **imago stock&people** (p. 211 centre: PhotoAlto); **interfoto e.k.** (p. 15 Mahatma Gandhi: Sammlung Rauch; p. 44: Sammlung Rauch; p. 50: Writer Pictures Ltd/Rogan Coles; p. 52: Writer Pictures Ltd/Derek Adams; p. 79: Mary Evans/Nigel Sorrell Collection; p. 94 C: SuperStock; p. 105: CLASSICSTOCK/R. KRUBNER);

Nick Kim, Wellington (p. 298); **laif** (p. 28 left: UPI; p. 93 bottom right: Luke Duggleby 2010/Redux; p. 102: Polaris; p. 151 top: eyevine/©Antonio Olmos); **LOOK-foto** (p. 150 bottom: Glasshouse Images); **mauritius images:** (p. 27 centre: alamy stock photo/Bruce McGowan, bottom: Photononstop/Till Jacket; p. 41: alamy stock photo/brenton west; p. 56 bottom: Alamy/Justin Kase z12z; p. 57 bottom: Alamy; p. 63 bottom: alamy stock photo/Yanice Idir; p. 69: alamy stock photo/amer ghazzal; p. 88 top left: imageBroker/Olaf Krüger, bottom right: alamy stock photo/Louise Batalla Duran; p. 95 D: alamy stock photo/Archive Pics, F: alamy stock photo/David R. Frazier Photolibrary, Inc.; p. 113: Cultura; p. 129 Made in U.S.A.: alamy stock photo/Independent Picture Service, Made in India: alamy stock photo/Carolyn Jenkins; p. 137 right: Luka Storm/Cultura/Luka Storm; p. 159 left: alamy stock photo/Holger Burmeister; p. 162: alamy stock photo/Roger Bamber; p. 173 right: alamy stock photo/Robert Landau; p. 181 top: alamy stock photo/Mick Sinclair; p. 188: alamy stock photo/Carol and Mike Werner; p. 195 top: Alamy, bottom: Raimund Linke/All mauritius images; p. 202 B: alamy stock photo/doug steley, p. 203 C: alamy stock photo/Robin Galloway, E: alamy stock photo/Northern Ireland; p. 210 alamy stock photo/Richard Levine; p. 211 bottom: alamy stock photo/Marvin Dembinsky Photo Associates; p. 216: alamy stock photo/M.Sobreira; p. 219 top: alamy stock photo/jeremy sutton-hibbert; p. 230: Malcolm Park/Loop Images/Loop Images/Malcolm Park; p. 237 right: Luka Storm/Cultura/Luka Storm; p. 271 bottom right: alamy stock photo/The Protected Art Archive; p. 202/203 C: alamy stock photo/Robin Galloway; **Amy Mohammed** (p. 186 top); **REUTERS** (p. 28 right: STAFF/Clement Rossignol; p. 74 A; p. 118 A: Johannes Eisele; p. 119 E: Pawel Kopczynski; p. 158 top: Fred Prouser); **Royal Shakespeare Company** (p. 39: Manuel Harlan; p. 43: Hugo Glendinning; p. 45: Sheila Burnett; p. 228 top: Hugo Glendinning); **Science Photo Library** (p. 152 bottom: SILVAIN BONNIOL/EURELIOS/LOOK AT SCIENCES); **Shutterstock:** p. 14 A: Photographee.eu, C: Zurijeta, D: Marc Bruxelle; E: LightField Studios; p. 16: marekuliasz; p. 17: littlesam; p. 20: Sorelyn Medina; p. 21: Rawpixel. com; p. 29: GoodStudio; p. 30 1., 2., 3 from top, bottom: GoodStudio, words: Tupungato; p. 31 top: Herr Loeffler, bottom right: gazanfer, bottom left: Titima Ongkantong; p. 32 bottom right: phloxii, bottom left: topinambur; p. 34 frame (M): Radu Bercan; p. 36: Rolau Elena; p. 40: chbaum; p. 46 hand: Peshkova; p. 47: iofoto; p. 49 Shakespeare image (M): Stefanina Hill, t-shirt (M): Syda Productions; p. 54/55 flag (M): Rsinha; p. 56 top: jorgen mcleman; p. 57 top: Ivan Marc; p. 60 top: Dan Breckwoldt; p. 61 like, unlinke: Alhovik, crown: Sashkin, bottom: Songquan Deng; p. 64: Maran Garai; p. 66: supervector555 ; p. 68: Frank L Junior; p. 70: Reservoir Dots; p. 75 C: JeremyRichards, D: gnomeandi, E: India Picture; p. 78 Ellora Caves: JeremyRichards, Sanchi: saiko3p, Chola Temples: msankar4, Taj Mahal: RuthChoi, railways: Attila JANDI, Qutb Minar: Chris Pole, map: Tupungato; p. 80: Ktkrypton; p. 81: Vectomart; p. 87: Mikhail Klyoshev; p. 91: ChiccoDodiFC; p. 93 top: pinana_treeangle, satellite dishes: MarcelClemens, food: Joe Gough, India map on screen (M): Katsiaryna Pleshakova, camera: photka; p.95 Statue of Liberty (M): Marcio Jose Bastos Silva; p.98 bottom: Boris15; p.100: Gustavo Frazao; p.103 top: Andy Dean Photography; p.108: arloo; p.111: Markus Mainka; p.118 B: Marko Aliaksandr; p.124: Pedro Rufo; p.128 e-mail icon (M): Pishchala Maksym, ear icon (M): Irina Medvedeva Mejg, TV icon (M): Vector, pullover icon (M): Ira Yapanda, masks icon (M): Vadim Almiev, USA icon (M): pinta.t.s, factory icon (M): VectorsMarket, test tube icon (M): inspiron.dell.vector, shopping basket icon (M): Anastasia_B, earth icon (M): Macrovector; p.129 Made in China: STILLFX; p.130: Akarat Phasura; p.132: vintagio; p.134: 3D_Render_Art; p.135: PrinceOfLove; p.138 D: WhiteDragon, E: Fisher Photostudio, G: Shevs, H: Vuk Varuna; p.141: Vuk Varuna; p.150 top: molekuul_be; p.151 bottom: Kateryna Kon; p.152 top: Natali_ Mis; p.153 top: ktsdesign; p.159 right: metamorworks; p.160 A: Lurin, B: AVAVA; p.161 C: Jon Rehg; p.165: PaO_ STUDIO; p.167: Gustavo Frazao; p.170: RTimages; p.171: Robert Kneschke; p.176 bottom: Andrei Mayatnik, top: takayuki; p.177: Gustavo Frazao; p.178: FPWing; p.180: Goodluz; p.182 top: Iconic Bestiary; p.183: Rawpixel; p.186 bottom: Photographee.eu; p.192 icons (left): Palsur, light bulb icon (M): Alvaro Cabrera Jimenez, board (M): Nerthuz; p.193 top: tmcphotos; p.194 camera (M): Vasin Lee, classroom (M): Monkey Business Images; p.202 A: stocker1970, D: Dan Thornberg; p.206 A: Paul Daniels, B: Ryan DeBerardinis; p.207: Tero Hakala; p.209 top: gpointstudio; p.212: Sky and glass; p.213: s4svisuals; p.214: PRESSLAB; p.219 bottom: Michael Shake; p.220: Sascha Burkard; p.224: everything possible; p.247 bottom: tassel78; p.250: Featureflash; p.253: emin kuliyev; p.262: Stokkete; p.272: Maxx-Studio; p.274: Syda Productions; p.278: Bluehousestudio; p.280: igor kisselev; p.281: favorita1987; p.282: Ozz Design; p.294: ibreakstock; p.308: bikeriderlondon; p.309: Ron Ellis; p.311 top: Ed Samuel, p.312: alexwhite; p.318: hxdbzxy; p.321: Lorelyn Medina; p.324: Andrey_Popov; p.328 top: pui_bunny; p.328 bottom: Alexandr III; p.329: Alexandr III; **stock.adobe.com** (p.14 F: Syda Productions; p.26: higyou; p.33 top: Tim, bottom: Paylessimages; p.35 background (M): striZh; p.63 top: determined; p.73: Wayne Shakell; p.89: paul_brighton; p.90: Andrew Lever; p.118 C: Lance Bellers; p.119 D: william87, globe: niroworld; p.121: koya979; p.126: Kzenon; p.129 Made in Bangladesh: Jörg Lantelme; p.138 B: Africa Studio, C: Sergey Nivens; p.139 F: Andrea Danti; background (M): joephotostudio; p.148: freshidea; p.156 centre: luigi giordano, top: luigi giordano, bottom: luigi giordano; p.181 bottom: peshkova; p.209 bottom: Jeanette Dietl; p.221 bottom: Patrik Stedrak, top: pavel vashenkov; p.238: science photo; p.242: Andrea Danti; p.248: Claudio Divizia; p.254: visceralimage; p.255: digitalstock; p.257: sgursozlu; p.264: fottoo; p.267: Natalia Bratslavsky; p.269 bottom: dbrnjhrj, centre: Darren Green; top: Bikeworldtravel; p.271 top: Andrei Nekrassov, bottom left: Brian Jackson; p.300: rasstock; p.310: dzmitry; p.316: Syda Productions;); **The Bush Theatre** (p.67: nabokov; p.228 bottom: Sheila Burnett); **TopicMedia** (p.192 frame (M): Simon Belcher); **VISUM** (p.15 John F. Kennedy: Ted Spiegel/The Image Works, Albert Einstein: Beeldunie.nl, Margaret Thatcher: Wolfgang Steche, Franklin D. Roosevelt: Andia; p.74 B: Philippe Lissac/Godong/Panos Pictures; p.110: Panos Pictures/Chris Stowers; p.137 left: Panos Pictures/Anti-Slavery International; p.237 left: Panos Pictures/Anti-Slavery International); **yourphoto today** (p.184: /KTS/A1PIX/KTSDESIGN/SCIENCE PHOTO LIBRARY).

Context

- ▸ Aktuelle lehrplangerechte Materialien für die Oberstufe
- ▸ Konsequente Kompetenzorientierung
- ▸ Ausgewiesene Differenzierung in allen Bereichen
- ▸ Aufbau von Sprachbewusstheit, interkultureller Handlungsfähigkeit und Sprachlernkompetenz
- ▸ Nutzung verschiedener Formen des Feedbacks für den Lernprozess

Cornelsen

ISBN 978-3-06-036475-6

9 783060 364756